THE TWILIGHT ZONE COMPANION

"You unlock this door with the key of imagination. Beyond it is another dimension . . .

. . . a dimension of sound . . .

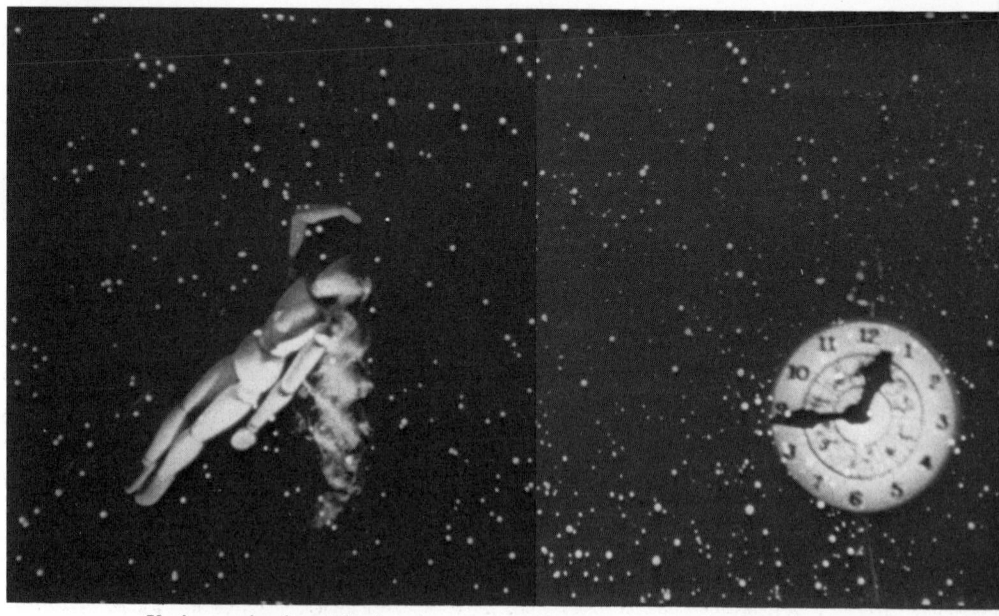

. . . You're moving into a land of both shadow and substance . . .

. . . of things and ideas . . .

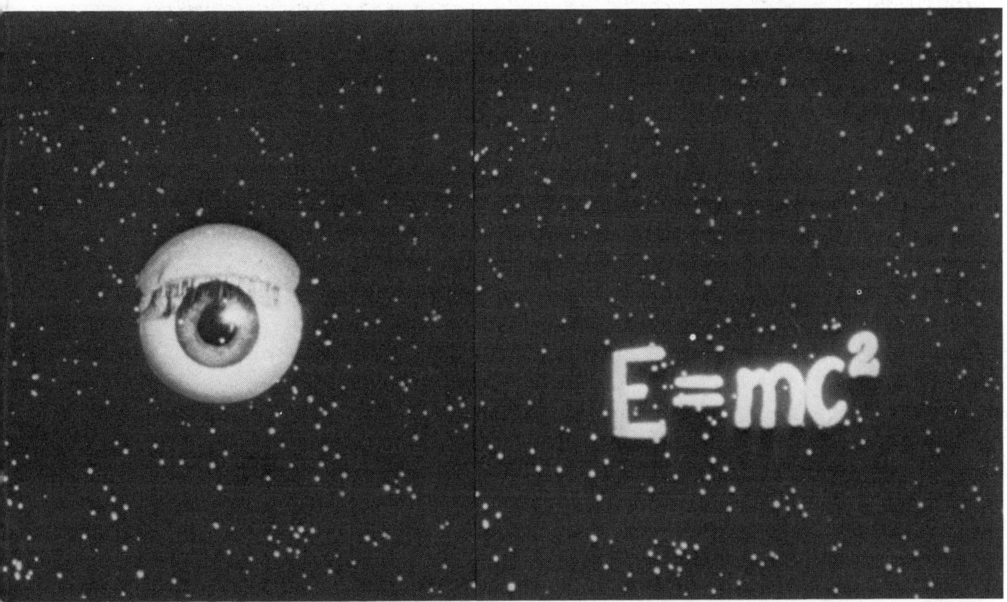

. . . a dimension of sight . . .

. . . a dimension of mind . . .

. . . You've just crossed over . . .

. . . into the Twilight Zone."

THE TWILIGHT ZONE COMPANION

SECOND EDITION

Marc Scott Zicree

SILMAN-JAMES PRESS
Los Angeles

To Gloria Zicree,
mother and true friend

First Silman-James Press Edition 1992

20 19 18 17 16 15 14 13

Library of Congress Cataloging-in-Publication Data

Zicree, Marc Scott
The twilight zone companion / by Marc Scott Zicree.
p. cm.
Includes index.
1. Twilight zone (Television program) I. Title.
PM1992.77.T87Z52 1992 791.45'72—dc20 92-23881

ISBN: 1-879505-09-6

Printed and bound in the United States of America

SILMAN-JAMES PRESS
1181 Angelo Drive
Beverly Hills, CA 90210

CONTENTS

PHOTO CREDITS

Photo courtesy Chris Beaumont—p. 152

Photos courtesy Bob Burns—pp. 142, 143, 146, 174, 175, 202, 235, 248, 278, 289, 377, 403, 407

Photos courtesy Bob Burns and Bob Skotak—pp. 73, 204, 206

Photo courtesy Cosimo Studios—pp. iv, v, 29, 133, 213, 295, 361

Photo courtesy Joe Dante—p. 443

Photo courtesy Bert Granet—p. 18

Photo courtesy Bill Mumy—p. 191

Photos courtesy Tim Murphy—pp. 45, 49, 60, 81, 90, 99, 106, 120, 124, 128, 149, 155, 185, 195, 219, 221, 226, 232, 241, 247, 254, 259, 268, 271, 279, 281, 291, 326, 333, 336, 347, 351, 357, 375, 384, 389, 405, 414, 417, 419, 426

Photo courtesy Maurita Pittman—pp. 215, 216, 246

Photo courtesy *Rod Serling's The Twilight Zone Magazine*—pp. 137, 207, 344, 367, 369, 370, 378, 380, 382, 396, 411

Photo courtesy Carol Serling—pp. 4, 5, 8, 22, 23, 37, 40, 41, 42, 47, 50, 58, 68, 70, 78, 79, 82, 85, 91, 100, 103, 104, 109, 113, 115, 117, 119, 132, 135, 136, 144, 157, 162, 169, 171, 187, 188, 189, 298, 430

Photo courtesy the Serling Archives, Ithaca College School of Communications—pp. ii, iii, 31, 38, 53, 63, 65, 66, 69, 88, 92, 94, 97, 102, 111, 112, 118, 122, 160, 166, 177, 178, 197, 198, 223, 228, 229, 231, 237, 239, 242, 255, 257, 261, 267, 270, 275, 276, 280, 284, 285, 300, 302, 304, 306, 313, 317, 320, 322, 324, 331, 343, 349, 363, 365, 372, 376, 385, 390, 393, 394, 397, 400, 408

Photo courtesy Sonny Fox Productions—p. 12

Photo courtesy Marc Scott Zicree—pp. 2, 9, 48, 55, 72, 74, 126, 139, 141, 151, 158, 164, 173, 181, 183, 200, 217, 224, 249, 263, 265, 286, 309, 315, 339, 366, 373, 392, 402, 410, 413, 420, 421, 424, 433

ACKNOWLEDGMENTS

First of all, thanks must be made to George Clayton Johnson, who first gave me the idea; to my wife Elaine, who talked me into doing it, then selflessly aided and supported me throughout; and to Carol Serling, without whose enormous kindness and assistance this book would not have been possible.

Beyond them, I must express my gratitude to the numerous people connected with *The Twilight Zone* or its creators, who generously provided me with information, photographs and production materials: Buck Houghton, William F. Nolan, Chris Beaumont, George T. Clemens, Richard Matheson, again George Clayton Johnson, Maurita Pittman, Earl Hamner, Jr., Anne Serling, Jodi Serling, Robert J. Serling, Herbert Hirschman, Bert Granet, William Froug, Jerry Sohl, Damon Knight, Jerome Bixby, John Tomerlin, Bill Idelson, John Brahm, James Sheldon, Buzz Kulik, Lamont Johnson, Ralph Nelson, Tony Leader, Richard L. Bare, Alvin Ganzer, Allen Reisner, the late Boris Sagal, Perry Lafferty, Ralph Senensky, Jack Smight, Elliot Silverstein, E. Jack Neuman, Reginald Rose, Lucille Fletcher, Martin Goldsmith, Harlan Ellison, Lillian Gallo, John Erman, Dick Berg, Bill Self, John Conwell, George Ambrose, Phil Barber, OCee Ritch, Bill Mumy, Anne Francis, Robert Lansing, John McLiam, Robert Ellis Miller, Bjo Trimble, Theodore Sturgeon, David Greene, Ben Wright, Norman Corwin, Pat Hingle, Richard Donner, Robert Stevens, Forrest J Ackerman, Ira Steiner, Ray Russell, Edward Denault, Charles Aidman, Liam Sullivan, George Takei, Burgess Meredith, Maxine Stuart, Keenan Wynn, John Hoyt, Ross Martin, Kevin McCarthy, Nehemiah Persoff, Kellam deForest, Richard Corben, William Windom, Richard Kiley, William Shatner, Barney Phillips, John Anderson, Wah Ming Chang, James Gregory, Murray Matheson, Don Gordon, Hollywood Silver Screen, Inc. and Kirk Douglas.

Finally, I must express my appreciation to those people who either lent me equipment, trusted me with irreplaceable items from their collections, provided me with encouragement or in some other way helped the process along: Sam Oldham, Tim Murphy, Bob Burns, Christine Rongone of the Wisconsin Center for Film and Theater Research, the UCLA Television Archive, Minnie Fuhrman, Abe Fuhrman, Judy Fuhrman, Bel Krieger, J. P. Heyes, Marian Powell, Stuart Shostak of Shokus Video, David Abelar, Tova Feder, Erin King, Teddy Tsoneff, Sally and Paul Rubidoux, Neal Mendelsohn, Janet English, Sonny Fox Productions, Elliott Eklund, Betty Steinberg, Bob Costa, Ken Hollywood, J. Michael Reaves, Pat Pedersen, Diane Corwin, Terry Hodel, Lola Johnson, Howard Turner, the crew at Alan's Custom Lab, David Kishiyama, Jerry Neeley, Jim Doherty, Juliette Anthony of the UCLA Theatre Arts Reading Room, Robert Butler, Lisa Mateas and Delores Foster of KTLA, Jim Rondeau, David Ichikawa, Bob Skotak, Henry Holmes, Patricia Murphy, Irwyn Applebaum, Jim Mathenia, Richard Mason, Barbara Benom and the Serling Archives, Ithaca College School of Communications.

A new edition requires additional thanks be made to a number of kind souls. Kevin Fong, Richard A. Mason, Jr., Dennis McGrew, Scott Pitzer, and Howard H. Prouty all provided indices from which the current, improved index derived much of use. Others who provided information, assistance, or other good deeds include L. Dan Rector, Walter E. Thayer, Jr., Robert Anderson, Alan Brennert, Michael Cassutt, Joe Dante, Jim Doherty, Kathryn Drennan, Joel Engle, David Keil, Mark Lungo, Jeffrey S. Menkes, J. D. Feigelson, Harlan Ellison, George R. R. Martin, Mary Radford, Linda Salzman, Edward H. Schwartz, Scott Shen, Ron Cobb, Robin Love, Mark Shelmerdine, J. Michael Straczynski, Karen Weber, and Lawrence T. Wetzel.

In closing, special attention must be accorded to Candace Monteiro, my agent, and Lou Aronica and Betsy Mitchell of Bantam Books, without whom this edition would not have been attempted.

Author's Note on the Second Edition

When I first began researching *The Twilight Zone*, the year was 1977. There was no *Twilight Zone Magazine*, no feature film, no bumper sticker. There was only my own curiosity—and 156 episodes of a television series that had ceased production thirteen years earlier.

To satisfy that curiosity, I spent five years asking questions, screening episodes, burrowing through dusty files, reading teleplays, transcribing tapes and making thousands of pages of notes. The result was this book, which was rejected by more than twenty-five publishers—then went on to become a best-seller and garner an American Book Award nomination.

Admittedly, by the time I'd written the book, my curiosity on the subject had been sated. The hot August day that I completed the manuscript, I turned to my lovely, long-suffering wife (who, without ever really *wanting* to, now knew every episode by title, plotline, and major star) and said, "Honey, let's go to a movie and *forget* about *The Twilight Zone*."

An hour later, we were sitting in an air-conditioned theater, Coke and popcorn in hand. The house lights dimmed. Suddenly, an all-too-familiar voice intoned, "Imagine if you will . . ." It was a trailer for the film *Neighbors* and utilized a Rod Serling soundalike for its pitch.

Clearly, although I thought I was through with *The Twilight Zone*, *it* was not through with *me*.

Since publication of the first edition of *The Twilight Zone Companion*, I've been interviewed by dozens of newspapers, magazines, radio shows and TV programs. Invariably, the question would be asked, "Why, after all these years, is *The Twilight Zone* still popular?"

Particularly when you're on the air live, to hesitate is to be lost, so I'd prepared a ready answer: "I agree with *Twilight Zone* writer Earl Hamner: 'They're great stories well told.' "

Unfortunately, some rude, perceptive fellows would persist. "Yes, but why *Twilight Zone* specifically? What makes it unique?"

"Uh, well, er . . ."

Eventually, it dawned on me that I would actually have to *think* about it. And gradually, an answer came.

After World War II, triumphant soldiers came flooding back home, married their sweethearts and settled into tract homes to raise their kids. The extended family became a thing of the past—and alienation became the great dilemma of our age.

The Twilight Zone was the first, and possibly only, TV series to deal on a regular basis with the theme of alienation—particularly urban alienation. From "Where Is Everybody?" to "The Monsters Are Due on Maple Street," Rod Serling's "fear of the unknown working on you, which you cannot share with others" became the dominant motif. Like the old woman in "Nothing in the Dark," many of us barricade ourselves in our homes, our neighbors strangers, loneliness and fear our only companions. All too often, television itself has been an accomplice in this tragic process, providing anonymous oblivion in its unending, kaleidoscopic parade.

Happily, *The Twilight Zone* proved an exception. Repeatedly, it states a simple message: The only escape from alienation lies in reaching out to others, trusting in their common humanity. Give in to the fear and you are lost.

In the hundreds of letters I've received and the calls I've taken on radio shows, there runs a common thread: an abiding desire to share the ways in which *The Twilight Zone* has touched and enriched people's lives. (Perhaps my favorite came from a young man who confided that *The Twilight Zone* so scared him as a child that, for years, his nightmares featured Rod Serling as host.) At a summer camp, a boy, having taken a bet not to speak for a day, attempts to pantomime the plot of "The Silence." In Washington, a pastor shows episodes to his congregation in order to raise theological questions. In East L.A., an elementary school teacher uses *The Twilight Zone* to spark discussion among his honor students. One day, the principal reads a proclamation: The children have been judged obsolete; they must leave Earth or face liquidation. Their assignment: write a paper detailing their escape route.

In "Kick the Can," Charles Whitley asserts that "there *is* magic in the world." He's right, of course—the magic lies in the caring. In transporting us to other worlds and dimensions, *The Twilight Zone* has brought us face-to-face with ourselves . . . and we are the wiser for the journey.

"This highway leads to the shadowy tip of reality; you're on a through route to the land of the different, the bizarre, the unexplainable . . . Go as far as you like on this road. Its limits are only those of the mind itself. Ladies and gentlemen, you're entering the wondrous dimension of imagination. Next stop—*THE TWILIGHT ZONE*."

—Twilight Zone *opening by Rod Serling;* never used.

INTRODUCTION

If you've bought this book, or if you're reading this introduction in a bookstore, you are reading it for one reason and one reason only: Rod Serling's *The Twilight Zone* entertained you, touched you, and left its mark. You are not alone in this. During its original five-year run on CBS from 1959 to 1964, *The Twilight Zone* attracted an average weekly audience of close to eighteen million people, and since then the numbers that have watched it in syndication have added countless millions more.

When *The Twilight Zone* debuted in 1959, it was a flower blooming in a television desert, made vacant by an endless number of situation comedies, westerns, and cop shows. To its faithful viewers, *The Twilight Zone* offered far more than empty laughs or a lesson in urban or frontier justice. Instead, at its best, it lived up to the promise of its opening narration, revealing a vista of realities not weighed down by the merely probable. At a time when the rest of television was hammering home the unstated but nonetheless apparent message that the realities and expectations of life were bracketed within very narrow borders, *The Twilight Zone* presented a universe of possibilities and options. Most importantly, with few exceptions the characters inhabiting *The Twilight Zone* were average, ordinary people: bank clerks, teachers, petty hoods, salesmen, executives on the rise or decline. It took no great leap for us to identify ourselves with these frail and vulnerable souls and imagine that perhaps in some flight of fancy, some slight tangent from the reality of the ordinary routine, what happened to these characters might very well happen to us.

In the next several hundred pages, we will look behind the magician's curtain, peek into the top hats and under the tables, and learn all the secrets. With minor magic tricks, revelation brings only disappointment, but with luck, examination of *The Twilight Zone*'s grander wizardry will bring greater understanding and appreciation of the intricacies behind the art. The first object of our scrutiny will be the Grand Sorcerer of the Twilight Zone himself, master of ceremonies and principal sleight-of-hand artist. Ladies and gentlemen . . . Mr. Rod Serling.

I / ROD SERLING

If the name Rod Serling were to pop up in some nationwide word association test, virtually everyone in America would venture the automatic response, "*The Twilight Zone*," such is the degree to which Serling's name is attached to his creation. But during the 1950s, prior to *The Twilight Zone,* Serling's name summoned up references of an entirely different nature. He was counted one of a small, elite group of young and innovative writers, among them Paddy Chayefsky and Reginald Rose, whose works were defining television as a dramatic art form, one with a realism surpassing movies and an immediacy rivalling the stage. To public and press alike, Serling was viewed as video's equivalent of Arthur Miller or Tennessee Williams. One commentator even compared him to Sophocles.

Rod Serling

Given this, it came as quite a shock when Serling announced in 1959 that he was going to devote all his energies to a weekly series of science-fiction and fantasy stories.

"To go from writing an occasional drama for *Playhouse 90,* a distinguished and certainly important series, to creating and writing a weekly, thirty-minute television film," he conceded, "was like Stan Musial leaving St. Louis to coach third base in an American Legion little league."

Worse than the change in length, however, was the seemingly 180-degree shift in subject matter. It was as though Serling were saying that he was going to stop commenting on the human condition and go play in a field of daisies. To many, science fiction was considered three notches below grafitti in terms of literary importance. During an interview with Serling on September 22, 1959, TV newsman Mike Wallace said, ". . . [Y]ou're going to be, obviously, working so hard on *The Twilight Zone* that, in essence, for the time being and for the foreseeable future, you've given up on writing anything important for television, right?"

At the time, Serling's harshest critics made the assumption that *The Twilight Zone* was not only a step down but a choice made entirely out of the blue. To any astute observer, however, his decision should have come as no surprise, for it was a totally logical and predictable progression in his career. Like an Agatha Christie mystery, clues leading to Rod Serling's involvement in *The Twilight Zone* were sprinkled throughout his youth and early works.

Rodman Edward Serling was born in Syracuse, New York, on December 25, 1924 ("I was a Christmas present that was delivered unwrapped," he later said). Shortly thereafter, Rod and his family—his brother Robert, seven years his senior, and his parents, Samuel Lawrence Serling, a wholesale meat dealer, and Esther Cooper Serling—moved to Binghamton, a small city in upstate New York where, throughout his childhood, Rod's imagination and creativity were allowed to flourish.

"He was about the greatest extrovert you could ever hope for," says Bob Serling, now a successful novelist (*The President's Plane Is Missing*). "He was a good-looking kid and he knew it. Very popular, very articulate, very outspoken. He had no arrogance—it was confidence. There was a hell of a difference.

"We were fairly close as kids and we played together a hell of a lot, despite the seven-year difference. The two of us used to read *Amazing Stories, Astounding Stories, Weird Tales*—all of the pulps. If we saw a movie together, we'd come home and act it out, just for the two of us. Our bikes became airplanes with machine guns on them. We were always playing cowboys."

Rod Serling, his mother and father

Rod was not bookish by any means; he was outgoing, enthusiastic, loved to be center stage. "His mouth was hinged open like the front end of a steam shovel running amok," Bob Serling recalls. "The big treat for the family was to drive from Binghamton to Syracuse, which was seventy miles away, and my father once tipped us off that nobody was to say a word from the start of the trip *until Rod stopped talking*. Now, in those days it took approximately two and a half hours to drive the seventy miles and, so help me, he never stopped talking from the time he got into the car to the time we arrived in Syracuse. My mother and father were in absolute hysterics. He must have been six or seven years old. He was in a world all by himself. He'd sing, he'd act out dialogue, he'd talk to us without waiting for answers. He just kept talking.

"He was that way all through school, that I can remember. A class leader, always into dramatics. He'd try out for anything. There was some kind of compulsion in him to do something that nobody else—the ordinary kid—wouldn't do. And this included joining the paratroopers in World War II. He was a damn fool to do it."

The day he graduated high school, Rod enlisted in the U.S. Army 11th Airborne Division paratroopers. During basic training, he took up boxing for extra pay and privileges, winning seventeen out of eighteen bouts.

Following basic training, he was sent into combat in the Pacific. In 1945, while Rod was fighting in the Philippines, his father died of a heart attack at the age of fifty-two. When Rod was finally able to return to Binghamton, it was to a home lacking forever the security and stability he had known as a child.

Without World War II, there is no way of knowing whether or not Serling would have become a writer, but the war both broadened his experience and placed an emotional pressure on him that demanded catharsis. "I had been injured with the paratroopers [a severe shrapnel wound in the wrist and knee requiring hospitalization] and I was bitter about everything and at loose ends when I got out of the service. I think I turned to writing to get it off my chest."

Upon his discharge from the Army in 1946, Rod enrolled at Antioch College in Yellow Springs, Ohio, on the G.I. Bill. "I really didn't know what the hell I wanted to do with my life, but I went to Antioch because my brother [had gone] there. I majored in physical ed that first year because I was interested in working with kids." But physical education couldn't fill the pressing need he had for self-expression. He soon changed his major to language and literature. During the war he had written scripts for Armed Services Radio, as well as lots of bad poetry. Now radio seemed the ideal medium. He became manager of the Antioch Broadcasting System's radio workshop and wrote, directed and acted in weekly, full-scale productions which were broadcast over radio WJEM, Springfield. During the 1948–49 school year, the entire output of the workshop was written by Serling, and, with the exception of one adaptation, all the scripts were entirely original. Later, he would call this work "pretty bad stuff," adding, "Style is something you develop by copying the style of someone who writes well. For a while you're a cheap imitation. I was a Hemingway imitator. Everything I wrote began, 'It was hot.'" However, he was getting invaluable training and discipline, plus his first taste of practical business matters: every script he wrote he mailed out to at least one national radio show for consideration.

In the fall of 1946, Rod met Carolyn Louise Kramer, a strikingly attractive, articulate, no-nonsense young lady of seventeen, majoring in

The Serling family

education and psychology. Serling was twenty-one. Says Carol of their first meeting, "He struck me as being very intelligent, with a wonderful sense of humor. And there was something about him that fascinated me. I had never met anyone who was as self-assured before."

Initially, Carol was a little wary of Rod. "He had the reputation at Antioch College of being quite a ladies' man," she recalls. "He had dated just about every other girl in the school before he got to me." Soon it became clear to both that theirs was more than just a passing college romance. In the summer of 1948, the two were married. It was a marriage that would last until Serling's death twenty-seven years later.

Marriage did little to tone Serling down. If anything, the emotional security of a wife increased his creativity and his determination to succeed. Also undiminished was his often outrageous sense of humor.

Carol Serling: "I remember one time it was dark and we were in a trailer which had two hatches in the top which could be opened to let in fresh air. I had to go out for a moment and when I returned Rod had disappeared. Then I looked up and there was this head hanging through the open hatch. In the darkness of the trailer it looked horrible and I screamed.

"It was Rod hanging upside down on top of the trailer . . . He got stuck in the hatch and friends had to free him. I thought he really deserved it."

Serling's first big break came on March 16, 1949, while he was still a college student. *Dr. Christian,* a radio show that obtained all its scripts through an annual contest (its slogan was "the only show on radio where the audience writes the scripts") sent him a telegram informing him that his script, "To Live a Dream," had won second prize. "The prizes included five hundred dollars cash and an all-expense-paid trip to New York for me and Carol," Serling recalled. "By the time we were dizzily installed in a big suite of rooms in a plush midtown hotel I felt like Norman Corwin!" Carol Serling noted, "The college newspaper ran a story about it with a headline that said, 'Serling Goes to Christian Reward.'"

"To Live a Dream," was about a prizefighter slowly dying of leukemia who keeps a stiff upper lip while starting a younger fighter on the road to the top. That same year, Rod sold two radio scripts to *Grand Central Station,* and the following year, his first television script, "Grady Everett for the People," to *Stars Over Hollywood* for one hundred dollars.

Upon graduation, Rod and Carol moved to Cincinnati, where Rod got a job as a staff writer with WLW radio. His duties, though numerous, were less than fulfilling. He provided folksy banter for two entertainers he described as "a hayseed M.C. who strummed a guitar and said 'Shucks, friends,' and a girl yodeler whose falsetto could break a beer mug at twenty paces." He composed phony testimonials for a patent medicine remedy

("It had about twelve percent alcohol by volume and, if the testimonials were to be believed, could cure everything from arthritis to a fractured pelvis"). He wrote documentaries honoring local towns, of which he said: "In most cases, the towns I was assigned to honor had little to distinguish them save antiquity. Any dramatization beyond the fact that they existed physically, usually had one major industry, a population and a founding date was more fabrication than documentation."

Rod was desperate to break away from this and devote all his energies to writing things he sincerely cared about, but at the same time he was a married man with responsibilities. At best, freelance writing was a tremendous financial risk, one he was extremely hesitant to take. So, for a short time, his schedule went like this: write all day at WLW, come home, have dinner and write all evening on his own projects. "It was during this double-shift period that I collected forty rejection slips in a row. Nobody but a beginning writer can realize just how crushing this is to the ego."

Clearly, this was an impossible situation. "The process of writing cannot be juggled with another occupation," Serling wrote in 1957. "Writing is a demanding profession and a selfish one. And because it is selfish and demanding, because it is compulsive and exacting, I didn't embrace it. I succumbed to it." Rod quit his job at WLW. "For lush or lean, good or bad, Sardi's or malnutrition, I'd launched a career."

Fortunately for Serling, his timing couldn't have been better. In 1951, television was much easier to break into than it is today. Today, there are virtually no anthology shows, but in 1951 they were all over the dial. If one show rejected his script, Rod could send it, with no changes whatsoever, to another. During his first year freelancing, he earned just under $5,000, selling scripts to such shows as *Hallmark Hall of Fame*, *Lux Video Theater*, *Kraft Television Theater*, *Suspense*, and *Studio One*. It was hard work, but it was a living—and Serling was his own man.

A lot of these early scripts were rough, underdeveloped, hurried; some, admittedly, were still "pretty bad stuff." But to be fair, it should be said that if they were bad at least they were bad in the right direction. A quality which could be seen in these scripts, even as it can be seen in Serling's later scripts for *The Twilight Zone*, was that even the worst of them revealed a primary concern for people and their problems. Sometimes the situations were clichéd, the characters two-dimensional, but always there was at least some search for an emotional truth, some attempt to make a statement on the human condition.

Needless to say, this is *not* what most television concerned itself with in the early fifties (or today, for that matter). For example, take this television guide from the Cincinnati *Times-Star* of November 12, 1953, reprinted verbatim. These program listings include time and channel, and were listed under the heading *DRAMA:*

6:30 12—Superman's secret identity is threatened by a gangster's dog.

7:00 9—Captain Video advises Rangers to blast at full space speed.

7:30 9—Tom Conway stars as Inspector Mark Saber.

8:00 5—Joan complicates Brad's hobby of collecting tropical fish.

8:30 9—Colonel Flack outswindles a tout at the racetrack.

8:30 5—"My Little Margie" causes "A Slight Misunderstanding" worth $35,000.

9:00 5—Cincinnatian Rod Serling's "A Long Time Till Dawn", story of tumultuous conflict in a young poet, is produced.

Given this kind of comparison, it's easy to see why young Serling, only twenty-eight in 1953, quickly gained the notice of both the public and a number of television critics.

James Dean in "A Long Time Till Dawn"

Rod Serling

On Wednesday, January 12, 1955, *Kraft Television Theater* presented Serling's seventy-second television script. To Rod and Carol, at the time, the script seemed little different from the seventy-one before it and they expected it to receive no greater reaction. Says Carol of that evening, "I remember that we had some business to do in upstate New York—we were living in Connecticut—and we got a babysitter for our daughter, Jodi, and said, 'We just moved into Connecticut. No one will call us, nothing will happen.' And while we were in upstate New York, the show was on."

The name of the show was "Patterns."

"One minute after the show went off the air my phone started to ring," Serling said seven years later. "It's been ringing ever since."

"Patterns" dramatized a struggle for power involving three men: Ramsey, the ruthless president of a major corporation (superbly played by Everett Sloane); Andy Sloane (Ed Begley), the aging vice-president Ramsey wants to pressure into resigning; and Fred Staples (Richard Kiley), the unwitting but basically decent young hotshot brought in to replace Andy. It was simple, direct, and tremendously powerful. The reaction to it was overwhelming.

"Nothing in months has excited the television industry as much as the Kraft Television Theater's production of 'Patterns', an original play by Rod Serling," Jack Gould wrote in the *New York Times*. "The enthusiasm is justified. In writing, acting, and direction, 'Patterns' will stand as one of the high points in the TV medium's evolution. . . . For sheer power of narrative, forcefulness of characterization and brilliant climax, Mr. Serling's work is a creative triumph that can stand on its own." Gould's reaction was typical. From coast to coast, newspaper critics hailed Serling a brilliant new find.

On February 9, 1955, a little under a month after the original broadcast, "Patterns" was again performed live, by popular demand. This was unprecedented. On March 17, 1956, "Patterns" won for Serling the first of what would eventually be six Emmys. And on March 27, 1956, a little over a year after the initial airing, the movie version of "Patterns" was released. It was directed by Fielder Cook, who had directed the television show, and starred Everett Sloane, Eg Begley, and, in the Kiley role, Van Heflin.

Thanks to "Patterns," Serling was now a "hot" property. In two weeks after its initial broadcast, he received twenty-three firm offers for television writing assignments, three motion picture offers, fourteen requests for interviews from major newspapers and magazines, two offers of lunch from Broadway producers, and two offers to discuss novels with publishers.

Accordingly, Serling took a lot of these people up on their offers: ". . . I was the hungry kid left all alone in the candy store. Man, I just *grabbed*!" That season alone, he had twenty of his plays telecast, earning him eighty thousand dollars. Most of these scripts were ones he had written in college and just afterward in Cincinnati for a local television program called *The Storm*.

"I found I could sell everything I had—and I did," Serling said later. "I realize now I was wrong; a lot of them should have stayed in the trunk . . . I had three bad shows on the air in [one] two week period. Not since the British raided Cologne had so many bombs landed in such a small space in such a short time."

The movie offers were taken up, too. The first script that Serling worked on was 20th Century-Fox's *Between Heaven and Hell,* which was eventually done by six other writers. Serling: "I turned in a script that would conservatively have run for nine hours on the screen. I think it was about 500 pages long. I didn't know what the hell I was doing. They just said, 'Here's fifteen hundred a week,' and so I just wrote and wrote. I lay claim to the fact that there were some wonderful moments in it—but in nine hours of film, my God, there *has* to be a couple of wonderful moments if a guy just blows his nose!"

Serling wrote a handful of screenplays during this period which were never made, including an adaptation of John Christopher's science fiction novel *No Blade of Grass*. Other than *Patterns,* only one Serling script *was* produced, a western called *Saddle the Wind,* of which he later said, "I gave better dialogue to the horses than the actors."

This is not to say everything Serling wrote during this period was bad. His screenplay for *Patterns,* in which he expanded his original script from a running time of fifty-three minutes to eighty-four minutes, was skillful and intense. Then, too, there was "The Rack," an hour-long drama on the *United States Steel Hour,* which was an honest and powerful investigation into the after-effects of mental torture on American POWs in Korea (later made into a film starring Paul Newman, with a script by Stewart Stern). But nothing he wrote during the year or so following "Patterns" seemed to have either the same dramatic punch or the power to remain long imbedded in the public mind. This point was driven home to Serling when, during a network interview, he was introduced as "Rod Serling, the man who wrote 'Patterns' and" (a long pause) ". . . and . . . well . . . here he is—Rod Serling."

The pressure was on. "I had something to prove, first to others and then to myself. I had to prove that 'Patterns' wasn't all I had. There had been other things before and there would be other things to follow."

On October 4, 1956, CBS debuted a ninety-minute, weekly series called *Playhouse 90*. The aim of the show was ambitious: to recruit the best actors, writers and directors and to air shows of a quality never before seen on television. In this aim, they were largely successful. Stars on *Playhouse 90* included Paul Muni, Charles Laughton, Melvyn Douglas, Cliff Robertson, Jason Robards, Ethel Barrymore, Shirley Booth, Boris Karloff, Franchot Tone, Geraldine Page and Sterling Hayden. Original presentations included "The Miracle Worker," "Judgment at Nuremberg," and "The Days of Wine and Roses"—all later made into films. Three out of every four shows were to be live, with the fourth on film. Budget was set at $100,000 per episode.

The first episode was "Forbidden Area," with a script by Serling from a novel by Pat Frank. The cast consisted of Charlton Heston, Vincent Price, and Tab Hunter. If either Serling or the executives behind *Playhouse 90* expected to have their reputations made by this show, they were quickly disillusioned. The reviews were not glowing, nor should they have been, considering the plot of this Cold War "thriller." Air Force nuclear bombers are mysteriously being blown up in flight. One-eyed Major Charlton Heston suspects sabotage. Ultimately, the enemy within is uncovered. Tab Hunter, a cook in the Strategic Air Command kitchen, has been smuggling bombs inside the coffee Thermoses the bomber pilots have been taking with them on their flights! "It presented a war drama that ran the gamut of hokum," wrote a less-than-enthusiastic Jack Gould in the *New York Times*. "Mr. Serling's script had everything in it but the proverbial kitchen sink." Clearly, this was not the play to top "Patterns."

But as it turned out, the second *Playhouse 90* was.

"Requiem for a Heavyweight," the first original ninety-minute show ever written for television, aired October 11, 1956. An enormously touch-

Keenan Wynn, Jack Palance and Ed Wynn in "Requiem for a Heavyweight"

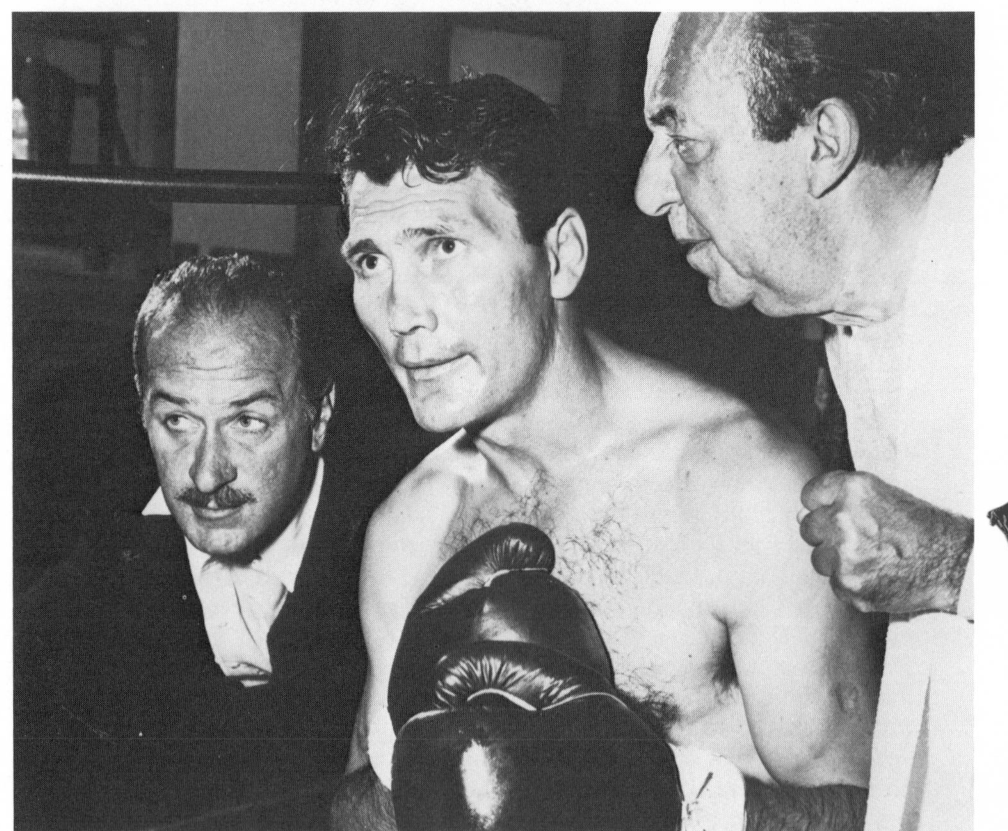

ing story, it starred Jack Palance as Harlan "Mountain" McClintock, a fighter on the rapid and ugly decline, Keenan Wynn as his unscrupulous manager, Ed Wynn as his sympathetic trainer and Kim Hunter as a concerned social worker.

Serling's close friend, producer Dick Berg, was with Rod that evening. "I spent the night with him at his house in Connecticut with our respective wives the night that 'Requiem' ran, and I must say he was quite uncertain as to what the reception would be. Those were the live television days and you waited until the *New York Times* arrived the next morning before you could determine whether or not you had a good show. And while we felt rather warmly toward it, there was no persuading Rod that it worked until Jack Gould of the *New York Times* told him it worked.

"And in fact, our morning *New York Times* arrived and the review was missing, because Gould simply wanted more time. And when the later edition came with the review, it was the first of thousands all over the country—and, of course, it was the accolade of the decade."

"Requiem for a Heavyweight" swept the 1956 Emmy Awards, winning for best single show of the year, best teleplay, best direction (Ralph Nelson), best single performance (Jack Palance), and best art direction (Albert Heschong). Serling was also awarded the Sylvania Award, the Television–Radio Writers Annual Award for Writing Achievement, and the George Foster Peabody Award (the first writing award ever given in the seventeen-year history of the Peabodys).

The years that followed were bright for Serling. In 1957, his adaptation of Ernest Lehman's short story, "The Comedian," starring Mickey Rooney, won him his third Emmy. "The Dark Side of the Earth," about the unsuccessful Hungarian revolt against Russia, won critical acclaim. So, too, did "A Town Has Turned to Dust" and "The Rank and File" in 1958 and "The Velvet Alley," his partially autobiographical story of a TV writer's rise to the top, in 1959. All of these were scripts for *Playhouse 90* and each one brought him $10,000. In January of 1958, he signed a contract with MGM to write four screenplays for a total of $250,000. In February, he, Carol, and daughters Jodi and Anne, ages five and two respectively, moved into a sumptuous, two-story house in Pacific Palisades.

Artistically and financially, Serling was a very successful man. So why then, in 1957, did he begin looking for an alternative to *Playhouse 90* and motion pictures, an alternative that would eventually become *The Twilight Zone?*

Perhaps a small part of the answer comes from this seemingly trivial fact: prior to the initial broadcast of a show he'd written, it was decided that the Chrysler Building had to be painted out of New York skyline as seen through an office window on the set because the sponsor of the show was the Ford Motor Company.

Or this: on a program called *Appointment with Adventure,* the words "American" and "lucky" were stricken from his script and "United States" and "fortunate" put in their place because the sponsor was a tobacco company concerned that the words might remind viewers of rival brands of cigarettes.

Or this: prior to the broadcast of "Requiem for a Heavyweight," the line "Got a match?" was struck because the sponsor was Ronson lighters.

Or, more importantly, *this:* in 1956, Serling wrote "Noon on Doomsday" for *United States Steel Hour*. The plot concerned a violent neurotic who kills an elderly Jew and then is acquitted by residents of the small town in which he lives.

Before the show was broadcast, a reporter asked him if the script was based on the Emmett Till case, in which a black, fourteen-year-old boy was kidnapped and murdered in Mississippi and the murderers were acquitted by an all-white local jury. Serling replied, "If the shoe fits . . ." *Variety* and others reported that "Noon on Dooomsday" *was* based on the Till case. Three thousand letters poured into the offices of U.S. Steel threatening a boycott. "I asked the agency men at the time how the problem of boycott applied to the United States Steel company," Serling later wrote. "Did this mean that from then on that all construction from Tennessee on down would be done with aluminum? Their answer was that the concern of the sponsor was not so much an economic boycott as the resultant strain in public relations."

U.S. Steel demanded changes in the script. The town was moved from an unspecified area to New England. The murdered Jew was changed to an unnamed foreigner. Bottles of Coca-Cola were removed from the set and the word "lynch" stricken from the script (both having been determined "too Southern" in their connotation). Characters were made to say "This is a strange little town" or "This is a perverse town," so that no one would identify with it. Finally, they wanted to change the vicious, neurotic killer into "just a good decent, American boy momentarily gone wrong." Serling: "It was a Pier 6 brawl to stop this alteration of character." When it was finally aired in April of 1956, "Noon on Doomsday" was so watered down as to be meaningless.

Two years later, Serling made another stab at an Emmett Till kind of story with "A Town Has Turned to Dust" for *Playhouse 90*. He fared no better.

"By the time 'A Town Has Turned to Dust' went before the cameras, *my* script had turned to dust," said Serling. "Emmett Till became, as *Time* noted, a romantic Mexican who loved the storekeeper's wife, but 'only with his eyes.' My sheriff couldn't commit suicide because one of our sponsors was an insurance firm and they claimed that suicide often leads to complications in settling policy claims. The lynch victim was called Clemson, but we couldn't use this 'cause South Carolina had an all-white college by that name. The setting was moved to the Southwest in the 1870s . . . The phrase 'Twenty men in hoods' became 'Twenty men in homemade masks.' They chopped it up like a roomful of butchers at work on a steer."

In the introduction to his 1957 collection of television plays, *Patterns,* Serling related a series of events which occurred during the production of "The Arena," a show for *Studio One* dealing with the United States Senate. As usual, absurd demands were made. ". . . I was not permitted to have my Senators discuss any current or pressing problem. To talk of tariff was to align oneself with the Republicans; to talk of labor was to suggest control by the Democrats. To say a single thing germane to the current political scene was absolutely prohibited. So, on television in April of 1956, several million viewers got treated to an incredible display on the floor of the United States Senate of groups of Senators shouting, gesticulating and talking in hieroglyphics about make-believe issues, using invented terminology, in a kind of prolonged, unbelievable double-talk."

In general, Serling's experiences on "The Arena" were little different from those he'd had on "Noon on Doomsday" or "A Town Has Turned to Dust." What *was* different was his conclusion: "In retrospect, I probably would have had a much more adult play had I made it science fiction, put it in the year 2057, and peopled the Senate with robots. This would probably have been more reasonable and no less dramatically incisive." To go from this reasoning to *The Twilight Zone* took no great mental leap. It was an option Serling greeted with relief.

"I don't think it far-fetched that he should have been as impressed as he was by science fiction," says producer Dick Berg, "particularly because he had much on his mind politically and in terms of social condition, and science fiction—and *Twilight Zone* specifically—gave him as much flexibility in developing those themes as he might have had anywhere else at that time. Within the parameters of his own store, such as he enjoyed on *Twilight Zone,* he could do anything he wanted. He could do a story about Nazis, about racism in general, about economic plight, about whatever, and fit it within the framework. So it became a natural habitat for him creatively."

Other factors contributed to Serling's decision to enter into series television. By the late 1950s, live television was a dying art form. The basic economic reality was inescapable: a live show could be aired only once while a show on film could be shown again and again. Dick Berg: "I think it's important to understand that in the life of one of the more significant guys of the mid–twentieth century, this science-fiction series was a kind of life raft, an escape hatch. It was an arena for self-expression such as he was no longer able to enjoy with the demise of the live anthology shows on television. And when eight of them went off the air in a twelve- or eighteen-month period, *Twilight Zone* provided Rod with the most satisfying replacement possible for that anthology market."

So, on a day in 1957, Serling went to his file cabinet and pulled out a half-hour script he had written shortly after graduating college. It was "The Time Element," an imaginative time-travel fantasy that had been aired on *The Storm* in Cincinnati. He expanded the script to an hour and had his secretary type these words on the front page:

"THE TWILIGHT ZONE"
THE TIME ELEMENT
BY
ROD SERLING

Then he submitted it to CBS.

II / ENTERING THE TWILIGHT ZONE

"Let's not kid ourselves about *Twilight Zone*. A lot of luck was involved in selling that to anyone. It was a show no one wanted to buy." **—ROD SERLING**

To say that CBS greeted "The Time Element" with less than open arms would be an understatement. They did buy the script, but then promptly shelved it. And it would undoubtedly have remained on the shelf to this day, gathering dust like so many other worthy projects, had it not been for the efforts of a man named Bert Granet.

Even today, Granet seems a tough, hard-nosed realist who fights hard for the things he wants. In 1958, he was producing *Westinghouse Desilu Playhouse*, a series featuring pedestrian dramas three weeks out of four and situation comedies starring Lucille Ball and Desi Arnaz every fourth week. In years past he had encountered his share of difficulties while producing motion pictures such as *Berlin Express*, directed by Jacques Tourneur, and *The Marrying Kind*, directed by George Cukor and starring Judy Holliday, but on *Desilu Playhouse* he faced a new problem: how to lend prestige to a television show that had absolutely no pretensions to great art.

Granet went about solving his problem in two ways: first, by securing big-name film actors to star and, secondly, by buying up scripts from top television writers. Rod Serling was definitely a name he wanted on the credits of his show.

Through a mutual friend, television and film director Robert Parrish (who later directed "One for the Angels," "A Stop at Willoughby," "Mr. Bevis," and part of "The Mighty Casey" for *The Twilight Zone*), Granet was introduced to Serling. "Rod remembered that he had once sold something to CBS, and CBS wasn't doing anything with it," Granet recalls. "So, using great persuasion, I found out what it was, got to CBS, and bought it for what was a lot of money at that time—ten thousand dollars."

"The Time Element" was put on the production schedule of *Desilu Playhouse* for the 1958–59 season. As with every other script of the series, McCann-Erickson, the advertising agency representing Westinghouse, the show's sponsor, had script approval. Granet recalls their reaction. "I got a

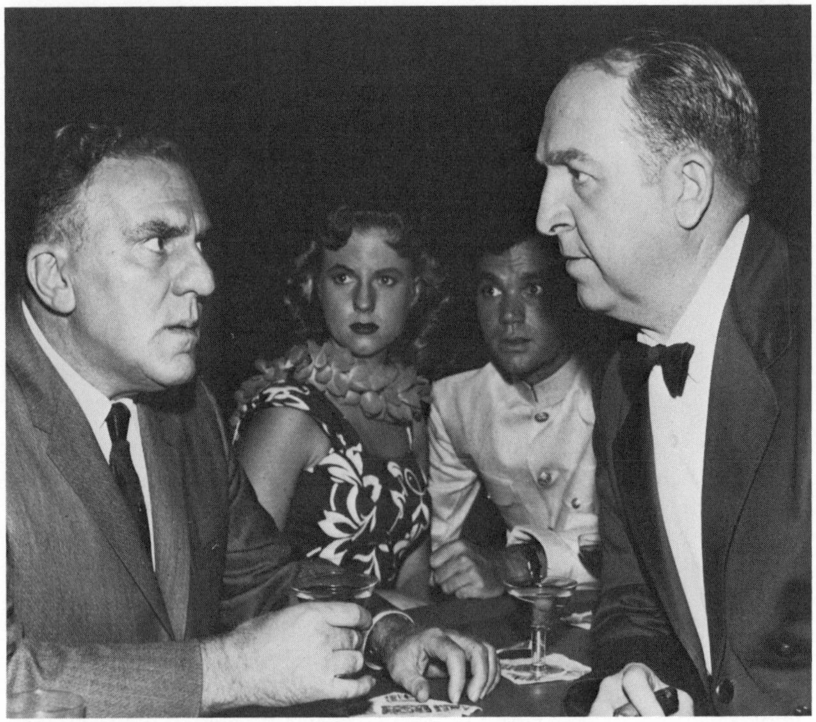

William Bendix, Carol Kearney, Darryl Hickman and Jesse White

call from New York: 'Absolutely, flatly no.' They didn't want any unfinished stories. They wanted neat bows at the end where each story wrapped up, unlike *Twilight Zone* stories which gave you many outs, many possibilities of using the imagination.

"So I said, 'Well, I want to do it.' And with that, they flew out about four important vice-presidents to tell me why not. And I must say, at this point all it would have meant was swallowing ten thousand dollars in not doing it. But [Desi] Arnaz backed me up."

Reluctantly, McCann-Erickson relented, but not before setting up a few conditions. "They said if we did it I had to make a blood promise that I would *never* do that kind of a story again." Then there was the matter of the script itself. In Serling's original draft, the main character tries unsuccessfully to warn the Army of the impending attack on Pearl Harbor. But Westinghouse had a number of government contracts; they couldn't risk offending the Pentagon. The character would *not* try to warn the Army.

Once past this point, the production moved ahead smoothly. Granet hired director Allen Reisner, a talented man who had worked with Serling material before. Together, they assembled a cast of strong professionals, with William Bendix in the lead, supported by Martin Balsam, Darryl Hickman, and Jesse White. The budget was approximately $135,000.

On November 24, 1958, "The Time Element" was aired on CBS. The story, as finally presented, was an intriguing one. Pete Jenson (Bendix), a "part-time unsuccessful bookie," card dealer and bartender, seeks out the aid of Dr. Gillespie (Balsam), a psychiatrist. He explains that he's been having a recurring dream in which he finds himself in Honolulu on December 6, 1941—the day before the attack on Pearl Harbor. In his dream, he tries to warn a number of people of the attack, including a young naval ensign (Hickman) and his bride (Carol Kearney), and a newspaper editor (Bartlett Robinson). Predictably, no one takes him seriously.

Dr. Gillespie understands perfectly how this could be a most unpleasant dream, but he is astounded when Jenson reveals that he believes these events are real, that he is in fact going back in time! The doctor tries to explain to Jenson the plain impossibility of time travel, but Jenson counters with:

"I've never been in Honolulu in my whole life before, except during that dream. So after the first couple of times I dreamed this I decided I'd put it to a test. I knew the ensign's last name. It was an odd one: Janosky. He told me that he and his girl had come from a little town called White Oak, Wisconsin. I placed a call there. There was only one Janosky in the book. A woman answered the phone. She told me she was his mother. I told her that I was an old friend of his from Honolulu and I asked was he there . . . And then she told me that her son and his wife were killed in Honolulu on December seventh, 1941."

On the psychiatrist's couch, Jenson falls asleep. His dream picks up where it last left off, on the morning of December 7, 1941. Through the French doors of his hotel room he sees a number of Japanese planes coming in for a bombing run. Jenson cries out, "I told you! Why wouldn't anybody listen to me?" His only answer comes with the sound of an explosion, as the panes of the French doors shatter and the room comes down on top of him.

In his office, Dr. Gillespie lifts his head with a start. He is alone. Vaguely, he knows something is amiss, but *what*? He checks his appointment book; no appointments today. To steady himself, he goes into a bar down the street and orders a drink. On the wall behind the bar, he notices a picture of Pete Jenson. For some reason he can't quite put his finger on, he feels a sense of disquiet.

"Who's the guy in the picture?" he asks the bartender (Paul Bryer).

"Oh, that's Pete Jenson," the bartender answers. "He used to tend bar here. Know him?"

"No." Gillespie shrugs. "Just looked familiar, that's all. Where is he now?"

"He's dead," the bartender replies. "He was killed at Pearl Harbor."

But the episode doesn't end there. Apparently, the sponsor was still extremely nervous about the ambiguous ending, and so at the end of the show Desi Arnaz stepped out and offered his "rational" explanation of the events: "We wonder if Pete Jenson did go back in time or if he ever existed. My personal answer is that the doctor has seen Jenson's picture at the bar sometime before and had a dream. Any of you out there have any other answers? Let me know." This prompted one irate journalist to write, "GO HOME, DESI!"

Compared with *Twilight Zone* episodes to come, "The Time Element" stands as no great masterpiece of television. The direction is competent but not brilliant. The acting, though sincere, is unconvincing. And although Nick Musuraca (*Cat People, Curse of the Cat People, The Spiral Staircase*) was director of photography, the episode looks flat and featureless, typical television drab. The importance of "The Time Element" lay not in what it *was*, but rather in what it *did*.

"The Time Element" received more mail than any other episode of *Desilu Playhouse* that year, and the newspaper reviews were universally good. This was enough to convince CBS that it had made an error in shelving Serling's script. It was decided that a pilot of *The Twilight Zone* would be made.

William Dozier, vice-president in charge of West Coast Programming for CBS, assigned William Self, a recent recruit to the CBS corporate hierarchy, to oversee the project. It was a good choice; just prior to joining CBS, Self had spent four years as producer of *Schlitz Playhouse of Stars*, a successful half-hour anthology series.

In order to make a pilot, the first thing Self needed was a script. Serling had written "The Time Element" intending it to be the pilot, but since it had just been done as a *Desilu Playhouse* it was no longer available. So Serling wrote a new script entitled "The Happy Place." An hour in length, this script dealt with a totalitarian society of the future in which people who reach the age of sixty are routinely escorted to concentration camps, euphemistically referred to as "The Happy Place," and exterminated.

The main characters of the piece are Dr. Harris, a fifty-eight-year-old surgeon who remembers the good old days of freedom and justice for all; his son Steven, director of one of the camps (which, by the way, appear in every way to be ideal retirement communities—except that the old folks go into elevators and never emerge); and his grandson Paul, a Hitler Youth type, thoroughly propagandized. Because of his outspokenness against the

State, Dr. Harris's records are changed so that his age is listed as sixty. The order goes out to have him brought in for execution. Although Steven is unwilling to resign from his post in order to save his father, he is sympathetic to the point where he is willing to bring clothing, food, and a gun to his father's hiding place. But just as father and son meet, the police burst in and fatally shoot the elder man.

In the final scene of the script, we learn that it was Paul who, as a good citizen of the State, informed the police of his grandfather's whereabouts. In closing, Paul tells his father the extermination age is too high; it should be fifty. Nervously, Steven replies, "Now you're getting close to my age, Paul." To which Paul, the hope of the future, replies, *"I know!"*

William Dozier gave the script to Bill Self and asked for an opinion. "It was, I thought, very downbeat and depressing," Self recalls. "An interesting episode, but it would never sell as a series. I reported this to Dozier, who said, 'Oh Jesus, what are we going to do with Serling? He loves it!' I said, 'Well, I don't know Serling, but why don't we have a meeting?'

"So we had a meeting, and I told Rod that I didn't like it and why I didn't like it, and rather than being belligerent about it, which Dozier had anticipated he might be, he said, 'Okay, then I'll go write another one.' And he went away and he wrote a completely new script."

The new script Serling turned in bore the title "Where Is Everybody?" and it proved an ideal selection. Its plot was utterly straightforward, dealing with an amnesiac who is unable to locate any other human beings in a small town. Ultimately, it is revealed that the entire sequence of events has been hallucinated by the main character, whose mind has snapped during an isolation experiment. "Where Is Everybody?" was a thoroughly rational story draped in the trappings of science fiction. If anything would allay the fears of science-fiction-leery network and advertising executives, this would.

Robert Stevens, a friend of William Dozier's and veteran director of numerous episodes of *Alfred Hitchcock Presents,* was hired to direct the pilot. Earl Holliman was cast as Mike Ferris. It was vital that the look and sound of the show match the peculiar mood of the writing, so special care was taken in the selection of a director of photography and a composer. Cinematographer Joseph La Shelle (*Laura, Marty, The Apartment,* and *The Chase*) was elected to capture *The Twilight Zone* on film and composer Bernard Herrmann (*Citizen Kane, Psycho, The Day the Earth Stood Still,* and *North by Northwest* just scratch the surface of his credits) was chosen to give music to *The Twilight Zone.* (Herrmann's original theme music for the show—a subtle and lovely piece scored for strings, harp, flute and brass—survived through most of the first season, then was replaced by the more familiar rythmic theme by French avant-garde composer Marius Constant.) Because they offered the numerous backlot sets needed for the episode, the facilities of Universal International Studios were chosen for the shooting of the pilot.

The pilot was an expensive one, and this concerned a number of network executives. "My impression is that the budget was somewhere around $75,000," says Bill Self, "which in those days was very high for a half-hour pilot. Today, a half-hour pilot's like $225,000 to $250,000, so it seems cheap by today's standards."

Rehearsal and shooting of the pilot took a total of nine days. The film was dubbed, scored and edited in three, and then flown immediately to New York to be screened for prospective sponsors. There, it took only six hours to sell. On March 8, 1959, General Foods, represented by the Young and Rubicam agency, signed with CBS as the primary sponsor of *The Twilight Zone*. Soon after, Kimberly-Clark, makers of Kleenex products, signed on as secondary sponsor. "It was all very smooth," Self remembers. "It was not a hard sale. It was a good pilot, as you know."

A contract was drawn up between CBS and Serling. It stipulated that *The Twilight Zone* would be produced by Serling's company, Cayuga Productions (named after Cayuga Lake in upstate New York, where Serling and family vacationed each summer) and that Serling would write eighty percent of the first season's scripts. In return for this service, Serling would own fifty percent of the series plus the original negatives, with CBS owning the other fifty percent. Within two months of the signing of the contracts, the series had a full crew assigned to it, with production of the first season's episodes under way.

"WHERE IS EVERYBODY?" (originally broadcast 10/2/59)

Earl Holliman

Written by Rod Serling
Producer: William Self
Director: Robert Stevens
Director of Photography: Joseph La Shelle
Music: Bernard Herrmann

Cast:
Mike Ferris: Earl Holliman
Air Force General: James Gregory
With: John Conwell, Paul Langton, James McCallion, Jay Overholts, Carter Mulavey, Jim Johnson, and Gary Walberg

"The place is here, the time is now, and the journey into the shadows that we're about to watch could be our *journey."*

Mike Ferris, an amnesiac in an Air Force jumpsuit, finds himself in a town strangely devoid of people. But despite the emptiness, he has the odd feeling that he's being watched. As he inspects the town's cafe, phone booth, police station, drugstore and movie theater, his desperation mounts. Finally he collapses, hysterically pushing the "walk" button of a stoplight again and again. In reality, the "walk" button is a panic button, and Ferris is an astronaut-trainee strapped into an isolation booth in simulation of a moon flight. After 484 hours in the booth, he has cracked from sheer loneliness. His wanderings in the vacant town have been nothing more than an hallucination.

"Up there, up there in the vastness of space, in the void that is sky, up there is an enemy known as isolation. It sits there in the stars waiting, waiting with the patience of eons, forever waiting . . . in the Twilight Zone."

"Where Is Everybody?" aired October 2, 1959, as the premier episode of *The Twilight Zone.* But the film that was shown that evening, and

Earl Holliman

continues to be shown in syndication to this day, differed in several significant ways from the film that was shown to the sponsors months before—and all of these differences could be discerned within the first minute of the show. For one thing, the visual opening was different: images of galaxies dissolve into one another until finally out of a spiral galaxy, in heavy, seemingly three-dimensional block letters (*a la* every science-fiction movie of the 1950s), the words "TWILIGHT ZONE" appear. No doubt this sequence was abandoned because even then that kind of opening was clichéd.

Then there was the matter of the opening narration, which ran: "There is a sixth dimension, beyond that which is known to man. It is a dimension as vast as space and as timeless as infinity. It is the middle ground between light and shadow, and it lies between the pit of man's fear and the sunlight of his knowledge. This is the dimension of imagination. It is an area that might be called *The Twilight Zone*."

Bill Self took particular exception to the opening line, "There is a sixth dimension . . ." "I said 'Rod, what is the *fifth* one?' And he said, 'I don't know. Aren't there five?' I said, 'I can only think of four.' So we rewrote it and rerecorded it and said, 'There is a fifth dimension, beyond that which is known to man . . .'" Serling made several other slight revisions in the opening, changing the line "sunlight of his knowledge" to "summit of his knowledge" and "It is an area that might be called *The Twilight Zone*" to "It is an area which we call *The Twilight Zone*," as well as adding a line that the Twilight Zone was the middle ground "between science and superstition."

Asked how he came up with the title *The Twilight Zone*, Serling said, "I thought I'd made it up, but I've heard since that there is an Air Force term relating to a moment when a plane is coming down on approach and it cannot see the horizon, it's called the twilight zone, but it's an obscure term which I had not heard before."

Undoubtedly, the most significant change made was in the identity of the narrator. Originally, the narrator was not Rod Serling. "That came about accidentally and out of necessity, I guess," says Self. "It was from the outset decided that there would be a narrator, someone who would set the stage or wrap it up. The first person we used was Westbrook Van Voorhis, who had done *The March of Time* and had that kind of big voice. But when we listened to it we decided it was a little too pompous-sounding."

At the screenings of the pilot in New York, all agreed that a different narrator had to be found. Ira Steiner, then of the Ashley-Steiner Agency, which represented Serling, remembers the general consensus: "Orson Welles was the choice for the narrator, he was everybody's *numero uno*. That is, he was everybody's choice but one; Rod was not at all thrilled with the idea of having Orson Welles narrate *The Twilight Zone*. But Welles sat well with the agency, sat well with the sponsor, sat well with the network—except for one little problem. I don't even know how far it got as far as Welles was concerned, but he was quoted at a price which took the show to a point more than Young and Rubicam and General Foods had in mind as a budget."

Many narrators were suggested who would be within the budget, but no choice was satisfactory to all concerned. Bill Self recalls, "Finally, Rod himself made the suggestion that maybe he should do it. It was received with skepticism. None of us knew Rod except as a writer. But he did a terrific job."

Because Serling wanted to give "Where Is Everybody?" his best shot, he invested much from personal experience into the script. The original idea came from two separate sources. Serling read an item in *Time* magazine that isolation experiments were being performed on astronaut-trainees. This was then coupled with a purely subjective experience on his part: "I got the idea while walking through an empty lot of a movie studio. There were all the evidences of a community—but with no people. I felt at the time a kind of encroaching loneliness and desolation, a feeling of how nightmarish it would be to wind up in a city with no inhabitants."

Then there's the scene in which Ferris, believing himself trapped in a phone booth, pushes and pushes on the door, only to find that the door *pulls* open. "That's dummy me," Rod recalled in 1975. "The reason I put that in was because I was once in a phone booth, trying to catch a plane, and I heard the loudspeaker and I started to push on the door and I couldn't get out and I got panicky. I started to yell at people, 'Could you do this?' Suddenly, some guy comes along and kicks it with his foot. I wanted to die."

Over the years, Serling became increasingly dissatisfied with "Where Is Everybody?", commenting in 1975 that "unlike good wine, this film hasn't taken the years very well at all . . ." Certainly, almost as soon as he finished writing the episode he must have been unhappy with the totally straightforward ending, devoid of any twists or surprises, for when he adapted the script into a short story for his collection *Stories From The Twilight Zone* (Bantam, 1960), he altered it, beginning at the point where Ferris enters a movie theater. "When he goes into the theater," Serling later explained, "there's nobody giving tickets. So he reaches in and takes a ticket, and he walks in and he tears off the stub and he drops one in the little reticule there and he puts the other stub in his pocket. And then you play the whole thing, and when he gets out of the isolation booth and they're carrying him on the [stretcher], he reaches into his pocket and there's a theater stub. Now, it doesn't mean anything except, 'Wait a minute'—Bwaang!—'What happened here?' It's a fillip upon a fillip."

Particularly galling to Serling later was a dramatic device that he employed in the episode in order to advance the plot, that of an endless monologue on the part of the main character.

Serling recounted a way in which, in retrospect, he would have made it more plausible. "Seat (Ferris) on the counter. Take a shot through the door and there's a little white cloth that moves, like the apron of a cook. And you say, 'Hey buddy, I'd like ham and eggs. . . . You got quite a town here. You like this music? . . .' Finally, he goes over and it's an apron hanging from a [hook], blowing in a fan. But you can't continue to make this man talk to a ghost and get any sense of reality at all, and it gets a little ludicrous after a while."

For all its faults, "Where Is Everybody?" accomplished one thing that perhaps no other episode of *The Twilight Zone* could have done: it sold the series. A number of other episodes might have been superior in terms of drama or imagination, but they would almost certainly have seemed too far out to ever sell this unique series to such conservative executives. Even as it was, there were questions as to whether *The Twilight Zone* was really viable. Says agent Ira Steiner, "While it was a stunning pilot, it nevertheless was—I guess in today's words—a little 'freaky' in terms of the kind of show that was usually brought in for viewing."

"My only concern about it," says Bill Self, "which I think was everybody's, was that, being an anthology, there were no recurring elements other than the concept. You couldn't say, 'Gee, Earl Holliman's great, he'll be back next week,' you could say, 'Earl Holliman's great, but he *won't* be back next week.' So we felt that it was a very good film but whether the sponsors would believe we could duplicate it, with different stories and different actors, was the question in everybody's mind."

With all these concerns, it should come as no surprise to learn that those involved hold different opinions as to why the pilot *did* sell. Rod Serling believed that a large portion of it was luck. Buck Houghton, soon to be the producer of *The Twilight Zone* and a man with forty years worth of savvy in the motion picture and television business, believes that *The Twilight Zone* sold primarily due to Serling's reputation. "You see, Rod had muscle from the *Playhouse 90*s he'd done and the network wanted to hold on to him. And if he'd said, 'I want to do a series about a tightrope walker,' they'd have said, 'Let's indulge this guy because he's very important. We'll let him write this thing and we may even make a pilot, and then we'll say, "Well, Rod, while we think about this, how about adapting this John Steinbeck novel for us?"' This has been done many times before, where a man has a certain strength and you induce him to join your club with all sorts of promises, intending to use him in his area of strength and indulge him in the areas he's interested in but nobody gives a shit about. Nobody but a guy with the muscle that Rod had could have gotten a science-fiction series launched. They were very, very touchy about it."

Bill Self disagrees. "The reason it sold was, first, it was a very good show, and, secondly, CBS wanted it on the air. They wanted it because they thought that it was good. If it hadn't been good, they wouldn't have put it on. Rod's written a lot of pilots that didn't get on."

The most obvious and likely answer is that it was a combination of all three—luck, Serling's name, and the quality of the show—that sold *The Twilight Zone*. And perhaps a fourth factor should be added to that list: push. A number of people besides Serling had to push with all their talent, influence, and gall to get this series on. The first man to push for *The Twilight Zone* was Bert Granet, producer of *Westinghouse Desilu Playhouse*, producer of "The Time Element." And what does he have to say about *The Twilight Zone*? "I can't make any comment, except I was the first to like it, basically. I fought very hard because it was very difficult to get it on the air. It's questionable whether *Twilight Zone* would have ever existed if I hadn't beat down McCann-Erickson . . . because they did not want that show nohow. At any rate, the rest of it just became history."

THE FIRST SEASON: 1959–1960

Producer: Buck Houghton
Executive Producer: Rod Serling
Production Manager: Ralph W. Nelson
Director of Photography: George T. Clemens
Assistant Directors: Edward Denault, Kurt Neuman, Jr., Joe Boyle and Don Klune
Casting: Mildred Gusse and John Erman
Art Directors: George W. Davis, William Ferrari and Merrill Pye
Editors: Joseph Gluck, Bill Mosher, Lyle Boyer and Fred Maguire
Makeup: Bob Keats
Special Effects: Virgil Beck
Camera Operators: Jack Swain, Paul Uhl and John Travers Hill
Sound: Franklin Milton, Jean Valentino and Philip N. Mitchell
Theme Music: Bernard Herrmann, Marius Constant
Set Direction: Rudy Butler, Henry Grace, Keogh Gleason and Budd S. Friend
Animated Title: U.P.A.
Filmed at Metro–Goldwyn–Mayer

III / THE FIRST SEASON

"A year ago, when the first publicity came out on the series, I was inundated by submissions from agents offering me six foot nine actors with long necks to which electrodes could easily be attached. One agent told me that he had an actor so versed in horror movies that he'd taken to sleeping in a box in the basement." —ROD SERLING

With the go-ahead from the network to produce the first twenty-six episodes of *The Twilight Zone,* Rod Serling asked Bill Self to stay on as producer of the show. Self declined, preferring his executive position with the network. As his replacement, he suggested Buck Houghton, a producer who had been his script editor on *Schlitz Playhouse of Stars*. Serling had no objections and so, as Houghton recalls, "Bill Self called me up and asked if I was free, and fortunately I just happened to be at that moment. So he sent me a couple of Rod's *Twilight Zone* scripts, then arranged for a meeting with Rod. I must say, the first two scripts were really very striking, and my enthusiasm showed, and they said, 'Fine, let's go.'"

For the first three years of *The Twilight Zone*—undeniably the best years of the series—Houghton was the single man most responsible for translating the visions of Serling and the other writers on the show from paper to film. From the purchasing of scripts (other than Serling's) to casting to scoring to cutting, no decision was made without Houghton's approval. And, as the series itself testifies, no abler, more imaginative man could have possibly been found for the job.

Douglas Heyes, director of some of *The Twilight Zone*'s finest episodes, including "The After Hours," "The Howling Man," and "The Invaders," holds Houghton in high esteem. "I think Buck was the best producer I ever worked with. He would listen to suggestions and try to support the director or the actor or whomever in their own originality as much as he could. He brought out the best in everyone and he made me feel like I wanted to do innovations and do exciting things for *Twilight Zone,* much more than I ever felt for any other series."

Buck Houghton was born Archible Ernest Houghton, Jr., on May 4, 1919, in Denver, Colorado. The nickname "Buck" was tacked on at such

A SELECTION OF TWILIGHT ZONE OPENINGS

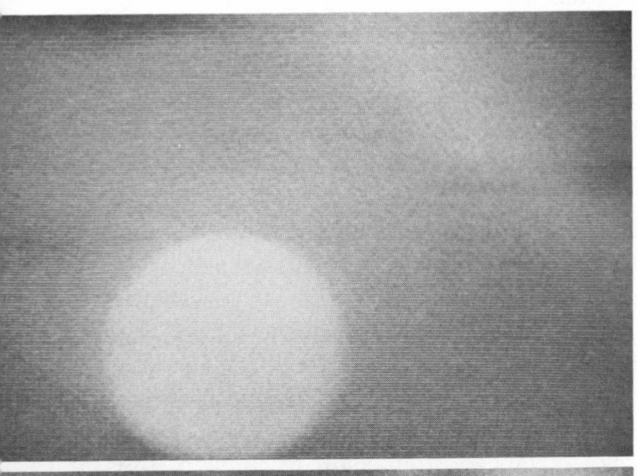

"You're travelling through another dimension, a dimension not only of sight and sound but of mind; a journey into a wondrous land whose boundaries are that of imagination. That's the signpost up ahead— your next stop, the Twilight Zone!"

"There is a fifth dimension beyond that which is known to man. It is a dimension as vast as space and timeless as infinity. It is the middle ground between light and shadow, between science and superstition, and it lies between the pit of man's fears and the summit of his knowledge. This is the dimension of imagination. It is an area which we call the Twilight Zone."

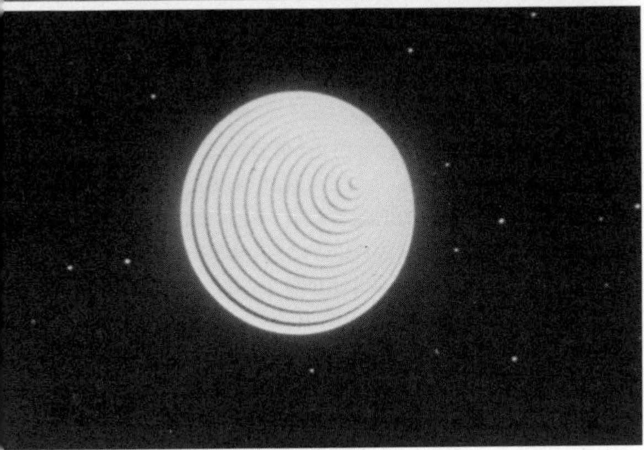

"You're travelling through another dimension, a dimension not only of sight and sound, but of mind; a journey into a wondrous land whose boundaries are that of imagination—Next stop, the Twilight Zone!"

an early age that Houghton isn't really sure where it came from but says, "I think I had buck teeth when I was a kid." When he was eight, he and his parents moved to Los Angeles, where he grew up in the shadow of Hollywood. From his early years, Houghton intended a career in film. His majors at UCLA were economics and English, but only because "there wasn't a theater department there then."

College behind him, he landed a job as a reader for Val Lewton, then working as a story editor for David Selznick at Selznick International Pictures. Of Lewton, Houghton says, "I didn't know him from a hole in the fence. I just wrote him a letter, saying that I was an English major from UCLA and that I thought I was reasonably articulate and fairly perceptive and I'd love to work for him. So he called me in and we chatted and he gave me a book to write a report on. By the time he had the third or fourth report, he thought I was pretty good."

Since the job as a reader consisted of piece work and didn't bring a steady income, Buck had to take on an additional job working in the mailroom at Paramount Studios. Eventually, he was promoted to the studio's casting office and, after a year, into the budget office.

With the advent of World War II, Buck attempted to join the Army but, failing the physical, ended up working for the Office of War Information, making propaganda shorts for European distribution. "It was fun," says Houghton. "I had come from an industry that figured that you couldn't take the lens cap off the camera without forty fellas standing around. I found out you could do it with three and a station wagon, which is what we did."

After the war, Houghton got a job working as an assistant to Jack Gross, an executive producer at RKO. Coincidentally, one of the producers Gross was working with at the time was Val Lewton, for whom Buck had worked before the war. As a result of this, Houghton was in on the production of a number of Lewton films which are today considered classics of the horror genre: *Curse of the Cat People*, *The Body Snatchers*, and *Bedlam*. Certainly, this experience didn't hurt him when it came time to produce *The Twilight Zone*.

After four years at RKO, Houghton moved to MGM as an assistant story editor. Two years later, he got his first job in television, as story editor on *Schlitz Playhouse of Stars*. After three years, he decided it was time to move up. "Having worked in both story department and budget department, I knew how to handle money and I knew how to handle writers, so it was more or less natural that I'd want to produce. My first experience of that was on *China Smith*."

China Smith was a syndicated television series starring Dan Duryea in the title role as a renegade Irishman in Singapore, a private-eye type with "good, entertainingly seedy connections." For the freshman producer,

China Smith was a harsh proving ground. Over a period of a year and a half, fifty-two episodes were made. Of these, the first thirteen had shooting schedules of two days each, with no rehearsal. For the rest, Houghton was allowed a more leisurely pace: an extra half day.

After *China Smith,* Houghton produced *Wire Service,* a weekly, hour-long series with a rotating cast featuring Mercedes McCambridge, George Brent, and Dane Clark as reporters. After that came *Meet McGraw,* starring Frank Lovejoy as a private eye; followed by *Yancy Derringer,* a western set in New Orleans starring the pre-Tarzan Jock Mahoney as a gentleman riverboat gambler; and in 1958, *Man With a Camera,* starring Charles Bronson as an intrepid and persistent freelance photographer (with choice lines like "I've been trying to shoot this guy all day, and I'm *going* to shoot him!").

Then came *The Twilight Zone.*

Houghton's first order of business was the selection of a studio. The pilot had been shot at Universal, but that had been done simply as a courtesy to CBS, as Universal did not rent its facilities to outside production companies. Houghton decided to rent space and facilities at Metro–Goldwyn–Mayer. "I knew it had the best storehouse of sets in town. MGM traditionally kept everything they ever made. Just about everything you could ever wish for in an anthology was there, including the back lot, which had New York streets and forests and lakes and you name it." The "you name it" included small towns from Middle America and the Old West, a European village, a frontier fort, facades of tenements, shops, and movie theaters, a courthouse, a state capitol, a park with bandstand, a jungle, a river, a dock, a cruise ship, a paddleboat, a three-masted schooner, modern and nineteenth-century trains and train stations, various roads, a gas station, and southern mansions.

Next came the hiring of a production crew. From the MGM makeup department came Bob Keats and from the art department came art director William Ferrari, an Oscar winner for the movie *Gaslight* (and later to do *The Time Machine*). From his associations on *Schlitz Playhouse of Stars,* Houghton hired production manager Ralph W. Nelson and director of photography George T. Clemens. Clemens—a distant relative of Samuel Langhorne Clemens (aka Mark Twain) and a cameraman on *High Noon,* Chaplin's *The Great Dictator,* the Fredric March *Dr. Jekyll and Mr. Hyde,* and the Valentino *Blood and Sand,* among a multitude of others—would prove particularly vital to the series, establishing a look that was unique in television. For casting director, network boss William Dozier suggested Mildred Gusse, someone Houghton had never heard of. But Dozier's suggestion "was a handshake and welcome aboard," says Buck, "because you didn't call up Bill Dozier and say, 'I think you're wrong.'" But the choice proved a good one. "She just turned out brilliantly. She fought for who she thought were the right people, didn't just bring the lists. She was thoroughly effective."

Before production began, Serling, Houghton, and George Clemens had a meeting to discuss directors, in order to have a list at hand as the various episodes came due for production throughout the season. Houghton strongly believes that directors should be cast with every bit as much thought as goes into the casting of actors. "So often it happens that the best efforts of people come from their enthusiasm, not from their saying, 'Fine, it was a good job of work. I'll go ahead and connect the pipes and then turn on the water and there won't be any leaks, don't worry about a thing'—you know, a good journeyman job. So the problem then is to arrange it so that a director is just *enthused* about what he must do."

Clemens recalls the meeting. "Rod had a couple of favorite directors that Buck and I didn't like at all, and we had a couple of favorite directors that he wasn't too happy with. So we made a compromise: 'We won't use him if you don't use *him*.' So it worked out fine."

Together, the three pooled their considerable knowledge of directors into a list that represented some of the most talented men to ever work in film and television. The majority were primarily television directors but several were men who had distinguished themselves in film. Most notable among these, at least to Houghton, was Mitchell Leisen, who had directed, among many, many other things, the classic fantasy *Death Takes a Holiday*, starring Fredric March. To Houghton, hiring Leisen held a special importance.

"Well, that was pure hero worship," he explains. "When I was a kid at Paramount, he was making the biggest pictures in town—Fred MacMurray–Barbara Stanwyck dramas, *The Big Broadcast of 1937* and *1938*. Some way or another, he lost all his money, and he was a very merry, pleasant fellow who just said, 'Well, if they don't want me in pictures then the hell with it, I'll direct television.' So I called him up and I said, 'Mitch, you won't remember me because I was a fourth assistant director on one of your pictures, but are you honest-to-God doing television?' He says, 'You bet your ass. What have you got?' I was delighted because, God, this was a guy I had tiptoed around when I was a kid."

Hiring movie directors to do television didn't always go smoothly, however. Robert Parrish had been an Oscar-winning editor with credits that included *Body and Soul*, *A Double Life* and *All the King's Men*, and had also worked as a movie director, but the direction of the *Twilight Zone* episode "One for the Angels," starring Ed Wynn, was something totally new to him. Houghton recalls: "He was a friend of Rod's and Rod suggested him. And Bob said, 'My God, I don't know anything about television! I've got a thirty-page script. I only shoot five pages a day. That's fifteen pages and this is thirty pages. How am I going to do this in three days?'

"I said to him, 'Bob, forget it's television. Just take the script and bring me a list of all the camera setups you want, just like you had six days to do it, five pages a day, thirty pages.'

"The next day he brought in a legal-size piece of paper with all of his setups. I said, 'Now cross off all the shots that represent two ways of doing it. All right. Now cross off all the shots that are redundant, that give you a choice between over-shoulders and closeups.' Then I said, 'How many are left?' He said, 'I can do these in three days.'"

With the rental of space and facilities at MGM, the hiring of a production crew and selection of directors, *The Twilight Zone* settled into a regular routine. Each episode was given what was—for television at least—an extremely generous schedule: one full day of rehearsal plus three shooting days. Full production began in June. Twenty episodes would be made before those working on the show would have the slightest inkling of the public's reaction.

As for Serling, his commitment to the show was total. During the early months, he was working twelve to fourteen hours a day, seven days a week. "He would get up very early," Carol Serling remembers, "grab a cup of coffee, and be out there at the crack of dawn. In his office in back of the house, he'd dictate his scripts into a tape machine. Often, if the weather was nice, he'd take the machine outside with him and sit by the pool" (prompting writer Mary Wood to observe, "He's the only person I know who can get a tan and make money at the same time"). "Usually," says Carol, "he finished writing at twelve or one o'clock; he'd written himself out. Rod would then drive from Pacific Palisades to MGM in Culver City. There, he would work on until late into the evening."

"Rod was around all the time," recalls assistant director Edward Denault, now a vice-president with Lorimar Productions. "He was instrumental in the development of the scripts and in the rewrites, was in on the post-production, always looked at the dailies. If we got in a jam and something had to be rewritten in an effort to get the show finished on time or if we were short of minutes, he was always ready and could knock off a scene very quickly. He was very, very much involved."

For all his involvement, Serling also knew his own limitations. And although he was credited as executive producer, he had no pretensions of being a producer. "You see, Rod had a very short span of attention," explains Buck Houghton. "He was a very intense guy and he worked very hard and he drove himself very hard and he was very short of patience. He was not *im*patient; patience was not something he had. A ten-minute story conference with him was the limit, then he'd want to go out and get an ice-cream soda or a shoeshine. So, as far as sitting through a dubbing session or going through the casting lists or sitting and cueing the music with a composer, that sort of thing: no thanks. And that's not to derogate the title of executive producer; he *did* have the final say. If things had started to come apart, I'm sure he would have leapt in there one way or another. But in what I consider the producer's function, which is to bring creative forces together and make the most out of them, that was not his intention nor did he try to do it."

Edward Denault believes that Houghton and Serling made a perfect team. "Buck complemented Rod in those areas where Rod did not have the expertise. Because Buck understood production, you could go to him and explain a problem, and then he would go to Rod and say, 'We've got a problem and here it is and I think we can resolve it this way.' He satisfied both sides, and I think he was very good for Rod."

Over a nine-month period, Serling produced twenty-eight of the first season's scripts. These scripts fell into three basic categories: science fiction, horror, and fantasy—all employing the surprise twist ending which came to characterize *The Twilight Zone*.

"I am writing faster now than ever before," Serling said at the time. "Some of the plays I did for *Playhouse 90* took me from six months to a year to complete. Each *Twilight* script took from thirty-five to forty hours."

Yet none of this was hack work. The scope and variety of *The Twilight Zone* scripts were amazing. How was Serling able to accomplish it? "First, I've been wanting to do a show of this kind—a series of imaginative tales that are not bound by time or space or the established laws of nature—for many years. So I had a backlog of story ideas. You could say many of the stories were written in my mind.

"Second, there is the fact that with a half-hour show you have fewer alternatives in approach to consider. This is important. If a story can be handled in only one way, you sit down and write it. If you can develop a story in many different ways, you've got problems."

Then there was the fact that Serling dictated his scripts. "At one time I used a typewriter [prior to the success of 'Patterns'], but I found that I think faster than I can type. The typewriter held me up."

On *The Twilight Zone*, Serling's writing followed a rigid pattern. "I dictate the first draft and have a secretary type it up. Then I will sit down and decide what has to be rewritten. The rewrite is usually to tighten up the rough draft to solve the time problem. Most of my first drafts run too long.

"I usually don't have to do a second rewrite. Of course, after the director and cast have seen the script, there will be some last-minute pencilled changes. That's only to be expected." (Not all the scripts Serling wanted to do came to fruition. Early in the year, he tried to buy three classic science-fiction stories to adapt—Heinlein's "Life-Line," Arthur C. Clarke's "The Nine Billion Names of God," and Phillip K. Dick's "The Imposter"—but for various reasons was unable to acquire the rights.)

Serling's commitment to the series and the dazzling quality of his work fired up the enthusiasms of others on the show. "We used to put in some very long hours," says Edward Denault, "yet there was a lot of excitement. Each script was different, something unusual that had never been done before, and you looked forward to it in anticipation of what was coming up next. I am very happy that I was a part of it."

"THE LONELY" (11/13/59)

Jack Warden and Jean Marsh

Written by Rod Serling
Producer: Buck Houghton
Director: Jack Smight
Director of Photography: George T. Clemens
Music: Bernard Herrmann

Cast:
James A. Corry: Jack Warden
Alicia: Jean Marsh
Capt. Allenby: John Dehner
Adams: Ted Knight
Carstairs: James Turley

"Witness if you will a dungeon, made out of mountains, salt flats and sand that stretch to infinity. The dungeon has an inmate: James A. Corry. And this is his residence: a metal shack. An old touring car that squats in the sun and goes nowhere—for there is nowhere to go. For the record let it be known that James A. Corry is a convicted criminal placed in solitary confinement. Confinement in this case stretches as far as the eye can see, because this particular dungeon is on an asteroid nine million miles from the Earth. Now witness if you will a man's mind and body shrivelling in the sun, a man dying of loneliness."

Allenby, the captain of a supply ship that travels the solar system, takes pity on Corry, who's serving a fifty-year sentence for murder, and leaves him a box containing Alicia, a robot that looks and sounds exactly like a woman. Initially, Corry is repelled by the robot, but eventually his heart melts and he falls deeply in love with her. Eleven months pass. Then one day the supply ship lands. Allenby tells Corry he's received a full pardon, and that they've come to get him. But there's a hitch: Corry can only take fifteen pounds of gear, and Alicia weighs more than that. Corry refuses to leave her behind, claiming that she's a *woman*. Reluctantly, Allenby draws his gun and shoots Alicia full in the face, revealing a mass of smoldering wires. He tells Corry, "All you're leaving behind is loneliness." Stunned, Corry replies, "I must remember that. I must remember to keep that in mind."

"On a microscopic piece of sand that floats through space is a fragment of a man's life. Left to rust is the place he lived in and the machines he used. Without use, they will disintegrate from the wind and the sand and the years that act upon them; all of Mr. Corry's machines—including the one made in his image, kept alive by love, but now obsolete . . . in the Twilight Zone."

The first episode ready to go before the cameras was "The Lonely," which presented a unique problem for Buck Houghton: Where to find an asteroid?

The answer was Death Valley. "It was supposed to be an asteroid and look as kooky as possible," says Houghton, "and Death Valley is about as kooky as you can find. It's barren and deserted. That *must* be the way Mars looks."

Alicia revealed

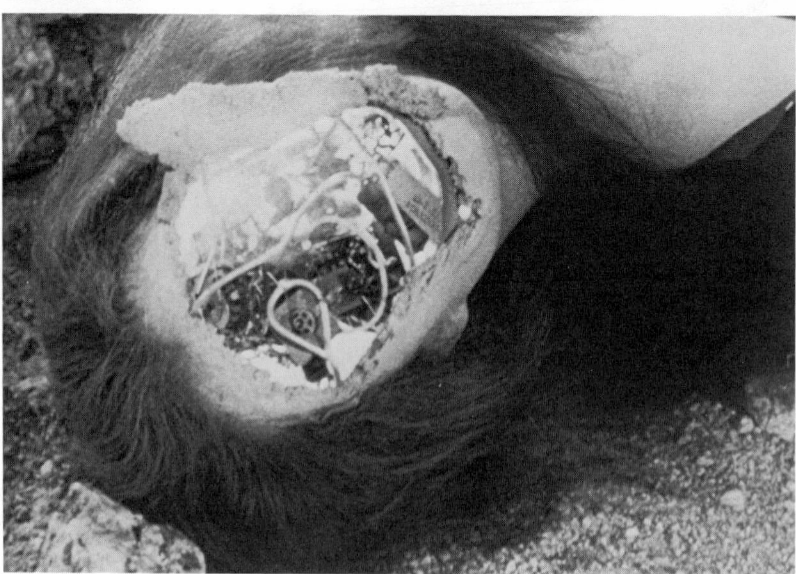

So on the second week of June, 1959, Houghton, director Jack Smight (whose film credits now include *Harper, The Illustrated Man, No Way to Treat a Lady,* and *Midway*), actors Jack Warden, Jean Marsh (later to co-create and star in the *Masterpiece Theatre* presentation *Upstairs, Downstairs*), John Dehner, Ted Knight (later of *The Mary Tyler Moore Show*), and James Turley, set out with the production crew for the lowest, driest, hottest place in the United States. The maiden voyage proved a trial by fire.

"That was unbelievable heat when we shot out there," says Jack Smight. "The temperature was around 130 degrees. One day the caterer very foolishly served a very heavy meal for lunch, and about eight crew members just dropped in the afternoon. George Clemens actually fell off the camera crane right into the sand. I thought he was having a heart attack, because he was up on the crane, we were setting up a shot, and he just toppled off."

"We had a nurse with us and she kept pushing lukewarm water," Buck Houghton recalls. "And once in a while a guy would say, 'Well, don't worry about *me,*' and put down a quart of nice, cold chocolate milk. In about a half hour, he'd turn green and have to lie down in the truck."

Edward Denault recalls being called on to do double duty. "As well as being the assistant director, I wound up doing script work and was the sound boom man for a couple of shots. Everybody was filling in for somebody else because people were just dropping off like flies."

Buck Houghton: "One time, Jean Marsh lay down in the shot that's the tag of the picture. We put a thermometer down beside her. It was 140 degrees where she was lying."

The incredible heat also created technical problems. "There's a funny problem that nobody but someone connected with motion pictures would ever think of," explains George Clemens. "When we want to show heat, to make people look like they're sweating, we spray them with a composition of oil and water. Each makeup artist has a different thing that he puts on. Of course, you always darken under the arms and so forth to make it look like they're sweating like hell. Well, in Death Valley, we wanted to convey this idea, but I don't care what we put on them, before we'd start the camera it was gone—they were just as dry as you or me. We ended up putting about ninety percent oil and a little water on their faces, and the oil would stay in little droplets."

Finally, Death Valley proved too much. After two days of shooting, Houghton and Smight decided—to the relief of cast and crew alike—to return to MGM, reconstruct the interior of the metal shack in which the convict in the story lives, and shoot the final day's scenes under comparatively cool klieg lights. Smight undoubtedly speaks for all concerned when he says, "It was just too hot."

"ESCAPE CLAUSE" (11/6/59)

David Wayne

Written by Rod Serling
Producer: Buck Houghton
Director: Mitchell Leisen
Director of Photography: George T. Clemens
Music: stock

Cast:
Walter Bedeker: David Wayne
Mr. Cadwallader: Thomas Gomez
Ethel Bedeker: Virginia Christine
Adjuster #1: Dick Wilson
Adjuster #2: Joe Flynn
Judge: George Baxter
Doctor: Raymond Bailey
Cooper: Wendell Holmes
Guard: Nesdon Booth
Subway Guard: Allan Lurie
Janitor: Paul E. Burns

"You're about to meet a hypochondriac. Witness Mr. Walter Bedeker, age forty-four, afraid of the following: death, disease, other people, germs, drafts and everything else. He has one interest in life, and that's Walter Bedeker. One preoccupation: the life and well-being of Walter Bedeker. One abiding concern about society: that if Walter Bedeker should die, how will it survive without him?"

Bedeker makes a deal with Mr. Cadwallader, an impeccably-dressed, jovial fat man who also happens to be the Devil. Bedeker will receive immortality and indestructibility in exchange for his soul. An escape clause is provided, however; if at any time he tires of life, all he need do is summon Cadwallader. Soon after the deal is struck, Bedeker realizes he's been taken. Nothing can harm him, true—but nothing thrills him either. He throws himself in front of subway trains and buses, drinks poison, all without the slightest ill effect. Finally he decides to jump off the top of his apartment building. In trying to stop him, his wife accidentally falls off the building to her death. Realizing that this gives him a unique opportunity to experience the electric chair, Bedeker confesses to murdering his wife. He receives a shock of a different kind, however, when the judge sentences him to life imprisonment without chance of parole. Cadwallader appears and grants him a reprieve, in the form of a fatal heart attack.

"There's a saying, 'Every man is put on Earth condemned to die, time and method of execution unknown.' Perhaps this is as it should be. Case in point: Walter Bedeker, lately deceased, a little man with such a yen to live. Beaten by

the Devil, by his own boredom—and by the scheme of things in this, the Twilight Zone."

Of this second episode in the production schedule, *Daily Variety* said, "Here was a little gem. Good work, Rod Serling. This little piece about a hypochondriac who gets tangled up with an obese, clerical devil ranked with the best that has ever been accomplished in half-hour filmed television." High praise for an episode that was really par for the course during the first season.

"WALKING DISTANCE" (10/30/59)

Gig Young

Written by Rod Serling
Producer: Buck Houghton
Director: Robert Stevens
Director of Photography: George T. Clemens
Music: Bernard Herrmann

Cast:
Martin Sloan: Gig Young
Martin's Father: Frank Overton
Martin's Mother: Irene Tedrow
Martin as a boy: Michael Montgomery
Charlie: Byron Foulger
Soda Jerk: Joseph Corey
Wilcox Boy: Ronnie Howard
Mr. Wilson: Pat O'Malley
Mr. Wilcox: Bill Erwin
Teenager: Buzz Martin
Woman: Nan Peterson
Attendant: Sheridan Comerate

"Martin Sloan, age thirty-six. Occupation: vice-president, ad agency, in charge of media. This is not just a Sunday drive for Martin Sloan. He perhaps doesn't know it at the time—but it's an exodus. Somewhere up the road he's looking for sanity. And somewhere up the road, he'll find something else."

On a drive in the country, world-weary advertising executive Martin Sloan leaves his car at a gas station and sets off on foot to his home town, Homewood, where he finds things are exactly the same as when he was a child. Soon he realizes that he has somehow gone back in time. He confronts his parents but only succeeds in convincing them he's a lunatic. And when he tries to catch up with himself as a child—wanting only to tell the young Martin to savor his youth—the frightened boy falls off a merry-go-round and breaks his leg. Later, Martin's father, who has gone through Martin's wallet and now realizes Martin *is* his son, tells him he must leave, that there is "only one summer to every customer." Reluctantly, Martin returns to the present—with a limp he got from falling off a merry-go-round when he was a child.

"Martin Sloan, age thirty-six, vice-president in charge of media. Successful in most things, but not in the one effort that all men try at some time in their lives—trying to go home again. And also like all men perhaps there'll be an occasion—maybe a summer night sometime—when he'll look up from what he's doing and listen to the distant music of a calliope, and hear the voices and the laughter of his past. And perhaps across his mind there'll flit a little errant wish, that a man might not have to become old, never outgrow the parks and the merry-go-rounds of his youth. And he'll smile then too because he'll know it is *just an errant wish, some wisp of memory not too important really, some laughing ghosts that cross a man's mind—that are a part of the Twilight Zone."*

"I think probably 'Walking Distance' was as good as any we made," says Buck Houghton. "It may be personal but I don't think so, because I'm not beleaguered by my work."

With "Walking Distance," Rod Serling took a fantasy journey to the

Michael Montgomery

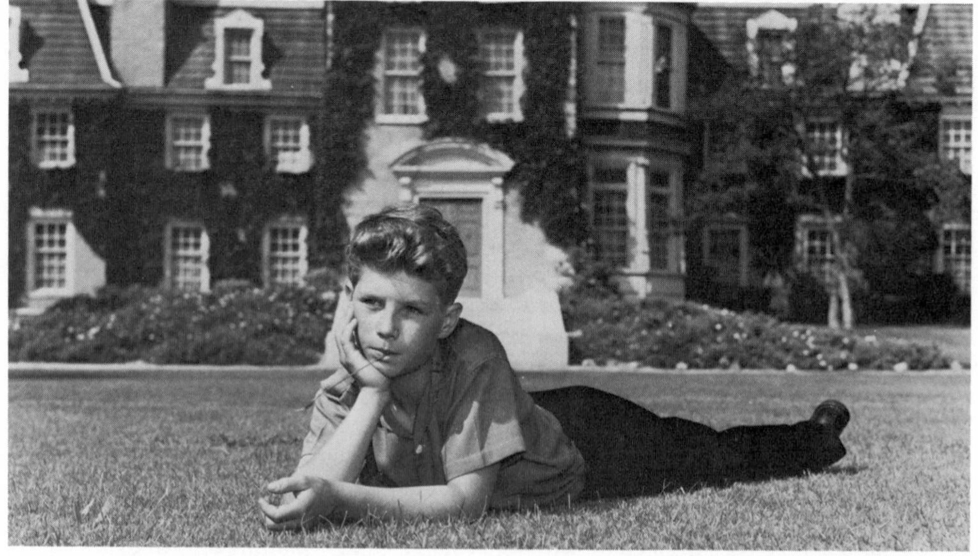

Binghamton of his youth and invited us along for the ride. "Not long ago," he told Kay Gardella of the New York *Daily News* in 1959, "I was walking on a set at MGM when I was suddenly hit by the similarity of it to my home town. Feeling an overwhelming sense of nostalgia, it struck me that all of us have a deep longing to go back—not to our home as it is today, but as we remember it. It was from this simple incident that I wove the story 'Walking Distance' . . ."

Upon the recommendation of CBS management, who were much pleased by the job he had done on the pilot, director Robert Stevens was hired to direct. Gig Young was cast in the lead, with Frank Overton and Irene Tedrow as his parents. Ronnie Howard (later of the long-running *Happy Days*) was also cast, as a neighborhood child. Houses originally built on MGM's Lot 3 for the movie *Meet Me in St. Louis* were magically transformed into the homes of Homewood. From an outside firm, a gorgeously detailed carousel was rented and set up on a backlot park.

From the first, there was a feeling that "Walking Distance" was something special. Says Buck Houghton, "There was a fortunate conspiracy of all sorts of arts and crafts that came to bear on that picture: the good fortunes of casting, the good fortunes of direction. Gig Young was just superb. The sets were absolutely magnificent for a half-hour show. There were a lot of good vibes coming out of the material as you encountered it, all the way up and down the line. It's a beauty."

"Walking Distance" makes no pretense at being science fiction; it's clearly a fantasy. Nowhere is this delineation so clear as in Martin's entrance into the past. Rather than using a time machine, Serling and Stevens employ a visual allusion to *Through the Looking Glass*. In the present, Martin heads down a dirt road toward his home town. The camera pans over to a mirror in which we see his reflection. This cuts to a reflection of Martin in a drugstore mirror in the past, just as he enters. A similar device was used for the return to the present. Martin jumps on a spinning merry-go-round which cuts to a record spinning in a jukebox in the present-day version of the same drug store.

Serling realized that the harsh, hard-edged style of writing he'd used in "Where Is Everybody?" and "The Lonely" wouldn't do here. Instead, he used a style that was wistful, nostalgic. A longing for the past fills this episode, and that longing is communicated more through words than action. Nowhere is Serling's command of the language more in evidence. Take for example this scene near the end of the show, between Martin and his father:

FATHER: Martin, you have to leave here. There's no room, there's no place. Do you understand that?

MARTIN: I see that now, but I don't understand. Why not?

FATHER: I guess because we only get one chance. Maybe there's only one summer to every customer. That little boy, the one I know, the one who belongs here, this is *his* summer, just as it was yours once—don't make him share it.

MARTIN (Bitterly): All right.

FATHER: Martin, is it so bad where you're from?

MARTIN: I thought so, Pop. I've been living at a dead run and I was tired. Then one day, I knew I had to come back here. I had to come back and get on a merry-go-round and eat cotton candy and listen to a band concert, to stop and breathe and close my eyes and smell and listen.

FATHER: I guess we all want that. Maybe when you go back, Martin, you'll find that there are merry-go-rounds and band concerts where you are. Maybe you haven't been looking in the right place. You've been looking behind you, Martin. Try looking ahead.

Then, too, there is Serling's closing narration, perhaps the most touching and beautifully written of any episode of *The Twilight Zone*.

"Walking Distance" is also a prime example of how greatly a musical score can benefit a piece of drama. Bernard Herrmann, with movie credits including *The Ghost and Mrs. Muir, The Seventh Voyage of Sinbad, Journey to the Center of the Earth, The Three Worlds of Gulliver, Mysterious Island,* and *Jason and the Argonauts,* was one of the great composers of fantasy film music. Here, his gentle and evocative score permeates the episode, omnipresent yet unobtrusive. Listening to this score, composed specifically for this episode, it is hard to believe any composer—particularly one with such distinguished credits in feature films—would bother to take such pains. In mood, if not in specifics, the score is reminiscent of much of Herrmann's superb score for François Truffaut's *Fahrenheit 451,* which he composed seven years later. But to Buck Houghton, there's no mystery behind the excellence of the "Walking Distance" score. "When you have a good rough cut, a musician does a better job than he would with a less distinguished picture. Bernie responded very strongly to things that he thought were good. It's a *great* score."

This episode was certainly Serling's most personal and undoubtedly one of the series' most finely crafted. Surprisingly, for all its beauty and lyricism, "Walking Distance" caused Houghton and Serling some problems. Following the production and sale of the pilot, but before regular production of the series began, network vice-president William Dozier was given several of Serling's *Twilight Zone* scripts to read. Buck Houghton explains where the trouble came in: "The pilot could have happened. This was about a guy in a space machine who got claustrophobia to a point where he thought he was the only man in the world. That was one of the two or three *Twilight Zones* that *could* have happened. The next script that Bill Dozier read was 'Walking Distance,' about a guy who walks into his own home town hale and hearty and comes back with a limp that he got as a child, and Dozier said, 'Bullshit! This doesn't work. Who the fuck's going to believe this, Rod?'

"I remember Rod and I spending a couple of two-hour-long sessions with Bill Dozier saying, 'It's just that people won't swallow this!' And Rod said, 'Bill, that's *The Twilight Zone*, that's what imaginative fiction is about. It's like the one I'm writing, in which a guy falls in love with a girl and, sure enough, she's a mechanical girl, just like it says on the label.' And Bill said, 'Oh shit, you're kidding. Is this what this is all going to be about?'

"We got through the two-hour conferences, and the next time I heard of it, Bill was totally supportive. He'd been convinced to jump off the deep end and he was with it. So when sponsors started to say, 'Hey, what's *this*?' he said, 'Well, that's what you *bought*.' He acted just like he'd never had any objections himself, which was great."

"MR. DENTON ON DOOMSDAY" (10/16/59)

Jeanne Cooper and Dan Duryea

Written by Rod Serling
Producer: Buck Houghton
Director: Allen Reisner
Director of Photography: George T. Clemens
Music: stock

Cast:
Al Denton: Dan Duryea
Hotaling: Martin Landau
Pete Grant: Doug McClure
Henry J. Fate: Malcolm Atterbury
Liz: Jeanne Cooper
Charlie: Ken Lynch
Leader: Arthur Batanides
Doctor: Robert Burton
Man: Bill Erwin

"Portrait of a town drunk named Al Denton. This is a man who's begun his dying early—a long, agonizing route through a maze of bottles. Al Denton, who would probably give an arm or a part of his soul to have another chance, to be able to rise up and shake the dirt from his body and the bad dreams that infest his consciousness. [Shot of Henry J. Fate.] In the parlance of the times, this is a peddler, a rather fanciful-looking little man in a black frock coat. [A six-gun materializes beside Denton.] And this is the third principal character of our story. Its function: perhaps to give Mister Al Denton his second chance."

The setting is the old west. Al Denton—once a feared gunslinger, now the town drunk—is forced to draw against Hotaling, a sadistic bully. But on that same day, Henry J. Fate rides into town. Somehow, Fate's glance gives Denton's hand a life of its own, and Denton gets off two miraculous shots, disarming his tormentor and regaining the respect of the town. His dignity renewed, he swears off liquor. But all too soon, he finds himself in the same trap that drove him to the bottle in the first place: his newly-won reputation causes a young hotshot to challenge him to a duel. Denton discovers, however, that his old ability is completely gone, and in desperation he buys a potion from Fate guaranteed to give him ten seconds of deadly accuracy. The moment his opponent enters the saloon, Denton downs the potion—and sees the other man doing exactly the same thing! The two shoot the guns out of each other's hands, each sustaining an injury that will never allow him to shoot again. Denton, freed of ever having to face down another man, tells his adversary that they've both been blessed.

"Mr. Henry Fate, dealer in utensils and pots and pans, liniments and potions. A fanciful little man in a black frock coat who can help a man climbing out of a pit—or another man from falling into one. Because, you see, Fate can *work that way . . . in the Twilight Zone."*

Serling followed up "Walking Distance" with the first of what would be three strong and moving fantasies in a row. Originally, his idea for the story was something entitled "You Too Can be a Fast Gun," about a meek schoolteacher who achieves his wish to be a gunfighter by way of a magic potion, but eventually Serling rethought the story and opted for something a little less superficial. "Mr. Denton on Doomsday" explores a theme that writers would touch on often on *The Twilight Zone,* that of a person magically granted a second chance.

Cast as Denton was Dan Duryea, with whom Houghton had worked on *China Smith.* Years before, Duryea had made his reputation in films playing thoroughly detestable weasel types. Here he had a chance to play a

Dan Duryea, original advertisement

good guy, and he gave a performance of wisdom, strength, and humility (*and* believability—Denton genuinely looks like a man at the bottom of the barrel). Ably supporting him were Jeanne Cooper as a *Twilight Zone* version of *Gunsmoke*'s Miss Kitty, Malcolm Atterbury as Fate, and, as two gunslingers who play key roles in the action, a young (and wonderfully sadistic) Martin Landau and a *very* young Doug McClure. Allen Reisner, director of "The Time Element," skillfully guided this episode away from the clichéd and maudlin, and as a result Serling's story emerges as truly poignant.

"ONE FOR THE ANGELS" (10/9/59)

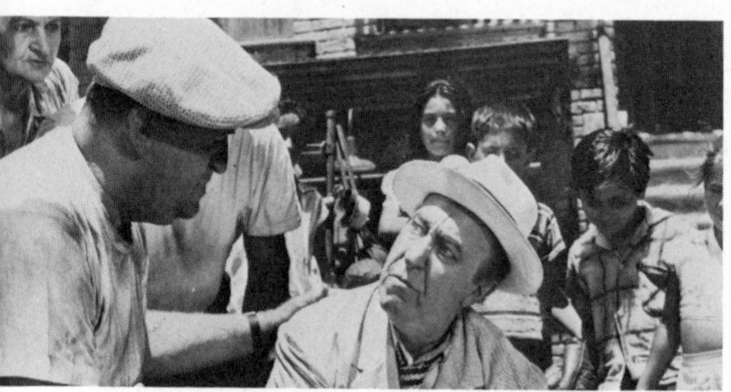

Merrit Bohn, Ed Wynn and Dana Dillaway

Written by Rod Serling
Producer: Buck Houghton
Director: Robert Parrish
Director of Photography: George T. Clemens
Music: stock

Cast:
Lew Bookman: Ed Wynn
Mr. Death: Murray Hamilton
Maggie: Dana Dillaway
Truck Driver: Merritt Bohn
Doctor: Jay Overholts
Little Boy: Mickey Maga

"Street scene: Summer. The present. Man on a sidewalk named Lew Bookman, age sixtyish. Occupation: pitchman. Lew Bookman, a fixture of the summer, a rather minor component to a hot July, a nondescript, commonplace little man whose life is a treadmill built out of sidewalks. And in just a moment, Lew Bookman will have to concern himself with survival—because as of three o'clock this hot July afternoon he'll be stalked by Mr. Death."

Sidewalk salesman Lew Bookman is confronted by Mr. Death, who informs him that he is to die at midnight. A persuasive man, Bookman succeeds in convincing Death to let him stay on Earth until he has had a chance to do his masterpiece, the Big Pitch—"one for the angels." But Bookman has no intention of *ever* making that pitch. Realizing he must now take someone in Bookman's place, Death arranges for a truck to hit Maggie, a neighborhood child. The substitution is proceeding nicely; all that remains is that Death must be in the dying girl's room at precisely midnight to claim her. Bookman, determined that Death not take Maggie, makes a pitch so enthralling that Death misses his deadline. The child is saved. Having made his one Big Pitch, Bookman leaves with Mr. Death.

"Lewis J. Bookman, age sixtyish. Occupation: pitchman. Formerly a fixture of the summer, formerly a rather minor component to a hot July. But, throughout his life, a man beloved by the children, and therefore a most important man. Couldn't happen, you say? Probably not in most places—but it did *happen in the Twilight Zone."*

Just after college, Serling wrote a teleplay entitled "One for the Angels," which was aired on *The Storm* in Cincinnati and later nationwide on *Danger*. The plot concerned an unsuccessful sidewalk pitchman who tries

Dana Dillaway and Ed Wynn

to save his two-bit punk brother from a couple of hitmen by giving a pitch so beguiling that they will always be surrounded by a crowd. Serling wanted to write a special *Twilight Zone* for Ed Wynn and he felt that this character would suit him ideally. So he borrowed the main character and title from the earlier work and wove an entirely new—and superior—story.

Director Robert Parrish's problems with this episode have already been discussed, but not those of Wynn. Although the episode was written specifically for him, he seems an odd choice for the role of a fast-talking pitchman, what with his lisp and extremely deliberate way of talking.

"It was exactly what Rod thought he could do," says Buck Houghton. "And Ed said, 'My God, I can't say all those words!' Rod said, 'Well, Ed, just concentrate. This is film, you know. We can stop it and pick it up again.'"

Despite Serling's assurances, Wynn was unable to overcome his inadequacies as a fast-talker, and as a result what was intended to be a spellbinding pitch comes across as thoroughly unconvincing. Fortunately,

Wynn's compensatory strengths as an actor make this a moot point, and "One for the Angels" emerges as a moving commentary on mortality and self-sacrifice.

As a concession to Wynn's age, all of the episode's night scenes were shot during the day. This was accomplished by pulling tarpaulins over the backlot tenement street, giving the illusion of night. But don't let this give the impression that everyone was bending over backwards for Wynn. On the contrary, it was he who extended himself to the fullest. "He was outstanding," says assistant director Edward Denault. "He was very prompt, knew his lines. I remember his chair was very close to the camera at all times, so it was never, 'I'll be in my dressing room,' or anything like that. You turned around when you were ready and Ed was sitting right there. He was a real joy to work with, a real pleasure."

"JUDGMENT NIGHT" (12/4/59)

Nehemiah Persoff

Written by Rod Serling
Producer: Buck Houghton
Director: John Brahm
Director of Photography: George T. Clemens
Music: stock

Cast:
Lanser: Nehemiah Persoff
Captain Wilbur: Ben Wright
First Officer: Patrick MacNee
Lt. Mueller: James Franciscus
Mr. Potter: Hugh Sanders
Maj. Devereaux: Leslie Bradley
Barbara: Diedre Owen
Bartender: Kendrick Huxham
First Steward: Richard Peel
Second Steward: Donald Journeaux
Engineer: Barry Bernard
Little Girl: Debbie Joyce

"Her name is the S.S. Queen of Glasgow. *Her registry: British. Gross tonnage: five thousand. Age: indeterminate. At this moment she's one day out of Liverpool, her destination New York. Duly recorded on this ship's log is the sailing time, course to destination, weather conditions, temperature, longitude and latitude. But what is never recorded in a log is the fear that washes over a deck like fog and ocean spray. Fear like the throbbing strokes of engine pistons, each like a heartbeat, parceling out every hour into breathless minutes of*

watching, waiting and dreading. For the year is 1942, and this particular ship has lost its convoy. It travels alone like an aged blind thing groping through the unfriendly dark, stalked by unseen periscopes of steel killers. Yes, the Queen of Glasgow *is a frightened ship, and she carries with her a premonition of death."*

On board the *Glasgow* is a German named Carl Lanser, with no memory of how he got there, yet with the feeling that he's met all the passengers somewhere before. Things are made even more mysterious by Lanser's certainty that an enemy sub is stalking the ship, and by his premonition that *something* is going to happen at 1:15 A.M. His fear proves correct: at one-fifteen a U-boat surfaces. Peering through binoculars, Lanser sees that its captain is . . . himself! The U-boat sinks the helpless freighter, then crew members machine-gun the survivors. Lanser sinks beneath the waters. Later, on board the sub, a lieutenant suggests they might all face damnation for their action. Kapitan Lanser discounts this theory—not realizing that he is, in fact, doomed to relive the sinking of that ship for eternity.

"The S.S. Queen of Glasgow, *heading for New York, and the time is 1942. For one man, it is* always *1942—and this man will ride the ghost of that ship every night for eternity. This is what is meant by paying the fiddler. This is the comeuppance awaiting every man when the ledger of his life is opened and examined, the tally made, and then the reward or the penalty paid. And in the case of Carl Lanser, former Kapitan Lieutenant, Navy of the Third Reich, this is the penalty. This is the justice meted out. This is judgment night in the Twilight Zone."*

"Judgment Night" is a *Flying Dutchman* variation involving a Nazi submarine commander, persuasively portrayed by Jerusalem-born Nehemiah Persoff. The episode also boasts a pre–*Mr. Novak* James Franciscus in a bit role as a nervous lieutenant under Persoff's command, demonstrating for all to hear that a convincing German accent is beyond his reach. Numerous sets are employed from *The Wreck of the Mary Deare,* a film starring Gary Cooper and Charlton Heston that Metro had just completed. Authentic footage of a U-boat crew in action was convincingly integrated into the film, as well.

This nautical, fog-enshrouded ghost story, well-written by Serling, was the first episode directed by German-born director John Brahm. Previously, Brahm had directed the movie *The Brasher Doubloon,* an adaptation of Raymond Chandler's *The High Window,* as well as *The Lodger* and *Hangover Square,* two effectively scary films starring Laird Cregar (Cregar's last two films, in fact). It was on the basis of the two Cregar films that Houghton hired Brahm, feeling that the mood he had created in them would be perfect for *The Twilight Zone*. It was. In all, Brahm would direct twelve episodes for the series, more than any other director.

"Judgment Night" marked the first (and only reported) case of censorship on *The Twilight Zone*. In his original script, Serling had the ship's first officer (Patrick MacNee, later the inimitable Mr. Steed of *The Avengers*) order up a cup of tea to the bridge. General Foods, whose Sanka coffee commercials were sponsoring the show, objected to this reference to what they perceived as a competitor. The line was changed to ordering "a tray" be sent up. (It's fortunate that apparently no one at General Foods realized that on occasion people will drink water, too, or the episode might have had to take place on dry land!)

Serling encountered another problem on "Judgment Night," albeit a tiny one, regarding the reading of the narration. "One of the first lines I had to say was, 'Next week, we invite you to take a trip on a tramp steamer.' And of course I said, 'Next week, we invite you to take a trip on a stamp treamer.' And of course we had to do it over."

SERLING AS NARRATOR

Serling had more problems in adjusting to his on-camera role than just stumbling over the occasional word. His last acting had been in college, and it hadn't been to an audience of twenty million. During the first season, Serling's narrations were off-camera, his sole on-camera appearance being at the end of each show to announce next week's program. During the second season, this role was expanded to include an on-camera appearance at the beginning of every show, as well.

"Rod was a very nervous man before the camera," explains director Lamont Johnson, who would come on the scene during the second season. "When he had to do his lead-ins he would go through absolute hell. He would sweat and sputter and go pale. He was terribly ill at ease in front of the camera."

Johnson resorted to a number of devious devices in order to relax Serling. "I'd clown around with him and roll the camera without letting him know and I'd say, 'What was that you said?' And he would sort of snap off the thing at me as though, 'Smart ass, I'll show you.' The crew was with me on that; they'd shut up and be quiet, otherwise we'd never get a take under those circumstances."

One director who actually enjoyed and felt challenged in directing Serling was Douglas Heyes. With each new episode he would try to think up a novel and surprising way of introducing Serling into the scene. In "The Eye of the Beholder" we see the bizarre and distorted silhouette of a figure walking behind a screen. When the figure emerges, it is Serling. In

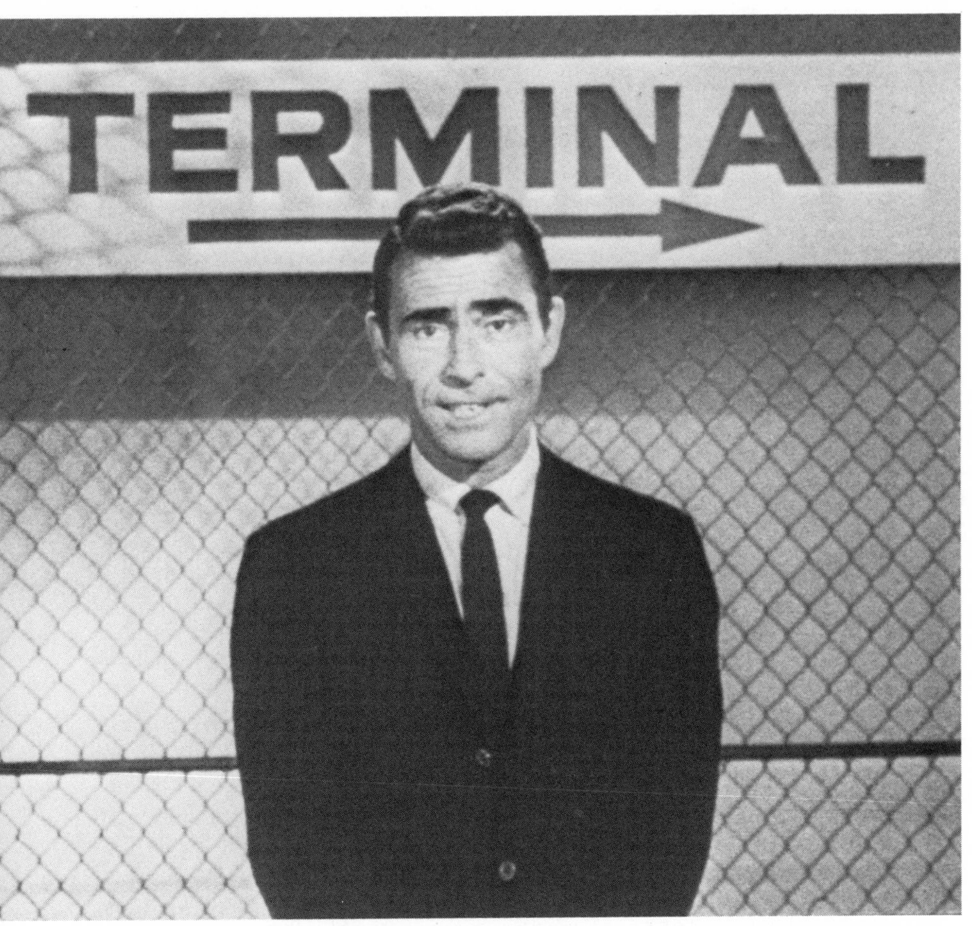

Rod Serling introducing "Nightmare at 20,000 Feet"

"Dust," a weighted bag has a noose fitted around it on a gallows. The trap is sprung, the weight falls and jerks to a halt directly behind Serling. In "Nervous Man in a Four Dollar Room," we see a down-shot of a tiny room looking directly from the ceiling. Serling enters the frame—at such an angle that he would have to be standing straight out from one of the walls! (This was accomplished by using rear projection of the room behind Serling.)

The directors weren't the only ones to film Serling's spots. In fact, during the fourth season, producer Herbert Hirschman often took on the assignment. Generally, however, the chore would fall to an assistant director.

"I remember the first time that I directed him," says assistant director Edward Denault. "You know, Rod always talked out of the corner of his mouth, and I felt that that didn't look right for camera and I tried and tried, as nicely as I could, to get him to be relaxed and to get him to deliver in such a way that he would open his mouth, because he also talked through his teeth. And I got to the point where I felt that I was beginning to make him nervous because I was trying to change him. So finally, I said, 'Rod, you've got to do it the way you feel comfortable.' So all I did then was try to put him in a comfortable setting and maybe have him walk from one thing to another if the timing looked right or felt right. And he went ahead and he talked the way he talked and did it, and he always did it the same way and it became a trademark, really."

Serling said of being chosen to host *The Twilight Zone*, "[They] looked at me and said, 'Hell, at least he's articulate and he speaks English, so let's use him.' Only my laundress knows how frightened I am!"

RICHARD MATHESON

Appearing on camera wasn't the only new consideration Serling had to deal with on *The Twilight Zone*. Contractually, he was bound to write eighty percent of the scripts; but since it was *his* show he had to make certain that the other twenty percent were of the same high quality. For the first time, he had the responsibility of hiring other writers.

Initially, he decided to try something new. "Before we started out on this show of mine, I'd been screaming loudly on behalf of new talent. For years, I'd been bellowing about how new talent wasn't getting a chance.

"So I opened up the show for unsolicited manuscripts. 'Come on, fellers,' I yelled. 'Send 'em in. If you think you have a talent for writing and you know the special demands of this show, let's hear from you.'

"I got fourteen thousand manuscripts in the first five days. Of those fourteen thousand, I and members of my staff read about five hundred. And four hundred and ninety-eight of those five hundred were absolute trash; hand-scrawled, laboriously written, therapeutic pieces of writing from sick people. Of the two remaining scripts, both of professional quality, neither fitted the show."

Obviously, more traditional methods would have to be used to obtain the needed scripts. A screening of the pilot was held, to which established writers were invited. Out of that screening, two writers were selected who, with Serling, provided all but one of the first season's scripts.

Richard Matheson and Charles Beaumont were men whose work was amazingly similar but who couldn't have been more different as people. Matheson, to this day, is a very private man, soft-spoken, disciplined, very family-oriented. Beaumont, on the other hand, was tremendously outgo-

Richard Matheson today

ing, energetic, and disorganized. Writer William F. Nolan, co-author of the novel *Logan's Run* and a friend to both, compares the two: "Dick was Mr. Dependable, Mr. Resolute, Mr. Solid, Mr. Take-care-of-the-family-on-Sunday, and he's still like that. Chuck was Mr. Will-o'-the-wisp. You never even knew if he was in the city or not. He was supposed to be going to dinner with his wife and he was in Chicago or something."

Yet the two, for all their differences, were very close. "Chuck Beaumont was my best friend for many years," says Matheson. "We wrote together for a period of time when we first went into television (until we decided that we would do better each going solo) and acted as 'spurs' to each other creatively. I had sold my first collection of short stories before Chuck, which spurred him on to get his first collection. (Matheson's *Born of Man and Woman* [Chamberlain Press, 1954], Beaumont's *The Hunger and Other Stories* [G. P. Putnam's Sons, 1958].) We both wrote 'mainstream' novels about the same time (Beaumont's *The Intruder* [G. P. Putnam's Sons, 1959], Matheson's *The Beardless Warriors* [Little, Brown & Company, 1960].) We both went into TV at the same time. We both wrote films in the same period of time. There was competition but only of the friendliest sort. We were not jealous of each other but happy for each others' success."

Richard Burton Matheson was born in Allendale, New Jersey, on February 20, 1926, the son of Norwegian immigrants. Of his early upbringing, Matheson notes that there was little to turn him toward writing. "I believe that environment is less a factor than most in the formation of a writer. I don't think I became a writer because my environment made me introspective. I believe I was born to be introspective for various reasons (among them astrological) and therefore reacted to my environment accordingly. I do not feel it is environmental that the first book I borrowed from the library at age seven was a fantasy novel; that my first poems and stories at age seven were of a fantasy nature. In essence, I was 'born' to be a writer, and probably a fantasy writer predominantly."

Following a childhood in Brooklyn, combat in Germany in World War II (from which experience he wrote his novel *The Beardless Warriors*), and college at the University of Missouri (majoring in journalism), Matheson emerged determined to have a writing career. But it didn't come easy. "After I got out of college, I couldn't get a job on a newspaper or a magazine," he says. "Donald Berwick, an editor at *Esquire*, suggested that I get a night job and work in the daytime since I wanted to write. So I got a night job typing up address plates for magazines at a place my brother ran, then started writing short stories. Within a few months, I sold 'Born of Man and Woman.'"

"Born of Man and Woman" appeared in the Summer 1950 issue of *The Magazine of Fantasy and Science Fiction*. A gruesome yet sensitive story told first person from the viewpoint of a hideously malformed mutant child kept chained in a basement, it gained Matheson instant notoriety and has come to be recognized as a classic of the field. In succeeding years, Matheson gathered extensive credits, selling to most of the major science fiction magazines, as well as writing numerous film and television scripts. Occasionally, these areas of interest overlapped: what initially brought him out to Hollywood was to adapt his novel *The Shrinking Man* (Fawcett, 1956) into Universal's *The Incredible Shrinking Man*.

Matheson's stories, particularly his horror stories, were remarkably powerful—and their effect was considerable. Writer Stephen King says of Matheson, "He was the first guy that I ever read who seemed to be doing something that Lovecraft wasn't doing. It wasn't eastern Europe—the horror could be in the Seven-Eleven store down the block, or it could be just up the street. Something terrible could be going on even in a G.I. Bill–type ranch development near a college, it could be there as well. And to me, as a kid, that was a revelation, that was extremely exciting. He was putting the horror in places that I could relate to."

Matheson's approach to writing was one that suited *The Twilight Zone* perfectly: "To me, fantasy at its best (strictly personal, of course) consists of putting in one drop of fantasy into a mixture which is, otherwise, completely factual, realistic. And, once that drop of fantasy has been put into the mixture, I try to forget that I am writing a fantasy and write as realistic a story as I can, recalling, of course, that the springboard has been some offbeat concept."

The transition to writing for *The Twilight Zone* went very smoothly. "Chuck and I pitched ideas and then started writing scripts," says Matheson. "For a long time it was just the two of us and Rod."

It should be noted that during the years that Matheson and Beaumont were regular contributors to *The Twilight Zone* they were also busy writing short stories, novels, teleplays for other series, and screenplays. The films Matheson wrote scripts for during the *Twilight Zone* years include *House of Usher, The Pit and the Pendulum, Master of the World, Tales of Terror, The Raven, The Comedy of Terrors,* and (with Beaumont and George Baxt) *Burn, Witch, Burn*. Beaumont's film scripts include *The Intruder, The Premature Burial* (with Ray Russell), *The Wonderful World of the Brothers Grimm* (with David P. Harmon and William Roberts), *The Haunted Palace,* and *The Seven Faces of Dr. Lao*.

"THE LAST FLIGHT" (2/5/60)

Kenneth Haigh

Written by Richard Matheson
Producer: Buck Houghton
Director: William Claxton
Director of Photography: George T. Clemens
Music: stock

Cast:
Flight Lt. Decker: Kenneth Haigh
Major Wilson: Simon Scott
General Harper: Alexander Scourby
Air Marshal Mackaye: Robert Warwick
Stunt Pilot: Frank Gifford Tallman
Corporal: Harry Raybould
Guard: Jerry Catron
Jeep Driver: Paul Baxley
Truck Driver: Jack Perkins

"Witness Flight Lieutenant William Terrance Decker, Royal Flying Corps, returning from a patrol somewhere over France. The year is 1917. The problem is that the Lieutenant is hopelessly lost. Lieutenant Decker will soon discover that a man can be lost not only in terms of maps and miles, but also in time—*and time in this case can be measured in eternities."*

While on a World War I flying mission, Decker experiences a fit of cowardice and deserts his best friend, who is surrounded by enemy planes. In his panic, he flies through a strange white cloud—and lands at a modern-day American air base in France. He is immediately taken into custody by a major and led into the office of the base's commanding general. At first, both officers doubt Decker's authenticity, but slowly the major comes to believe his story. In turn, Decker discovers that the man he left to die survived, went on to become a hero in World War II, and is due to inspect the base that very day. Realizing that his trip in time has been for a purpose—to give him a second chance—Decker overpowers the major, escapes to his plane and takes off, disappearing into the same white cloud. Later that day, Decker's former friend, now a flight marshal in the RAF, arrives at the base. From him we learn that Decker *did* return to save him—at the cost of his own life.

"Dialogue from a play, Hamlet to Horatio: 'There are more things in heaven and earth than are dreamt of in your philosophy.' Dialogue from a play written long before men took to the sky. There are more things in heaven and earth, and

in the sky, that perhaps can *be dreamt of. And somewhere in between heaven, the sky, the earth, lies the Twilight Zone.*"

The first non-Serling script to go into production was Richard Matheson's "The Last Flight." While the episode is thoroughly as effective as anything Serling wrote for the series, it is totally different in its emphasis. Matheson had none of Serling's sentimentality or nostalgia and none of his affection for "the little people," those insignificant, slightly eccentric characters so in evidence in many of Serling's scripts. Rather, his strength lay in the power of his plotting, the inexorable way in which his stories unfold. This is particularly evident in such episodes as "The Invaders" (Agnes Moorhead menaced by tiny spacemen) and "Nightmare at 20,000 Feet" (the gremlin on the wing), but it holds true for "The Last Flight," as well. We watch not because of any particular warmth we feel for the characters but because the story is so *interesting.*

This strength in plotting not only helped Matheson sell the concept of "The Last Flight" to the viewers, but to Serling and Houghton as well. Normally, the procedure for a first-time contributor to the show would have been to write an outline before going to script, but in this case, Matheson just told them the idea. "That was one of those cases," he explains, "where the idea is so vivid—a World War I pilot lands and he's on a modern airbase—it gives you a vision so immediately that they responded to it."

"The Last Flight" was filmed on location at Norton Air Force Base in San Bernardino, California. Director William Claxton sent actors Kenneth Haigh, Simon Scott, Alexander Scourby, and Robert Warwick through the motions with as little trickery and embroidery as possible, with the result that the drama of the piece emerges out of its utter straightforwardness. The vintage 1918 Nieuport biplane used in the episode was both owned and flown by Frank Gifford Tallman, a veteran motion picture pilot. As for the plane, it too had been previously before the cameras in such films as *The Dawn Patrol, Lafayette Escadrille, Men with Wings,* and *The Lost Squadron.* "As a matter of fact," Tallman remarked in 1959, "this particular airplane has appeared in more World War I motion pictures than any other plane."

When Tallman landed the biplane at Norton Air Force Base, he discovered that the allure resulting from the juxtaposition of two time-frames extended beyond Matheson's teleplay. Director of photography George Clemens recalls, "When he landed at this airport and taxied up, you've never seen people come around a thing—like kids around a new toy—as these modern-day jet pilots. They looked in the cockpit and felt the wings. They'd never seen anything like that!" This attention was so enthusiastic the plane had to be roped off and special guards posted to protect it from damage.

It is a mark of both the quality of the writing and the respect in which the written word was held on *The Twilight Zone* that Matheson's script was filmed almost exactly as written. The only change was one of title, from "Flight" to "The Last Flight."

"I had double meanings in many of my titles," says Matheson, "and I wanted it to refer not only to the flight of the airplane but to the protagonist's flight from the situation he was in. I suppose it still had a similar meaning. It was the last time he ran away as a coward."

"AND WHEN THE SKY WAS OPENED" (12/11/59)

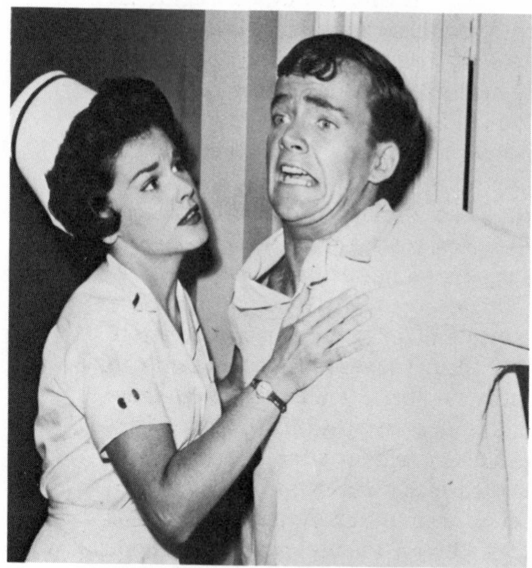

Sue Randall and James Hutton

Written by Rod Serling
Based on the short story "Disappearing Act" by Richard Matheson
Producer: Buck Houghton
Director: Douglas Heyes
Director of Photography: George T. Clemens
Music: Leonard Rosenman

Cast:
Col. Clegg Forbes: Rod Taylor
Col. Ed Harrington: Charles Aidman
Maj. William Gart: James Hutton
Amy: Maxine Cooper
Girl in Bar: Gloria Pall
Bartender: Paul Bryar
Nurse: Sue Randall
Investigator: Logan Field
Officer: Oliver McGowan
Medical Officer: Joe Bassett
Mr. Harrington: S. John Launer
Nurse Two: Elizabeth Fielding

"Her name: X–20. Her type: an experimental interceptor. Recent history: a crash landing in the Mojave Desert after a thirty-one-hour flight nine hundred miles into space. Incidental data: the ship, with the men who flew her, disappeared from the radar screen for twenty-four hours. . . . But the shrouds that cover mysteries are not always made out of a tarpaulin, as this man will soon find out on the other side of a hospital door."

Three astronauts have returned from this first space flight. Major Gart is hospitalized with a broken leg, but the other two, Colonels Harrington and

Forbes, go off for a night of revelry. In a bar, Colonel Harrington suddenly gets a strange feeling. He calls his parents. They tell him that they *have* no son. Suddenly, mysteriously, Harrington disappears, with no one but Colonel Forbes remembering that he ever existed. When Forbes tells Gart the story at the hospital, Gart says he doesn't know any Ed Harrington either. Suddenly, Forbes gets a peculiar feeling of euphoria. He shakes it off, screams, "I don't want this to happen!" and runs out of the room. By the time Gart gets to the hallway, Forbes too has disappeared, and nobody else has any memory of *him*. Then Gart disappears, and with him their ship, wiping the last evidence of their existence off the face of the earth.

"Once upon a time, there was a man named Harrington, a man named Forbes, a man named Gart. They used to exist, but don't any longer. Someone—or something—took them somewhere. At least they are no longer a part of the memory of man. And as to the X–20 supposed to be housed here in this hangar, this too does not exist. And if any of you have any questions concerning an aircraft and three men who flew her, speak softly of them . . . and only in the Twilight Zone."

Serling's script for "And When the Sky Was Opened" was ostensibly based on Matheson's short story, "Disappearing Act" (which appears in his collection, *Third From the Sun*), but the connection was very thin. The original story concerns an unsuccessful writer who finds that the people in his life, one by one, are disappearing, and only he remembers them. Ultimately, of course, he too disappears. In comparing the episode with his short story, Matheson says, "My feeling about it is like my feeling about the second version of my novel, *I Am Legend* [filmed as *The Omega Man*]: it's so far removed that there's nothing to judge by."

"And When the Sky Was Opened" marked director Douglas Heyes's entry into *The Twilight Zone*. Neither Serling nor Houghton had ever worked with him before, but his work on a number of episodes of *Maverick* convinced Houghton to hire him. "I was taken with Doug's direction right off the bat," says Houghton. "And When the Sky Was Opened" is a beautiful job of directing, wonderfully executed in handling of both actors and equipment. Houghton made it a point to use Heyes on episodes where something imaginative in the way of direction was needed, such as "Eye of the Beholder," in which none of the characters' faces could be seen until the very end, or "Nervous Man in a Four Dollar Room," in which the entire show is a dialogue between a man and his mirror image.

Heyes found the challenge invigorating. "Buck and Rod Serling both were extremely encouraging as to finding unusual and new ways to do things. They didn't say, 'Stick to the script,' to me or to any director.

They'd say, 'Think of something to make it *Twilight Zone,* to make it unusual.'"

With "And When the Sky Was Opened," Heyes took the initiative in two specific scenes. Cast as the three astronauts (in order of disappearance) were Charles Aidman, Rod Taylor, and Jim Hutton. The climactic moment of the episode comes when Taylor, after trying futilely to convince those around him that there was a third astronaut on the mission, begins to feel himself disappearing. "Originally," says Heyes, "Rod's disappearance or the feeling that he was going was written as a very painful experience, but I decided to make it a very *euphoric* experience. Instead of playing it for terror or agony—everything had been fear up till then, fear of disappearance, fear of the unknown, and so forth—I said to Rod Taylor, 'Let's play this as if this is the most marvelous thing that ever happened.' We took an angle on him and we lowered the camera as he was talking, so the effect was that he seemed to be rising while he was talking."

The other departure was far less euphoric. Heyes explains, "Rod Taylor is searching for Charles Aidman, who disappeared in a telephone booth in a bar while they were talking. Taylor gets drunk and he comes to this bar which is now closed and forces his way in. Now, it's not written in the script, but because Rod encouraged me to do things like that, I simply had him walk through the glass door, sort of spin and crash through it into the bar. It was an unexpected entrance and Rod Serling liked it very much."

"And When the Sky Was Opened" is a frightening episode, and not inadvertently so. Serling had thought long and hard on the subject of fear. "In making a judgment, or any analysis or inventory," he once said, "of what are the degrees of emotional reaction and indeed types of emotional reaction, I think there is a universality of reaction to certain given prods. Now, our reaction to fear of a mugging, I think, is relatively universal. There are maybe eight different types of reactions, but I think you could almost categorize them and put them in a textbook.

"The worst fear of all is the fear of the unknown working on *you,* which you cannot share with others. To me, that's the most nightmarish of the stimuli." Serling had defined a fear that was universal and basic. This fear would be exploited repeatedly on *The Twilight Zone,* and not just by Serling. Here, it is used to particular advantage.

Of course, what makes the threat of disappearance so believable lies mostly in the performances of Hutton, Aidman, and Taylor. All three react with an uneasiness that grows to near-hysteria as the reality—or unreality—of the situation sinks in. Australian-born Rod Taylor, so very fine in the movies *The Birds* and *The Time Machine,* is the focal character of the episode, and his performance is intelligent, appealing, and powerful. His is a most difficult task, to make us believe that the impossible is happening—and he succeeds admirably.

"And When the Sky Was Opened" is a flawed episode, however, and this flaw lies in its resolution. Like "Where Is Everybody?" it sets up the question "What is going on here?"—then fails to satisfactorily answer it. In this case, an answer isn't even attempted; the astronauts are simply yanked out of existence with no explanation at all, like an old vaudevillian getting the hook from a stagehand in the wings. Serling didn't feel that this was particularly significant, though. "My feeling here was that the bizarre quality of what occurred so out-shadowed the required rationale that we didn't have to worry about it."

One consideration perhaps should soften any dissatisfaction with "And When the Sky Was Opened." In a sense, the episode was made in a different era. We *know* that when astronauts go into outer space they don't cease to exist—we've done it. But when Serling wrote the script, no one could be certain *what* would happen when men first ventured into space. In his script, he was trying to capture that dread of the unknown, and in that, at least, he succeeded.

"THE HITCH-HIKER" (1/22/60)

Leonard Strong and Inger Stevens

Written by Rod Serling
Based on the radio play "The Hitch-Hiker" by Lucille Fletcher
Producer: Buck Houghton
Director: Alvin Ganzer
Director of Photography: George T. Clemens
Music: stock

Cast:
Nan Adams: Inger Stevens
Hitch-Hiker: Leonard Strong
Sailor: Adam Williams
Mechanic: Lew Gallo
Highway Flag Man: Dwight Townsend
Counterman: Russ Bender
Waitress: Mitzi McCall
Gas Station Man: George Mitchell
Mrs. Whitney: Eleanor Audley

"Her name is Nan Adams. She's twenty-seven years old. Her occupation: buyer at a New York department store, at present on vacation, driving cross-country to Los Angeles, California, from Manhattan. . . . Minor incident on Highway 11 in Pennsylvania, perhaps to be filed away under accidents you walk away

from. But from this moment on, Nan Adams's companion on a trip to California will be terror; her route—fear; her destination—quite unknown."

Following a blowout in Pennsylvania, Nan Adams repeatedly sees the same ominous hitch-hiker. Frightened by the fact that the man seems to be beckoning to her, she tries to run him over, only to be told by a sailor to whom she's given a lift that there was no hitch-hiker on the road. Finally she calls home—and learns her mother has suffered a nervous breakdown following the death of her daughter six days earlier in an automobile accident in Pennsylvania. Strangely devoid of emotion, Nan returns to her car where the hitch-hiker—whose identity and purpose she now understands—awaits.

"Nan Adams, age twenty-seven. She was driving to California, to Los Angeles. She didn't make it. There was a detour—through the Twilight Zone."

Death personified made his second appearance on *The Twilight Zone* in "The Hitch-Hiker." People generally credit Serling with originating the story, but in truth he only adapted it, and very well indeed, from a radio play by Lucille Fletcher, author of the famous radio play *Sorry, Wrong Number*.

"The Hitch-Hiker" was the first and only radio play to be made into a *Twilight Zone* episode. In 1941, Serling had heard the original broadcast of "The Hitch-Hiker" on *The Mercury Theatre on the Air*, starring Orson Welles in the lead (Welles reprised the role at least once, on *Suspense*). The play stuck with him and when *The Twilight Zone* came along, he contacted Lucille Fletcher and bought the rights. He then reworked the play, changing the first name and gender of the main character (from Ronald Adams to Nan Adams), but otherwise leaving the basic plot intact.

A press release on the episode, written in 1960, claims that Serling wrote the script of "The Hitch-Hiker" in just six hours—which, considering Serling's average output, is entirely within the realm of possibility. As for the change in name, Serling named the character after his daughter, Anne, whose family nickname is Nan. "That one always bothered me," says Anne. "I thought, why did he have to use *that* name?"

"I was not asked to adapt the play to television," says Lucille Fletcher, "nor was I asked about the change of gender in the main character. If I had been, I would never have approved of it, for good though Inger Stevens's performance was, I don't think a female in the part added anything to my play. In fact, I think that the dramatic effect was minimized."

Curiously, although Serling was unaware of it when he changed the main character to a woman, "The Hitch-Hiker" was based on an incident that

"Going my way?"

happened to the author herself. She explains, "I first got the idea for 'The Hitch-Hiker' in 1940, when I crossed the country—from Brooklyn to California—with my first husband, Bernard Herrmann (who wrote the music for the radio play, incidentally)*—and we saw an odd-looking man, first on the Brooklyn Bridge and then on the Pulaski Skyway. We never saw him again. However, I didn't quite know what to do with the idea until a year later, when, shortly after my first daughter was born, I conceived the idea of doing it as a ghost story. After that I wrote it in a couple of days, during the afternoon, when my newborn baby was taking a nap.

"It reached radio and Orson Welles, because Benny, my husband, was musical director of the *Mercury Theatre on the Air*. I knew Orson, and in fact, had done a lot of publicity on him, when I was working at CBS before my marriage to Benny. I wrote the show for him, designing the narration more or less to fit his style and manner of speaking. Welles did it eloquently and imaginatively and I was very pleased with the result."

Despite Ms. Fletcher's preferences, the fact remains that it is the *Twilight Zone* version of "The Hitch-Hiker" which is remembered today, and judged on its own merits it proves quite effective. Inger Stevens plays her role with an extreme nervousness which, when coupled with the

*Although the *Twilight Zone* version of "The Hitch-Hiker" bears no music credit (which indicates that, rather than having music composed specifically for this episode, music from the CBS music library was used), most if not all of the episode's music was unmistakably composed by Herrmann, as well. In fact, several phrases heard in the *Twilight Zone* episode can be discerned in the original *Mercury Theatre* version, too.

deadpan calm of Leonard Strong as the hitch-hiker (Mr. Death), makes for a great deal of tension. Director Alvin Ganzer adds to this tension by setting up a number of shots so that the face of the hitch-hiker suddenly and unexpectedly comes into view. Very creepy stuff—surrounded by a cemetery chill.

At one point, Ganzer's inventiveness almost brought several camera technicians face to face with their *own* hitch-hikers. A certain scene called for Nan Adams's car to stall on the railroad tracks with a train bearing down on her (finally, the car starts and she backs it off the tracks, just in time). Ganzer couldn't rent a train, so he had to set up his equipment by a railroad crossing and wait for a regularly scheduled train to go by. Initially, it occurred to him that it might be exciting to film the train coming dead-on. "We had the camera on the tracks," he explains, "and we were going to pull it off. Luckily, a train went the opposite direction and we realized how fast the train went through that intersection. When we saw that, we thought three times and put the camera on the side of the tracks."

"TIME ENOUGH AT LAST" (11/20/59)

Burgess Meredith

Written by Rod Serling
Based on the short story "Time Enough at Last" by Lynn Venable
Producer: Buck Houghton
Director: John Brahm
Director of Photography: George T. Clemens
Music: Leith Stevens

Cast:
Henry Bemis: Burgess Meredith
Mr. Carsville: Vaughn Taylor
Helen Bemis: Jacqueline deWit
Woman in Bank: Lela Bliss

"Witness Mr. Henry Bemis, a charter member in the fraternity of dreamers. A bookish little man whose passion is the printed page but who is conspired against by a bank president and a wife and a world full of tongue-cluckers and the unrelenting hands of a clock. But in just a moment Mr. Bemis will enter a world without bank presidents or wives or clocks or anything else. He'll have a world all to himself—without anyone."

Mild-mannered and myopic, bank teller Henry Bemis loves to read, but neither his shrewish wife nor efficiency-minded boss give him much chance. Sneaking into the vault on his lunch hour to read, he is knocked unconscious by a mammoth shock wave. When he comes to, he discovers that the world has been devastated by a nuclear war and that he, having been protected by the vault, is the last man on Earth. He decides to commit suicide, but at the final moment his eyes fall on the ruins of a library. For him, it is paradise. Gleefully he piles the books high, organizing his reading for the years to come. But as he settles down to read the first book, his glasses slip off his nose and smash, trapping him forever in a hopelessly blurry world.

"The best-laid plans of mice and men—and Henry Bemis, the small man in the glasses who wanted nothing but time. Henry Bemis, now just a part of a smashed landscape, just a piece of the rubble, just a fragment of what man has deeded to himself. Mr. Henry Bemis . . . in the Twilight Zone."

If "The Hitch-Hiker" demonstrated Rod Serling's ability to use restraint in adapting a work of merit, then the next episode demonstrated that he also knew when *not* to.

"Time Enough at Last" began as a six-page short story by Lynn Venable in the January, 1953, issue of *If* magazine. It told in a clipped, bland manner the story of a harassed little bookworm who survives a nuclear war and is faced with a blissful future of solitude in which to read . . . only to break his glasses. The story was cute, clever—and forgettable.

What Serling did with this piece was to expand it, flesh out its characters (the short story has almost no dialogue) and transform it into a show that is unforgettable in its humor, its humanity, and its tragedy. Central to this transformation was Serling's delineation of Mr. Bemis. In the short story, he is just a chess piece moved from square to square. But in the show, Serling takes the time to acquaint us with this mild, introspective and funny man, to get to know and like him, so that when disaster befalls him, we feel an overwhelming sympathy. Take, for example, this piece of dialogue, original with Serling, that does nothing to advance the plot, but much to reveal the character. The scene is the bank in which Bemis works. He is counting money out to a customer:

BEMIS: Mrs. Chester, have you ever read *David Copperfield*?

MRS. CHESTER: How's that?

BEMIS: It's a wonderful book. There's this poor little fella, and his father has passed away and his mother has married this miserable man called Murdstone. Isn't that a villainous name? *Murd*stone. Well, this Murdstone has a sister called Jane—

MRS. CHESTER: Mr. Bemis, you shortchanged me again! You owe me one more dollar! See? There's only twenty-four here and there *should* be twenty-five!

BEMIS: Oh! I'm terribly sorry, Mrs. Murd—er, uh, Mrs., uh, *Chester* . . .

Playing Bemis is Burgess Meredith, star of the film adaptation of *Of Mice and Men,* and two-time Oscar nominee (for *Day of the Locust* and *Rocky*). It is the first of four episodes he will do for *The Twilight Zone,* and his performance shines. John Brahm, director of "Time Enough at Last," says of working with Meredith, "It is so easy. He understands immediately. You respect him. Actually, one can say that everything moves right, from the beginning, without much talk. Burgess Meredith is in a class by

Burgess Meredith

"The best laid plans of mice and men . . ."

himself." Mention should also be made of the wonderfully obnoxious performances turned in by Vaughn Taylor and Jacqueline deWit as Bemis's monstrous, anti-literate boss and wife, respectively.

A great deal of ingenuity went into the making of "Time Enough at Last." To give Meredith a properly bookwormish appearance, he was given a fake moustache and tremendously thick glasses (two pairs were actually used; one with thick, distorting lenses for the closeups, and another with window glass so that Meredith could see on the long shots). To get across the idea of a nuclear attack, all clichés were avoided. There are no stock shots of mushroom clouds nor of real destroyed cities. Instead, the focus is moved in close. Bemis is in the bank vault, eating his lunch. He glances down casually at a book lying on the floor next to his pocket watch. Suddenly, the book flips open. The glass in the watch shatters. Then the concussion hits. To accomplish this last effect, George Clemens had the entire set built on springs, so that both the camera and the set could shake at the same time.

The after-the-Bomb sets were also particularly striking. Two different sets were used. One was a seemingly huge Bomb-wrecked landscape, complete with stormcloud-filled skies. In reality, this set was built on a soundstage, with a sky originally painted for a motion picture. In order to bring out the clouds even more, Clemens decided to use a blue filter, which was quite unorthodox—so unorthodox, in fact, that when he had to take off half a day to go to court and had to explain the procedure to a replacement, Clemens remembers, "He was scared to death!"

The other set was an enormous flight of steps, representing the sole remains of a massive library. In reality, these impressive steps were a standing set on the MGM backlot. Generally, actors would be filmed standing on or walking up the steps, and then a painting of a state capitol or some such building would be matted in. These same steps can be seen in the episode "A Nice Place to Visit," also directed by Brahm, and in George Pal's *The Time Machine*. It was Brahm's idea to place Meredith on the steps. "I had the idea to put him there, all by himself, after this end of the world, so to speak. In other words, the emptiness was shown. Everything was gone."

"Time Enough at Last" remains one of the best-remembered and best-loved episodes of *The Twilight Zone*. Few can watch it and not be seduced by its simplicity and its pathos.

"The only thing I can tell you about that particular episode," says Meredith, "is that I've heard more about that than any of [the other three *Twilight Zone* episodes], and indeed almost more about it than anything else I've done on television. I think it must have had a great impact on people. I don't suppose there's a month goes by, even to this day, that people don't come up and remind me of that episode."

"PEOPLE ARE ALIKE ALL OVER" (3/25/60)

Roddy McDowall and Susan Oliver, original advertisement

Written by Rod Serling
Based on the short story "Brothers Beyond the Void" by Paul Fairman
Producer: Buck Houghton
Director: Mitchell Leisen
Director of Photography: George T. Clemens
Music: stock

Cast:
Sam Conrad: Roddy McDowall
Warren Marcusson: Paul Comi
Teenya: Susan Oliver
Martian #1: Byron Morrow
Martian #2: Vic Perrin
Martian #3: Vernon Gray

"You're looking at a species of flimsy little two-legged animal with extremely small heads whose name is Man. Warren Marcusson, age thirty-five. Samuel A. Conrad, age thirty-one. . . . They're taking a highway into space, Man unshackling himself and sending his tiny, groping fingers up into the unknown. Their destination is Mars, and in just a moment we'll land there with them."

When their ship crashes on the Martian surface, Marcusson—the optimist who believes people are alike all over, even on Mars—is killed. Left alone is Sam Conrad, who does *not* share Marcusson's philosophy and who is terrified when he hears someone banging on the outside of the ship. His terror turns to relief, however, when he ventures out and sees that the Martians are indeed human, albeit telepathic, and that they appear extremely friendly. The next morning, the Martians present him with a surprise, a house built to look exactly like one on Earth. Pleased by this, Conrad is left alone inside. But very soon, Conrad comes to the shocking realization that the house has no windows and all the doors are locked. Suddenly, a wall slides upward, revealing vertical bars beyond which stands a crowd of gaping Martians. Conrad is in a zoo. He cries out, "Marcusson, you were right—people *are* alike everywhere!"

"Species of animal brought back alive. Interesting similarity in physical characteristics to human beings in head, trunk, arms, legs, hands, feet. Very tiny undeveloped brain; comes from primitive planet named Earth. Calls himself Samuel Conrad. And he will remain here in his cage with the running water and the electricity and the central heat as long as he lives. Samuel Conrad has found *the Twilight Zone."*

"People Are Alike All Over" is adapted from Paul Fairman's "Brothers Beyond the Void," which originally appeared in the March, 1952, issue of *Fantastic Adventures* and is included in August Derleth's anthology *Worlds of Tomorrow* (Berkley, 1953). In the original story, however, it is Marcusson alone who goes to Mars; Sam Conrad is an older friend who stays at home. As for the Martians, they are four-and-a-half feet tall, "not ugly or especially beautiful," and they certainly don't look like Susan Oliver (something that is undoubtedly the Martian's loss).

In scripting this for *The Twilight Zone,* Serling put added emphasis on the irony of the piece by making Sam Conrad initially afraid of the Martians and then being reassured by Marcusson's conviction that people are "the same all over"—a cosmic truth that ultimately brings about his downfall. Particularly nice is the show's opening shot. It is the night before the launch. Marcusson and Conrad stand behind a metal fence looking up at their ship; their hands idly grasp the metal links. They look, for all the world, like animals in a cage.

"THIRD FROM THE SUN" (1/8/60)

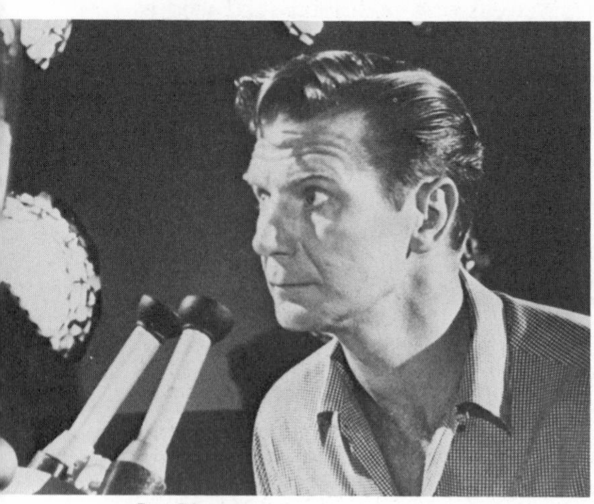
Joe Maross

Written by Rod Serling
Based on the short story "Third From the Sun" by Richard Matheson
Producer: Buck Houghton
Director: Richard L. Bare
Director of Photography: Harry Wild
Music: stock

Cast:
William Sturka: Fritz Weaver
Jerry Riden: Joe Maross
Carling: Edward Andrews
Eve: Lori March
Jody: Denise Alexander
Ann: Jeanne Evans
Guard: Will J. White
Loudspeaker Voice: S. John Launer

"5:30 P.M.: Quitting tine at the plant. Time for supper now. Time for families. Time for a cool drink on a porch. Time for the quiet rustle of leaf-laden trees that screen out the moon. And underneath it all, behind the eyes of the men, hanging invisible over the summer night, is a horror without words. For this is the stillness before storm. This is the eve of the end."

Scientist William Sturka, certain that an all-out nuclear war is imminent, plots with test pilot Jerry Riden to steal an experimental spaceship and escape with their families to a planet eleven million miles away. They are almost stopped by a slimy government stooge named Carling, but they manage to overpower him, board the ship, and take off. In space, they wonder what their new home will be like. From radio broadcasts, they know it is inhabited by people like themselves, and that its name is . . . Earth!

"Behind a tiny ship heading into space is a doomed planet on the verge of suicide. Ahead lies a place called Earth, the third planet from the sun. And for William Sturka and the men and women with him, it's the eve of the beginning . . . in the Twilight Zone."

Serling adapted Richard Matheson's short story "Third from the Sun" (which appears in Matheson's collection of the same name), retaining both the title and the basic plot.

Fritz Weaver, Edward Andrews and Joe Maross

A neat little scientific inaccuracy crops up in this episode. At one point, Maross mentions that the distance from his planet to the Earth is 11 million miles. Considering the fact that Venus is our closest neighbor at 24,600,000 miles (at its nearest), then either a number of astronomers are nearsighted or Serling didn't do his homework.

In order to set the stage for the final twist, director Richard L. Bare resorted to some pretty tricky uses of the camera. Only a handful of shots were filmed straight-on: most were distorted, tilted this way or that. And that wasn't all: "I shot every scene with an extremely wide-angle lens," Bare explains. "Even on close-ups, which are normally shot with a 75mm or 100mm lens, I used a 28mm."

Buck Houghton elaborates. "He used wide-angle lenses all the time on the theory that if you were going to tell people in the end that they weren't on Earth, you should have a peculiar feeling while you're getting there, you should have been made a little restless or uncomfortable. And while Dick was a very straightforward sort of director—he'd have to have a big reason not to use an eye-level camera—he was shooting up under tables and past flashlights to people's faces and all that sort of thing, which I thought was very clever of him. It was an idea of his that I applauded."

CHARLES BEAUMONT

The thirteenth episode to be produced by Cayuga Productions, "Perchance to Dream," was the first script written for *The Twilight Zone* by the late Charles Beaumont. As did Matheson, Beaumont produced stories totally unlike Serling's, displaying virtually no sentimentality but revealing a strong morbidity and an almost clinical fascination with the horrific.

"Chuck was the perfect *Twilight Zone* writer," says writer William F. Nolan, "more than Matheson or Rod Serling, even. Matheson is very much of a realist who can mentally lose himself in those worlds. He doesn't live in them the way Chuck lived in them. Chuck actually lived in the Twilight Zone."

Charles Beaumont in 1960

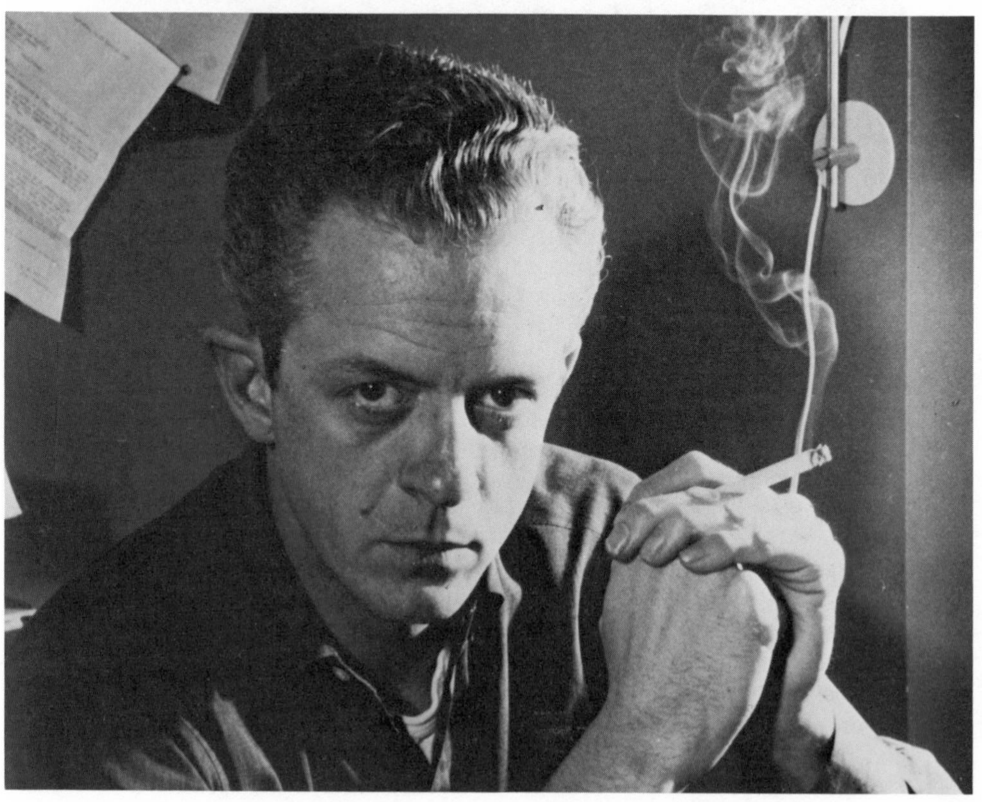

Charles Beaumont was second only to Serling in production of *Twilight Zone* scripts and was responsible for some of the series' most memorable episodes, including "Long Live Walter Jameson" and "The Howling Man." In his brief, fourteen-year career, he wrote and sold ten books, seventy-three short stories, twenty-two articles and profiles, fourteen columns, thirteen screenplays and sixty-eight teleplays. Five men would not be writers today if not for Beaumont and at least that many consider him the best friend they ever had—and the single most powerful influence on their lives.

"He was tremendously magnetic," says Richard Matheson. "I am a quiet person—although there is an antic spirit underneath the surface which some people see, most normally my family. Chuck was a meteoric type of person. His sense of humor was devastating. He was a very funny, very witty person. He had interests in so many things and pursued them all fully. So there was, I suppose, some aspect in which I enjoyed all these things and was exposed to them through him; lived them vicariously through him."

Who was this remarkable man?

Charles Beaumont was born Charles Leroy Nutt on January 2, 1929, on Chicago's North Side. In 1954, he wrote of his childhood, "Football, baseball and dimestore cookie thefts filled my early world, to the exclusion of Aesop, the Brothers Grimm, Dr. Doolittle, and even Bullfinch. The installation by my parents of 'library wallpaper' in the house ('a roomfull of books for only seventy cents a yard!') convinced me that literature was on the way out anyway, so I lived in illiterate contentment until laid low by spinal meningitis. This forced me to less strenuous forms of entertainment. I discovered Oz; then Burroughs; then Poe—and the jig was up."

The light tone of this statement belies the truth of Beaumont's childhood, however. In reality, it was almost certainly one of oppressive peculiarity and morbidity (Beaumont once described it as being "one big Charles Addams cartoon"). On one occasion, Beaumont confided to William F. Nolan that his classic short story, "Miss Gentillbelle"—in which a deranged woman dresses her eight-year-old boy as a little girl and sadistically murders all his pets—was more than mere fancy: his mother *had* dressed him as a little girl and, at least once, had killed one of his pets as a punishment.

"His mother was totally crazy," Beaumont's son, Chris, remembers. "I only met her once, when she came out to California to visit. I was five or six, so I don't remember much, but from what little I remember and from what my father told me about her, I know she was very unstable. She didn't have a very firm foundation in reality and was not terribly responsible as a mother."

Because of his mother's instability, Beaumont was put in the care of his aunts. In 1960, he told the *San Diego Union,* "I lived with five widowed aunts who ran a rooming house near a train depot in the state of Washington. Each night we had a ritual of gathering around the stove and there I'd hear stories about the strange death of each of their husbands."

This is not to say that Beaumont's childhood was all death and deprivation. In the rooming house, he had one relative, either a grandmother or an aunt (memories differ on this point) of whom he was very fond and from whom he inherited his diabolical sense of humor, as he related in an unpublished story:

"Her sense of humor ran slightly to the macabre . . . [Once] I accidentally broke off the blade of the bread knife. We managed to make it stand up on her chest so that the knife appeared to be imbedded almost to the hilt in her. Then I was commanded to rip her clothes a bit and empty a whole bottle of ketchup over her and the linoleum. Then she lay down and I ran screaming, 'Somebody come quick! Somebody come quick!' It was gratifying that Aunt Dora fainted away completely, though the others saw through the joke at once."

In his teens, Beaumont was an avid fan of science fiction, publishing his own fanzine, *Utopia,* and writing endless letters to pulp magazines. Predictably, school did little to capture his interest or his energies. "[I] barely nosed through the elementary grades and gained a certain notoriety in high school as a wastrel, dreamer, could-do-the-work-if-he'd-only-tryer and general lunkhead." Accordingly, he dropped out of high school in the tenth grade and joined the Infantry. "I served valorously for three months," he later wrote, "before they eased me out." It should be noted that his discharge was medical—back trouble—rather than dishonorable.

After a short-lived stage career in California, Beaumont tried his hand at commercial illustration. Although only a mediocre artist, he met with some degree of success, selling illustrations to a number of pulp magazines and the first edition of *Out of the Unknown,* a collection of short stories by husband-and-wife team A. E. van Vogt and E. Mayne Hull. As Charles Leroy Nutt was not a terribly suitable name for an artist (and even less so for a writer—"Hey, you seen that Nutt's story in *Amazing*?"), he changed it to Charles *Mc*Nutt, then later, when collaborating with another artist, to E. T. Beaumont (possibly from Beaumont, Texas, he later said), and finally, legally, to Charles Beaumont.

At the age of nineteen, while working as a railroad clerk in Mobile, Alabama, Beaumont met Helen Broun, an intelligent, sensitive, and attractive twenty-year-old. A year later, they were married and moved to California. Little more than a year after that, Christopher was born, the first of four children. Beaumont now had a family to support. Toward that end, he worked as a piano player (with "an immensely talented right hand

and a nowhere left"), an animator at MGM, a disc jockey, an usher, a dishwasher, an editor at a comic book company (helping "to guide the destinies of such influential literary figures as Bugs Bunny, Mickey Mouse, Donald Duck and Andy Panda"), and a mimeograph operator.

During this entire time, Beaumont was writing feverishly, but meeting with little success. His agent at the time, Forrest J. Ackerman (later editor of *Famous Monsters of Filmland* magazine), was unable to sell any of his first seventy-two short stories. Says Ackerman, "I consider it more a criticism of short-sighted editors that they passed by most of those seventy-two stories, because eventually I think he sold about every word he ever wrote. But in the beginning I couldn't *give* them away."

Finally, in 1950, Beaumont sold his first short story, "The Devil, You Say?" (appearing in the January, 1951, issue of *Amazing Stories,* and adapted in 1962 into the *Twilight Zone* episode "Printer's Devil.")

In September, 1954, Beaumont's short story, "Black Country," appeared in *Playboy*. A *tour de force* about a terminally ill jazz musician, it was a turning point in his career. His stories began to appear regularly in the most widely read and best-paying magazines in the nation. *Playboy* put him on a five-hundred-dollar monthly retainer for first refusal rights to his manuscripts, and listed him as a contributing editor. In April, 1958, G. P. Putnam's Sons published his first collection, *The Hunger and Other Stories,* to good reviews. Beaumont had arrived.

By 1958, Beaumont had also managed to gain a considerable foothold in film and television. Over the previous four years, he had sold a number of scripts to such shows as *Suspense, Have Gun Will Travel, Wanted, Dead or Alive,* and *One Step Beyond,* among others, and had had one film script produced, *The Queen of Outer Space,* an atrocious movie about which he said, "I wrote the thing as a big spoof. Only trouble was the director and some of the cast didn't realize it."

Rod Serling first met Beaumont at a party around this time. "This was right after 'Velvet Alley,'" he recalled in 1963, "and Chuck Beaumont, whom I didn't even know, in a very tasteful way—nothing offensive in the way he did it—he said, 'Quite honestly, I must tell you to your face, it's the worst piece of writing I've ever seen.' I didn't rebel at this at all, but to this day I lay claim that Chuck is absolutely wrong . . . Anyway, it put Chuck and me on a very good basis, because I feel now not only the right but the obligation to speak to Chuck honestly."

Buck Houghton found Beaumont thoroughly impressive, too. "He was very sure of himself," he says. "He talked a story as though he had it licked and maybe he did in his mind, maybe he didn't at that point—I don't know. But I'll tell you this: if there hadn't been a writing profession he'd have been busy at something else. He was really a goer and a doer and a shaker and a mover."

"PERCHANCE TO DREAM" (11/27/59)

Suzanne Lloyd and Richard Conte

Written by Charles Beaumont
Based on the short story "Perchance to Dream" by Charles Beaumont
Producer: Buck Houghton
Director: Robert Florey
Director of Photography: George T. Clemens
Music: Van Cleave

Cast:
Edward Hall: Richard Conte
Dr. Rathmann: John Larch
Maya/Miss Thomas: Suzanne Lloyd
Girlie Barker: Eddie Marr
Rifle Range Barker: Russell Trent
Stranger: Ted Stanhope

"Twelve o'clock noon. An ordinary scene, an ordinary city. Lunchtime for thousands of ordinary people. To most of them, this hour will be a rest, a pleasant break in the day's routine. To most, *but not all. To Edward Hall, time is an enemy, and the hour to come is a matter of life and death."*

Hall, a man with a cardiac condition, has sought out the aid of Dr. Rathmann, a psychiatrist. He explains that he's been dreaming in chapters, as if in a movie serial. In his dream Maya, a carnival dancer, lures him into a funhouse and onto a roller coaster with the express intention of scaring him to death. If he goes to sleep, he knows he'll return to the dream and will have a fatal heart attack. On the other hand, if he stays awake much longer, the strain will be too much for his heart. Realizing that Rathmann can't help him, he starts to go, but stops when he realizes that the doctor's receptionist is a dead ringer for the girl in his dream. Terrified, he runs back into Rathmann's office and jumps out the window to his death. The doctor calls his receptionist into his office—where Hall lies on the couch, his eyes closed. Rathmann tells the receptionist that Hall came in, lay down, immediately fell asleep—and then a few moments later, let out a scream and died.

"They say a dream takes only a second or so, and yet in that second a man can live a lifetime. He can suffer and die, and who's to say which is the greater reality: the one we know or the one in dreams, between heaven, the sky, the earth . . . in the Twilight Zone."

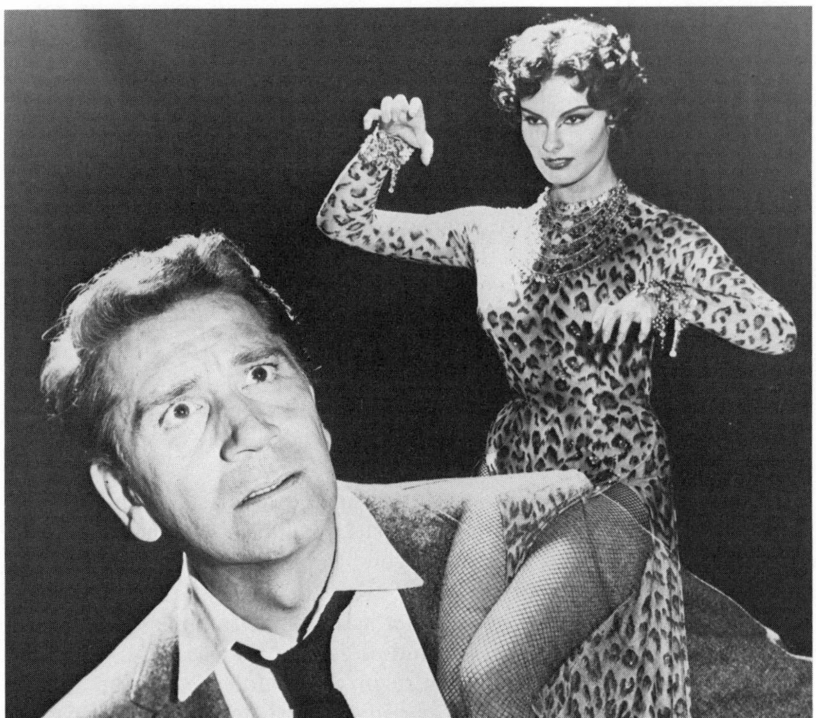

Richard Conte and Suzanne Lloyd

With "Perchance to Dream," Beaumont entered *The Twilight Zone* at full throttle. The show is adapted from his short story of the same name, which originally appeared in the November, 1958, issue of *Playboy*, and can be found in two of his collections (both, unfortunately, out of print): *Night Ride and Other Journeys* (Bantam, 1960), and *The Magic Man* (Fawcett, 1965).

Directed by Robert Florey (director of the movie *The Beast With Five Fingers* and the first Marx Brothers film, *The Cocoanuts*, co-director of *Monsieur Verdoux*, and co-scripter of *Frankenstein*) and starring Richard Conte (*The Godfather*, *Call Northside 777*), the episode hurls forward with incredible velocity. The feeling of inevitable and inexorable momentum is built layer by layer, beginning with Beaumont's tightly-conceived script, intensified by Florey's taut direction and Conte's intense performance, framed by George Clemens's claustrophobic and disorienting camera work, and capped off by Van Cleave's shrill, twitchy, deliberate and disturbing score. Conte's appearance in "Perchance to Dream" represents a perfect job of casting. His breathless, staccato delivery was one ideally suited to the role, giving the character an agitated, urgent quality that lends credence to the story.

In "Perchance to Dream," the dominant image is that of the seductive and frightening nightmare world of the amusement park, an image that was more than an expedient construct to its creator. For Charles Beaumont, both dreams and amusement parks had potent personal meaning. He shared with the lead character of "Perchance" the trait of dreaming in chapters. "He was always frightened of dreams," William F. Nolan observes. "He always felt that dreams and reality impinged on each other, and this is just another version of his own fear. He was also terrified of roller coasters. He would ride a roller coaster but he would be terrified while he was doing it and he would always say afterwards that it was the last time he'd ever ride one."

Nolan recalls an incident that occurred several years prior to the writing of "Perchance to Dream" that well illustrates the mixture of attraction and horror that amusement parks held for Beaumont.

"We went down to Pacific Ocean Park to go through the funhouse," he explains. "We both loved amusement parks as kids so we thought, look, we were in our twenties, we haven't gone through a fun house for years, let's just go through the old fun house. Well, the guy at the fun house gate was a young punk kid wearing a leather jacket and cleaning his fingernails with a switchblade knife, and he kind of gave us a look.

"About ten minutes later, we were in the middle of the fun house, groping our way along one of these corridors, and Chuck said, 'I think that kid's in here with us.' I said, 'What are you talking about? What kid, Chuck?' 'The kid with the knife,' he said, 'I just think he's in here with us. I've got a feeling that that leather-jacketed son-of-a-bitch with the knife is in here with us.' I said, 'Oh, come on, Chuck. He's out *there*. He's got to take the tickets.' He said, 'Who knows the fun house better than that kid? He's been here by day and by night, he's been here when the lights were on. He could kill us so quick in the dark. How many bodies have been washed under the pier?'—We were on the pier and we could hear the water lapping—'How many trapdoors have opened and how many people have gone in one end of this fun house and never come out the other?' I said, 'I guess that kid could be in here all right.' 'Did you see the look he gave me? He didn't like me,' he said. 'He'd put me away like *that*!' And he had me convinced that that kid was in there with the knife, and by the time he had finished talking we were running through the fun house to try to get out before the kid could get us. And I said, 'Here, this way, Chuck, this way!' And he'd say, 'Over here! Over here!' And when we got out, we *ran* out—and the kid was still there at the ticket stand and he was still picking his nails. And I looked at him, and Chuck looked at me and he said, 'Well, I *could* be wrong.'"

"THE SIXTEEN-MILLIMETER SHRINE" (10/23/59)

Ida Lupino and John Clarke

Written by Rod Serling
Producer: Buck Houghton
Director: Mitchell Leisen
Director of Photography: George T. Clemens
Music: Franz Waxman

Cast:
Barbara Jean Trenton: Ida Lupino
Danny Weiss: Martin Balsam
Marty Sall: Ted de Corsia
Sally: Alice Frost
Jerry Hearndan: Jerome Cowan
Hearndan in Film: John Clarke

"Picture of a woman looking at a picture. Movie great of another time, once-brilliant star in a firmament no longer a part of the sky, eclipsed by the movement of earth and time. Barbara Jean Trenton, whose world is a projection room, whose dreams are made out of celluloid. Barbara Jean Trenton, struck down by hit-and-run years and lying on the unhappy pavement, trying desperately to get the license number of fleeting fame."

Aging actress Barbara Jean Trenton secludes herself in a private screening room, where she watches her old films. Gently but desperately, her agent tries to coax her out into the real world by arranging a part for her in a film and by bringing a former leading man to visit her. But these acts only drive her further into the past. Bringing her a meal, the maid finds the screening room empty—and is horrified by what she sees on the screen. She summons the agent, who turns the projector back on. On the screen he sees the living room of the house, filled with stars as they appeared in the old films. Barbara Jean is the center of attention. He pleads with her to come back, but she only throws her scarf toward the camera and departs. The film runs out. In the living room, the agent finds Barbara Jean's scarf. "To wishes, Barbie," he says. "To the ones that come true."

"To the wishes that come true, to the strange, mystic strength of the human animal, who can take a wishful dream and give it a dimension of its own. To Barbara Jean Trenton, movie queen of another era, who has changed the blank tomb of an empty projection screen into a private world. It can *happen—in the Twilight Zone."*

"The Sixteen-Millimeter Shrine" marked director Mitchell Leisen's third and last *Twilight Zone*—and his best. "I thought it was very well directed," says Buck Houghton, "largely because Mitch had a feeling for how people could get that way. He undoubtedly reminisced about situations that he'd been in when he was on top."

Perhaps this *Sunset Boulevard*–cum–*Twilight Zone* struck Leisen even closer to home than Houghton might suspect. "He still lived in the past," explains George Clemens. "Drove his Rolls-Royce, had a chauffeur, insisted on a lot pass and so forth. He wasn't getting enough money to live that way! But he was a real talented man in his day—well, always talented—but he wasn't able to adjust to television. He wanted to make television like a feature picture."

Under Leisen's sure hand, Ida Lupino (star of the movies *High Sierra* and *They Drive by Night*) and Martin Balsam, as her agent, give performances of a subtlety, control, and conviction that are astounding for a half-hour television show. Jerome Cowan also appears in the episode, as a shockingly aged former leading man. Cowan too harkened back to the golden age of movies. In *The Maltese Falcon,* he played Miles Archer, Sam Spade's murdered partner, for whom Mary Astor takes the fall.

Bitterness and nostalgia pervade the episode, but are balanced so perfectly that neither becomes overpowering. Topped off with a fine and evocative score by Franz Waxman (*Sunset Boulevard, The Bride of Frankenstein, Rebecca*), "The Sixteen-Millimeter Shrine" stands as a moving statement on the ones who are (to quote the episode) "eclipsed by the movement of Earth and time"—both in front of and behind the camera.

"THE MIGHTY CASEY" (6/17/60)

Robert Sorrells and Don O'Kelly

Written by Rod Serling
Producer: Buck Houghton
Directors: Robert Parrish and Alvin Ganzer
Director of Photography: George T. Clemens
Music: stock

Cast:
Mouth McGarry: Jack Warden
Casey: Robert Sorrells
Dr. Stillman: Abraham Sofaer
Monk: Don O'Kelly
Doctor: Jonathan Hole
Beasley: Alan Dexter
Commissioner: Rusty Lane

"What you're looking at is a ghost, once alive but now deceased. Once upon a time, it was a baseball stadium that housed a major-league ballclub known as

the Hoboken Zephyrs. Now it houses nothing but memories and a wind that stirs in the high grass of what was once an outfield, a wind that sometimes bears a faint, ghostly resemblance to the roar of a crowd that once sat here. We're back in time now, when the Hoboken Zephyrs were still a part of the National League and this mausoleum of memories was an honest-to-Pete stadium. But since this is strictly a story of make-believe, it has to start this way: Once upon a time, in Hoboken, New Jersey, it was tryout day. And though he's not yet on the field, you're about to meet a most unusual fella, a left-handed pitcher named Casey."

In order to test the skills of Casey, a human-looking robot he has invented, Dr. Stillman arranges with Mouth McGarry, manager of the broken-down Hoboken Zephyrs, to have him signed up as the team's star pitcher. The Zephyrs zoom to fourth place, thanks to Casey's ability to pitch shut-outs. But when he's beaned by a ball, a doctor discovers the pitcher has no heart. The rules of baseball clearly state that nine *men* make up a team, and without a heart Casey is not a man. The baseball commissioner rules that unless Casey is given a heart, he will not be allowed to play. Dr. Stillman happily complies, but the now-compassionate Casey has too much heart—literally—to strike out the other team's players. The Zephyrs lose the pennant and Casey is washed up as far as baseball is concerned. As a memento, Stillman gives McGarry Casey's blueprints. Looking at them, McGarry gets a sudden inspiration. Shouting Stillman's name, he chases after him.

"Once upon a time there was a major league baseball team called the Hoboken Zephyrs who, during the last year of their existence, wound up in last place and shortly thereafter wound up in oblivion. There's a rumor, unsubstantiated of course, that a manager named McGarry took them to the West Coast and wound up with several pennants and a couple of world's championships. This team had a pitching staff that made history. Of course, none of them smiled very much, but it happens to be a fact that they pitched like nothing human. And if you're interested as to where these gentlemen came from, you might check under 'B' for baseball—in the Twilight Zone."

The Fates were not kind to "The Mighty Casey," a comedy by Serling involving a losing baseball team that acquires a robot player. Cast in the lead as the manager of the team was Paul Douglas, a burly actor who had distinguished himself in a number of films, including *The Solid Gold Cadillac*.

"I loved Paul Douglas," said Serling. "There was something gutsy and ballsy about this guy and you could always count on him."

Nevertheless, Serling had his reservations about Douglas. "He had had a reputation for being heavy on the bottle, but it had been somewhat dispelled over the last two or three years . . . and his agent guaranteed us that he would not drink or was not drinking during that time.

"Anyway, we look at the first day's rushes and Paul Douglas looks, even in black and white, mottled . . . high color, semi-diffuse, a breath so short that he couldn't continue one short staccato sentence without [gasping for breath]. So right away I make the assumption that he's drunk, he's drinking, and I blew my top and I called his agent and I said, 'This is very unethical of you. You assured me he wasn't drinking.'

"His agent said, 'To the best of my knowledge, he's not drinking.'

"Well, we finished the show and it was a disaster. We finished shooting, I think, on a Thursday and Saturday morning Douglas was dead. What he had been suffering, of course, was an incipient coronary and we were watching him literally die in front of us.

"Well . . . we did a rough cut of the film, and I took it over to CBS and said to them, "Well, gentlemen, this is the one substantial piece of celluloid you're going to have to eat, because there's nothing funny about this show . . .' And they looked at it and they allowed that it wasn't the funniest thing, but they didn't feel that they could afford additional money to get another actor and shoot around and put in new stuff."

Out of pocket, Serling spent $27,000 to recast, reshoot, and re-edit the show. Jack Warden was brought in to replace Douglas. Alvin Ganzer had directed the earlier sequences; Robert Parrish directed the latter. Cast and crew returned to the Hollywood Baseball Park and duplicated actions they had originally made eight months before. In reshooting, as little was filmed as possible. Footage was taken off the cutting-room floor and reinserted into the episode.

"The Mighty Casey" was broadcast June 17, 1960, as the next-to-last episode of the first season. As with most of Serling's *Twilight Zone* comedies, the show emerged as rather heavy-handed and only mildly amusing. But, thanks to Serling, the episode was not a disaster. Had he not been willing to put himself—and his money—on the line, it would have been another story entirely.

"THE FOUR OF US ARE DYING" (1/1/60)

Don Gordon, Ross Martin, Phillip Pine and Harry Townes

Written by Rod Serling
Based on an unpublished story by George Clayton Johnson
Producer: Buck Houghton
Director: John Brahm
Director of Photography: George T. Clemens
Music: Jerry Goldsmith

Cast:
Arch Hammer: Harry Townes
Hammer as Foster: Ross Martin
Hammer as Sterig: Phillip Pine
Hammer as Marshak: Don Gordon
Maggie: Beverly Garland
Pop Marshak: Peter Brocco
Penell: Bernard Fein
Detective: Milton Frome
Trumpet Player: Harry Jackson
Man in Bar: Bob Hopkins
Man Two: Pat Comiskey
Busboy: Sam Rawlins

"His name is Arch Hammer. He's thirty-six years old. He's been a salesman, a dispatcher, a truck driver, a con man, a bookie, and a part-time bartender. This is a cheap man, a nickel-and-dime man, with a cheapness that goes past the suit and the shirt; a cheapness of mind, a cheapness of taste, a tawdry little shine on the seat of his conscience, and a dark-room squint at a world whose sunlight has never gotten through to him. But Mr. Hammer has a talent, discovered at a very early age. This much he does *have. He can make his face change. He can twitch a muscle, move a jaw, concentrate on the cast of his eyes, and he can change his face. He can change it into anything he wants. Mr. Archie Hammer, jack of all trades, has just checked in at three-eighty a night, with two bags, some newspaper clippings, a most odd talent—and a master plan to destroy some lives."*

Relying on newspaper photographs, Hammer impersonates trumpet player Johnny Foster in order to get Foster's girlfriend Maggie, a sultry torch singer, to agree to run away with him. He later impersonates Virgil Sterig, a murdered gangster, in order to squeeze some money out of Mr. Penell, the thug who had Sterig killed. His plan backfires when Penell sees through the deception and sends a couple of strong-arm men after him. In order to escape from them, Hammer assumes the face of boxer Andy Marshak, which he takes from a weathered fight poster. But then he runs into Marshak's father, who mistakes him for the son who broke his mother's heart and did dirt to a sweet little girl. Hammer pushes the man aside and returns to his hotel room. Later, however, when he resumes Marshak's face in order to evade a police detective, he runs into Marshak Senior again—only this time the old man has a gun. Frantically Hammer tries to convince him that he's making a mistake, that he can prove he's not the boxer if he just has a moment to *concentrate* . . . but the old man fires. As Hammer lies dying, his features shift from one face to another, until he dies—again wearing his *own* face.

"He was Arch Hammer, a cheap little man who just checked in. He was Johnny Foster, who played a trumpet and was loved beyond words. He was Virgil Sterig, with money in his pocket. He was Andy Marshak, who got some of his agony back on a sidewalk in front of a cheap hotel. Hammer, Foster, Sterig, Marshak—and all four of them were dying."

Early in 1959, George Clayton Johnson, a young writer and friend of Charles Beaumont, wrote a story entitled "All of Us Are Dying," about a young man who capitalizes on the fact that people see him as whomever they most want to see in the world (his downfall occurs when he pulls into a gas station and the attendant recognizes him as a man he's wanted to kill for ten years). Johnson submitted the story to a certain agent.

"After the agent read it," Johnson recalls, "he scrubbed out the title with a ballpoint pen and wrote in *Rubberface!* He then sent it to Rod Serling."

Serling liked Johnson's original title and the idea of a man who could change his face. He bought the story, entitling his teleplay adaptation "The Four of Us Are Dying." What he then did was to write a totally different story of his own.

Having a character with four similar but different-looking faces was no easy job to cast. In December, 1959, casting director Millie Gusse told Peg Stevens of the Syracuse *Post-Standard,* "First I thought we could use one actor and have him change his appearance. But this was ruled out when we timed it. The actor would be in the makeup room longer than he would be before the cameras."

Buck Houghton remembers the casting as one big headache. "It's bad enough when you've got two look-alikes to work with, but when you get four it's a nightmare. I think we wound up with three blonds at one time and couldn't find a fourth that was anywhere in the ballpark, so three guys were out of a job."

As an alternative, men with dark hair and brown eyes were called in. Millie Gusse explained, "They were all told to dress alike—dark suits and ties, white shirts. I'm sure they all thought they were going to a wedding.

When they arrived, we immediately eliminated two of them because of their light eyes. And then we changed the interviewing procedure we usually follow. It's our custom to interview each individually.

"This time, we lined them up in chairs against one wall and allowed them to ask us questions, like 'What's this story all about?' or 'Why will four of us be needed for one role?' After the questioning period ended we knew the four who were similar enough in drive and ability to play the roles."

Cast in the lead were Harry Townes as Arch Hammer (the central figure), Ross Martin, Phillip Pine, and Don Gordon. Two other actors were used in a scene early in the show in which Hammer's face changes twice while he's shaving. This is a beautiful sequence, done in one continuous shot. Hammer (Townes) is shaving. The camera pans over to the mirror, which reveals a different face (the "mirror" being nothing more than an empty frame behind which a second actor stands). Hammer goes to flick ash from his cigarette into an ashtray. The camera follows his hand. When it rises back to the glass, the face is once again different.

"The Four of Us Are Dying," despite a basically absurd premise (after all, even if a man *could* change his face, how could he possibly imitate the voices and mannerisms of men he never met?), is a powerful show. Serling's writing is harsh and spare, telling the story of a merciless man who comes to a merciless end. John Brahm's direction is ingenious without being obviously so. The acting of Townes, Martin, Pine, Gordon, and Beverly Garland as a torch singer is cool and controlled. Particularly notable is the fine percussive score by Jerry Goldsmith (*Planet of the Apes, Alien, Star Trek: The Motion Picture*). Made up of piano, drum, xylophone, trumpet and flute, it is all hard edges and sharp movement, perfectly fitted to and enhancing the story. "The Four of Us Are Dying" is a tough story about tough people, and it presented some difficult problems. But, once again, an unusual challenge was overcome with talent, imagination and enthusiasm.

"THE PURPLE TESTAMENT" (2/12/60)

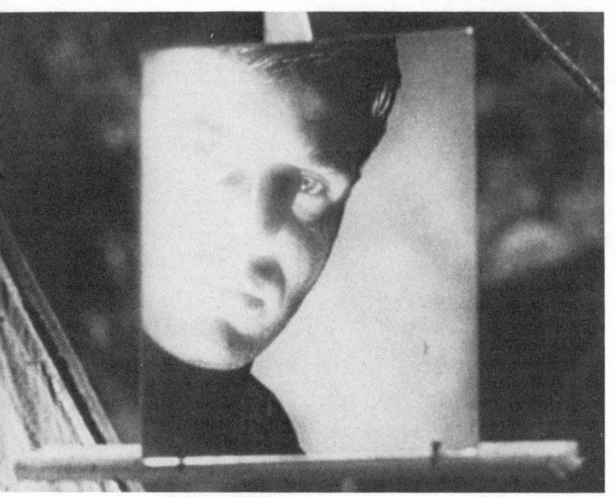

William Reynolds

Written by Rod Serling
Producer: Buck Houghton
Director: Richard L. Bare
Director of Photography: George T. Clemens
Music: composed by Lucien Morawack; conducted by Lud Gluskin

Cast:
Lt. Fitzgerald: William Reynolds
Capt. Riker: Dick York
Capt. Gunther: Barney Phillips
Jeep Driver: Warren Oates
Smitty: Michael Vandever
Sergeant: William Phipps
Orderly: Paul Mazursky
Freeman: Marc Cavell
Colonel: S. John Launer
Man with Harmonica: Ron Masak

"Infantry platoon, U.S. Army, Phillipine Islands, 1945. These are the faces of the young men who fight. As if some omniscient painter had mixed a tube of oils that were at one time earth brown, dust gray, blood red, beard black, and fear—yellow white, and these men were the models. For this is the province of combat and these are the faces of war."

Lieutenant Fitzgerald is a man who has found his own special war-time hell. Looking into the faces of his men prior to a battle, he sees a peculiar light on the faces of those who are to die. Captain Riker, his close friend and superior officer, scoffs at this—until "Fitz" sees the odd light on *his* face. Nevertheless, Riker feels duty-bound; he goes into combat and is killed. Soon after, Fitz is relieved to hear that he is being sent back to division headquarters. Packing to go, he glances in a mirror and is horrified to see the same terrible light on his face as on the others. As he gets into a jeep, a sergeant cautions the driver that there are mines in the road. "Relax," the driver tells Fitz. "We've got a four-hour drive ahead of us." Fitz replies, "I doubt it." A while later, the sergeant and his men hear the sound of a distant explosion.

"From William Shakespeare, Richard the Third, *a small excerpt. The line reads, 'He has come to open the purple testament of bleeding war.' And for Lieutenant William Fitzgerald, A Company, First Platoon, the testament is closed. Lieutenant Fitzgerald has* found *the Twilight Zone."*

The "look of death" on the soldiers' faces in "The Purple Testament" was an especially eerie effect, accomplished simply by suddenly shifting the emphasis of the lighting and overexposing the film.

A special irony attended this production. Director Richard L. Bare recalls, "The evening that it was to be aired first-run, Bill Reynolds and I were in the middle of the Caribbean swimming for our lives, with three broken legs between the two of us." Bare and Reynolds had just finished making *The Islander,* a pilot for MGM, and were flying back to Miami. At three hundred feet, both engines quit and the plane went down in the ocean, killing one of the five people on board. Although Bare had two broken legs, he decided that he and Reynolds should try and make for shore.

"We were four miles off the coast of Jamaica, swimming on our backs toward shore, about forty feet apart, when I yelled over to Bill and said, 'Bill, how are you doing?' He answered, 'I'm making it.' A little later, I called over again. 'You know what's playing tonight?' He said, 'Yeah, "The Purple Testament."' And I said, 'Bill, please *don't* look at me!'" Both Bare and Reynolds survived and recovered fully. Bare went on to direct 158 episodes of *Green Acres,* Reynolds to star in *The FBI.*

William Reynolds, whose wife had had a baby just two weeks earlier, adds an interesting postscript. "Buck Houghton took the show off the air that night, because he didn't know whether I was a survivor or not from the first news reports. But I thought it was indicative of the class of that production company that they not only did not make capital of the fact, which might have been the obvious thing to do, but they took the show off the air. I was pleased that they didn't subject my family to that."

"THE MONSTERS ARE DUE ON MAPLE STREET" (3/4/60)

Claude Akins and Jack Weston

Written by Rod Serling
Producer: Buck Houghton
Director: Ron Winston
Director of Photography: George T. Clemens
Music: composed by Rene Garriguenc; conducted by Lud Gluskin

Cast:
Steve Brand: Claude Akins
Charlie: Jack Weston
Mr. Goodman: Barry Atwater
Tommy: Jan Handzlik
Tommy's Mother: Mary Gregory
Mrs. Brand: Anne Barton
Mrs. Goodman: Lea Waggner
Pete Van Horn: Ben Erway
Don: Burt Metcalfe
Charlie's Wife: Lyn Guild
Woman Next Door: Joan Sudlow
Man One: Jason Johnson
Woman One: Amzie Strickland
First Alien: Sheldon Allman
Second Alien: William Walsh

"Maple Street, U.S.A. Late summer. A tree-lined little road of front porch gliders, barbecues, the laughter of children, and the bell of an ice-cream vendor. At the sound of the roar and the flash of light, it will be precisely 6:43 P.M. on Maple Street. . . . This is Maple Street on a late Saturday afternoon, in the last calm and reflective moment—before the monsters came."

After what is at first taken to be a meteor speeds overhead, Maple Street experiences a total power failure—appliances, telephones, even cars. Pete Van Horn sets off on foot to find out the cause, but Tommy, a young reader of sci-fi, says *he* knows—human-looking aliens have infiltrated Maple Street. At first, this is laughed off, but when Mr. Goodman's car inexplicably starts up for a few seconds, suspicion falls on him—bolstered by the fact that a neighbor has seen him looking up at the stars late at night. As evening falls, Steve Brand tries to get others to remain calm. But when a mysterious figure walks toward them in the dark, panic breaks out. Charlie Farnsworth grabs a neighbor's rifle and fires, killing the menace, who turns out to be the returning Pete Van Horn. Madness prevails. Charlie is accused of being the alien, then Tommy. As the lights of various houses flash on and off, full-scale rioting breaks out. From nearby, two aliens watch these events unfold. One explains to the other that by manipulating electricity, it is easy to turn neighbor against neighbor. Maple Street is typical—and only the beginning.

"The tools of conquest do not necessarily come with bombs and explosions and fallout. There are weapons that are simply thoughts, attitudes, prejudices—to be found only in the minds of men. For the record, prejudices can kill and suspicion can destroy, and a thoughtless, frightened search for a scapegoat has a fallout all its own—for the children, and the children yet unborn. And the pity of it is that these things cannot be confined to the Twilight Zone."

"The Monsters Are Due on Maple Street" is Serling's chilling commentary on how easily neighbor can be turned against neighbor when brought up against inexplicable events—in this case, manipulated by aliens in outfits from *Forbidden Planet*. (The final shot of the episode shows the

Jack Weston leads his hysterical Maple Street neighbors

aliens' ship flying through outer space, away from the camera. In fact, this is a shot from *Forbidden Planet,* shown upside-down and backwards.)

The real star of the show is the mob itself, and in all its individual parts it is convincing and frightening (ironically, the episode was shot on MGM's *Andy Hardy* street). Directed with intensity by newcomer Ronald Winston, the episode is filled with dark power reminiscent of Fritz Lang's fine 1936 anti-lynching film *Fury,* starring Spencer Tracy. Here, the brute group entity is dissected, and Serling reveals it for what it is: a violent chaotic force, powered by fear and nurtured by irrationality.

Curiously, just prior to the broadcast of the episode, a number of papers, including the *Miami Herald,* misquoted Serling as saying that "The Monsters Are Due on Maple Street" was his commentary on the fact that "the minorities always need a scapegoat to explain their own weaknesses." Serling's point had been borne out even before the show had aired—prejudice *can't* be confined to *The Twilight Zone.*

"LONG LIVE WALTER JAMESON" (3/18/60)

Kevin McCarthy

Written by Charles Beaumont
Producer: Buck Houghton
Director: Anton Leader
Director of Photography: George T. Clemens
Music: stock
Makeup: William Tuttle

Cast:
Prof. Walter Jameson: Kevin McCarthy
Prof. Samuel Kittridge: Edgar Stehli
Laurette Bowen: Estelle Winwood
Susanna Kittridge: Dody Heath

"You're looking at Act One, Scene One, of a nightmare, one not restricted to witching hours or dark, rainswept nights. Professor Walter Jameson, popular beyond words, who talks of the past as if it were the present, who conjures up the dead as if they were alive . . . In the view of this *man, Professor Samuel Kittridge, Walter Jameson has access to knowledge that couldn't come out of a volume of history, but rather from a book on black magic, which is to say that* this *nightmare begins at noon."*

In class, Jameson—Kittridge's colleague for twelve years and prospective son-in-law—reads aloud from the Civil War journal of Union officer Hugh

Skelton. That evening, when Jameson arrives at his house for dinner, Kittridge reveals that he has looked Skelton up in a book of Mathew Brady photographs—and found him to be a dead ringer for Jameson, down to the mole on his face and the ring on his finger! Jameson confides in Kittridge—he *is* Skelton, but his secret is an even darker one. More than two thousand years ago, he paid an alchemist for the gift of immortality, but soon he found that it was no gift at all. Down the long years, he has seen wives, children, friends, all grow old and die. Now he longs for an end, but he lacks the courage to kill himself. Kittridge forbids Jameson to marry his daughter, but Jameson—realizing the woman would think her father a madman if he tried to tell her the truth—convinces her to elope with him that very night. Going home to pack, Jameson is surprised by a hideously withered old woman in his study. A wife he long ago abandoned, she saw the notice of his engagement in the paper and has come to stop the wedding. When he refuses, she grabs a revolver off his desk and shoots him. Hearing the shot, Kittridge rushes in—just in time to see Jameson age and turn to dust.

"Last stop on a long journey, as yet another human being returns to the vast nothingness that is the beginning and into the dust that is always the end."

The twentieth episode of *The Twilight Zone* (nineteenth under Houghton) was the most technically demanding yet attempted. To accomplish the climactic effect of Jameson aging and turning to dust a close collaboration was required between Kevin McCarthy, director of photography George Clemens, and William Tuttle, head of the MGM makeup department. Fortunately, a more talented man than Tuttle could not have been present. Five years later, he became the first makeup artist to receive an Academy Award, for his superb work on Tony Randall in *The Seven Faces of Dr. Lao* (which, coincidentally, was also scripted by Beaumont). His credits range all the way from *The Wizard of Oz* (uncredited) to *Young Frankenstein, The Fury* and *Love at First Bite.*

McCarthy's metamorphosis consisted of three separate and distinct age makeups, each older than the one before it. For the first change, a trick was employed which Clemens had first encountered while working on the Fredric March *Dr. Jekyll and Mr. Hyde* in 1931. This consisted of drawing lines on the actor's face—in this case age lines—in red makeup. The set was then lit with key lights with red filters over them so that the set was bathed in a red light, rendering the lines invisible. As the scene progressed, the red lights were dimmed while simultaneously lights with green filters were raised. Now in a green light, the lines suddenly became visible. Since the film is in black and white, the color change is undetecta-

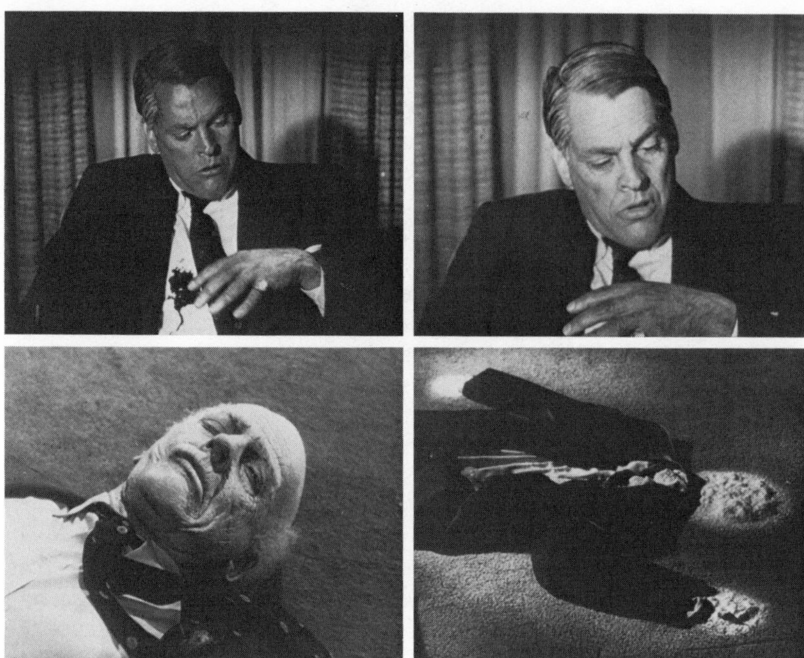

Walter Jameson turns to dust

ble. What appears to happen is an apparent miracle in which a complete makeup change has occurred on camera with no cuts.

Considerably heavier makeup was required for the second and third changes. Prior to the shooting, a life mask was made of McCarthy. Onto that, folds and wrinkles were modeled in Plasticine, an oil-based clay that never dries out. For each various component of the makeup (forehead, cheeks, chin, neck, and upper lip), a separate mold was made. Foam rubber pieces were cast from the molds and glued onto McCarthy's face. What emerges is a sequence in which the illusion of someone rapidly aging is rendered quite convincingly, while leaving McCarthy still recognizable throughout (something that wouldn't have been possible had they just substituted *real* old men for McCarthy).

Like "Perchance to Dream," "Long Live Walter Jameson" is basically a dialogue between two men (in the former, between the main character and a psychiatrist; in the latter, between the two professors), but whereas the former sustains itself with its tremendous velocity, the strength of the latter lies in the allure of its concept and the virtuosity of Beaumont's writing. Like so many of the more memorable episodes of *The Twilight Zone,* it cues into a basic universal fantasy and brings us to a revelation about that fantasy. Who, in his mind, has not dreamed about immortality, longed for it, wondered about it? In "Walter Jameson," these dreams are realized and taken to their logical, inevitable, and dreadful conclusion.

The challenge in "Walter Jameson" was to present a character claiming to be immortal and not have the audience immediately reject the notion out of hand as absurd. This was accomplished through the utter seriousness with which McCarthy, Stehli, and Winwood played their roles. Nothing is tongue in cheek here, nor condescending. Director Tony Leader, previously a producer-director of radio's *Suspense* and later director of the motion picture *Children of the Damned,* keeps the proceedings down-to-earth, which lends credence to the fantastic subject matter.

Much of the credit for the episode's success must go to McCarthy and his ability to play a man centuries old. Leader says of him, "To work with McCarthy was a pleasure. You worked very hard, he worked very hard, and he was always trying. There was no sloughing it off, no superficiality, if he could help it and you could help *him.*"

McCarthy, the star of the 1956 filming of *Invasion of the Body Snatchers,* gave considerable thought to playing Jameson and decided that the most credible way to play an immortal lay in underplaying everything. "Part of it," he explains, "is that he had to be modest and unassuming. He didn't want to call any attention to himself . . . He always sort of fades into the landscape."

Since doing "Walter Jameson," McCarthy has come to feel that his role in it may have been typecasting of an entirely unforeseen kind. "I did a little segment in the new *Invasion of the Body Snatchers,* and they said, 'My God, except that your hair has changed color, you look the same as you did when you did it twenty years ago! What is this anyway?' My own kids, I can see, are very young looking, they don't have faces or physiques that denote the passage of time so easily. So I say to myself, 'Maybe I *am* going to live to be two thousand years old.'"

THE TWILIGHT ZONE DEBUTS

It's very likely that during the making of "Long Live Walter Jameson" there was a certain nervousness on the set, but it wasn't over the prospect of having to turn a man to dust. Rather, it stemmed from the fact that on that Friday, October 2, 1959, *The Twilight Zone* was to be unveiled to the public. For four months, Serling, Houghton, and the crew had labored in the dark, with no idea as to what the reaction, if any, would be. *The Twilight Zone* wasn't the only series with such concerns. This season also marked the debut of *The Untouchables, Bonanza, Dennis the Menace,* and *The Many Loves of Dobie Gillis* (They were just the successes; ever hear of

The Alaskans or *Staccato*?). Going in, *The Twilight Zone* would face tough competition: on NBC, *People Are Funny* and (in the East) Friday night prize fights; on ABC, *77 Sunset Strip* for the first two weeks and then *The Detectives,* starring Robert Taylor.

Before the debut of the series, Serling embarked on a media blitz, writing magazine articles and granting newspaper and television interviews. The purpose of this was twofold: first, to explain his reasons for entering into series television, and secondly, to define the series itself. Regarding the former, he told TV newsman Mike Wallace, "I don't want to fight anymore. I don't want to have to battle sponsors and agencies. I don't want to have to push for something that I want and have to settle for second best. I don't want to have to compromise all the time, which in essence is what the television writer does if he wants to put on controversial themes." To the Marion, Indiana, *Leader-Tribune,* he gave the positive side of the coin: "This is something I've wanted to do for years. Television hasn't touched it yet. Sure, there have been science-fiction and fantasy shows before, but most of them were involved with gadgets or leprecauns." He went on to explain, "*The Twilight Zone* is about people—about human beings involved in extraordinary circumstances, in strange problems of their own or of fate's making." In an article in *TV Guide,* he enlarged upon the subject. "Here's what the program isn't: it's not a monster rally or a spook show. There will be nothing formula'd in it, nothing telegraphed, nothing so nostalgically familiar that an audience can usually join the actors in duets." Serling knew that science-fiction fans were a tiny minority, too small to ever make much of a television audience. If *The Twilight Zone* was to succeed, it had to appeal to people who had never read a word of science fiction, nor ever wanted to.

The second of October came and went. It wasn't a promising start.

"Unfortunately, the debut title 'Where Is Everybody?' posed a question that could best be answered by another network," wrote Harvey Karman of the *Hollywood Reporter,* "but when word gets around, *Twilight* should give the competition a run for their ratings."

Two groups were immediately enthralled by the show: television critics—and children. "The appeal to children was a complete surprise to us," says Buck Houghton. "We never thought of that. I don't think CBS did, either; it was on at ten o'clock. We got a lot of nasty notes from parents, saying, 'You're keeping the kids up.'"

As for the critics, they couldn't have been more enthusiastic. Cecil Smith of the *Los Angeles Times* called *The Twilight Zone* "the finest weekly series of the season, the one clear and original light in a season marked by the muddy carbon copies of dull westerns and mediocre police shows." John Crosby of the *New York Herald Tribune* agreed, saying it was "certainly the best and most original anthology series of the year." *Time* commented, "Whether the hero is an Air Force officer suffering hallucinations after more than 400 hours of isolation, or a tired old pitchman bargaining with 'Mr. Death,' tales from *The Twilight Zone* are proof that a little talent and imagination can atone for a lot of television." Probably the greatest compliment came from Terry Turner of the *Chicago Daily News*, who wrote, ". . . *Twilight Zone* is about the only show now on the air that I actually look forward to seeing. It's the one series that I will let interfere with other plans."

Meanwhile, production of episodes continued. October found the crew back in Death Valley, filming "I Shot an Arrow Into the Air."

"I SHOT AN ARROW INTO THE AIR" (1/15/60)

Dewey Martin

Written by Rod Serling
Based on an idea by Madelon Champion
Producer: Buck Houghton
Director: Stuart Rosenberg
Director of Photography: George T. Clemens
Music: stock

Cast:
Corey: Dewey Martin
Col. Donlin: Edward Binns
Pierson: Ted Otis
Brandt: Leslie Barrett
Langford: Harry Bartell

"Her name is the Arrow One. She represents four and a half years of planning, preparation and training, and a thousand years of science and mathematics and the projected dreams and hopes of not only a nation but a world. She is the first manned aircraft into space. And this is the countdown, the last five seconds before man shot an arrow into the air."

But something goes wrong; the Arrow One disappears off the radar screen and crashes. Three of the eight astronauts survive the wreck. They find themselves on what they take to be an asteroid, with only five gallons of water between them. Corey intends to kill Pierson and Donlin for their water, but before Pierson dies he manages to crawl to the top of a mountain, look over it, and draw a peculiar symbol in the sand. Corey, paying this no mind, kills Donlin. But when he climbs the mountain, he finally sees what the symbol meant: telephone poles. They've been on Earth the entire time—in the Nevada desert.

"Practical joke perpetrated by Mother Nature and a combination of improbable events. Practical joke wearing the trappings of nightmare, of terror, of desperation. Small human drama played out in a desert ninety-seven miles from Reno, Nevada, U.S.A., continent of North America, the Earth, and of course—the Twilight Zone."

"I Shot An Arrow Into the Air" represents the only time that Serling was approached in a social setting with an idea for a *Twilight Zone* episode that excited him. "Madelon Champion said to me, 'What would happen if three guys landed on what they thought was an asteroid and it turned out to be outside of Las Vegas? I paid five hundred dollars for that one on the spot. But it never happened again."

On a dramatic level, the episode is fairly effective, but, as with many of *The Twilight Zone*'s forays into science fiction, on a scientific level it's utterly ludicrous. Any astronaut who crash lands on a body within our solar system that has the same gravity and atmosphere as Earth and doesn't immediately realize he's *on* Earth, had better go back to astronaut school.

The filming took the crew back to Death Valley. Buck Houghton recalls, "The weather was no better, but we knew better how to deal with it. Dietetically speaking, our meals were much more on the salads—very satisfying but light. Also, we said to the crew, 'Look, we're going to have a two-hour lunch. We're going to go back to the hotel and serve lunch around the pool. You can go to your room. And don't let's have any horseplay about the union and the overtime and all that jazz because you know very well that it's the best thing to do for all of us, and you'll still come out the same number of pay hours as if we gave you the forty-five-minute lunch out here on location and made you sweat through it and work on till six.' And they all said, 'Hail!'"

"WHAT YOU NEED" (12/25/59)

Ernest Truex

Written by Rod Serling
Based on the short story "What You Need" by Lewis Padgett (pseudonym of Henry Kuttner and C. L. Moore)
Producer: Buck Houghton
Director: Alvin Ganzer
Director of Photography: George T. Clemens
Music: Van Cleave

Cast:
Fred Renard: Steve Cochran
Pedott: Ernest Truex
Girl in Bar: Arline Sax
Lefty: Read Morgan
Bartender: William Edmonson
Woman on Street: Judy Ellis
Man on Street: Fred Kruger
Hotel Clerk: Norman Sturgis
Waiter: Frank Allocca
Photographer: Mark Sunday

"You're looking at Mr. Fred Renard, who carries on his shoulder a chip the size of the national debt. This is a sour man, a friendless man, a lonely man, a grasping, compulsive, nervous man. This is a man who has lived thirty-six undistinguished, meaningless, pointless, failure-laden years and who at this moment looks for an escape—any escape, any way, anything, anybody—to get out of the rut. . . . And this little old man is just what Mr. Renard is waiting for."

Pedott is a sidewalk salesman with the uncanny ability to tell what people will need before they need it. To Fred Renard, a two-bit thug, he gives a pair of scissors—scissors that save Renard's life when his tie gets caught in the doors of an elevator. But Renard wants more, *much* more. Sensing that unless he acts, Renard will eventually kill him, Pedott gives him a pair of shoes. Renard slips them on. Suddenly, a truck rounds the corner, heading directly for him. Renard tries to run, but the new soles are slippery and he can't get any traction on the wet pavement. He is struck and killed . . . and Pedott's safety is assured.

"Street scene. Night. Traffic accident. Victim named Fred Renard, gentleman with a sour face to whom contentment came with difficulty. Fred Renard, who took all that was needed . . . in the Twilight Zone."

For "What You Need" the crew returned to the comfortable backlots of Metro. The original story by Henry Kuttner and C. L. Moore (under the pseudonym of Lewis Padgett) concerned a scientist who invented a machine that could read people's probable futures and who then gave them what they needed to be guided in a certain direction. Serling liked the idea but not the scientist or the machine, so he instead crafted a story about an elderly sidewalk peddler who can see into the future and sells people seemingly trivial items (spot remover, scissors, a ticket to Scranton, Pennsylvania) which ultimately prove essential to them.

Unfortunately, the show suffers from lackluster direction and performances, but the ending is cleverly set up, with the threatened old man giving the thug the pair of slippery shoes. He puts them on and stands in the street. "Come on, old man," he says. "Tell me. Are these what I need?"

"I didn't say they were," the peddler replies. "But I'll tell you something—they happen to be what *I* need."

Cosmic justice—from the Twilight Zone.

"A WORLD OF DIFFERENCE" (3/11/60)

Howard Duff and Eileen Ryan

Written by Richard Matheson
Producer: Buck Houghton
Director: Ted Post
Director of Photography: Harkness Smith
Music: Van Cleave

Cast:
Arthur Curtis: Howard Duff
Marty: Frank Maxwell
Nora: Eileen Ryan
Brinkley: David White
Sally: Gail Kobe
Endicott: Peter Walker
Kelly: William Idelson
Marian: Susan Dorn

"You're looking at a tableau of reality, things of substance, of physical material: a desk, a window, a light. These things exist and have dimension. Now, this is Arthur Curtis, age thirty-six, who is also real. He has flesh and blood, muscle and mind. But in just a moment we will see how thin a line separates that which we assume to be real with that manufactured inside of a mind."

Businessman Arthur Curtis is surprised to find the phone in his office dead—but he's even more surprised when he hears a voice behind him shout, "Cut!" and turns to see that his office is actually a set on a soundstage. What's more, everyone on the set insists that Curtis is actually Jerry Raigan, a drunken movie star on the decline, and that "Arthur Curtis" is the character Raigan plays in the movie! Determined to assert his identity, Curtis commandeers the car of Raigan's shrewish ex-wife and drives to where his home *should* be. There, he finds no trace of his wife or daughter, or his house, or even the street they live on. Later, at Jerry Raigan's house, Curtis calls information for the number of the company he's worked at for the past seven years—no listing. Thinking his client is having a nervous breakdown, Raigan's agent tries to reassure him, telling him he needn't return to the picture, that the studio has cancelled the production. The sets are being dismantled. Realizing that the only fragile link to *his* world—the office set—is about to be destroyed, Curtis races to the studio. Just in time, he dashes onto the set and pleads with some unseen force not to maroon him in this uncaring place. The sounds of studio hustle-bustle fade away. Curtis finds himself back in the office he knew, complete with four solid walls. Meanwhile, the agent arrives on the soundstage—and finds that Jerry Raigan is nowhere to be found.

"The modus operandi *for the departure from life is usually a pine box of such and such dimensions, and this is the ultimate in reality. But there are other ways for a man to exit from life. Take the case of Arthur Curtis, age thirty-six. His departure was along a highway with an exit sign that reads: 'This way to escape.' Arthur Curtis, en route to . . . the Twilight Zone."*

The nature of identity (or "Am I who I think I am?") was a theme *The Twilight Zone* would explore many times.

Of "A World of Difference," Richard Matheson says, "I liked that one. It's one of those Kafkaesque ideas that you get, that a man goes to his office, thinks he's living his normal life, and suddenly finds out that he's an actor on a set."

To effect the transition from one reality (the office—business as usual) to the other (the soundstage), director Ted Post (whose movie credits include *Magnum Force, Hang 'em High,* and *Beneath the Planet of the Apes*) employed an ingenious visual trick. The scene in the show goes as follows, in one continuous shot: businessman Arthur Curtis enters his office. We see all four walls, establishing its solidity and reality. Curtis sits down at his desk and picks up the phone—only to find that the line is dead. Suddenly, he hears someone say, "Cut!" As he turns to look in the direction of the voice, the camera follows his gaze to reveal that one wall has disappeared, revealing a soundstage with a full production crew looking on.

To accomplish this shot, one wall was built on rails and removed during the scene. Because it was one continuous shot, the wall had to move silently, which it did. Buck Houghton was totally supportive of this procedure, explaining, "If you're going to prove something, it's better to prove it in a continuous shot so that people are really nailed."

"THE FEVER" (1/29/60)

Written by Rod Serling
Producer: Buck Houghton
Director: Robert Florey
Director of Photography:
George T. Clemens
Music: stock

Cast:
Franklin Gibbs: Everett Sloane
Flora Gibbs: Vivi Janiss
Drunk: Art Lewis
Public Relations Man:
William Kendis
Floor Manager: Lee Sands
Cashier: Marc Towers
Photographer: Lee Millar
Sheriff: Arthur Peterson
Girl: Carole Kent
Croupier: Jeffrey Sayre

"Mr. and Mrs. Franklin Gibbs, from Elgin, Kansas, three days and two nights, all expenses paid, at a Las Vegas hotel, won by virtue of Mrs. Gibbs's knack with a phrase. But unbeknownst to either Mr. or Mrs. Gibbs is the fact that there's a prize in their package neither expected nor bargained for. In just a moment one of them will succumb to an illness worse than any virus can produce, a most inoperative, deadly, life-shattering affliction known as The Fever."

Tight-fisted Franklin Gibbs is not at all pleased when his wife Flora wins the trip for two to Las Vegas, nor when a noisy drunk gives him a silver dollar and forces him to put it in a one-armed bandit. But things change when he pulls down the lever and it pays off. He begins to hear the machine calling his name, and develops a mania to play—until he's soon down to his last dollar. When he feeds this into the slot, the machine inexplicably jams. Certain that it has done so in a deliberate effort not to pay out a big jackpot, he pushes it over, hysterically screaming, "Give me back my dollar!" Later upstairs in his room with Flora, he believes he sees the machine coming for him. Terrified, he takes a fatal fall out the window.

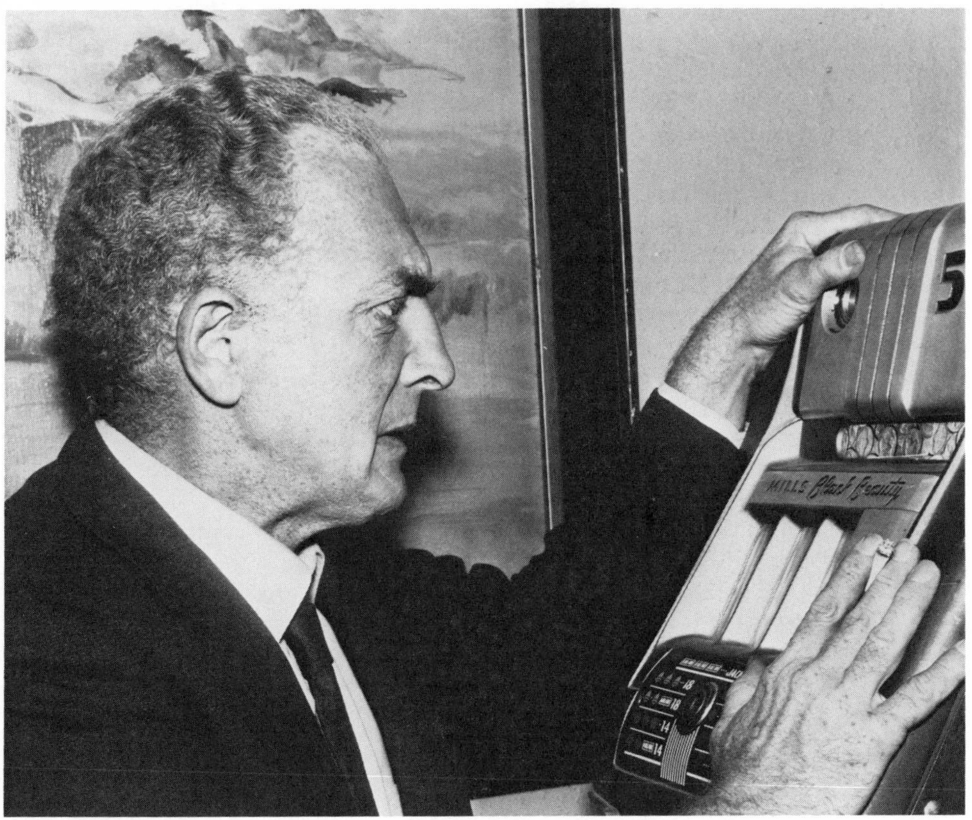

Everett Sloane

On the pavement, the triumphant machine rolls up to him and spits out his dollar.

"Mr. Franklin Gibbs, visitor to Las Vegas, who lost his money, his reason, and finally his life to an inanimate metal machine variously described as a one-armed bandit, a slot machine or, in Mr. Franklin Gibbs's words, a monster with a will all its own. For our purposes we'll stick with the latter definition—because we're in the Twilight Zone."

As far as the human performers in "The Fever" went, Serling had nothing to worry about. Everett Sloane, who had done so well for him in "Patterns," was cast in the lead as Franklin Gibbs. Playing his browbeaten wife, Flora, was Vivi Janiss, an actress of intelligence, subtlety, and depth.

Serling's problem lay in casting the role of the slot machine. In the show, the machine comes alive, calling Franklin's name, beckoning him. Now, how to give a slot machine a voice—and make it *sound* like a slot machine?

The initial problem was getting a slot machine at all. "Gambling machines were illegal in California," explains Buck Houghton. "A prop house couldn't even have them. So we had to get one-armed bandits from the police department where they were impounded. It was just like a machine gun, you had to have a policeman along with it. There was a policeman on the set at all times, to make damn sure that somebody didn't take one off and set it up in his uncle's barber shop."

It was decided that the most effective voice would be one that sounded like tinkling coins—the sound a machine makes when it pays off. The first step in the process was to tape the sound of metal coins. Says Buck Houghton, "We made it as metallic as we could. We put hundreds of dimes and quarters—not nickels, because they were lead and didn't make the same sound—down a metal chute. So we just had yards and yards and yards of coins running down metal."

Next, a human subject was chosen. Two small speakers were strapped to either side of his esophagus. The sound of tinkling coins was played out through the speakers, to the effect that when the man opened his mouth, the sound came from his throat. This sound could then be shaped into words by using the tongue and lips just as with sounds from the larynx. But he himself made no use of his own voice whatsoever; the tape provided all the sound. And *voilá*—one talking slot machine.

"ELEGY" (2/19/60)

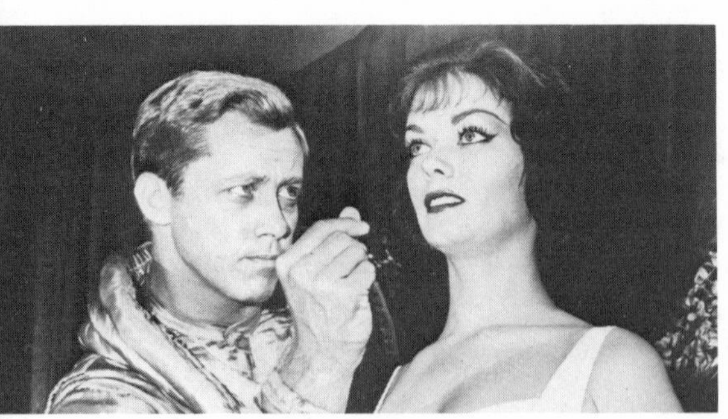

Don Dubbins

Written by Charles Beaumont
Based on the short story "Elegy" by Charles Beaumont
Producer: Buck Houghton
Director: Douglas Heyes
Director of Photography: George T. Clemens
Music: Van Cleave

Cast:
Jeremy Wickwire: Cecil Kellaway
Capt. James Webber: Kevin Hagen
Kurt Meyers: Jeff Morrow
Peter Kirby: Don Dubbins

"The time is the day after tomorrow. The place: a far corner of the universe. The cast of characters: three men lost amongst the stars, three men sharing the common urgency of all men lost—they're looking for home. And in a moment

they'll find home, not a home that is a place to be seen but a strange, unexplainable experience to be felt."

Their ship almost out of fuel, astronauts Webber, Meyers, and Kirby set down on a remote asteroid—and run smack into a mystery. The place is quite Earthlike, down to the buildings and the people, *but no one moves.* The men witness a number of inanimate tableaux: a full marching band, a man being elected mayor, a card table at which one of the players holds four aces, a romantic liaison in a hotel suite, complete with violinists, and a homely woman winning a beauty contest. The three are startled when they find someone who *does* move—Jeremy Wickwire, caretaker of the place. He explains that the entire asteroid is an exclusive cemetery where the dear departed can realize their greatest wish in life, after they die. He serves the men wine and asks what *their* greatest wish would be. All three reply that they would like to be on their ship, heading for home. Too late, they realize that Wickwire, who is a robot, has poisoned their drinks. Having thus insured the continuing tranquility of Happy Glades, Wickwire installs the inanimate, embalmed figures of the three men back in their ship.

"Kirby, Webber, and Meyers, three men lost. They shared a common wish, a simple one, really—they wanted to be aboard their ship, headed for home. And fate, a laughing fate, a practical jokester with a smile that stretched across the stars, saw to it that they got their wish, with just one reservation: the wish came true, but only in the Twilight Zone."

While "The Fever" presented the problem of bringing an inanimate object to life, "Elegy," Charles Beaumont's third *Twilight Zone,* presented exactly the opposite problem. A large percentage of the show was devoted to the exhibiting of various tableaux, including a full marching band, all utterly frozen. "We did not use dummies once," says director Douglas Heyes. "We used real people."

Using real people brought its own share of problems. No matter how still a person tries to be, there are always small movements. To minimize audience awareness of these, Heyes utilized a little technical sleight-of-hand. "If you'll notice on 'Elegy,' when you see those characters, the camera is almost always in movement, moving backwards and forwards, panning, and so forth." Despite this, the motions of the actors are still noticeable and this works against the episode's credibility. Later, when Heyes was brought back to do "The After Hours," another episode demanding inanimate human figures, he would remember this experience and take an entirely different approach.

Heyes had no objections to most of the tableaux in Beaumont's script, but there was one that he felt was totally unworkable: an automobile race. Auto racing was one of Beaumont's hobbies and very probably to him it was the most personally appealing of all the tableaux. But whatever its appeal, Heyes knew it would not translate effectively to film. "To me," he says, "stationary cars don't seem to be frozen in movement; they just seem to be parked cars." In its place, he substituted the beauty contest, which remains perhaps the single most memorable image of the entire episode.

As for Beaumont, he wasn't happy with the change. "Charles never liked anything I did with any story he ever wrote," says Heyes, "but continued to be friends with me, assuming apparently that we had the right to be different. Rod would endorse what I had done in terms of changes on his stories enthusiastically, while Charles would say, 'I don't think you did my story any good at all.'"

Unquestionably, what saves "Elegy" from becoming unbearably morbid is Cecil Kellaway's performance as Wickwire, the robot caretaker. Short and cute and likeable, his many fine performances in films such as *I Married a Witch, The Postman Always Rings Twice,* and *Harvey* (plus two Oscar nominations, for *The Luck of the Irish* and *Guess Who's Coming to Dinner*) had proved him inimitable. Says Buck Houghton, "You couldn't really feel too depressed about these fellows in the care of such a fine old fellow, I don't think."

In "Elegy," *The Twilight Zone* was once again on shaky ground scientifically. According to the script, the asteroid circles twin stars 655 million miles from Earth. Quite a trick, considering the fact that the nearest star to our solar system is approximately twenty-six *trillion* miles away. In fact, if these stars were actually where claimed, they would be closer to our sun than is the planet Saturn.

"MIRROR IMAGE" (2/26/60)

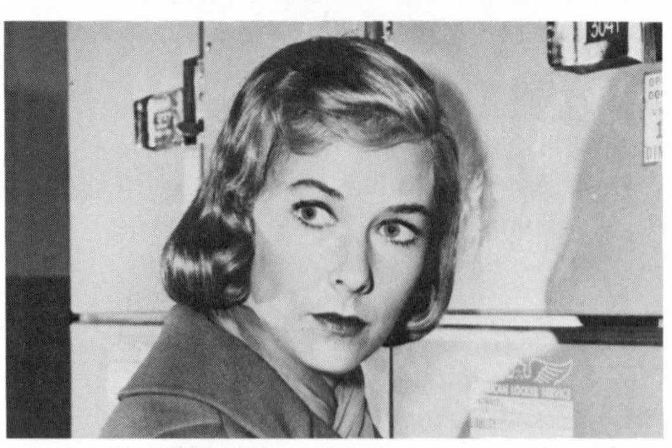

Vera Miles

Written by Rod Serling
Producer: Buck Houghton
Director: John Brahm
Director of Photography: George T. Clemens
Music: stock

Cast:
Millicent Barnes: Vera Miles
Paul Grinstead: Martin Milner
Ticket Agent: Joe Hamilton
Woman Attendant: Noami Stevens
Husband: Ferris Taylor
Old Woman: Terese Lyon
Bus Driver: Edwin Rand

"Millicent Barnes, age twenty-five, young woman waiting for a bus on a rainy November night. Not a very imaginative type is Miss Barnes, not given to undue anxiety or fears, or for that matter even the most temporal flights of fancy. Like most young career women, she has a generic classification as a, quote, girl with a head on her shoulders, end of quote. All of which is mentioned now because in just a moment the head on Miss Barnes's shoulders will be put to a test. Circumstances will assault her sense of reality and a chain of nightmares will put her sanity on a block. Millicent Barnes, who in one minute will wonder if she's going mad."

Millicent suspects the bus station is run by lunatics: snappishly, the ticket taker tells her that she's repeatedly asked when the bus will arrive, adding that her suitcase has *already* been checked. In the washroom, the attendant claims she was there only a moment before. Yet she's done none of these things. She realizes that it is not *their* sanity which is in question when, in the washroom mirror, she spies a duplicate of herself sitting in the waiting room. Rushing out, she finds the room empty. A short time later, Millicent elicits the sympathy of Paul Grinstead, an amiable businessman also waiting for the bus. When it arrives, the two of them start to get on, but Millicent flees back into the station when she sees that the *other* her has already boarded. Concerned, Paul misses the bus to remain with the distraught Millicent, who says she now knows what is occurring—a mirror image of her from a parallel world has somehow slipped into this world, and must take her place to survive. Certain she's mentally ill, Paul summons the police, who take Millicent away. But a few minutes later, he has reason to regret his decision: chasing an elusive figure he believes has stolen his case, he sees that the man's mockingly grinning face is—his own!

"Obscure metaphysical explanation to cover a phenomenon, reasons dredged out of the shadows to explain away that which cannot be explained. Call it parallel planes or just insanity. Whatever it is, you find it in the Twilight Zone."

With "Mirror Image," Serling took the loss-of-identity theme and raised it to even greater heights of paranoia. "I was in an airport in London," he once recalled. "I was sitting there very quietly, with my topcoat in hand and a briefcase at my feet. And I looked up and across the room there stood a man five foot six, my identical height, wearing the identical topcoat, with a briefcase of identical cowhide. And I kept staring and staring, with this funny ice-cold feeling that if he turns around and it's me, what will I do?

"Well, in point of fact, he did turn around and he was ten years younger and far more attractive. But this did leave its imprint sufficiently to write a story about it."

"Mirror Image" represents *The Twilight Zone* at its most malevolent, presenting a world where threatening, destructive forces hold the upper hand and where the best intentions of people bring only disaster. The moral, stated previously in other episodes, is clear: without trust or belief, there can be no survival.

FIRST SEASON HIATUS

With the beginning of November, 1959, production of *The Twilight Zone* came to a halt. Twenty-six episodes had been produced. Now the network was going to see whether the show could attract a sizeable enough audience to warrant renewing it for the remainder of the season.

Serling continued his campaign to publicize the unique qualities of the show. "I make no bones about taking every opportunity to blatantly plug my show," he said. Clever turns of phrase came as readily to him in conversation as they did when he was alone with his Dictaphone. Reporters quoted him in hundreds of newspapers across the country.

Nervously, Serling watched the ratings. It was touch and go all the way. "I don't believe them. I don't think they're statistically accurate. But, boy, am I on the phone waiting to hear them . . ." Doom-criers predicted an early cancellation. In the L.A. *Mirror-News,* Hal Humphrey reported one sooth-sayer as dismissing the show with, "It's a think show, and viewers don't want to think."

One person who almost certainly must have agreed with that statement was one of the show's sponsors, called "the Old Man" by the crew. "He used to call up the agency on Monday morning and demand to know what Friday's script had been all about," Serling told *TV Guide.* "Then he'd demand an explanation of the explanation. I guess he figured if he couldn't understand it, neither could the people who bought his products. The funny part was that although every renewal was right at the wire—one day I got eight phone calls, four telling me we were off the air and four more telling me we were back on—the Old Man stuck for a whole season before he decided he couldn't stand it any longer."

Within two months, the Nielsen ratings showed *The Twilight Zone* ahead of its competition. The series was attracting a weekly audience of close to twenty million, and while it was never a runaway hit, its audience did prove loyal—and vociferous. Serling: "We got almost six thousand pieces of mail in eighteen days. A lot of teenagers wrote, which surprised us, and a lot of doctors and professional people, people who ordinarily would never write a letter to a show." The letters ranged all the way from scholarly analyses of various episodes to out-and-out hero worship, the purest example of the latter being one that began, "Dear Mr. Serling; I think of you like most people think of God, but this is not intended as a fan letter . . ." Another letter, this one to a newspaper, praised Serling for his "fictitious imagination."

On February 10, 1960, the suspense was broken. CBS announced in a press release that the series would continue for the rest of the season, with both General Foods and Kimberly-Clark staying on as sponsors. Heaving a collective sigh of relief, Cayuga Productions got back down to business.

"EXECUTION" (4/1/60)

Albert Salmi

Written by Rod Serling
Based on an unpublished story by George Clayton Johnson
Producer: Buck Houghton
Director: David Orrick McDearmon
Director of Photography: George T. Clemens
Music: stock

Cast:
Joe Caswell: Albert Salmi
George Manion: Russell Johnson
Johnson: Than Wyenn
Reverend: Jon Lormer
Judge: Fay Roope
Elderly Man: George Mitchell
Bartender: Richard Karlan
Cowboy: Joe Haworth

"Commonplace-if-somewhat-grim unsocial event known as a necktie party, the guest of dishonor a cowboy named Joe Caswell, just a moment away from a rope, a short dance several feet off the ground, and then the dark eternity of all evil men. Mr. Joe Caswell, who, when the good Lord passed out a conscience, a heart, a feeling for fellow men, must have been out for a beer and missed out. Mr. Joe Caswell, in the last quiet moment of a violent life."

In 1880, Joe Caswell is about to be hanged for shooting a man in the back. But as the noose tightens around his neck, Caswell disappears—and reappears in the modern laboratory of Professor Manion, inventor of the time machine that has saved his neck by plucking him at random out of the past. Seeing the rope burns and surmising that Caswell is one of life's more dangerous people, Manion attempts to send him back. The two men struggle. Caswell hits Manion over the head with a heavy lamp and runs out onto a busy city street. Overwhelmed by the lights and the noise, Caswell soon returns to the laboratory to seek Manion's aid, but his blow has killed the scientist. Then Paul Johnson, a petty thief, enters the lab. Caswell grapples with him for his gun. Johnson strangles Caswell with the drawcord of a curtain. But in looking for a hidden safe, Johnson unwittingly activates the time machine. He is sent back to 1880, appearing in the noose meant for Caswell and meeting the fate intended for the other man.

"This is November, 1880, the aftermath of a necktie party. The victim's name—Paul Johnson, a minor-league criminal and the taker of another human life. No comment on his death save this: justice can span years. Retribution is not subject to a calendar. Tonight's case in point in the Twilight Zone."

The first episode produced in February (number twenty-seven in order of production), "Execution," proved one of Serling's lesser efforts. In George Clayton Johnson's original unpublished story, two modern scientists use a time machine to yank a nineteenth-century killer out of a hangman's noose and into the present. Soon, the scientists realize that they've made a mistake and have unwittingly let loose a violent primitive. Ultimately, the man is shot to death by a policeman and reappears back in the noose, the cycle complete. In adapting the story into a teleplay, Serling added verbiage and contrivance, eliminating one of the scientists (in the show, the remaining scientist is played by Russell Johnson, later the Professor on *Gilligan's Island*) and adding a modern-day criminal, who strangles the man from the past with ludicrous ease. In particular, Serling's addition of the burglar, obviously intended as Caswell's modern counterpart, makes the piece seem cluttered and unbalanced.

Playing nineteenth-century killer Joe Caswell was Albert Salmi, a fine character actor who deserves better roles than he usually gets. Here, he gives Caswell an air of authenticity, speaking with an archaic accent and moving with the menacing body language of a man long used to violence. His is a faultless performance, but it is not enough to overcome a poorly adapted script.

"THE BIG TALL WISH" (4/8/60)

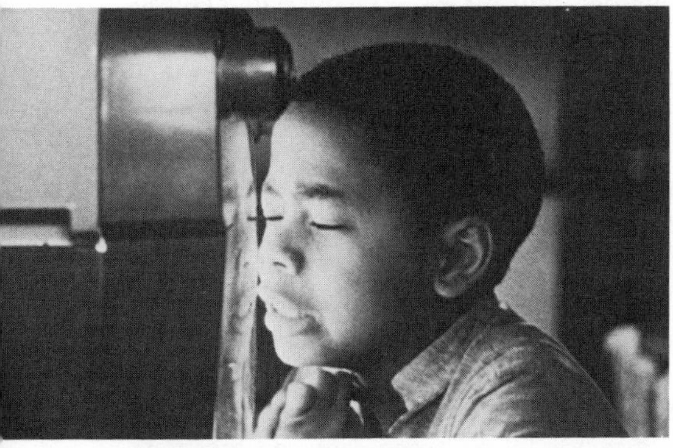

Steven Perry

Written by Rod Serling
Producer: Buck Houghton
Director: Ron Winston
Director of Photography: George T. Clemens
Music: Jerry Goldsmith

Cast:
Bolie Jackson: Ivan Dixon
Henry: Steven Perry
Frances: Kim Hamilton
Mizell: Walter Burke
Thomas: Henry Scott
Other Fighter: Charles Horvath
Announcer: Carl McIntire
Referee: Frankie Van

"In this corner of the universe, a prizefighter named Bolie Jackson, one hundred eighty-three pounds and an hour and a half from a comeback at St. Nick's arena. Mr. Bolie Jackson, who by the standards of his profession is an aging, over-the-hill relic of what was, and who now sees a reflection of a man who has left too many pieces of his youth in too many stadiums for too many years before too many screaming people. Mr. Bolie Jackson, who might do well to look for some gentle magic in the hard-surfaced glass that stares back at him."

Although Jackson breaks his hand prior to the fight, he wins it because Henry—a little boy who adores the fighter and who believes utterly in magic—has made the "big, tall wish." Unfortunately, after the fight the boxer refuses to believe in the magic, insisting it was his own ability that won the match. In anguish, the child tells him, "If you don't believe, it won't be true!" But the fighter has been battered and beaten for so long that he *can't* believe. Suddenly, Jackson finds himself back in the ring, flat on his back and counted out. When he returns to Henry, the child tells him that he won't be making any more wishes. "I'm too old for wishes," he says, "and there ain't no such thing as magic, is there?" "Maybe there is magic," says Bolie. "Maybe there's wishes, too. I guess the trouble is, there's not enough people around to believe."

"Mr. Bolie Jackson, one hundred eighty-three pounds, who left a second chance lying in a heap on a rosin-spattered canvas at St. Nick's arena. Mr. Bolie Jackson, who shares the most common ailment of all men, the strange and perverse disinclination to believe in a miracle, the kind of miracle to come from a little boy, perhaps only to be found in the Twilight Zone."

The theme of "The Big Tall Wish" was nothing new, being simply a reiteration of the old saw about the washed-up fighter and the adorable little boy the lug's just gotta win the big fight for, but Serling had a couple of twists in mind. For one, the central drama of the piece revolved around a belief in magic. For another, both the fighter and the little boy, along with the boy's mother and all the people in the neighborhood, were played by black actors. In 1960, casting blacks in a dramatic show not dealing with racial issues was something practically unheard of, but this was a deliberate move on Serling's part. "Television, like its big sister, the motion picture, has been guilty of a sin of omission," he said at the time. "Hungry for talent, desperate for the so-called 'new face,' constantly searching for a transfusion of new blood, it has overlooked a source of wondrous talent that resides under its nose. This is the Negro actor."

Originally cast in the lead was boxer Archie Moore, but when he couldn't keep up the pace casting director John Erman replaced him with Ivan Dixon, whom he had seen on the New York stage. Dixon, unfortunately best known as a regular on *Hogan's Heroes*, is an extremely talented actor, and he turns in a delicately balanced performance of both strength and vulnerability. Also excellent is Steven Perry as Henry, the little boy. His is an agonized performance—and it *is* a performance, not just a bland recitation of lines, as is so often the case with child actors.

The director of "The Big Tall Wish" was Ron Winston, and he was met with problems here far removed from those he had encountered on "The

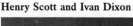

Henry Scott and Ivan Dixon

Monsters Are Due on Maple Street." One of these was one shared by every television director who's ever had to stage a prize fight: how to give the feel of a crowded arena without being able to hire several hundred extras. To overcome this, in "The Big Tall Wish" the camera comes in close. We see the hands of the spectators as they react in various ways to the fight. One man eats popcorn, a woman peeks out from behind spread fingers, a man's fists mimic the blows he sees falling in the ring. Through these few shots a composite impression is formed of a larger reality.

Winston was particularly skilled at dealing with fragile, intangible emotions which are at the heart of this piece—notably the hope, love and faith of the little boy. Says Buck Houghton, "It was sentimental and he was sentimental. He was very good at extracting sentiment without getting sugary about it, very restrained."

"A NICE PLACE TO VISIT" (4/15/60)

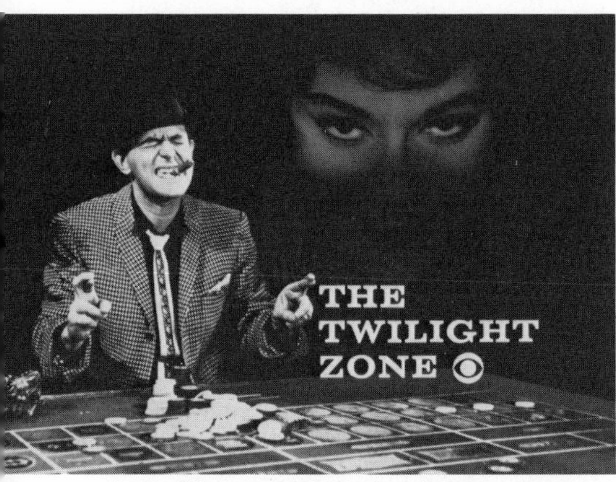

Larry Blyden, original advertisement

Written by Charles Beaumont
Producer: Buck Houghton
Director: John Brahm
Director of Photography: George T. Clemens
Music: stock

Cast:
Rocky Valentine: Larry Blyden
Mr. Pip: Sebastian Cabot
Policeman: John Close
Croupier: Wayne Tucker
First Beautiful Girl: Sandra Warner
Dancing Girl: Barbara English
Crap Dealer: Peter Hornsby
Midget Policeman: Nels Nelson
Parking Attendant: Bill Mullikin

"Portrait of a man at work, the only work he's ever done, the only work he knows. His name is Henry Francis Valentine but he calls himself Rocky, because that's the way his life has been—rocky and perilous and uphill at a dead run all the way. He's tired now, tired of running or wanting, of waiting for the breaks that come to others but never to him, never to Rocky Valentine . . . A scared, angry little man. He thinks it's all over now, but he's wrong. For Rocky Valentine, it's just the beginning."

After being shot to death by a policeman, petty thief Rocky Valentine revives to find himself unhurt—and in the company of a seemingly good-natured, white-haired fat man named Pip. Pip explains that he is Valentine's "guide," and that he has been instructed to supply him with whatever he wishes. At first, Valentine is suspicious—to the point of shooting Pip point-blank in the head. But when Pip isn't harmed at all by this, Rocky concludes that Pip must be his guardian angel, and *he* must be in Heaven! Accordingly, he goes on a good-time spree filled with gambling and beautiful women. The only problem is that everything is *too* good: Rocky wins at every game, and any woman he wants is his for the asking. All of this very quickly becomes insufferably stifling. Rocky pleads with Pip to be sent to "the Other Place." With a gleeful ferocity, Pip replies, "This *is* the Other Place!"

"A scared, angry little man who never got a break. Now he has everything he's ever wanted—and he's going to have to live with it for eternity . . . in the Twilight Zone."

Charles Beaumont's fourth and final first-season entry was his weakest. It's basically a prolonged one-liner. However, as regarded the casting of the lead, Beaumont had something truly original and bizarre in mind. He wrote Serling: "I've had an absolutely screwball idea. Your first reaction will be one of dumb astonishment, followed by rapid blinking and fantods. If for any reason we can't get Mickey Rooney for 'The Other Place' [the script's original title], why don't *you essay the role of Rocky yourself*? (Dumb astonishment? Rapid blinking? Fantods?) When I mentioned it to Helen, she said, 'Swell, now he'll think you consider him the cheap crook type.' I cuffed her lightly about the ears, explaining that if I know writers, it's a good bet Old Rod has the same secret ambition I do . . . to wit, to act. We're all hams, in our own ways, each of us planning to write himself into a part some day; is it not so? My opinion is that it would be a lot of fun all around, that if you can indeed act you'd be keen in the role, and that the concomitant publicity would be unbad."

Serling passed on the idea, instead casting Larry Blyden. Unfortunately, Blyden's performance seriously mars the episode. Although he is likeable, his broad portrayal of Valentine comes across like a third-rate composite impression of James Cagney, Edward G. Robinson and George Raft.

Buck Houghton feels that the material dictated Blyden's approach. "You had to do something extravagant to keep it from just laying there. If he had just gone for it and said, 'Gee, that's a great broad. You mean she's mine?' it would have been about as interesting as yesterday's fish. But he said, 'Hoo boy! *Really?!* Ha ha!!' It may not have been the *right* thing to do, but it was something to do."

If there is a saving grace in this episode, it must surely lie in the cultured and malevolent performance of Sebastian Cabot as Pip, Valentine's guardian "angel." This part demanded a great sacrifice of Cabot, though. His black hair and neatly groomed black beard were among his trademarks—but they just wouldn't do for a character presumed to be an angel throughout most of the show. His hair would have to be white.

"That was quite a chore," Buck Houghton remembers. "It's very hard to whiten hair. What they usually use is thinned zinc oxide and it *looks* like thinned zinc oxide. It's bad. And yet this fellow had to have white hair, it really made a big difference. And what they do to really make it white is they bleach it and it ain't very good for your hair. We really had to talk Sebastian into doing it, because then he had to be white-haired for three months, until it grew out. That was a major task, to get him to do that."

"NIGHTMARE AS A CHILD" (4/29/60)

Terry Burnham and Janice Rule

Written by Rod Serling
Producer: Buck Houghton
Director: Alvin Ganzer
Director of Photography: George T. Clemens
Music: Jerry Goldsmith

Cast:
Helen Foley: Janice Rule
Markie: Terry Burnham
Peter Selden: Shepperd Strudwick
Doctor: Michael Fox
Police Lt.: Joe Perry
Little Girl: Suzanne Cupito

*"Month of November, hot chocolate, and a small cameo of a child's face, imperfect only in its solemnity. And these are the improbable ingredients to a human emotion, an emotion, say, like—*fear. *But in a moment this woman, Helen Foley, will realize fear. She will understand what are the properties of terror. A little girl will lead her by the hand and walk with her into a nightmare."*

Coming home from work, schoolteacher Helen Foley encounters Markie, a strangely-serious little girl, on the stairs outside her apartment. She invites her in for a cup of hot chocolate and finds that the child seems to *know* her—and is particularly insistent on jogging her memory about a vaguely familiar-looking man she saw earlier that day. This does not seem important until the same man arrives at Helen's door. Frightened, Markie runs out the back way. The man is Peter Selden, who worked for Helen's mother when Helen was a child and who claims to have been the first to find her mother's body after she was murdered—an event Helen witnessed but has blocked from her conscious mind. When she mentions Markie, Selden remarks that this was *Helen's* nickname as a child and shows her an old photo of herself. She and Markie are one and the same! After Selden leaves, Markie reappears. She *is* Helen, and she's here for a reason: to force Helen to remember her mother's death. Just then, Selden returns. He confesses to the murder and explains that he has tracked Helen down in order to get rid of the sole witness to his crime. He lunges at her, but she manages to get out to the hallway and push him down the stairs—to his death. Thanks to the intervention of Markie—who was, in fact, no more than the part of herself that *did* remember, trying desperately to save her—Helen survives.

"Miss Helen Foley, who has lived in night and who will wake up to morning. Miss Helen Foley, who took a dark spot from the tapestry of her life and rubbed it clean—then stepped back a few paces and got a good look at the Twilight Zone."

Immediately on the heels of "A Nice Place to Visit" came two original fantasies by Serling, one dealing with confrontation, the other with escape.

The story of "Nightmare as a Child," when stripped to its essentials, seems compelling, but in execution, the episode falls flat. Part of this must certainly be attributed to poor casting. The character played by Miss Rule (who, incidentally, was named Helen Foley, after one of Serling's favorite high school teachers) seems hard and unsympathetic, and the child is little more than harsh and irritating. Neither Serling's script nor Alvin Ganzer's direction do much to bring the story alive, either.

But then perhaps a major part of the trouble resides in the fact that the story isn't really much of a fantasy. If you assume that the appearance of the child is a hallucination on Helen's part, manufactured by her subconscious in attempt to bring her to a realization about the identity of the killer, then the episode isn't fantasy at all. Like "Where Is Everybody?" "Nightmare As a Child" is totally rational. And for *The Twilight Zone*, anything that remains so grounded in reality must be considered a disappointment.

"A STOP AT WILLOUGHBY" (5/6/60)

James Maloney and James Daly

Written by Rod Serling
Producer: Buck Houghton
Director: Robert Parrish
Director of Photography: George T. Clemens
Music: Nathan Scott

Cast:
Gart Williams: James Daly
Jane Williams: Patricia Donahue
Mr. Misrell: Howard Smith
Conductor #1: Jason Wingreen
Conductor #2: James Maloney
Helen: Mavis Neal
Boy One: Billy Booth
Boy Two: Butch Hengen
Trainman: Ryan Hayes
Man on Wagon: Max Slaten

"This is Gart Williams, age thirty-eight, a man protected by a suit of armor all held together by one bolt. Just a moment ago, someone removed the bolt, and Mr. Williams's protection fell away from him and left him a naked target. He's been cannonaded this afternoon by all the enemies of his life. His insecurity has shelled him, his sensitivity has straddled him with humiliation, his deep-rooted disquiet about his own worth has zeroed in on him, landed on target, and blown him apart. Mr. Gart Williams, ad agency exec, who in just a moment will move into the Twilight Zone—in a desperate search for survival."

During a meeting, Mr. Misrell, Williams's boss, savagely dresses him down for losing an important automobile account. Riding home on the train, Williams has a dream in which he is on a very different train in July of 1880, entering a restful little town named Willoughby, a place (as the conductor tells him) "where a man can slow down to a walk and live his life full measure." He realizes that he isn't made for the competitive life, that Willoughby is where he belongs. But when he tries to explain this to his wife—an acquisitive woman who sorely regrets her choice of husband—he receives only ridicule. Ultimately, the pressure of his job causes Williams to crack. When he calls his wife to tell her that he's quitting and to beg her to wait at home for him, she hangs up. On the commuter train, Williams feels devastated, his life a shambles. Miraculously, he suddenly finds himself back in Willoughby, where the townsfolk greet him warmly by name—he's home to stay. Meanwhile, the commuter train has come to a full stop. It seems that Mr. Williams, a regular passenger, shouted something about "Willoughby," then jumped off the train to his death. The body is loaded into a hearse. The sign on the back—"Willoughby Funeral Home."

"Willoughby? Maybe it's wishful thinking nestled in a hidden part of a man's mind, or maybe it's the last stop in the vast design of things—or perhaps, for a man like Gart Williams, who climbed on a world that went by too fast, it's a place around the bend where he could jump off. Willoughby? Whatever it is, it comes with sunlight and serenity, and is a part of the Twilight Zone."

"A Stop at Willoughby" can be considered a companion piece to "Walking Distance." Like its predecessor, it concerns a middle-aged advertising executive near the breaking point. What differentiates this episode from "Walking Distance," and what allows the ending to be happy instead of melancholy, is the fact that Willoughby, unlike Martin Sloan's Homewood, is clearly a fantasy. Gart Williams doesn't travel into the past. Instead, he escapes into a dream. This point is made clear by the fact that everyone in town knows Williams's name and that the entire place seems oriented specifically to him (as a nice touch of irony, when he returns to Willoughby to stay, the band in the park strikes up "Beautiful Dreamer").

"A Stop at Willoughby" is one of the most enduring episodes of *The Twilight Zone*, but not so much due to specific characters or situations. In "And When the Sky Was Opened" and "Mirror Image," Serling had tapped into a universal fear. Here, he did the opposite. In creating and defining Willoughby, he stumbled upon an area of universal desire. Virtually all people find themselves in pressure situations at least sometime in their lives, times when they feel ill-equipped to come up to the demands

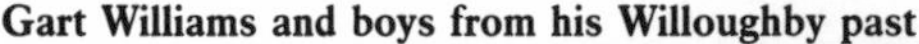
Gart Williams and boys from his Willoughby past

placed upon them. Who at these times wouldn't like to escape to a paradise with no pressures or demands?

"THE CHASER" (5/13/60)

George Grizzard and Patricia Barry

Written by Robert Presnell, Jr.
Based on the short story "The Chaser" by John Collier
Producer: Buck Houghton
Director: Douglas Heyes
Director of Photography: George T. Clemens
Music: stock

Cast:
Roger Shackleforth: George Grizzard
Prof. Daemon: John McIntire
Leila: Patricia Barry
Homburg: J. Pat O'Malley
Blonde: Barbara Perry
Fat Lady: Marjorie Bennett
Bartender: Duane Grey
Tall Man: Rusty Wescoatt

"Mr. Roger Shackleforth. Age: youthful twenties. Occupation: being in love. Not just *in love, but madly, passionately, illogically, miserably, all-consumingly in love—with a young woman named Leila who has a vague recollection of his face and even less than a passing interest. In a moment you'll see a switch, because Mr. Roger Shackleforth, the young gentleman so much in love, will take a short but meaningful journey into the Twilight Zone."*

Desperate to win his Leila's affections, Roger obtains a love potion from an enigmatic professor named A. Daemon. Visiting Leila's apartment, he manages to slip her the potion in a glass of champagne. It works—but too well. After six months of marriage, Roger is so sick of Leila's nauseatingly intense devotion that he resolves to do her in. Returning to the professor Roger pays a thousand dollars for a dose of his guaranteed "glove cleaner" ("no trace, no odor, no taste, no way to detect its presence—and it's sure"). At home, he slips the liquid into Leila's champagne. But upon hearing that she is expecting a baby, his shock is so great that he drops the glass. Outside on the patio, Prof. Daemon reclines on a deck chair, smoking a cigar. He blows a heart-shaped smoke ring and disappears.

"Mr. Roger Shackleforth, who has discovered at this late date that love can be as sticky as a vat of molasses, as unpalatable as a hunk of spoiled yeast, and as

all-consuming as a six-alarm fire in a bamboo and canvas tent. Case history of a lover boy who should never have entered the Twilight Zone."

Very little distinguishes "The Chaser" other than the fact that it was the only episode of the first season not written by Serling, Beaumont, or Matheson. Adapted by Robert Presnell, Jr., from a superior and much shorter story by John Collier, this script was originally written for and aired live on *The Billy Rose Television Theatre* in 1951. Collier's story, in its entirety, consists simply of a dialogue between two men—one young, one old—in a tiny, sparsely furnished room. The young man has come to buy a love potion. The old man sells it to him for a dollar, darkly hinting that in years to come, when he is more prosperous, he will no doubt return to buy the five-thousand-dollar "spot remover" (". . . quite imperceptible to any known method of autopsy").

In enlarging this piece for television, a number of scenes between the young man and the object of his affection, both before and after administration of the potion, were added. This had the unfortunate result of obscuring and trivializing what is essentially a beautifully conceived vignette. However, the final shot of the episode, Professor Daemon blowing a heart-shaped smoke ring that rises into the night sky as it dissipates, is not without its charm. This shot was accomplished by first filming John McIntire pretending to blow a smoke ring and then superimposing a shot of a smoky-looking heart airbrushed on a black card. The card was moved back and forth in front of the camera and made to appear to dissipate by simply taking it out of focus. A clever bit of camera magic in an episode with little magic itself.

"A PASSAGE FOR TRUMPET" (5/20/60)

Jack Klugman and Mary Webster

Written by Rod Serling
Producer: Buck Houghton
Director: Don Medford
Director of Photography: George T. Clemens
Music: Lyn Murray

Cast:
Joey Crown: Jack Klugman
Gabe: John Anderson
Nan: Mary Webster
Baron: Frank Wolff
Truck Driver: James Flavin
Pawnshop Owner: Ned Glass
Woman Pedestrian: Diane Honodel

"Joey Crown, musician with an odd, intense face, whose life is a quest for impossible things like flowers in concrete or like trying to pluck a note of music out of the air and put it under glass to treasure. . . . Joey Crown, musician with an odd, intense face, who in a moment will try to leave the Earth and discover the middle ground—the place we call the Twilight Zone."

Convinced that he'll never amount to anything—never even have a girlfriend—Joey has taken to the bottle, with the result that he can't get a gig anywhere. Deciding to commit suicide, he throws himself in front of a truck. When he regains consciousness, he finds himself alone on the street at night. Visiting several of his regular haunts, he is unable to locate anybody he knows, and the people who are there can neither see nor hear him. When he notices that he casts no reflection in a mirror, Joey concludes that he must be a ghost. Reflecting back on his life, he realizes that, contrary to what he previously believed, it was actually filled with any number of small joys. Drawn by the sound of a trumpet being played, Joey meets a tall, elegant man in a tuxedo who, surprisingly, can see and hear him—*and* knows his name. The man tells him that it is the *other* people who are dead, that Joey is in a limbo between life and death, and the choice of which way to go is his. Joey opts for life. As the man departs, Joey asks his name. The answer: "Gabriel." Joey finds himself back on the pavement, just an instant after being hit by the truck, alive and unharmed. That night, while playing trumpet on a rooftop, he meets Nan, a newcomer to the city, who shyly asks if Joey could show her the sights. Enthusiastically, he accepts the offer.

"Joey Crown, who makes music, and who discovered something about life; that it can be rich and rewarding and full of beauty, just like the music he played, if a person would only pause to look and to listen. Joey Crown, who got his *clue in the Twilight Zone."*

Two newcomers to *The Twilight Zone* arrived with "A Passage for Trumpet." The first was director Don Medford, whose credits since have included such action series as *The Fugitive, The Man From U.N.C.L.E., The F.B.I.,* and *Baretta*. In all, he would direct this and four other *Twilight Zone* episodes: "The Man in the Bottle," "The Mirror," "Deaths-head Revisited," and "Death Ship." Says Buck Houghton, "Don was especially useful where you needed to be very, very gripping and where violence of nature had something to do with it. I don't mean violence in the sense of a baseball bat hitting a guy's head, I mean the tensions that go around violence. Don appreciates those, he likes them, and he struggles for them."

If Medford liked intensity, then the leading man he had to work with suited him ideally. Playing trumpeter Joey Crown was Jack Klugman, an actor rarely matched for power and subtlety of performance. This is the first of Klugman's four starring roles on *The Twilight Zone*, a number equalled only by Burgess Meredith, and it is a minor masterpiece. Perhaps better than any other actor, Klugman was able to exemplify the urban loser, the underdog struggling to improve himself but knowing deep down that the odds are overwhelmingly against him.

Several factors raise Klugman's performance here above the merely competent. The first is his total dedication to the part. Buck Houghton recalls: "Klugman took pains, for instance, to learn how to finger a trumpet. He got a good trumpeter to teach him how to do it."

Another major factor is one hard to define, but an example is easily given. Here is an excerpt from the final scene of Serling's original script, reprinted verbatim. Joey has opted to stay alive. He sits on the roof of a building, playing his trumpet. From out of the shadows appears Nan (again that name!), a pleasant-looking young woman who has just arrived in New York. They exchange names, then:

NAN: Will you play some more, Joey?

JOEY: Sure. Sure I'll play some more. I'll play whatever you like. For as *long* as you like. You know . . . You know, you may like it here. It's not a bad town.

John Anderson

to be returned to the way he was before—broke, jobless, and with no place to live. Hempstead complies, but he arranges for Bevis's jalopy to be given back to him undamaged. He is *still* Bevis's guardian angel, and will continue to help him in small ways.

"Mr. James B. W. Bevis, who believes in a magic all his own. The magic of a child's smile, the magic of liking and being liked, the strange and wondrous mysticism that is the simple act of living. Mr. James B. W. Bevis, species of twentieth-century male, who has his own private and special Twilight Zone."

Angels made another appearance in the episode produced directly after "A Passage for Trumpet." Originally, Serling intended "Mr. Bevis" as a pilot for a series starring Burgess Meredith, wherein each week the angel would get Bevis out of yet another scrape. But Meredith was unwilling to commit himself to a series and turned the offer down. As a result, Serling abandoned the idea of doing "Bevis" as a series and the script was filmed simply as a one-shot *Twilight Zone* episode, with Orson Bean as Bevis and Henry Jones as J. Hardy Hempstead, Bevis's guardian angel.

Considering what *was* filmed, it seems just as well that the series was never made. "That was one of my least favorite," says Buck Houghton. "Somehow, it just didn't come together. It was apples and oranges. I didn't think there was any excitement or interest. You just wondered, why watch it?"

As with most of Serling's attempts at comedy, the humor here seems artificial and strained. The jokes rarely work and the material flows sluggishly. Weighting down the comedy even further are the direction of William Asher (*I Love Lucy*) and the performance by Orson Bean as Bevis. While Burgess Meredith might have fleshed out the main character, as he did in "Time Enough at Last" (whose main character, certainly not coincidentally, was named *Bemis*), Bean just amiably strolls through the part. His Bevis is palpably a loser, a man using eccentricity as a blind behind which he can hide from a world hopelessly beyond his ability to cope. Certainly, Meredith would have presented a character with more backbone, one who, despite his eccentricities, was undeniably a survivor. Bean's Bevis has charm but no substance, and without that he can seem no more than silly and trivial. Consequently, so does the episode.

"THE AFTER HOURS" (6/10/60)

James Milhollin and Anne Francis

Written by Rod Serling
Producer: Buck Houghton
Director: Douglas Heyes
Director of Photography: George T. Clemens
Music: stock
Makeup: William Tuttle

Cast:
Marsha White: Anne Francis
Saleswoman: Elizabeth Allen
Armbruster: James Millhollin
Elevator Operator: John Conwell
Miss Pettigrew: Nancy Rennick
Sloan: Patrick Whyte

"Express elevator to the ninth floor of a department store, carrying Miss Marsha White on a most prosaic, ordinary, run-of-the-mill errand. . . . Miss Marsha White on the ninth floor, specialty department, looking for a gold thimble. The odds are that she'll find it—but there are even better odds that she'll find something else, because this isn't just *a department store. This happens to be the Twilight Zone."*

Marsha finds the ninth floor to be a disturbingly barren place where the *only* piece of merchandise is a single gold thimble. This is sold to her by an overly familiar, strangely insolent saleslady. Returning to the main floor, Marsha notices that the thimble is scratched—but when she goes to complain she's told that there *is* no ninth floor. Spotting the salesgirl, Marsha points her out—and is horrified to see that the figure is a mannequin! Shaken, she is assisted by store personnel to an inner office where she falls asleep. When she awakens, she finds the store closed and herself a prisoner within. As she wanders in the dark, she hears voices speaking to her which seem to come from the mannequins. Terrified, she backs into an elevator—which takes her to the ninth floor. The mannequins are there, and one by one they come to life, including the saleslady and the elevator operator who originally conducted her to the ninth floor. Under their probing, Marsha remembers that she too is a mannequin. Each of them is allowed a month's sojourn among the humans, but Marsha forgot her true identity and did not return on time. With melancholy resignation, Marsha apologizes, then reverts to her original—and inanimate—form.

"Marsha White in her normal and natural state: a wooden lady with a painted face who, one month out of the year, takes on the characteristics of someone as

normal and as flesh and blood as you and I. But it makes you wonder, doesn't it? Just how normal are we? Just who are the people we nod our hellos to as we pass on the street? A rather good question to ask—particularly in the Twilight Zone."

One of the high points of the first season was Serling's bizarre and frightening "The After Hours." The biggest challenge of this episode was to construct mannequins which would look like the principal actors, yet still be clearly recognizable as mannequins. "I was very concerned about that one being technically good," says Buck Houghton, "because I felt it would fall right on its face if those models weren't awfully good. And we debated whether to have Anne Francis do it herself in some sort of frozen pose and we talked about waxing her face and doing a lot of things to make her look like a mannequin, but we felt that wouldn't work. I remember going round and round on how to make that so solid that nobody would laugh at it or say, 'Oh, I caught them doing their tricks.'"

What was finally done was that William Tuttle and his assistant Charles Schram made molds of the faces of the three principals, Anne Francis, Elizabeth Allen, and John Conwell. From these, duplicate heads were cast in plaster and painted with acrylics. The heads were then affixed to mannequin bodies. With that, "The After Hours" had three superb-looking props.

But a good prop does not necessarily a good show make, and for that the best efforts of Serling, Anne Francis, and director Douglas Heyes were required. For his part, Serling once again utilized "the fear of the unknown working on you, which you cannot share with others." Who, after all, can't identify with a woman trapped all alone in a department store with something chasing her?

From there, Douglas Heyes elaborated upon the script and gave the thing a spooky, unspoken, oppressive quality. He was fortunate to be able to work within a truly enormous set. "We inherited a huge basic set from some feature picture which had been a big newspaper office," Heyes remembers, "and we converted it into a big department store." Given this kind of space, Heyes could make use of a wide variety of shots to create tension: long shots of silhouetted figures, closeups of Anne Francis's feet as she walks down darkened aisles, shots through pebbled glass of her face—and through all of this, the camera is almost always in motion, as though it were itself a character, nervously stalking.

No amount of visual flair could make this episode work without a strong central presence, and this is where the contribution of Anne Francis comes in. As a rule, women in *The Twilight Zone* generally come across as drab, colorless, uninteresting. Think of Vera Miles in "Mirror Image" or Janice

Rule in "Nightmare as a Child." Possibly this was due to a chauvinism on the part of Serling, possibly to the sexism of the times. But Ms. Francis is an exception. There's an energy about her and a freshness, an individuality. Her performance is exciting, her reactions genuine. Says Douglas Heyes, "I think the casting of Anne Francis in that role was unbelievably good." Apparently, this opinion is shared by many others, for Anne Francis observes, "I still have people who walk up to me and say, 'The favorite show that I ever saw that you were in was that.' It did make a mark, it did make an impression."

"A WORLD OF HIS OWN" (7/1/60)

Keenan Wynn and Phyllis Kirk

Written by Richard Matheson
Producer: Buck Houghton
Director: Ralph Nelson
Director of Photography: George T. Clemens
Music: stock

Cast:
Gregory West: Keenan Wynn
Victoria West: Phyllis Kirk
Mary: Mary La Roche

*"The home of Mr. Gregory West, one of America's most noted playwrights. The office of Mr. Gregory West. Mr. Gregory West—shy, quiet, and at the moment very happy. Mary—warm, affectionate . . . And the final ingredient—*Mrs. *Gregory West."*

Victoria West is surprised when she looks in the window of her husband's study and sees him sharing a drink with Mary, an attractive blonde. But she's even more surprised when she barges in a moment later and finds the woman gone without a trace. Gregory explains that simply by describing something—or somebody—into his dictation machine, he can cause that thing to materialize in his office. To make it disappear, all he need do is throw the tape in the fireplace. He demonstrates both these actions, first with Mary, and then—when Victoria attempts to run off—with a full-grown elephant in the hallway. Despite the evidence of her own senses, Victoria informs Gregory she is convinced he is insane and intends to have him committed. In reply, Gregory removes an envelope from a wall safe. He tells her it contains the length of tape on which *she* is described. Believing none of this, Victoria snatches the envelope away from him and throws it on the fire. She has just enough time to register astonishment before she disappears. Gregory rushes to the tape machine and frantically begins to redescribe Victoria . . . then reconsiders and describes instead Mrs. *Mary* West. The loving—and far less temperamental—Mary appears, contentedly mixing her husband a drink.

"Leaving Mr. Gregory West, still shy, quiet, very happy—and apparently in complete control of the Twilight Zone."

The final episode of the first season, both in order of production and broadcast, was Richard Matheson's "A World of His Own." This comedy, about a playwright who can make his characters come to life by describing them into a Dictaphone, had a curious genesis. Matheson recalls, "Actually, the first outline I submitted was a serious one in which it became very nightmarish to him when his characters came to life. I guess it was a little melodramatic for them, so they suggested that I try to lighten it up, and I redid it as a comedy, which I think worked out well."

The casting couldn't have been better: Keenan Wynn as the playwright, Phyllis Kirk as his volatile wife, and Mary La Roche as his long-suffering mistress. From start to finish, the episode is wonderfully funny and sophisticated. Director Ralph Nelson (*Lilies of the Field, Charly* and *Requiem for a Heavyweight*) viewed his task, and rightly so, as akin to "keeping one of those glass bubbles on top of a fountain."

"A World of His Own" employed one of the largest props used in any episode of the series. For one key scene, the playwright had to summon up an elephant in his hallway to block his wife from leaving the house. Rear projection or stock footage of an elephant just wouldn't be convincing; a real elephant had to be brought onto the set.

Buck Houghton remembers the episode with amusement. "I came around the stage corner and there was the elephant. And the elephant man was having him go on his nose and then on his back legs, and on his nose and then on his back legs, and then his nose—I stood there wondering what this guy was beating this poor elephant to death for. Finally—he didn't give the next order—the elephant shit a bale of hay. And he says, 'Now he's good for two hours.' So I went in and I told Nelson, 'You've got two hours to use the elephant or we're in trouble.'"

One of the series' finest jokes and a perfect capper to the first season was the final gag of the show. For this, Serling makes his first on-camera appearance in an episode. Serling strolls on-camera and addresses the audience. "We hope you enjoyed tonight's romantic story on *The Twilight Zone*. At the same time, we want you to realize that it was, of course, purely fictional. In real life, such ridiculous nonsense—"

"Rod, you shouldn't!" says West. He walks over to the wall safe and pulls out an envelope marked "Rod Serling." "I mean, you shouldn't say such things as 'nonsense' and 'ridiculous'!" He pulls the tape out of the envelope and throws it on the fire.

Serling looks at this for a moment, says, "Well, that's the way it goes," and promptly disappears.

It's an ending that pleases Richard Matheson greatly. "I think I was the only one who ever was able to add a sequence where Rod Serling was made to disappear, too. It was the last show of the season, so they felt they could do that."

TAKING ACCOUNT OF THE FIRST SEASON

Production of the first season came to a halt early in April of 1960. In all, thirty-six episodes had been produced, and they had been of such quality that had the series ended right there, *The Twilight Zone* would still have been a television landmark. This fact was not lost on those at the time. In the spring of 1960, John Brahm won a Directors Guild Award for "Time Enough at Last." Buck Houghton picked up a Producers Guild Award for Best Produced Series. The show won awards from *Limelight, Radio and Television Daily,* and *Motion Picture Daily*. Perhaps most significantly, the Eighteenth World Science Fiction Convention voted *The Twilight Zone* the prestigious Hugo Award for best dramatic presentation—the first of three such awards the series would win. In April, Bantam Books released *Stories From The Twilight Zone,* a paperback collection containing Serling's adaptations of six of his *Twilight Zone* teleplays. The stories were "The Mighty Casey," "Escape Clause," "Walking Distance," "The Fever," "Where Is Everybody?" and "The Monsters Are Due on Maple Street." Bantam had contracted with Serling to do the book even before the series started filming. Originally, Bantam intended to release the book several months earlier, but wisely delayed the release until the series had attracted a larger audience. Without exception, the reviews were favorable and the book sold well.

On May 11, 1960, CBS announced that *The Twilight Zone* had been renewed for a second season, with General Foods and Colgate-Palmolive as sponsors. *The Twilight Zone* had survived its infancy.

Another measurement of the series' success related specifically to Serling. Perhaps he first became aware of it while walking down the street or going into a restaurant or theater. Since "Patterns," his name had been well-known, but not his face. Now all that was changed. Rod was a TV star.

Fame was not without its drawbacks. Serling: "Now people see me on the street and they say, 'Why, we thought you were six foot one' or 'We thought you looked like a movie actor,' and then they look at me and say, 'Why, God, this kid is five foot five and he's got a broken nose.' I photograph far better than I look, and that's the problem."

Serling's children were also having troubles as a result of their father's fame. "I think I was about eight when I realized that Daddy didn't just work, Daddy really did something," Anne recalls. "And kids used to say to me, 'Are you something out of the Twilight Zone?' What can you say?"

Another problem was that outside of the house, the children could never have their father to themselves. Says Jodi, "I was very annoyed by people coming up and saying, 'You're Rod Serling.' And so I used to ask him, 'Please, just say you're somebody else.' He never would, and he was always very kind to people."

Despite these difficulties, Serling's close friend, producer Dick Berg, thinks he enjoyed his new-found celebrity status. "He was a writer for the masses and he wanted to persuade them, entertain them, and be loved back by them. And part of that love came, on a personal level, through recognition, so that actually he was almost a hyphenated writer-actor, if you will, and he rather enjoyed that. There were many of his snotty friends who thought that was sellout time or childish, but actually he was merely living out their fantasies. He figured, if you're gonna do it, be the best, and the best known, and the most highly paid. And all of those came about through this star status which he helped create."

On the afternoon of June 21, 1960, Serling prepared to attend the annual Emmy Awards presentation. He was nominated for his fourth Emmy, for his writing on *The Twilight Zone,* but he had no expectations of winning. He was up against two very prestigious shows: James Costigan's adaptation of *The Turn of the Screw* on *Ford Startime,* starring Ingrid Bergman, and Loring Mandel's "Project Immortality" on *Playhouse 90.* Had he thought he might win, he would have shaved prior to the broadcast, but as he was just going to be another face in the crowd applauding the winner, he really didn't see any necessity for it.

For the most part, the winners were as expected. Laurence Olivier won for *The Moon and Sixpence,* Ingrid Bergman for *The Turn of the Screw,* Robert Stack for *The Untouchables.* And then came the Emmy for Outstanding Writing Achievement in Drama. And the winner was . . . Rod Serling!

To say it came as a surprise to him that he won would be an understatement. When he got up onto the stage and accepted the award, he had this to say: "I don't know how deserving I am but I do know how grateful I am." Afterwards, he told reporters, "Actually, it was probably the happiest moment of my professional career."

A year before, Serling had stepped onto a tightrope that no one had ever tested before. Had he fallen, it would have been a long drop, both in terms of prestige and money. But back in September, he'd told Mike Wallace, ". . . I'm not nearly as concerned with the money to be made on this show as I am with the quality of it, and I can prove that. I have a contract with Metro–Goldwyn–Mayer which guarantees me something in the neighborhood of a quarter of a million dollars over a period of three years. This is a contract I'm trying to break and get out of, so I can devote time to a series which is very iffy, which is a very problematical thing. It's only guaranteed twenty-six weeks, and if it only goes twenty-six and stops, I'll have lost a great deal of money. But I would rather take the chance and do something I like, something I'm familiar with, something that has a built-in challenge to it."

Serling had taken the chance, and won.

Rod Serling after winning his fourth Emmy, first for *The Twilight Zone*

THE SECOND SEASON: 1960–1961

Producer: Buck Houghton
Associate Producer: Del Reisman
Production Manager: Ralph W. Nelson
Director of Photography: George T. Clemens
Assistant Directors: E. Darrell Hallenbeck and Lindsley Parsons, Jr.
Casting: Ethel Winant and Stalmaster-Lister
Art Directors: George W. Davis and Phil Barber
Editors: Bill Mosher, Leon Barsha and Jason H. Bernie
Makeup: Bob Keats
Special Effects: Virgil Beck
Camera Operators: Fred Mandl and Bill Rand
Sound: Franklin Milton, Charles Sheid and Bill Edmondson
Theme Music: Marius Constant
Set Direction: Henry Grace and H. Web Arrowsmith
Titles and Opticals: Pacific Title
Mr. Serling's Wardrobe: Kuppenheimer
Filmed at Metro–Goldwyn–Mayer

Videotape Credits:
Producer: Buck Houghton
Associate Producer: Del Reisman
Assistant to the Producer: Lennie Horn
Production Assistant: Lillian Gallo
Associate Director: James Clark
Casting: Ethel Winant
Art Director: Robert Tyler Lee
Technical Director: Jim Brady
Lighting Director: Tom D. Schamp
Set Decorators: Buck Henshaw and Art Parker
Makeup: Bud Sweeney
Special Effects: Bob Waugh

IV / THE SECOND SEASON

With the debut of the second season, Serling could rest assured that *The Twilight Zone* had found its audience. "On *The Twilight Zone*," he wrote, "we now hit approximately five hundred letters a week. We have fan clubs in thirty-one states. And we get an average of fifty story ideas submitted to us each week from people who 'dig' fantasy, the unusual, the imaginative." And this was not a frugal audience: by November, 1960, sales of *Stories From The Twilight Zone* exceeded 400,000 copies. There were more *Twilight Zone* products to come this year: a comic book (with each story introduced by a comic-book version of Serling); a record album (featuring the Muzak of Marty Manning and his orchestra and billed as "An Adventure in the Space of Sound"); a board game, in which players moved their pieces down various maze-like "roads to reality"; and Serling's *More Stories From The Twilight Zone*, which went into a second printing two weeks after it was released. Where the products left off, the inventiveness of the fans took over. A black Model A Ford was seen outside a Los Angeles high school with the words "The Twilight Zone" painted in white across its side. And in Teaneck, New Jersey, "The Twilight Zone" coffee house opened its doors for business.

The show's popularity brought production bonuses, too. "After the first year, there was no trouble getting a cast," George Clemens recalls. "The producer would suggest a name to somebody and they'd say, 'Oh, well, you can't get *him*. The money is way out of this world.' But they'd come in and do *Twilight Zone* for a half of what they would normally get because it was prestige and it was fun for them."

Despite all of this, this season saw only twenty-nine episodes produced, down seven from the previous year. "In the second season," says Buck Houghton, "it seems to me that CBS was more concerned about the cost of the shows in relation to the rating it was getting than they were in either the first season or the third season. Indeed, that's the only reason we taped, to save some money." The taping that Houghton refers to is the videotaping of six episodes which was done as a cost-cutting measure—a subject we will deal with later in this chapter.

"*KING NINE* WILL NOT RETURN" (9/30/60)

Robert Cummings

Written by Rod Serling
Producer: Buck Houghton
Director: Buzz Kulik
Director of Photography: George T. Clemens
Music: Fred Steiner

Cast:
Capt. James Embry: Bob Cummings
Doctor: Paul Lambert
Psychiatrist: Gene Lyons
Nurse: Jenna McMahon
British Officer: Seymour Green
British Man: Richard Lupino

"This is Africa, 1943. War spits out its violence overhead and the sandy graveyard swallows it up. Her name is King Nine, *B-25, medium bomber, Twelfth Air Force. On a hot, still morning she took off from Tunisia to bomb the southern tip of Italy. An errant piece of flak tore a hole in a wing tank and, like a wounded bird, this is where she landed, not to return this day, or any other day."*

Captain James Embry regains consciousness beside the wreckage of the *King Nine*, utterly alone. He recalls crashing with the rest of the crew, but after that—nothing. His duty is clear; he must find his men and get them to safety. But where are they? He sees the grave of one, mirages of the entire crew, and—most peculiar of all—*jet* aircraft flying overhead. However, there is no trace of his men, and no indication why they left him behind. At his wits' end, Embry collapses—and awakens in a hospital bed. In truth, the year is 1960. Seventeen years earlier, Embry fell ill and missed the last flight of the *King Nine*. Since then, he has carried within him an enormous feeling of guilt. Spying a headline that the wreck of the *King Nine* had been found in the desert, he fell into a state of shock. His trip back to his plane has been an hallucination. That would *seem* to account for everything . . . but how on earth did Embry get all that sand in his shoes?

"Enigma buried in the sand, a question mark with broken wings that lies in silent grace as a marker in a desert shrine. Odd how the real consorts with the shadows, how the present fuses with the past. How does it happen? The question is on file in the silent desert, and the answer? The answer is waiting for us in—the Twilight Zone."

Like "Where Is Everybody?" the first season opener, "*King Nine* Will Not Return," concerns a character who finds himself all alone in bizarre surroundings with no memory of how or why he got there. And as with the previous story, this too had its basis in a factual event.

In May, 1959, a team of British geologists exploring the Libyan desert for oil stumbled upon the wreckage of the *Lady Be Good*, an American B-24 bomber that had disappeared on April 4, 1943. The geologists inspected the plane and found the water jugs full and the guns and ammunition intact—but no trace of the nine-man crew. The Air Force labeled the discovery "one of the greatest mysteries in aviation history."

This was far too intriguing for Serling to pass up.

In adapting this story for *The Twilight Zone,* Serling rechristened the plane the *King Nine* and deposited the ship's captain (Robert Cummings) in the middle of the mystery, searching desperately for his lost crew in the desert amid the wreckage. The mystery of the disappearing men is never resolved, but the captain's dilemma is. And unlike "Where Is Everybody?" in "*King Nine*" Serling was allowed his final twist.

An unusual episode, the casting of the lead in "*King Nine*" proved unusual as well. "I wanted Rod to do a script for me to use on one of my specials," Cummings explained at the time. "Money is useless in a situation like that. The man is so busy that he can't be tempted with money. It was then that we worked it out—he would supply a script and I would open the new season of *Twilight Zone.*"

Except for the final scenes in the hospital, "*King Nine*" was shot entirely on location in the desert near Lone Pine, California. A war surplus B-25 was bought from the Air Force for $2500 (down from an original cost of $345,000) disassembled, flown to the location, and reassembled there.

Robert Cummings and crew

Production manager Ralph W. Nelson then ingeniously solved the challenge of transporting the cast and crew by arranging for a DC-3 to land on the highway right next to the location.

Director Buzz Kulik was a newcomer to *The Twilight Zone* with "*King Nine,*" but he soon proved himself one of the series' ablest directors. Kulik's great strength as a director lay in his ability to work with actors, a fact borne out by his television work since *The Twilight Zone,* which has included *Kill Me If You Can* (the story of Caryl Chessman, starring Alan Alda) and *Brian's Song*. Since "*King Nine*" was virtually a one-man show, Kulik's attention to characterization and his willingness to engage in lengthy rehearsal greatly enhanced the production. Additionally challenging was the fact that during most of the show Cummings's lines were contained in voice-over interior monologues (obviously Serling's alternative to the clumsy verbal monologues in "Where Is Everybody?"). In order to allow Cummings's facial expressions to match his thoughts, the voice-overs were pre-recorded at MGM and then played back on location.

The attention to detail payed off. As Hank Grant wrote in the *Hollywood Reporter,* "This was a *tour de force* for Robert Cummings, an extremely difficult role that ran the gamut from relief to joy to panic to crazed hysteria—a performance that should merit serious consideration when Emmy time comes around."

"NERVOUS MAN IN A FOUR DOLLAR ROOM" (10/14/60)

Joe Mantell

Written by Rod Serling
Producer: Buck Houghton
Director: Douglas Heyes
Director of Photography: George T. Clemens
Music: Jerry Goldsmith

Cast:
Jackie Rhoades: Joe Mantell
George: William D. Gordon

"This is Mr. Jackie Rhoades, age thirty-four, and where some men leave a mark of their lives as a record of their fragmentary existence on earth, this man leaves a blot, a dirty, discolored blemish to document a cheap and undistinguished sojourn amongst his betters. What you're about to watch in this room is a strange and mortal combat between a man and himself, for in just a moment Mr. Jackie Rhoades, whose life has been given over to fighting adversaries, will find his most formidable opponent in a cheap hotel room that is in reality the outskirts of the Twilight Zone."

Sitting in a stuffy, dingy, unbearably hot little room, Jackie finds himself in a terrible predicament. George, a gangster for whom he has done various nickel-and-dime jobs, has ordered him to murder the owner of a bar, an uncooperative old man, at two A.M. Jackie—a nervous, frightened, nail-biting mouse of a man—knows that he's done for. He hasn't the backbone to refuse George, and if he commits the murder it's a certainty he'll be caught. Looking for a match, Jackie is terrified to see that his mirror image is already smoking a lighted cigarette. The reflection is actually a *different* Jackie, intelligent, strong, self-assured. It is the man Jackie could have been had he chosen a better path and it wants *out*, it wants to take over before it's too late. Jackie tries to bolt, but he comes face to face with mirrors in the closet, the bathroom and the hallway. There is no escape. Later, George arrives to deal with Jackie, who has not done the job, but he gets a surprise: *this* Jackie Rhoades says he's resigning, beats him up, and throws him out. The old Jackie is now in the mirror, and Mr. *John* Rhoades—a nervous man no longer—is checking out.

"Exit Mr. John Rhoades, formerly a reflection in a mirror, a fragment of someone else's conscience, a wishful thinker made out of glass, but now made out of flesh and on his way to join the company of men. Mr. John Rhoades, with one foot through the door and one foot out—of the Twilight Zone."

Although "*King Nine* Will Not Return" was the first episode aired this season, it was not the first produced. That distinction belonged to another virtual one-man show scripted by Serling—one man, but *two* characters. Once again, Serling was dealing with a type with whom he was seemingly very familiar: the anonymous, insecure, unimportant little man struggling desperately against enormous odds. Here the conflict is a basic one, the internal combat between an individual's weaknesses and fears on the one hand, and his will to rise to the occasion and take control on the other.

Taking place entirely in a tiny hotel room, "Nervous Man in a Four Dollar Room" centers around the dialogue between the main character and his alter ego, who appears in a variety of mirrors. The standard operating procedure here would have been for the actor to play to his mirror image, using split screen. But director Douglas Heyes felt that this would limit the movements of both camera and actor and that it would eliminate the performer's sense of playing *to* someone. Instead, Heyes decided to use rear projection. This was done by filming Mantell as the mirror-self first. All of the mirrors in the hotel room set were actually rear projection screens on which the previously-shot footage was projected. So what Mantell as the "real" Jackie Rhoades sees and reacts to is exactly what we see in the finished product.

"Joe played all the scenes in this room just as if he was playing with another actor," says Heyes. "He could walk up to the guy, walk away from him, cross him, he could do everything. And he could maintain eye contact with him, also, because he was looking right at himself in his 'mirror.'"

Joe Mantell is an actor not generally known, but he should be. You can find him if you look for him. For instance, he's Jack Nicholson's partner in *Chinatown,* the one who sums up the movie at the end with, "C'mon, Jake. It's . . . Chinatown." In "Nervous Man in a Four Dollar Room," Mantell demonstrates a tremendous range. In reality, he's playing two parts: the "real" Jackie, described in the show as "always look[ing] like somebody's squeezing [him] through a door"; and the mirror image, calm, self-assured, commanding, and intelligent. And, wonder of wonders, both are completely believable. (Mention must be made of Jerry Goldsmith's excellent score; his theme for the "real" Jackie is ideal—nervous, quick, with a rhythm that sounds like scissors cutting.)

Perhaps the most amazing achievement of Mantell's performance is a simple, wordless reaction shot. The hit hasn't been done. Jackie is in his room, sitting on the bed, his head in his hands. The gangster who ordered him to do the job (William D. Gordon) comes in and says, "Whatta you got to say for yourself, crumb?" Slowly, Jackie raises his head. In an instant, before he's said a single word, we know that a transformation has occurred, that this is the mirror image, and that Jackie has been given a second chance.

"THE MAN IN THE BOTTLE" (10/7/60)

Joseph Ruskin

Written by Rod Serling
Producer: Buck Houghton
Director: Don Medford
Director of Photography: George T. Clemens
Music: stock

Cast:
Arthur Castle: Luther Adler
Edna Castle: Vivi Janiss
Genie: Joseph Ruskin
Mrs. Gumley: Lisa Golm
Man From the IRS: Olan Soule
German Officer: Peter Coe
German Officer #2: Albert Szabo

"Mr. and Mrs. Arthur Castle, gentle and infinitely patient people, whose lives have been a hope chest with a rusty lock and a lost set of keys. But in just a

moment that hope chest will be opened, and an improbable phantom will try to bedeck the drabness of these two people's failure-laden lives with the gold and precious stones of fulfillment. Mr. and Mrs. Arthur Castle, standing on the outskirts and about to enter the Twilight Zone."

After taking pity on an old woman and giving her a dollar for a seemingly worthless bottle she fished from the trash, impoverished curio shop owner Arthur Castle is amazed to see emerge from it a dapper genie in modern dress, who informs him that he and his wife have been granted four wishes. Unbelieving, Castle wishes for the cracked glass in a display case to be fixed. In an instant, it is done. His next wish is considerably grander: a million dollars in cash. But after giving thousands away to the folks in the neighborhood, he and his wife have a nasty shock; income taxes take all but five dollars of what's left. For his third wish, Castle comes up with what he thinks is foolproof. He wishes to be ruler of a foreign country sometime in the twentieth century, one who can't be voted out of office. Laughing, the genie willingly complies. All is exactly as Castle specified, but it is certainly *not* what he desired. The country is Germany, it is the end of World War II, and he is Adolf Hitler! Frantically, he uses the final wish to return to his old life. The genie is gone, the wishes expended, and Castle is back where he started. And yet, somehow, life doesn't seem so bad.

"A word to the wise now to the garbage collectors of the world, to the curio seekers, to the antique buffs, to everyone who would try to coax out a miracle from unlikely places. Check the bottle you're taking back for a two-cent deposit. The genie you save might be your own. Case in point, Mr. and Mrs. Arthur Castle, fresh from the briefest of trips into the Twilight Zone."

The second episode to be produced, written by Serling, was a pretty pale affair.

There are a couple of nice special effects shots—a broken glass display case heals itself and the shards of a bottle reassemble into an unblemished whole—and Joseph Ruskin, in modern dress, makes a dapper and menacing genie, but overall the episode isn't terribly interesting.

"MR. DINGLE, THE STRONG" (3/3/61)

Burgess Meredith

Written by Rod Serling
Producer: Buck Houghton
Director: John Brahm
Directors of Photography: George T. Clemens and William Skall
Music: stock

Cast:
Luther Dingle: Burgess Meredith
Bettor: Don Rickles
O'Toole: James Westerfield
Callahan: Edward Ryder
1st Martian: Douglas Spencer
2nd Martian: Michael Fox
Abernathy: James Millhollin
Boy: Jay Hector
1st Venusian: Donald Losby
2nd Venusian: Greg Irvin
1st Man: Phil Arnold
2nd Man: Douglas Evans
3rd Man: Frank Richards
Nurse: Jo Ann Dixon
Photographer: Bob Duggan

"Uniquely American institution known as the neighborhood bar. Reading left to right are Mr. Anthony O'Toole, proprietor, who waters his drinks like geraniums but who stands foursquare for peace and quiet and for booths for ladies. This is Mr. Joseph J. Callahan, an unregistered bookie, whose entire life is any sporting event with two sides and a set of odds. His idea of a meeting at the summit is any dialogue between a catcher and a pitcher with more than one man on base. And this animated citizen is every anonymous bettor who ever dropped rent money on a horse race, a prize fight, or a floating crap game, and who took out his frustrations and his insolvency on any vulnerable fellow barstool campanion within arm's and fist's reach. And this is Mr. Luther Dingle, a vacuum-cleaner salesman whose volume of business is roughly that of a valet at a hobo convention. He's a consummate failure in almost everything but is a good listener and has a prominent jaw. . . . And these two unseen gentlemen are visitors from outer space. They are about to alter the destiny of Luther Dingle by leaving him a legacy, the kind you can't hardly find no more. In just a moment, a sad-faced perennial punching bag who missed even the caboose of life's gravy train will take a short constitutional into that most unpredictable region that we refer to as the Twilight Zone."

As an experiment, a couple of Martians (two heads, but *one* body) give Dingle the strength of three hundred men. Discovering his new power,

Dingle performs various tricks—lifting a statue, tearing boulders in two, and so on—and gains the notice of both the newspapers and the general public. In the bar, he prepares to perform an amazing feat not only for those assembled but also for a live TV audience: he plans to lift the entire building. Just then, the Martians, appalled by his foolish behavior, remove his strength. Unable to make good his claims, Dingle is made a laughing stock. As the Martians exit, they encounter two Venusians in search of an Earthling on whom to perform an intelligence experiment. The Martians recommend Dingle. Shining a ray on him, the Venusians boost his intelligence three-hundred fold—and away we go again.

"Exit Mr. Luther Dingle, formerly vacuum-cleaner salesman, strongest man on Earth, and now mental giant. These latter powers will very likely be eliminated before too long, but Mr. Dingle has an appeal to extraterrestrial note-takers as well as to frustrated and insolvent bet-losers. Offhand, I'd say that he was in for a great deal of extremely odd periods, simply because there are so many inhabited planets who send down observers, and also because of course Mr. Dingle lives his life with one foot in his mouth—and the other in the Twilight Zone."

A year before, in an article about *The Twilight Zone*, a reporter had mistakenly referred to the main character of "Mr. Denton on Doomsday"

Burgess Meredith and Venusians

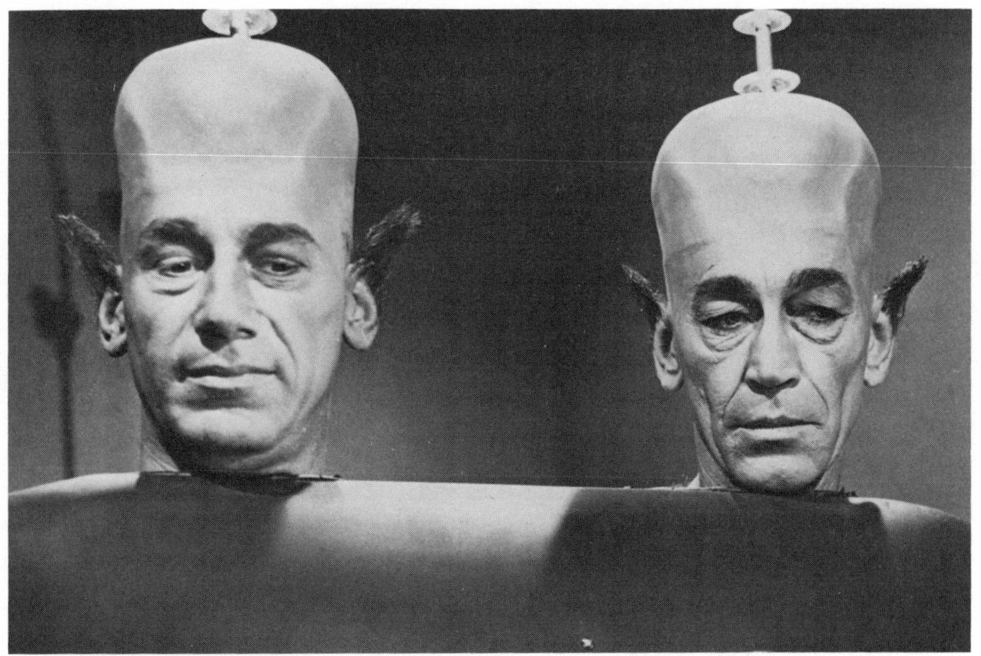

Mr. Dingle's Martians

as "Mr. Dingle." Serling must have liked the name, for he created "Mr. Dingle, the Strong."

As with "Mr. Bevis," Serling once again threw all sensitivity for his characters out the window in an effort to achieve out-and-out boffo comedy. Consequently, Mr. Dingle is little more than a bland punching bag of a character, whom virtually anyone and everyone can walk over.

This isn't to say that "Mr. Dingle, the Strong" is without interest, though. The Martian might not be a terribly convincing alien, but with its two high-domed heads—one with a turning radar dish, the other with a blinking light—pointed ears, and central pedestal, it's certainly peculiar enough to grab our attention. And, at the end of the episode, there are two equally bizarre Venusians, played by a couple of nine-year-olds wearing moustaches, eye stalks, and bald caps with cones of foam rubber under them.

Then there are the various strong-man tricks that Dingle performs. Engineered by special-effects man Virgil Beck, these include reaching over to turn off his alarm clock and inadvertently squashing it, lifting a woman on a park bench with one hand, tearing a statue from its base, and ripping rocks and a phone book in half.

"THE EYE OF THE BEHOLDER" (11/11/60)

William D. Gordon and Maxine Stuart

Written by Rod Serling
Producer: Buck Houghton
Director: Douglas Heyes
Director of Photography: George T. Clemens
Music: Bernard Herrmann
Makeup: William Tuttle

Cast:
Janet Tyler (under bandages): Maxine Stuart
Janet Tyler (revealed): Donna Douglas
Doctor: William D. Gordon
Janet's Nurse: Jennifer Howard
Leader: George Keymas
Reception Nurse: Joanna Heyes
Walter Smith: Edson Stroll

"Suspended in time and space for a moment, your introduction to Miss Janet Tyler, who lives in a very private world of darkness, a universe whose dimensions are the size, thickness, length of a swath of bandages that cover her face. In a moment we'll go back into this room and also in a moment we'll look under those bandages, keeping in mind, of course, that we're not to be surprised by what we see, because this isn't just a hospital, and patient 307 is not just a woman. This happens to be the Twilight Zone, and Miss Tyler, with you, is about to enter it."

Lying in a darkened hospital room, her head entirely wrapped in bandages, Janet Tyler, whose hideously abnormal face has made her an outcast all her life, waits to see if the last treatment has succeeded in making her look normal. This is her eleventh hospital visit—the maximum allowed by the State. If it is a failure, she will be sent to a village where others of her kind are segregated. Unseen by her, only heard, the shadowy figures of her doctor and her nurse come and go. On televisions throughout the hospital, the Leader of the State speaks of "glorious conformity," as Miss Tyler's bandages are gradually removed. Revealed, her face is extremely beautiful. The doctor draws back in horror. The treatment has been a failure! As the lights are turned on, we see the faces of the others: misshapen, asymmetrical, like something out of a nightmare. Crying hysterically, Miss Tyler runs from her room, down several hallways, and finally into a room where she comes face to face with another "freak"—Walter Smith, a strikingly handsome man in charge of an outcast village in the north. He has come to take her there. Gently, he assures her that she will come to have a sense of belonging and that she will be loved. He advises her to remember the old saying: "Beauty is in the eye of the beholder."

"Now the questions that come to mind. Where is this place and when is it, what kind of world where ugliness is the norm and beauty the deviation from that norm? The answer is, it doesn't make any difference. Because the old saying happens to be true. Beauty is *in the eye of the beholder, in this year or a hundred years hence, on this planet or wherever there is human life, perhaps out among the stars. Beauty is in the eye of the beholder. Lesson to be learned . . . in the Twilight Zone."*

After "Mr. Dingle, the Strong," Serling demonstrated that he hadn't lost his touch with "The Eye of the Beholder," an episode that is indisputably one of the series' finest.

What makes this episode remarkable is the artistry of its creators: the delicacy and sensitivity of Serling's writing, the directorial imagination and control of Douglas Heyes, the superb delivery of all the actors, the visual beauty and technical perfection of George Clemens's camera work, the alien and moody score by Bernard Herrmann, and the brilliant makeup work by William Tuttle.

From the first, Buck Houghton realized that this script required a great deal of imagination and innovation if it was to succeed. "I think that 'Eye of the Beholder' is probably the most difficult director's job that ever came down the pike. I was scared to death of that, the problems of making that picture in such a way that the tag wasn't foreseen long before you got there." To Houghton, Douglas Heyes was the obvious and immediate choice for this most difficult of shows.

Essential to the credibility of the piece was that the makeup revealed at the climax be both repulsive and convincing. "Production manager Ralph Nelson saw that we got the time," William Tuttle recalls. "Now, this is something that I can't recall any of the other television productions doing. They'd come in the day before and expect a miracle for the next morning."

From the beginning, Heyes and Tuttle worked together closely. "As a matter of fact," says Heyes, "the first problem on the makeup on that was that it was going to be too expensive." Fortunately, Heyes had had experience in this area. "I had started as a cartoonist at Walt Disney's and had been an art director and so on. When we did those faces for 'Eye of the Beholder,' Tuttle had just done *The Time Machine*, and he had created those Morlocks. When he told me the problem as far as cost, I went down to his department and I saw some of the pieces that he had put the Morlocks together with, and I said, 'Bill, why can't we do something like this, just make some pieces and paste them on?'"

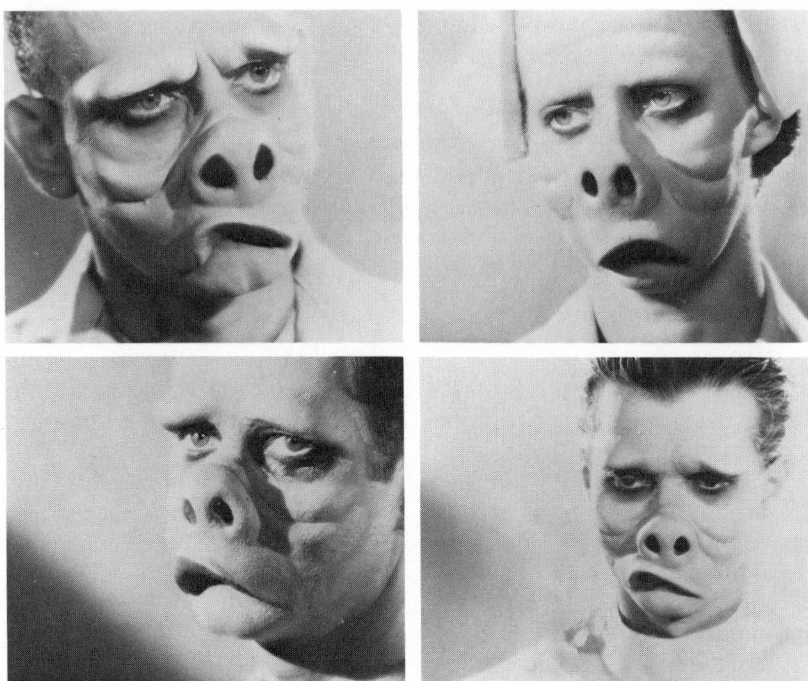

"Beauty is in the eye of the beholder"

The idea was sound, and the final makeup consisted of variations of a brow piece and a large piece that covered the nose, cheeks and upper lip. These were cast in foam rubber and attached to the actors' faces with spirit gum. To remove them, acetone was used.

The physical appearance of the "uglies" also involved a collaboration between Tuttle and Heyes. "Doug came up and got his fingers in the clay," Tuttle remembers. "We'd model some things, and then he'd take a look and offer some suggestions, and it sort of evolved from that."

As for the initial concept, Tuttle explains, "The idea was to make them look like pigs, with the big nostrils and the piglike nose."

Heyes elaborates: "The important thing about that group of people was that although they had to look slightly different, they had to conform, they had to be the same species. They couldn't all be different monsters."

In all, about twelve actors portrayed the uglies. "We didn't take masks of each one," says Tuttle, "but we took three or four different ones and modelled them so they looked different, and then before they'd cast the people we'd try them on, see if one would fit another one. In other words, we didn't have to do twelve different ones. On a thing like this, the more distortion you get the better."

In the end, Heyes was glad that what was originally planned had been too expensive. "They were thinking of doing complete makeups on everything, and actually it was better not to, because the individual characteristics of the actors could still show up—*their* cheekbones, *their* jawlines, *their* ears. Another thing is that by doing that, I was able to photograph the backs of heads and ears and things like that, which were perfectly normal. It was only frontally that they looked different." What emerged was a makeup that was horrifying, unique, and unforgettable.

In Serling's original script, the doctors and nurses were presented as unsympathetic, but Heyes felt that portraying them as such would be a tip-off, so he decided to take a different approach. "I cast the show without looking at the actors. I kept my back to them until after I'd heard them, because what I wanted from the doctors and the nurses were the most sympathetic voices that I could hear."

The only major role left to cast was that of Janet Tyler, the main character, and that presented a major problem: "The important surprise is that the girl who emerges from the bandages is incredibly beautiful by our standards," says Heyes. "So it doesn't really matter, I said, if that girl is a great actress or not so long as she's a great beauty. It *does* matter that the girl under bandages is a great actress, but we're not going to be able to see her. Now, it's very difficult to find a great beauty who is that great an actress, so my original concept was that it would be easier to find a great actress who could do the voice and then find a great beauty who could look like that."

Accordingly, Heyes cast two actresses to play the lead. The first was Maxine Stuart, as the woman "under wraps." Heyes cast her "because of her voice, because her voice did not suggest a beautiful girl—it suggested a strong, harsh, realistic woman, and therefore the unveiling would be a surprise."

Maxine Stuart, who today is still active on stage and television, finds it ironic that she was cast to play only part of the role. "It's absolutely right for Hollywood to do a script about conformity and then demand that your leading lady conform to a standard of beauty. I do understand that, though. They were saying something. They wanted a really *beautiful* beauty to point up the difference."

Nevertheless, Ms. Stuart found the role a delight, particularly the fact that her entire head was covered and that she could not see the other actors. "It was heaven," she says. "It was like I was in my little womb. I was acting all alone. I didn't have to be bothered with all those others." (Ironically, Serling's original title for the script was "A Private World of Darkness.")

"God, she gave a fantastic performance," says Douglas Heyes. "I figured this was strictly a vocal performance, but she also did great gestures.

Her hands were terribly expressive. I later used her in other things, but this was the first time I'd ever worked with her."

The other actress cast in the lead—the "beauty"—was Donna Douglas. Although not well-known at the time, she soon would be, as Jed Clampett's daughter Ellie on *The Beverly Hillbillies*. "She was not yet known to anybody, but she was absolutely beautiful," says Heyes. "So I said, 'You'll have a few lines, but later Maxine Stuart will dub them in her voice.'

"It turned out that Donna was a very good actress, and she hung around during the entire performance, the playing of scenes under bandages, and when it came to the time that she was unveiled and she had these words to say, she did them so accurately in the same voice that we never dubbed her."

The single most difficult aspect in filming "The Eye of the Beholder" lay in hiding the faces of the doctors and nurses without limiting camera movement. To accomplish this, Heyes and George Clemens worked together to block every movement of camera and actor perfectly. As a result, "The Eye of the Beholder" is choreographed as meticulously as a ballet.

"The trick in that," Heyes recalls, "was to keep you from seeing them for a great part of the story, yet I didn't want it to be obvious that I was only using hands and inserts and hearing dialogue. So I evolved a very complicated camera movement, by which you were seeing these doctors and nurses all the time but actually they would be passing one another at exactly the same moment that the camera would be, so that you wouldn't really see their faces, or they'd go behind a pillar just as they were turning toward the camera and so on—and the place was shadowed. And my justification for playing it that way was that the girl who was under bandages couldn't really see them, so I was using it as her viewpoint. In other words, she knew that they were there, but she didn't know what they looked like. So in a kind of way it made that credible, the fact that we didn't know what they looked like, either, because she didn't."

Heyes recalls the particular challenge of the crucial scene when the bandages are being removed from Janet Tyler's head. "While they were unwrapping her, I wanted the effect of her point of view as the layers of gauze became less and less until, little by little, she was able to see outlines of shapes and so forth.

"I told George Clemens what I wanted. I said, 'I want to have something in front of the camera so that it will be her point of view.' Well, that was one of the advantages of rehearsing with the crew before we shot, because Clemens got a fish bowl and hung it in front of the camera, and wrapped the fish bowl. So the lens was shooting from inside the fish bowl, and when the bandages were unwrapped over the fish bowl you saw layer by layer beginning to get less and less until you began to see outlines."

Says Clemens, "It was one of the few pictures that I remember Heyes working nights on. We worked till midnight or one o'clock one night to finish it."

Finally, filming was completed. But what everyone, especially Buck Houghton, wanted to know was, would it work?

"I remember the first time I had a chance to try that on somebody who was completely fresh to it was Lud Gluskin, who was in charge of music for CBS and a very, very bright man about the musical scoring problem," Houghton remembers. "Lud had a lot to do, he didn't read the scripts or anything. He came to a final cut and would talk about how to do the music. He was a very imperturbable old German. At the time, Lud must have been sixty-five, and he was pretty hard to move. And at the end of that he said, 'Je-*sus* Christ! Really?!' So I knew we had a pretty good picture."

"NICK OF TIME" (11/18/60)

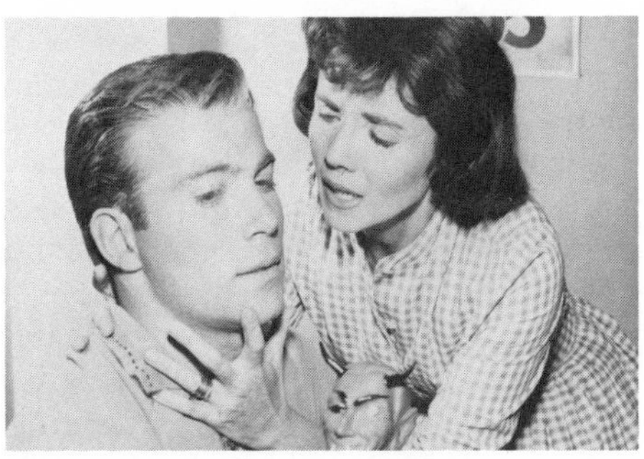

William Shatner and Patricia Breslin

Written by Richard Matheson
Producer: Buck Houghton
Director: Richard L. Bare
Director of Photography: George T. Clemens
Music: stock

Cast:
Don Carter: William Shatner
Pat Carter: Patricia Breslin
Counter Man: Guy Wilkerson
Mechanic: Stafford Rep
Desperate Man: Walter Reed
Desperate Woman: Dee Carroll

"The hand belongs to Mr. Don S. Carter, male member of a honeymoon team en route across the Ohio countryside to New York City. In one moment, they will be subjected to a gift most humans never receive in a lifetime. For one penny, they will be able to look into the future. The time is now, the place is a little diner in Ridgeview, Ohio, and what this young couple doesn't realize is that this town happens to lie on the outskirts of the Twilight Zone."

While waiting for their car to be repaired, the couple decide to grab a meal in a local diner. Don, superstitious by nature, is intrigued by a table top fortune-telling machine that dispenses little cards answering yes or no questions. Although the answers are extremely general, he soon becomes convinced that the machine has correctly predicted two events: his promotion to office manager and a close call he and Pat have while crossing the street. Rushing back to the diner, he begins to furiously feed pennies into the machine, totally unable to make a single decision for himself. At this point, Pat—who has been skeptical all along and is dismayed at the machine's power over her husband—rebels, telling Don he mustn't waste his life on a cheap machine, that they must make their futures themselves. Buoyed by her love and by her confidence in him, Don is able to shake off the machine's influence—and his own superstitions. They exit the diner, free to determine their own destinies. Just then, another couple, looking worn and harried, enters and proceeds to the same machine. Desperately, they ask when they might be allowed to leave the town. Like Don and Pat, they have been snared—but they *haven't* escaped.

"Counterbalance in the little town of Ridgeview, Ohio. Two people permanently enslaved by the tyranny of fear and superstition, facing the future with a kind of helpless dread. Two others facing the future with confidence—having escaped one of the darker places in the Twilight Zone."

Richard Matheson's "Nick of Time" is one of *The Twilight Zone*'s subtlest episodes.

The idea came from a simple source. Says Matheson, "My wife and I were in San Fernando, going to a movie, and there was a little fortune-telling machine like that in the booth in the café." As with his previous scripts, this too had a title with a double meaning. "They're rescued in the nick of time and there's also time—the nick—how it cuts into your life."

In "Nick of Time," nothing is overt, all is suggestion. Maybe the machine is predicting the future, maybe not—which, of course, is the uncertainty underlying all superstitious belief. The point that Matheson succeeds in making is that whether or not there is magic at work, the effect is the same: a loss of free will and independence of action.

The fact that all is inferred places a tremendous burden on the actors. There are no special effects to carry the show, nothing mysterious or majestic. This is a story of character, of things said and unsaid, of nuance. Luckily, the actors are up to this demand. "I thought the two performances were marvelous," says Matheson. "They played together so well. And the direction was nice. I thought it worked beautifully."

Matheson let "Nick of Time" end happily for his main characters, but he felt obliged to put a final little twist on the story. Thanks largely to the courage and determination of his wife, Don Carter has broken free of the machine's influence. He says (more to the machine than to his wife) "We'll drive out of this town and go where we want to go—anytime we please." The two exit, their will power restored. At the same moment, another couple enters. Nervously, they sit themselves down at the same booth and feverishly begin feeding pennies into the machine. Yin and yang, even in *The Twilight Zone*.

"THE HOWLING MAN" (11/4/60)

H. M. Wynant, Robin Hughes and John Carradine

Written by Charles Beaumont
Based on the short story "The Howling Man" by Charles Beaumont
Producer: Buck Houghton
Director: Douglas Heyes
Director of Photography: George T. Clemens
Music: stock

Cast:
David Ellington: H. M. Wynant
Brother Jerome: John Carradine
The Howling Man: Robin Hughes
Brother Christophorus: Frederic Ledebur
Housekeeper: Ezelle Poule

"The prostrate form of Mr. David Ellington, scholar, seeker of truth and, regrettably, finder of truth. A man who will shortly arise from his exhaustion to confront a problem that has tormented mankind since the beginning of time. A man who knocked on a door seeking sanctuary and found instead the outer edges of the Twilight Zone."

During a walking trip of central Europe following World War I, Ellington gets caught in a storm and loses his way. Exhausted and on the edge of delirium, he comes to a remote hermitage. At first, he is turned away, but when he passes out the monks are forced to take him in. Upon reviving, he hears a bizarre howling—one which the brothers feign not to hear. Drawn by the sound, he comes upon a gentle-seeming bearded man locked in a cell. He has been imprisoned by Brother Jerome, the head of the order, whom the bearded man claims is insane. The prisoner begs to be released. Ellington confronts Jerome, who makes a startling revelation: the creature howling in the cell is no *man*, but the Devil himself! He has been kept there for five years, held in place by the "staff of truth" that bars the cell door. Ellington tells Jerome that he accepts this explanation and pledges not to reveal this secret to the outside world, but as soon as he has a chance he sneaks away to the cell and releases the prisoner—who immediately transforms into the Devil and disappears in a flash of light and a puff of smoke. Soon after, World War II erupts. Realizing what he has done, Ellington devotes his life to recapturing the Devil. Finally, he succeeds. As he leaves to make preparations to ship his captive back to the hermitage, he cautions his housekeeper to pay no heed to the howling which will issue from behind the door secured with a tiny staff. As soon as he leaves, however, she lifts the small piece of wood away. Ominously, the door swings open.

"Ancient folk saying: 'You can catch the Devil, but you can't hold him long.' Ask Brother Jerome. Ask David Ellington. They know, and they'll go on knowing to the end of their days and beyond—in the Twilight Zone."

For *his* first script of the season, Charles Beaumont decided to pull out all the stops. In "Nick of Time," there was a devil's head atop the fortune-telling machine, but in "The Howling Man" we got the real thing.

Charles Beaumont and Robin Hughes

The show is an improvement over the original short story of the same name, which appeared in *Night Ride and Other Journeys*. In the original, a young American tourist falls ill while bicycling through post–World War I Germany and is tended in a remote abbey. There, he hears continual, crazed shrieking. Investigating, he finds a naked, filthy man being kept prisoner. When he confronts the abbot, he is told that the prisoner is Satan himself. The young man rejects this as the delusion of a religious fanatic and releases the prisoner. Shortly thereafter, World War II breaks out. Finally, after the war, the man receives a postcard from Germany which reads, "Rest now, my son. We have him back with us again." But whether the prisoner really was the Devil is left to the judgment of the reader.

For his *Twilight Zone* script, Beaumont kept the basic story, except for the fact that the young man becomes obsessed with the idea of recapturing the escapee and sending him back to the abbey. However, he decided to leave no ambiguity as to the identity of "the Howling Man." In the scene where the Devil escapes, Beaumont wrote in one visual element—a cloven hoof—that left no doubt. As things went, however, this was never used.

Director Douglas Heyes explains, "In my literal kind of visual sense, I wanted to see him turn into the Devil, I felt the audience would feel cheated unless they saw that. And Beaumont didn't want them to see it, he just wanted the expression on Wynant's face as he chased after him and reached up as the man went over a wall. All he wanted was to see the hand touching a cloven hoof just as it went over the wall.

"When I did the literal translation of showing him visually turn into the Devil, Beaumont didn't like that. He liked better the way he had written it and that was what he wanted to see. But I have a funny feeling as a director. I started as an artist and I like to *see* things. If I promise the audience something, if I say there are three thousand Indians on the other side of that hill, I don't want to see one feather poke up behind a rock—I want to see three thousand Indians!"

Heyes's literal transformation of Robin Hughes into the Devil involved two different approaches. The first occurs as the prisoner steps from his cell. The lighting shifts, and suddenly his face is subtly but dramatically changed. Before, his face had looked benevolent; now it looks *evil*. What has occurred, all in one shot with no cuts, is a complete makeup change. This was done with George Clemens's red-green filter trick, which he had used before on "Long Live Walter Jameson."

The second approach was much more complicated. Heyes explains, "I had seen many transitions—*Dr. Jekyll and Mr. Hyde* or *The Wolf Man* or something—in which they would suddenly become immobile and the makeup would change and then they would start moving. 'I don't want to do that,' I said. 'I want to see him moving all the time the makeup is changing.'

"So what we did is that we had a long corridor, and from the time that he started the makeup change I had him walk, very fast, down the corridor. At the end of the corridor, he turns and he is now transformed completely into the Devil, and he dissolves in a puff of smoke.

"I had the camera on a dolly, and we timed it so that we ran it exactly the same speed every time. Now, between us and him were a series of pillars. He would make the entire walk at full speed, and we would go with him at full speed all the way in every makeup. But when it was cut together, we cut from makeup to makeup as we were passing the pillars, so that in the blur of the foreground pillar, which was only a matter of the most split of seconds, he would be in the next makeup, and the illusion was that he never stopped moving and the camera never stopped moving. It was just 'Zooooom!'—he flashed down that corridor, and as he was moving very fast, the makeup was changing."

Sad to say, the final makeup achieved is *too* literal. With his absurdly long nose, pointed ears, and horns, the Devil looks more foolish than frightening. The only makeup that strikes a truly satanic mood is the first and most subtle change.

Despite this, "The Howling Man" succeeds as a gloriously melodramatic piece in the mold of all those simply awful but wonderful horror films of the thirties and forties. The prologue sets the tone, as David Ellington (Wynant, in very convincing age makeup) says to the camera, "I know it's an *incredible* story—I, of all people, know this—and you won't believe me, no, not at first, but I'm going to tell you the whole thing. Then you'll believe, because you must. You *must* believe!" Dissolve to a flashback, as a much younger Ellington arrives at the hermitage.

Ellington may be the main character, but the real star of the show is Brother Jerome (John Carradine), head of the order, a man who dresses, sounds, and acts like Moses. Casting Carradine, with his basso voice and commanding presence, was an inspiration. Says Heyes, "That was one case where John Carradine was able to do his stuff, full out, because it called for it. In this, I said, '*Go,* because this guy is weird, wild.'"

As with "The Eye of the Beholder," Heyes decided that "The Howling Man" required elaborate camera movement. Throughout much of the piece, Ellington is in a state bordering on delirium. Heyes decided that the camera should reflect his inner lack of equilibrium. As a result, whenever Ellington feels dizzy, which is quite often, the camera tilts severely. If he's walking and the camera is tilting one way, when he turns a corner the camera tilts in the opposite direction. Although this effect was difficult to orchestrate, requiring two operators on the camera, it proved well worth it. The mood produced is a disquieting one, queasy and disorienting.

An aspect of the show which caused some concern was the howling, which in the end sounded more like a dog than a man. "The howling aspects of the thing were hard to sell," Heyes recalls. "Now, when you mention howling in a story—you hear this crazy howling off in the distance all the time, this man in the cell is howling—that's all right in a story. Very hard to translate to the screen. It's hard to believe that that man who is in that cell would make those howling noises. I don't think we ever actually saw him howling, we only heard him, because to see him howling would have been very, very hard to buy."

A visitor to the set at the time was Beaumont's friend, William F. Nolan. "I remember how concerned they were about the kind of cries and howlings, how demonic to make them," says Nolan. "So they played endless tape recordings of howls to see which howl they liked the best, and they'd all sit around and say, 'Well, that howl is not satanic enough,' and 'That howl is too high, it's almost like a woman,' and 'Maybe if we took that howl and this howl . . .' We had a big howl session."

One aspect of Beaumont's script that Douglas Heyes was sure wouldn't work was the prop that all the brothers in the hermitage were supposed to carry—a large wooden cross. "I said, 'Chuck, I'm worried about them having the crosses, because the minute you do that you make them some sort of Christian sect, and the minute you do *that* you're in danger from all kinds of religious groups who resent the fact that you're using a Christian symbol.' So I said, 'Let's find something else,' and I substituted the staff for the cross, which he didn't like, either."

"A MOST UNUSUAL CAMERA" (12/16/60)

Jean Carson

Written by Rod Serling
Producer: Buck Houghton
Director: John Rich
Director of Photography: George T. Clemens
Music: stock

Cast:
Chester Diedrich: Fred Clark
Paula Diedrich: Jean Carson
Woodward: Adam Williams
Waiter: Marcel Hillaire
Racetrack Tout: Artie Lewis

"A hotel suite that in this instance serves as a den of crime, the aftermath of a rather minor event to be noted on a police blotter, an insurance claim, perhaps a three-inch box on page twelve of the evening paper. Small addenda to be added to the list of the loot: a camera, a most unimposing addition to the flotsam and jetsam that it came with, hardly worth mentioning really, because cameras are

cameras, some expensive, some purchasable at five-and-dime stores. But this *camera, this one's unusual, because in just a moment we'll watch it inject itself into the destinies of three people. It happens to be a fact that the pictures that it takes can only be developed in the Twilight Zone."*

After burglarizing a curio shop, Chester Diedrich and his wife Paula discover that one of the items they've stolen is a camera that takes instant pictures of events five minutes in the future. When Paula's brother Woodward, an escaped convict, arrives—as predicted by the camera—Chester gets the idea of taking the camera to the races and using it to bet on the winning horses. The trio makes a killing, but then a waiter in their hotel informs them that a French inscription on the camera says, "Ten to an owner." The three argue over how best to use the remaining pictures. Chester and Woodward get into a fight and fall out the window to their deaths. From the window Paula takes a picture of the bodies below, to keep as a souvenir. She begins to gather up the loot. Just then, the waiter enters. He has discovered that the three guests are crooks, and wants to take the loot for himself. He looks at the photograph Paula has just taken—and notes that it shows more than two bodies. Paula rushes to the window, trips on a cord, and falls out. Now, however, the waiter realizes that the picture shows not three but *four* bodies. With a shout, he falls out the window, too.

"Object known as a camera, vintage uncertain, origin unknown. But for the greedy, the avaricious, the fleet of foot who can run a four-minute mile so long as they're chasing a fast buck, it makes believe that it's an ally, but it isn't at all. It's a beckoning come-on for a quick walk around the block—in the Twilight Zone."

Directed limply by John Rich, who would later direct and produce *All in the Family,* "A Most Unusual Camera," never really goes anywhere. What's oddest about the episode is its finale, when the waiter realizes, to his horror, that there are *four* bodies in the photo—at which point the camera delicately moves in on the "most unusual" camera, and we hear him shout and tumble out the window. Now how did *he* fall out?

"A THING ABOUT MACHINES" (10/28/60)

Richard Haydn

Written by Rod Serling
Producer: Buck Houghton
Director:
David Orrick McDearmon
Director of Photography:
George T. Clemens
Music: stock

Cast:
Bartlett Finchley: Richard Haydn
TV Repairman: Barney Phillips
Edith: Barbara Stuart
Intern: Jay Overholts
Girl on TV: Margarita Cordova
Policeman: Henry Beckman
Telephone Repairman: Lew Brown

"This is Mr. Bartlett Finchley, age forty-eight, a practicing sophisticate who writes very special and very precious things for gourmet magazines and the like. He's a bachelor and a recluse with few friends, only devotees and adherents to the cause of tart sophistry. He has no interests save whatever current annoyances he can put his mind to. He has no purpose to his life except the formulation of day-to-day opportunities to vent his wrath on mechanical contrivances of an age he abhors. In short, Mr. Bartlett Finchley is a malcontent, born either too late or too early in the century, and who in just a moment will enter a realm where muscles and the will to fight back are not limited to human beings. Next stop for Mr. Bartlett Finchley—the Twilight Zone."

From his behavior—kicking in picture tubes, throwing radios down stairs, demolishing chiming clocks—it is clear that Finchley *hates* machines. What Finchley doesn't realize is that the feeling is mutual. For several months, odd things have been happening. His television, radio, and clock have all awakened him in the middle of the night. But when his secretary quits, things come to a head. By itself, the typewriter types, "GET OUT OF HERE, FINCHLEY." The television broadcasts the same message, as does the telephone. Snakelike, his electric razor slithers down the stairs toward him. Frightened, Finchley runs from his house, only to be pursued by his car, which chases him to the edge of his swimming pool. He falls in, plummets straight to the bottom—and stays there.

"Yes, it could be. It could just be that Mr. Bartlett Finchley succumbed from a heart attack and a set of delusions. It could just be that he was tormented by an imagination as sharp as his wit and as pointed as his dislikes. But as perceived by those attending, this is one explanation that has left the premises

with the deceased. Look for it filed under "M" for machines—in the Twilight Zone."

Although the concept of "A Thing About Machines," is a clever one and some of the effects are fun (who couldn't help but love the image of an electric shaver slithering down a flight of stairs?), neither the writing, direction, nor performances are able to give the show any real vitality.

"THE PRIME MOVER" (3/24/61)

Christine White, Dane Clark, Jane Burgess and Buddy Ebsen

Written by Charles Beaumont
Based on an unpublished story by George Clayton Johnson (uncredited)
Producer: Buck Houghton
Director: Richard L. Bare
Director of Photography: George T. Clemens
Music: stock

Cast:
Jimbo Cobb: Buddy Ebsen
Ace Larsen: Dane Clark
Kitty Cavanaugh: Christine White
Big Phil Nolan: Nesdon Booth
Sheila: Jane Burgess
Trucker: Clancy Cooper
Croupier: Joe Scott
Hotel Manager: Robert Riordan
Desk Clerk: William Keene

"Portrait of a man who thinks and thereby gets things done. Mr. Jimbo Cobb might be called a prime mover, a talent which has to be seen to be believed. In just a moment, he'll show his friend and you *how he keeps both feet on the ground—and his head in the Twilight Zone."*

When a car careens into some power lines, amiable Jimbo Cobb, co-owner of a café, is forced to reveal his psychokinetic power in order to save those within. Volatile Ace Larsen, his partner and a compulsive gambler, soon realizes that Jimbo is as adept at moving dice as he is at moving automobiles. With Jimbo in tow, Ace and his girlfriend Kitty set off for Las Vegas. In an evening, Ace and Jimbo win $200,000. But Ace isn't satisfied; he intends to keep on gambling. Disgusted by his behavior, Kitty angrily returns home. Spurned, Ace takes up with Sheila, a flashy cigarette girl. The next morning he contacts highroller Phil Nolan, a Chicago gangster, and invites him to his hotel room to shoot dice. Initially, he wins every roll, thanks to Jimbo. But when Sheila enters and wraps herself around Ace, Jimbo tries to get him to stop gambling. Ace ignores this and bets everything on a final roll. He loses. Jimbo explains that he "blew a fuse." They're poor again, but Ace, his sense of balance restored, is able to laugh it off. He returns to the café and proposes to Kitty, who accepts. This so surprises Jimbo that he drops a broom. Making sure no one is looking, Jimbo uses his power—which he never *really* lost—to retrieve it.

"Some people possess talent, others are possessed by it. When that happens, a talent becomes a curse. Jimbo Cobb knew, right from the beginning. But before Ace Larsen learned that simple truth, he had to take a short trip through the Twilight Zone."

Based on the credits, one would assume that "The Prime Mover" was an original piece written entirely by Charles Beaumont. Actually, this engaging script was based on an unpublished story by George Clayton Johnson. Explains Johnson, "Charles Beaumont could get an assignment, he needed a story, he didn't have a story, none of his stories seemed suitable. He therefore bought from me my story. He paid me six hundred dollars for it. My name never ended up on the screen, it was an accident of production for which Buck Houghton apologized. I felt bad that my name wasn't on it, but I thought it was a good show."

In adapting the story, Beaumont retained Johnson's basic plot but added a love interest and a Chicago gangster (named Phil Nolan, a Beaumont in-joke on his friend William F. Nolan). In the original, the pair simply make their winnings at various local floating crap games, but Beaumont rightly conceived that placing the action in Las Vegas would add a greater dramatic tension. As for the two central characters, they remained the same, a Mutt and Jeff pair—Dane Clark nervous and quick-tempered, Buddy Ebsen slow and infinitely calm.

"BACK THERE" (1/13/61)

Russell Johnson

Written by Rod Serling
Producer: Buck Houghton
Director:
David Orrick McDearmon
Director of Photography:
George T. Clemens
Music: Jerry Goldsmith

Cast:
Peter Corrigan: Russell Johnson
William: Bartlett Robinson
Police Sergeant: Paul Hartman
Policeman: James Gavin
John Wilkes Booth: John Lasell
Patrolman: James Lydon
Jackson: Raymond Greenleaf
Millard: Ray Bailey
Whittaker: John Eldredge
Attendant 1865: Fred Kruger
Mrs. Landers: Jean Inness
Lieutenant: Lew Brown
Lt.'s Girl: Carol Rossen
Chambermaid: Nora Marlowe
Attendant 1961: Pat O'Malley

"Witness a theoretical argument, Washington, D.C., the present. Four intelligent men talking about an improbable thing like going back in time. A friendly debate revolving around a simple question: could a human being change what happened before? Interesting and theoretical, because who ever heard of a man going back in time—before tonight, that is. Because this is . . . the Twilight Zone."

It is April 14, 1961. After discussing time travel at his men's club, Peter Corrigan suddenly feels an inexplicable dizziness. When it clears, he sees that he has moved back in time to April 14, 1865—the date of Lincoln's assassination. In attempting to warn those at Ford's Theater, he succeeds only in getting himself arrested as either a drunk or a lunatic. A "Mr. Wellington" asks that Corrigan be remanded to his custody. Soon, his motives become clear: Wellington is actually John Wilkes Booth, and he wants no interference. He takes Corrigan to his room and drugs him. By the time Corrigan revives, it is too late; Lincoln has been shot. He returns to the present, intent on telling his friends that the past *can't* be changed. But at the men's club he gets a shock: William, formerly the attendant, is now a wealthy man. It turns out that his great-grandfather—the only policeman who believed Corrigan—gained a name for himself in trying to stop Lincoln's assassination, rose in politics, and became a millionaire. Corrigan *has* changed the past, but not in the way he intended.

"Mr. Peter Corrigan, lately returned from a place 'back there,' a journey into time with highly questionable results, proving on one hand that the threads of history are woven tightly and the skein of events cannot be undone, but on the other hand there are small fragments of tapestry that can be altered. Tonight's thesis to be taken as you will, in the Twilight Zone."

In "Execution," Russell Johnson played a man who invented a time machine but did not himself travel through time. In Serling's "Back There," the eleventh episode produced this season, he got the chance—though here the agent that propels our Mr. Corrigan through time is not a machine but rather a highly theoretical discussion.

For all the intellectual fascination of its premise, however, "Back There" is a dramatic failure. The reason is obvious: from the outset, the conclusion is known; Lincoln *was* assassinated, therefore Corrigan won't be able to intercede. Says Buck Houghton, "I think that when you play ducks and drakes with the shooting of Lincoln, your suspension of disbelief goes to hell in a bucket."

One and only one aspect of "Back There" deserved better than it got, and that was Jerry Goldsmith's original and haunting score. Fortunately, pieces of it were used to great effect in later episodes, notably "Death Ship" and "Nightmare at 20,000 Feet."

"DUST" (1/6/61)

Vladimir Sokoloff and Thomas Gomez

Written by Rod Serling
Producer: Buck Houghton
Director: Douglas Heyes
Director of Photography: George T. Clemens
Music: Jerry Goldsmith

Cast:
Sykes: Thomas Gomez
Sheriff Koch: John Larch
Gallegos: Vladimir Sokoloff
Luis Gallegos: John Alonso
Mr. Canfield: Paul Genge
Estrelita: Andrea Margolis
Mrs. Canfield: Dorothy Adams
Rogers: Duane Grey
Man #1: John Lormer
Man #2: Daniel White
Farmer Boy: Douglas Heyes, Jr.

"There was a village, built of crumbling clay and rotting wood, and it squatted ugly under the broiling sun like a sick and mangy animal waiting to die. This village had a virus, shared by its people. It was the germ of squalor, of hopelessness, of a loss of faith. For the faithless, the hopeless, the misery-laden, there is time, ample time, to engage in one of the other pursuits of men—they begin to destroy themselves."

On the day that Luis Gallegos is to be hanged for drunkenly running over and killing a little girl with his wagon, a conscienceless peddler named Sykes—who has sold the hangman some brand-new five-strand hemp for the noose—sells the condemned man's father a small bag of "magic dust" that can turn hate into love. In reality, it is no more than common dirt, but the anguished father pays Sykes one hundred pesos for it. In front of the gallows, he throws the dust on the waiting crowd, crying, "You must pay heed to the magic!" It seems to have no effect. The noose is fitted around Luis's neck, the trap is sprung—and as if by magic, the rope breaks! The bereaved parents of the little girl, deciding that there has been enough death, pardon Luis, who leaves with his grateful father. The crowd disperses. Astounded by what he has seen, Sykes stares at the broken rope—then tosses the hundred pesos to Luis's young siblings. The magic has worked on *him*, too.

"It was a very small, misery-laden village on the day of a hanging, and of little historical consequence. And if there's any moral to it at all, let's say that in any

quest for magic, in any search for sorcery, witchery, legerdemain, first check the human heart. For inside this deep place there's a wizardry that costs far more than a few pieces of gold. Tonight's case in point—in the Twilight Zone."

Although competently written, "Dust" lost much of its dramatic punch due to the conception of the episode by director Douglas Heyes. When it came to difficult, tricky episodes, Heyes had no equal. But "Dust" had no trickery, it was a simple straightforward western, with a little bit of magic. Here's how Heyes conceived of the episode: "'Dust' was about a town that had sunk into the dust, in effect. It had no energy. The people there were listless. They were going to allow this man to be hanged simply because it was easier than not doing that."

In keeping with his conception, Heyes directed all the actors, with the exception of Vladimir Sokoloff, Thomas Gomez, and John Alonso, to play their roles with a lethargy bordering on the catatonic. A case in point was John Larch, who played the sheriff. "John Larch came in and I changed him quite a bit," says Heyes, "because he was written as a strong sheriff and I played him as a sheriff who had no energy at all, who represented the listlessness of that town. It was hard for John to do, because he's a man *with* energy."

For all its faults, "Dust" remains an entertaining episode, thanks to the performances of Gomez and Sokoloff. Both had long and distinguished film careers (Sokoloff's credits include *The Life of Emile Zola*, *Juarez*, and *For Whom the Bell Tolls*) and knew how to milk a part for all it was worth. As Sykes (in a part very different from the urbane Devil he portrayed in "Escape Clause"), Gomez is so rotten you can almost smell him, and Sokoloff, as the father, gives a performance of enormous anguish and dignity.

GEORGE CLAYTON JOHNSON

Of the core of writers that shaped and guided *The Twilight Zone*, only one has not been really introduced to this point. George Clayton Johnson's output on *The Twilight Zone* was relatively small when compared with Serling, Beaumont, and Matheson—only four stories ("Execution," "The Four of Us Are Dying," "The Prime Mover," and "Ninety Years Without Slumbering") and four teleplays ("A Penny For Your Thoughts," "A Game of Pool," "Nothing in the Dark," and "Kick the Can"), with the first teleplay being in the second season—but that output was of such quality that it must be put on a level with the work of the other three. And while the visions of Johnson meshed perfectly on an artistic and thematic level with the others, his approach was such that he mapped out a territory all his own.

"George is very sentimental," says Buck Houghton, "and he manages to bring that off pretty well without getting mawkish about it. He keeps his feet on the ground while he's being sentimental. And that's not a tap you can just turn on, not something you can say, 'Well hey, George, that's swell. Give us some more.' If you could get a guy that'd do 'A Game of Pool' and 'Nothing in the Dark' five times a year, you'd be in clover. But it wasn't in George to do that. It's a trick that's not that easy to work."

Considering his background, it's remarkable that George Clayton Johnson was able to emerge as a writer at all, and absolutely astounding that he was able to produce works of such sensitivity and merit. Johnson was born in a barn outside of Cheyenne, Wyoming, on July 10, 1929. At the time, his father was in the Army but later worked as an occasional day laborer and small-time bootlegger. When Johnson was young, his parents were divorced. He and his older brother were left in the care of their alcoholic mother, but because of her drinking Johnson was shuttled between aunts and cousins who treated him as a sort of charity case, wearing hand-me-downs and receiving little affection.

Robert Redford and George Clayton Johnson

When he was seven, Johnson was hospitalized for nearly a year as the result of a broken leg. It was an isolated, lonely existence with no one to talk to and precious little to do. Once a week, his mother would visit.

"I kept telling her to get me pulp magazines," he recalls, "but she couldn't understand what I meant. I kept trying to tell her it was a big, fat, thick book with a lot of stories in it, fantasy stories, but she never bought them for me. So I stayed in this place, and about the only thing I had to do was to daydream, to reverie, to sleep. So I did that."

After his hospital stay, Johnson returned to school, but having missed the second grade he was hopelessly behind. Succeeding years only made things worse. He flunked the sixth grade and dropped out of school entirely in the eighth. At fourteen, the courts took him away from his mother and placed him in the state orphanage in Casper. After a year, his mother was able to convince the courts to return custody to her. But things did not go well.

"We went back to Cheyenne, my mother and I," Johnson remembers, "and she started up her old tricks again, she started drinking. When she was drinking, my mother just didn't seem to see disorder or dirt, and little elements like was there any way of building a fire or was there any food in the house just didn't seem to bother her too much, she went away without worrying about that.

"So I asked her if I could leave. Finally, she said okay."

So before he was sixteen Johnson was on his own. In Casper he got work in a shoeshine parlor, but very quickly, he felt the limitations of his situation. "This was no kind of life. It depended entirely upon strangers giving me quarters, and it was also a cold, barren little town."

At seventeen, he enlisted in the Army and almost immediately realized that it was a mistake. But in the Army he did learn drafting, which enabled him to make a living afterwards. Upon his discharge, he came to California, got married, had a son and a daughter, and worked designing houses and doing architectural renderings. By this time, however, he had decided that he wanted to be a writer. He closed his drafting office and began to associate with Beaumont and his circle of writer friends. For five long, lean years, Johnson struggled to make his first sale. Finally, he sold "All of Us Are Dying," then "Execution." But those were stories; Johnson had never sold a teleplay. The year was 1960, and the script that changed all that was "A Penny For Your Thoughts."

Johnson recalls that the impetus to write the script came from his friends. "We had a practice of going out in a car and shmoozing while we just drove interminably out along the beach and here and there. And I was having some very strong opinions about science fiction and about stories and about what was art, and John Tomerlin [later to work with Beaumont on "Number Twelve Looks Just Like You"] was writing the *Lawman* series and Beaumont was writing *The Twilight Zone* and *Naked City* and *Have Gun Will Travel* and a couple of things like that, and I was writing *nothing*, except those two short stories which I had sold. So Chuck said to me, 'George, you ought to put your money where your mouth is. It's one thing for you to have all these opinions about what's good and what's bad and to put us down in various ways, but then you've got to prove that you can do it better or else we can't take you seriously.' So I decided then that nothing would stop me from finishing the work I was doing, which was 'A Penny For Your Thoughts.'"

Because of Beaumont's rebuke, Johnson was determined to make good, and when Buck Houghton offered to buy the story rights to "A Penny For Your Thoughts," Johnson was adamant that he be allowed to take the story through at least a first draft teleplay himself. It took Houghton a week and a half to agree, but it was a decision he never regretted.

Johnson sums up his approach to fantasy in this way: "For me, fantasy must be about something, otherwise it's foolishness. If it's not about something then it's just oddballsville for oddballsville's sake. If anything is possible, then nothing is interesting. The game must be like a game of chess, it must have restrictions set on it. A man with one miraculous talent but not two. A man with one miraculous talent, *however*—there are certain kinds of imposed rules on how that works and what it must be about, and ultimately it must be about human beings, it must be about the human condition, it must be another look at infinity, it must be another way of seeing the paradox of existence."

"A PENNY FOR YOUR THOUGHTS" (2/3/61)

June Dayton and Dick York

Written by
George Clayton Johnson
Producer: Buck Houghton
Director: James Sheldon
Director of Photography:
George T. Clemens
Music: stock

Cast:
Hector B. Poole: Dick York
Miss Turner: June Dayton
Mr. Bagby: Dan Tobin
Mr. Smithers: Cyril Delevanti
Mr. Sykes: Hayden Rorke
Mr. Brand: Harry Jackson
Driver: Frank London
Newsboy: Anthony Ray

"Mr. Hector B. Poole, resident of the Twilight Zone. Flip a coin and keep flipping it. What are the odds? Half the time it will come up heads, half the time tails. But in one freakish chance in a million, it'll land on its edge. Mr. Hector B. Poole, a bright human coin—on his way to the bank."

After paying for his morning paper with a coin that lands on edge, mild bank clerk Hector Poole finds he has the power to read people's minds—but it gives him nothing but trouble. His revelation that Sykes, a businessman applying for a sizeable loan, intends to bet it on the horses in a desperate attempt to repay embezzled funds results in the man storming out of the bank—an act that greatly displeases Bagby, Poole's boss. Then Poole "overhears" Smithers, an old and trusted bank employee, thinking about going into the vault, filling his briefcase with money, and escaping to Bermuda. Poole tells Bagby, who searches Smithers's briefcase and finds travel folders, a sandwich, and a pair of socks. Smithers's thoughts were no more than a recurring daydream. Poole is fired. Miss Turner, a fellow-employee who has a crush on Poole, tries to console him, but she doesn't know what to think of his claim that he's telepathic. Just then, Bagby rushes up. Sykes has been arrested—Poole was right. He offers Poole his old job. Miss Turner sends Poole the thought that he should press for a promotion. Using information he's gained telepathically about Bagby's weekend plans with his mistress, he blackmails Bagby into making him an office manager—*and* giving Smithers a free trip to Bermuda. Leaving with Miss Turner, Poole buys an evening paper from his usual newsstand, where the newsboy has been keeping his earlier miracle-coin standing on edge all day. But the coin Poole now tosses knocks over the other—and his telepathic powers are gone.

"One time in a million, a coin will land on its edge, but all it takes to knock it over is a vagrant breeze, a vibration or a slight blow. Hector B. Poole, a human coin, on edge for a brief time—in the Twilight Zone."

The first of George Clayton Johnson's four Twilight Zone scripts was his lightest, but the easy tone doesn't detract from it. The episode is charming and funny, and it does have a point: that people do things without thinking about them and think things without having the slightest intention of doing them. Or rather, that telepathy isn't all it's cracked up to be.

The humor in this piece is precarious, requiring just enough exaggeration to be funny but not so much as to seem ridiculous. Fortunately, both the acting and direction were up to the task. Dick York (pre-*Bewitched*), June Dayton, Dan Tobin and the utterly delightful Cyril Delevanti all perform their roles with just the proper sense of self-satire.

This was the first of six episodes directed by James Sheldon. Beyond guiding the episode, Sheldon also conceived two funny bits of business. In the first, Hector Poole overhears some sympathetic thoughts about himself and at first believes them to be coming from a bust of George Washington—when they're actually from Miss Turner. In the second, Poole, deliberately eavesdropping on the thoughts of the bank's customers, idly strolls up to a woman who is smiling blissfully and holding a stack of money—only to find that she's thinking absolutely nothing.

On the set during the filming were George Clayton Johnson and his wife Lola. He recalls that the reaction to his story was very favorable. "Dan Tobin said that it was a darn clever idea. He thought that it would make a series, of what would happen to people who came into contact with that coin. So I wrote a presentation called *A Penny For Your Thoughts,* and I wrote a story about a gambler who got the coin which allowed him to read thoughts. He was in a big poker game and he knew he was going to win, he'd won one poker game and another and another, because he could read the minds of the other players. Now it's finally the biggest poker game of all, and it's all very obscure. He is taken to this very special place to meet with this very famous gambler, and the very famous gambler is an Oriental—and the Oriental thinks in Chinese when he's watching the cards!"

The dearest memory that Johnson holds regarding "A Penny For Your Thoughts" stems from another incident that occurred during the filming. "I felt sort of like a stranger on the set," he recalls. "It was the *Twilight Zone* set, not mine, and I felt like I was being allowed to eavesdrop by even being allowed to be there while it was done. And while this was happening, Rod came through with a couple of people, visitors that he had brought on, and he saw me and Lola and he stopped to introduce us to these people. And his attitude toward me was one of great respect. It wasn't like, 'I'm Rod Serling and this is one of the flunkies on the set,' it was more like, 'Look, here's the man who wrote this absolutely wizard thing that we're making right now.' It really built my ego and made me feel worthwhile."

"THE TROUBLE WITH TEMPLETON" (12/9/60)

Brian Aherne and Pippa Scott

Written by E. Jack Neuman
Producer: Buck Houghton
Director: Buzz Kulik
Director of Photography: George T. Clemens
Music: Jeff Alexander

Cast:
Booth Templeton: Brian Aherne
Laura Templeton: Pippa Scott
Barney Flueger: Charles S. Carlson
Willis: Sydney Pollack
Freddie: Larry Blake
Sid Sperry: King Calder
Marcel: Dave Willock
Ed Page: John Kroger
Eddie: David Thursby

"Please to present for your consideration Mr. Booth Templeton, serious and successful star of over thirty Broadway plays, who is not quite all right today. Yesterday and its memories is what he wants, and yesterday is what he'll get. Soon his years and his troubles will descend on him in an avalanche. In order not to be crushed, Mr. Booth Templeton will escape from his theater and his world and make his debut on another stage in another world—that we call the Twilight Zone."

Feeling very old and very tired, Templeton longs for those years in the twenties when his beloved wife Laura was alive—the only truly happy time in his life. When Willis, a brash young director, severely dresses him down for arriving late to the first rehearsal of a new play, he rushes from the theater—and finds himself back in 1927. Searching, he locates Laura in a speakeasy. Although as lovely as he remembered, her manner is quite the opposite; she is flirtatious, vulgar, and self-centered. His idyllic memories destroyed, he returns to the theater—and the present. But he has inadvertently brought back a memento: several sheafs of paper Laura was fanning herself with. Inspecting them, he sees they are pages of a script, entitled "What To Do When Booth Comes Back." Realizing the entire thing was staged for his benefit—so that he would stop dwelling on his past and get on with *living* his life—Templeton is filled with a new self-confidence. Commanding Willis's respect, he plunges energetically into rehearsing the new play.

"Mr. Booth Templeton, who shared with most human beings the hunger to recapture the past moments, the ones that soften with the years. But in his case,

the characters of his past blocked him out and sent him back to his own time, which is where we find him now. Mr. Booth Templeton, who had a round-trip ticket . . . into the Twilight Zone."

"The Trouble With Templeton" marked the only contribution to *The Twilight Zone* of E. Jack Neuman, a friend of Buck Houghton's and writer-producer of eleven pilots which have become TV series, among them *Mr. Novak, Dr. Kildare, Petrocelli,* and *Police Story.*

Of "Templeton," Neuman says, "I had often toyed with the notion of 'You can't go home again,' and it should have been, 'You *shouldn't* go home again, ever,' which is what I was trying to say here." Although the script is beautifully written, Neuman wasn't able to labor on it long. "I wrote it in about a day," he recalls.

Cast as Templeton was Brian Aherne, and a better choice could not have been made. Like Templeton, Aherne had been a great actor, superb as the Emperor Maximilian in the movie *Juarez.* At fifty-eight, he was still a remarkably handsome man and a perceptive and skillful performer. But when he received the *Twilight Zone* script, he didn't know what to make of it. "When I first read the script I thought the writer must surely be out of his head," he said at the time. "Then Rod Serling . . . suggested I have a look at one of the earlier shows. I'd never seen it before, as I'm not much of a TV fan. Then I realized what 'twilight zone' meant, and that the script was really as excellent one."

"Brian Aherne was just a charming, wonderful, delightful man, a terribly professional man, and one of the nicest people that I've ever worked with," says Director Buzz Kulik. "He was very touched by what he had to do. It was very, very real to him." As for himself, Kulik admits that he too was moved by the material. "Maybe it was because it was about show business, maybe because I could relate to it myself much more than most things, but I've always had a very special affection for that show."

"The Trouble With Templeton" has in it one of the most visually beautiful scenes of the entire series. This occurs in the crowded, smoke-filled speakeasy in which Templeton finds Laura (very well played by Pippa Scott). The place is loud with conversation and raucous music. At one point, Laura breaks into an absurd-looking Charleston. Templeton tries to grab her, to stop her. She slaps him and says, "Why don't you go back where you came from? We don't want you here!" She returns to her dancing. The camera follows the devastated Templeton as he rushes out. The moment he exits, all those in the speakeasy immediately fall silent and still. The smoke which had suggested gaiety a moment before now suggests a ghostliness. The camera pans across the room back to Laura. She steps forward. The expression on her face is one we have not seen before, one we immediately realize reflects her *true* nature: beautiful, intelligent, full of sorrow and longing. The lights behind her dim, leaving her alone in space. Then the light goes down on her, and all is black.

"The biggest concern we had," says Kulik, "was that we would make sure that everybody understood that she was playing a part, that she was really forcing herself to do this to get him to go back, you see." He adds modestly, "It seemed to work."

Also cast in "The Trouble With Templeton" was Sydney Pollack, a friend of Kulik's who is today a top film director with credits which include *They Shoot Horses Don't They?*, *The Way We Were*, and *The Electric Horseman*. Ironically, the part Pollack played in "Templeton" was that of an abrasive young stage director. Buzz Kulik admits that the role had a bit of a private joke to it. "He and I knew a producer-director in New York, and I didn't think very kindly of this man, he and I had had our struggles through the years, and so had Sydney. And the thing about this fellow—this man we were *vaguely* imitating—was that he came from Georgia. He had lost his accent, much of it, except that when he became angry or uptight or nervous, he fell back into his youthful patois. We had to give this character some kind of additional color, so we thought, let's make him this fellow that we both knew."

"THE INVADERS" (1/27/61)

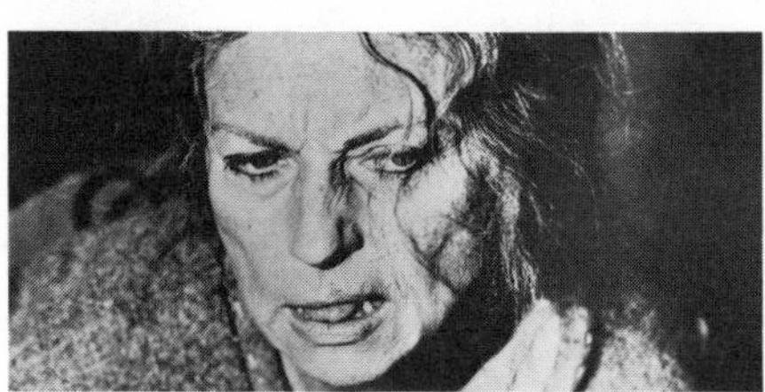
Agnes Moorhead

Written by Richard Matheson
Producer: Buck Houghton
Director: Douglas Heyes
Director of Photography: George T. Clemens
Music: Jerry Goldsmith

Cast:
Woman: Agnes Moorhead
Voice of Astronaut: Douglas Heyes

"This is one of the out-of-the-way places, the unvisited places, bleak, wasted, dying. This is a farmhouse, handmade, crude, a house without electricity or gas, a house untouched by progress. This is the woman who lives in the house, a woman who's been alone for many years, a strong, simple woman whose only problem up until this moment has been that of acquiring enough food to eat, a woman about to face terror which is even now coming at her from . . . the Twilight Zone."

Hearing a strange sound on her roof, the woman goes up to investigate—and sees a miniature flying saucer out of which emerge two tiny, robot-like creatures. A battle for survival ensues, with the creatures tormenting the woman with a ray gun and one of her own kitchen knives. Finally, she manages to grab hold of one, battering it into lifelessness. With an ax, she destroys the saucer and the remaining creature within. Before he is killed, he sends a message to his home planet not to send more ships to this world of giants. The lettering on the side of the saucer reads—U.S. Air Force!

"These are the invaders, the tiny beings from the tiny place called Earth, who would take the giant step across the sky to the question marks that sparkle and beckon from the vastness of the universe only to be imagined. The invaders, who found out that a one-way ticket to the stars beyond has the ultimate price tag. And we have just seen it entered in a ledger that covers all the transactions of the universe, a bill stamped 'paid in full,' and to be found . . . in the Twilight Zone."

It's been mentioned previously that Richard Matheson was, and is, a master of the horror form, yet none of his *Twilight Zone* scripts to this point had explored this genre—not until "The Invaders."

Again, Buck Houghton looked to Douglas Heyes to pilot a difficult episode. Immediately, Heyes had a number of suggestions. For the lead he wanted Agnes Moorhead, an actress who, during her long career, played everything from Orson Welles's mother in *Citizen Kane* to Elizabeth Montgomery's in *Bewitched*. "The reason that I suggested her," says Heyes, "was that she had done a radio show called 'Sorry, Wrong Number,' which was a half-hour *tour de force* where she used nothing *but* her voice, and I said, 'Here's a half-hour *tour de force* where the woman doesn't use her voice at all!'"

All might have seemed clear to Heyes, but not to Agnes Moorhead. "She looked at me very curiously when she came in," Heyes recalls. "I said, 'What is it?' She said, 'Well, I've been reading the script and I've been trying to find my part!' There was only one woman, and there were no lines, and most actresses skimming through a script look to see what the woman has to say. She'd looked through the whole part and couldn't find anything the woman had to say!"

So Heyes had his lead, but what about the others, the little men? "I didn't want to do this with process photography or with tricks, a la *Dr. Cyclops* or something," says Heyes. He decided that the tiny creatures should be the exact size they were shown to be. "By having them that size, she was able to grab them physically and hurl them across the room, which made it far more interesting than if you were using process and she couldn't really touch them."

With his art background, Heyes had no difficulty in making a sketch of what he wanted. "These characters were then made, oddly enough, by the makeup department. They modelled them from my drawing, which was sort of based on the Michelin Tire Man. The reason I made them this kind of bulky round shape is that, first of all, they should not look like human beings, but secondly, after the fact, you had to say they *were* human beings. Ah hah! Then therefore, they were in inflated spacesuits, right?"

Agnes Moorhead and the invader

Agnes Moorhead and the invading ship

The figures that were crafted were made of foam rubber and painted gold to give them a metallic sheen. Watching the episode, one would assume that they were given movement by some internal mechanism, but this wasn't the case. Heyes reveals that there was a slit up the back of each figure, through which a person could insert his hand. To walk, the person put his fingers in the hollows of the legs. To raise the arms, the fingers went in there. Consequently, the figures could not move their arms and legs at the same time. A little ray gun was made to light up by running a wire to an external battery with a button on it. The same was done with an antenna on one of the creature's heads. To disguise the arm sticking out of the back, Heyes claims that the operator wore a black sleeve, making it invisible against a dark background. And he should know—he was the operator!

Heyes not only gave movement to the tiny figures, he gave them voice as well. Apart from Serling's narration, there is only one speech in the entire

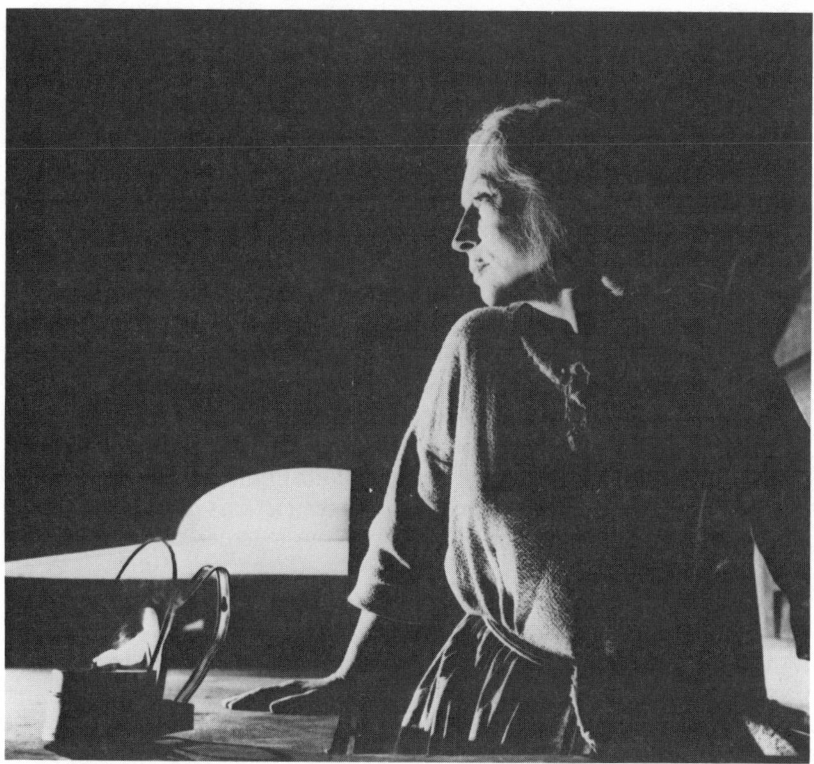

show, that of the remaining, dying astronaut warning Earth. "That was my voice," says Heyes, "because I was those little guys."

There were still plenty of challenges left to overcome. The flying saucer the little men land in was easy; simply pull the miniature ship from *Forbidden Planet* out again (although a rougher model was made for those shots in which the woman attacks it with an ax). Then there was the interior of the cabin. Since at the end it was revealed to be on an alien planet, nothing could be obviously of Earth origin, yet nothing should be so peculiar as to telegraph the ending. "So we used just the basic things," says Heyes. "A curtain was just basically a curtain, a chair was just the shape of a chair. There was no style that could be attributed to any particular period in history or place, yet basically it came down to what would be on a farm in the most primitive type of communities."

The cabin used was a small one, and was a considerable challenge. Among those responsible was director of photography George Clemens, whose moody camera work adds immensely to the suspense. Most challenging to him was a scene in which Moorhead had to carry a candle from room to room, with the candle supposedly the only light source. "I would say that was a problem," says Clemens. "To truly make it look right, you have to visualize where your shadows change lights." Clemens put lights all over the set with dimmer switches, and dimmer boys to work them. "In that particular picture, I had to take over a couple of dimmers myself, being able to know just what I wanted and the time to make the moves. But I think I had about six dimmer boys, six lights, and all that had to be synchronized. One source would come up and the other would go out as she went from room to room. I was very happy with the result I was able to achieve, because it looked real to me after I finally got it."

Shooting went quickly and easily. "By being able to incorporate my little guys in with her and so forth, I was able to keep it down to a minimum of cuts," says Heyes. "I would rehearse for about a half a day with her and with the camera for one piece of film, and then we would do it. It would take like four hours of rehearsal and then four minutes to shoot it. Then another long, long period of rehearsing and then a short piece of film. And when the seven or eight pieces of film were put together, we had our half-hour show."

Surprisingly, one person not enamored of this episode is Richard Matheson. "I never liked it," he says. "I don't like it today. For one thing, I think it's incredibly slow-moving. My script had twice as much incident as they used in the final version; it moved like a shot. The teaser alone, of the woman cutting vegetables and then hearing the noise, it seems like it takes her forever to get up to the roof.

"Also, I thought those little roly-poly dolls were ridiculous looking. The way I had written it, you would only catch very quick views of them and never anything clear. To see these little things waddling across the floor was about as frightening as Peter Rabbit coming at you."

Although Matheson is no fan, "The Invaders" does have its admirers. One of these is writer Theodore Sturgeon. "I loved *The Twilight Zone*," says Sturgeon, "and I think of all the episodes the one I liked the most was 'The Invaders.' Years ago, a producer—happened to be a very schlock producer, but he knew what he was talking about—said that if a blind man sits in front of a television set listening to a drama and he can tell you afterwards what it was about, then the director, the producer, the writer and everybody else have failed. Likewise, if a deaf man watches a television show and can tell you what the whole thing was about, then it has succeeded. This is a way of underlining the fact that it's a *visual* medium. Well, Matheson wrote that one without one word of dialogue. There were some grunts and screams in it, but no dialogue whatsoever. And it really and truly came to fruition as the kind of visual medium that it is."

"THE ODYSSEY OF FLIGHT 33" (2/24/61)

Written by Rod Serling
Producer: Buck Houghton
Director: Justus Addiss
Director of Photography: George T. Clemens
Music: stock

Cast:
Capt. Farver: John Anderson
1st Officer Craig: Paul Comi
Flight Engineer Purcell: Harp McGuire
2nd Officer Wyatt: Wayne Heffley
Navigator Hatch: Sandy Kenyon
Paula: Nancy Rennick
Jane: Beverly Brown
RAF Man: Lester Fletcher
Lady on Plane: Betty Garde
Passenger: Jay Overholts

"You're riding on a jet airliner en route from London to New York. You're at 35,000 feet atop an overcast and roughly fifty-five minutes from Idlewild Airport. But what you've seen occur inside the cockpit of this plane is no reflection on the aircraft or the crew. It's a safe, well-engineered, perfectly designed machine, and the men you've just met are a trained, cool, highly efficient team. The problem is simply that the plane is going too fast and there is nothing within the realm of knowledge or at least logic to explain it. Unbeknownst to passengers and crew, this airplane is heading into an unchartered region well off the track of commercial travelers—it's moving into the Twilight Zone. What you're about to see we call 'The Odyssey of Flight 33.'"

After picking up a freak tail wind that accelerates the plane past three thousand knots and through a shock wave, the crew of Global 33 is unable to raise anyone on the radio. Descending below the cloud cover to get a bearing, they see a Manhattan Island devoid of buildings and populated by dinosaurs. Somehow, they have gone back in time. Their only chance to return to their own time is to try to recapture that tail wind. They succeed in this, and when they descend again they see the familiar skyline of New York City. But all is not well—when they raise La Guardia Tower, the voice on the other end claims never to have heard of radar or jet aircraft. In the distance, the crew spies the Perisphere and Trylon of the 1939 New York World's Fair. Flight 33 has come back—but not far enough. Running low on fuel, the plane ascends in one final attempt to get back home.

"A Global jet airliner, en route from London to New York on an uneventful afternoon in the year 1961, but now reported overdue and missing, and by now searched for on land, sea, and air by anguished human beings fearful of what they'll find. But you and I know where she is, you and I know what's happened. So if some moment, any moment, you hear the sound of jet engines flying atop the overcast, engines that sound searching and lost, engines that sound desperate, shoot up a flare or do something. That would be Global 33 trying to get home—from the Twilight Zone."

On the day that Serling first conceived of the episode—one of the series' most effective and authentic—his brother, then an aviation writer for United Press International, was visiting from back East. Rod had taken him to MGM. Robert J. Serling recalls, "There was some mail on his desk at Cayuga Productions, and on the top was an envelope from American Airlines, and he opened that just about first. It was a brochure offering a mockup of a 707 passenger cabin to any studio that was going to film a scene. It was something they used in stewardess training and they decided to build another one. They had this one on the West Coast and they were going to rent it out or sell it.

"We go back out of the studio and he hasn't opened one goddamn piece of mail except this. We get to the car and he says, 'You drive,' and I thought, Oh God, something's wrong, because he never let me touch one of his cars, he wouldn't even let me put my finger on it let alone drive it.

"We're driving and he's still looking at this brochure. All of a sudden, he

The dinosaur spotted by the crew of Flight 33

closes it and says, 'Bob, suppose you had a jet over the Atlantic and it picked up a freak tail wind of such velocity that its ground speed was something like eight thousand miles an hour and it went so fast that it went through a time barrier, and when it came in over Idlewild Airport there wasn't any more airport, they were back in prehistoric times.' This was 'The Odyssey of Flight 33.'"

Bob Serling's involvement with the episode didn't end there. "He calls me up about two weeks later—I was back in Washington—and he says, 'Hey, I need cockpit dialogue for that jet that goes back in time.' I said, 'You need *what*?' 'Cockpit dialogue, what happens in the cockpit when they pick up the tail wind.' I said, 'Rod, you've got an impossible, implausible situation to begin with, so how in the hell can I give you the cockpit dialogue?' He said, 'Well, give me something about the radio checkpoints they try to reach, something about what would be happening in the airplane, the groundspeed versus the true airspeed and all that stuff.' I said, 'Okay, I'll try.'

"There was a TWA International captain living in Washington. He commuted up to New York to take his flights out. I called him. He came over to the house one night and I guess we killed a bottle of bourbon between us and came up with the dialogue in the cockpit. I kept telling him the story and we'd act out the roles. Then I called Rod back—I never could write to him, I always had to call him, he was always in a hurry—and gave him the dialogue over the phone.

"Somewhere, he's got letters from some pilots who said it was the most technically accurate piece that anybody had ever done on an airplane flight. It was. The checkpoints were perfect; the dialogue was just what a crew would say."

Under Justus Addiss's direction, John Anderson, Paul Comi, Harp McGuire, Wayne Heffley, and Sandy Kenyon, as captain and flight crew, give performances that are cool, understated, and credible. Aerial stock footage of the 1939 New York World's Fair is well integrated into the episode. Of course, the real shocker of the show is contained in two brief but very convincing shots—bird's-eye views of a brontosaurus. These wonderful shots were accomplished using a tabletop landscape and a miniature, jointed model of a brontosaurus, moved frame by frame in the classic technique known as stop-motion animation.

"The dinosaur was one of the puppets used in the Jack Harris picture, *Dinosaurus*, for which Project Unlimited did the special effects," explains special-effects wizard Wah Chang. "The partners in Project were Gene Warren, Tim Barr, and myself. We also did the effects for *The Time Machine, Seven Faces of Dr. Lao, Wonderful World of the Brothers Grimm,* as well as the TV series *Outer Limits,* some of the effects for *Star Trek,* and many more."

"The most expensive piece of film ever shot for *Twilight Zone* was the dinosaur watching the plane go by," says Buck Houghton. It cost us $2500 and, God, Business Affairs raised hell with me about it."

Thanks to this kind of attention to detail, "The Odyssey of Flight 33" has left an indelible impression on many. John Anderson, the captain (and previously the angel Gabriel in "A Passage for Trumpet,"), recalls: "Waiting to tee off at a golf course several years ago, a man from the foursome behind us approached and said, 'Didn't you do that *Twilight Zone* about the flight that got lost in time?' I said, 'Guilty.' And he came back with, 'That's one of my favorite of all these shows,' and added, 'I fly for United and you know, sometimes up there during a long flight you do get crazy thoughts like what happened to your ship on that flight.'"

VIDEOTAPE INVADES THE TWILIGHT ZONE

In November of 1960, *The Twilight Zone* tried an experiment. So far, sixteen episodes of the second season had been filmed, but all was not well. Says Buck Houghton, "We were inching up to around $65,000 an episode, which at that time was frightening." In an attempt to cut costs, the network suggested that six episodes be done on videotape rather than film. Tape was less expensive than film, and the editing costs were negligible since most editing was done on the spot, switching from camera to camera as in live TV. Ultimately, the shows would be transferred from tape to sixteen-millimeter film for broadcast. If the experiment succeeded, more episodes would be done on tape, thus keeping costs under control.

This method had its limitations, though. At the time, tape was still at an extremely primitive stage of its development. Except for the integration of stock footage, none of the taped shows could have any exterior locations; everything had to be shot on a soundstage. Also, since tape couldn't be edited as cleanly as film, there could be fewer different camera setups and fewer complex camera movements. Obviously, this limited the range of story possibilities. Serling wasn't happy about this but, the network being the network, he agreed to give it a try.

Doing a show on tape was closer in procedure to live TV than to film, so Houghton was careful to only hire directors who had experience in live television. Instead of one day of rehearsal and three shooting days, the tape shows had four days of rehearsal and two days of taping. "We actually rehearsed them like we were doing a live show," says Jack Smight, director of three of the six. "Then we'd go into the studio and block it and have a run-through, a dress rehearsal, and then actually tape it."

The six shows were taped at CBS Television City in Los Angeles. They had no director of photography as such. Instead, a technical director sat up in a booth with the director. On the set were the actors, a lighting man, sound men, and four cameramen. The four cameras were hooked up to monitors in the booth. As taping progressed, the technical director, at the command of the director, would switch from one camera to another. Today this is standard procedure for nearly all situation comedies, but in 1960 tape was something quite innovative. "Actually," says Buck Houghton, "I enjoyed the experience on tape. It was like getting a new set of toys that were different than I'd used before."

"THE LATENESS OF THE HOUR" (12/2/60)

John Hoyt and Inger Stevens

Written by Rod Serling
Producer: Buck Houghton
Director: Jack Smight
Videotape—no director of photography
Music: stock

Cast:
Jana: Inger Stevens
Dr. Loren: John Hoyt
Mrs. Loren: Irene Tedrow
Nelda: Mary Gregory
Robert the Butler: Tom Palmer
Gretchen: Doris Karnes
Suzanne: Valley Keane
Jensen: Jason Johnson

"The residence of Dr. William Loren, which is in reality a menagerie for machines. We're about to discover that sometimes the product of man's talent and genius can walk amongst us untouched by the normal ravages of time. These are Dr. Loren's robots, built to functional as well as artistic perfection. But in a moment Dr. Loren, wife, and daughter will discover that perfection is relative, that even robots have to be paid for, and very shortly will be shown exactly what is the bill."

Dr. Loren lives in what he feels is the ideal environment: a house built to his specifications staffed by human-looking robot servants. But his daughter Jana feels the sanctuary is actually a prison, and that her parents' reliance on the robots is turning them into vegetables. She gives her father an ultimatum: either he dismantles the robots or she leaves home. Reluctantly, Loren complies. Jana is ecstatic, but when she tells her parents that soon she'll meet a young man and have children, their alarmed expressions fill her with a terrible suspicion. Frantically, she searches in vain through the family photo album for pictures of herself as a child. The truth becomes evident: Jana is a robot. Sobbing uncontrollably, she collapses at the top of the stairs. Realizing that things will never be the same, Dr. Loren erases Jana's memory and reprograms her—as a maid.

"Let this be the postscript: should you be worn out by the rigors of competing in a very competitive world, if you're distraught from having to share your existence with the noises and neuroses of the twentieth century, if you crave serenity but want it full time and with no strings attached, get yourself a workroom in a basement and then drop a note to Dr. and Mrs. William Loren. They're a childless couple who made comfort a life's work, and maybe there are a few do-it-yourself pamphlets still available—in the Twilight Zone."

In the first of the tape shows, Serling tried to overcome the physical limitations imposed on him by making physical limitation a theme of the script.

"I thought it had a good atmosphere to it," says director Jack Smight. "That's really what we were working on. I don't think the plot was that good really, but when we were rehearsing it we were working on atmosphere more than anything else, and I think we accomplished that." Then there's the ending of the episode, in which Jana, having discovered the truth about herself, is reprogrammed as a mindless maidservant. It's a surprising shock, and it packs a wallop.

Particularly welcome is the presence of John Hoyt as Dr. Loren. With a career that spans more than five decades, Hoyt is one of that small band of character actors who infuse individuality into every role they play, never letting a character become invisible or anonymous. Here he brings a cool and superior bearing, seeming totally believable as a restrained and brilliant inventor who is almost always in control.

"STATIC" (3/10/61)

Dean Jagger and Carmen Mathews

Written by Charles Beaumont
Based on an unpublished story by OCee Ritch
Producer: Buck Houghton
Director: Buzz Kulik
Videotape—no director of photography
Music: stock

Cast:
Ed Lindsay: Dean Jagger
Vinnie Broun: Carmen Mathews
Prof. Ackerman: Robert Emhardt
Mrs. Nielsen: Alice Pearce
Roscoe Bragg: Arch W. Johnson
Boy: Stephen Talbot
Miss Meredith: Lillian O'Malley
Mr. Llewellyn: Pat O'Malley
Junk Dealer: Clegg Hoyt
Rock & Roll Singer: Jerry Fuller
Real Estate Pitchman: Eddie Marr
Girl in Commercial: Diane Strom
Disc Jockey: Bob Crane
TV/Radio Announcer: Roy Rowan
Man #1: Bob Duggan
Man #2: Jay Overholts

"No one ever saw one quite like that, because that's a very special sort of radio. In its day, circa 1935, its type was one of the most elegant consoles on the market. Now, with its fabric-covered speakers, its peculiar yellow dial, its serrated knobs, it looks quaint and a little strange. Mr. Ed Lindsay is going to find out how *strange very soon—when he tunes in to the Twilight Zone."*

Disgusted by television, Lindsay, a cantankerous old bachelor, retrieves his old radio from the basement of the boardinghouse in which he lives and installs it in his room. He soon finds that it can receive programs from the past, but only when he's alone. Vinnie Broun, an old maid to whom he was once engaged, is convinced he hears the shows only in his mind, the result of a profound nostalgia for the good old days when the two of them had a chance for happiness. Lindsay utterly rejects this view and isolates himself with the radio. Concerned for his sanity, Vinnie gives the radio to the junk dealer. Furious, Lindsay retrieves it, praying that it still works. It does indeed—when he calls Vinnie to come hear, it is an adoring, younger version who appears. The year is 1940, and Lindsay—himself a young man again—has been given a second chance.

"Around and around she goes, and where she stops nobody knows. All Ed Lindsay knows is that he desperately wanted a second chance and he finally got it, through a strange and wonderful time machine called a radio . . . in the Twilight Zone."

In anyone who mourns the demise of the old radio shows and the advent of television, this story of a radio that receives Tommy Dorsey, Major Bowes, and Fred Allen must surely strike a responsive chord.

"Static" was based on a story by OCee Ritch, a friend of Charles Beaumont. The idea for it came from a party given by Richard Matheson attended by both Ritch and a fan of old-time radio who performed bits of radio nostalgia. "At the time," Ritch recalls, "I think I said something like, 'Hey man, wouldn't it be great if you could just tune in those old things?' So I went home and wrote a story called 'Tune in Yesterday.' It was Chuck's suggestion that I make it into a *Twilight Zone* instead of submitting it as a short story. I submitted it to *Twilight Zone* and they accepted it as a story on Chuck's recommendation and asked him to do a teleplay based on it."

In reworking Ritch's story, Beaumont made substantial alterations. While the original concerned a middle-aged, unhappily married man who uses the radio to escape into the past, Beaumont's script deals with a sour, aging bachelor who lives in a boardinghouse under the same roof with the woman who might have been his wife had things not gone wrong. The magic radio gives the man a second chance, transporting him to an idyllic past in which he and his beloved did not let life pass them by.

"Static" also gave Beaumont a chance to take a few satiric jibes at television, utilizing the medium itself. Although not figuring at all in the original story, in Beaumont's teleplay television is presented as an antagonist, a destructive and stupefying force. The TV shows and commercials in "Static" are fictitious, but they bear a striking resemblance to reality:

ANNOUNCER'S VOICE

GREEN . . . green, cool grass, the touch, the smell of green, cool grass, now brought to you for the first time in GREEN, the new chlorophyll cigarette, the smoke that doesn't smell like tobacco, but smells good, green, cool, like grass . . .

And this:

PITCHMAN'S VOICE

(*Hard sell*) . . . if you act now, you can get your acreage

> in Splendid Flats for the fantastic, the unbelievable price of twenty-five cents an acre! A week! Look at this land! It's flat! It's gray! It's undeveloped! But within ten years with the coming of water and people, it will be a veritable oasis of loveliness! Get in on it now, folks! Before the land value skyrockets!

Most of all, "Static" is a loving remembrance of something dear that is gone. In his book of nostalgic essays, *Remember? Remember?* (Macmillan, 1963), Beaumont wrote, "The world of radio was real to us. There are squirts and small fry today who will soon be as old as the Us of Then, and I know some who haven't turned a radio on in their entire lives. I try to tell them what it was like, but they don't understand. They can't believe I'm talking about the little plastic box in the kitchen that plays rock-'n-roll and gives us the news, and I'm not sure I believe it, either. Television is the substitute for what we had, and I deem it a bad one. It inspires neither loyalty nor awe. It does not thrill, transport, terrify or enchant. It only entertains . . ." The point is made even more succinctly by a line that Lindsay says in the episode: "Radio is a world that has to be believed to be seen." It's true, and "Static" reminds us of that.

"THE WHOLE TRUTH" (1/20/61)

Nan Peterson and Jack Carson

Written by Rod Serling
Producer: Buck Houghton
Director: James Sheldon
Videotape—no director of photography
Music: stock

Cast:
Harvey Hunnicut: Jack Carson
Honest Luther Grimbley: Loring Smith
Irv: Arte Johnson
Nikita Khrushchev: Lee Sabinson
Old Man: George Chandler
Young Man: Jack Ging
Young Woman: Nan Peterson
Translator: Patrick Westwood

"This, as the banner already has proclaimed, is Mr. Harvey Hunnicut, an expert on commerce and con jobs, a brash, bright, and larceny-loaded wheeler and dealer who, when the good lord passed out a conscience, must have gone for a beer and missed out. And these are a couple of other characters in our story: a

little old man and a Model A car—but not just any old man and not just any Model A. There's something very special about the both of them. As a matter of fact, in just a few moments they'll give Harvey Hunnicut something that he's never experienced before. Through the good offices of a little magic, they will unload on Mr. Hunnicut the absolute necessity to tell the truth. Exactly where they come from is conjecture, but as to where they're heading for, this we know, because all of them—and you—are on the threshold of the Twilight Zone."

After buying the Model A, which its elderly owner assures him is haunted, Hunnicut, an unscrupulous used-car dealer, finds he is compelled to tell the absolute truth. Consequently, he can't sell a single car on the lot. When a local alderman who is up for re-election expresses his interest in buying the car (to give the illusion he is not getting rich off his constituents), Hunnicut tells him of the spell it casts. Realizing that any politician who told the whole truth would very quickly be out of a job, he immediately changes his mind. Instead, he names several of his colleagues whom he would love to hear tell the truth for once. This gives Hunnicut an idea. Using the ruse that, if presented as the typical car of the average American, the Model A could be effective in anti-U.S. propaganda, Hunnicut manages to unload the car on someone he thinks will be much embarrassed by the truth—Nikita Khrushchev!

"Couldn't happen, you say? Far-fetched? Way-out? Tilt-of-center? Possible. But the next time you buy an automobile that happens to look as if it had just gone through the Battle of the Marne, and the seller is ready to throw into the bargain one of his arms, be particularly careful in explaining to the boss about your grandmother's funeral when you were actually at Chavez Ravine watching the Dodgers. It'll be a fact that you are actually the proud possessor of an instrument of truth manufactured and distributed by an exclusive dealer . . . in the Twilight Zone."

"The Whole Truth" was an odd choice, both for videotape and for *The Twilight Zone*. Although the used car lot is supposed to be outside, the illusion is not convincing. And the subject matter reveals that even Serling was not immune to some of the more pervasive prejudices of the day.

"NIGHT OF THE MEEK" (12/23/60)

Art Carney

Written by Rod Serling
Producer: Buck Houghton
Director: Jack Smight
Videotape—no director of photography
Music: stock

Cast:
Henry Corwin: Art Carney
Mr. Dundee: John Fiedler
Burt: Burt Mustin
Officer Flaherty: Robert Lieb
Sister Florence: Meg Wyllie
Bartender: Val Avery
Elf: Larrian Gillespie
Fat Woman: Kay Cousins

"This is Mr. Henry Corwin, normally unemployed, who once a year takes the lead role in the uniquely American institution, that of department-store Santa Claus in a road-company version of 'The Night Before Christmas.' But in just a moment Mr. Henry Corwin, ersatz Santa Claus, will enter a strange kind of North Pole which is one part the wondrous spirit of Christmas and one part the magic that can only be found in . . . the Twilight Zone."

Showing up at the department store drunk on Christmas Eve, Corwin is fired by Dundee, the manager. Still dressed in his moth-eaten Santa suit, he wanders aimlessly—until he comes upon a magic bag that can dispense any gift that's asked of it. Corwin sets off to spread joy to one and all, but he soon runs into Officer Flaherty, who assumes the gifts are stolen and hauls him off to the station where a vengeful Dundee awaits. But when Dundee tries to remove the "stolen merchandise," all he finds is a stray cat and some garbage. Corwin explains that it's "a most unusual bag." Facetiously, Dundee asks for a bottle of cherry brandy, vintage 1903. To his astonishment, Corwin supplies it. For the rest of the night, Corwin distributes presents. At midnight, the bag is empty. Burt, a friendly bum, notes that Corwin has taken no present for himself. He replies that his only wish would be to do this every year. The wish comes true: in an alley, Corwin comes upon an elf, sleigh and reindeer—all waiting to take him to the North Pole.

"A word to the wise to all the children of the twentieth century, whether their concern be pediatrics or geriatrics, whether they crawl on hands and knees and wear diapers or walk with a cane and comb their beards. There's a wondrous magic to Christmas, and there's a special power reserved for little people. In

short, there's nothing mightier than the meek, and a merry Christmas to each and all."

"Once in a while, Rod would have an enthusiasm," Buck Houghton recalls. "He'd say to himself or to me or to Carol or whomever, that he particularly liked somebody. There was a Christmas show that we did just because he wanted to see Art Carney play Santa Claus."

Sentimental, touching, and timeless, "Night of the Meek" is filled with holiday magic. As Corwin (named after Serling's idol, writer Norman Corwin) Carney is wonderful, providing just the right balance between comedy and drama. Supporting him in grand style are John Fiedler, as Corwin's quick-tempered boss, and Burt Mustin, as a friendly skid-row

Santa and two of his neighborhood children

bum. This is a genuinely funny episode, with the humor flowing naturally and enhancing the characters. There are no boffo laughs but rather many pleasant little moments, such as when Fiedler is in a police station berating Carney for distributing what he believes to be the store's merchandise, not noticing that the "gifts" he's removing from the bag as he talks are in fact empty tin cans—until he removes a cat.

Taped just three weeks before Christmas, "Night of the Meek" had a special effect on the cast and crew, and especially on the many children on the set. Production assistant Lillian Gallo, today a producer, recalls, "There were more children performing on that show as extras than on the other tape shows, and I remember their excitement and their joy. Sometimes, it was difficult for them to contain themselves during the times that you have to be quiet during the show. There was a different atmosphere throughout that shooting schedule."

This isn't to say that "Night of the Meek" pleased everybody. One viewer was so enraged at the "blasphemy" of presenting a drunk as Santa Claus that he sent outraged letters to Serling, the network, and several newspapers.

"TWENTY-TWO" (2/10/61)

Barbara Nichols

Written by Rod Serling
Based on an anecdote in *Famous Ghost Stories,* edited by Bennett Cerf
Producer: Buck Houghton
Director: Jack Smight
Videotape—no director of photography
Music: stock

Cast:
Liz Powell: Barbara Nichols
Doctor: Jonathan Harris
Nurse/Stewardess: Arline Sax
Barney: Fredd Wayne
Night Duty Nurse: Norma Connolly
Day Duty Nurse: Mary Adams
Ticket Clerk: Wesley Lau
Ticket Clerk #2: Joe Sargent
P.A. Voice: Jay Overholts
Double for Sax: Carole Conn

"This is Miss Liz Powell. She's a professional dancer and she's in the hospital as a result of overwork and nervous fatigue. And at this moment we have just

finished walking with her in a nightmare. In a moment she'll wake up and we'll remain at her side. The problem here is that both Miss Powell and you will reach a point where it might be difficult to decide which is reality and which is nightmare, a problem uncommon perhaps but rather peculiar to the Twilight Zone."

In the hospital, Miss Powell has a recurring vision in which she follows a nurse to room 22—the morgue—at which point the nurse, who is disturbingly beautiful, throws open the door, smiles ominously, and says, "Room for one more, honey." Miss Powell is convinced that these events are real, but her doctor and her agent believe they are no more than a bad dream. This seems even more certain when it is pointed out that the morgue's night nurse is *not* the woman she saw. Finally, Miss Powell is discharged from the hospital. Arriving at the airport to board a nonstop flight to Miami, she has a dreadful sense of *déjà vu*—the plane is flight *22*! Boarding, she is horrified to see that the stewardess is the nurse in her vision. The woman smiles at her and says, "Room for one more, honey." Screaming hysterically, Miss Powell runs back to the airport lounge. The plane takes off without her—and explodes in mid-air.

"Miss Elizabeth Powell, professional dancer. Hospital diagnosis: acute anxiety brought on by overwork and fatigue. Prognosis: with rest and care, she'll probably recover. But the cure to some nightmares is not to be found in known medical journals. You look for it under 'potions for bad dreams'—to be found in the Twilight Zone."

Rod Serling adapted "Twenty-Two" from a short anecdote in *Famous Ghost Stories,* edited by Bennett Cerf (Random House, 1944). In the original, an attractive young New York girl visits the Carolina plantation of some distant relatives. On two successive nights, just as she is getting into bed, she looks out the window to see "a magnificent old coach, drawn by four coal-black horses" pull up outside. The coachman, a ghastly-looking fellow, jumps off the coach, points a finger at her and says, "There is room for one more!" This so unnerves the girl that she packs her bags and heads back to New York, where she goes to see a doctor. The doctor dismisses the entire thing as an hallucination, but just as she is about to board the elevator to return to the ground floor of the medical building, she hears a familiar voice, saying, "There is room for one more!" The elevator operator is the same man as the coachman! The girl screams and draws back. The cables on the elevator break and all the passengers plummet to their deaths.

In adapting the story, Serling kept the basics but changed the setting from plantation to hospital and the vision from coach to morgue (an impressive set utilizing forced perspective). As for the elevator, that's transformed into the airliner that explodes upon takeoff (an effect that was accomplished with a model hanging from a wire and rigged with explosives).

"Twenty-Two" was not one of the more shining examples of *The Twilight Zone*. Barbara Nichols, Fredd Wayne, and Jonathan Harris (later Dr. Smith on *Lost in Space*) give performances which are shrill, shallow, and hard, and the theme of the episode, with its garbled premonitions and disbelieving bystanders, seems much better suited to a show like *One Step Beyond*. In the end, no one connected with the show felt very warmly toward it. Says director Jack Smight, "I just didn't think it had the quality of some of the others."

"LONG DISTANCE CALL" (3/3/31)

Lili Darvas and Billy Mumy

Written by William Idelson and Charles Beaumont
Producer: Buck Houghton
Director: James Sheldon
Videotape—no director of photography
Music: stock

Cast:
Billy Bayles: Billy Mumy
Grandma Bayles: Lili Darvas
Chris Bayles: Philip Abbott
Sylvia Bayles: Patricia Smith
Shirley: Jenny Maxwell
Dr. Unger: Henry Hunter
Mr. Peterson: Reid Hammond
Attendant: Lew Brown
1st Fireman: Bob McCord
2nd Fireman: Jim Turley
Nurse: Jutta Parr

"As must be obvious, this is a house hovered over by Mr. Death, that omnipresent player to the third and final act of every life. And it's been said, and probably rightfully so, that what follows this life is one of the unfathomable mysteries, an area of darkness which we the living reserve for the dead—or so it is said. For in a moment, a child will try to cross that bridge which separates light and shadow, and of course he must take the only known route, that indistinct highway through the region we call the Twilight Zone."

For his fifth birthday, Grandma Bayles gives her loving grandson Billy—

whom she possessively thinks of as "her son"—a toy telephone, then promptly takes sick and dies. For a short time, Billy is despondent, but he quickly seems to recover, spending virtually all his time talking animatedly into the toy. He claims Grandma is on the other end, that she is lonely and wants him to come visit, but his parents dismiss this as a child's imaginings—at first. But when Billy throws himself in front of a speeding car, narrowly avoiding being killed, then claims "someone" *told* him to do it, his mother has a dread suspicion. Hearing Billy talking on the toy late that night, she grabs it from him—and hears breathing on the other end! Screaming that she broke his telephone, Billy runs from the house and tries to drown himself in the fish pond. A fire rescue team tries frantically to resuscitate him, but with no response. At his wits' end, Billy's father goes into the child's room and speaks into the toy telephone. He pleads with his mother to let Billy live, arguing that if she really loves Billy she'll let him grow up and experience the world. Suddenly, Billy begins to respond. Grandma has finally loosened her grip on Billy . . . and given him back to the living.

"A toy telephone, an act of faith, a set of improbable circumstances, all combine to probe a mystery, to fathom a depth, to send a facet of light into a dark after-region, to be believed or disbelieved depending on your frame of reference. A fact or a fantasy, a substance or a shadow—but all of it very much a part of the Twilight Zone."

As with "Static," the idea for this morbid and effective little ghost story originated with one of Charles Beaumont's friends, in this case William Idelson. In his youth, Idelson had been an actor (he was a regular on radio's *Vic and Sade*); later he would be a top TV comedy writer-producer, with credits including *Love American Style* and *The Bob Newhart Show.* But at the time he was selling real estate and desperately trying to break into writing for television.

Of "Long Distance Call," Idelson says, "It grew out of a true situation which I expanded and fictionalized. It was after the birth of my first kid, a little boy. It was just the situation in the house with my mother there and my wife there, and she had given my kid a toy telephone for his second birthday, and I saw her call him on the phone. It's so hard to know how ideas come, but it was like a flash."

Richard Matheson, another of Idelson's friends, submitted his script to *The Twilight Zone*. Initially, it was rejected, but Beaumont heard about the script and liked the idea. Upon his promise that he would rewrite the script with Idelson, Cayuga bought it. And Idelson had made his first sale.

"Long Distance Call" also marked the debut on *The Twilight Zone* of a gifted young actor who would ultimately be featured in three episodes. Today, Billy Mumy is primarily remembered for his role as Will Robinson on *Lost in Space*, but in reality his career has been a long and varied one, including such films as *A Child is Waiting* and *Papillon*.

What makes "Long Distance Call" truly frightening is the horrifying concept of a dead relative guiding a child toward suicide. The total vulnerability of the child and the utter helplessness of the parents to intercede (until the end) cannot help but involve us emotionally. It was a theme that concerned some of those on the set as well. "I remember my mother was really upset with the suicide scenes," says Mumy, "thinking that it might make some type of weird impression on me to get something out of them by maybe pulling a stunt like that." One scene in particular must have caused a great deal of anxiety. "When I tried to commit suicide in the pond," Mumy recalls, "we shot a whole thing there with me floating in the water. I don't think that that was on camera, but I remember doing it. I was a real good swimmer then."

One of the factors that might originally have dissuaded Cayuga from buying Idelson's script was the less-than-successful climactic scene, in which the child's father picks up the toy telephone and pleads with his dead mother to return the boy. Here's how it appeared in the original script:

> Ma! Ma, if you can hear me, give him back to us. You said you loved me, and I know you did. I remember so many things. Remember that funny little dog I had? You let me keep him even when he tore up all the furniture. Pa wanted to give him away, but you said no. And remember the first day of school? How scared I was . . . and you sat in the back of the room all morning so I wouldn't cry? And that first pair of long pants. And the time I broke the window with the ball? You hid me under the bed when the policeman came. My graduation . . . and that first date I had, you remember? With that skinny redhead, how mad you were? We had lots of fights, but I always knew you loved me. And I loved you, too, so very, very much. I never really got a chance to tell you. Oh, Ma, please, give him back to us, so we can love him too. Give him back to us.

"Chuck Beaumont and I were on the set while they were shooting the show," says Idelson, "and Rod came down and said, 'I don't like this last speech. I want you to change it.' Chuck and I went into an office and changed it, on the spot."

What emerged was a speech (beautifully performed by Philip Abbot) in which the focus was moved away from the father and put where it rightly belongs—on the child:

> Mother, if you can hear me, listen. You said you loved Billy. At his birthday you picked him up and you hugged him—and you said he gave you life again. If you really love Billy, give him *back*. He's only five. He hasn't even started. He doesn't know anything about going to school. Or girlfriends. Or wearing long pants. Even pitching a baseball. He's hardly been out of this room, out of this house. There's a whole world he hasn't even touched. Mother, you said Billy gave you life again—now you can give *him* life. If you really love him, let him live. Give him *back. Give him back, Ma!*

"When the show went on the air," says Idelson, "they all came over to my house—Chuck, Dick Matheson, Bill Nolan—and they were all very complimentary. It was a tremendous thrill for me."

TAKING STOCK

"Long Distance Call" was the last episode of *The Twilight Zone* to be videotaped. In all, Cayuga had saved five thousand dollars per episode, but for a series that required the entire universe as a stage, the limitations of tape far outweighed the advantages. In 1972, Serling finally made public his feelings on the subject. In an interview with Douglas Brode in *Show* magazine, he said, "I never liked tape because it's neither fish nor fowl. You're bound to the same kind of natural laws as in live TV, but they try to mix it with certain qualities of film. . . . on *Twilight Zone* we tried six shows on tape, and they were disastrous."

Although Serling and company were done with the six tape episodes, others were not. Both "Static" and "Long Distance Call" resulted in lawsuits against Cayuga by writers who had submitted stories to *The Twilight Zone*, one of which utilized a magical toy telephone, the other a magical radio. Unfortunately, because *The Twilight Zone* was essentially a show that relied on various supernatural or scientific gimmicks, it left itself wide open to such charges.

"There were accusations floating around all the time that Rod was stealing every story that was ever written, and Rod was very self-conscious about it," says Buck Houghton. "[Science fiction] is a limited field, and you can't write in it without stepping on somebody's former idea. It's like saying that every love story is a steal of *Romeo and Juliet*. You know, boy gets girl, boy loses girl, boy wins girl is not copyrightable. But there was this feeling." Ultimately, settlements were made in both cases.

Following the tape shows, Cayuga broke for the remainder of the winter. For most of the production crew, this meant a well-deserved vacation, but not for Serling. If anything, his work load increased, preparing six of the remaining seven scripts of the season. Shooting of film episodes resumed at the beginning of March, 1961, with two very different stories of time travel, both by Serling.

"A HUNDRED YARDS OVER THE RIM" (4/7/61)

Miranda Jones and Cliff Robertson

Written by Rod Serling
Producer: Buck Houghton
Director: Buzz Kulik
Director of Photography: George T. Clemens
Music: Fred Steiner

Cast:
Christian Horn: Cliff Robertson
Joe: John Crawford
Mary Lou: Evans Evans
Doctor: Ed Platt
Martha Horn: Miranda Jones
Sheriff: Robert L. McCord III
Charlie: John Astin

"The year is 1847, the place is the territory of New Mexico, the people are a tiny handful of men and women with a dream. Eleven months ago, they started out from Ohio and headed west. Someone told them about a place called California, about a warm sun and a blue sky, about rich land and fresh air, and at this moment almost a year later they've seen nothing but cold, heat, exhaustion, hunger, and sickness. This man's name is Christian Horn. He has a dying eight-year-old son and a heartsick wife, and he's the only one remaining who has even a fragment of the dream left. Mr. Chris Horn, who's going over the top of a rim to look for water and sustenance and in a moment will move into the Twilight Zone."

Scouting a hundred yards over the rim, Horn is shocked to see a paved highway lined with telephone poles—and the wagons he left behind only minutes before completely gone! A huge truck—which Horn takes for a monster—thunders by. He throws himself to the ground and his rifle discharges into his arm. Stumbling along the road, he comes to a diner run by Joe and Mary Lou (a former nurse's aide). Mary Lou treats Horn's arm and gives him a bottle of penicillin pills. The couple find the stranger extremely odd, and Horn finds both them and the restaurant totally inexplicable—until he spies a calendar dated September, 1961. The couple summon a doctor who questions Horn and finds that his "delusions" have their own peculiar rationality, lent credence by his clothes, his gun, and the old-fashioned fillings in his teeth. Joe, realizing this is all beyond him, calls the sheriff to take Horn away. Horn emerges from the other room. He has looked in an encyclopedia and found that his son grew up to be a renowned physician. He realizes that his journey through time has been for a purpose. As the sheriff arrives, Horn runs from the diner. Joe and the sheriff give chase, but Horn tops the rim and returns to 1847—armed with penicillin for his boy and the knowledge of nearby water and game. All that is left in 1961 is his rifle, which suddenly looks as though it has been rotting in the desert for a hundred years.

"Mr. Christian Horn, one of the hardy breed of men who headed west during a time when there were no concrete highways or the solace of civilization. Mr. Christian Horn, family and party, heading west, after a brief detour through the Twilight Zone."

In order to save money, whenever possible Buck Houghton liked to schedule two shows utilizing similar locations back to back, so that the crew would only have to make one trip outside the studio. Both "A Hundred Yards Over the Rim" and "The Rip Van Winkle Caper" were shot in the desert near Lone Pine, California.

First to be filmed was "A Hundred Yards Over the Rim." The episode boasts many good performances, but it is the powerful central performance of Cliff Robertson that holds the show together. As Chris Horn, he plays his role with intelligence and conviction, seeming in movement, expression, and even accent every bit the nineteenth-century man.

Director Buzz Kulik recalls being impressed with Robertson's methods. "He came to me while we were rehearsing with an eight- or nine-page analysis of his character that he had written, and he said, 'Will you read this and see if you agree or disagree or if there's anything you can add.' Well, we used to do that when we were all kids just out of acting school, but very few people take the time to do that."

In his striving for authenticity, Robertson sometimes went to lengths that people on the set found curious. Both Kulik and Robertson wanted the main character to look not like a cowboy, but rather to wear what actually might have been worn by an Easterner on his way west. Says director of photography George Clemens, "Do you remember he wore a big stovepipe hat? It was Cliff's idea and I was so scared that we'd be laughed off the screen on the first scene. In fact, Rod was back in

Interlaken [town in upstate New York bordering Cayuga Lake] and I even insisted that Buck call him and talk to him. Comedy and drama are so close that if you step over one side you get a laugh and you ruin the whole effect of the drama. But I was wrong, and I was the first guy that admitted it. Cliff was a great guy, and I thought he did a hell of a job."

"THE RIP VAN WINKLE CAPER" (4/21/61)

Oscar Beregi, John Mitchum, Lew Gallo and Simon Oakland

Written by Rod Serling
Producer: Buck Houghton
Director: Justus Addiss
Director of Photography: George T. Clemens
Music: stock

Cast:
Farwell: Oscar Beregi
DeCruz: Simon Oakland
Brooks: Lew Gallo
Erbie: John Mitchum
Man on Road: Wallace Rooney
Woman on Road: Shirley O'Hara
Brooks's Stunt Double: Robert L. McCord III
DeCruz's Stunt Double: Dave Armstrong

"The time is now and the place is a mountain cave in Death Valley, U.S.A. In just a moment, these four men will utilize the services of a truck placed in cosmoline, loaded with a hot heist cooled off by a century of sleep, and then take a drive into the Twilight Zone."

After robbing a bullion train bound from Fort Knox to California, four thieves stow their million dollars' worth of gold bricks in a cave and, utilizing a gas invented by Farwell, the ringleader, enter glass cases and go into suspended animation. While asleep, one is killed by a falling rock. But the others awake a hundred years later, hale and hearty—and free from all possible pursuit. They soon find, though, that they have not escaped their own greed. Hot-tempered DeCruz, eager to lessen the number of partners, uses the truck to run over and kill Brooks. But then the truck goes out of control and is wrecked. DeCruz and Farwell must walk through the desert to the nearest town, carrying as much gold as they can. Farwell, the older of the two, quickly becomes parched and exhausted. After losing his canteen, he is forced to pay DeCruz one gold bar for each sip of water. When the price goes up to *two* gold bars, Farwell lashes out, striking

DeCruz with one of the gold bricks and killing him. Weak and dehydrated, Farwell trudges along the highway weighted down by the golden burden he is unwilling to abandon. Finally, he collapses. A futuristic car drives up. Farwell offers his gold to the couple inside in exchange for a drink of water and a drive into town, but he is already too far gone. He dies—never knowing that years earlier a way of manufacturing gold was found . . . making his precious loot utterly worthless.

"The last of four Rip Van Winkles who all died precisely the way they lived, chasing an idol across the sand to wind up bleached dry in the hot sun as so much desert flotsam, worthless as the gold bullion they built a shrine to. Tonight's lesson . . . in the Twilight Zone."

Two performances raised "The Rip Van Winkle Caper" above the mundane: Simon Oakland, as a sadistic and greedy thug, and Oscar Beregi, as the brains of the operation. Together, the two generate a lot of electricity. This episode also adds another fine ironic ending to the catalogue of *The Twilight Zone*.

"SHADOW PLAY" (5/5/61)

Dennis Weaver

Written by Charles Beaumont
Producer: Buck Houghton
Director: John Brahm
Director of Photography: George T. Clemens
Music: stock

Cast:
Adam Grant: Dennis Weaver
Henry Ritchie: Harry Townes
Paul Carson: Wright King
Jiggs: William Edmondson
Carol Ritchie: Anne Barton
Coley: Bernie Hamilton
Phillips: Tommy Nello
Priest: Mack Williams
Judge: Gene Roth
Attorney: Jack Hyde
Jury Foreman: Howard Culver
Guard: John Close

"Adam Grant, a nondescript kind of man found guilty of murder and sentenced to the electric chair. Like every other criminal caught in the wheels of justice he's scared, right down to the marrow of his bones. But it isn't prison that scares

him, the long, silent nights of waiting, the slow walk to the little room, or even death itself. It's something else that holds Adam Grant in the hot, sweaty grip of fear, something worse than any punishment this *world has to offer, something found only in the Twilight Zone."*

What has Grant so scared is his certainty that all of this is a dream he's having, a recurring nightmare that has him waking up screaming every single night. District Attorney Ritchie rejects this as preposterous, but his friend Paul Carson, a newspaper editor, isn't so sure—and he's terrified that when Grant is electrocuted all of them will cease to exist. Carson convinces Ritchie to visit Grant in his cell, but Ritchie is not swayed by the fact that Grant is expecting him, nor by Grant's ability to lip-sync his every word. Grant offers to prove the world is all his invention; when Ritchie goes home he finds that the roast his wife put in the oven has inexplicably changed into a steak—yet he still refuses to accept Grant's claim. As midnight draws near, Carson pleads with him to call the governor for a stay of execution, arguing that Grant is clearly a mental incompetent. Reluctantly, Ritchie picks up the phone. But it is too late. As the switch is pulled on Grant, Ritchie and Carson disappear—as does everything else in their world. For a moment, all is blackness, then suddenly Grant is back in the courtroom being sentenced. Some of the characters are different, but the scenario is the same—and the nightmare is starting over.

"We know that a dream can be real, but who ever thought that reality could be a dream? We exist, of course, but how, in what way? As we believe, as flesh-and-blood human beings, or are we simply parts of someone's feverish, complicated nightmare? Think about it, and then ask yourself, do you live here, in this country, in this world, or do you live instead . . . in the Twilight Zone."

As in "Perchance to Dream," Charles Beaumont once again explored the shadow realm of the nightmare in "Shadow Play."

Although somewhat stereotypical, the episode is suspenseful. Will Adam Grant be able to convince the D.A. that this is all a dream, or will he go to the chair? It's a race to the wire. Dennis Weaver, then known principally as Matt Dillon's limping right-hand man Chester, gives an intense if broad performance. Directing this was John Brahm, and he was a good choice, having directed many segments of *Alfred Hitchcock Presents*. One sequence seems particularly Hitchcockian: Grant is describing to a fellow prisoner the long walk to the electric chair. He concludes his monologue with, "Then they drop the mask. It's musty, it smells like an old sofa. Then you wait, every muscle tense, straining. Any second, any second. Then you can almost hear it. They pull the switch . . ." Quick cut to a closeup of a stove as the D.A.'s wife pulls a sizzling steak from the broiler. Effective black humor.

Perhaps best of all, "Shadow Play," like "Mirror Image" and a number of others, was an episode that could easily set a viewer's mind to thinking, to questioning the nature of reality. Or perhaps it should be put like this: Are you really reading this page, or is someone *dreaming* you reading this page?

"THE SILENCE" (4/28/61)

Franchot Tone and Jonathan Harris

Written by Rod Serling
Producer: Buck Houghton
Director: Boris Sagal
Director of Photography: George T. Clemens
Music: stock

Cast:
Col. Archie Taylor: Franchot Tone
Jamie Tennyson: Liam Sullivan
George Alfred: Jonathan Harris
Franklin: Cyril Delevanti
1st Man: Everett Glass
2nd Man: Felix Locher
3rd Man: John Holland

"The note that this man is carrying across a club room is in the form of a proposed wager, but it's the kind of wager that comes without precedent. It stands alone in the annals of bet-making as the strangest game of chance ever offered by one man to another. In just a moment, we'll see the terms of the wager and what young Mr. Tennyson does about it. And in the process, we'll witness all parties spin a wheel of chance in a very bizarre casino called the Twilight Zone."

Aristocratic Archie Taylor wants nothing more than to enjoy a little peace and quiet at his men's club, but this is made impossible by the incessant chatter of fellow member Jamie Tennyson. Filled with contempt, he offers Tennyson a wager: if Tennyson can remain silent for a year, he will pay him half a million dollars. In order to insure his unbroken silence, he will be housed in the club's basement. Hopelessly in debt, in love with a wife with expensive tastes, Tennyson reluctantly agrees. As the weeks roll by, it becomes clear that Tennyson is determined to win. Taylor offers him a thousand dollars to call off the bet. When this fails, he uses every dirty trick he can think of to get Tennyson to speak, including making insinuations that his wife is being unfaithful to him. Finally, the year is over. Tennyson emerges from the basement and puts out a hand for his winnings. A broken man, Taylor reveals that he lost his fortune years before, that he never had any intention of paying off the bet. Tennyson is clearly devastated by this news, but he enigmatically remains silent. The truth becomes horribly clear when he writes a note and hands it to Taylor. It reads: "I knew I would not be able to keep my part of the bargain, so one year ago I had the nerves to my vocal chords severed!"

"Mr. Jamie Tennyson, who almost won a bet, but who discovered somewhat belatedly that gambling can be a most unproductive pursuit, even with loaded dice, marked cards, or in his case some severed vocal chords. For somewhere beyond him a wheel was turned and his number came up black thirteen. If you don't believe it, ask the croupier, the very special one who handles roulette—in the Twilight Zone."

"The Silence" is a curiously atypical episode. It has no supernatural nor science-fictional elements, nor is there even the suggestion of any, as in "Where Is Everybody?" In every aspect, the story seems more suited to *Alfred Hitchcock Presents* than to *The Twilight Zone.*

Although it isn't credited, "The Silence" is almost certainly based on "The Bet," a short story by Anton Chekhov, in which a banker bets a young lawyer a huge sum of money that he will not be able to stay in solitary confinement for a period of fifteen years. Fifteen years pass during which the banker suffers numerous setbacks. If he pays the bet he will be ruined, so he determines to murder the lawyer in his sleep. Fortunately, over the years the lawyer has come to the conclusion that material goods are without value. To prove this, he decides to disappear just before the fifteenth year expires, thus forfeiting the bet and saving the banker—and himself, though he doesn't know it.

Appropriate or not, the story did present its share of challenges. The first headache went to George Clemens. The set where Sullivan was to be imprisoned was made up entirely of panes of glass! "When I saw the set, I pretty near lost my lunch," Clemens recalls. "How in the world am I going to get a light in there, and show light, without getting reflections?" But Buck Houghton had hired the right man, and Clemens persevered. "Once I started on the thing," he says, "I think I only had to take two panes of glass out in the whole picture."

The first day's shooting went just fine. The opening and closing scenes of the episode, both of which take place in the main room of the men's club, were completed. The company broke for the weekend. But the biggest problem was yet to come.

"On the second day of shooting, Franchot Tone didn't show up," Serling recalled years later. "And we waited and we waited. The call is six in the morning. When it got to be ten A.M. and everybody had been sitting there in their own smoke waiting and no Franchot Tone, we get his agent who tracks him down. He's in a clinic."

Stories differ. According to Liam Sullivan, Tone told him that he'd been at a party and, in attempting to pick a flower for his date off a bush on the terrace, had fallen down a hillside and landed on the driveway of the house next door. According to Serling, Tone had approached a girl in the parking lot of a restaurant and her boyfriend had taken offense and beaten him up. Whatever the truth, the result was still the same: half of Tone's face was scraped raw.

With one day's shooting in the can, recasting was out of the question. Serling: "I said, 'So be it. Come on in, Franch, and we'll shoot the other side of your face,' which we did."

The result was indeed odd. During the opening scene of the episode, we see Tone full face. When the scene changes to the glass cage in which Sullivan is imprisoned, we only see Tone's face in profile or with half of it obscured. Then in the final scene, we see Tone full-face again.

Surprisingly, the effect works to the episode's advantage. The scenes in the middle are those in which Tone tries to convince Sullivan to break his silence, using every dirty trick he can think of, including relaying ugly rumors about Sullivan's wife. Speaking out of the corner of his mouth, only half-turned toward Sullivan, Tone seems predatory and sly, what he says takes on an added suggestiveness. The impact was not lost. In fact, director Boris Sagal once recalled that at the time a number of critics complimented him on the effect!

"THE MIND AND THE MATTER" (5/12/61)

Shelley Berman

Written by Rod Serling
Producer: Buck Houghton
Director: Buzz Kulik
Director of Photography: George T. Clemens
Music: stock

Cast:
Archibald Beechcroft: Shelley Berman
Henry: Jack Grinnage
Rogers: Chet Stratton
Landlady: Jeane Wood

"A brief if frenetic introduction to Mr. Archibald Beechcroft, a child of the twentieth century, a product of the population explosion, and one of the inheritors of the legacy of progress . . . Mr. Beechcroft again. This time act two of his daily battle for survival. And in just a moment, our hero will begin his

personal one-man rebellion against the mechanics of his age, and to do so he will enlist certain aids available only in the Twilight Zone."

Beechcroft detests *people,* but he feels he has no alternative but to suffer the crowds and the noise—until an office boy, trying to make up for spilling coffee on his suit, gives him a book on mind power. After reading this, Beechcroft is convinced that concentration can do anything, and he proves it by making his landlady disappear, followed by everybody else in the world! The next day, he finds his office barren, quiet—and lonely. Suddenly, he gets a brainstorm: he'll repopulate the world with men and women who look, act, and sound exactly like *him.* But when he does this he finds to his dismay that these duplicates are relentlessly sour, snappish, and self-centered. "A lot of me is just as bad as a lot of them," he concedes. Perhaps a little more forgiving of the faults of others, he returns things to the way they were originally, determined never to play God again.

"Mr. Archibald Beechcroft, a child of the twentieth century, who has found out through trial and error—and mostly error—that with all its faults it may well be that this is the best of all possible worlds. People notwithstanding, it has much to offer. Tonight's case in point . . . in the Twilight Zone."

"The Mind and the Matter" is filled with any number of clever little gags, such as when Archibald Beechcroft (comedian Shelley Berman), after having made everyone else in the world disappear, arrives at his empty office and notices a ticking clock. "That'll be just about enough of *that,*" he says, at which point the clock immediately stops. Or when, out of boredom, he idly says, "Although if the truth be known, I would like a little diversion of some kind, any sort of diversion. . . . Like, um, like . . . an earthquake." Immediately, the office begins to shake violently. "For goodness sake!" cries Beechcroft in dismay. "No! No! Not that!" The quake subsides. "How about a nice little electrical storm?" The lights in the office dim. Outside, thunder and lightning do their damndest. "Forget it!" he says.

Bored and lonely, Beechcroft finally decides to repopulate the world—with himself. The results are bizarre and hilarious as Beechcroft has to contend with sour and obnoxious people who look and sound just like him. On the elevator, a woman (played by Berman) snaps at him, "Will you please get off my foot, you ugly little man?" Arriving at his office, Beechcroft scans his co-workers seated at their desks (in a seemingly continuous pan, technically superb): all are played by Berman.

"The noise, the miserable noise!" grouses the first. "I'll go out of my mind, I'll go out of my ever-lovin' mind!"

"A sty, that's what it is," says the second. "Nothing but people, and people are pigs."

"People, people, people, people!" comments the third. "Is there no respite? Is there no relief?"

"Herds, droves, hosts, and bevies of people," says the fourth.

"Will you people stop muttering back there?" snarls the fifth. "I'm trying to work!"

One effect which didn't quite come off was a sequence in which Beechcroft was to enter an elevator crammed with exact duplicates of himself. In the finished product, what we see is that with the exception of Shelley Berman as Beechcroft, all the rest are clearly actors in ill-fitting Shelley Berman masks. These were crafted by William Tuttle.

"The first batch he made just didn't seem to look like Shelley at all," says director Buzz Kulik. "And I'm not sure that they ever looked like Shelley. The problem is, when you do television you can't say, 'Let's wait another three or four weeks and take another shot at it.'"

"WILL THE REAL MARTIAN PLEASE STAND UP" (5/26/61)

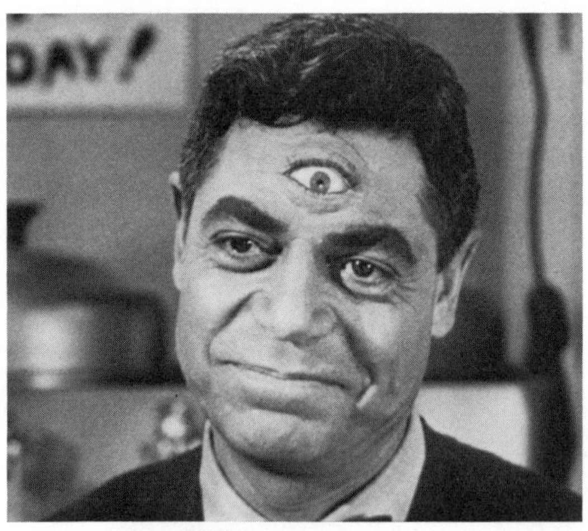
Barney Phillips

Written by Rod Serling
Producer: Buck Houghton
Director: Montgomery Pittman
Director of Photography: George T. Clemens
Music: stock
Makeup: William Tuttle

Cast:
Ross: John Hoyt
Haley: Barney Phillips
Avery: Jack Elam
Trooper Dan Perry: Morgan Jones
Trooper Bill Padgett: John Archer
Olmstead: Bill Kendis
Ethel McConnell: Jean Willes
Peter Kramer: Bill Erwin
Rose Kramer: Gertrude Flynn
George Prince: Ron Kipling
Connie Prince: Jill Ellis

"Wintry February night, the present. Order of events: a phone call from a frightened woman notating the arrival of an unidentified flying object, and the check-out you've just witnessed with two state troopers verifying the event, but with nothing more enlightening to add beyond evidence of some tracks leading across the highway to a diner. You've heard of trying to find a needle in a

haystack? Well, stay with us now and you'll be part of an investigating team whose mission is not to find that proverbial needle, no, their task is even harder. They've got to find a Martian in a diner, and in just a moment you'll search with them, because you've just landed in the Twilight Zone."

Troopers Perry and Padgett follow the tracks from a frozen pond in which something *may* have landed. In the diner they encounter a soda jerk, a bus driver and his seven passengers—all of whom seem perfectly human. Only problem is that the driver is certain only *six* people originally got on his bus. Someone is not what he seems. Two married couples are automatically eliminated from suspicion because there is only *one* extra person. That leaves three suspects: an edgy, middle-aged businessman impatient to make his meeting in Boston, an attractive "professional dancer" who has no identification, and a wild-eyed, eccentric old man. The troopers try to narrow it down even further but are hampered by a jukebox starting up, lights flickering on and off, and items on the tables flipping over—all seemingly of their own accord. A call comes from the county engineer. A decaying bridge has been declared safe; the bus can continue on its way. Reluctantly, the troopers give up the chase (". . . you can't hold somebody on suspicion of being a monster"). The passengers board the bus and depart, escorted by the troopers' patrol car. A little later, the businessman returns. The bridge *wasn't* safe; it collapsed and he alone survived. The phone call was merely an illusion. *He* is the Martian, advance scout of an invasion force. Smugly, he drinks a cup of coffee and smokes a cigarette, using all *three* of his arms. But the soda jerk has a surprise for him: he's a Venusian, and *his* invasion force has intercepted the Martian fleet. Grinning from ear to ear, he removes his cap, revealing a third eye. The real Martian has stood up—and had the rug pulled out from under him.

"Incident on a small island, to be believed or disbelieved. However, if a sour-faced dandy named Ross or a big, good-natured counterman who handles a spatula as if he'd been born with one in his mouth, if either of these two entities walks onto your premises, you'd better hold their hands—all three of them—or check the color of their eyes—all three of them. The gentlemen in question might try to pull you into . . . the Twilight Zone."

In a story precis written October 12, 1958, titled "The Night of the Big Rain," Serling laid down the basics of this story, with one big difference—the alien turns out to be a stray dog that the operator of the diner has adopted. In the intervening years, sanity must have prevailed, for when Serling wrote the script (originally titled "Nobody Here But Us Martians") he played fair with the audience and revealed one of the people in the diner as the Martian. This didn't stop him from putting in a twist, though, and having the fellow who runs the diner reveal himself as a Venusian!

Directed with style and humor by Montgomery Pittman, "Will the Real Martian Please Stand Up" is genuinely entertaining. Veteran character actor Jack Elam, made up as an old man, performs outrageously and wonderfully, spouting lines like, "She's just like a science fiction, that's what she is! A regular Ray Bradbury!" With his wild eyes and exaggerated movements, he seems every bit the Martian, which is exactly what he's supposed to seem. Actually, he's just a decoy.

In the end, we see how the Martian differs from an Earthling as he lights a cigarette and drinks a cup of coffee using three hands instead of two. The effect was easy to accomplish: someone crouched behind John Hoyt, reaching an arm around and under one of Hoyt's real arms. The arm was clothed in the same materials as Hoyt's arms and an overcoat was draped over Hoyt's shoulders to obscure the fact that the extra arm didn't originate from his body. With plenty of rehearsal to insure a fluidity of movement between the three hands, the illusion was complete—and perfect.

John Hoyt as the real Martian reveals his third arm

Not so successful was the way in which the Venusian (Barney Phillips) differed. In the end, he pushes back his soda jerk's hat to reveal a third eye. Unfortunately, it looked pretty much like one you might buy in a joke shop. It didn't come that easy, though. Barney Phillips reveals, "They had run a wire over my head concealed in my hair and one of the property men was concealed behind me, manipulating the trigger on the wire to effectuate the rolling of the eyeball in the socket. They had done a very big makeup job. They made a cast of the eye socket. I guess they must have spent well over a day working with me fitting that device prior to the actual shooting of the show."

Says Buck Houghton of the third eye, "We tried that two ways. We had the actor with an eye in his head, and we were also going to try it with a double exposure. But the double exposure didn't work at all because you could still see through it. And it wouldn't have allowed for hardly any movement, but we could have had it blink, which we couldn't do with the other one."

In spite of its failings, the third eye definitely had an impact. Says Barney Phillips, "Every time that that particular segment is televised, without exception, the next day I'm greeted by somebody, some total stranger along the way, who says, 'My God, where's the third eye?'"

"THE OBSOLETE MAN" (6/2/61)

Fritz Weaver

Written by Rod Serling
Producer: Buck Houghton
Director: Elliot Silverstein
Director of Photography: George T. Clemens
Music: stock

Cast:
Romney Wordsworth: Burgess Meredith
Chancellor: Fritz Weaver
Subaltern: Joseph Elic
Guard: Harry Fleer
1st Man: Barry Brooks
2nd Man: Harold Innocent
Woman: Jane Romeyn

"You walk into this room at your own risk, because it leads to the future, not a future that will be but one that might be. This is not a new world, it is simply an extension of what began in the old one. It has patterned itself after every dictator who has ever planted the ripping imprint of a boot on the pages of history since the beginning of time. It has refinements, technological advances,

and a more sophisticated approach to the destruction of human freedom. But like every one of the superstates that preceded it, it has one iron rule: logic is an enemy and truth is a menace. . . . This is Mr. Romney Wordsworth, in his last forty-eight hours on Earth. He's a citizen of the State but will soon have to be eliminated, because he's built out of flesh and because he has a mind. Mr. Romney Wordsworth, who will draw his last breaths in the Twilight Zone."

In this future society, all books have been banned, along with all religion. Wordsworth, a God-fearing librarian, is judged obsolete by a chancellor of the State and sentenced to be executed in a manner of his own choosing. He is granted three requests: that only his assassin know the method of his death, that he die at midnight the next day, and that he have an audience. Forty-five minutes before he is to die, he invites the Chancellor to his room and reveals that he has chosen to be killed by a bomb set to explode precisely at twelve. He then locks the door, trapping the Chancellor. A TV camera will broadcast all that transpires—and Wordsworth will prove which is stronger, the will of the State or that of the individual. At first, the Chancellor hides behind his bravado, but soon it becomes clear that no one is coming to save him. Wordsworth calmly reads from a forbidden Bible. The minutes tick by. Finally, the Chancellor cries out, "In the name of God, let me out!" Wordsworth hands him the key and the Chancellor bolts from the room—none too soon. The bomb explodes and Wordsworth is killed. But he has triumphed; when the Chancellor returns to his court, he finds he has been judged obsolete and replaced. Loyal members of the State surround him and tear him to pieces.

"The Chancellor—the late *Chancellor—was only partly correct. He* was *obsolete. But so was the State, the entity he worshipped. Any state, any entity, any ideology that fails to recognize the worth, the dignity, the rights of man, that state is obsolete. A case to be filed under 'M' for mankind . . . in the Twilight Zone."*

The final show of the second season was "The Obsolete Man," Serling's cautionary tale of a neo-Nazi super-state of the near future. Although it is well acted, Serling has stacked the deck *too* much, presenting the story in such black-and-white terms that there is no controversy. The viewer can sit at home smug and comfortable, certain that *he* would never be part of such a State.

These criticisms notwithstanding, "The Obsolete Man" is still a remarkable episode, thanks in large part to the contribution of director Elliot Silverstein. Silverstein had come from live theater, and later he would direct such films as *Cat Ballou* and *A Man Called Horse*. In this, the first of four *Twilight Zone* episodes he would direct, he imposes upon the proceedings his own unique theatricality. From the first, he made it clear what he wanted.

Says Silverstein, "It was vaguely reminiscent of some of the German films of the twenties, and there was a certain amount of expressionism in the style of the performances and the sets." Indeed, the major set of the piece, the room in which Meredith is judged, is quite unlike anything seen before on *The Twilight Zone*. The walls are completely covered with black velvet. There is a single, long, narrow table. At the end of it is an immensely tall, narrow lectern, behind which the Chancellor stands elevated and apart. The only other feature of the room is the door, which opens from the middle. Like the table and the lectern, it is long and narrow.

"That was very tough to do," says Silverstein, "because a door that high had never been built in television before. It was twenty-five feet, an enormously high thing. I had done some work like that in the theater before I came to Hollywood, so it was a very natural thing for me to just automatically adapt what I had already done and use it in this."

The people too are unusual. Starkly uniformed, they stand at attention on either side of the table, arms at their sides, their shapes mirroring the shapes of the table, the lectern and the door. The lighting is harsh, casting long, narrow shadows. The first words of the episode come from the subaltern (Joseph Elic). "*Words*worth. *Rom*ney. *Ob*solescence." A curiously harsh monotone, that Silverstein reveals was inspired by the sound of Joseph McCarthy's voice during the Army-McCarthy hearings.

One sequence of events which occurred during the making of "The Obsolete Man" has had repercussions that have extended far beyond *The Twilight Zone*. Silverstein explains: "There was a key scene and a key moment in the expressionistic sequence, when these two high, vertical doors open and Fritz Weaver comes in to be addressed and judged, and the place was ringed by automaton-like witnesses. Now, it was reminiscent, of course, both in structure and in my view of it, of Franz Kafka's *The Trial*. Vaguely reminiscent, not in the story but in the feeling.

"Sometime before this, I had a nightmare that involved sound, a group of people standing and looking at someone and just going, deep-throated, 'Aaahhhh . . .' and it would grow stronger in intensity and move very slowly up the chromatic scale as it grew in intensity, but it had to grow in intensity first. I tried to reproduce that sound with this chorus which surrounded Fritz Weaver. I wanted them to do absolutely nothing but stand there and start this deep-throated, growl-like 'Aaahhhh,' until it reached a pitch of volume that required something else to happen, like a cover on boiling water; until the water boils high enough, the cover won't move.

"So they started. 'Aaaahhh*hhhhhh* . . .' making their voices get lower rather than higher as they went louder, and they stared at him with a kind of insane fury. Then, when they could go neither lower nor louder, I had them start moving slowly forward, and as they reached him they leaped on him like a pack of mad dogs and dragged him along the table.

"The editor was working very well with me until we came to that moment. He showed me this rough assembly and he had them moving immediately, as soon as they started to growl. I said, 'No, no, you don't understand. You see, in the master shot I have them standing there.' He said, 'Well, so what?' I said, 'Well, that is how I staged the scene. I want them standing there until their voices reach a certain pitch. The master is a message to you and to everybody else.' He said, 'Well, I don't want to cut it that way.' I remember very clearly, I felt my temperature and my blood pressure go up. I said, 'You *what*?' 'I don't want to cut it that way. It's ridiculous.' I said, 'It's only ridiculous because you haven't done it before. I want it this way.' He said, 'I won't do it.'

"I went to Buck Houghton, who resolved it with a compromise. However, it *was* a compromise. It never did what I wanted it to do, which was to have everybody in the audience saying, 'Why aren't they moving? Why are they all just doing this strange thing?' And I wanted the sound of the voices on chorus to rise until the hackles rose on the back of your neck. So, the compromise was, I suppose, the best of what Buck could achieve in trying to be fair to an editor with whom he had to work again and a director who was being very adamant.

"I didn't forget that, and I felt that therein lay a reason why so many shows that I'd seen on television had seemed stamped out. There was no individual style.

"As a direct result of that very genuine anger, I called up Buzz Kulik and Lamont Johnson and all those guys, and we all got together. I told them what I just told you, and I said, 'Have you guys had similar experiences?' You should have heard the roar that Sunday morning! I said, 'Why aren't we doing something about it?' and we all agreed that we could. I said, 'Let's form a committee to assist the Guild to start taking positions with Management that will protect our rights as artists!' They all agreed, and that's begun a campaign that's still not ended."

Thanks to Silverstein's actions, significant changes have been made. "Today, that could never happen," he says. "If an editor said, 'I won't cut it that way,' he'd be fired right there on the spot, or if he weren't fired somebody else would be called in. He would just simply have to do it, there would be no question about it, none."

END OF YEAR TWO

For Serling, the spring of 1961 was like a replay of the previous year. Again there were the host of awards including another Hugo, and the 1961 Unity Award for Outstanding Contributions to Better Race Relations. Then in May, another Emmy, again for Outstanding Writing Achievement in Drama. In accepting, Serling held up the award and addressed the show's other writers, saying, "Come on over, fellas, and we'll carve it up like a turkey."

Serling wasn't the only *Twilight Zone* member to pick up an Emmy that year. George Clemens nabbed one for Outstanding Achievement in Cinematography for Television. No one could possibly have deserved the award more.

The spring of 1961 also found CBS toying for the first time with the idea of expanding *The Twilight Zone* from a half hour to an hour. True, just two years earlier the network had made Serling alter his concept of the series from an hour to a half hour, but now the network reasoned that a bigger *Twilight Zone* would attract a bigger audience. Ultimately, CBS decided not to lengthen *The Twilight Zone* during its third season. "Frankly, I'm glad of it," Serling said at the time. "We can keep that vignette approach . . ." Little did he know that less than a year later he, Beaumont and Matheson would be busy crafting hour-length scripts.

Thus *The Twilight Zone* survived its second year. So far, sixty-five episodes had been produced. The worst had been no less than entertaining and the best had been unforgettable. Soon, the quality of the show would begin to slip, but for now the series was at its peak, a peak which few television series before or after would attain.

THE THIRD SEASON: 1961–1962

Producer: Buck Houghton
Production Manager: Ralph W. Nelson
Director of Photography: George T. Clemens
Story Consultant: Richard McDonagh
Assistant Director: E. Darrell Hallenbeck
Casting: Stalmaster-Lister and Robert Walker
Art Directors: George W. Davis, Phil Barber and Merrill Pye
Editors: Jason H. Bernie and Bill Mosher
Makeup: Bob Keats
Special Effects: Virgil Beck
Camera Operators: Charles Wheeler and Jimmy King
Sound: Franklin Milton and Bill Edmondson
Theme Music: Marius Constant
Set Direction: H. Web Arrowsmith, Keogh Gleason and Henry Grace
Titles and Opticals: Pacific Title
Mr. Serling's Wardrobe: Eagle Clothes
Filmed at Metro–Goldwyn–Mayer

V / THE THIRD SEASON

"Next year, I'm going to do the commercials—
'In the Twilight Zone, nine out of ten doctors recommend you smoke . . .' They'll say I've really sold out."

—ROD SERLING

"I've never felt quite so drained of ideas as I do at this moment," Rod Serling said in April of 1961. "Stories used to bubble out of me so fast I couldn't set them down on paper quick enough—but in the last two years I've written forty-seven of the sixty-eight *Twilight Zone* scripts, and I've done thirteen of the first twenty-six for next season. I've written so much I'm woozy."

For Serling, fatigue was finally beginning to overcome his enthusiasm. "It's just more than you really should do," he said. "You can't retain quality. You start borrowing from yourself, making your own clichés. I notice that more and more."

Other of Serling's talents than writing were just being called into service, however. With the start of the third season, the American Tobacco Company replaced General Foods as a sponsor alternating every other week with Colgate-Palmolive. As a part of the deal, it was arranged that Serling would do a plug for the cigarette sponsor at the end of every show sponsored by American Tobacco. A typical plug went like this: "Very often, when you write for a living you run across blocks, moments when you can't think of the right thing to say. Now, happily, there are no blocks to get in the way of the full pleasure of Chesterfield. Great tobaccos make it a wonderful smoke. Try 'em, they satisfy."

"TWO" (9/15/61)

Elizabeth Montgomery

Written and Directed by
Montgomery Pittman
Producer: Buck Houghton
Director of Photography:
George T. Clemens
Music: Van Cleave

Cast:
Man: Charles Bronson
Woman: Elizabeth Montgomery
Stunt Double: Sharon Lucas

"This is a jungle, a monument built by nature honoring disuse, commemorating a few years of nature being left to its own devices. But it's another kind of jungle, the kind that comes in the aftermath of man's battles against himself. Hardly an important battle, not a Gettysburg or a Marne or an Iwo Jima. More like one insignificant corner patch in the crazy quilt of combat. But it was enough to end the existence of this little city. It's been five years since a human being walked these streets. This is the first day of the sixth year—as man used to measure time. The time: perhaps a hundred years from now. Or sooner. Or perhaps it's already happened two million years ago. The Place? The signposts are in English so that we may read them more easily, but the place—is the Twilight Zone."

While searching for food, a young woman wearing the tattered uniform of the invading army encounters an enemy soldier—one intent on declaring peace. Initially, she is violently distrustful of him—a situation which only intensifies when they remove two working rifles from a pair of skeletons. Later, though, when she admires a dress in a store window, he removes it and gives it to her. She goes into a recruiting office to slip it on. Unfortunately, the propaganda posters within rekindle the old hatreds; she rushes out and fires off several rounds at him. The next day, the man returns, dressed in ill-fitting civilian clothes. To his surprise, the woman is wearing the dress. Finally having put aside the war, she joins him and the two of them set off, side by side.

"This has been a love story, about two lonely people who found each other . . . in the Twilight Zone."

"Two," the third season opener, was both written and directed by Montgomery Pittman (1920–1964), a man whose talents in both departments were considerable. His first assignment on *The Twilight Zone* had been directing "Will the Real Martian Please Stand Up," but it was "Two" that demonstrated the full range of his abilities.

Born in Louisiana and raised in Oklahoma, Pittman had a wide variety of experiences before becoming a director. As a teenager, he joined a travelling medicine show with his older brother. Eventually, his travels took him to New York where he became an actor, associating with the likes of Marlon Brando and Steve Cochran. Arriving in California in 1949, he decided to forsake acting for writing. He wrote several films, including a script (uncredited) for Antonioni's *Il Grido.* In television, his credits included *Schlitz Playhouse of Stars,* where he met Buck Houghton. Finally, exasperated by the way in which his scripts had been mangled by incompetent directors, Pittman turned to directing in order to insure that his work would get from his brain to the screen with the least amount of muddle.

In "Two," Pittman gives us an optimistic tale set in an extremely bleak world. The time is presumably after World War III, the setting a devastated town inhabited only by the dead, with the exception of two enemy soldiers. It is fairly clear that Bronson represents an American soldier and Montgomery a Russian. In fact, her single line is *"Precrassny"*—Russian for "pretty." This is a gritty and realistic story of survival, told with a minimum of dialogue yet with the emphasis always on characterization.

Charles Bronson

"We shot it at the old Hal Roach Studio when it was standing," Houghton continues. "It had weeds in the street, theater marquee letters hanging sideways, and we didn't have to do hardly a thing to it. At MGM, we'd have had to put out our own weeds and tear up our own windows and everything. This was an old backlot street that was about to be torn down, plowed under."

In "Two," the characters go against the stereotype. It is Bronson, broad and muscular, with a face like an eroded cliff, who is the pacifist. Montgomery is the one who is suspicious and quick to violent action. Those who remember her from *Bewitched* might be shocked by her appearance here: long brown hair, smudged face, pretty in a peasantish way but not at all the glamour girl.

"Liz Montgomery, at the time, was so dedicated to her art," Montgomery Pittman's widow, Maurita, recalls. "Most girls want to look really pretty for the camera. Monty had to fight her, really, because she wanted to make her eyes *really* black. She got too much makeup on, she was making herself *too* haggard."

Montgomery's dedication to the role shows, and it was not an easy part by any means. "You find yourself reacting to things you never reacted to before," she said at the time. "You find it difficult not to exaggerate every look, every action. You think nobody will notice you unless you ham it up. You have to underplay every scene in a play of this type. But I must say I never enjoyed doing a show as much as I did 'Two.'"

"THE ARRIVAL" (9/22/61)

Harold J. Stone

Written by Rod Serling
Producer: Buck Houghton
Director: Boris Sagal
Director of Photography: George T. Clemens
Music: stock

Cast:
Grant Sheckly: Harold J. Stone
Paul Malloy: Fredd Wayne
Bengston: Noah Keen
Airline Official: Robert Karnes
Ramp Attendant: Bing Russell
Dispatcher: Jim Boles
Tower Operator: Robert Brubaker

"This object, should any of you have lived underground for the better part of your lives and never had occasion to look toward the sky, is an airplane, its

official designation a DC–3. We offer this rather obvious comment because this particular airplane, the one you're looking at, is a freak. Now, most airplanes take off and land as per scheduled. On rare occasions they crash. But all airplanes can be counted on doing one or the other. Now, yesterday morning this particular airplane ceased to be just a commercial carrier. As of its arrival it became an enigma, a seven-ton puzzle made out of aluminum, steel, wire and a few thousand other component parts, none of which add up to the right thing. In just a moment, we're going to show you the tail end of its history. We're going to give you ninety percent of the jigsaw pieces and you and Mr. Sheckly here of the Federal Aviation Agency will assume the problem of putting them together along with finding the missing pieces. This we offer as the evening's hobby, a little extracurricular diversion which is really the national pastime in the Twilight Zone."

The mystery begins when Flight 107 out of Buffalo lands and taxis to a perfect stop, with no luggage, no passengers, no crew—and no pilot! Sheckly, an FAA investigator with a record of no unsolved incidents in twenty-two years, inspects the plane, accompanied by Malloy and Bengston, two executives with the airline. Although the names on the passenger manifest seem familiar to Sheckly, none of their relatives has contacted anyone at the airport. Even stranger is the fact that each of the men sees the plane's seats a different color and its serial code a different sequence. Sheckly is convinced the plane is an illusion. To prove it, he sticks his hand into one of its spinning propellors. The plane immediately disappears—as do the men who are with him! Sheckly finds Malloy and Bengston in the airport's operations room, but neither of them has any memory of the mystery; Flight 107 arrived right on schedule. Then Bengston remembers: a Flight 107 out of Buffalo *did* disappear, it was lost in the fog and never found—seventeen years earlier! It was the one case Sheckly never solved . . . and it has come back to haunt him.

"Picture of a man with an Achilles' heel, a mystery that landed in his life and then turned into a heavy weight, dragged across the years to ultimately take the form of an illusion. Now, that's the clinical answer that they put on the tag as they take him away. But if you choose to think that the explanation has to do with an airborne Flying Dutchman, *a ghost ship on a fog-enshrouded night on a flight that never ends, then you're doing your business in an old stand . . . in the Twilight Zone."*

The first show of the new season written by Serling (although the second aired) was "The Arrival," which sets up a nifty mystery but then cops out by making the whole thing a hallucination on the part of the investigator. In reviewing it, *Variety* pointed out something inexplicable in the show's conclusion: ". . . how does the FAA investigator, in his hallucination, know the names and faces of actual people (the airline's operation chief and p.r. director) he has never seen before?" The mystery is never explained. *Variety* added, "The show now seems to be feeding off itself. . . . Last Friday's episode, unless it proves to be an exception in the new skein, doesn't augur well for the future of the series. *Twilight Zone* seems to be running dry of inspiration."

"THE GRAVE" (10/27/61)

Lee Marvin and Ellen Willard

Written and directed by Montgomery Pittman
Producer: Buck Houghton
Director of Photography: George T. Clemens
Music: stock

Cast:
Conny Miller: Lee Marvin
Mothershed: Strother Martin
Johnny Rob: James Best
Steinhart: Lee Van Cleef
Ira Broadly: Stafford Rep
Ione: Ellen Willard
Jasen: William Challee
Corcoran: Larry Johns
Pinto Sykes: Richard Geary

"Normally, the old man would be correct: this would be the end of the story. We've had the traditional shoot-out on the street and the badman will soon be dead. But some men of legend and folk tale have been known to continue having their way even after death. The outlaw and killer Pinto Sykes was such a person, and shortly we'll see how he introduces the town, and a man named Conny Miller in particular, to the Twilight Zone."

After Sykes is gunned down by a group of townspeople, Miller—a gunman hired by the town to track Sykes down but who never caught up with him, perhaps by choice—learns that on his deathbed Sykes vowed to reach up and grab Miller if he ever came near his grave. Johnny Rob and Steinhart bet Miller he won't have the courage to visit Sykes's grave. Determined to win the bet, Miller goes to the grave, kneels down, and plunges a knife into the earth to prove he was there. But as he rises, something grabs him and pulls him down. The next morning, Johnny Rob, Steinhart and several others find Miller dead beside the grave. What happened seems clear: the wind blew Miller's coat over the grave, in the dark he stuck his knife through it, when he tried to rise his coat pulled on him—and the shock killed him. But then Sykes's sister Ione raises a disquieting fact: the previous night the wind was blowing *away* from the grave!

"Final comment: you take this with a grain of salt or a shovelful of earth, as shadow or substance, we leave it up to you. And for any further research check under 'G' for 'ghost' in the Twilight Zone."

"The Grave," a spooky story of the Old West, is moody and genuine, with many fine character performances by the likes of James Best, Lee Van Cleef, Strother Martin, and Stafford Repp. The man in the starring role, however, did cause some problems.

"We had a guy who was a little too heavy on the bottle," director of photography George Clemens remembers. "We weren't going to use him between four and the night, so he spent the time over at a bar very close to MGM. When we started that night he was so rough on this horse—I knew it—he backed the horse right up to a picket fence and then both of them went through and I thought he was going to kill himself! He got out and wanted to work!

"So we had to call the night's work off. And I told Buck, I sez, 'Fire the son of a bitch! Just recast.' But they wouldn't go for it and we went on. Eventually, it ended up as a very fine picture. . . . This is him—Lee Marvin."

To leave the story at this point would be to do Marvin a disservice. "The next day he apologized to the crew," Buck Houghton recalls, "because, he said, 'Everybody was ready to work and I wasn't, and I'm terribly sorry, and you just watch me go today.' And by God, he put in a day's work that would knock your hat off."

"NOTHING IN THE DARK" (1/5/62)

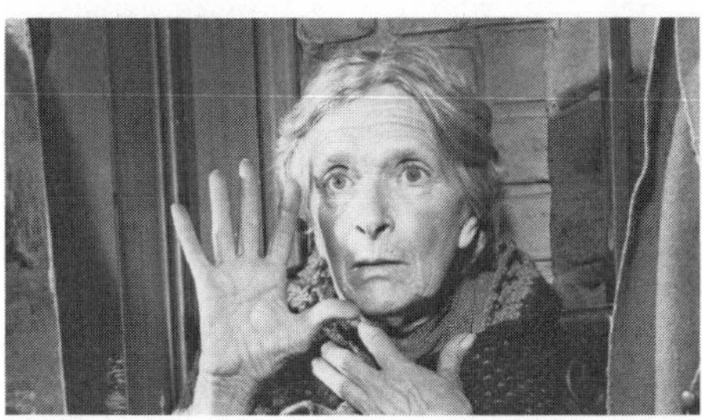
Gladys Cooper

Written by
George Clayton Johnson
Producer: Buck Houghton
Director: Lamont Johnson
Director of Photography:
George T. Clemens
Music: stock

Cast:
Wanda Dunn: Gladys Cooper
Harold Beldon: Robert Redford
Man: R. G. Armstrong

"An old woman living in a nightmare, an old woman who has fought a thousand battles with death and always won. Now she's faced with a grim decision—whether or not to open a door. And in some strange and frightening way she knows *that this seemingly ordinary door leads to the Twilight Zone."*

So terrified is elderly Wanda Dunn that "Mr. Death"—who can assume any number of disguises—will kill her with his touch that she has barricaded herself in her cold, dark tenement apartment for years. But when policeman Harold Beldon is shot just outside her door, she overcomes her fear and drags him inside. Later, a burly man breaks through her door. Wanda, thinking him Mr. Death, faints. Actually, he's merely a contractor hired to demolish the condemned building; he tells Wanda she must leave then he departs. Wanda realizes the contractor couldn't see Beldon—it is *Beldon* who is Mr. Death! But he has not come as a merciless destroyer. Gently, he bids her take his hand. She does—and is surprised to see her dead body across the room. No longer afraid, she allows Mr. Death to lead her outside . . . into the sunlight.

"There was an old woman who lived in a room and, like all of us, was frightened of the dark, but who discovered in the minute last fragment of her life that there was nothing in the dark that wasn't there when the lights were on. Object lesson for the more frightened amongst us—in or out of The Twilight Zone."

George Clayton Johnson's "Nothing in the Dark," is thematically similar, although superior to, Serling's "One for the Angels," and is also related to "The Hitch-hiker." Once again, Mr. Death makes an appearance.

For this episode, Buck Houghton hired a director with whom he had not worked before. Lamont Johnson (no relation to George Clayton Johnson) had previously been an actor (performing Tarzan's voice on the radio) and a stage director. In the years since *The Twilight Zone,* he has made a name for himself directing both feature films *(One on One, Lipstick)* and movies for television *(My Sweet Charlie, That Certain Summer, The Execution of Private Slovik, Fear on Trial).* "The whole mystique of *The Twilight Zone* appealed to me as a tremendous, drenching relief from the *Dr. Kildare*s and *Have Gun Will Travel*s and things that I was doing," he says. "These were wonderfully theatrical games for me, and it was a joy to do them."

For the lead in "Nothing in the Dark," Johnson recruited an actress he had directed on the stage. Gladys Cooper, a reigning beauty on the London stage in World War I, had come to America and played such roles as Joan Fontaine's sister-in-law in *Rebecca*, Bette Davis's mother in *Now Voyager,* and Rex Harrison's mother in *My Fair Lady.* "I insisted on Gladys for the role," says Lamont Johnson. "She was a great lady of the theater, and she had an elegant, polished London Mayfair kind of speech, but it seemed incongruous for that character, who's a sort of an Apple Mary character. Everybody said, 'Oh, she's such a great elegant *lady,* how could she possibly . . . ?' I said, 'She can do it.' And I talked to her, and she thought it was a terrific idea."

Gladys Cooper agreed with Lamont Johnson that her normal accent wouldn't fit this character. "So she tried various accents for me," recalls Johnson, "one a kind of North Country, which was still too fanciful, and then she had a nice kind of nasal, low London quality that was just a bit common and slightly whiney, which was just right."

George Clayton Johnson at first found this a dubious improvement. "When I heard her first talking with the cockney accent, I didn't think it would work. I thought she should play it with her own voice, an old woman's voice. But she said, 'No, no.' She started to do this strange British accent—and I fell right into believing it."

As Wanda, Gladys Cooper plays her part with a frailty that is real and immediate. Clearly, this is a character who is living solely by the strength of her determination *not* to die.

Another strong addition to the cast is R. G. Armstrong as the man contracted to demolish the tenement in which Wanda lives. Brutal and violent—although not by intention—it's *he* we at first mistake for Mr. Death. Soon, this misconception is dispelled. Nevertheless, it is he who mouths, by proxy, a defense of Mr. Death's actions (although, to him, he is merely defending his *own* job): "People get the idea that I'm some kind of destroyer, they think I get kicks out of tearing stuff down. That ain't the way it is. I just clear the ground so that other people can build. In a way, I help them do it. Look around, it's the way things are. A big tree falls and new ones grow out of the same ground. Old animals die and young ones take their places. Even people step aside when it's time."

What Johnson is getting at in his script is the notion that death, rather than being something frightening, is simply part of the natural process. Mr. Death turns out not to be the hard, uncaring construction man, but rather the sympathetic and angelic-looking cop. And when he finally does touch the old woman, her death comes so gently that at first she is unaware of it. "You see?" says Mr. Death. "No shock. No engulfment. No tearing asunder. What you feared would come like an explosion is like a whisper. What you thought was the end is the beginning."

If there is anything that mars the eloquence of "Nothing in the Dark," it is the presence of Robert Redford, who performs with all the emotion of a male mannequin—which he strongly resembles. Ironically, one of the lines he delivers, in a leaden monotone, is, "Am I really so bad?"

"He was very new," says Lamont Johnson. "I saw him on *Playhouse 90* in a one-scene part with Charles Laughton [in Serling's "In the Presence of Mine Enemies"], and I thought he was amazing. I mean, I thought he was amazing *looking*. I thought if you had somebody who had those kind of blazing eyes and that candor and that kind of American Beauty about him, he'd be great for this cop as I was reading it."

"Nothing in the Dark" is too well-written to be overwhelmed by one weak performance. It remains a thoughtful and moving statement on old age and the fear of death.

For all her involvement in the show, for all she gave to it, Gladys Cooper did not see the episode until a year later, when she was filming "Passage on the *Lady Anne*." John Conwell, then assistant to the producer: "I ran it for

Mr. Death, Robert Redford

her after we were through shooting that day. She didn't even relate to it as herself. She kept saying, 'Oh, look at that woman, look at that old lady.' She was very moved by it, but it was like she was not watching herself at all."

"IT'S A GOOD LIFE" (11/3/61)

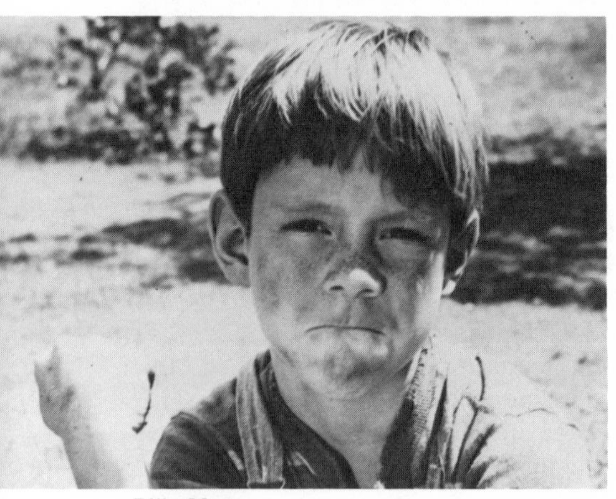

Billy Mumy

Written by Rod Serling
Based on the short story "It's a *Good* Life" by Jerome Bixby
Producer: Buck Houghton
Director: James Sheldon
Director of Photography: George T. Clemens
Music: stock

Cast:
Anthony Fremont: Billy Mumy
Mr. Fremont: John Larch
Mrs. Fremont: Cloris Leachman
Aunt Amy: Alice Frost
Dan Hollis: Don Keefer
Ethel Hollis: Jeanne Bates
Pat Riley: Casey Adams
Bill Soames: Tom Hatcher
Thelma Dunn: Lenore Kingston

"Tonight's story on The Twilight Zone *is somewhat unique and calls for a different kind of introduction. This, as you may recognize, is a map of the United States, and there's a little town there called Peaksville. On a given morning not too long ago, the rest of the world disappeared and Peaksville was left all alone. Its inhabitants were never sure whether the world was destroyed and only Peaksville left untouched or whether the village had somehow been taken away. They were, on the other hand, sure of one thing: the cause. A monster had arrived in the village. Just by using his mind, he took away the automobiles, the electricity, the machines—because they displeased him—and he moved an entire community back into the dark ages—just by using his mind. Now I'd like to introduce you to some of the people in Peaksville, Ohio. This is Mr. Fremont. It's in his farmhouse that the monster resides. This is* Mrs. *Fremont. And this is Aunt Amy, who probably had more control over the monster in the beginning than almost anyone. But one day she forgot; she began to sing aloud. Now, the monster doesn't like singing, so his mind snapped at her, turned her into the smiling, vacant thing you're looking at now. She sings no more. And you'll note that the people in Peaksville, Ohio, have to smile; they have to think happy thoughts and say happy things because, once displeased, the monster can wish them into a cornfield or change them into a grotesque,*

walking horror. This particular monster can read minds, you see. He knows every thought, he can feel every emotion. Oh yes, I did forget something, didn't I? I forgot to introduce you to the monster. This *is the monster. His name is Anthony Fremont. He's six years old, with a cute little-boy face and blue, guileless eyes. But when those eyes look at you, you'd better start thinking happy thoughts, because the mind behind them is absolutely in charge. This is the Twilight Zone."*

During a surprise party at the Fremont house, Dan Hollis receives a present of a Perry Como record—but he can't play it in front of Anthony for fear of what might happen. Resentful, he begins to drink heavily then breaks into song. The other adults are aghast as Anthony's attention turns on him. Frantically, Hollis pleads with the others to kill Anthony while he is distracted. However, none of them can summon the courage to act; Anthony turns Hollis into a huge jack-in-the-box, then dispatches the body to the cornfield. In the shocked moments that follow, Anthony causes snow to fall outside—something that will kill off half the crops. "But it's good that you're making it snow, Anthony, it's real good," says his father, with fear and a touch of hysteria, "And tomorrow—tomorrow's gonna be a *real good day*!"

"No comment here, no comment at all. We only wanted to introduce you to one of our very special citizens, little Anthony Fremont, who lives in a place called Peaksville in a place that used to be Ohio. And if by some strange chance you should run across him, you had best think only good thoughts. Anything less than that is handled at your own risk, because if you do meet Anthony you can be sure of one thing: you have entered the Twilight Zone."

The first Serling script to be produced this season was an adaptation of Jerome Bixby's classic short story, "It's a *Good* Life," which originally appeared in 1953 and was reprinted in *Science Fiction Hall of Fame* (Doubleday, 1971). Telling the story of a monstrous, conscienceless child with enormous powers and no restraints, it is truly a horrifying story.

"At this late date, I don't remember how the idea for 'It's a *Good* Life' came to me," says Jerome Bixby. "I wrote it over a weekend in 1953, with no sleep Saturday night.

"Oddly, Serling did the screenplay, *then* bought the rights to the story a few days later."

In adapting the story, Serling made a number of minor changes, but retained the essentials. The script is very well written, but the major accolades for the success of this show must go to director James Sheldon and to an extraordinary cast. The actors playing the townspeople of

Peaksville all seem as one, so uniform is the manner in which they present themselves: pleasantly bland on the surface, with a nervousness bordering on hysteria underneath. The impression given is that we are peeking into an ongoing reality, that these people are all acting in this narrow, constricting way because it is the only way they *can* act in order to survive.

Then there is Anthony himself. In the story, he is not described, save for the fact that he has a "wet, purple gaze." Something more specific than that would be needed for television. Departing from the story, James Sheldon cast Billy Mumy, depicting Anthony as an attractive child whose looks belie his actions. Whenever he was supposed to be doing something awful, Sheldon directed Mumy to make his eyes big and to stare unblinkingly. Says Sheldon, "Billy just loved doing that stuff with his eyes."

"Well, I had big eyes," says Mumy. "My face has kinda grown into my eyes a little bit, but you use what you've got. And it's *fun* to look scary when you're a kid."

"It's a Good Life" made a tremendous impression on Mumy. "I've always liked Anthony, and I've kept Anthony with me. I'll send people to the cornfield when I'm really pissed at them. I mean, I'll *do* it. Not that it works, but it's a release for me."

Buck Houghton recalls "It's a Good Life" with fondness. "It seemed to have caught on in a lot of ways. Around the set, when somebody would goof, people would say, 'Well, that's a good thing you did,' which they would always say to Billy Mumy when he killed a cow or whatnot—'That's a good thing you did.'"

"THE SHELTER" (9/29/61)

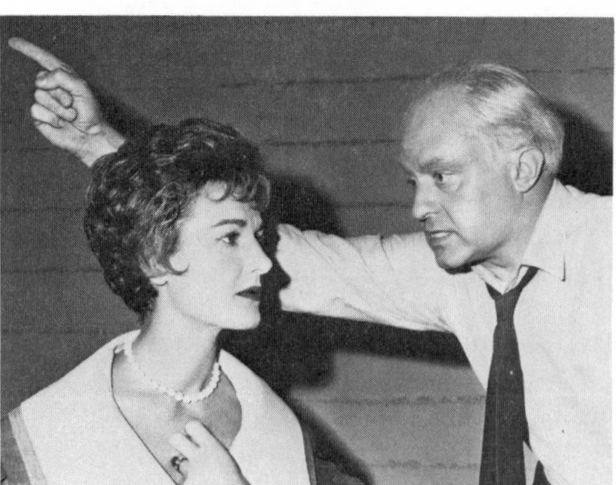

Peggy Stewart and Larry Gates

Written by Rod Serling
Producer: Buck Houghton
Director: Lamont Johnson
Director of Photography: George T. Clemens
Music: stock

Cast:
Dr. Stockton: Larry Gates
Jerry Harlowe: Jack Albertson
Marty Weiss: Joseph Bernard
Henderson: Sandy Kenyon
Man: John McLiam
Grace Stockton: Peggy Stewart
Paul Stockton: Michael Burns
Mrs. Harlowe: Jo Helton
Mrs. Weiss: Moria Turner
Mrs. Henderson: Mary Gregory

"What you are about to watch is a nightmare. It is not meant to be prophetic, it need not happen, it's the fervent and urgent prayer of all men of good will that it never shall happen. But in this place, in this moment, it does *happen. This is the Twilight Zone."*

On the evening of a surprise party for kindly, middle-aged Doc Stockton, the radio announces that radar has detected UFOs heading due southeast and that citizens are urged to go to their shelters. Doc promptly locks himself, his wife, and their twelve-year-old son inside the shelter he has built in his basement. His neighbors are unprepared, however; they beg Doc to let them and their families share the shelter. He refuses; there's only air and provisions for three. As the neighbors argue what to do, their bigotry and violence rise to the surface. Finally, they obtain a large length of pipe and use it to batter down the shelter door. Just then, the radio announces that the UFOs have been identified as harmless satellites. The neighbors, ashamed of their behavior, apologize for the damage they've done. But Doc is not mollified; he knows that though the missile alarm was a false one, the experience has destroyed them all.

"No moral, no message, no prophetic tract, just a simple statement of fact: for civilization to survive, the human race has to remain civilized. Tonight's very small exercise in logic from the Twilight Zone."

The plot of "The Shelter" is simple. Unfortunately, in making his point—which is that everyone is rotten in a crisis—Serling did not pay enough attention to logic and characterization. The people are clearly cardboard cutouts being moved around as the story dictates. One character (Joseph Bernard) violently objects to battering down the door of the shelter in order to get in, yet a moment later he is one of those manning the battering ram. This clearly is not a logical dramatic progression, but rather a too-obvious and heavy-handed manipulation by the writer.

"That was Rod in one of his messianic moods," says Lamont Johnson, the episode's director. "It was too uptight with its own self-righteousness, I think. I found it an interesting idea, I think the thesis was excellent, but I think its devices and its general style of writing were a little too pompous."

"DEATHS-HEAD REVISITED" (11/10/61)

Oscar Beregi

Written by Rod Serling
Producer: Buck Houghton
Director: Don Medford
Director of Photography: Jack Swain
Music: stock

Cast:
Becker: Joseph Schildkraut
Capt. Lutze: Oscar Beregi
Innkeeper: Karen Verne
Doctor: Ben Wright
Taxi Driver: Robert Boone
Dachau Victim: Chuck Fox

"Mr. Schmidt, recently arrived in a small Bavarian village which lies eight miles northwest of Munich, a picturesque, delightful little spot onetime known for its scenery but more recently related to other events having to do with some of the less positive pursuits of man: human slaughter, torture, misery and anguish. Mr. Schmidt, as we will soon perceive, has a vested interest in the ruins of a concentration camp—for once, some seventeen years ago, his name was Gunther Lutze. He held the rank of a captain in the S.S. He was a black-uniformed, strutting animal whose function in life was to give pain, and like his colleagues of the time he shared the one affliction most common amongst that breed known as nazis: he walked the Earth without a heart. And now former S.S. Captain Lutze will revisit his old haunts, satisfied perhaps that all that is awaiting him in the ruins on the hill is an element of nostalgia. What he does not know, of course, is that a place like Dachau cannot exist only in Bavaria. By its nature, by its very nature, it must be one of the populated areas of the Twilight Zone."

Reminiscing happily within the ruins of the concentration camp, Lutze comes upon Becker, a former inmate whom he takes for a caretaker. Becker, however, is actually a ghost, and he and the camp's other dead victims have risen up to judge Lutze and mete out justice. Following a trial in one of the barracks, Lutze is forced to experience the physical agonies of his victims—something that renders him permanently insane. Later, a doctor who examines him wonders what could have turned Lutze into a raving maniac in only two hours. Then he looks around him at the camp and is filled with an angry passion. "*Dachau,*" he says. "*. . . Why do we keep it standing?*"

"There is an answer to the doctor's question. All the Dachaus must remain standing. The Dachaus, the Belsens, the Buchenwalds, the Auschwitzes—all

of them. They must remain standing because they are a monument to a moment in time when some men decided to turn the Earth into a graveyard. Into it they shoveled all of their reason, their logic, their knowledge, but worst of all, their conscience. And the moment we forget this, the moment we cease to be haunted by its remembrance, then we become the gravediggers. Something to dwell on and remember, not only in the Twilight Zone but wherever men walk God's Earth."

In "Deaths-head Revisited," Serling's preachment fits the subject perfectly. This is an impressive episode in every way, including the set which doubles for Dachau. Buck Houghton explains, "CBS had made a pilot for a western, and they had built a four-sided frontier fort. It was a hundred-fifty or two-hundred-thousand-dollar set to pilot this western, and it was standing out on Lot 3 at MGM. We just had to downgrade it, it was nice and fresh, so we had to take some doors off the hinges and put some dust around and that sort of thing. As I recall, the look of it was quite splendid."

The ghosts of Dachau

As effective as the set, certainly, is Oscar Beregi as former S.S. Captain Lutze. In "The Rip Van Winkle Caper" he was saddled with a mediocre part. Here, he has a role with some meat on it, and he presents us with a complex and complete character: assured, cruel, callous, egocentric—but never so broad as to seem outlandish.

Then there is Joseph Schildkraut as Becker, the "caretaker" of Dachau, who turns out to be the ghost of an inmate. The man who played Dreyfus in *The Life of Emile Zola* (for which he won an Oscar) and Anne Frank's father in *The Diary of Anne Frank* here has the difficult role of playing a symbol, Serling's spokesman for all those killed in the concentration camps. A supremely professional actor, Schildkraut not only achieves this but manages to transcend the role, making the character both a symbol and an individual. As Becker, he is eloquent, wise, and infinitely sad. With his cultured European accent, he delivers speeches which could easily seem pompous, but which in his skilled hands seem the untainted Voice of Truth. The memories his words recall are not pleasant, but they are potent. "Ten million human beings were tortured to death in camps like this," he tells Capt. Lutze. "Men. Woman. Children. Infants. Tired old men. You burned them in furnaces. You shovelled them into the earth. You tore up their bodies in *rage*. And now you come back to your scenes of horror, *and you wonder that the misery that you planted has lived after you*?"

Beyond the words, "Deaths-head Revisited" has an energy to it, a power in its images and in its actions, thanks both to Serling and to director Don Medford. Repeatedly, there are shots that are disorienting, surprising, and powerful. For example, Schildkraut and Beregi are outside the barracks. Beregi runs past Schildkraut toward the camera, screaming in anger, until his bulk fills the screen, blacking out everything. Cut to Beregi's back as he runs away from the camera, still howling. But we see he is now inside one of the barracks, running toward an open door, which shuts just as he reaches it. He falls backward. Cut to his point of view, as we see, upside down, the faces of the dead inmates looking at him, judging him. The camera rotates so that now the faces are right side up. In another instance, Beregi, still inside, lunges with both hands for Schildkraut's throat. Cut to exterior as Beregi completes the movement, but instead of Schildkraut's throat, his hands grasp the post of a gallows.

"Don is very good with action things, startling things," says Buck Houghton. "He has a need for explosion of some sort. I was afraid that 'Deaths-head Revisited' was going to get a little talky. There were opportunities for people to appear in a way that would startle you, and there were all sort of confrontations that I thought could profit by a director whose taste was for violent action. And I think he delivered it. I think he did very well in that."

"YOUNG MAN'S FANCY" (5/11/64)

Rickey Kelman and Helen Brown

Written by Richard Matheson
Producer: Buck Houghton
Director: John Brahm
Director of Photography: George T. Clemens
Music: Nathan Scott

Cast:
Virginia: Phyllis Thaxter
Alex: Alex Nicol
Mr. Wilkinson: Wallace Rooney
Mother: Helen Brown
Alex (age 10): Rickey Kelman

"You're looking at the house of the late Mrs. Henrietta Walker. This is Mrs. Walker herself, as she appeared twenty-five years ago. And this, *except for isolated objects, is the living room of Mrs. Walker's house, as it appeared in that same year. The other rooms upstairs and down are much the same. The time, however, is not twenty-five years ago but* now. *The house of the late Henrietta Walker is, you see, a house which belongs almost entirely to the past, a house which, like Mrs. Walker's clock here, has ceased to recognize the passage of time. Only one element is missing now, one remaining item in the estate of the late Mrs. Walker: her son Alex, thirty-four years of age and, up till twenty minutes ago, the so-called 'perennial bachelor.' With him is his bride, the former Miss Virginia Lane. They're returning from the city hall in order to get Mr. Walker's clothes packed, make final arrangements for the sale of the house, lock it up and depart on their honeymoon. Not a complicated set of tasks, it would appear, and yet the newlywed Mrs. Walker is about to discover that the old adage 'You can't go home again' has little meaning in the Twilight Zone."*

Arriving at the house, Alex is overwhelmed with nostalgia for his boyhood. Virginia suspects the spirit of Alex's mother is exerting her influence, a suspicion supported by an old, supposedly-broken radio playing the woman's favorite song, a broken clock ticking, and the reappearance of long-gone furniture, appliances, magazines and home-made fudge. The allure of the past grows stronger: Alex refuses to sell the house. Then Alex's mother appears on the stairs and confronts Virginia. But it is not *her* wish to return to the past—it is Alex's. Alex changes back into a boy again, then tells Virginia to get out. She does—filled with a mixture of disgust, horror and loss.

"Exit Miss Virginia Lane, formerly and most briefly Mrs. Alex Walker. She has just given up a battle and in a strange way retreated, but this has been a

retreat back to reality. Her opponent, Alex Walker, will now and forever hold a line that exists in the past. He has put a claim on a moment in time and is not about to relinquish it. Such things do *happen—in the Twilight Zone."*

Richard Matheson's story is an interesting one, but somehow "Young Man's Fancy" never really hits the mark.

"The ending, I hated," says Matheson. "It was the way I wrote it, the story being that the boy was causing it, not the mother. It's just that the mother didn't look menacing, she just looked a little worn out, like Stella Dallas or something. It didn't have the impact it should have had. She should have been kind of horrifying, so that when Phyllis Thaxter started to tell her off you thought that there was a confrontation here like in *The Uninvited*. But there wasn't that feeling to it. And then the little boy came out and he wasn't very good either, which kind of blew the whole point of the show."

"FIVE CHARACTERS IN SEARCH OF AN EXIT" (12/22/61)

Susan Harrison, Kelton Garwood and Clark Allen

Written by Rod Serling
Based on the short story "The Depository" by Marvin Petal
Producer: Buck Houghton
Director: Lamont Johnson
Director of Photography: George T. Clemens
Music: stock
Makeup: William Tuttle

Cast:
The Major: William Windom
The Clown: Murray Matheson
The Ballerina: Susan Harrison
The Tramp: Kelton Garwood
The Bagpipe Player: Clark Allen
Little Girl: Mona Houghton
Woman: Carol Hill

"Clown, hobo, ballet dancer, bagpiper, and an army major—a collection of question marks. Five improbable entities stuck together into a pit of darkness. No logic, no reason, no explanation; just a prolonged nightmare in which fear, loneliness and the unexplainable walk hand in hand through the shadows. In a moment we'll start collecting clues as to the whys, the whats and the wheres. We will not end the nightmare, we'll only explain it—because this is the Twilight Zone."

The five characters find themselves trapped inside an enormous, featureless cylinder, with no memory of who they are nor how they got there. After various speculations on the nature of their imprisonment—including the theory that they might be in Hell—the Major hits on a plan of escape. With the other four forming a human ladder, he is ultimately able to reach the rim of the cylinder and climb over. Unfortunately, he loses his balance and falls into the snow far below. The truth is revealed: the five characters are actually nothing more than dolls; their prison a Christmas toy donation barrel. A little girl spies the Major and returns him to the barrel.

"Just a barrel, a dark depository where are kept the counterfeit, make-believe pieces of plaster and cloth, wrought in the distorted image of human life. But this added, hopeful note: perhaps they are unloved only for the moment. In the arms of children there can be nothing but *love. A clown, a tramp, a bagpipe player, a ballet dancer and a major. Tonight's cast of players on the odd stage known as the Twilight Zone."*

Rarely can the plot of an episode be summed up so completely in its title. "Five Characters in Search of an Exit" is a drama with the fewest possible of props. For most of the show, the five actors are all that can be seen, with the exception of the blank, curving wall of the cylinder.

"It was like a theater experience," says director Lamont Johnson, "like working on a unit set in the theater, and I've done a lot of theater so it didn't hold any particular problems for me."

As for the odd cylinder, Johnson says, "The barrel was two different sets. One was vertical, the other was horizontal or at an angle so that we could cant it and make it at whatever angle we felt we needed for the camera." Thus, when the characters stood on each other's shoulders, the set was actually tilted at a forty-five-degree angle, with a mattress at the bottom just in case anyone should accidentally slide down. As to what the set was made of, director of photography George Clemens says, "It was a round aluminum set that we just kept moving around. And I could not use direct lighting, I used what we call indirect lighting, reflected. I had a great big sheet that was treated so as to reflect light."

The greatest enjoyment from "Five Characters in Search of an Exit" stems from the dialogue between the ultra-serious, prone-to-hysteria Army Major and the ridiculous, ever-facetious, and utterly charming clown. In his white clown face, with potted plant for a hat, Murray Matheson is delightful, doing somersaults and fatalistically refusing to ever take matters too seriously. "I was upside-down for most of the time," Matheson recalls, "but I started as a dancer on the stage and so that part of it was easy for me."

As the Major, William Windom provides a perfect counterpoint to Matheson, loud, belligerent, impatient. Of the part, Windom says, "I just poured on the coal. You try to make it undoll-like as long as you can, which isn't hard to do, because they're all sort of strange people."

The people weren't the only strange thing—the dolls were, too. As the camera pans from doll to doll at the end of the episode, we see that the figures are clearly *not* the actors in makeup, yet their faces bear a marked resemblance to the actors. One would assume that tiny replicas were fashioned, but in reality, these figures were actually life-size copies of the actors. With each of them, a life mask was made, then painted to look like a doll. Says makeup artist William Tuttle, "They sent out and got some mannequin bodies, so that we just did the heads. Charlie Schram did most of them."

For Buck Houghton, "Five Characters in Search of an Exit" held special anxieties; the little girl who places the army-major doll back in the barrel at the end of the episode was played by his daughter Mona. "She was terribly nervous about the whole thing," he recalls, "and she was a very active child in the first place, she spent her days in motion. So I just took her out and walked her around the backlot until she was so goddamn tired that she couldn't be nervous. I must have walked her three miles."

"TO SERVE MAN" (3/2/62)

Richard Kiel

Written by Rod Serling
Based on the short story "To Serve Man" by Damon Knight
Producer: Buck Houghton
Director: Richard L. Bare
Director of Photography: George T. Clemens
Music: stock

Cast:
Chambers: Lloyd Bochner
Kanamit: Richard Kiel
Pat: Susan Cummings
Citizen Gregori: Theodore Marcuse
Reporter #1: Will J. White
Reporter #2: Gene Benton
Colonel #1: Bartlett Robinson
Colonel #2: Carlton Young
Secy. General: Hardie Albright
Senor Valdes: Robert Tafur
M. Leveque: Lomax Study
Scientist: Nelson Olmstead
Man #1: Charles Tannen
Man #2: James L. Wellman
Woman #1: Adrienne Marden
Woman #2: Jeanne Evans

"Respectfully submitted for your perusal—a Kanamit. Height: a little over nine feet. Weight: in the neighborhood of three hundred and fifty pounds. Origin: unknown. Motives? Therein hangs the tale, for in just a moment we're going to ask you to shake hands, figuratively, with a Christopher Columbus from another galaxy and another time. This is the Twilight Zone."

The Kanamits arrive on Earth with seemingly one purpose in mind: to aid mankind in every possible way using their superior technology. They end famine, supply a cheap power source and provide defensive force fields. Armies become obsolete. Although some distrust them, the Kanamits appear totally altruistic, a fact supported by a Kanamit book left at the U.N. Once translated, the title reads *To Serve Man.* Thousands book passage to the Kanamits' home planet, including Michael Chambers, a U.S. decoding expert. Meanwhile, however, his assistant Pat is trying to translate the Kanamit book's text. As Chambers prepares to board ship, Pat frantically rushes up. She's succeeded in her attempts—*To Serve Man* is a cookbook! Chambers tries to escape, but a Kanamit forces him into the ship, which then blasts off. Helplessly, Chambers finds himself bound for another planet—and some alien's dinner table!

"The recollections of one Michael Chambers, with appropriate flashbacks and soliloquy. Or more simply stated, the evolution of man, the cycle of going from dust to dessert, the metamorphosis from being the ruler of a planet to an ingredient in someone's soup. It's tonight's bill of fare on the Twilight Zone."

Adapted by Serling from the short story of the same name by Damon Knight (which is included in *The Best of Damon Knight* [Pocket Books, 1976]), "To Serve Man" has one of the most shocking punchlines of any episode.

Damon Knight: " 'To Serve Man' was written in 1950, when I was living in Greenwich Village and my unhappy first marriage was breaking up. I wrote it in one afternoon, while my wife was out with another man."

Serling kept the basics of Knight's story, but made some changes, the first of which was in the aliens themselves. In the story, the Kanamit (singular: Kanama) look "something like pigs and something like people." In his script, Serling made them nine feet tall and essentially humanoid, noting, "At the moment, no one knows whether we *cast* this part, or make it!" As they appear in the show, the Kanamits (singular: Kanamit) resemble angels gone to seed, with full-length robes, high-domed heads, and just a hint of corruption about the eyes and mouth. The effect is striking, with seven-foot-two Richard Kiel (later to play the character "Jaws" in several James Bond films) playing the various Kanamits.

Damon Knight found this all to his liking. "I thought the adaptation was kind of neat—it made me famous in Milford, Pennsylvania; suddenly everybody knew who I was. I didn't mind the aliens being acromegalic giants, because I knew they couldn't film my pig-people without making it look like a Disney film. The only thing that bugged me was Serling's treating the alien language as if it were just another kind of code."

In Knight's original story, a friend of the narrator's, both of whom are U.N. translators at the beginning of the story, manages to steal a Kanamit book. Using material from Kanamit bulletin boards and an extremely limited English-Kanamit dictionary issued by the aliens to the human staff members at the Kanamit Embassy, the two are able to translate the title of the book into *How to Serve Man*. The narrator goes off to a vacation in Canada. He returns to find that his friend has decoded the first paragraph of the book and discovered, of course, that it's a cookbook.

For some reason, Serling decided to change this. In the show, the Kanamit deliberately leaves the book at the U.N. A staff of cryptographers led by Lloyd Bochner attempts to decipher the alien language as though it were some secret code, which is utterly ludicrous. Without some sort of interplanetary Rosetta stone, deciphering an unknown language would be impossible.

This isn't to say that Knight's story isn't without dubious assertions, too, such as the fact that the word "serve" would have the same double meaning in Kanamit as in English. "About the double meaning of 'to serve,'" says Knight, "I tried to cover myself by having the narrator's friend remark that some of the idioms were very much like English. (In fact, French and Italian have the same double meaning, and in German and Swedish the word is almost the same; but I didn't know that then.)"

Finally, there is the curiously apt name of "Kanamit." But Knight asserts, "Kanamit isn't intentionally a pun on cannibal." Perhaps not—but then again . . .

"THE JUNGLE" (12/1/61)

John Dehner

Written by Charles Beaumont
Based on the short story "The Jungle" by Charles Beaumont
Producer: Buck Houghton
Director: William Claxton
Director of Photography: George T. Clemens
Music: stock

Cast:
Alan Richards: John Dehner
Doris Richards: Emily McLaughlin
Chad Cooper: Walter Brooke
Templeton: Hugh Sanders
Hardy: Howard Wright
Sinclair: Donald Foster
Taxi Driver: Jay Overholts
Derelict: Jay Adler

"The caracass of a goat, a dead finger, a few bits of broken glass and stone—and Mr. Alan Richards, a modern man of a modern age, hating with all his heart something in which he cannot believe and preparing—although he doesn't know it—to take the longest walk of his life, right down to the center of the Twilight Zone."

Returned home to New York from a hydroelectric project in Africa, engineer Alan Richards scoffs at the voodoo lion curse placed on him by a group of witch doctors who are angered because he plans to erect a dam on their ancestral land. However, he is taken aback when a dead goat appears on his doorstep. To protect him, his superstitious wife surreptitiously slips him an anti-lion charm, but he inadvertently leaves this in a bar late at night, then discovers his car won't start. A wind comes up, accompanied by jungle sounds. Feeling pursued, Richards boards a taxi, but when it stops at a red light the driver slumps over—dead. The sounds grow louder. Richards desperately races through the park on foot until he reaches his apartment. Inside, all is quiet. Then a low growl issues from the bedroom. A lion has killed his wife. Seeing him, the beast springs.

"Some superstitions, kept alive by the long night of ignorance, have their own special power. You'll hear of it through a jungle grapevine in a remote corner of the Twilight Zone."

Charles Beaumont's first contribution to the third season was this tension-filled little tale about a voodoo curse that reaches all the way from the heart of Africa to the streets of New York City. The original short story appeared in 1954 in *If* magazine and later in his collection *Yonder* (Bantam, 1958).

"The Jungle" takes place entirely in the city, and one senses that it might be more effective if we were shown a bit of Africa, in the beginning, so that the threat might seem less obscure. Even so, the episode has its effective moments, such as when John Dehner (last seen in "The Lonely") is riding in a cab that has stopped for a red light. A moment passes on the dark street. The light turns green. No movement. "Driver," says Dehner, "the light's green. You can go now." No reply, no movement. "Driver, the light's green—" Dehner reaches over to touch the man on the shoulder. The man slumps over sideways . . . dead.

Another forceful moment (well directed by William Claxton) is when Dehner finally reaches the sanctuary of his apartment. The drums have stopped, all is quiet. Out of breath but feeling secure, Dehner pours himself a drink. As he raises it to his lips, a low growl issues from the bedroom. Slowly, he opens the bedroom door. Sprawled on the bed is the dead body of his wife, above which stands a lion. The lion sees him and springs (a very effective point-of-view shot in which the lion jumped entirely *over* the camera).

"The Jungle" plays upon our instinctual fear of being alone, of being chased, of the darkness, of the night. More than most people, Charles Beaumont was especially in tune with these fears, having often experienced them himself. A glimpse is provided by William F. Nolan: "One night, I remember, we had gone to a late-night horror movie. I'd parked my car that night in the parking lot of one of the big stores along Wilshire. We came out of the theater and we were walking back to the car, two supposedly sophisticated adults. And we got ourselves so hyped up talking about the horror film that we'd seen and other horrors, and the kind of crazy people that are wandering the streets and can strike at you from the dark, from any building front, any alley, they could be there. Chuck was fascinated with all that stuff.

"When we got to the lot, we saw a car parked right next to mine. There were only two cars on the whole lot, my car and this other car, and some kind of figure was sitting there, kind of slumped over sideways and just kind of staring. I said, 'Oh shit, Chuck. That guy looks like some kind of maniac to me.' Chuck said, 'Here are the possibilities'—Chuck would always take his fingers—'He could be, one, *dead*. He could be a dead man, and we certainly don't want to get involved with that.' And I said, 'No, I don't want to get involved with some dead guy.' 'Two, he could be some kind of pervert or killer, waiting for us to get in your car to strike.' I said, 'It's possible he could be.'—I know this sounds crazy, but at that time of night, after what we'd gone through, it seemed perfectly logical— 'Or, three, he could be just an ordinary person waiting for his wife to come out of someplace. But if you were an ordinary person, *what are you doing in a parking lot alone at three in the morning*?' I said, 'I don't know, Chuck, but I tell you one thing: we're taking the bus home tonight!'"

Today, Nolan recalls such events only with fondness. "That's the kind of stuff you'd do with Beaumont. I would never do things like that with other people; I'd just go and get my car. But he made a drama out of everything, and that's why people loved to be with him. He brought just a walk home from a movie into the realm of the Twilight Zone. He utterly convinced me that if we went to that car, we would probably die."

"STILL VALLEY" (11/24/61)

Gary Merrill

Written by Rod Serling
Based on the short story "The Valley Was Still" by Manly Wade Wellman
Producer: Buck Houghton
Director: James Sheldon
Director of Photography: Jack Swain
Music: Wilbur Hatch

Cast:
Paradine: Gary Merrill
Old Man: Vaughn Taylor
Dauger: Ben Cooper
Sentry: Addison Myers
Lieutenant: Mark Tapscott
Mallory: Jack Mann

"The time is 1863, the place the state of Virginia. The event is a mass blood-letting known as the Civil War, a tragic moment in time when a nation was split into two fragments, each fragment deeming itself a nation. . . . This is Joseph Paradine, Confederate cavalry, as he heads down toward a small town in the middle of a valley. But very shortly, Joseph Paradine will make contact with the enemy. He will also make contact with an outpost not found on a military map—an outpost called the Twilight Zone."

Confederate scout Paradine ventures into town and finds it filled with Union soldiers—all frozen in place. They are under a spell cast by an old man wielding a book of black magic. Knowing he will soon die, the old man gives Paradine the book, urging him to use it to win the war. Paradine returns to camp and convinces his commanding officer to let him cast a spell that will freeze the entire Union Army. But when he starts to read it aloud, Paradine realizes it will force him to call upon the Devil and renounce God. He throws the book on the fire; if the Confederacy is to die, he wants it to be buried in hallowed ground.

"On the following morning, Sergeant Paradine and the rest of these men were moved up north to a little town in Pennsylvania, an obscure little place where a battle was brewing, a town called Gettysburg—and this one was fought without the help of the Devil. Small historical note not to be found in any known books, but part of the records in the Twilight Zone."

"Still Valley," Serling's adaptation of Manly Wade Wellman's short story, "The Valley Was Still," is a clichéd and unconvincing Civil War story. As in "Elegy," the illusion of stillness was accomplished by casting extras who could remain motionless and by using still photographs. In long shots this works, but in closeups it fails utterly. In the original story, the hero decapitates the old man who gives him a book of black magic, and this bit of gruesomeness might have added a little excitement had it been retained—but then almost anything would have helped. But as it is, "Still Valley" is merely a rehash of themes *The Twilight Zone* had done before, and better.

"A QUALITY OF MERCY" (12/29/61)

Dean Stockwell and Jerry Fujikawa

Written by Rod Serling
Based on an idea by Sam Rolfe
Producer: Buck Houghton
Director: Buzz Kulik
Director of Photography: George T. Clemens
Music: stock

Cast:
Lt. Katell/Lt. Yamuri: Dean Stockwell
Sgt. Causarano: Albert Salmi
Japanese Capt.: Jerry Fujikawa
Japanese Non-Com: Dale Ishimoto
Hansen: Leonard Nimoy
Watkins: Rayford Barnes
Hanacheck: Ralph Votrian
Jeep Driver: Michael Pataki

"It's August, 1945, the last grimy pages of a dirty, torn book of war. The place is the Philippine Islands. The men are what's left of a platoon of American Infantry, whose dulled and tired eyes set deep in dulled and tired faces can now look toward a miracle, that moment when the nightmare appears to be coming to an end. But they've got one more battle to fight, and in a moment we'll observe that battle. August, 1945, Philippine Islands. But in reality it's high noon in the Twilight Zone."

New to the battlefield and desperate to prove his manhood before the war ends, Lieutenant Katell orders his platoon to make a near-suicidal assault on a group of starved Japanese soldiers holed up in a cave. War-weary Sergeant Causarano tries to convince him to bypass the cave, but the lieutenant is determined to show the enemy no mercy. Suddenly, Katell finds himself on Corregidor on May 4, 1942. He is Lieutenant Yamuri, a Japanese officer, and his captain is about to order an assault on a cave holding a handful of wounded American soldiers. He pleads with the captain to show mercy and bypass the cave—to no avail. Abruptly, Katell is returned to the Philippines, just in time to hear that an A-bomb has been dropped on Japan; the platoon is to fall back and *not* attack the cave. Katell, having seen both sides of the coin, feels an overwhelming sense of relief.

" 'The quality of mercy is not strained, it droppeth as the gentle rain from heaven upon the place beneath. It blesseth him that gives and him that takes.' Shakespeare, The Merchant of Venice, *but applicable to any moment in time, to any*

group of soldiery, to any nation on the face of the Earth—or, in this case, to the Twilight Zone."

Shot on an already-standing jungle set on a soundstage at the Hal Roach Studios, "A Quality of Mercy" traverses much of the territory already covered by "The Purple Testament" (in which, coincidentally, Dean Stockwell was originally cast as the lead but was unable to appear). Again we are brought face to face with the grimness of war, the fatigue and the futility. Fortunately, this was a subject on which Serling was an expert, and so the material is well written. The character who gets to mouth most of Serling's sentiments on the subject is the war-weary sergeant, very well played by Albert Salmi (last seen in "Execution").

As for the lead, Dean Stockwell is a good choice, although curiously he gives a better performance as a Japanese soldier than as an American. The episode also boasts a bit part by a pre–*Star Trek* Leonard Nimoy, as an American soldier.

"THE HUNT" (1/26/62)

Arthur Hunnicut

Written by Earl Hamner, Jr.
Producer: Buck Houghton
Director: Harold Schuster
Director of Photography: George T. Clemens
Music: Robert Drasnin

Cast:
Hyder Simpson: Arthur Hunnicut
Rachel Simpson: Jeanette Nolan
Wesley Miller: Titus Moede
Tillman Miller: Orville Sherman
Rev. Wood: Charles Seel
Gatekeeper: Robert Foulk
Messenger: Dexter Dupont

"An old man and a hound dog named Rip, off for an evening's pleasure in quest of raccoon. Usually, these evenings end with one tired old man, one battle-scarred hound dog and one or more extremely dead raccoons, but as you may suspect that will not be the case tonight. These hunters won't be coming home from the hill. They're headed for the backwoods of the Twilight Zone."

When Rip dives into the water after a raccoon, Simpson dives in after him—but only the raccoon emerges. Next morning, man and dog awaken beside the water. Returning home, Simpson finds that neither his wife, the preacher, nor his neighbors can see or hear him—and they all seem to think he's dead! Walking along the road to the local graveyard, he encounters a fence he's never seen before and decides to follow it. Soon, he and Rip come to a gate. The gatekeeper explains it's the entrance to Heaven. Simpson is welcome, but dogs aren't allowed; Rip must stay outside. Infuriated, Simpson takes Rip and continues down the road. There, he meets an angel dispatched to bring him to Heaven. The gate was actually the entrance to Hell—and Rip wasn't allowed in because he would have smelled the brimstone and warned his master.

"Travellers to unknown regions would be well-advised to take along the family dog. He could just save you from entering the wrong gate. At least, it happened that way once—in a mountainous area of the Twilight Zone."

Naive, badly directed, only tolerably acted (with the exception of a fine characterization by Jeanette Nolan), "The Hunt" was the first of eight shows written by Earl Hamner, Jr. (whose other *Twilight Zone* credits include "A Piano in the House," "Jess-Belle," "Ring-a-ding Girl," "You Drive," "Black Leather Jackets," "Stopover in a Quiet Town," and "The Bewitchin' Pool"). Its failings, however, were not his fault. Born in Schuyler, Virginia, raised in the Blue Ridge Mountains, Hamner had an affection for these people and a special skill in setting them down as they really talked and acted.

Unfortunately, others connected with the show were not so familiar with these characters. The wardrobe is hillbilly, Hollywood style, thoroughly stereotypical, as are the sets, which include a log cabin. Perhaps most detrimental to the show is the performance of Arthur Hunnicut in the lead. Although speaking with his natural Arkansas drawl, he plays the Old Man leadenly and with no range.

"The actor played the role of the Old Man much too seriously," says Hamner. "He should have had fun with the role rather than treating it so literally. It required a kind of homespun, tongue-in-cheek approach, because the idea of a hillbilly angel immediately imposes a certain kind of fun. You know, 'Let's relax, this is a romp!'"

Years later, Hamner created a series based on his own family, in which his characters were presented in a more positive light. The name of the show was *The Waltons*. Notably, there is a strong similarity between the Old Man and the Old Woman of "The Hunt" and the characters of Grandma and Grandpa Walton. "The similarity is not accidental," says Hamner, "because at that time I was working on a series of short stories called 'The Old Man and the Old Woman.' Those characters which I used in 'The Hunt' also were later to become the Grandma and Grandpa Walton people." To put Hunnicut's performance in perspective, just imagine what Will Geer might have done with the part.

"The Hunt" was a curious thing for *The Twilight Zone* to do. It presented a fundamentalist Heaven and was completely opposite to the kind of urban-based and relatively cynical things being written by the other writers on the show. Hamner acknowledges the fact. "I was delighted and surprised, and I think it was probably simply the charm of the idea that attracted them. But I've found that true on many series, that they will occasionally break their mold."

How Hamner broke into *The Twilight Zone* is itself a remarkable story. "When I came to California, I had had an agent in New York who introduced me to an agent here, so I thought, Well fine, I'll go to work immediately, because I'm a hotshot writer. I spent the next six months trying to get writing assignments.

"The main problem was that producers would say, 'Yes, we've read your books,' or 'We've seen your name on tape television, but you've never done any film.' It was as if to do film there was some mystique to it that you had to absorb with the smog. Consequently, for six months I went without work when I first came to California, and we had spent most of my meager savings in renting a house and having our furniture shipped across the country. The money was simply drifting away, all because I didn't write film."

In 1947, Hamner had met Serling in New York when they were both winners of the *Dr. Christian* competition. Now desperate, he recalled that brief meeting. "I thought of a couple of *Twilight Zone* ideas, and I mailed them to Rod, and I received a very nice letter in which he said, 'Our decisions are usually made by a committee. I have passed on my recommendation to the other committee members and you'll be hearing from us.' Shortly after that, Buck Houghton called. Buck said, 'We like these stories but we understand that you don't write film. Would you like to write them up like little plays?' I said, 'No, I would like to write them up like little television scripts.'"

For all its faults, "The Hunt" has one memorable line. The Old Man, Hyder Simpson, has declined entering what he takes to be Heaven because it won't allow his dog to accompany him. Further down the Eternity Road, Simpson meets an angel who tells him that it was actually Hell he was almost tricked into entering. When he asks why they wouldn't let a dog in, the angel replies, "You see, Mr. Simpson, a man, well he'll walk right into Hell with both eyes open—but even the Devil can't fool a dog!"

"THE LAST RITES OF JEFF MYRTLEBANK" (2/23/62)

James Best

Written and Directed by
Montgomery Pittman
Producer: Buck Houghton
Director of Photography:
Jack Swain
Music: Tommy Morgan

Cast:
Jeff Myrtlebank: James Best
Comfort Gatewood:
Sherry Jackson
Orgram Gatewood: Lance Fuller
Mr. Peters: Dub Taylor
Pa Myrtlebank: Ralph Moody
Ma Myrtlebank: Ezelle Poule
Ma Gatewood: Helen Wallace
Liz Myrtlebank: Vickie Barnes
Rev. Siddons: Bill Fawcett
Doc Bolton: Edgar Buchanan
Mrs. Ferguson: Mabel Forrest
Mr. Strauss: Jon Lormer
Tom: Pat Hector
Jerry: Jim Houghton

"Time, the mid-twenties. Place, the Midwest—the southernmost section of the Midwest. We were just witnessing a funeral, a funeral that didn't come off exactly as planned, due to a slight fallout—from the Twilight Zone."

During his funeral, Jeff Myrtlebank abruptly sits up in the coffin, alive, well, and even hungry. Jeff claims to be the same as always, but as time goes by others have doubts, fueled by the fact that Jeff exhibits new traits: a love of hard work, skill at fisticuffs and the ability to make freshly-picked flowers wilt in his grasp. After Jeff bests Orgram Gatewood, the brother of his fiancée Comfort, in a fight, a group of townspeople come to the conclusion that Jeff is actually an evil spirit. They decide to run him out of the county. Although previously frightened of Jeff, Comfort rushes off to warn him. Jeff demands that Comfort decide whether she'll stick by him. As the men arrive, Comfort agrees to marry him. Jeff tells the men that he and his wife-to-be intend to stay. If he *is* Jeff Myrtlebank they have nothing to worry about; but if he's a supernatural being then they'd better treat him and his family well—for with his magic he can cause them no end of distress. Feigning that they are reassured, although actually they are terrified, the townfolk depart. Jeff explains to Comfort that he lied to them; he's as human as she is. But while he says this, he lights a match—without striking it!

"Jeff and Comfort are still alive today, and their only son is a United States senator who's noted as an uncommonly shrewd politician—and some believe he must have gotten his education in the Twilight Zone."

An episode with many of the Earl Hamner trademarks was "The Last Rites of Jeff Myrtlebank," a lighthearted backwoods tale of an intense young man (James Best, seen previously in *The Grave* and later of *The Dukes of Hazard*) who has trouble being accepted by his fellow townspeople after he seemingly returns from the dead. In actuality, the episode was written and directed by Montgomery Pittman, who, as has already been mentioned, was also from the South.

"I liked it very much," Buck Houghton says of this episode. "It was well done, very entertaining. Wonderful country humor. Some of those names:

James Best and Sherry Jackson

'Orgram.' And I thought James Best was just wonderful—'I feel *real* hungry!' And that came out of Monty. James could do it, but Monty had to ask for it. And for that old man to be reading that Montgomery Ward catalogue and just sort of pawing through it. His wife says, 'I hope that new one arrives 'cause you've got that one worn out with looking through it.' I mean, two lazy people sitting there saying, 'I don't know when I've seen Jeff use so much energy as he has of late.' And you can see that they haven't had any energy for years!"

In casting, Pittman selected character actors who could handle the light touch necessary for this kind of country humor. Edgar Buchanan (later Uncle Joe on *Petticoat Junction*), Dub Taylor, and Jon Lormer are the most vocal and ignorant townspeople. Sherry Jackson, Pittman's step-daughter and a regular on *Make Room for Daddy* as a child, plays Comfort, the sweet and innocent love interest. Lance Fuller is quite funny as Comfort's brother Orgram, a fellow who seemingly has a force-field of stupidity surrounding him.

"THE FUGITIVE" (3/9/62)

J. Pat O'Malley and Susan Gordon

Written by Charles Beaumont
Producer: Buck Houghton
Director: Richard L. Bare
Director of Photography: Jack Swain
Music: stock

Cast:
Old Ben: J. Pat O'Malley
Jenny: Susan Gordon
Mrs. Gann: Nancy Kulp
1st Man: Wesley Lau
2nd Man: Paul Tripp
Howie: Stephen Talbot
Pitcher: Johnny Eiman
Doctor: Russ Bender

"It's been said that science fiction and fantasy are two different things: science fiction, the improbable made possible; fantasy, the impossible made probable. What would you have if you put these two different things together? Well, you'd have an old man named Ben who knows a lot of tricks most people don't know and a little girl named Jenny who loves him—and a journey into the heart of the Twilight Zone."

Two men are looking for Old Ben, a mysterious fellow who can transform himself into anything, from mouse to fly to hideous monster from outer space. Ben confides to his friend Jenny, a little girl who lives with her aunt and wears a leg brace, that he is a fugitive from outer space; the men are his pursuers. Before fleeing, Ben uses a device to fix Jenny's leg. The two men arrive and use a similar device to make Jenny deathly ill. The trap works; Ben is forced to return and heal Jenny. The truth then becomes clear: Ben is not a fugitive from justice but the beloved monarch of an alien planet; the two men subjects sent to plead with him to return to the throne. Reluctantly, Ben agrees. But the men refuse to let Jenny come along. Suddenly, Jenny has an idea; Ben is allowed a minute alone with her. The men return to find two *Jennys*! Afraid to take the wrong one, they are forced to take both.

"Mrs. Gann will be in for a big surprise when she finds this [*photo of a handsome young man*] *under Jenny's pillow, because Mrs. Gann has more temper than imagination. She'll never dream that this is a picture of Old Ben as he* really *looks, and it will never occur to her that eventually her niece will grow up to be an honest-to-goodness queen—somewhere in the Twilight Zone."*

Charles Beaumont's "The Fugitive" is a sort of Cinderella story about Jenny, a beautiful but crippled little girl (charmingly played by Susan

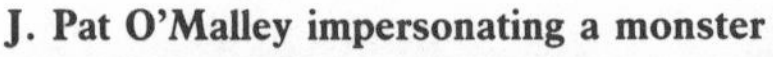

J. Pat O'Malley impersonating a monster

Gordon) and Old Ben (J. Pat O'Malley), a friendly neighborhood codger who, with his ability to change his appearance at will as well as being able to bat fly balls out of sight, is just about the greatest grandfather-figure you could ever hope for. Rounding out this very fine cast is Nancy Kulp (later Miss Hathaway on *The Beverly Hillbillies*) as Mrs. Gann, Jenny's sour and unhappy guardian.

Here, Beaumont is clearly making a case for the superiority of fantasy over reality. Mrs. Gann represents the sensible, down-to-earth type we've all come to know and hate in our daily lives, as personified by dialogue like this:

> MRS. GANN: Who're you talkin' to?
>
> JENNY: Myself.
>
> MRS. GANN: Cut it out. You can go crazy that way.

In the end, as in any fairy tale, good overwhelmingly triumphs. We can definitely assume Ben and Jenny will live happily ever after—away from all the Mrs. Ganns of this world.

"A GAME OF POOL" (10/13/61)

Jonathan Winters and Jack Klugman

Written by
George Clayton Johnson
Producer: Buck Houghton
Director: Buzz Kulik
Director of Photography: Jack Swain
Music: stock

Cast:
Jesse Cardiff: Jack Klugman
Fats Brown: Jonathan Winters

"Jesse Cardiff, pool shark, the best on Randolph Street, who will soon learn that trying to be the best at anything carries its own special risks in or out of the Twilight Zone."

Alone in Clancy's pool hall, Jesse voices his dearest wish: that he be allowed to play the late Fats Brown and prove that he, not Fats, is really the world's greatest pool player. Fats appears and challenges Jesse to a game—with Jesse's life as the stakes. A game of skill, nerve and bluff commences, with Fats seeming to hold the upper hand. But at last, Jesse has only one easy ball to sink to win the game. Fats warns him that he might win more than he bargains for, but Jesse disregards this and sinks the ball. After he dies, however, he realizes the meaning of Fats's words: it is now *he* who must wearily rise to every challenge from ambitious players on Earth.

"Mr. Jesse Cardiff, who became a legend by beating one, but who has found out after his funeral that being the best of anything carries with it a special obligation to keep on proving it. Mr. Fats Brown, on the other hand, having relinquished the champion's mantle, has gone fishing. These are the ground rules in the Twilight Zone."

Jack Klugman's second appearance on *The Twilight Zone* was in George Clayton Johnson's "A Game of Pool," a tautly written piece dealing with the ramifications of winning and losing—and being the best. This episode should be shown to anyone who thinks that in order to have dramatic tension one needs car chases, explosions and guns, for it packs more drama than any ten cop shows combined.

For this one show, Johnson abandoned his usual sentimentality and wrote with a realism and hardness that makes his dialogue crackle. Reprinting the entire script would be impractical, but we can provide a sniff of the cork, as it were. Here, Fats has just materialized in the poolroom:

JESSE (*Incredulous*): It's impossible!

FATS: Nothing's impossible. Some things are less likely than others, that's all.

JESSE: It isn't a rib. It's you. You're—

FATS: James Howard Brown. Known to my friends as "Fats." I know it's a shock, but then you called me—I didn't call you.

JESSE: Well, I didn't mean anything. You see, it was just I was trying to—

FATS: Oh sure, sure, I understand. It was just big talk, is that it? You like to play with fire but you don't like to cook. You're not as good as you claim and you know it. Deep down, you know that you're second rate.

JESSE: Now wait a minute!

FATS: Are you afraid? Look, I've come a long way, boy, and not to be fooled with. I've seen your kind before—a little skill, a knack, a style, but when the heat's on, you fold.

JESSE: That isn't fair. You've never seen me play. Maybe I can beat you. It's possible, isn't it?

FATS: It's possible. Things change. Records get higher. But you'll never get the job done with your mouth.

JESSE: All right, fat boy, dead or alive, let me tell *you* something. Maybe you are some kind of a legend—a tin god. You know what you are to me? You're a big balloon waiting for someone to stick a needle in it. (*Indicating his pool cue*) Well, I'm the someone and here's the needle.

As Jesse, Klugman is intense, thoughtful, and complex. More than that, he is *real.* As for Winters, well, first of all he is not the "ponderous man with a neat fringe of beard" described in Johnson's script.

Director Buzz Kulik explains the reasoning behind the casting of Winters. "With a guy like Jack Klugman, you go out and get Jack Warden or somebody like that. However, we determined that here was this guy who was such a brilliant talent, who would bring a kind of freshness, because this was his first time as a dramatic actor. He'd never even been on film before."

For Winters, appearing in "A Game of Pool" was anything but a lark. "He was very anxious to do this well," says Kulik, "and yet he was kind of embarrassed because he felt, 'My God, here are all these professional people, this crew and cast, and here I am.' And not only did he have to work his dialogue but he had to play pool! So, whenever he'd blow a line or make a mistake, in order to cover his embarrassment he would go on for like ten, fifteen minutes, in the character, doing some of the wildest, funniest, most marvelous things you'd ever seen."

Curiously, the conclusion of the show was *not* the original ending. "We had a heck of a time with the ending on that," says Buck Houghton. "I don't know that it ever was satisfactory. It seems to me we reshot that about three different times. We never could wrap that up to our satisfaction."

As for George Clayton Johnson, he greatly prefers the ending he wrote in the script, in which Jesse *loses* the game. Here it is, in its entirety:

TWO SHOT FEATURING JESSE

With a final look at Fats he bends to the table. He

carefully sights. It is absolutely silent as he takes two tentative passes at the cue ball and shoots. The cue ball hits the 15 ball. It rolls toward the pocket, hooks the corner and bounds back. He has missed.

FATS STEPS INTO F.G.

Bends, sights, shoots and sinks the ball. He turns slowly to face Jesse. Jesse stands frozen. He is struck dumb with terror. It is time to pay off the bet.

JESSE: (*Hysteria*) What are you waiting for? Get it over with!

Fats continues to look at him without moving.

JESSE (CONT'D): You said life or death!

CLOSE SHOT FATS

FATS: Do you really expect me to kill you?

CLOSE SHOT JESSE

Confused. He had expected sudden horrible death. Not this.

JESSE: You said if I won I'd live. If I lost I'd die!

CLOSE SHOT FATS

FATS: And you will—as all second-raters die—you'll be buried and forgotten without me touching you. If you'd beaten me you'd have lived forever.

CLOSE SHOT JESSE

Reacting. At first with sudden relief as he realizes that Fats has no intention of taking his life, and then with anger because he has been tricked.

JESSE: You tricked me!

CLOSE SHOT FATS

FATS: You had to prove yourself under pressure. Any man can be a marksman if the target doesn't shoot back.

TWO SHOT

Jesse looks at him in bewilderment as Fats packs his cue

back into its case. Fats turns and walks into the shadows at the rear of the poolroom. He turns, nods and vanishes. Jesse shakes himself, blinks. With a cry he runs to the spot where Fats disappeared.

JESSE: Wait!

He looks wildly around.

CLOSE SHOT JESSE

JESSE: Wait! It isn't over! Do you hear? I haven't given up! I'll practice—day and night if necessary! I'm still alive! I can get better! I *will* get better!

He cocks his head listening . . . Silence. And then, slowly, he turns.

ANOTHER ANGLE

As he walks back to the table, picks up his stick and begins to practice combination shots.

JESSE: (*Under his breath*) You'll hear from me again, Fats Brown!

SERLING'S VOICE: *Lives of great men all remind us:*
We can make our lives sublime
And, departing, leave behind us
Footprints on the sands of time.
On the Earth as we know it,
And in The Twilight Zone.

FADE TO BLACK

Whichever ending one prefers, "A Game of Pool" is top-flight in every regard. Who wins the game is not as important as the game itself. In one guise or another, it is a game most of us have played at least once in our lives.

"THE PASSERSBY" (10/6/61)

James Gregory, Joanne Linville and Warren Kemmerling

Written by Rod Serling
Producer: Buck Houghton
Director: Elliot Silverstein
Director of Photography: George T. Clemens
Music: Fred Steiner

Cast:
Lavinia: Joanne Linville
The Sergeant: James Gregory
Abraham Lincoln: Austin Green
Charlie: Rex Holman
The Lieutenant: David Garcia
Jud: Warren Kemmerling

"This road is the afterwards of the Civil War. It began at Fort Sumter, South Carolina, and ended at a place called Appomattox. It's littered with the residue of broken battles and shattered dreams. . . . In just a moment, you will enter a strange province that knows neither North nor South, a place we call the Twilight Zone."

A Confederate sergeant with a wooden leg stops to rest in front of the burnt-out mansion of Lavinia Godwin. He strikes up a conversation with Lavinia, who feels certain her beloved husband Jud, a Confederate officer, is dead. Loneliness and sense of loss have bred hatred in her, and when a blinded Union lieutenant pauses for a drink of water she shoots him point-blank with a rifle—to no effect. The lieutenant departs, and the sergeant begins to draw a frightening conclusion: that everyone on the road, including himself and Lavinia, are dead. Suddenly, Jud arrives and confirms this fact. Lavinia cannot accept the revelation. She begs Jud to stay with her, but he is compelled to continue, promising to meet her at the end of the road. As he walks away, a figure draws near who is the last man on the road—and the last casualty of the Civil War—Abraham Lincoln. Gently, he consoles Lavinia. Finally accepting the truth, she runs off to join her husband.

"Incident on a dirt road during the month of April, the year 1865. As we've already pointed out, it's a road that won't be found on a map, but it's one of many that lead in and out of the Twilight Zone."

"The Passersby," is one of the weakest shows of the first three seasons. The direction by Elliot Silverstein is competent and the acting is fine, although James Gregory (later of *Barney Miller*) seems too old for the role of a sad balladeer who went off to war to become a man. The episode also has a very pretty score by Fred Steiner. What makes this an embarrassing episode is Serling's script. Turgid, verbose, posturing, it takes a long time for the widow and the sergeant to realize what is obvious almost from the beginning.

James Gregory recalls a humorous incident from the shooting. "On 'The Passersby,' I put my belt buckle on upside down, a big 'C.S.A.' The director saw it and remarked about it, and I told him, 'But don't you see, Elliot, these people are dead, and the buckle upside down indicates that status?' Well, he gave me a funny look and then, 'Ah, yes, Jim, I see what you mean. Good touch.' I don't think either of us truly understood, but it was good for a laugh."

"THE MIDNIGHT SUN" (11/17/61)

Lois Nettleton

Written by Rod Serling
Producer: Buck Houghton
Director: Anton Leader
Director of Photography: George T. Clemens
Music: Van Cleave

Cast:
Norma: Lois Nettleton
Mrs. Bronson: Betty Garde
Intruder: Tom Reese
Neighbor: Jason Wingreen
Neighbor's Wife: June Ellis
Refrigerator Repairman: Ned Glass
Policeman: John McLiam
Doctor: William Keene
Announcer: Robert J. Stevenson

"The word that Mrs. Bronson is unable to put into the hot, still, sodden air is 'doomed,' because the people you've just seen have been handed a death sentence. One month ago, the Earth suddenly changed its elliptical orbit and in doing so began to follow a path which gradually, moment by moment, day by day, took it closer to the sun. And all of man's little devices to stir up the air are now no longer luxuries—they happen to be pitiful and panicky keys to survival. The time is five minutes to twelve, midnight. There is no more darkness. The place is New York City and this is the eve of the end, because even at midnight it's high noon, the hottest day in history, and you're about to spend it in the Twilight Zone."

While most people have left New York in a desperate attempt to reach cooler climates, Norma and her neighbor Mrs. Bronson remain in their apartment building, trying as best they can to cope with irregular electricity and the ever-increasing heat. A thirst-crazed man breaks into Norma's apartment and gulps down her water, then regains his senses, begs her forgiveness and departs. A little later, Mrs. Bronson becomes delirious and then dies. As the temperature rises, Norma's paintings melt and run off the canvas and the thermometer bursts. Norma screams and collapses. When she revives, it is cool, dark and snowing outside. It was all a feverish delusion; the Earth is not heading *toward* the sun—it's heading *away* from it!

"The poles of fear, the extremes of how the Earth might conceivably be doomed. Minor exercise in the care and feeding of a nightmare, respectfully submitted by all the thermometer-watchers in the Twilight Zone."

During the first season, Serling had explored the end of the world in "Time Enough at Last." In "The Midnight Sun" he returned to that theme, but the catalyst is no longer nuclear war. Instead, the world he depicts is one in which the Earth's orbit has changed, bringing it daily closer to the sun. Coincidentally, the plot is remarkably similar to a film shot that same year in Great Britain, *The Day the Earth Caught Fire*. Both depict the utter breakdown of society, scarcity of water, people trying to get to cooler regions of the planet, deserted cities, and the hysteria that sets in when the death of a world seems inevitable. But *The Day the Earth Caught Fire* had the budget and shooting schedule of a feature film, while "The Midnight Sun" had only three shooting days and $52,577 to portray the total destruction of the Earth. Remarkably, a pretty convincing picture is presented.

"With a very limited budget and facilities, we had to do a lot of improvising," recalls director Tony Leader, who had done so very well on "Long Live Walter Jameson." "We had to use every means available to us to project the fear of this developing heat and this cataclysmic ending to the world. I think we did a pretty good job."

Many visual effects lend credence to the feeling of terrible heat: the sweaty-looking makeup on the actors, their matted hairdos, mercury boiling and breaking the glass in a thermometer, a painting melting and running down the canvas (which was accomplished by painting a picture in wax on the surface of a hotplate and then turning the hotplate on). The actors are also very skilled at presenting the illusion of a doomed world, particularly Lois Nettleton in the lead as Norma and Betty Garde as her landlady, Mrs. Bronson.

Tony Leader recalls an additional factor that helped put the actors into the spirit of the thing. "In those days, they had no air conditioning on the set and we shot in summer, so it was hot enough to give you the initial feeling. I remember that there were a couple of scenes in which I asked the electrical grip to add heat, not so much heat that it would show on the film, but heat that we would feel on the set. It made us distinctly uncomfortable, but I think it helped us develop the feeling that we had of heat. I didn't do that throughout, because its effect would have been lost eventually. We would have just been plain simply miserable and angry with each other for being involved in this thing."

The finale Serling cooked up was pure *Twilight Zone.*

"Mrs. Bronson, I had such a terrible dream," Norma tells her landlady. "It was so hot. It was daylight all the time. There was a midnight sun, there was no night at all. . . . Mmm, isn't it wonderful to have darkness and coolness?"

With an expression of dread expectation, Mrs. Bronson answers, "Yes, my dear—it's wonderful."

"THE MIRROR" (10/20/61)

Peter Falk

Written by Rod Serling
Producer: Buck Houghton
Director: Don Medford
Director of Photography: George T. Clemens
Music: stock

Cast:
Ramos Clemente: Peter Falk
Cristo: Tony Carbone
D'Allesandro: Richard Karlan
Tabal: Arthur Batanides
General DeCruz: Will Kuluva
Priest: Vladimir Sokoloff
Garcia: Rodolfo Hoyos
Offstage Voice: Robert McCord III
Offstage Voice: Jim Turley
Stunt Double: Dave Armstrong
Guard: Val Ruffino

"This is the face of Ramos Clemente, a year ago a beardless, nameless worker of the dirt who plodded behind a mule, furrowing someone else's land. And he looked up at a hot Central American sun and he pledged the impossible. He made a vow that he would lead an avenging army against the tyranny that put the ache in his back and the anguish in his eyes, and now one year later the

dream of the impossible has become a fact. In just a moment we will look deep into this mirror and see the aftermath of a rebellion . . . in the Twilight Zone."

After seizing power, Clemente is told by General DeCruz, the deposed tyrant, that a magic mirror in his office reveals the faces of one's assassins. Looking into it, Clemente sees his compatriots advancing on him with machine gun, knives and poison. He kills them all but this brings him no sense of security. When a priest tells him that the people are appalled by the round-the-clock executions he has ordered, Clemente replies that the people are not his concern, that he sees assassins everywhere and is constantly afraid. The priest tells him that tyrants have only one real enemy, "the one they never recognize—until too late." He exits. All alone, Clemente spies his own reflection in the mirror, shatters it, then shoots himself. The priest rushes in. "The last assassin," he says. "And they never learn. *They never seem to learn!*"

"Ramos Clemente, a would-be god in dungarees, strangled by an illusion, that will-o'-the-wisp mirage that dangles from the sky in front of the eyes of all ambitious men, all tyrants—and any resemblance to tyrants living or dead is hardly coincidental, whether it be here or in the Twilight Zone."

The "tyrants living or dead" invoked at the end of "The Mirror" was clearly a reference to Fidel Castro, whom Falk, as Clemente, is made up to resemble. This, however, is not one of Falk's shining moments: he rants, raves and struts through a thoroughly superficial portrayal.

"This was our impression of Castro at that time," says Buck Houghton. "He was a very flamboyant Latin, which Peter isn't. It goes back to all those banana-boat republic strong-arm men."

The chill wind of the Cold War blows through this one-sided episode, and it does Castro a disservice, merely reinforcing the prejudices of the audience for whom it was intended. In retrospect, Buck Houghton admits, "I think we had a fairly simplistic view of Castro at that time." "The Mirror" holds up an imperfect mirror to the real world and in doing so presents more distortion than reflection.

"ONCE UPON A TIME" (12/15/61)

Stanley Adams and Buster Keaton

Written by Richard Matheson
Producer: Buck Houghton
Director: Norman Z. McLeod (one sequence by Les Goodwins; uncredited)
Director of Photography: George T. Clemens
Music: composed by William Lava; played by Ray Turner

Cast:
Woodrow Mulligan: Buster Keaton
Rollo: Stanley Adams
Repair Man: Jesse White
Prof. Gilbert: Milton Parsons
Clothing Store Manager: Warren Parker
Policeman 1890: Gil Lamb
Policeman 1962: James Flavin
2nd Policeman 1962: Harry Fleer
Fenwick: George E. Stone

"Mr. Mulligan, a rather dour critic of his times, is shortly to discover the import of that old phrase, 'Out of the frying pan, into the fire'—said fire burning brightly at all times in the Twilight Zone."

Disgruntled over the clamor and high prices of 1890, janitor Woodrow Mulligan uses a time helmet invented by his employer, Professor Gilbert, to travel to 1962, which he assumes will be a utopia. Once there, he realizes the error of his assumptions and is eager to get back to 1890, but the helmet has been damaged—and in only fifteen minutes he will be unable to return. He meets Rollo, an electronics scientist, who takes the helmet to a repair shop. Once fixed, Rollo's motives become clear: he intends to use the helmet himself! Mulligan grabs hold of him and the two materialize in 1890. Mulligan is overjoyed, but Rollo soon becomes dissatisfied; to him, 1890 is hopelessly backward. Mulligan plops the helmet onto Rollo's head and ships him back to 1962.

" 'To each his own'—so goes another old phrase to which Mr. Woodrow Mulligan would heartily subscribe, for he has learned—definitely the hard way—that there is much wisdom in a third old phrase which goes as follows: 'Stay in your own back yard.' To which it might be added, 'and if possible, assist others to stay in theirs'—via, of course, the Twilight Zone."

Richard Matheson's "Once Upon a Time" is a slapstick comedy starring Buster Keaton. "I met Buster Keaton through Bill Cox, a writer friend of mine," relates Richard Matheson, "and I thought, Gee, that would be wonderful if we could get Keaton into a *Twilight Zone*."

To oversee this episode, Buck Houghton turned to Norman Z. McLeod, an old-time director who was in semi-retirement. McLeod's credits read like a history of film comedy: *Monkey Business, Horse Feathers, It's a Gift, Topper, The Secret Life of Walter Mitty,* and *The Paleface* (McLeod also directed the disastrous 1933 *Alice in Wonderland*). "He wasn't working a lot, he didn't want to," says Buck Houghton. "But he thought, My God, work with Buster Keaton? Lead me to it."

"The experience with Keaton was absolutely wonderful," says Houghton. "Here's a legend in his own time, for goodness sake, and he was exactly as reported. He was very sober about comedy. He'd take me out on the street and say, 'Buck, you can't do it that way. If I start *here,* then the gag works, but if I start there you can never make it work.' Such things as walking behind a policeman in step and disappearing down a manhole just before the bird comes, you know, those Rube Goldberg devices that the picture was full of. He knew right down to the jot what made it work. It was fascinating, too, to be walking around the backlot and have the art director say, 'You know, this section of street was built for a Buster Keaton comedy in 1921.'"

Sad to relate, the humor in "Once Upon a Time" is not very funny. The sequences in 1890 at the beginning and end are silent, with cards replacing dialogue. A typical gag shows Keaton walking past chickens and pigs on the street. A card appears which reads "Oink, oink . . . cluck, cluck." Robert Benchley, it ain't.

Some of the show's problems were apparent from the first. "This thing sat in the cutting room for weeks and weeks while [editor] Jason Bernie and I wondered how to get the goddamn thing to work better," says Buck Houghton, "because it seemed to go kind of slowly, as if there's *one* apple . . . and *two* apples . . . and *three* apples—and by then you're bored to hear me talk about the fourth apple. So it needed a goose."

The solution that Houghton and Bernie arrived at was to print only two out of every three frames in the silent sequences. This sped everything up and gave a jerky look to every movement, similar to early, hand-cranked silent films.

"Having done that and found that it was a good notion," says Houghton, "the episode needed an added sequence, and that sequence in the repair shop was directed by somebody else [Les Goodwins] months later."

Richard Matheson was not pleased with the results. "I had so much more going on, it was so much funnier, what I had written. Obviously because of cost reasons, the second act became this interminable scene in this repair shop, but I had it a chase from beginning to end, with him going through a car wash and a supermarket on a bike. It never stopped for a moment. After he meets Stanley Adams, though, it just stagnates."

When all is said and done, Keaton's presence alone makes "Once Upon a Time" worth watching. For all its faults, it is a warm reunion with a man who, long ago, made us laugh long and hard and well.

"KICK THE CAN" (2/9/62)

Ernest Truex

Written by
George Clayton Johnson
Producer: Buck Houghton
Director: Lamont Johnson
Director of Photography: George T. Clemens
Music: stock

Cast:
Charles Whitley: Ernest Truex
Ben Conroy: Russell Collins
Mr. Cox: John Marley
David Whitley: Barry Truex
Carlson: Burt Mustin
Mrs. Summers: Marjorie Bennett
Frietag: Hank Patterson
Mrs. Wister: Anne O'Neal
Agee: Earle Hodgins
Mrs. Densley: Lenore Shanewise
Nurse: Eve McVeagh
Boy #1: Gregory McCabe
Boy #2: Marc Stevens

"Sunnyvale Rest, a home for the aged—a dying place—and a common children's game called kick-the-can that will shortly become a refuge for a man who knows he will die in this world if he doesn't escape into . . . the Twilight Zone."

After his son refuses to take him in, Charles Whitley—a resident of Sunnyvale Rest Home—begins to brood, ultimately concluding that the secret of eternal youth lies in *acting* young. He tries to convince the other residents of this—much to the dismay of his lifelong friend, Ben Conroy, now a sour old man. Late one night, Whitley awakens the others and pleads with them to join him in a game of kick-the-can. Touched by his sincerity, all agree but Ben, who runs off to rouse Mr. Cox, the home's superintendent, in order to stop the game. But when the two rush outside, all they find is children; the magic has worked. Ben pleads with Whitley—now a boy—to take him along . . . but it is too late. The children run off into the bushes, leaving Ben behind.

"Sunnyvale Rest, a dying place for ancient people who have forgotten the fragile magic of youth. A dying place for those who have forgotten that childhood, maturity and old age are curiously intertwined and not separate. A dying place for those who have grown too stiff in their thinking to visit the Twilight Zone."

George Clayton Johnson's final script for *The Twilight Zone* was "Kick the Can," an enormously moving piece about youth, old age, death, and friendship.

As Charles, Ernest Truex is passionate and persuasive. In "What You Need," he had been rather forgettable, but here his performance is superb. This is an extremely sentimental show, and without the right balance it could have been cloying. But Truex throws himself into the part wholeheartedly.

The others in the cast are very fine as well, notably Russell Collins as Charles's sour and unbelieving friend Ben, John Marley as the superintendent of the home and Burt Mustin as one of the residents. Snatches of Bernard Herrmann's lovely score for "Walking Distance" are heard throughout and contribute much to the feelings of nostalgia and longing.

Johnson's writing in "Kick the Can" is marvelous for its brevity and accuracy. In one effective scene, Whitley had awakened the other residents, all but Ben. He pleads with them to come out on the lawn with him to play kick-the-can. At first, they're extremely resistant. He says to them, "Look! Think! Feel!" He presses an old tin can into their hands. "Here, hold it. Doesn't that wake some sleeping part of you? Listen, can't you hear it? Summer, grass, run, jump—youth! Wake up! Wake up! Oh, this is your last chance!" Finally, in desperation, he cries out, *"I can't play kick-the-can alone!"* This does the trick; the others rise out of their seats to play.

Lamont Johnson remembers the experience of working with these actors. "I find old people, if they're turned on, to have a curious kind of wonderful daring and madness and commitment, because they say, 'Why the hell not? What have I got to lose?' Middle-aged and younger actors are far more uptight. They really had such fun. It was such joy to them to be released into a kind of fanciful thing."

As the others ready themselves to play, Whitley goes to wake Ben to plead with him to join in the game. Ben is adamant in his refusal. Whitley says, "Ben, you're afraid. You're afraid of a new idea. You're afraid to look silly. You're afraid to make a mistake. You decided that you were an old man, and that has *made* you old." Reluctantly, Whitley goes off to play kick-the-can without him.

"Kick-the-Can" is not an escapist fantasy, instead it makes a point that has tremendous validity: that the key to youth lies in taking risks, in commitment, in extending oneself; and that old age is the price of being judgmental and opinionated, of playing it safe, of living a sedentary life. When George Clayton Johnson wrote this he was only thirty-two, but he had a wisdom beyond his years. Whitley recaptures his youth, but only because the others regard him highly enough to risk looking foolish. The magic lies in the caring.

"ONE MORE PALLBEARER" (1/12/62)

Joseph Wiseman

Written by Rod Serling
Producer: Buck Houghton
Director: Lamont Johnson
Director of Photography: George T. Clemens
Music: stock

Cast:
Paul Radin: Joseph Wiseman
Mr. Hughes: Gage Clark
Mrs. Langford: Katherine Squire
Col. Hawthorne: Trevor Bardette
Policeman: Ray Galvin
Electrician #1: Joseph Elic
Electrician #2: Robert Snyder

"What you have just looked at takes place three hundred feet underground, beneath the basement of a New York City skyscraper. It's owned and lived in by one Paul Radin. Mr. Radin is rich, eccentric and single-minded. How rich we can already perceive; how eccentric and single-minded we shall *see in a moment, because all of you have just entered the Twilight Zone."*

Radin invites three people to the elaborate bomb shelter he's constructed: high school teacher Mrs. Langford, who flunked him; Colonel Hawthorne, who court-martialed him; and the Reverend Mr. Hughes, who made public a scandal involving a girl who committed suicide over him. Using bogus sound effects and radio announcements, he convinces them that all-out nuclear war is moments away; they can remain in the shelter if only they apologize to him for their past actions. The three refuse, valuing honor higher than life itself, and then depart. Suddenly, the sound of a tremendous explosion shakes the shelter. Radin takes the elevator to the surface and is devastated to see that nuclear war *has* occurred—the world is in ruins. In reality, however, there has been no war; Radin, shattered by the failure of his hoax, has lost his mind.

"Mr. Paul Radin, a dealer in fantasy, who sits in the rubble of his own making and imagines that he's the last man on Earth, doomed to a perdition of unutterable loneliness because a practical joke has turned into a nightmare. Mr. Paul Radin, pallbearer at a funeral that he manufactured himself . . . in the Twilight Zone."

In "One More Pallbearer," the audience is clearly supposed to sympathize with the authority figures of the preacher, the colonel, and the schoolteacher; however, it just doesn't come off. Joseph Wiseman plays his role as the neurotic millionaire with such vulnerability and the others their roles with such unfeeling coldness that we cannot help but feel pity for him and contempt for the others. The dialogue doesn't help dissuade us from these feelings:

COLONEL: Are we to understand, Mr. Radin, that you will permit us this luxury, you will allow us to stay?

RADIN: Of course, colonel. As a matter of fact, it's precisely why I've asked you to come. Each of you in his own way has tried to destroy me, but I'll not repay the compliment. That is to say, I will not require an eye for an eye, nothing as primitive or as naked as that.

COLONEL: What is your price, Mr. Radin? I'd be interested.

RADIN: The colonel would be interested. I presume the reverend and the schoolmarm would be interested. I submit, dear friends, you're not just interested. It's probably the only thing in God's Earth that has any meaning left at all! But the price, colonel. You will beg my pardon, you will ask for my forgiveness, and if need be you will get down on your hands and knees to perform the function.

TEACHER: Pretty please with sugar on it.

RADIN: What's that, teacher?

TEACHER: Pretty please with sugar on it. It's what children say to exact a favor. I don't want your favor, Mr. Radin, let me out of here! If I'm to spend my last half hour on Earth, I'd rather spend it with a stray cat, or alone in Central Park, or in a city full of strangers whose names I'll never know.

REVEREND: The door, Radin, will you open the door now?

COLONEL: Open up, Radin!

RADIN: You're too blind or you're too stupid, because none of you seem to understand. All you have to do, literally all you have to do, is to say a sentence. Just a string of silly, stupid words, like a command, colonel, or like a lesson, teacher, or like a prayer, reverend—all you have to do is say you're sorry!

Needless to say, they don't apologize. In the end, Radin goes mad, and the three escape untouched, either physically or emotionally, safe in their sanctimonious hypocrisy, to destroy yet more people's lives. Unintentionally an unhappy ending . . . in the Twilight Zone.

"DEAD MAN'S SHOES" (1/19/62)

Warren Stevens and Joan Marshall

Written by Charles Beaumont and OCee Ritch (credited solely to Beaumont)
Producer: Buck Houghton
Director: Montgomery Pittman
Director of Photography: George T. Clemens
Music: stock

Cast:
Nate Bledsoe: Warren Stevens
Chips: Ben Wright
Wilma: Joan Marshall
Sam: Harry Swoger
Maitre D': Eugene Borden
Dagget: Richard Devon
Dagget's Woman: Florence Marly
Ben: Ron Hagerthy
Jimmy: Joe Mell

"Nathan Edward Bledsoe, of the Bowery Bledsoes, a man once, a specter now. One of those myriad modern-day ghosts that haunt the reeking nights of the city in search of a flop, a handout, a glass of forgetfulness. Nate doesn't know it but his search is about to end, because those shiny new shoes are going to carry him right into the capital of the Twilight Zone."

After slipping on a pair of expensive shoes he's removed from the body of a murdered gangster, Bledsoe is taken over by the spirit of the dead man—a spirit intent on revenge. He locates the killer—Dagget, the deceased's former business partner—and tries to shoot him, but is instead gunned down himself. Before he dies, the ghost inside Bledsoe makes a pledge: to keep coming back until he succeeds in killing Dagget. Bledsoe's body is dumped in an alley. Assuming Bledsoe is asleep, a fellow vagrant steals the fancy shoes—and the cycle begins anew.

"There's an old saying that goes, 'If the shoe fits, wear it.' But be careful. If you happen to find a pair of size nine black-and-gray loafers, made to order in the old country, be very careful—you might walk right into the Twilight Zone."

Originally, the idea of this episode was to have the haunted item be a cowboy hat, but this was soon altered. "I think it was a good change," says Buck Houghton, "because it seems to me that shoes would take you places you weren't intending to go, whereas a hat wouldn't."

Although the show is credited to Charles Beaumont, at the time Beaumont was too loaded down with other assignments to do the script, so he farmed the job out to OCee Ritch, who had originated the idea for "Static." At the very least, Ritch ghostwrote the entire first draft of the script, a fact of which Buck Houghton was totally unaware at the time. Perhaps as a result of all these subterranean dealings, the writing is very muddy, the characterizations extremely sketchy. The idea is a good one, but the story lacks a feeling of authenticity. The characters all feel like old carbon copies of various B-movie types, rather than being based on real people, and this is death for "Dead Man's Shoes."

"A PIANO IN THE HOUSE" (2/16/62)

Barry Morse

Written by Earl Hamner, Jr.
Producer: Buck Houghton
Director: David Greene
Director of Photography: George T. Clemens
Music: stock

Cast:
Fitzgerald Fortune: Barry Morse
Esther Fortune: Joan Hackett
Marge Moore: Muriel Landers
Marvin the Butler: Cyril Delevanti
Gregory Walker: Don Durant
Throckmorton: Phil Coolidge

"Mr. Fitzgerald Fortune, theater critic and cynic at large, on his way to a birthday party. If he knew what is in store for him he probably wouldn't go, because before this evening is over that cranky old piano is going to play 'Those Piano Roll Blues'—with some effects that could happen only in the Twilight Zone."

Fortune buys his wife a player piano for her birthday, then discovers it has magical properties—its music reveals people's hidden faces. A hard-hearted curio-shop owner gushes with sentimentality; a solemn butler bursts out with gales of laughter. Using it on his wife, Fortune discovers that she actually detests him. Fortune decides that the piano is the ideal tool to humiliate his wife's party guests. Under the music's spell, a seemingly jaded playwright admits to being passionately in love with Fortune's wife. A boisterous fat woman reveals fantasies of being a delicate, graceful little girl and a beloved, beautiful snowflake. Delighted with his cruel game, Fortune hands his wife another roll to put in the piano, but she substitutes a *different* piece, one that bewitches Fortune and strips him of his facade. In truth, he is no more than a frightened, sadistic child. Disgusted and embarrassed, the guests depart—along with Fortune's wife.

"Mr. Fitzgerald Fortune, a man who went searching for concealed persons and found himself—in the Twilight Zone."

Earl Hamner, Jr.'s "A Piano in the House" unfortunately suffers from superficial characterization. The main character is a sadistic theater critic (Barry Morse) with the unlikely name of Fitzgerald Fortune. He buys a magic player piano that has the ability to reveal people's inner selves and uses it to humiliate his wife (Joan Hackett) and various of her friends. In the end, of course, the piano is turned against Fortune himself and we see that he is nothing more than an ill-tempered child. The episode boasts competent performances by Joan Hackett as Fortune's wife and Cyril Delevanti as his butler, plus an exceptional performance by Muriel Landers as a fat woman with a fragile and secret soul.

Again the problem was the writer dealing with characters not at all connected with reality. Says Earl Hamner, "I'd never known a critic, but it was my idea of what a critic was like."

"SHOWDOWN WITH RANCE McGREW" (2/2/62)

Larry Blyden and Arch Johnson

Written by Rod Serling
Based on an idea by
Frederic Louis Fox
Producer: Buck Houghton
Director: Christian Nyby
Director of Photography:
George T. Clemens
Music: stock

Cast:
Rance McGrew: Larry Blyden
Jesse James: Arch Johnson
Director: Robert Cornthwaite
TV Jesse James: Robert Kline
Property Man: William McLean
Cowboy #1: Troy Melton
Cowboy #2: Jay Overholts
TV Bartender: Robert J. Stevenson
Old Man: Hal K. Dawson
Double for Rance: Jim Turley

"Some one-hundred-odd years ago, a motley collection of tough moustaches galloped across the West and left behind a raft of legends and legerdemains, and it seems a reasonable conjecture that if there are any television sets up in cowboy heaven and any of these rough-and-wooly nail-eaters could see with what careless abandon their names are bandied about, they're very likely turning over in their graves—or worse, getting out of them. Which gives you a clue as to the proceedings that will begin in just a moment, when one Mr. Rance McGrew, a three-thousand-buck-a-week phony-baloney discovers that this week's current edition of make-believe is being shot on location—and that location is the Twilight Zone."

Temperamental TV cowboy star McGrew is about to film a scene in which "Jesse James" shoots him in the back when he abruptly finds himself in a genuine Old West saloon. The *real* Jesse James enters and explains that he and the other famous desperadoes are dismayed at how they are portrayed on McGrew's show. He challenges McGrew—who's never shot a gun in his life—to a showdown. McGrew tries to run away, but Jesse corners him and draws. McGrew falls to his knees, saying he'll do anything if only Jesse will spare him. Jesse accepts; McGrew is returned to the set. But then McGrew's "agent"—Jesse himself—arrives. He intends to stay and insure that the outlaws consistently have the upper hand—beginning with the TV Jesse throwing McGrew through a plate-glass window.

"The evolution of the so-called 'adult' western, and the metamorphosis of one Rance McGrew, formerly phony-baloney, now upright citizen with a preoccupation with all things involving tradition, truth and cowpoke predecessors. It's the way the cookie crumbles and the six-gun shoots . . . in the Twilight Zone."

This is what Serling had to say about the episode: "Fred Fox had an interesting notion, which was quite serious, about a modern-day cowpoke, not a television star, who found himself living in the past. It had no sense of humor in it. It was a straightforward piece. But it struck me that it would be a terribly interesting concept to have a guy who plays the role of a Hollywood cowboy suddenly thrust into the maelstrom of reality in which he has to do all these acts of prowess against real people. . . . And it just occurred to me, My God, what would happen if the Rance McGrews of our time had to face this? I used to think this about John Wayne all the time, who had fought most of our major wars. In truth, of course, they were fought on the backlot of Warner Brothers, in which the most deadly jeopardy would be to get hit by a flying starlet. And I always wondered what Wayne's reaction would be if he ever had to lift up an M-1 and go through a bloody foxhole on attack sometime. But this is the element of humor that I was striving to get."

An intriguing concept, but "Showdown With Rance McGrew" fails to come off, specifically because the "real" Old West presented in the episode is every bit as TV-phony as the bogus Old West in the episode. The sets are identical and the look is the same. The "real" Jesse James is no closer to historical reality than the phony one. Had it been done correctly, with the Old West presented as it *really* was, the show probably would have been quite entertaining—and it might have helped to deflate a few myths. As it is, though, "Showdown With Rance McGrew" is just dated, tedious, and silly.

"THE LITTLE PEOPLE" (3/30/62)

Robert Eaton and Michael Ford

Written by Rod Serling
Producer: Buck Houghton
Director: William Claxton
Director of Photography: George T. Clemens
Music: stock

Cast:
Peter Craig: Joe Maross
William Fletcher: Claude Akins
Spaceman #1: Michael Ford
Spaceman #2: Robert Eaton

"The time is the space age, the place is a barren landscape of a rock-walled canyon that lies millions of miles from the planet Earth. The cast of characters? You've met them: William Fletcher, commander of the spaceship; his copilot, Peter Craig. The other characters who inhabit this place you may never see, but they're there, as these two gentlemen will soon find out. Because they're about to partake in a little exploration into that gray, shaded area in space and time that's known as the Twilight Zone."

After their ship is damaged by meteors, Fletcher and Craig set down in the canyon to effect repairs. While Fletcher works on the engines, Craig investigates the terrain—and discovers an Earth-type civilization populated by beings no larger than ants. Craig becomes a full-blown megalomaniac, terrorizing the little people by stamping on their city and proclaiming himself a god. When Fletcher informs him that the ship is fixed and that they can leave, Craig pulls a gun on him and orders him to depart alone; he intends to stay—and there's no room for *two* gods. Fletcher blasts off. But then *another* ship lands. Two spacemen emerge, bigger than mountains, towering over Craig. Hysterically, he screams at them to go away. Drawn by the sound, one of the spacemen picks Craig up, inadvertently crushing him to death.

"The case of navigator Peter Craig, a victim of a delusion. In this case, the dream dies a little harder than the man. A small exercise in space psychology that you can try on for size—in the Twilight Zone."

Of "The Little People," Buck Houghton remembers, "For the final shot we were having a hell of a time, because scale is very hard to achieve. And what we did was to take a shot that had been made for 'I Shot an Arrow Into the Air.' We were in Death Valley, and because the fellow in search of where the hell they were decided to go over that mountain and somebody said, 'Geez, we can't get over *that,*' we had a point-of-view shot straight up to the mountains, very tall, very ominous, shot quite close to the foot of it. I recalled a painting I once ran across, I forget by whom, a fairly famous painter of former times, that posed a genie who was looming up over mountains that gave him scale. So what we did was take an up shot of the two astronauts and matted this shot that we had of the mountains over it, so that they looked like they were standing over something that had some scale."

As far as science goes, "The Little People" is out-and-out fantasy. As height is squared, volume is cubed, meaning that weight increases at a much faster rate than size. Humans the size of those seen at the end of the episode couldn't possibly exist; their own weight would crush them. So if you come upon a race of intelligent little creatures and decide you might like to be their god, don't worry, no one significantly larger will come along to upstage you . . . at least, no one human.

"I SING THE BODY ELECTRIC" (5/18/62)

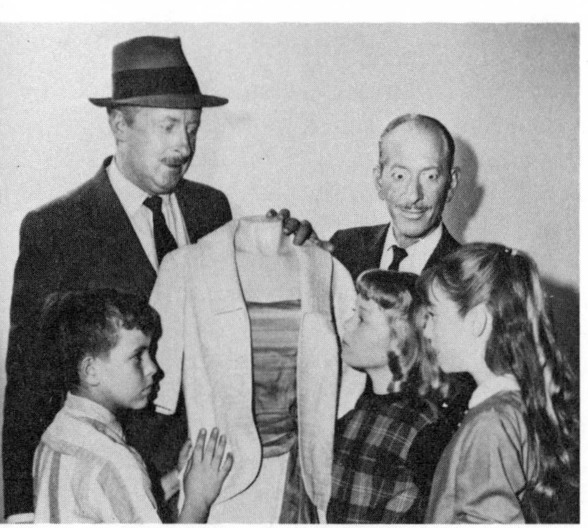

David White, Vaughn Taylor, Charles Herbert, Dana Dillaway and Veronica Cartwright

Written by Ray Bradbury
Based on the short story "I Sing the Body Electric" by Ray Bradbury
Producer: Buck Houghton
Directors: James Sheldon and William Claxton
Director of Photography: George T. Clemens
Music: Van Cleave

Cast:
Grandma: Josephine Hutchinson
Anne (age 11): Veronica Cartwright
Father: David White
Tom (age 12): Charles Herbert
Karen (age 10): Dana Dillaway
Salesman: Vaughn Taylor
Nedra: Doris Packer
Anne (age 19): Susan Crane
Tom (age 20): Paul Nesbitt
Karen (age 18): Judy Morton

"They make a fairly convincing pitch here. It doesn't seem possible, though, to find a woman who might be ten times better than mother in order to seem half as good—except, of course, in the Twilight Zone."

A widower buys a robot grandmother to act as a surrogate mother for his three children. Karen and Tom take to this intelligent, maternal machine almost instantly, but Anne steadfastly refuses to be won over. "Grandma" reminds Anne of her mother—a mother she bitterly resents for having died. When Anne blindly runs into the path of an oncoming van, Grandma throws herself in front of it, saving Anne's life. But Grandma isn't injured; being a robot has its advantages. Realizing that Grandma *can't* leave her as her mother did, Anne finally lets down her guard and reciprocates the robot's love. Years pass, during which the children grow up under Grandma's affectionate supervision. As Tom, Anne and Karen prepare to leave for college, Grandma tells them she is returning to Facsimile, Limited. She is well-satisfied that her job here is completed.

"A fable? Most assuredly. But who's to say at some distant moment there might not be an assembly line producing a gentle product in the form of a grandmother whose stock in trade is love. Fable, sure—but who's to say?"

"I Sing the Body Electric" encountered trouble almost from the beginning. Although Veronica Cartwright (who as an adult would have memorable roles in *Invasion of the Body Snatchers* and *Alien*) turns in a good performance as Anne, the other two children are poor. Also, director James Sheldon was strongly opposed to the casting of Hutchinson as the electronic grandmother. In retrospect this is curious, because with her warmth, maturity and intelligence she seems well-suited to the role.

Buck Houghton recalls that great pains were taken in an attempt to improve the episode. "We did retakes. We practically did that over. It just didn't work. The first thing was done in October of '61 and the next one was done in February of '62, and it was damn near a full re-do. Aunt Nedra was played by June Vincent in the original and Doris Packer in the second. It just wasn't an acceptable picture . . . and so we rewrote." Directing the retakes was William Claxton, director of "The Last Flight," "The Jungle," and "The Little People." "I guess Jim Sheldon wasn't available," says Houghton. "Normally, I'd have called him back."

The final version that was arrived at works fairly well; it's a pleasant story. But somehow one feels that it was meant to be more, to strike a warm chord of recognition, as "Walking Distance" had done, and in this area it misses the mark. Nevertheless, "I Sing the Body Electric" is that rarity on *The Twilight Zone,* an adaptation of a story by a famous science-fiction writer adapted by the writer himself, and that alone makes it notable.

It should be mentioned that initially it was intended for Ray Bradbury's involvement with *The Twilight Zone* to be far greater than just one script.

Prior to the show's debut, several articles even named him as a major contributor along with Matheson and Beaumont. Indirectly, Bradbury's influence on the series was significant. In an afterword to Beaumont's collection *The Magic Man,* Richard Matheson wrote, " . . . [It] was Ray who helped both Chuck and myself on the initial steps of our writing careers—as he had helped others. I was living in Brooklyn at the time, just graduated from college, and Ray was highly generous in his correspondence and encouragement. It meant a good deal to me. Chuck, fortunate enough to be living in Los Angeles, had more personal contact with Ray and accordingly enjoyed an even closer communication and a greater proportion of encouragement and inspiration. I know that it meant a good deal to him as well."

Bradbury's influence on Serling, although not a personal relationship as in the cases of Beaumont and Matheson, was still a major one. Serling's favorite science-fiction writers were Bradbury, Isaac Asimov, and Robert A. Heinlein. He had learned about the genre from reading their works. But beyond the field of science fiction, there was a more specific theme linking Bradbury and Serling. Serling had been born in Binghamton in 1924, Bradbury in Waukegan, Illinois, four years earlier. Both had wonderful small-town childhoods which left a permanent mark on their sensibilities and on their work. In Bradbury's nostalgic, small-town stories, Serling must have read much with which he wholeheartedly agreed. When he wrote "Walking Distance" and "A Stop at Willoughby," Serling realized that he was on Bradbury's turf, so to speak, and he made oblique acknowledgment of the fact by adding references to "Dr. Bradbury" in "Walking Distance" and "the Bradbury account" in "A Stop at Willoughby."

So the question arises: if Bradbury's influence on *The Twilight Zone* was so great, why was his participation so minimal? "I Sing the Body Electric" is his only episode, and that in the third season.

The answer is a complex one.

Bradbury was approached by Serling and Houghton before *The Twilight Zone* began production and seemed perfectly willing to be a major contributor. On July, 23, 1959, he submitted a full teleplay adaptation of his short story, "Here There Be Tygers" (which appears in his collection *R Is For Rocket*), with this cover letter:

> Dear Buck and Rod:
>
> I'd be happy to hear any suggestions you want to make about this: HERE THERE BE TYGERS. And as soon as you want me to, I'll start on another for you. I have several weeks of extra time starting now.
>
> Best,
> Ray

"Here There Be Tygers" concerns an expedition of space explorers that lands on a planet so idyllic that it seems almost impossible. The grass is short and smells newly mown. Streams are filled with white wine. Fish jump out of cold springs into hot springs and cook right before your eyes. Winds gently lift you so that you can fly like a bird. The men quickly realize that the entire planet is a single conscious entity, one willing to supply their slightest whim simply in return for kind treatment. The men take this in stride, enjoying the first-class treatment—all except Chatterton, the minerologist, whom the men call "Chat." He's wary of the planet and doesn't trust it. He warns the others, saying, "To quote a map I saw once in medieval history: 'Here There Be Tygers.' When you're all asleep, the tygers and cannibals will show up." Finally, Chatterton attacks the planet with a huge drill mounted on a tractor. The planet swallows the tractor in a tar pit, then summons up a tiger that kills Chatterton. The rest of the men hurriedly board their ship, all but one who elects to remain behind. From space, the explorers see the planet erupt in volcanoes, avalanches, and lightning storms, but this is only an illusion for their benefit. On the surface, the planet is serene. With a running start, the lone crewman leaps into the air and flies away from the camera, over the horizon to where the distant voices of laughing women can be heard.

Although a beautifully written script, Serling and Houghton passed on "Here There Be Tygers." A year and a half later, they *did* buy Bradbury's adaptation of his short story "A Miracle of Rare Device" (collected in *The Machineries of Joy*), which concerns two likeable tramps who attempt to homestead a mirage that assumes the appearance of any city the person looking at it has most wanted to visit. This too was quite well written. It got as far as having a director tentatively assigned to it, Tony Leader, who had done "Long Live Walter Jameson" and "The Midnight Sun." But like "Here There Be Tygers," it was never produced.

Why is it that the talents of Bradbury were utilized so little when they were so readily available?

Part of the answer might be found in something Serling said in 1975. "Ray Bradbury is a very difficult guy to dramatize, because that which reads so beautifully on the printed page doesn't fit in the mouth—it fits in the head. And you find characters saying the things that Bradbury's saying and you say, 'Wait a minute, people don't say that.'" Certainly, Bradbury's dialogue does lean to the poetic and this might have been a consideration.

Then, too, there were logistical considerations. In "Here There Be Tygers," there were five men flying, a spaceship landing and taking off, a futuristic mobile drill that is enveloped by tar and sinks out of sight, and scenes of planetary turmoil including volcanoes, lightning storms, avalanches, and monsters rising up. "Any one of those I would have tackled without any particular trepidation," says Buck Houghton, "but two of them would have been a worry and three of them would have been a deal-breaker."

As for Bradbury, his comments shed little light on the subject: "I would prefer not to write or talk much about *Twilight Zone* or my stories. The series is over and done, my work for it stands on its own. For various reasons two scripts were never done. I don't recall the reasons now, so many years later."

Perhaps in some alternate universe, Cayuga Productions bought "Here There Be Tygers." Perhaps in that parallel world there was a long and fruitful working relationship with Bradbury that included *Twilight Zone* adaptations of "Mars Is Heaven," "The Veldt," "A Sound of Thunder," "Kaleidoscope," and many, many more.

But not in this universe, and that's a shame.

"FOUR O'CLOCK" (4/6/62)

Theodore Bikel

Written by Rod Serling
Based on the short story "Four O'Clock" by Price Day
Producer: Buck Houghton
Director: Lamont Johnson
Director of Photography: George T. Clemens
Music: stock

Cast:
Oliver Crangle: Theodore Bikel
Mrs. Williams: Moyna MacGill
Mrs. Lucas: Phyllis Love
Hall: Linden Chiles

"That's Oliver Crangle, a dealer in petulance and poison. He's rather arbitrarily chosen four o'clock as his personal Götterdämmerung, *and we are about to watch the metamorphosis of a twisted fanatic, poisoned by the gangrene of prejudice, to the status of an avenging angel, upright and omniscient, dedicated and fearsome. Whatever your clocks say, it's four o'clock—and wherever you are it happens to be the Twilight Zone."*

Political fanatic Oliver Crangle keeps detailed files on people and makes phone calls and sends letters discrediting those he has determined are evil. By mystical and unspecified means, he determines to shrink every evil person in the world to a height of two feet tall at exactly four o'clock. But when the time rolls around, it is *he* who becomes two feet tall!

"At four o'clock, an evil man made his bed and lay in it, a pot called a kettle

black, a stone-thrower broke the windows of his glass house. You look for this one under 'F' for fanatic and 'J' for justice—in the Twilight Zone."

"Four O'Clock" was Serling's adaptation of a story by Price Day that appears in *Alfred Hitchcock Presents: 14 of My Favorites in Suspense* (Random House, 1959). Although dealing with a subject Serling felt strongly about, the writing is not sharp, and the characters are oversimplified to the point of caricature. As Crangle, Bikel is fun to watch, but one feels he could have done a much better job had Serling given him a more substantial character to work with.

"THE GIFT" (4/27/62)

Edmund Vargas

Written by Rod Serling
Producer: Buck Houghton
Director: Allen H. Miner
Director of Photography: George T. Clemens
Music: Laurindo Almeida

Cast:
Williams: Geoffrey Horne
Doctor: Nico Minardos
Pedro: Edmund Vargas
Manuelo: Cliff Osmond
Officer: Paul Mazursky
Guitarist: Vladimir Sokoloff
Rudolpho: Vito Scotti
Woman: Carmen D'Antonio
Sanchez: Henry Corden
Woman #2: Lea Marmer
Man #1: Joe Perry
Man #2: David Fresco

"The place is Mexico, just across the Texas border, a mountain village held back in time by its remoteness and suddenly intruded upon by the twentieth century. And this is Pedro, nine years old, a lonely, rootless little boy, who will soon make the acquaintance of a traveller from a distant place. We are at present forty miles from the Rio Grande, but any place and all places can be—the Twilight Zone."

After crash-landing outside the village, a human-looking alien accidentally kills one police officer, and is himself wounded by another. He stumbles to a village bar where he collapses. A sympathetic doctor removes two bullets from his chest. While recuperating, the alien—who calls himself "Mr.

Williams"—is befriended by Pedro, a somber orphan who sweeps up the bar. Williams gives Pedro a gift, which he says he will explain later. Meanwhile, the bartender has notified the army as to the alien's whereabouts. Williams tries to escape but is cornered by soldiers and villagers. He tells Pedtro to show them the gift, but it is snatched from him and set afire. The soldiers shoot Williams and kill him. The doctor takes the remnant of the gift from the fire. It reads, "Greetings to the people of Earth. We come . . . in peace. We bring you this gift. The following chemical formula is . . . a vaccine against all forms of cancer . . ." The rest is burned away.

"Madeiro, Mexico, the present. The subject: fear. *The cure: a little more faith. An Rx off a shelf—in the Twilight Zone."*

At some point prior to the filming of the *Twilight Zone* pilot, Rod Serling wrote an additional, hour-length pilot script that was never produced. Entitled "I Shot an Arrow Into the Air" (but bearing no relation to the first-season episode of the same name), the plot concerned an intelligent and sensitive little boy who was shunned by his peers because his father died in the explosion of a home-made rocket ship (his mother defends his father by explaining he was simply "a man whose dreams were just a little bigger than his knowledge"). The boy's solitude proves an asset, however, when he stumbles upon a wounded alien in the woods and befriends him. With his aid, the alien is able to return to his home planet. The boy grows up to be an astronaut and, years later, meets his friend once again, in space. Three years later, Serling cannibalized this script, changed the location to Mexico and shortened it into "The Gift."

"The Gift" is no gift to fans of *The Twilight Zone,* however. It is pretentious, stereotypical, and insulting, particularly to anyone of Mexican heritage. With the exception of Pedro, the doctor, and a blind guitar player (Vladimir Sokoloff), all the people in the village are presented as superstitious, fearful peasants who prefer to see the alien as an agent of the Devil rather than as a friendly emissary from "beyond the stars."

"The Gift" has a guitar score composed and performed by Laurindo Almeida, one of the great classical guitarists, and that's about all it has to recommend it. The child playing Pedro is a beautiful child, but as Buck Houghton freely admits, "He couldn't act at all." As the alien, Geoffrey Horne doesn't do much better, delivering his lines as though he wished he were serving tables somewhere instead.

"HOCUS-POCUS AND FRISBY" (4/13/62)

Frisby's alien

Written by Rod Serling
Based on an unpublished story by Frederic Louis Fox
Producer: Buck Houghton
Director: Lamont Johnson
Directors of Photography: George T. Clemens and Jack Swain
Music: Tom Morgan
Makeup: William Tuttle

Cast:
Frisby: Andy Devine
Alien #1: Milton Selzer
Alien #2: Larry Breitman
Mitchell: Howard McNear
Scanlan: Dabbs Greer
Old Man: Clem Bevans
Alien #3: Peter Brocco

"The reluctant gentleman with the sizeable mouth is Mr. Frisby. He has all the drive of a broken camshaft and the aggressive vinegar of a corpse. As you've no doubt gathered, his big stock in trade is the tall tale. Now, what he doesn't know is that the visitors out front are a very special breed, destined to change his life beyond anything even his *fertile imagination could manufacture. The place is Pitchville Flats, the time is the present. But Mr. Frisby's on the first leg of a rather fanciful journey into the place we call the Twilight Zone."*

Taking his self-aggrandizing tales at face value, aliens masquerading as humans spirit Frisby away to their flying saucer, with the intention of taking him home as a zoo specimen—after all, he advertised himself as the optimum human. Unable to convince them of their error, Frisby decides to relax by playing his harmonica—and discovers that the sound knocks the aliens out! Frisby escapes, and the frightened aliens hurriedly depart. Returning to the combination general store and gas station he owns, Frisby finds all his friends waiting for him; it's a surprise birthday party. But when he tries to tell them of his abduction—no one believes him!

"Mr. Somerset Frisby, who might have profited by reading an Aesop fable about a boy who cried wolf. Tonight's tall tale from the timberlands—of the Twilight Zone."

"Hocus-Pocus and Frisby" was a fairly funny piece. Andy Devine, with his scraped-wall of a voice, is well-cast as the big blowhard Frisby. The aliens, with their whole-head latex masks, aren't very convincing, but since this is a comedy that's not terribly important.

Andy Devine

"PERSON OR PERSONS UNKNOWN" (3/23/62)

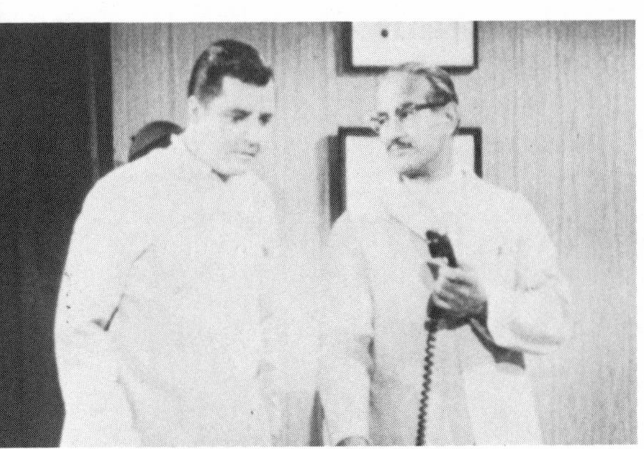

Richard Long and Frank Silvera

Written by Charles Beaumont
Producer: Buck Houghton
Director: John Brahm
Director of Photography: Robert W. Pittack
Music: stock

Cast:
David Gurney: Richard Long
Dr. Koslenko: Frank Silvera
Wilma #1: Shirley Ballard
Wilma #2: Julie Van Zandt
Woman Clerk: Betty Harford
Sam Baker: Ed Glover
Policeman: Michael Keep
Bank Guard: Joe Higgins
Mr. Cooper: John Newton

"Cameo of a man who has just lost his most valuable possession. He doesn't know about the loss yet. In fact, he doesn't even know about the possession. Because, like most people, David Gurney has never really thought about the matter of his identity. But he's going to be thinking about it a great deal from now on, because that *is what he's lost. And his search for it is going to take him into the darkest corners of the Twilight Zone."*

David Gurney wakes up to find that no one—not his wife, his fellow workers, his best friend, or even his own mother—knows him, and that all evidence of his identity has inexplicably disappeared. He's committed to an asylum but manages to escape and find a photograph of himself and his wife, *proving* that she must know him. But when the police arrive with a psychiatrist, the picture has changed and shows Gurney alone. He throws himself on the ground—and wakes up in bed. It was all a bad dream. His wife gets out of bed and talks to him from the bathroom as she removes cream from her face. But when she emerges, Gurney is horrified to see that, although she talks and acts the same as always, she doesn't look anything at all like the wife he knows!

"A case of mistaken identity or a nightmare turned inside out? A simple loss of memory or the end of the world? David Gurney may never find the answer, but you can be sure he's looking for it—in the Twilight Zone."

In Charles Beaumont's "Person or Persons Unknown," once again we have Serling's "fear of the unknown working on *you,* which you cannot share with others." This, more than any other kind of story, is what *The Twilight Zone* is all about.

If there is any weakness to "Person or Persons Unknown," it lies in its close similarity to Matheson's "A World of Difference," leaving one with the feeling that it had already been done before. However, this is more than made up for by any number of factors. Richard Long's acting is very good. He takes just long enough to realize that what is happening to him is no joke, and he acts in a perfectly natural manner. Everyone else in the cast acts just as you think they would, trying to see to it that Gurney's delusion disrupts their lives as little as possible. The direction by John Brahm is fine and unobtrusive. Finally, there is the show's subtle reaffirmation of a fact we all know very well—that you can act a hell of a lot crazier with people you know than with those you don't.

"LITTLE GIRL LOST" (3/16/62)

Tracy Stratford

Written by Richard Matheson
Based on the short story "Little Girl Lost" by Richard Matheson
Producer: Buck Houghton
Director: Paul Stewart
Director of Photography: George T. Clemens
Music: Bernard Herrmann

Cast:
Bill: Charles Aidman
Chris Miller: Robert Sampson
Ruth Miller: Sarah Marshall
Tina: Tracy Stratford
Tina's Voice: Rhoda Williams

"Missing: one frightened little girl. Name: Bettina Miller. Description: six years of age, average height and build, light brown hair, quite pretty. Last seen being tucked in bed by her mother a few hours ago. Last heard—aye, there's the rub, as Hamlet put it. For Bettina Miller can be heard quite clearly, despite the rather curious fact that she can't be seen at all. Present location? Let's say for the moment—in the Twilight Zone."

When his daughter Tina rolls underneath her bed and disappears, Chris Miller summons the aid of his friend Bill, a physicist—after which the family dog bolts under the bed and disappears, too. Bill suspects Tina has fallen through a hole into another dimension, a theory borne out when he puts his hand through a seemingly-solid wall. Chris reaches his arm through in an attempt to grab Tina and inadvertently pitches forward, halfway through the hole—and finds himself in a world of bizarre, distorted sights and sounds. He calls the dog, who brings Tina to him. Chris grabs hold of both Tina and the dog, and Bill pulls the three of them out. None too soon—the hole has closed; the wall is entirely solid. "Another few seconds," Bill tells Chris, "and half of you would have been here and the other half . . ."

"The other half where? The fourth dimension? The fifth? Perhaps. They never found the answer. Despite a battery of research physicists equipped with every device known to man, electronic and otherwise, no result was ever achieved, except perhaps a little more respect for and uncertainty about the mechanisms of the Twilight Zone."

Richard Matheson's final episode of the third season was "Little Girl Lost," a gripping science-fiction story about a little girl who falls through a hole between dimensions.

"That was based on an occurrence that happened to our daughter," says Matheson. "She didn't go into the fourth dimension, but she cried one night and I went to where she was and couldn't find her anywhere. I couldn't find her on the bed, I couldn't find her on the ground. She had fallen off and rolled all the way under the bed against the wall. At first, even when I felt under the bed, I couldn't reach her. It was bizarre, and that's where I got the idea."

Matheson wrote the original short story, which appears in his collection *The Shores of Space* (Bantam, 1957), in 1953. He tried to keep the feeling of it as real as possible, to the point that the wife is named Ruth and the daughter Tina—the names of his real-life wife and daughter. In adapting the story into a teleplay he strove to maintain this feeling of mundane reality gone askew.

Several things work against the credibility of the episode, however. For those scenes of her in the fourth dimension, the voice of Tina was supplied by adult actress Rhoda Williams, and it *sounds* like an adult impersonating a child. As the mother, Sarah Marshall is almost continuously hysterical, dishevelled and off-balance. Rather than contributing in a positive manner, she merely irritates with her emotionalism and incompetence. As for the father, played by Robert Sampson, he's all right in a bland way, except for the curious fact that before he checks to see if his daughter has somehow fallen under the house, he calls his friend Bill because he's a physicist and might know if she's in another dimension.

Two factors override all of these negatives. The first is Matheson's first-rate script, and the second is the bravura performance of Charles Aidman as the physicist friend of the little girl's father. In "And When the Sky Was Opened," Aidman made a fantastic concept—disappearing off the face of the Earth—seem altogether real. Here he accomplishes the same feat. In a role that affords no character whatsoever, that consists almost entirely of an extremely long and theoretical monologue on the nature of other dimensions, Aidman conveys intelligence and supreme competence. He is a rock, an anchor that holds the episode securely in place.

Creating the look and sound of the fourth dimension was an enjoyable challenge to those connected with the show. Bernard Herrmann's score, full of woodwinds and strings, is beautiful and strange. So too are several shots in which Charles Aidman's hand goes *through* a wall, into the other dimension. Amazingly, these shots were *not* double exposures. Director of photography George Clemens arranged that the wall be built with the center section parallel to but a foot behind the rest of the wall. The wall was then flooded with light to a degree that the separation was invisible. The camera was positioned at an angle to the wall. When Aidman placed his hand in the space between the sections of wall, his hand appeared to go through the wall and disappear. Says Clemens, "You look through the camera, you'd swear it was all one solid wall." Clemens recalls that a scene was filmed showing the little girl going through the wall into the other dimension, but it was not included in the finished episode.

Finally, there was the fourth dimension itself, a bizarre place of total distortion. "We did a lot of it with putting oil on glass and moving it in front of the camera," says Clemens, "and secondly, where we were unable to achieve all the results we wanted, we put it in the optical printer." Additionally, Clemens double exposed reflections from a mirrored ball onto these scenes.

"It was pretty nice," Richard Matheson says of the episode. "Aidman is a marvelous actor, and Paul Stewart directed it well. It had a nice feeling to it. The fourth dimension could have been a little stranger, but it wasn't bad at all; I was very pleased with it."

"THE DUMMY" (5/4/62)

Cliff Robertson

Written by Rod Serling
Based on an unpublished story by Lee Polk
Producer: Buck Houghton
Director: Abner Biberman
Director of Photography: George T. Clemens
Music: stock

Cast:
Jerry Etherson: Cliff Robertson
Frank: Frank Sutton
Willy (as ventriloquist): George Murdock
Georgie: John Harmon
Noreen: Sandra Warner
M.C.: Rudy Dolan
Doorkeeper: Ralph Manza
Chorus Girl: Bethelynn Grey
Chorus Girl: Edy Williams

"You're watching a ventriloquist named Jerry Etherson, a voice-thrower par excellence. *His alter ego, sitting atop his lap, is a brash stick of kindling with the sobriquet 'Willy.' In a moment, Mr. Etherson and his knotty-pine partner will be booked in one of the out-of-the-way bistros, that small, dark, intimate place known as the Twilight Zone."*

Jerry, who drinks more than is good for him, is convinced that Willie is alive—and malevolent. Frank, Jerry's manager, believes Jerry's problem is entirely in his mind, but Jerry refuses to listen to him. Instead, he determines to attempt to escape from Willie. When his act with Goofy Goggles—a dummy *without* a will of his own—is well-received, Jerry locks Willie in a trunk and departs the club with Goofy, intending to abandon Willie. But suddenly, Jerry hears Willie's voice, taunting him, and sees Willie's shadow on a wall. In a frenzy, he rushes back to the club, unlocks the trunk and smashes the dummy to pieces. To his horror, he sees it is *Goofy* he has destroyed. Willie laughs maniacally. Sometime later, Willie and Jerry play a club in Kansas City, but Willie has transformed into the ventriloquist—Jerry is the dummy!

"What's known in the parlance of the times as the old switcheroo, from boss to blockhead in a few easy lessons. And if you're given to nightclubbing on occasion, check this act. It's called Willie and Jerry, and they generally are

booked into some of the clubs along the 'Gray Night Way' known as the Twilight Zone."

In adapting "The Dummy" from a story by Lee Polk, Serling was greatly influenced by a sequence in the 1945 British film *Dead of Night,* in which Michael Redgrave plays a demented ventriloquist who believes his dummy is alive, and by "The Glass Eye," an episode of *Alfred Hitchcock Presents* concerning a woman who falls in love with a handsome ventriloquist only to discover that it is *he* who is the dummy and the "dummy" a dwarf ventriloquist. But Serling went these one better.

"The Dummy" was the first of four *Twilight Zone* episodes directed by Abner Biberman (the others were "The Incredible World of Horace Ford," "Number Twelve Looks Just Like You," and "I Am the Night—Color Me Black"). Previously, he had been an actor, appearing in such films as *Gunga Din, His Girl Friday, The Leopard Man,* and *Viva Zapata.* With "The Dummy," he demonstrated fine control as a director.

"The Dummy" has one of the most chilling final shots of any episode of *The Twilight Zone,* a slow camera pan from the grinning, now-human Willie to the dummy of Jerry. William Tuttle recalls that getting a ventriloquist's dummy to resemble Cliff Robertson was no mean feat. "That has quite a story connected with it," he says. "They wanted a caricature of

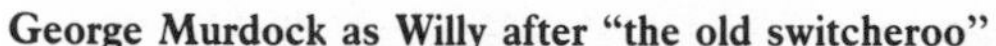

George Murdock as Willy after "the old switcheroo"

Robertson—a ventriloquist's dummy is a caricature, in a sense, it's not human—but they wanted it to look like him so that you could recognize it. They brought in a ventriloquist's dummy with the mechanics already in it, and I thought that was a good place to start and then build the caricature over that of Robertson. But I don't happen to be good at caricature in drawing, and we had to have something to work from.

"So I said to production manager Ralph Nelson, 'You need someone to do a caricature and I'm no good at it, I don't have the knack.' One of the greatest caricaturists is a man who calls himself T. Hee. He was one of the top men at Disney for many years. I first met him years ago. His name was Frank Campbell. He was a fantastic caricaturist. So I told Ralph Nelson all this, and he said, 'Well, maybe I can get in touch with him through Disney.' And they found him. He was living out in Mojave someplace.

"So I called him and I said, 'Frank, if you do some sketches, then we can work from the sketches.' We sent some pictures of Robertson out to him, and he made caricatures, and that's what we worked from."

"CAVENDER IS COMING" (5/25/62)

Jesse White, Carol Burnett and Albert Carrier

Written by Rod Serling
Producer: Buck Houghton
Director: Chris Nyby
Director of Photography: George T. Clemens
Music: stock

Cast:
Agnes Grep: Carol Burnett
Cavender: Jesse White
Polk: Howard Smith
Field Rep #1: William O'Connell
Field Rep #2: Pitt Herbert
Field Rep #3: John Fiedler
Field Rep #4: G. Stanley Jones
Stout: Frank Behrens
Frenchman: Albert Carrier
Bus Driver: Roy Sickner
Little Girl: Norma Shattuc
Little Boy: Rory O'Brien
Woman #1: Sandra Gould
Woman #2: Adrienne Marden
Truck Driver: Jack Younger
Child: Danny Kulick
Woman #3: Donna Douglas
Man #1: Maurice Dallimore
Matronly Woman: Barbara Morrison

"Small message of reassurance to that horizontal young lady: don't despair, help is en route. It's coming in an odd form from a very distant planet, but it's nonetheless coming. . . . Submitted for your approval, the case of one Miss Agnes Grep, put on Earth with two left feet, an overabundance of thumbs and a propensity for falling down manholes. In a moment she will be up to her jaw in miracles, wrought by apprentice angel Harmon Cavender, intent on winning his wings. And, though it's a fact that both of them should have stood in bed, they will tempt all the fates by moving into the cold, gray dawn of the Twilight Zone."

After losing her job as an usherette, clumsy-but-lovable Agnes Grep makes the acquaintance of Cavender, a bungling angel who has been assigned to help her as his last chance to win his wings. To alleviate her chronic unemployment, Cavender provides Agnes with a personal fortune and sets her up in a mansion. Unfortunately, a side effect of this is that none of the people in her old neighborhood—who previously adored her—now remember her. Preferring friends over riches, Agnes demands to be returned to her old life. Reluctantly, Cavender complies. Polk, Cavender's boss, is furious with him—until he notices that, back on Earth, Agnes is extremely happy. Given this, Polk decides that *other* mortals could use Cavender's services.

"A word to the wise now to any and all who might suddenly feel the presence of a cigar-smoking helpmate who takes bankbooks out of thin air. If you're suddenly aware of any such celestial aids, it means that you're under the beneficent care of one Harmon Cavender, guardian angel. And this message from the Twilight Zone: lotsa luck!"

During the first season, Serling had originally thought up "Mr. Bevis" with the intention of selling it as a pilot. With "Cavender Is Coming," he resurrected "Mr. Bevis," changed the gender of the main character, and gave it another shot. The basic plot, however, remains the same.

Playing the part of Agnes Grep, the main character in "Cavender," was Carol Burnett. "Rod was a great admirer of her," Buck Houghton recalls. "When he brought it up, saying, 'I'm going to do a picture for Carol Burnett,' I said, 'Who?' because I hadn't been seeing the variety show that established her. But he'd been an admirer of hers and apparently he had studied what it is that made her work."

In writing "Cavender Is Coming," Serling used material from Burnett's own life for certain sequences. At the beginning of the episode, Agnes is employed as an usherette. This was actually taken from one of Burnett's personal experiences. "The first day I went to work as an usherette," she related at the time, "the manager ran through a list of silent signals. Three fingers slapped on the wrist meant take a thirty-minute break. Opening your mouth like a fish and pointing to it meant you were thirsty. And when the manager poked his finger into the center of his palm, that meant he wanted a girl to stand in the center of the lobby to direct the patrons to the available seating. One of the girls worked up her own signal in reply to the boss's gestures. She poured a bag of buttered popcorn on his head and told him, 'That means I quit.'"

Unfortunately, the humor in "Cavender Is Coming" is so terminally unfunny that it would be better titled "Cadaver Is Coming." As the guardian angel, Jesse White tries his best, but the material is just too leaden. Throughout, Burnett seems utterly lost, making broad expressions in an effort to be funny, but never succeeding. Again, the fault lies with the writing.

Further hampering the episode is the inclusion of a laugh track, smeared over the action like a thick coat of paint.

Buck Houghton says of the laugh track, "That was CBS's idea, because they were in a pilot mood and they wanted to get a Jesse White thing going. I refused to go to the dubbing session with the canned laughter man there. I thought it was a dreadful idea."

Had "Mr. Bevis" sold, each week would have been a new adventure involving Bevis and his guardian angel. "Cavender Is Coming" took a different tack, in that each episode would have involved the guardian angel with a different human being. But although it got so far as to be considered a pilot, "Cavender Is Coming," like "Mr. Bevis," did not sell . . . a blessing as far as the American viewing public was concerned.

"THE CHANGING OF THE GUARD" (6/1/62)

Donald Pleasance and Philippa Bevans

Written by Rod Serling
Producer: Buck Houghton
Director: Robert Ellis Miller
Director of Photography: George T. Clemens
Music: stock
Makeup: William Tuttle

Cast:
Prof. Ellis Fowler: Donald Pleasence
Headmaster: Liam Sullivan
Mrs. Landers: Philippa Bevans
Graham: Bob Biheller
Butler: Kevin O'Neal
Boy #1: Jimmy Baird
Boy #2: Kevin Jones
Boy #3: Tom Lowell
Boy #4: Russell Horton
Boy #5: Buddy Hart
Boy #6: Darryl Richard
Boy #7: James Browning
Boy #8: Pat Close
Boy #9: Dennis Kerlee

"Professor Ellis Fowler, a gentle, bookish guide to the young, who is about to discover that life still has certain surprises, and that the campus of the Rock Springs School for Boys lies on a direct path to another institution, commonly referred to as the Twilight Zone."

Preparing to leave for Christmas vacation, Professor Fowler is informed by the Headmaster that, after fifty-one years of teaching, he is to be forcibly retired. Fowler is devastated by this news and begins to brood. That evening, having decided his teaching has accomplished nothing, he takes a pistol and walks back to the school, determined to commit suicide. Suddenly, he hears a school bell. He enters a classroom—and sees the ghosts of a number of his now-deceased students materialize. They're there for a purpose: to convince him that his lessons helped them to go on and commit acts of bravery. Fowler returns home, satisfied that he has made some mark in the world—and content now to retire.

"Professor Ellis Fowler, teacher, who discovered rather belatedly something of his own value. A very small scholastic lesson, from the campus of the Twilight Zone."

The theme of old age interested Rod Serling enough that he dealt with it in two scripts during the third season.

In "The Changing of the Guard," a saintly old schoolteacher *(á la Goodbye, Mr. Chips)* contemplates suicide after being forced into retirement. Well directed by Robert Ellis Miller (whose film work includes *The Heart Is a Lonely Hunter),* the episode boasts an enchanting performance by Donald Pleasance. In convincing age makeup by William Tuttle, he plays elderly Professor Ellis Fowler with grace and humility. It's not an easy role, as it is talky and clichéd, but Pleasance easily surmounts these obstacles.

One monologue is particularly memorable. After being informed of his termination, Fowler goes home and looks through old school yearbooks. He says to his housekeeper: "They all come and go like ghosts. Faces, names, smiles, the funny things they said or the sad things, or the poignant ones." He pauses thoughtfully. "I gave them nothing, I gave them nothing at all. Poetry that left their minds the minute they themselves left. Aged slogans that were out of date when I taught them. Quotations dear to me that were meaningless to them. I was a failure, Mrs. Landers, an abject, miserable failure. I walked from class to class an old relic, teaching by rote to unhearing ears, unwilling heads. I was an abject, dismal failure—I moved nobody. I motivated nobody. I left no imprint on anybody." He puts on his glasses and smiles. "Now, where do you suppose I ever got the idea that I was accomplishing anything?"

As performed by Pleasance, it's a poignant soliloquy, a summation of the life the main character now believes was utterly without worth. "Pleasance was an idea of the casting director's, I'd never heard of him," says Buck Houghton. "Boy, damn the expense; we brought him from England. He was just wonderful in it. He's a very nice man. I have a feeling it was his first time in this country professionally, and while he was a thoroughgoing professional with a huge experience in stage and everything else, he was a little apprehensive of this whole experience because he arrived on a given day and five days later it was all going to be over. So he had a lot to absorb. But Bob Miller is very together and gave him confidence and we were off and running."

"THE TRADE-INS" (4/20/62)

Joseph Schildkraut and Alma Platt

Written by Rod Serling
Producer: Buck Houghton
Director: Elliot Silverstein
Director of Photography:
George T. Clemens
Music: stock

Cast:
John Holt: Joseph Schildkraut
Marie Holt: Alma Platt
Mr. Vance: Noah Keen
Farraday: Theodore Marcuse
John Holt (young): Edson Stroll
Gambler #1: Terrence de Marney
Gambler #2: Billy Vincent
Receptionist: Mary McMahon
Attendant: David Armstrong

"Mr. and Mrs. John Holt, aging people who slowly and with trembling fingers turn the last pages of a book of life and hope against logic and the preordained that some magic printing press will add to this book another limited edition. But these two senior citizens happen to live in a time of the future where nothing is impossible, even the trading of old bodies for new. Mr. and Mrs. John Holt, in their twilight years—who are about to find that there happens to be a zone with the same name."

John and Marie Holt visit the New Life Corporation, hoping to transplant their personalities into youthful, artificial bodies. Unfortunately, they have only five thousands dollars—just enough for *one* body. Marie pleads with John—who is in constant pain—to have the operation himself, but he won't hear of it. Trying to double his money, John seeks out a poker game but succeeds only in losing the entire five thousand. Farraday, who runs the game, takes pity on him and gives him back his money. Finally overwhelmed by the pain, John submits to the operation. He emerges young and strong and free of pain. Enthusiastically, he tells Marie of their life to come, one filled with excitement and adventure. Suddenly, he stops, horrified in his realization that *she* is still old; the transformation has created a gulf between them. John returns to his old body, content that he and Marie will spend what time they have left . . . together.

"From Kahil Gibran's The Prophet: *'Love gives not but itself and takes not from itself, love possesses not nor would it be possessed, for love is sufficient unto love.' Not a lesson, just a reminder, from all the sentimentalists in the Twilight Zone."*

Joseph Schildkraut returned to *The Twilight Zone* in "The Trade-ins," a sensitive story by Serling. Alma Platt is excellent as Schildkraut's wife, but it is Schildkraut who makes the episode shine, portraying the main character, John Holt, as a strong, fine man beaten down by age and by excruciating pain. Ultimately, Holt yields to the pain, taking the transplant for himself (bolstered by his wife's insistent repetition of the word "yes" in an extremely moving scene). But when he emerges, young and healthy (and strangely minus his previous accent) in a new body (played by Edson Stroll), he runs smack into a painful truth: that where before he and his wife were united by age, now they are separated by it; he has gained a new world while she has lost the old. Holt returns to his old, pain-filled body, content in the knowledge that while the time he has left may not be great, it will not be lived in loneliness.

"The Trade-ins" is a story about love and courage, and Joseph Schildkraut does it up fine. But unbeknownst to all but those on the set, the same qualities were strongly at play within Schildkraut during the filming of the episode. Director Elliot Silverstein recalls, "He was undergoing a tragedy at the time . . . his own wife was dying. As a matter of fact, in the middle of the three-day schedule, his wife did in fact die. And he insisted that we not stop production for him; the Schildkraut family was a great theatrical family in Europe—he would finish the film and *then* mourn. He was in real tears, off-screen."

ESTABLISHMENT AND TRANSITION

By the close of the third season, *The Twilight Zone* had made cultural inroads beyond its status as a mere television series. In a world of ever-increasing oddness, "the twilight zone" was a phrase perfectly suited to describe any number of situations. "Dean Rusk, our Secretary of State, in a speech to the Senate, referred to 'the twilight zone in diplomacy,'" Serling noted. "When that happened, I thought, My gosh, we've arrived!"

Serling also must have chuckled when, during the 1962 California gubernatorial primaries, Governor Pat Brown said he was looking forward to the post-election TV logs reading, "Richard Nixon Returns to Twilight Zone."

In the spring of 1962, *The Twilight Zone* was late in finding a sponsor for its fourth season. As a result, CBS programmed a new show, *Fair Exchange,* into its time slot for the fall. Suddenly and without prior warning, *The Twilight Zone* was off the air. Serling's agent frantically attempted to work out some kind of deal with CBS so that the series could remain on television.

Meanwhile, Buck Houghton found himself without a job. At the same time, he received a very attractive offer from Four Star Productions. "During the last year at least and maybe before that," he recalls, "there were people that wanted me to work for them, and they were constantly saying, 'You can't tie your career to Rod's kite. Pretty soon you'll only be known as the producer of Rod Serling material,' and I said, 'No, I produced a lot of material before I ever met Rod.' But there were pressures to pull me away from there, and I knew that those pressures arose from the excellence of *Twilight Zone,* which in turn depended on Rod. So I thought, 'The hell with that, I'll stick with him.' And indeed I did, right up until it came to a position of fish or cut bait where I was really faced with the prospect of within a month turning down the Four Star deal and then having *Twilight Zone* not renewed, and losing both wasn't a choice I could conscientiously face myself with." He accepted the position with Four Star.

Eventually, CBS decided to renew *The Twilight Zone,* but in a different format. Eighteen episodes of the series were ordered, each an hour in length, to begin airing in January, 1963, as a mid-season replacement. At the recommendation of Serling and Houghton, CBS hired producer Herbert Hirschman to supervise these shows.

With the close of the third season, *The Twilight Zone* was losing more than just a producer. Together, Rod Serling and Buck Houghton had made the series what it was. They had given it an energy and an excitement unparalleled in series television. The two had complemented each other perfectly: Serling a cornucopia of ideas, characters, and stories; Houghton the master craftsman who lent concrete reality to Serling's fancies. They were a winning team. But in 1962, Houghton wasn't the only one who was leaving. Serling was leaving, too.

After CBS dropped *The Twilight Zone,* Serling accepted a teaching post at Antioch College, effective September, 1962, through January, 1963. The series' renewal made no change in this decision. Serling was tired of *The Twilight Zone* and burned out. Over the next two seasons, his involvement in the show would be greatly decreased. He would still host the show and contribute his share of scripts, but his input on the details of production would be minimal. Those decisions would be made by others.

Serling's reasons for going to Antioch pretty well illustrate his state of mind at the time. "I have three reasons," he said. "First is extreme fatigue. Secondly, I'm desperate for a change of scene, and third is a chance to exhale, with the opportunity for picking up a little knowledge instead of trying to spew it out. . . . At the moment, my perspective is shot. I think that is evident at times in the lack of quality in some of the *Twilight Zone* scripts. And frankly, I'd like to be able to do my best work all the time. Who wouldn't? For that matter, Antioch is liable to drop my option, too. I've never taught before. If that happens, and if CBS doesn't go ahead with the hour show, I may just go fishing the rest of my life."

Speaking of the early days of the show, Serling once said, "I think we had a very special quality on our show due to the personnel who worked on it. That makes the difference all the time. We used to finish up at two in the morning, have a beer in a place across the street and discuss the work. Everyone was interested, in other words." In the years to come, there would be no more two A.M beers with the crew.

Sensibilities other than those which had created *The Twilight Zone* would shape the series during its final two seasons, and this change would be apparent in the episodes produced. A number of memorable shows would be made, but none with the same innovation and freshness as those produced by Houghton and Serling in the first three years. Good or bad, after the spring of 1962, *The Twilight Zone* was a different show.

THE FOURTH SEASON: 1963

Producers: Herbert Hirschman and Bert Granet
Associate Producer: Murray Golden
Assistant to the Producer: John Conwell
Production Manager: Ralph W. Nelson
Directors of Photography: George T. Clemens and Robert W. Pittack
Assistant Directors: Ray de Camp and John Bloss
Art Directors: George W. Davis, William Ferrari, John J. Thompson, Paul Groesse and Edward Carfagno
Editors: Edward Curtiss, Richard W. Farrell, Eda Warren, Everett Dodd and Al Clark
Makeup: Bob Keats
Special Effects: Virgil Beck
Sound: Franklin Milton and Joe Edmondson
Theme Music: Marius Constant
Set Direction: Edward M. Parker, Henry Grace, Frank R. McElvy and Don Greenwood, Jr.
Titles and Opticals: Pacific Title
Mr. Serling's Wardrobe: Eagle Clothes
Filmed at Metro–Goldwyn–Mayer

VI / THE FOURTH SEASON

"Ours is the perfect half-hour show . . . If we went to an hour, we'd have to fleshen our stories, soap-opera style. Viewers could watch fifteen minutes without knowing whether they were in a *Twilight Zone* or *Desilu Playhouse*."

—ROD SERLING

Several ironies attended the rebirth of *The Twilight Zone* in January of 1963. The first was that it replaced *Fair Exchange*, the same series that had replaced it back in the fall (not to mention the aptness of title; this mid-season switch was indeed a fair exchange). The second was that with its return the series featured a new name: *Twilight Zone (sans The)*. Though CBS didn't know it, changing the show's name was particularly appropriate: with its new producer and expanded length, this series bore little relation to its predecessor.

During its first three seasons, *The Twilight Zone* had established a structure perfectly suited to its half-hour length. "The ideal *Twilight Zone*," notes Richard Matheson, "started with a really smashing idea that hit you right in the first few seconds, then you played that out, and you had a little flip at the end; that was the structure." In order for the payoff to be satisfactory the material preceding it had to move quickly and directly; the more time it took to get to the payoff, the bigger the payoff had to be. The hour length could not possibly sustain this structure. As Buck Houghton put it, "People will go along with an old gag. You say, 'Hey, I've got this fellow who can walk through walls.' 'Okay, what else you got?' By the time the fortieth minute comes along, you gotta be walking on water to keep an audience."

Clearly, the new producer had a job ahead of him.

Herbert Hirschman was a man up to the task. Like Buck Houghton, he had worked his way up in the business and knew his job inside out. Earning an M.F.A. in directing and producing at Yale Drama School, he landed a job first as a script reader at RKO, then as a stage manager on Broadway, and then moved into live television. After serving for five years as producer-director of *The Web*, a half-hour anthology show, he went on to direct episodes of *Studio One* and alternately work as story editor, director and associate producer on *Playhouse 90*. Film shows followed; he produced the third season of *Perry Mason*, the *Hong Kong* series, starring Rod

Taylor, and—finally—*Dr. Kildare,* casting Richard Chamberlain and setting the tone of the show. And then came *Twilight Zone*.

Luckily for Hirschman, production manager Ralph W. Nelson and director of photography George T. Clemens were staying put, allowing the show to maintain some sense of continuity. Clemens found Hirschman a man to his liking. "Hirschman and I got along great," he says. "He didn't try to change anything. He didn't come in with his own fixed ideas. He said, 'What you've been doing in the past has certainly worked. I'm going to keep it that way.'" Clemens also found Hirschman's experience as a director a welcome asset. "Whenever it came to a point where we had to make retakes or something, he wouldn't bring the director back, he'd come down and direct it himself, which was great for us because then we weren't dependent on one person."

The shooting schedule that greeted Hirschman on the hour shows was quite different from the half hours. Says George Clemens, "It was six days. There was a day of rehearsal and a day of set pickups. So I would work eight days and then I would have four days with the weekend off."

Since the shooting of episodes was scheduled back to back, and since preparation was needed prior to each episode's shooting, Clemens couldn't possibly be director of photography on all episodes. At his recommendation, Hirschman hired Robert W. Pittack (who had substituted for him on "Person or Persons Unknown") to alternate with him as director of photography every other episode.

As for scripts, when Hirschman entered the scene he had to start from scratch—almost. "There was only one script that actually had been prepared," he relates. "CBS gave me a script to read which fit into our format in a way. It was a story of a lot of scientists of the United States government vying with Russia to invent an anti-gravity device. It was a fascinating script by a very prominent screenwriter and it had been written as a pilot. The reason we finally didn't do it was that it was going to be so expensive to do, because of the various devices that had to be created when the government built this instrument, so that it could lift itself off the ground. It just got to be too cumbersome and expensive."

Meanwhile, Serling was off at Antioch, teaching "Mass Media" and "Writing in Dramatic Form" to undergraduates. But this was not turning out to be the vacation from writing he had intended. He was busy at work on the screenplay adaptation of *Seven Days in May.* In addition, Serling was turning out a number of *Twilight Zone* scripts. "He would mail me his scripts," says Hirschman, "and I would send him the other scripts that he himself hadn't written. Then we'd discuss his comments and notes on the phone."

Serling was busy, and his full attention was not on *Twilight Zone*. "We had a few fights," Hirschman admits. "Rod was a tremendously talented

Rod Serling with elements from the fourth season opening

writer and very, very facile. He was so much better than the average television writer that even half as good as he was capable of writing was better than most. I think it became easy for him. And our fights consisted of me saying, 'Rod, I think you can do better than this.' The scripts were pretty good by television standards, I just thought he was capable of better work, and he had to be flogged and kicked in the ass, frankly, and argued with to bestir him to improve on what was already pretty good. So any arguments we had were basically in those categories where he'd send me a script which, if it came from somebody else, I'd have been thrilled with, but I knew he was capable of better things."

Serling's presence in Yellow Springs also complicated his role as host-narrator on the show. Whenever he had to fly in to L.A. on other business, Hirschman made sure Rod came in to the studio and got in front of the cameras. "That was part of our day off," George Clemens recalls. "We'd get Serling out here and do as many as we could, three or four at a time. We'd do things before the picture was made and hope that the things that he spoke about would come to pass in the picture." Hirschman directed all of these openings, which were filmed with Serling standing in front of a gray background.

Hirschman recalls yet another uncredited contribution to the show. "I did, for good or bad, create the main title. You know, the clock ticking and the mannequin. I wanted to find some things that were interesting. I created that and I directed it. I supervised the making of the props and I came up with the notion of the things floating through the void. Rod wrote the narration and that sparked in me the symbols that I wanted to use."

Hirschman was determined that the hour shows have a fighting chance. He bought high-quality scripts from Matheson, Beaumont, Reginald Rose and Earl Hamner, Jr., and recruited *Twilight Zone* alumni directors Buzz Kulik, Don Medford, John Brahm and Abner Biberman. Production got under way at a brisk pace, as this passage in a letter from Hirschman to Serling, dated September 19, 1962, indicates: "We are very busy here today shooting scenes with Hitler on one stage, a spaceship on another, and a leopard on a third."

The new *Twilight Zone* debuted January 3, 1963. Serling was less than ecstatic about the scheduling. "The Thursday nine o'clock slot will eliminate a sizeable young audience that we had in the Friday night berth," he wrote the network, adding philosophically, "but I'm sure one can't expect everything."

Others on the show had even greater misgivings. "After about the fourth or fifth episode," recalls George Clemens, "I said, 'It'll die very quick.' I didn't think that the story material we had would carry for an hour."

But, as everyone realized, in the end that determination would have to be made by the audience.

"IN HIS IMAGE" (1/3/63)

George Grizzard

Written by Charles Beaumont
Based on the short story "In His Image" by Charles Beaumont
Producer: Herbert Hirschman
Director: Perry Lafferty
Director of Photography: George T. Clemens
Music: stock

Cast:
Alan Talbot/Walter Ryder, Jr.: George Grizzard
Jessica Connelly: Gail Kobe
Old Woman: Katherine Squire
Man: Wallace Rooney
Girl: Sherry Granato
Sheriff: James Seay
Driver: George Petrie
Hotel Clerk: Jamie Forster
Double for Grizzard: Joseph Sargent

"What you have just witnessed could be the end of a particularly terrifying nightmare. It isn't—it's the beginning. Although Alan Talbot doesn't know it, he is about to enter a strange new world, too incredible to be real, too real to be a dream. It's called the Twilight Zone."

Leaving his New York City hotel at 4:30 A.M., Alan Talbot enters a subway station. The only person there is an old woman, a religious fanatic who presses a pamphlet into his hands. Hearing odd electronic sounds in his mind, he pleads with the woman to leave him alone, but when she won't he throws her in the path of a speeding subway train. Niney minutes later, he arrives at the apartment of his fiancée, Jessica Connelly—whom he's known for only four days—with no memory of the murder. Together, they start the long drive to Coeurville, Alan's home town, to meet his Aunt Mildred. During the drive, Alan dozes off, mumbles something about "Walter" and, strangely, upon awakening, tells Jessica he knows no one of that name. Reaching Coeurville, Alan begins Jessica's tour and is met with a number of nasty surprises: there are buildings which he has never seen before which seemingly have been erected in the week he's been gone; his key doesn't fit the lock on Aunt Mildred's house, and the stranger who answers the door claims he's never heard of any such person; the university he works at is now an empty field; people he remembers seeing a week before have been dead for years; and in the graveyard, the tombstones marking his parents' graves are gone, replaced by those of a Walter Ryder and his wife. Jessica doesn't know what to make of this, but she loves Alan and intends to stick by him. But driving back to New York, Alan hears the odd noises and is filled with a murderous rage. He orders Jessica to stop, leaps from the car and demands she drive on. She obeys—unaware of Alan as he runs behind the car, insanely brandishing a large rock. Suddenly, another car rounds a bend and strikes him, putting a large gash in his arm. He looks down and sees, not blood, but lights, wires and transistors revealed just beneath his skin! Alan quickly covers the injury with a cloth, then has the driver drop him off at his hotel room. Looking in a phone book, he finds a listing for a Walter Ryder, Jr. He goes to the address and, disconcertingly, his key *does* fit this door. He steps inside and comes face to face with . . . Walter, a shy and lonely man who is his exact double! Walter explains that Alan is a robot that he created eight days ago. Although he left Coeurville twenty years earlier, he used his hazy recollections of the place to give Alan a fictitious past. His intention was to create an artificial man in his own image—but with none of the defects. However, Alan is flawed: a week ago, he attacked Walter with a pair of scissors, then fled. He's insane, and he can't be fixed. Desperate, Alan tells Walter of Jessica and insists—despite Walter's protests that it's not possible—that Walter make another Alan, a *perfect* one, for Jessica. He fishes the crumpled pamphlet out of his pocket and jots down her address, but the sight of the pamphlet triggers another fit; murderously, he attacks Walter. Later, answering a knock at her door, Jessica is relieved to see Alan, who reassures her that everything is going to be fine. Fortunately for her, this isn't *really* Alan—it's Walter. Alan is back in Walter's lab, deactivated—for good.

"In a way, it can be said that Walter Ryder succeeded in his life's ambition, even though the man he created was, after all, himself. There may be easier ways to self-improvement, but sometimes it happens that the shortest distance between two points is a crooked line—through the Twilight Zone."

Charles Beaumont's "In His Image" (based on the short story included in his collection *Yonder*) begins with youthful Alan Talbot (George Grizzard) pushing an old woman into the path of a speeding subway train—to the accompaniment of bizarre electronic noises in his head—then, only minutes later, cheerfully meeting with his fiancée. (Jay Fredericks, in his review of the episode in the Charleston, West Virginia, *Gazette-Mail,* jokingly noted that when the weird noises started, "I thought the Martians were arriving by subway.")

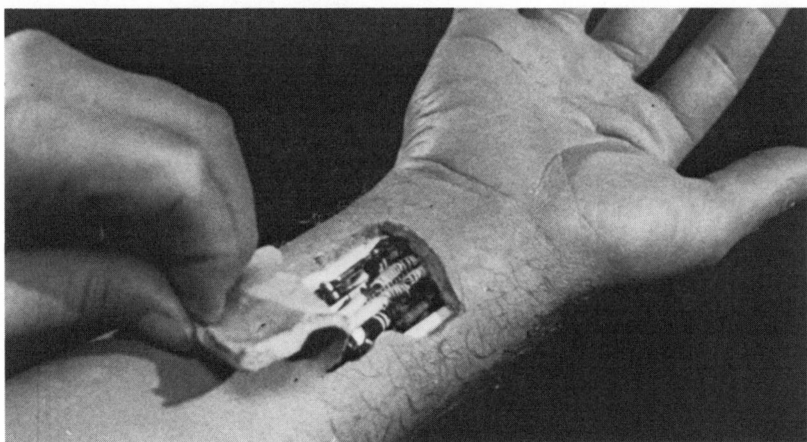

Alan Talbot discovers what he is made of

When the short story first appeared in the February, 1957, issue of *Imagination* (under the title "The Man Who Made Himself"), the main character's name was Pete Nolan, after Beaumont's friend William F. Nolan. But Beaumont, sensitive to the fact that Nolan might not like having a murderous robot with his last name plastered across the television screens of America, changed it when he wrote the script. Very possibly, the name Talbot came from another character with a dreadful inner secret—Lawrence Talbot, better known as "The Wolf Man."

In this episode, Beaumont's writing is some of his most thoughtful since "Long Live Walter Jameson." Particularly effective is a scene near the end, in which Alan confronts his creator, Walter Ryder. Here, Grizzard plays a dual role far removed from his part in "The Chaser." It is a *tour de force* of writing, directing and acting, for although Grizzard plays both Alan and Walter the illusion that this is a scene between two separate men is perfect. Grizzard presents two completely distinct characters. Alan—warm, intelligent and personable (if you can excuse the occasional lapses into psychosis); and Walter—bitter, lonely, full of self-loathing. The split screen when the two are talking to each other is indiscernable, and the double for Grizzard when either Walter or Alan is seen from the back (played by Joseph Sargent, later to turn director and do such films as *The Forbin Project* and *The Taking of Pelham One, Two, Three*) looks exactly like Grizzard from the back. Alan asks Walter the all-important question:

ALAN: Who am I?

WALTER: You're nobody, Alan, nobody at all.

ALAN (*Angrily*): Stop it, Walter!

WALTER: Well, who is this watch I'm wearing, ask me that. Who is the refrigerator in the kitchen? Don't you understand?

ALAN: No.

WALTER: You're a machine, Alan, a mechanical device.

ALAN: I don't believe it!

WALTER: I don't blame you, I wouldn't believe it either, but it's true. The fact is, you were born a long time ago, in my head. All kids have dreams, don't they? Well, you were mine. The others thought about joining the army or flying to Mars, and they finally grew up and forgot their dreams. I didn't. I thought about one thing and longed for one thing always. Just one. A perfect artificial man. Not a robot. A duplicate of a human being. Well, it was harmless, not even very imaginative for a child. But then I became an adult, only somewhere along the way I forgot to grow up—like most geniuses. I kept my dream. I created you, Alan, is that straight enough for you?

The finale that Beaumont provides is a happy one: the killer robot is destroyed; Walter, by impersonating his own creation, finds an escape from loneliness; and Jessica gets the man she loves—or, at least, someone mighty close. Beaumont tries to keep this a last-minute cliff-hanger by having Alan and Walter grapple in a fight to the death, so that when one of them subsequently knocks at Jessica's door, we are kept in suspense as to which it really is. But it isn't really much of a surprise. In order to present the alternative ending—an innocent young woman being left to the mercies of a clockwork maniac—*Twilight Zone* itself would have to have been demented. This does not matter, though. "In His Image" is exciting, suspenseful and thought-provoking. If this was to be a representative example of the hour-long shows, the series had nothing to worry about.

Unfortunately, such was not the case.

"THE THIRTY-FATHOM GRAVE" (1/10/63)

Written by Rod Serling
Producer: Herbert Hirschman
Director: Perry Lafferty
Director of Photography: George T. Clemens
Music: stock

Cast:
Chief Bell: Mike Kellin
Capt. Beecham: Simon Oakland
Doc: David Sheiner
McClure: John Considine
O.O.D.: Bill Bixby
Lee Helmsman: Tony Call
Helmsman: Derrick Lewis
Ensign Marmer: Conlan Carter
Sonar Operator: Charles Kuenstle
ASW Officer: Forrest Compton
Jr. O.O.D.: Henry Scott
Sailor #1: Vince Bagetta
Sailor #2: Louie Elias

*"Incident one hundred miles off the coast of Guadalcanal. Time: the present. The United States naval destroyer on what has been a most uneventful cruise. In a moment, they're going to send a man down thirty fathoms to check on a noise maker—someone or some*thing *tapping on metal. You may or may not read the results in a naval report, because Captain Beecham and his crew have just set a course that will lead this ship and everyone on it into the Twilight Zone."*

Onboard the destroyer, sonar picks up a sunken submarine on the ocean floor—and a persistent clanging coming from within the sub! One sailor jokingly says it's ghosts, a suggestion that causes Chief Bell—a man seemingly on the verge of a nervous breakdown—to faint. Diver McClure is sent down to investigate. He finds the sub considerably damaged, with evidence of having been strafed. Although it is of American design, the numbers on it are inaccessible. McClure taps on the outside and gets a tapping response from within: someone definitely seems to be inside. And yet no subs are listed as being in that area. Later, the sub shifts slightly and its numbers become legible; it *is* an American sub, sunk by the Japanese on August 7, 1942—over *twenty years ago*! Meanwhile, in sick bay, Chief Bell feels some mysterious force beckoning to him. Looking in the mirror and down the corridor, he sees the ghosts of young seamen, their clothes drenched, motioning for him to join them. The doctor dismisses this as an hallucination, but he has no explanation for the seaweed he finds in the corridor! Then McClure discovers something beside the sub: dogtags with Chief Bell's name on them. Bell confesses to Captain Beecham that he was assigned as a signalman on the sub during World War II, and that it was sunk because *he* accidentally dropped a signal lamp, knocking off its red filter and exposing light to the enemy. He alone survived and now, burdened by tremendous guilt, he feels that the ghosts of his crewmates are calling muster on him. Beecham argues that the sub was surrounded; it wasn't Bell's fault. Bell doesn't seem to hear. Hysterical, he slips the dogtags on, rushes from the room, runs to the side of the ship, dives overboard and drowns. Later, a team of divers enters the sub. McClure reports to the captain that a sheared section of periscope was swinging, and *that,* no doubt, accounted for the sounds. Very probably, but then what about the disquieting fact that one of the dead men had a hammer in his hand . . . ?

"Small naval engagement, the month of April, 1963. Not to be found in any historical annals. Look for this one filed under 'H' for haunting—in the Twilight Zone."

Executed as a half-hour show, "The Thirty-Fathom Grave" might have been effectively eerie, in the tradition of "Judgment Night," but at an hour it is impossibly padded. Rather than having the story develop at a normal pace, each new piece of information is revealed with all the urgency of sap dripping from a tree. Having divers investigate the sub once would suffice dramatically; here they go down *three* separate times. The writing borders on self-parody, as in this snatch of dialogue between the destroyer's captain (Simon Oakland) and the officer of the day (Bill Bixby):

O.O.D. (*Reacting to the clanking sound coming over the speaker from the sonar shack*): It's wild.

CAPTAIN: That it is, Lieutenant.

O.O.D.: But if it isn't a sub, sir, what is it?

CAPTAIN: Maybe it's a Spanish galleon with a treasure chest and a loose lid that's off its hinges. *(Meaningfully)* Or maybe it's—maybe it's just our imaginations.

And later, when they discover that the ship was sunk in 1942:

OFFICER: Well, that was twenty years ago! Captain

Beecham, who's down there? Who's inside that sub?

CAPTAIN: Somebody who dies *damn* hard.

As the spooked bosun's mate, Mike Kellin (later to get an Oscar nomination for his role as the father in the movie *Midnight Express*) gives a convincing performance, as does Simon Oakland. But their efforts are in vain. As *Variety* noted in its review of the episode (regrettably drawing conclusions about the series as a whole), "In a show where the imagination has been given freedom to run riot, it has chosen to plod along a well-marked groove."

"MUTE" (1/31/63)

Ann Jillian

Written by Richard Matheson
Based on the short story "Mute"
by Richard Matheson
Producer: Herbert Hirschman
Director: Stuart Rosenberg
Director of Photography:
Robert W. Pittack
Music: Fred Steiner

Cast:
Ilse Nielsen: Ann Jillian
Harry Wheeler: Frank Overton
Cora Wheeler: Barbara Baxley
Miss Frank: Irene Dailey
Prof. Karl Werner: Oscar Beregi
Frau Nielsen: Claudia Bryer
Holger Nielsen: Robert Boon
Frau Maria Werner: Eva Soreny
Tom Poulter: Percy Helton

"What you're witnessing is the curtain-raiser to a most extraordinary play; to wit, the signing of a pact, the commencement of a project. The play itself will be performed almost entirely offstage. The final scenes are to be enacted a decade hence and with a different cast. The main character of these final scenes is Ilse, the daughter of Professor and Mrs. Nielsen, age two. At the moment she lies sleeping in her crib, unaware of the singular drama in which she is to be involved. Ten years from this moment, Ilse Nielsen is to know the desolating terror of living simultaneously in the world—and in the Twilight Zone."

In Germany in 1953, a group of people pledge that, in order to develop their mental powers, they and their children will communicate solely through telepathy. The Nielsen family then moves to German Corners, Pennsylvania. Ten years later, their house burns down. Prof. Nielsen and his wife are killed; their last act: to telepathically warn their daughter Ilse, who escapes unharmed. Sheriff Harry Wheeler and his wife take Ilse in, but they are appalled to find she cannot speak, read or write—the result, they assume, of maltreatment by her reclusive parents. Ilse, a highly-developed telepath, can read the thoughts of those around her, but their speech is a hopeless garble. She is marooned, with no way to communicate. Cora, whose own daughter drowned, is determined to keep Ilse. When Harry writes letters about Ilse to a German address found amongst Prof. Nielsen's papers, Cora surreptitiously destroys them. Wanting Ilse to learn to talk, Harry sends her to a class taught by Miss Frank, who tries to get Ilse to say her own name by having the entire class repeat it in unison. When this fails, she realizes that Ilse can read her thoughts. Miss Frank's father had tried to make her into a medium when she was a child; she assumes this has happened to Ilse, too. Over a period of days, Miss Frank has her class *think* Ilse's name—which Ilse finds deafening. Meanwhile, Prof. Werner and his wife arrive in town from Germany, concerned that they have not heard from the Nielsens in months. At the Wheeler house, they discover that Miss Frank's methods have destroyed Ilse's telepathic ability; their thoughts are a painful jumble to her. Hysterically, she cries out, "My name is Ilse!" again and again. Cora tells the Werners that she loves Ilse and won't let them take her. Realizing that Ilse would now be an outcast in a community of telepaths, the Werners let the Wheelers keep her. But Frau Werner tells her husband it is no tragedy; Ilse's real parents saw her only as an experiment. But now she will be loved.

"It has been noted in a book of proven wisdom that perfect love casteth out fear. While it's unlikely that this observation was meant to include that specific fear which follows the loss of extrasensory perception, the principle remains, as always, beautifully intact. Case in point, that of Ilse Nielsen, former resident of the Twilight Zone."

In 1962, Richard Matheson wrote a novelette entitled "Mute." Initially, it was published in *The Fiend in You*, edited by Charles Beaumont, then subsequently in Matheson's *Shock II* (Dell, 1964). The story concerns a telepathic boy who, following the death of his parents, must contend with well-meaning adults who mistake his silence for traumatized muteness.

Matheson adapted the story for *Twilight Zone*, retaining the basic story but changing the gender of the child. What emerged was an episode that was crushingly pro-conformity.

What is so disturbing—particularly to anyone who believes that talent and individuality are sacred items—is the *manner* in which the story evolves. With the exception of the child herself (Ann Jillian, years later to play a sexpot on TV's *It's A Living*), virtually all of the main characters are either brutishly insensitive or cruelly neurotic. As Sheriff Harry Wheeler, Frank Overton exhibits none of the warmth and perceptiveness he showed as the father in "Walking Distance"; instead, he is cool and undemonstrative. His wife Cora is a selfish, hysterical woman who professes to love Ilse but is actually maniacally intent on keeping possession of a child she irrationally feels is her own daughter returned to her. Then there is Miss Frank (Irene Dailey), the schoolteacher. She spells her character out clearly to her class when she says of Ilse, "We are going to work with her until she's *exactly* like everybody else." In the end, when Ilse is traumatized into screaming "My name is Ilse!" over and over again, it is a triumph of sadistic and misguided teaching methods.

Paradoxically, this is treated as a happy ending. And to allay any suspicions that what we have been watching is actually a tragedy, Matheson provides a final scene involving the German couple who were participants in the original telepathy experiment. Having come with the intention of taking Ilse to join others of her kind, they change their minds when they see that now, although she has lost her telepathic ability, she has gained love ("and that is so much more important than telepathy"). This convenient reverse is neither satisfying nor convincing.

Without intending to, "Mute" focuses in on a terrible aspect of real life: those adults who commit secret atrocities against children, whose deeds never come to light, who are never punished for their actions. As most often in real life, the villains get away scot-free, their brutalities utterly successful in destroying a special—and vulnerable—talent. The problem with "Mute" is that instead of taking a moral stand against this behavior, it rationalizes these monstrous acts. As Richard Matheson himself says, "It's not that bad because she's found a home and found loving parents, which she did lose, you know. So it's six of one, half dozen of the other."

There is one issue that "Mute" fails to answer. Love may be more important than telepathy, but what kind of life will Ilse have with such parents and such a teacher?

"JESS-BELLE" (2/14/63)

James Best, Laura Devon and Anne Francis

Written by Earl Hamner, Jr.
Producer: Herbert Hirschman
Director: Buzz Kulik
Director of Photography: Robert W. Pittack
Music: Van Cleave

Cast
Jess-Belle: Anne Francis
Billy-Ben Turner: James Best
Ellwyn Glover: Laura Devon
Granny Hart: Jeanette Nolan
Ossie Stone: Virginia Gregg
Luther Glover: George Mitchell
Mattie Glover: Helen Kleeb
Obed Miller: Jim Boles
Minister: Jon Lormer

"The Twilight Zone has existed in many lands, in many times. It has its roots in history, in something that happened long, long ago and got told about and handed down from one generation of folk to the other. In the telling the story gets added to and embroidered on, so that what might have happened in the time of the Druids is told as if it took place yesterday in the Blue Ridge Mountains. Such stories are best told by an elderly grandfather on a cold winter's night by the fireside—in the southern hills of the Twilight Zone."

In the Blue Ridge Mountains of Virginia, Billy-Ben Turner proposes to Ellwyn Glover, the pretty daughter of a successful farmer. But Jess-Belle Stone, a poor-but-beautiful girl Billy-Ben passionately romanced on the sly before falling in love with Elly, is determined the marriage never take place. In desperation, she seeks the aid of Granny Hart, who is rumored to be a witch. Granny has a love potion. Having no money, Jess offers to pay for it with her silver hair pin; but Granny is inexplicably repulsed by the object—there'll be *another* price, one that Jess will soon know. Jess drinks down the potion. The magic works: the moment Billy sees her, he forgets utterly about Elly and belongs totally to Jess. Jess is joyful, but come midnight she learns the terrible price she has paid for her beloved prize: she transforms into a leopard and prowls until dawn. Granny Hart *is* a witch, and now so is Jess. She has bartered away her soul and is doomed to become a cat every night. In anguish, Jess initially rejects Billy's pleas to marry him. But eventually her love for Billy triumphs over her apprehension; she accepts his proposal. Before they can be wed, though, a hunting party is organized to track down what the community assumes to be a wildcat. The menfolk corner the leopard in the Glovers' shed and fire at it.

It disappears in a cloud of smoke—and Jess's spell over Billy is broken. A year passes and Billy is now preparing to marry Elly. He assumes that Jess is dead, but he soon finds he's sadly mistaken. At the wedding, a spider appears on Elly's gown—one that vanishes in smoke and flame when Billy tries to crush it! When Billy and Elly return to his cabin, an unseen force grabs Elly's arm, then a rat pushes over a grandfather clock, narrowly missing them. Elly is terrified. Billy tells her to sit in a chair, read the Bible and *not move*. He rushes to Granny Hart's cabin and demands to know the method for killing a witch. Granny asks for a lock of his hair so *she* can bewitch him, but he's too smart for her; he pays her in coin—and learns that Jess can be killed by stabbing one of her dresses through the heart with silver. From Jess's mother, he gets Jess's intended wedding dress and silver hair pin. These in hand, he returns home and finds Elly waiting for him outside the door. But when she opens her mouth, her voice is Jess-Belle's—Elly is possessed! Hurriedly, Billy slips the dress on a form and stabs it. Jess materializes in the dress then disappears, vanquished for good. Billy is relieved to see that Elly is herself again. Strolling outside, they see a falling star—sure sign that a witch has just died.

"Jess-Belle" has no closing narration by Serling. Instead, it ends with a repeat of a folk song heard at the beginning:

"Fair was Elly Glover,
Dark was Jess-Belle.
Both they loved the same man,
And both they loved him well."

"Jess-Belle," Earl Hamner, Jr.'s, finest *Twilight Zone* episode, is a classic tale of love and witchcraft.

The story behind the creation of "Jess-Belle" is as remarkable as the episode itself. "Herb Hirschman called me on a Friday," Earl Hamner recalls, "and he said, 'I've just had a script knocked out from under me, we can't do it. By a week from today I need an hour-long script. I know you are interested in folklore and backwoods-type stories, and I just have the feeling that maybe you could have a script for me in a week.'

"I said, 'Herb, it usually takes me a week to think of an idea. I have to scratch my head and get drunk and sleep and wrestle and walk before that kind of idea will come.' He said, 'Well, think about it until Monday and call me on Monday.'

"So on Monday I called and said, 'Herb, I do have an idea,' and I outlined it briefly, and it was 'Jess-Belle.' He said, 'Can you have it for me by Friday?' I said, 'Well, that will mean that I'll have to write an act a day, and I also want to write a folk song to go along with it.' And I could hear the hopelessness in his voice, but he said, 'Well, go ahead and try it.' So I did, and I delivered it that Friday, having written one act each day, and it was one of those cases where I really fell in love with the script."

Another person much taken with "Jess-Belle" was its director, Buzz Kulik. "I loved it," he says, "because I thought it was such a well-written piece. I always liked what Hamner did if he stayed in his own back yard. He had such a good ear for these people, they all rang true."

Created with great precision, Hamner's characters speak with a charming authenticity. Hamner also makes clever use of language with double meanings. Jess-Belle goes to Granny *Hart* for a love potion. After she's cursed, Billy-Ben refers to her as a "hellcat," completely unaware that the term is quite literally accurate. Then, when Jess-Belle is temporarily banished, cancelling her influence over Billy-Ben, Billy sidles up to Elly and says, "I'm enduring glad to see ya, Elly . . . It's been a long spell," again unaware that his words are much more than just a quaint colloquialism.

The complexity of "Jess-Belle" adds greatly to its effectiveness. Jess-Belle is never presented as wholly evil. Rather, she is a victim. Tricked out of her soul, forever under a terrible curse, she is a tragic figure. Especially moving is a scene between Jess, who has finally discovered the full cost of her actions, and the bewitched Billy-Ben:

BILLY-BEN: Hold out your hand. I got somethin' for you. (*He gives her the ring*)

JESS-BELLE: Elly's ring.

BILLY-BEN: Jess-Belle's ring. Belongs to the one I love, and the one I love is you. Every minute I'm away from you is a sufferin' and a torment.

JESS-BELLE: Sufferin' and torment. You know what sufferin' and torment means?

BILLY-BEN: Sure. It's havin' a girl that your heart's cravin' and have her keep puttin' the weddin' day off.

JESS-BELLE: All kinds of torment in this world, I reckon.

BILLY-BEN: What would you know of torment, girl?

JESS-BELLE: It's the torment comes from buyin' somethin', findin' out the price is dear.

BILLY-BEN: Well, what did you buy that cost so dear?

JESS-BELLE: Somethin' I love.

BILLY-BEN: You still love it though the price was high?

JESS-BELLE: Better than life.

BILLY-BEN: Better than me?

JESS-BELLE (*Bittersweet smile*): Ain't nothin' I love better than you.

"Basically, all she wanted was to love someone," says Hamner of Jess-Belle. "But it goes back to Faust: if you sell your soul, forget it."

In the leads, Anne Francis and James Best are wonderful. There is a feeling of past history between them that makes the characters' relationships believable.

The single most striking performance in "Jess-Belle" is that of Jeanette Nolan as Granny Hart. Speaking with the same authentic-sounding backwoods accent she used in "The Hunt," she is a truly marvelous character. Our introduction to her comes in the opening shot of Act One. We see her in extreme closeup, stirring a bubbling kettle and looking for all the world like a witch. A black hood covers her head. Several white strands escape from under the cloth and straggle down her face. She mumbles an incantation under her breath. Suddenly, there's a knock at the door. She stands up and throws the black cloth back, off her head, draping it over her shoulders. We see that she wears a white frilled blouse and that her hair is neatly braided around her head. She no longer resembles something out of *Macbeth,* but rather seems an attractive, utterly presentable woman.

Later, she reveals more of her character. When Jess-Belle discovers she's under a curse, she hurries back to Granny's cabin. She knocks on the door. Granny Hart ignores it. Jess storms in. "Didn't you hear me knockin'?" she asks.

"I never let trouble in the door if I can he'p it," she answers.

"How do you know I'm trouble?"

Granny smiles. "Why child, there ain't much I don't know." She tells Jess that she herself is a witch and that she has turned Jess into a witch, too. Jess begs to be changed back, but Granny tells her that she'll remain as she is until she dies.

"I hope I die soon," says Jess.

"Why, you're lookin' at it all wrong," says Granny Hart. "*Be* a witch. Take a witch's pleasure." She grins. "Take the man you bargained for—*give him witch's love*!"

"DEATH SHIP" (2/7/63)

Ross Martin, Jack Klugman and Fredrick Beir

Written by Richard Matheson
Based on the short story "Death Ship" by Richard Matheson
Producer: Herbert Hirschman
Director: Don Medford
Director of Photography: Robert W. Pittack
Music: stock

Cast:
Capt. Paul Ross: Jack Klugman
Lt. Ted Mason: Ross Martin
Lt. Mike Carter: Fredrick Beir
Ruth: Mary Webster
Jeannie: Tammy Marihugh
Kramer: Ross Elliott
Mrs. Nolan: Sara Taft

"Picture of the spaceship E–89, cruising above the thirteenth planet of star system fifty-one, the year 1997. In a little while, supposedly, the ship will be landed and specimens taken: vegetable, mineral and, if any, animal. These will be brought back to overpopulated Earth, where technicians will evaluate them and, if everything is satisfactory, stamp their findings with the word 'inhabitable' and open up yet another planet for colonization. These are the things that are supposed *to happen . . . Picture of the crew of the spaceship E–89: Captain Ross, Lieutenant Mason, Lieutenant Carter. Three men who have just reached a place which is as far from home as they will ever be. Three men who in a matter of minutes will be plunged into the darkest nightmare reaches of the Twilight Zone."*

When Lieutenant Mason's monitor shows something glinting on the surface of the planet, Captain Ross brings the ship in for a landing. They are shocked by what greets them: a wrecked duplicate of their own ship, and inside it what appear to be their own dead bodies, identical down to the identification cards in their pockets! Mason and Carter are convinced that they are dead, but the strong-willed Captain Ross rejects this utterly. Back on board their ship he offers his own theory: somehow they have gone through a time warp and witnessed a possible future in which their ship crashed on takeoff and they were killed. If they don't try to go back up, they won't die. Mason objects: Ross has no one waiting back on Earth for *him*, he says. There's an even more serious consideration, though; this is a harsh planet, and their food and power supplies will soon be depleted. Carter wearily rubs his eyes—and finds himself back on Earth, being greeted by Mr. Kramer and Mrs. Nolan, two of his neighbors. Eager to see his wife, he rushes home. Though he doesn't find her, he does find a veiled black hat, black gloves and a black purse on the bed, plus a telegram informing his wife that her husband has died. Abruptly Ross's voice brings him back to the ship. He tells the Captain of his bizzare experience—and suddenly remembers that both Mr. Kramer and Mrs. Nolan are dead. Ross glances over to the bunk where Mason is napping, and is amazed to see that he's disappeared! As for Mason, he's awakened back on Earth, and is joyously reunited with his wife and daughter, both previously killed in an automobile accident. Suddenly, Ross appears on the scene. He grabs Mason, they struggle—and both of them are back on the ship. Ross now has a *new* theory: the wrecked ship and the scenes back on Earth are illusions designed by telepathic aliens in order to stop them from reporting to Earth about this planet. In order to prove it, Ross takes the ship back up into space. There is no malfunction and no crash. Mason and Carter gladly concede that Ross must have been right after all. But then Ross orders them to prepare to land; they've got orders to collect samples, and he's determined to prove that there is *no* wrecked ship. Certain that if they try to land they'll crash, Carter tries to wrest the controls away. The ship plunges out of control. Ross and Mason manage to land the ship safely. But when they open the window ports, they see the same wrecked ship outside. Carter is in despair; he's sure that the next time they take off they *will* crash. But Mason, drained of all but hopelessness, corrects him: they won't crash . . . because they already *have* crashed. They *are* dead. He pleads with Ross to let them go, but Ross refuses. "*We are going to go over it again!*" he says. Abruptly, all three find themselves back at the beginning, with Mason spotting a strange glint on his screen . . .

"Picture of a man who will not see anything he does not choose to see—including his own death. A man of such indomitable will that even the two men beneath his command are not allowed to see the truth; which truth is, that they are no longer among the living, that the movements they make and the words they speak have all been made and spoken countless times before—and will be made and spoken countless times again, perhaps even unto eternity. Picture of a latter-day Flying Dutchman, *sailing into the Twilight Zone."*

Richard Matheson's short story "Death Ship" first appeared in the March, 1953, issue of *Fantastic Story Magazine*. Later it was included in his collection *Shock!* (Dell, 1961). In it, a three-man spaceship crew sights something glinting on the surface of an unexplored planet. Going down to investigate, they find the wreckage of a ship identical in design to their own and, inside it, dead duplicates of their *own* bodies. Eventually, the realization dawns on these men that they are ghosts. The story is short, precise and effective.

In making the adaptation for *Twilight Zone,* Matheson had to expand it considerably. But rather than bloating the story, the greater length allowed him to add complexity to the plot, flesh out the characters and introduce scenes that vastly enhance the drama. "Death Ship" is a fine melding of the science fiction and horror genres, and it touches on many fears: fear of the unknown, fear of loss, fear of death. The old dark house is turned into the ruined, dark spaceship and the monsters lurking within are the astronauts own corpses. In a way, these dead bodies are the most dreadful of all threats; a confrontation with an anonymous horror offers the possibility of death—but the discovery of your own lifeless form guarantees it.

Directed by Don Medford ("A Passage for Trumpet," "Death's-head Revisited"), "Death Ship" is filled with what might be called *emotional* violence, and flashes with the sparks that fly when three men are in bitter conflict, two aching to slide gently into death, the other holding them back, in defiance of reality. The balance of temperaments is excellent: Jack Klugman as the bull-headed Captain Ross, Ross Martin as the intellectual and melancholy Lieutenant Mason, and Fredrick Beir as the young, enthusiastic Lieutenant Carter.

Spaceship E-89 lands

Included in "Death Ship" are a number of visually impressive futuristic props, including the spaceship itself (a leftover from the movie *Forbidden Planet*) and an on-bridge device that scans the planet's surface. Realistic paintings depict the wrecked spaceship and the exterior of a house back on Earth. Also worth noting are the day and night shots of the spaceship landing and taking off. "The MGM special-effects department did this," Herbert Hirschman recalls. "I supervised the construction and told them what I wanted. We built a miniature to show the ship landing and taking off. It was on a table with sand and little plants. The ship was suspended from invisible wires. And as the ship was slowing in the descent, I wanted to see the sand billowing up. It was very expensive, but I felt that it was essential to the credibility of the show." The attention to detail was well worth the effort; it's a beautiful effect. "It was an awful lot of fun," says Hirschman, "I kept asking for more and they kept doing it."

Perhaps the episode's finest scene—and one of *Twilight Zone*'s most powerful emotional moments—occurs when Ross Martin, having gone to sleep in the ship, wakes to find himself apparently back on Earth, resting on the shore of a quiet lake. Out of the bushes, his daughter (Tammy Marihugh) appears, laughingly calling, "Oh Daddy, I thought I'd never find you!" Tears roll down Martin's face. His expression is one of elation and wonderment, suffused with an intensity of longing. It is clear from his reaction that the little girl *must* be dead; only such a reunion could bring so powerful and immediate a reaction. It is a magnificent, eloquent, unspoken moment.

At the time, Martin was separated from his own daughter, who was with his first wife in New York. In 1979, he recalled how he prepared for this scene. "I had found that certain personal things with regard to my own daughter motivate me or drive me or move me. Years ago, I was in a class taught by Marty Ritt, who is now a brilliant director, and one of the exercises we had was to move a distance of something like eighteen feet in three steps and sit in a chair. I mean, just *move,* three steps and you're sitting in the chair. And I said, 'It just can't be done.' He said, 'You give yourself something that'll *make* you do that.'

"So I pictured my daughter under certain circumstances. Now, it's horrible to me even now, as I mention it—but the truth is that I pictured her at a window, inside a burning building, calling to me in near panic, 'Daddy! Daddy!' *And I took those steps!* It was *effortless* to stride the length of a man's body. It was almost as though I had been shot out of a cannon, but that was because *that* was meaningful to me. And I used similar circumstances involving my own daughter, in my mind, in preparation for that scene, so that when I turned and saw her my heart just broke. The *joy,* the joy at seeing her!"

"VALLEY OF THE SHADOW" (1/17/63)

David Opatoshu, Dabbs Greer and Jacques Aubuchon

Written by Charles Beaumont
Producer: Herbert Hirschman
Director: Perry Lafferty
Director of Photography: Robert W. Pittack
Music: stock

Cast:
Philip Redfield: Ed Nelson
Ellen Marshall: Natalie Trundy
Dorn: David Opatoshu
Father: James Doohan
Girl: Suzanne Cupito
Evans: Dabbs Greer
Connelly: Jacques Aubuchon
Gas Attendent: Sandy Kenyon
Man #1: Henry Beckman
Man #2: Bart Burns
Man #3: King Calder
Man #4: Pat O'Hara

"You've seen them. Little towns, tucked away far from the main roads. You've seen them, but have you thought about them? What do the people in these places do? Why do they stay? Phillip Redfield never thought about them. If his dog hadn't gone after that cat, he would have driven through Peaceful Valley and put it out of his mind forever. But he can't do that now, because whether he knows it or not his friend's shortcut has led him right into the capital of the Twilight Zone."

Lost and nearly out of gas, reporter Philip Redfield pulls into Peaceful Valley, a small town that seems quite commonplace—until his dog gives chase to a cat and a little girl uses a bizarre gizmo to make the hound disappear. The child's father returns the dog, claiming it simply ran around the side of the house, but Redfield is not convinced. Stopping at the local hotel to get his dog a steak, he makes the acquaintance of Ellen Marshall, an attractive town resident. Disturbingly, Redfield finds that the hotel has no guests and that the most recent paper dates from 1953. Ellen tries to convince him that the hotel is full, then asks him to leave town. Angrily, Redfield departs—and drives smack into an invisible wall that wrecks his car and kills his dog. A number of townspeople come to his aid and, once he is out of sight, one of them uses a device to bring the dog back to life. Redfield is taken to the town chambers, where he meets Dorn, Evans and Connelly, three men who tell him he is never going to leave Peaceful Valley. Redfield tries to escape, but Dorn uses a device to teleport him from the doorway to a chair. He then explains that, one hundred years earlier, a stranger—who may or may not have been from outer space—arrived in town. He brought with him the equations for a miraculous new energy source, along with a number of devices made possible by these equations, including the force field that stopped Redfield from leaving, instruments to move matter and reshape it, even devices to reverse the flow of time. The people of Peaceful Valley are free to use these for their benefit, but forbidden to reveal them to the outside world until such time as the Earth is at peace. Redfield argues that the townspeople have a moral responsibility to share their secrets, but they won't hear of it. They give him two choices: stay in Peaceful Valley . . . or die. Naturally, Redfield elects to stay. Kept prisoner in a house by a force field, he pleads with Ellen—who has fallen in love with him—to help him escape. Later, he finds the force field down and Ellen waiting for him in his car. Redfield rushes to the town chambers, removes the contents of the safe where the equations are supposedly stored, uses a machine to create a .38 pistol, and shoots Dorn, Evans and Connelly when they try to stop him. Once they're outside the town, Ellen tells Redfield to look at the papers he's taken. The pages are all blank. She teleports him back to the town chambers, where Dorn, Evans and Connelly are waiting. It was all a test—and Redfield has failed. The men aim a device at him, and he finds himself back in his car. The time is just prior to the moment Redfield's dog jumped out to chase the fateful cat, and he retains no memory of the experiences he's had in Peaceful Valley. From a distance, Ellen watches him as he drives out of town.

"You've seen them. Little towns, tucked away far from the main roads. You've seen them, but have you thought about them? Have you wondered what the people do in such places, why they stay? Philip Redfield thinks about them now and he wonders, but only very late at night, when he's between wakefulness and sleep—in the Twilight Zone."

Charles Beaumont's "Valley of the Shadow" presents an anonymous-looking town that proves to be anything but mundane. Philip Redfield learns that Peaceful Valley has any number of wonderful machines, including an instrument that can create anything out of thin air (even a ham sandwich) and others that can reverse time and bring the dead back to life. (This last bit of scientific magic is demonstrated in a way that's a little hard to swallow: a member of the town council calmly allows himself to be stabbed in the chest with a letter opener. Now, speaking realistically, even if you knew the effects were not going to be permanent, would you let someone stab *you* in the chest?)

Most of the effects in the episode were accomplished easily, by reversing the footage so that blood seems to flow backward and disappear, or by jump-cutting from a shot of a person standing in the middle of a room to a shot of the exact same scene minus the person, giving the illusion that the person has been teleported. But director Perry Lafferty recalls an effect that wasn't quite so simple: "The script required us to create the illusion of an automobile driving down a country road and hitting an invisible wall, causing the car to be more or less demolished. We got a very effective sequence out of it by buying two old identical cars and wrecking the front of one of them. Through a series of cuts, the car was made to appear to slam into the unseen obstruction. The critical portion of the sequence was achieved by putting a one-inch chain around the back axle and running it with about twenty feet of slack, to a steady nearby tree where it was tied off. By framing a portion of the road, a stunt man drove the car into the frame of the camera and, when the slack was used up, was slammed against the steering wheel. The camera was undercranked, thereby giving the impression of considerably more speed than the 12 mph the car was travelling. We then put the leading actor in the car and made a quick cut of him going forward precisely when the car hit the wall. We then switched the 'good' car for the identical wrecked one and made another angle head on to the car showing the front end pushed in. The only thing humorous about this whole episode, and it is slightly grisly, is that the professional stunt man hired to do the gag went into the steering wheel so hard (even at 10 or 12 mph) that we had to call an ambulance and cart him off to the hospital."

Although "Valley of the Shadow" is entertaining, the story is so lacking in nuance and background detail that it never totally involves the viewer. We are told that Peaceful Valley is a town whose inhabitants live rich, full lives, but we are never shown how they *do* live. We see less than a dozen of the 981 people, and none in their normal, day-to-day routines. The characters are cardboard through and through, and while this does not ruin the story, it does tend to make it more theoretical than dramatic.

Another problem is that some of the twists and turns of plot are a little hard to follow, especially in the ending. Redfield is told he is to be executed but is instead simply sent back in time, to the point prior to when his dog jumped out of the car. But the dog doesn't jump this time, and so Redfield never learns about this secretive town. Apparently, this final twist lost a number of people, including Fran Conklin of the Orlando, Florida, *Sentinel,* who wrote, "We have just struggled and suffered in silence through sixty minutes (including commercials) of *Twilight Zone* only to learn that the strange happenings were but the daydreams of the newspaperman involved."

"HE'S ALIVE" (1/24/63)

Dennis Hopper

Written by Rod Serling
Producer: Herbert Hirschman
Director: Stuart Rosenberg
Director of Photography:
George T. Clemens
Music: stock

Cast:
Peter Vollmer: Dennis Hopper
Ernst Ganz: Ludwig Donath
Adolf Hitler: Curt Conway
Frank: Paul Mazursky
Nick: Howard Caine
Stanley: Barnaby Hale
Heckler: Bernard Fein
Gibbons: Jay Adler
Proprietor: Wolfe Brazell

"Portrait of a bush-league fuehrer named Peter Vollmer, a sparse little man who feeds off his self-delusions and finds himself perpetually hungry for want of greatness in his diet. And like some goose-stepping predecessors he searches for something to explain his hunger, and to rationalize why a world passes him by without saluting. That something he looks for and finds is in a sewer. In his own twisted and distorted lexicon he calls it faith, strength, truth. But in just a moment Peter Vollmer will ply his trade on another kind of corner, a strange intersection in a shadowland called the Twilight Zone."

Vollmer, the leader of a small band of American neo-nazis, wants *power*—but all his racist, streetcorner speeches net him are verbal abuse and fistfights. After one such speech, he seeks solace from Ernst Ganz, an elderly concentration camp survivor who has known him since he was an abused child and who has been like a father to him. Although Ernst despises Peter's views, he takes pity on him and lets him stay the night. Later, however, Peter is awakened by someone outside his window, a man who says he shares his philosophy and wants to help him. Staying in the shadows, he advises Peter on how to sway a crowd and win it over. Peter quickly adapts; soon, his speeches are filling a hall. His shadowy benefactor reappears, supplying money with which to pay the rent on the hall and offering new and shocking advice: the movement now needs a martyr. Peter complies; he orders Frank, a loyal deputy, to murder Nick, a devoted but stupid follower. The deed is done—and Peter's audience grows. Dismayed by this turn of events, Ernst interrupts one of Peter's speeches and denounces him. Peter pleads with him to stop; when Ernst refuses, he slaps him viciously. Ernst departs, but his strategy has worked:

the crowd no longer sees Peter as a charismatic leader. Peter is left alone in the hall. The shadowy figure enters, furious that Peter so utterly bungled the confrontation with Ernst. Angrily, Peter demands that the figure emerge from the shadows and reveal himself. He does. It is Adolf Hitler himself! Now *he'll* give the orders. He throws Peter a Luger and commands him to kill Ernst. Believing himself to be made of steel, Peter enters Ernst's apartment and shoots him. Later, a detective and a policeman arrive at the hall to arrest Peter for complicity in Nick's murder. He tries to run, then shoots at them. They return the fire and Peter collapses, bleeding from a bullet wound. Unbelieving, Peter says, "There's something wrong here . . . *Don't you understand that I'm made out of steel?*"

"Where will he go next, this phantom from another time, this resurrected ghost of a previous nightmare—Chicago; Los Angeles; Miami, Florida; Vincennes, Indiana; Syracuse, New York? Anyplace, everyplace, where there's hate, where there's prejudice, where there's bigotry. He's alive. He's alive so long as these evils exist. Remember that when he comes to your *town. Remember it when you hear his voice speaking out through others. Remember it when you hear a name called, a minority attacked, any blind, unreasoning assault on a people or any human being. He's alive because through these things we keep him alive."*

With "He's Alive," Serling again made a *Twilight Zone*–style investigation of nazism, but unlike "Death's-head Revisited," in which the drama carries the piece, this is just one long editorial. Here the intention is to examine the motivations of a young American neo-nazi, to reveal the banality of his thoughts and the immorality of his actions. Certainly, this theme has dramatic validity. Unfortunately, "He's Alive" lacks a feeling of reality. The characters are all stick figures and do not seem at all based on actual people. From the beginning we are supposed to accept that Peter Vollmer (Dennis Hopper, later to co-star in the movie *Easy Rider*) is deeply committed to the fascist organization of which he is the leader, while also accepting his claim that "the only thing in the world I've ever loved" is an elderly concentration camp survivor.

Although directed by Stuart Rosenberg (later to direct such films as *Cool Hand Luke* and *The Amityville Horror*), "He's Alive" never manages to work up much steam. Austrian actor Ludwig Donath is fairly good as the old man, but Dennis Hopper lacks the personal magnetism to be believable as a charismatic leader. Speeches which are intended to be hypnotic seem merely shrill, although the audience is clearly supposed to be mesmerized. As for Adolf Hitler, when actor Curt Conway stands in front of an enormous blowup of the *real* Hitler, the illusion that he is the ghost of Hitler is immediately destroyed. The physical resemblance is practically nil.

Herbert Hirschman recalls an interesting effects shot involving the main character. "The director came up with this notion that while he was lying in bed with his eyes open or after he woke up, you could see the swastika in the pupil of his eye, and it took a lot of work with the light and cutout swastika to project on the eye and trying to get the camera in tight enough to see it. I remember having arguments with Stuart Rosenberg about whether it was worth the time and trouble and whether it was proper emotionally, because I felt it was a trick, really, more than a natural part of the dramatics of the picture." Ultimately, the shot was not used.

"MINIATURE" (2/21/63)

Robert Duvall

Written by Charles Beaumont
Producer: Herbert Hirschman
Director: Walter E. Grauman
Director of Photography: Robert W. Pittack
Music: Fred Steiner

Cast:
Charley Parkes: Robert Duvall
Mrs. Parkes: Pert Kelton
Myrna: Barbara Barrie
Buddie: Len Weinrib
Dr. Wallman: William Windom
Museum Guard: John McLiam
The Doll: Claire Griswold
The Maid: Nina Roman
The Suitor: Richard Angarola
Diemel: Barney Phillips
Harriet: Joan Chambers
The Guide: Chet Stratton

"To the average person, a museum is a place of knowledge, a place of beauty and truth and wonder. Some people come to study, others to contemplate, others to look for the sheer joy of looking. Charley Parkes has his own reasons. He comes to the museum to get away from the world. It isn't really the sixty-cent cafeteria meal that has drawn him here every day, it's the fact that here in these strange, cool halls he can be alone for a little while, really and truly alone. Anyway, that's how it was before he got lost and wandered in—to the Twilight Zone."

Charley, a shy bachelor who lives with his mother, goes to the museum cafeteria, only to find it closed for alterations. Suddenly, he is caught up in a tour group and carried along to a different part of the museum. Extricating himself, he finds himself facing an elaborate nineteenth-century dollhouse—and is astounded to see inside a lifelike, mechanical doll, a beautiful woman playing Mozart's Piano Sonata in A Major on a miniature harpsichord! Curious, he asks a friendly museum guard about the mechanism, and is told that the doll is carved from a solid piece of wood and *doesn't* play any music! Returning late to work, Charley is fired by his boss, mainly for being someone who doesn't quite fit into the life of the office—"a square peg." In the days that follow, however, he doesn't search for another job; instead, he spends all his time at the museum, watching the doll—whom everyone else sees as totally inanimate—go through a routine of eating her meals, playing music, being groomed by her maid, reading, and greeting a miniature gentleman caller—all in pantomime. He has fallen in love with the doll, but he keeps this a secret. His mother, sister Myrna and brother-in-law Buddie are dismayed by his solitary habits. Trying to help Charley break out of his cocoon, Myrna sets him up with a co-worker named Harriet. But the date ends in disaster—when *Harriet* makes a pass! Next day, Charley is back at the museum, absorbed in his dollhouse. Suddenly, the tiny gentleman caller barges drunkenly into the dollhouse, knocking the maid away and carrying the terrified doll out of sight. Desperate to protect her honor, Charley grabs a nearby stone cherub and smashes the glass case surrounding the dollhouse—an act that lands him in an asylum. Eventually, Charley is able to convince Dr. Wallman, a psychiatrist, that he is cured of his delusion that the doll is alive. He is released back to his family, but the first chance he gets, he sneaks back to the museum. There, in the dollhouse, he finds the doll weeping tears of loneliness. He tells her that he understands; he, too, has been alone all his life. Together, they could understand, help and love each other. Frantic to find him, Dr. Wallman, Charley's family and the police search the museum. But there is no sign of him. Then the museum guard peers into the dollhouse, and is surprised to see *two* miniature figures. One is the doll . . . and the other is Charley!

"They never found Charley Parkes, because the guard didn't tell them what he saw in the glass case. He knew what they'd say, and he knew they'd be right, too, because seeing is not always *believing—especially if what you see happens to be an odd corner of the Twilight Zone."*

With "Miniature," Charles Beaumont crafted a most peculiar and touching love story.

"I consider it Beaumont's best script, period," says William F. Nolan. "He said it was based on me. It was about kind of a shy guy who had problems with women, which I've always had, I've never been a womanizer."

"I don't remember the genesis of the story," says Herbert Hirschman. "I remember reading a story once in some anthology of God reaching down and grabbing someone, and that image of a real person in a gigantic hand may have been part of the concept and inception of the thing. I thought it was a delightful story, and it was fun to make it work." The "real person in a gigantic hand" refers to the scene in which a psychiatrist places the tiny doll in Charley's palm to prove it is not a real woman. As seen from Charley's point of view, though, the little figure he holds is clearly alive.

Throughout "Miniature," Charley Parkes visits the dollhouse and watches a pantomime melodrama unfold as the girl is served by her maid and courted by a suitor whose intentions are most assuredly *not* honorable. In order to accomplish this, a four-room dollhouse *and* a full-size, identical replica were constructed. It was expensive, but well worth the effort.

"Miniature" is a fragile and wonderful story, a fairy tale about a man who just does not fit in with the rest of the world. Robert Duvall, a

Claire Griswold and Robert Duvall inside the dollhouse

marvelous chameleon of an actor, plays Charley as an intelligent and likeable man who is never at ease with other people. He is not a nonconformist so much as an alien. As his mother, Pert Kelton is a perfect caricature of the doting, possessive mother, speaking with a nasal voice that sounds like it's buzzing through a comb wrapped in wax paper, making him hot chocolate, and demanding to take off his shoes for him.

Above all, "Miniature" is a gentle story with gentle humor. A prime example is when Charley returns home after being committed to a mental institution as a result of his "delusions" concerning the doll. Charley is still crazy as a bedbug (at least as defined by the rest of society) but he's determined to convince everyone that he's fine—so that he'll have the opportunity to get back to the museum. Sipping hot chocolate, he says to his mother, "I sure missed this. No one makes cocoa the way you can."

"Did they hurt you, Charley?" his mother asks.

He replies, "Well, they were afraid they were gonna have to use shock treatment, and I hear that hurts quite a bit, but they decided not to when I got well."

Of all the hour-long *Twilight Zone* episodes, "Miniature" is the only one never put into syndication. The reason is that when the series was originally syndicated, "Miniature" was involved in a lawsuit. A script entitled "The Thirteenth Mannequin" had been submitted to Cayuga Productions prior to "Miniature." The script concerned an old man who preferred the company of store mannequins—mannequins who ultimately come to life. The suit claimed that since both works dealt with main characters becoming involved inanimate human figures who come to life, "Miniature" had stolen the idea.

Ultimately, the case was dismissed, both by the initial judge and on appeal. "The Thirteenth Mannequin" was no ancestor of "Miniature." The curious thing about this whole affair is that if any *Twilight Zone* episode was similar to "The Thirteenth Mannequin," it was Serling's "The After Hours"—and that was written long before anyone at Cayuga ever heard of "The Thirteenth Mannequin." Even when it was submitted, "The Thirteenth Mannequin" was not unique; *The Twilight Zone* had already explored its central idea.

Still, the damage was done. Because of the suit, "Miniature" was aired only once. A sad finale to a moving—and unique—episode.

"PRINTER'S DEVIL" (2/28/63)

Patricia Crowley, Robert Sterling and Burgess Meredith

Written by Charles Beaumont
Based on the short story
"The Devil, You Say?" by
Charles Beaumont
Producer: Herbert Hirschman
Director: Ralph Senensky
Director of Photography:
George T. Clemens
Music: stock

Cast:
Mr. Smith: Burgess Meredith
Douglas Winter: Robert Sterling
Jackie Benson: Patricia Crowley
Mr. Franklin: Ray Teal
Andy Praskins: Charles Thompson
Landlady: Doris Kemper
Molly: Camille Franklin

"Take away a man's dream, fill him with whiskey and despair, send him to a lonely bridge, let him stand there all by himself looking down at the black water, and try to imagine the thoughts that are in his mind. You can't, I can't. But there's someone who can*—and that someone is seated next to Douglas Winter right now. The car is headed back toward town, but its real destination is the Twilight Zone."*

Doug Winter, dedicated editor of the *Danzburg Courier,* is being driven out of business by the *Gazette,* which is owned by a big newspaper syndicate. When linotype operator Andy Praskins resigns in order to work for the *Gazette,* Doug is certain the *Courier*'s had it. He gets drunk and contemplates jumping off a bridge. He is interrupted in this by Mr. Smith, an ironic, cigar-smoking fellow who offers to work as both reporter and linotype operator for free—then pulls out five thousand dollars cash to pay off the *Courier*'s debts. Jackie Benson, Doug's girlfriend and devoted employee, is suspicious of Smith's motives, but Doug—seeing this as his paper's only chance—hires Smith on. Soon Smith is turning out editions with sensationalistic headlines that cause readership to soar. But when a fire destroys the *Gazette* building and the *Courier* reports the story within thirty minutes of the event, Doug suspects Smith may be doing more than just *reporting*. This is confirmed when Smith shows Doug his next scoop, all about a local sweepstakes win—written before the winner himself knows! Smith then produces a contract. The terms: his services in exchange for Doug's soul. Smith, it seems, is the Devil! Doug scoffs at this, but—fearful of losing Smith and having to face the bridge again—he signs.

Soon, however, he has reason to regret it, as Smith gleefully brings about a wave of disasters in order to fill the *Courier*'s front page. When Doug pleads with him to stop, Smith makes a counter-offer: he'll stop—if Doug kills himself. He then produces an added inducement: a story he's set on the linotype machine saying that Jackie will be seriously hurt in a car crash that evening. Smith has made modifications in the machine. Whatever is typed on it comes to pass—and the only thing that will save Jackie is Doug's death. As Doug ponders what to do, Smith asks Jackie to drive him out of town. He then takes the wheel, intending to steer headlong into an oncoming car. With only minutes to go, Doug gets a brainstorm. He sets in type a story stating that his contract with Smith is rendered null and void, and that Smith is banished. Just in time, Smith vanishes. Jackie's car sideswipes the other vehicle and Jackie escapes uninjured. Doug intends to battle the *Gazette* without Smith's aid from now on—and the first order of business is to get rid of that linotype machine!

"Exit the infernal machine, and with it his satanic majesty, Lucifer, prince of darkness—otherwise known as Mr. Smith. He's gone, but not for good; that wouldn't be like him—he's gone for bad. *And he might be back, with another ticket to—the Twilight Zone."*

Burgess Meredith made his fourth and final *Twilight Zone* appearance in Charles Beaumont's "Printer's Devil," playing a character far removed from the good and gentle men he had played in the previous three. "Printer's Devil" was based on Beaumont's first sale, a clever short story entitled "The Devil, You Say?" that appeared in the January, 1951, issue of *Amazing Stories*. In it, a young man inherits an unsuccessful newspaper from his father. On the day that he decides to close down the paper, a nattily-dressed old man appears in his office. The old man explains that long ago he made a deal with the man's father: the father would receive $150 per month plus be allowed to put out the newspaper . . . in exchange for his immortal soul. The old man is the Devil!

The contract had another stipulation, however. The son, too, must be made happy in order to close the deal. The Devil sets about doing just that, by making audacious things happen and then putting out editions of the paper with such incredible but true headlines as "MAYOR'S WIFE GIVES BIRTH TO BABY HIPPOPOTAMUS," "FARMER BURL ILLING COMPLAINS OF MYSTERIOUS APPEARANCE OF DRAGONS IN BACK YARD," "S.S. QUEEN MARY DISCOVERED ON MAIN STREET," and "BANK PRESIDENT'S WIFE CLAIMS DIVORCE—EXPLAINS CAUGHT HUSBAND TRIFLING WITH THREE MERMAIDS IN BATHTUB." Soon it becomes obvious that the

Devil is having such a good time making these events occur that he's no longer at all concerned about whether the young man is happy or not. Our hero decides that the Devil must be gotten rid of. With the aid of a lovely blonde reporter who's come from New York to interview him—and with whom he's fallen in love—he lures the Devil away from the press long enough to feed in a story that includes the Devil returning to Hell, his father escaping to Heaven, the newspaper office disappearing, and himself getting a job as a reporter on a large metropolitan newspaper. All of these things come to pass, but he suddenly realizes something: he forgot to mention the lady reporter. He finds her working for the same paper, but things have changed ("'Don't you remember, honey? You were doing me a favor, coaxing the devil to buy you a few drinks . . .' It was there in her eyes. She could have been staring at an escaped orangoutang"). Dejectedly, he realizes that he should have left things just as they were. "It wasn't very peaceful," he says, "but so what. I ask you, so what?"

In adapting the story, Beaumont removed the character of the lady reporter and changed the astonishing headlines to merely sensational ones: murders, robberies, fires, and the like. This had the effect of reducing "Printer's Devil" to a fairly run of the mill deal-with-the-Devil story. One of the few positive changes was the more appropriate title: "printer's devil" is a term that applies to a printer's apprentice or errand boy.

The best thing about the show, however, and the thing that saves it, is Meredith's bravura performance as Mr. Smith. With his hair cut in a widow's peak, his eyebrows pointing slightly upward, a twisted cigar in his mouth, he certainly looks the part. He is a grinning, leering Devil, full of subtleties. His interpretation goes well beyond the lines.

"The problem was to get him so that he was witty [while] still being menacing," Meredith says of the characterization, "and charming without losing his danger. I think it was a rich part. You know, you can't do anything if the possibilities are not there."

"I remember going to Wardrobe the day that Burgess came in for wardrobe," recalls the episode's director, Ralph Senensky (*Star Trek*, *The Waltons*, etc.), "and that was a revelation, to watch this man, because he stood in front of the mirror and put on all the possibilities and he just *changed*. He put on different items and you could see that he was feeling whether that would work for him. I'm sure that most of the wardrobe, in black and white, didn't really register, but it was important to him, because he drew from it and it was just a part of his putting together the character."

One item Meredith had to wear definitely was *not* his idea. In an early scene, Smith, lacking a match to light his cigarette, snaps his fingers and one of them bursts into flame. "They had him wired," explains Ralph Senensky. "There was a wire that went onto a battery and ran up his pant leg through his shirt to his hand. Then they stuck his finger into a coffee can of ice water. It would just get good and cold. They poured lighter fluid over it and then, when he did *this* [snaps his fingers], they would hit the switch, the spark would ignite it, and the lighter fluid would burn. The finger was literally a step from being frozen, so that it wouldn't hurt."

Unlike the original story, in "Printer's Devil" it is the main character—not his father—who makes the deal with the Devil. A high point in the episode comes when Smith, having saved the paper, confronts Winter and lays his cards on the table:

SMITH: Now first of all, I should like to ask whether or not you're happy with the way things have been going.

WINTER: Just what are you leading up to, Mr. Smith?

SMITH: A simple proposition. I hereby guarantee—understand? *guarantee*—that you will become the most successful newspaper editor in the world, if you will affix your signature to this little document. (*Hands the document to him*)

WINTER (*Reading*): "I, Douglas Winter, agree to relinquish my immortal soul to the bearer upon my death, in exchange for his services." (*Starts to laugh*) You're the Devil!

SMITH (*Laughs*): Mr. Winter, as a sophisticated, intelligent twentiety-century man, you *know* that the Devil does not exist. True?

WINTER: True.

SMITH: But you also know that the world is full of eccentric, *rich* old men, crazy old men who do all kinds of things for crazy reasons. Now, why don't you think of me like that? Here's a pen. (*Hands it to him*)

WINTER: This is ridiculous!

SMITH (*Chuckling*): Yes, isn't it . . . You don't really believe I'm the Devil, do you?

WINTER: No.

SMITH: Well then, why don't you put it this way. You're humoring me. After all, what good is the soul, anyway? It's sort of like an appendix these days, particularly since it doesn't exist in the first place.

WINTER: Well, just for the sake of argument, why do you want *mine*?

SMITH: Well, for the sake of argument, let's say I'm something of a connoisseur. You have a very choice soul, and as the vintners say—it's a good year.

WINTER: Well then again, just for sake of argument, why don't you just take it? Now, if you're the Devil, as you say you are, well you can do everything.

SMITH: Unhappily, not everything. I am bound by certain rules, and I do have my limitations.

WINTER: You're nuts.

SMITH: Yes, let's drink to that. I think I should warn you, however, that if you do not sign this, then the certain gloomy predictions you made about the *Courier*'s future will certainly come to pass. I'll have to resign, and—Well, let's not even *consider* such a proposition. After all, you don't want to go visiting that bridge again, do you?

WINTER: Hardly.

SMITH: No. Now, why not humor an old man? It would mean such a lot to me. And if you don't sign it, it would be admitting fear and belief. You're not afraid, are you?

WINTER: No. (*He raises the pen to sign, then hesitates*)

SMITH (*Taunting*): Fancy that—a grownup man who believes in the Devil!

WINTER (*Angrily*): This stupid thing! (*He signs furiously*) There. Now let's not hear any more about this, shall we?

In handling the striking of the bargain in this fashion, "Printer's Devil" avoids all the clichés. "Beaumont has done it so cleverly," says Ralph

Senensky, "because the Devil tricks him into doing it, predicated not on that he *believes,* but that he can't be foolish enough to believe. It's a marvelous approach."

Senensky has a final recollection regarding "Printer's Devil," one that seems particularly apt. "On that last confrontation between Smith and Doug, I shot the master, shot the two closeups, and with this whole soundstage full of people we didn't know until we went to the dailies the next day that this strange little man from the printing house that we had borrowed equipment from, who had been around observing, was standing back in the doorway, over Bob Sterling's shoulder. Nobody had seen him, including the operator, who sat and looked at this long closeup, never saw him. We went to the dailies and there he was, just as big as life. It almost seemed ghostlike—he *looked* like a ghost! So we had to do pickups of that shot."

"NO TIME LIKE THE PAST" (3/7/63)

Dana Andrews

Written by Rod Serling
Producer: Herbert Hirschman
Director: Justus Addiss
Director of Photography: Robert W. Pittack
Music: stock

Cast:
Paul Driscoll: Dana Andrews
Abigail Sloan: Patricia Breslin
Harvey: Robert F. Simon
Japanese Police Captain: James Yagi
***Lusitania* Captain:** Tudor Owen
Bartender: Lindsay Workman
Prof. Eliot: Malcolm Atterbury
Mrs. Chamberlain: Marjorie Bennett
Hanford: Robert Cornthwaithe
Horn Player: John Zaremba

"Exit one Paul Driscoll, a creature of the twentieth century. He puts to a test a complicated theorum of space-time continuum, but he goes a step further—or tries to. Shortly, he will seek out three moments of the past in a desperate attempt to alter the present—one of the odd and fanciful functions in a shadowland known as the Twilight Zone."

Sick to death of the constant threat of nuclear obliteration in the modern world, Driscoll utilizes a time machine in order to change past events. He soon finds, however, that it isn't as simple as he had thought: a Japanese police captain steadfastly refuses to believe that Hiroshima is about to have an atom bomb dropped on it; his assassination attempt on Adolf Hitler is foiled when a German maid summons the Gestapo; and the captain of the *Lusitania* rejects his claims that the ship is going to be torpedoed as the ravings of a lunatic. Driscoll returns to his own time, convinced that the present can't be changed. Frustrated, he decides to escape into an idyllic past. He uses the time machine to transport him back to Homeville, Indiana, on July 1, 1881. Finding the town lovely and serene, he checks into the local boardinghouse and meets Abigail Sloan, an attractive schoolteacher. Driscoll intends to stay, and is determined not to interfere with events; when he realizes that President Garfield is shortly to be assassinated, he keeps mum. All goes well for two days, but then Driscoll refers to a book of Midwestern history he's brought along with him and discovers that a kerosene lantern is about to be thrown from a runaway wagon, setting Abigail's school building afire and seriously injuring twelve children. Driscoll feels compelled to intervene. Seeing Professor Eliot's medicine wagon near the school, he pleads with Eliot to unhitch the horses. When Eliot refuses, he tries forcibly to unhitch them himself. Eliot, in trying to knock Driscoll away with his whip, frightens the horses and they run out of control. The lamp is thrown from the wagon and the school burns. In trying to stop the fire, Driscoll has *caused* it. Driscoll bids Abby farewell, telling her that he can be no part of her world. He returns to the present, content to leave the yesterdays alone—and determined to work on changing the tomorrows.

"Incident on a July afternoon, 1881. A man named Driscoll who came and went and, in the process, learned a simple lesson, perhaps best said by a poet named Lathbury, who wrote, 'Children of yesterday, heirs of tomorrow, what are you weaving? Labor and sorrow? Look to your looms again, faster and faster fly the great shuttles prepared by the master. Life's in the loom, room for it—room!' Tonight's tale of clocks and calendars—in the Twilight Zone."

Time travel was a subject that repeatedly fascinated Serling. With "No Time Like the Past," he again explored the potentials. Unfortunately, the story is chock full of illogic and dramatic cheats. Driscoll arrives in Hiroshima only six hours before it is bombed. Even if his warnings were believed, they would accomplish no more than a futile, hysterical prelude to the horror to come. As it turns out, he gets to the police chief of Hiroshima only minutes before the blast. In spite of this, he delivers his forecast, which he claims comes from "the Voice of History." In another scene, Driscoll is in a hotel room, kneeling by a window, looking through the telescopic sight of a high-powered rifle. Through the sight we see Adolf Hitler. The year is 1939, the place Germany. Driscoll aims and slowly squeezes the trigger. *Click*. It was just a test run.

This is the worst kind of cheat. No assassin in his right mind would get his intended victim centered in the cross hairs of his rifle without intending to fire. He would know that he might not get a second chance—as indeed Driscoll does not.

Despite a few bright moments, such as when Driscoll argues with a belligerent Homeville resident over nineteenth-century American military policy, "No Time Like the Past" fails to present a thoughtful, speculative story. Some months after its broadcast Serling summed it up quite succinctly like this: "On *Twilight Zone* . . . we've run the time travel theme to death . . ."

"I DREAM OF GENIE" (3/21/63)

Patricia Barry and Howard Morris

Written by John Furia, Jr.
Producer: Herbert Hirschman
Director: Robert Gist
Director of Photography: George T. Clemens
Music: Fred Steiner

Cast:
George P. Hanley: Howard Morris
Ann: Patricia Barry
Roger: Mark Miller
Genie: Jack Albertson
Watson: Loring Smith
Starlet: Joyce Jameson
Masters: James Millhollin
Clerk: Robert Ball
Sam: Bob Hastings

"Meet Mr. George P. Hanley, a man life treats without deference, honor or success. Waiters serve his soup cold. Elevator operators close doors in his face. Mothers never bother to wait up for the daughters he dates. George is a creature of humble habits and tame dreams. He's an ordinary man, Mr. Hanley, but at this moment the accidental possessor of a very special gift, the kind of gift that measures men against their dreams, the kind of gift most of us might ask for first and possibly regret to the last, if we, like Mr. George P. Hanley, were about to plunge head-first and unaware into our own personal Twilight Zone."

Searching for a birthday present for Ann, an attractive secretary at the office where he works as a bookkeeper, George is suckered into buying a tarnished Arabian lamp for twenty dollars. When Roger, a handsome, aggressive co-worker, gives Ann a revealing negligee, George is too embarrassed to present his own gift. Feeling very much the sap, he takes the lamp home and tries to shine it up with a rag. Suddenly, a genie appears—speaking in modern slang and wearing modern clothes (with the exception of his curl-toe shoes). George is allowed only *one* wish, so he must ponder it carefully. The genie returns to the lamp to give George time to think it over. At first, wishing for love appeals to him. He fantasizes being married to Ann, now become a movie star. Unfortunately, she's so famous and busy that she has no time for him—and then he discovers that she's having an affair with Roger, her leading man! The next day at work, he daydreams about wishing for great wealth. He is G. Peter Hanley, magnanimous industrialist. Ann is his secretary, Roger his chauffeur. Filled to the brim with charity, he gives a bedraggled newsboy a hundred dollar bill for a paper. But when he tries to donate $1,200,000 to his alma mater, his gesture is labeled ostentatious—and when he decides to stop buying things he's called subversive! Clearly, wealth is *not* the answer. Finally, George imagines what it would be like to wish for *power.* He is George P. Hanley, President of the United States. When Ann, now an elderly mother, pleads mercy for her son, who is about to be hanged for falling asleep on guard duty, George grants the boy a pardon. But then Roger, a four-star general, barges in with a group of presidential advisors. Alien spaceships have been sighted on radar; George must decide whether to shoot them out of the sky or let them land and risk possible invasion. The responsibility is too great, George *can't* decide—and power isn't the answer, either. But George has decided on his wish at last. Later, a bum fishes the lamp from a trash can and rubs it tentatively with a rag. A genie appears, dressed in turban and traditional Arabian garb. *This* genie offers three wishes—and his name is George P. Hanley!

"Mr. George P. Hanley. Former vocation: jerk. Present vocation: genie. George P. Hanley, a most ordinary man whom life treated without deference, honor or success, but a man wise enough to decide on a most extraordinary wish that makes him the contented, permanent master of his own altruistic Twilight Zone."

"It was a comedy that wasn't as funny as it might have been."

Herbert Hirschman's opinion of John Furia, Jr.'s, "I Dream of Genie" is unfortunately correct. The idea was certainly full of potential. As Hanley, comic actor Howard Morris has lots of charm—and he makes the material work better than it otherwise would have—but he is sabotaged by a weak script.

Part of the problem is that at the very beginning the genie *tells* George that neither love nor wealth will work as wishes, making two of the three fantasy sequences completely redundant. Another aspect that fails to work is the character of the genie, played by Jack Albertson. Dressed in modern clothes, talking in slang, extremely abrasive, he is anything but the traditional genie.

The best moments in "I Dream of Genie" come when Morris assumes the fantasy roles of industrialist and President, poking fun at the clichés of magnanimous billionaire and kindly head of state. As in a comedy skit, Morris knows exactly how far to exaggerate without going over the line. Here, he is a busy President in the Oval Office:

MAY: Your appointment schedule, Mr. President.

HANLEY: Thank you, May. Move the press conference to after lunch. I need a haircut.

MAY: Yes, sir.

HANLEY: I'll make the U.N. speech. Tell Lawrenson to whip up a draft and remind him: jokes!

MAY: Yes, Mr. President.

HANLEY: *Who* are Sonny and Mickey?

MAY: They're the cub scouts who wrote you the letter on citizenship. You asked to be reminded when they came into the capitol. Of course, there's no time—

HANLEY: Make time! We'll have our haircuts together.

MAY: Yes, sir. Oh, it's almost ten o'clock.

HANLEY (*He walks over to a large switch and throws it*): Twenty million kilowatts for the southwest. Too bad I can't make all these dedications in person!

"THE INCREDIBLE WORLD OF HORACE FORD"
(4/18/63)

Pat Hingle and Jim E. Titus

Written by Reginald Rose
Producer: Herbert Hirschman
Director: Abner Biberman
Director of Photography: George T. Clemens
Music: stock

Cast:
Horace Ford: Pat Hingle
Laura Ford: Nan Martin
Mrs. Ford: Ruth White
Leonard O'Brien: Phillip Pine
Betty O'Brien: Mary Carver
Mr. Judson: Vaughn Taylor
Horace (child): Jim E. Titus
Hermy Brandt: Jerry Davis

"Mr. Horace Ford, who has a preoccupation with another time, a time of childhood, a time of growing up, a time of street games, stickball and hide-'n-go-seek. He has a reluctance to go check out a mirror and see the nature of his image: proof positive that the time he dwells in has already passed him by. But in a moment or two he'll discover that mechanical toys and memories and daydreaming and wishful thinking and all manner of odd and special events can lead into a special province, uncharted and unmapped, a country of both shadow and substance known as . . . the Twilight Zone."

Toy designer Horace Ford, emotionally little more than an oversized child, lives with his wife Laura and his mother. He spends most of his time reminiscing about what he recalls as an idyllic childhood that was all play and no responsibility. Several evenings before his thirty-eighth birthday—for which Laura has planned a surprise party—Horace pays a nostalgic visit to his old neighborhood on Randolph Street. To his amazement, it is exactly as he remembered it, down to the clothes the people wear and the pushcart man selling hot dogs for three cents apiece. Suddenly, a group of young boys rush past. One of them bumps into Horace, knocking his pocket watch out of his hands. The boy turns and grins. Horace is astonished to see it is Hermy Brandt—who was a child when *he* was a child! Horace gives chase, but loses him. Returning home, he tries to tell Laura and his mother of the experience, but finds them extremely dubious. Then the doorbell rings. Laura answers it—and finds herself face to face with Hermy Brandt, who hands her Horace's watch, then runs away. Drawn by the mystery, Horace returns to Randolph Street the next night and finds the sequence of events identical. Only this time, he manages to catch up with the boys and overhears them angrily discussing some unnamed person who has slighted them by not inviting them to his birthday party. Horace comes back to his apartment, certain he has witnessed a recurring pattern—one in which he is inexplicably a part. This conviction is only strengthened when, as before, Hermy Brandt returns his watch and runs off. Obsessed by these events, Horace neglects his work. Sensing he is not well, Mr. Judson, his boss, orders him to take a leave of absence and see a psychiatrist. Furious, Horace refuses, and Judson is forced to fire him. When Horace tells his mother of this, she breaks down into hysterical tears of self-pity. Horace is filled with envy of the kids he's seen on Randolph Street: *they* don't have to support a wife and mother— all they have to do is have fun! He storms out of the apartment and races back to Randolph Street. There the events repeat themselves, but this time the boys' conversation continues and it becomes clear that the person who has offended them is Horace! He pleads with them to forgive him, but is ignored. Suddenly, he is a child again. Viciously, they jump on him and beat him up. Back at the apartment, Laura and the party guests wait for Horace's return. When the doorbell rings, the door is thrown open and they all yell "Surprise!"—but the surprise is on them. It's not Horace, it's Hermy Brandt, and *this* time the object he holds out is a Mickey Mouse watch! Horrified, Laura rushes to Randolph Street. It is quiet, empty of people, the stands covered over with cloths. Horace, still a little boy, lies unconscious on the ground, bleeding and bruised. Sobbing, Laura turns away from him. When she turns back, Horace is a man again. He revives, and tells her that what he found on Randolph Street put the lie to what he had remembered; in reality, his childhood was a terrible time. Now, finally, he is able to put it behind him. There's a party waiting for him at home. He and Laura leave Randolph Street—not noticing that high above them, atop a streetlamp, sits a grinning Hermy Brandt.

"Exit Mr. and Mrs. Horace Ford, who have lived through a bizarre moment not to be calibrated on normal clocks or watches. Time has passed, to be sure, but it's the special time in the special place known as—the Twilight Zone."

On June 13, 1955, *Studio One* presented "The Incredible World of Horace Ford" by Reginald Rose, writer of the film *Twelve Angry Men* and later to create the television series *The Defenders*. Starring Art Carney, the show concerned an overwhelmingly nostalgic toy designer who returns to the street of his childhood and finds it exactly as it was when he was a child—including the very same children! This was no "Walking Distance," however. His old neighborhood is a Lower East Side slum and the people turn out to be anything but friendly.

"What I meant to do with 'The Incredible World of Horace Ford,'" Rose wrote in 1956, "was to tell a simple horror story about an everyday man with a somewhat exaggerated but everyday kind of problem and, in so doing, point out that the funny, tender childhood memories we cling to are often distorted and unreal. What happened to Horace when he finally made it back to his childhood was typical of what actually happened to so many of us again and again when we were children. He was ridiculed, rejected, beaten up. These are all familiar experiences to us, yet somehow we tend only to remember, as Horace did, the joys of swiping pomegranates from Ippolito's."

Herbert Hirschman remembered this fantasy, thought it would be ideal for *Twilight Zone,* and bought it from Rose. He then hired Abner Biberman to direct.

One day, Biberman was in the MGM commissary and he happened to spot Pat Hingle, an accomplished Broadway actor with credits including *J.B., Cat on a Hot Tin Roof, The Glass Menagerie,* and *That Championship Season* (and later to play the father in the movie *Norma Rae*). Biberman approached Hingle and offered him the part. He accepted. Cast as his wife was Nan Martin, who had played his wife in *J.B.*

As Horace Ford, Pat Hingle gives a striking performance, his gestures and stride exaggerated, boyish. "I realized that he was like a man/boy or boy/man," says Hingle. "In many ways, his spirit had not grown up." Also very good are Nan Martin and, as Horace's mother, Ruth White.

Reginald Rose prefers the finale of the original "Horace Ford," which ends with Horace transforming into a child, being beaten up, and Hermy Brandt delivering a Mickey Mouse watch to the astonished Laura. "I was writing something quite strange, a realistic fantasy, and I wanted a shocking, impossible ending. Horace turns into a kid again and finds it to be not glorious, as he had always remembered, but dreadful. When *Twilight Zone* wanted to buy it, Herb Hirschman asked for another ending. He wanted it more upbeat. I obliged. The work had already been done the way I saw it, and therefore it didn't bother me to change the ending."

"THE BARD" (5/23/63)

John Williams and Jack Weston

Written by Rod Serling
Producer: Herbert Hirschman
Director: David Butler
Director of Photography: George T. Clemens
Music: Fred Steiner

Cast:
Julius Moomer: Jack Weston
William Shakespeare: John Williams
Rocky Rhodes: Burt Reynolds
Mr. Shannon: John McGiver
Gerald Hugo: Henry Lascoe
Cora: Judy Strangis
Bramhoff: Howard McNear
Sadie: Doro Merande
Secretary: Marge Redmond
Bus Driver: Clegg Hoyt
Dolan: William Lanteau

"You've just witnessed opportunity, if not knocking, at least scratching plaintively on a closed door. Mr. Julius Moomer, a would-be writer who, if talent came twenty-five cents a pound, would be worth less than car fare. But, in a moment, Mr. Moomer, through the offices of some black magic, is about to embark on a brand-new career. And although he may never get a writing credit on *the Twilight Zone, he's to become an integral character* in *it."*

So eager is agent Gerald Hugo to get sincere and talkative Julius out of his office that he promises to submit a script for Julius as a pilot for a black magic series—*if* Julius can get the script to him by Monday. Eager to research the subject, Julius immediately enters a used bookstore. Suddenly, an ancient book of black magic removes itself from the shelf and falls to the floor. Taking it home, he tries to invoke one of its spells, using materials at hand in place of those dictated by the formula in the book. His attempts produce no result at all. Dejectedly, he sits down. "Who do they think I am?" he says. "William Shakespeare?" Immediately, there is an explosion. When the smoke clears Julius is astounded to see that he has inadvertently summoned up William Shakespeare! Seizing on this golden opportunity, he enlists Shakespeare as a ghost writer. Shakespeare quickly turns out a teleplay entitled "The Tragic Cycle," which Shannon Foods buys for airing on the TV show it sponsors. The script is of such brilliance that, even before the show is aired, Moomer becomes a celebrity. Shakespeare is enraged that Julius has taken sole credit for the script. He decides to attend one of his play's rehearsals and see if it is being performed faithfully. When Shakespeare arrives at the studio, Julius explains to the sponsor and advertising executives that he is actually Julius's mad cousin, who believes he's William Shakespeare this week. Shakespeare is appalled by the changes the sponsor has made in his script: The lead has been rewritten to suit Rocky Rhodes, a method actor acclaimed for his performance in *A Streetcar Named Desire;* a love scene takes place in a subway station instead of on a balcony; and a female character, instead of committing suicide, runs off with one of Artie Shaw's musicians! When Shakespeare protests, Rhodes sidles up to him and asks what he's got against Stanislavsky. "*You,*" Shakespeare replies, and lands a mighty punch that decks the actor. Then he storms out—for good. Moomer's next assignment is a two-and-a-half-hour American history spectacular, but without Shakespeare he figures his career is at an end—until he remembers the book of black magic. Proudly, Julius troops into Gerald Hugo's office with his new writing staff: Robert E. Lee, Ulysses S. Grant, George Washington, Abraham Lincoln, Pocahontas, Daniel Boone, Theodore Roosevelt and Benjamin Franklin!

"Mr. Julius Moomer, a streetcar conductor with delusions of authorship. And if the tale just told seems a little tall, remember a thing called poetic license—and another thing called the Twilight Zone."

With "The Bard," Serling pokes fun at the medium of television—the writers, the actors, the agents, the executives and sponsors. Serling is on his home turf here, and one feels he took a delicious pleasure in writing this delightful episode.

Would-be writer Julius Moomer (Jack Weston) dreams of someday winning the "Wurlitzer" prize ("*Pulitzer,*" a little girl corrects him). He is bursting with ideas, but none of them are selling, and with good reason. Among them: a zombie story ("about this dame who marries a guy who walks around on his heels all the time. She thinks he's punchy but it turns out he's dead—all the time they're married, she don't know he's dead!"), a love story ("where the lady scientist falls in love with a robot"), a western ("where the president of the Western Pacific Railroad turns out to be Belle Starr"), a weekly series ("*Boy Meets Girl!* Every week we have a different boy and a different girl!"), and the idea of changing *The Millionaire* into *The Multi-Millionaire* and making an hour show of it. Moomer is short on originality, but long on enthusiasm, as when he's talking to a Hollywood agent:

JULIUS: If this one ain't sure fire, I'll cut off both my hands, I'll absolutely cut off both my hands! You ready? Are you ready? *Champion of the World*. Kirk Douglas, maybe. Burt Lancaster. You want to make him younger? Tony Curtis, I give you Tony Curtis . . . So now he's champion of the world, but he's made a promise to this girl never to fight again. You know, like a vow. A vow, Mr. Hugo, that's like a promise, I mean like *solemn*. And now, Mr. Hugo, comes the meat, this is what grabs you *right here*. Now, he's gotta fight but he promised his girl, and when he *tells* her he's gonna fight, she's aghast, I mean this broad is palpitating! She calls the champeen a filthy, rotten, dirty—

MR. HUGO: She's adamant, is that what you mean?

JULIUS: Oh ho ho ho ho, is this girl adamant! She's adamant like nobody ever was adamant! . . . You see, the beauty of the story is you can couch it in so many terms. So maybe he ain't a prizefighter, maybe he's a cowboy, a top gun, and maybe he promised his girl never to carry a gun again, and maybe it's the girl's *kid brother* who has this incurable disease . . . Say, how about if it was a science-fiction piece? This rocket man makes a promise to his girl never to go up in a spaceship again—

MR. HUGO: Julius, you've been here all morning. Now, I'll give you this: I've been an agent twenty-three years, never, never heard of so many variations of the same story!

Moomer's luck changes radically when, while researching a script dealing with black magic, he reads aloud from a book of incantations and inadvertently summons up William Shakespeare (John Williams). Realizing his opportunity, he decides to utilize Shakespeare's abilities as a ghost writer (literally!). Moomer quickly gains a reputation as a top-flight TV writer. Ah, but what happens to Shakespeare's writing!

Nicely directing all of this is David Butler, an old-time director whose films include some of Shirley Temple's best (*Bright Eyes, The Little Colonel, The Littlest Rebel, Captain January*), plus the rarely-seen 1930 science-fiction musical *Just Imagine*. Jack Weston, who was such a slimy character in "The Monsters Are Due on Maple Street," is loads of fun as the bungling Moomer. John Williams, perhaps best remembered as the Inspector in Hitchcock's *Dial M for Murder,* makes a fine—and *veddy* British—Shakespeare. A humorous running gag is one in which Shakespeare repeatedly quotes lines from his plays, including title, act and scene. At one point, he turns to Julius, says, "To be or not to be, Mr. Moomer, *that*—" pauses, looks confused, can't recall the rest, and exits.

Definitely the greatest surprise in "The Bard" lies in the character of the leading man chosen to star in Shakespeare's first—and last—TV show. This dialogue between an executive on the show and the sponsor should give some clue as to *who* this leading man is supposed to be:

BRAMHOFF: Mr. Shannon, we feel ourselves extremely fortunate to secure the services of Rocky Rhodes.

SHANNON: Rhodes, shmodes, I sell soup! I don't know nothin' about actors. Which one is Rhodes?

BRAMHOFF: He's the attractive one in the sweatshirt.

SHANNON: That's an actor?

BRAMHOFF: Well, he was brilliant in *Streetcar Named Desire*.

SHANNON: *Streetcar Named Desire*? What was he—a conductor?

Then there's this conversation, between Rhodes and the director of the show:

RHODES: What is my tertiary motivation here? I mean, like I walk through the door and I see *her.* Why?

DIRECTOR (*Very confused*): Why what, Rocky? What's the question?

RHODES: Exactly. What is the question? I mean, like any slob can walk through a door, I mean like I do it every day. But well now, maybe I shouldn't walk through the door at that moment. So I gotta ask myself, 'Would I walk through that door?' It's on the basis of that answer that I find my motivation. So the question is, what's my motivation?

DIRECTOR (*Humoring him*): Well, Rocky baby, why don't we just run through it and see how it plays?

"Burt Reynolds had a small part that was supposed to be like Marlon Brando," assistant to the producer John Conwell explains. "He was an old friend of mine, and I asked him if he would do it, because he looked very much like Brando at that time and did a marvelous imitation of him." Despite Reynolds's precise—and very funny—impersonation, and Serling's deliberate satirical intent, some people missed the point entirely. One reporter referred to Rhodes as "a beatnik leading man who did an imitation of the stories one used to hear about Rod Steiger . . ."

Serling was trying for a real grabber to close the episode, so he pulled out all the stops, but one feels that it would have been more logical for Julius to call upon Mark Twain, Bret Harte, James Fenimore Cooper, Stephen Crane, and Ambrose Bierce, since his problem wasn't an inability to research but rather an inability to *write*. Nevertheless, "The Bard" remains an episode that is both entertaining and accurate.

John Williams and Burt Reynolds

MID-SEASON CHANGES

On January 1, 1963, Herbert Hirschman's contract with CBS expired. At the same time, Hirschman received an offer from Herbert Brodkin, with whom he'd worked on *Playhouse 90*. Brodkin's company, in cooperation with Sir (now Lord) Lew Grade, was about to begin production in London on *Espionage,* a series to be aired both on NBC in America and on British television. Brodkin wanted Hirschman as producer of the show. Hirschman accepted. "The opportunity of going to Europe—I'd never lived or worked there before—superceded my interest in doing another three or four *Twilight Zones*."

Twilight Zone needed a new producer, and fast. Various names were suggested, including Perry Lafferty, who had directed "In His Image," "The Thirty-Fathom Grave," and "Valley of the Shadow." The man chosen was one who had, in a way, already produced a *Twilight Zone* episode: Bert Granet, producer of "The Time Element." Granet accepted, and production continued.

"PASSAGE ON THE *LADY ANNE*" (5/9/63)

Joyce Van Patten and Lee Philips

Written by Charles Beaumont
Based on the short story "Song For a Lady" by Charles Beaumont
Producer: Bert Granet
Director: Lamont Johnson
Music: composed by Rene Garriguenc, conducted by Lud Gluskin

Cast:
Allan Ransome: Lee Philips
Eileen Ransome: Joyce Van Patten
McKenzie: Wilfrid Hyde-White
Burgess: Cecil Kellaway
Millie McKenzie: Gladys Cooper
Capt. Protheroe: Alan Napier
Mr. Spiereto: Don Keefer
Officer: Cyril Delevanti

"Portrait of a honeymoon couple getting ready for a journey—with a difference. These newlyweds have been married for six years, and they're not taking this honeymoon to start *their life but rather to* save *it, or so Eileen Ransome thinks. She doesn't know why she insisted on a ship for this voyage, except that it would*

give them some time and she'd never been on one before—certainly never one like the Lady Anne. *The tickets read 'New York to Southampton,' but this old liner is going somewhere else. Its destination . . . the Twilight Zone."*

Driven by his ambition, Allan Ransome now seems to care only about business. When he has to travel to England, his wife Eileen—seizing this as a last-ditch opportunity to save her marriage—demands she be taken along *and* be allowed to choose the mode of transportation. Mr. Spiereto, a travel agent, reluctantly tells her of the *Lady Anne,* supposedly the slowest boat in the water. Much to Allan's dismay, Eileen books two passages on the *Lady Anne*. But when they arrive at the ship, they encounter McKenzie and Burgess, two elderly passengers who attempt to dissuade them from sailing—and then offer them ten thousand dollars in exchange for their tickets. Angrily, the Ransomes refuse. Initially, however, the cruise turns out not to be the salvation Eileen hoped for. Although the ship's decor is both opulent and beautiful, Allan remains cold and short-tempered. This only intensifies when they discover that everyone else on the ship—both passengers and crew—is over seventy-five years of age! The Ransomes get into an argument which culminates in their agreeing to get a divorce as soon as they reach England—a decision that causes Eileen considerable heartache. To while away the time, they become friendly with McKenzie and Burgess, as well as McKenzie's wife Millie. From them, they learn that long ago the *Lady Anne* was a boat reserved specifically for lovers. This is her last voyage, and those who fell under her spell years before have reunited for this final trip. McKenzie and Burgess explain that initially they viewed the Ransomes as interlopers, but now they see them as a symbol of young love—the perfect symbol for the *Lady Anne*. When Eileen begins to cry, however, the old people begin to suspect all is not well with her marriage. Burgess suggests the Ransomes step outside for a breath of fresh air. Leaning on the railing, Allan notices that the sun is behind them: they're heading north rather than east! Suddenly, Eileen is gone. Fearing that she's fallen overboard, Allan begins a frantic search; Eileen appears to be nowhere on the ship. Burgess and the McKenzies aren't terribly concerned; they seem to know something Allan doesn't. At his wits' end, Allan goes to his room—and finds Eileen there, dressed in a lovely nightgown that Mrs. McKenzie wore on *her* honeymoon. Eileen claims to have been in the room all the time, even though Allan searched the room earlier and found it empty. But that doesn't matter; the experience has rekindled Allan's love for her—and he won't forget the lesson. The next evening, the Ransomes are enjoying a shipboard party when the captain of the *Lady Anne* appears—and demands that they leave the ship! At gunpoint, he forces the couple into a lifeboat stocked with provisions as the rest of the passengers look on . . . with great affection. The captain tells them that their position has been radioed, and then they are set adrift. The *Lady Anne* sails off into the fog.

"The Lady Anne *never reached port. After they were picked up by a cutter a few hours later, as Captain Protheroe had promised, the Ransomes searched the newspapers for news—but there wasn't any news. The* Lady Anne *with all her crew and all her passengers vanished without a trace. But the Ransomes knew what had happened, they knew that the ship had sailed off to a better port—a place called the Twilight Zone."*

"Passage on the *Lady Anne*" was based on Charles Beaumont's short story, "Song For a Lady" (originally included in his collection *Night Ride and Other Journeys*).

In its heyday, the *Lady Anne* was a ship for young lovers, "an enchanted gondola," as one of the passengers put it.

"The family went to Europe in 1957 and we went across on the *Queen Elizabeth,*" Charles Beaumont's son Chris remembers. "There were a lot of old people aboard. My father got the idea aboard ship."

The major pleasure in "Passage on the *Lady Anne*" stems from a marvelous supporting cast of elderly British Empire actors, including Wilfrid Hyde-White, Cecil Kellaway, Gladys Cooper, Alan Napier and Cyril Delevanti. Old school all, full of charm and polish, they lend the episode dignity and grace. There is the feeling that these characters have a long history—which, in fact, they did.

"It was a joy to reunite with these great old characters and character actors," says director Lamont Johnson. "That was the chief attraction to do it. I loved hearing their anecdotes. Wilfrid Hyde-White and Gladys Cooper would sit around and gossip maliciously with enormous relish about people alive and dead, and some particularly scandalous thing that was happening currently in England or in the British colonies would send them into absolute flushes of youth. Their eyes would glow and their skin would take on a ruddy tone. They would just come alive with gossip."

"OF LATE I THINK OF CLIFFORDVILLE" (4/11/63)

Julie Newmar and Albert Salmi

Written by Rod Serling
Based on the short story "Blind Alley" by Malcolm Jameson
Producer: Bert Granet
Director: David Lowell Rich
Director of Photography: Robert W. Pittack
Music: stock

Cast:
Bill Feathersmith: Albert Salmi
Miss Devlin: Julie Newmar
Deidrich: John Anderson
Hecate: Wright King
Gibbons: Guy Raymond
Joanna: Christine Burke
Clark: John Harmon
Cronk: Hugh Sanders

"Witness a murder. The killer is Mr. William Feathersmith, a robber baron whose body composition is made up of a refrigeration plant covered by thick skin. In a moment Mr. Feathersmith will proceed on his daily course of conquest and calumny with yet another business dealing. But this one will be one of those bizarre transactions that take place in an odd marketplace known as the Twilight Zone."

The killing is a financial one: Mr. Diedrich, who has known and disliked Feathersmith since they were both young men in Cliffordville, Indiana, has taken out a three-million-dollar loan to aid his tool and die company; Feathersmith has bought up the loan and calls the note due—Deidrich is forced to sell him the company in order to avoid bankruptcy. Late that night, Feathersmith is drinking alone in his office when Mr. Hecate, a custodian for forty years who is also from Cliffordville, enters. Feathersmith tells him that, having reached the top, he's now bored. He'd like to be able to go back to the Cliffordville of his past and start all over again, re-experience the thrill of acquisition. A few minutes later, Feathersmith is surprised when the elevator deposits him not in the lobby, but on the floor of the Devlin Travel Agency. Miss Devlin, an attractive young lady with two horns sprouting from her head, offers him a unique service: she'll return him to the Cliffordville of 1910. He'll look young and his memory of the present will be unimpaired. The price is *not* his soul—they already *have* that—but his enormous fortune, all but fourteen hundred dollars. Feathersmith agrees, and shortly finds himself in Cliffordville. He expects nothing but success, but he is done in by his own faulty memory. He goes courting the daughter of Gibbons the banker and finds that she is not lovely, as he had remembered, but unspeakably homely. He uses his entire fourteen hundred to buy oil-rich land from Gibbons and Deidrich, not realizing that it is inaccessible to the drills of 1910. Finally, he tries to convince machinists to build a variety of modern-day inventions, but is unable to recall their workings specifically enough to draw blueprints. All this serves only to exhaust him utterly. With a shock, he realizes he's been tricked: he *looks* thirty, but internally he's still seventy-five! Miss Devlin appears. Feathersmith begs her to return him to 1963. She tells him that a special train is leaving immediately for the present and that Feathersmith is welcome to board—for forty dollars. Just then, Mr. Hecate happens by; Feathersmith sells him the deed to the oil-rich land for forty dollars. Then he returns to the present, but it is a present substantially altered by Feathersmith's dealings in the past. *Feathersmith* is now the janitor of forty years—and Hecate the wealthy financier!

"Mr. William J. Feathersmith, tycoon, who tried the track one more time and found it muddier than he remembered—proving with at least a degree of conclusiveness that nice guys don't always finish last, and some people should quit when they're ahead. Tonight's tale of iron men and irony, delivered f.o.b. from the Twilight Zone."

In 1963, Serling purchased "Blind Alley," a short story written in 1943 by Malcolm Jameson, for his anthology *Rod Serling's Triple W: Witches, Warlocks, and Werewolves* (Bantam, 1963). The story concerned an elderly, unscrupulous millionaire industrialist who, on his last legs, makes a deal with the Devil to go back in time forty years to Cliffordville, the town of his boyhood, with the intention of starting over. Only trouble is that he forgot to mention that he wanted to be young again (foolishly assuming it was part of the deal), so that he arrives in town old and sick and dies soon after. It was an adequate gimmick story, but no classic. Serling adapted this story into "Of Late I Think of Cliffordville," making numerous changes, but keeping some of the basics.

Directed by David Lowell Rich, (*A Family Upside-Down*, and *The Defection of Simas Kudirka*) "Of Late I Think of Cliffordville" remains static and uninvolving. The age makeup on several actors is mediocre, and Salmi never makes a convincing seventy-five-year-old man. Likewise, the final revelation of Feathersmith being an old man in a young man's skin is a bit contrived. At no point prior to this has Feathersmith shown any sign of infirmity; he seems vigorous and self-assured. More than that, the revelation is unnecessary. Feathersmith doesn't fail because of his chronological age; it is Feathersmith's *mind* that defeats him, not his body.

"THE PARALLEL" (3/14/63)

Steve Forrest

Written by Rod Serling
Producer: Bert Granet
Director: Alan Crosland
Director of Photography: Robert W. Pittack
Music: stock

Cast:
Robert Gaines: Steve Forrest
Helen Gaines: Jacqueline Scott
Col. Connacher: Frank Aletter
Maggie Gaines: Shari Lee Bernath
General Eaton: Philip Abbott
Captain: Morgan Jones
Project Manager: William Sargent
Psychiatrist: Paul Comi

"In the vernacular of space, this is T minus one hour, sixty minutes before a human being named Major Robert Gaines is lifted off from the Mother Earth and rocketed into the sky, farther and longer than any man ahead of him. Call this one of the first faltering steps of man to sever the umbilical cord of gravity and stretch out a fingertip toward an unknown. In a moment we'll join this astronaut named Gaines and embark on an adventure, because the environs overhead—the stars, the sky, the infinite space—are all part of a vast question mark known as the Twilight Zone."

While orbiting the Earth, Gaines's capsule inexplicably disappears from the radar screens. Gaines wakes up in a hospital. He was found in his capsule forty-six miles from point of lift-off. The capsule—which had no gear for landing on solid ground—was completely undamaged. It is a mystery for which Gaines has no explanation. He soon finds, however, that it is but the first of a number of mysteries: Colonel Connacher claims not to have called Gaines's wife Helen prior to the launch when Gaines is certain that he did; Gaines's house has a white picket fence he's never seen before; and everyone says he's a colonel when he *knows* he's a major. Both his wife and his daughter Maggie sense something strangely *different* about him. Doubting his own mind, he visits the Army Psychiatric Division. A psychiatrist finds Gaines's delusions peculiar, particularly his belief that the President of the United States is John Kennedy—someone no one else has ever heard of! Later, Gaines tells Connacher that he's looked through a set of encyclopedias and found a number of historical facts subtly altered, as though this is a world *parallel* to the one he knows. Connacher finds this all hard to swallow. To prove his point, Gaines asks Maggie *who he is*. She doesn't know—all she knows is that he's not her daddy! Meanwhile, back at the base, scientists have discovered that the capsule in which Gaines was found is *not* the one they sent up, but rather an almost-identical duplicate. Asking Gaines to identify it, he runs toward the capsule—and abruptly finds himself back in orbit, bringing his capsule in for a splash-down. In the hospital, Gaines learns that he was out of radar contact for six hours. He tells General Eaton and Colonel Connacher that he was in a parallel world populated by duplicates of all of them, in which *he* was a colonel. The others dismiss this as a bizarre delusion, but then an officer rushes up to them with the news that just moments ago the Cape picked up an unidentified spacecraft on radar for a period of ninety seconds—accompanied by a radio transmission from a *Colonel* Robert Gaines!

"Major Robert Gaines, a latter-day voyager just returned from an adventure. Submitted to you without any recommendations as to belief or disbelief. You can accept or reject; you pays your money and you takes your choice. But credulous or incredulous, don't bother to ask anyone for proof that it could happen. The obligation is a reverse challenge: prove that it couldn't. This happens to be . . . the Twilight Zone."

Although an interesting concept, "The Parallel" suffers from flat acting, particularly in the lead. As a result, what might have been as engrossing as "And When the Sky Was Opened" never generates much energy. (The same theme was explored in *Journey to the Far Side of the Sun,* a 1969 film starring Roy Thinnes.)

There were other problems, too. "Censorship was so strict at that time," Bert Granet recalls. "We tried something that was a shade too subtle, but basically I didn't want him to find out he was on the wrong planet until he went to bed with [the woman he thought was his wife]. The sexual habits were different. There's a suggestion of it but it's insufficient. Unless you're looking for it, I don't think you'll find it."

"THE NEW EXHIBIT" (4/4/63)

Bob Mitchell, Milton Parsons, David Bond and Rod Serling

Written by Jerry Sohl
Plotted by Charles Beaumont and Jerry Sohl (show credited solely to Beaumont)
Producer: Bert Granet
Director: John Brahm
Director of Photography: George T. Clemens
Music: stock

Cast:
Martin Lombard Senescu: Martin Balsam
Mr. Ferguson: Will Kuluva
Emma Senescu: Maggie Mahoney
Dave: William Mims
Henri Desire Landru: Milton Parsons
Jack the Ripper: David Bond
Albert W. Hicks: Bob Mitchell
Burke: Robert L. McCord
Hare: Billy Beck
Gas Man: Phil Chambers
Van Man: Lennie Breman
Sailor: Ed Barth
Guide: Marcel Hillaire
2nd Sailor: Craig Curtis

"Martin Lombard Senescu, a gentle man, the dedicated curator of murderers' row in Ferguson's Wax Museum. He ponders the reasons why ordinary men are driven to commit mass murder. What Mr. Senescu does not know is that the groundwork has already been laid for his own special kind of madness and torment—found only in the Twilight Zone."

Mr. Ferguson tells Martin that, as the result of poor attendance, he has been forced to sell the wax museum; it is to be demolished and a supermarket built in its place. Martin has been his employee for thirty years, and five of the figures have come to have special meaning for him, almost as though they were close friends. They are Jack the Ripper, Burke and Hare, Albert W. Hicks (who, one day in 1860, killed every member of a ship's crew with an ax) and Henri Desire Landru—all notorious murderers and all the handiwork of the great Henri Guilmont. Martin pleads to be allowed to house the figures in his basement; perhaps he will be able to get backers to open his *own* wax museum. Reluctantly, Ferguson agrees—to the dismay of Martin's wife Emma. As the weeks pass, Martin is unable to get backers, and the electricity bills to keep the basement air conditioned are staggering. The Senescus are broke. Nevertheless, Martin's obsession with the figures continues to grow; he spends all his waking hours down with them, grooming and attending them. Desperate to return to some kind of normalcy, Emma asks her brother Dave for advice. He suggests sabotage; disconnect the air conditioner and soon the wax figures won't be a problem. Late that night, Emma sneaks down to the basement to pull the plug. But suddenly, Jack the Ripper comes to life and murders her. Next morning, Martin discovers the body and sees blood on Jack's knife. Realizing that the police would never believe that a wax dummy killed his wife, Martin buries Emma in the basement and covers the grave with cement. But when Dave shows up, Martin has another problem: Dave won't swallow his story that Emma's gone to visit his sister, particularly when he hears the air conditioner going full blast downstairs! Dave sneaks into the basement—and is promptly dispatched by an ax wielded by Albert W. Hicks. Now Martin has to dig a second grave! Sometime later, Mr. Ferguson arrives with the news that he intends to sell the five figures to the Marchand Museum in Brussels. Although Martin protests, Ferguson remains adamant. When Martin goes upstairs to prepare some tea, Landru strangles Ferguson with a garrote. Returning, Martin is appalled to find Ferguson dead. Enraged, he tells the figures that he's going to destroy them. They come alive and draw near him, speaking to Martin in his mind, telling him that it is *he*, not they, who committed the murders. Later, at the Marchand Museum, a guide leads a group of the curious through the murderers' row, luridly relating the terrible deeds of each of the figures. Finally, he comes to the row's newest addition, a man who murdered his wife, brother-in-law and employer. It is the figure of Martin Lombard Senescu!

"The new exhibit became very popular at Marchand's, but of all the figures none was ever regarded with more dread than that of Martin Lombard Senescu. It was something about the eyes, people said. It's the look that one often gets after taking a quick walk through the Twilight Zone."

In "The New Exhibit," Martin Balsam does an excellent job playing a quiet little man with a most grisly hobby. As for the wax figures of the murderers, these are played by live actors, shown still-frame in closeups; the waxen makeup and their ability to stand very still creating a convincing illusion that they are actually inanimate wax. Where the story falls down is in its denouement. Although we *see* Jack the Ripper kill Martin's wife, Hicks his brother-in-law and Landru his boss, at the end the murderers reveal that it is Martin who committed the murders. This just does not wash. Had there been a greater subtlety in the murder scenes, merely suggesting that the murders were committed by the figures without actually showing them, this ambiguity might have allowed for such a conclusion. But such is not the case.

Although Charles Beaumont is credited as the sole writer on "The New Exhibit," it was actually ghostwritten, in its entirety, by Jerry Sohl, a man who had been a staff writer on *Alfred Hitchcock Presents* and the author of numerous novels, including *Costigan's Needle* and *Point Ultimate* (later, he would write the novel *The Lemon Eaters* and pen episodes for *The Outer Limits, Star Trek* and *The Invaders*). A year earlier, Beaumont had farmed out the writing of "Dead Man's Shoes" to OCee Ritch because he had been overwhelmed by his numerous writing commitments.

But now, the reason was quite different.

"He was never well," Beaumont's friend William F. Nolan comments. "He was always thin. He almost always had a headache. He used Bromo like somebody would use water. He had his Bromo bottle with him all the time. He'd buy it in those giant sizes, what he called 'window sizes,' and he'd empty one of those a month.

"Everybody kept saying, 'Chuck's working too hard. He's taking on too many jobs. He's stretching himself too thin. He's not sleeping enough.' And the headaches got worse, and we thought, well sure, they'd get worse. If I was doing seventy scripts instead of two, I'd have a headache, too. Sometimes, he'd have as many as ten projects going on at once in '62. He'd have like five different TV scripts, a movie script that he's supposed to be working on—and each one, the producers thought Beaumont was working on exclusively. But meanwhile, he'd have OCee Ritch holed up in one part of the city writing a draft of one, he'd have Jerry Sohl holed up writing a draft of another, John Tomerlin would be writing a draft of a third, I'd be polishing a magazine article for him, he'd be trying to get the movie written, Ray Russell would be working with him on a Roger Corman project, and he'd just be running and running, making different appointments. He'd say, 'I'll be at Dupar's and we'll have a ten-minute conference on the script, but I can't give you more than ten minutes, because I've got to be over at Ray's at four-thirty to meet *him*.' So you'd go, 'Chuck! Chuck!' and you'd try to fit yourself into this wild schedule. And I said to myself, 'Man, he's just going to kill himself doing that!' He was pushing himself *way* too hard. Nobody could survive that kind of pressure."

Soon, the pressure seemed to be taking its toll. "By '63, he was drinking an awful lot, which Chuck never used to do," says Nolan. "Every lunch hour, he had to have two or three martinis, and he would invite you over and it wouldn't be coffee anymore, it would be a martini or brandy or something. And his voice began to get slower, it began to get kind of loggy. We'd be calling up at ten in the morning, and he'd say, '*Yesss,* this is ol' Beaumont!' And I'd say to myself, 'My God, he must have started drinking at ten o'clock today! He just woke up an hour ago; he sounds fogged out already!'"

Yet, for all of this, it turned out that the drinking was merely a reaction to something much, much worse that was happening to Beaumont. Says John Tomerlin, "I was spending a great deal of time with Chuck at that time and was close enough to know that what he was drinking could not possibly account for the odd mental set that he had taken. He had a distorted view of his relationships with people, in business and personally. By distorted, I mean they were kind of just a half-notch off center, they were almost right, but not quite. He became extremely deliberate about his speech, and there would be pauses sometimes between syllables and words, and then at other times he would simply lose the thread of what he was saying and look at you rather bemusedly, as though he was waiting to hear whatever it was *you* were saying. It was kind of a frightening experience, because one realized that there was something wrong and it was impossible at that point to tell what it was."

There were other, extremely mysterious symptoms not attributable to drinking. Says director Douglas Heyes, "I didn't understand what was happening. Each time I'd see him, he'd seem so much older than I knew he was. I'd say, 'God, Chuck has aged a lot!'" It was true. In a photograph published in *Playboy* at the time, Beaumont—then thirty-three—appears at least fifty.

"The last half of '63, he couldn't write," says William F. Nolan. "He was drunk all the time—or so we thought. He would go out unshaven to meetings, and the meetings would be disastrous. He couldn't come up with ideas in front of producers. You've got to have the ability to think on your feet. If they don't like the purple elephant, you'd better think of a red giraffe to throw in there. If you can't think of the red giraffe, the guy says, 'Well, I don't want the purple elephant. What else you got?' Chuck would say, 'I . . . don't . . . have . . . anything . . . else!' And they'd say, 'Well, we're sorry, Mr. Beaumont, but we don't like the script.'"

While all this was going on, Beaumont's wife was desperately trying to understand what was happening and treat it. Beaumont's son Chris explains, "Because he worked very, very hard, we thought maybe it was just overwork, so we sent him to places where he could rest, hoping he would come back the man that we knew. When he didn't, it was very frustrating, because we thought each time we tried out one of these therapies that it would work. It was a great disappointment every time he would come home from whatever it was and he would be not only no better, he would be worse."

Bill Idelson, with whom Beaumont collaborated on "Long Distance Call," takes up the story. "I was in analysis at that time and I sent Beaumont there, because people thought it was an emotional thing. My analyst saw him and he said, 'I can't do anything for this man, because he's too ill—*physically* ill."

Nolan: "Finally, he went to UCLA for a battery of tests in about May of '64." The doctors diagnosed Beaumont as having one of two diseases: Alzheimer's Disease or Pick's Disease. Which one could only be discerned by an autopsy, but both had this much in common: they were degenerative diseases of the brain, popularly known as presenile dementia. The cause was unknown. The symptoms included acceleration of the aging process and a progressive loss of mental functions, including intellect, memory and coordination. Nolan recalls, "They sent him home, saying, 'There's absolutely no treatment for this disease. It's permanent and it's terminal. He'll probably live from six months to three years with it. He'll decline and he'll get where he can't stand up. He won't feel any pain. In fact, he won't even know this is happening.'"

Time had run out for Beaumont, at the age of thirty-five. The drinking had been merely an effort to cloud his mind to a point where he was unaware that his mind was clouded for *other* reasons, as yet unnamed, terrifying in their implication. By the time he was properly diagnosed, he was too far gone to understand the truth. Says John Tomerlin, "I think it just kind of faded out on him."

"The only time that he ever seemed to be aware of something dark and awful really happening to him," says William F. Nolan, "was one night, late in '63, when John Tomerlin and I and Chuck went to Musso and Frank's in Hollywood. We were going to have dinner and go to a movie. And I remember that night, he put his head in his hands and he said, 'I can't go to the movies, guys.' We said, 'What's wrong?' He said, 'I just can't go to any more movies. I can't think about them. I can't follow them. I can't stay there and watch all that. I don't know what's wrong with me.' And he just started to cry, and he said, 'I love you guys, but I just can't go to any more movies with you,' and going to movies was one of the things that we all loved to do.

"That was a very sad night. Driving home, we dropped him off, John and I, and we said, 'Shit, something is horribly wrong with Chuck, and I wish to God we knew what it was.'"

Charles Beaumont died February 22, 1967, at the age of thirty-eight. "When he died," says his son Chris, "he was physically a ninety-five-year-old man and *looked* ninety-five and was, in fact, ninety-five by every calendar except the one on your watch." Writer Brian Aldiss commented that Beaumont died "in the old age of his youth." Says William F. Nolan, "Like his character Walter Jameson, he just dusted away."

In early 1963, all of this was in the future. For now, there were only early, minor symptoms, and Beaumont needed a ghost writer for *Twilight Zone*.

Although it was against Writers Guild rules, Jerry Sohl agreed, splitting the money fifty-fifty with Beaumont. Over the next year or so, he wrote five *Twilight Zone* scripts, three of which were produced, teleplays for *Route 66, Naked City,* and *Alfred Hitchcock Presents,* plus articles for *Playboy*—all under Beaumont's name. "It was ridiculous of me to do this," says Sohl, "because he was just using me and I was not getting any pension money, I was not getting any health money, and it was perfectly dumb. On the other hand, I didn't have to deal with Bert Granet, I didn't have to deal with Rod Serling, I didn't have to do anything but write. What more could you ask? He was the one who went in and fought the battles, you see."

About "The New Exhibit," Sohl says, "One of the men in the script is the man that gave Chuck the idea for the script itself, Albert W. Hicks, the ax murderer. So we got to talking about, 'Well, supposing that someone had an exhibit wherein this murderer was, and he came alive and did all this and then went back to the exhibit after he had committed the murder. The police would never be able to find him.' This is the way that our minds went. Then we decided to change that and make it that they were *all* murderers, this is the murderers' exhibit. In other words, all this evolved."

Sohl's script went before the cameras virtually unchanged, with no rewrites at all. This was the case with most of the scripts he ghosted. "They went right in, and the reason is that Chuck Beaumont scripts were always so great that they didn't have to do anything."

During the shooting of "The New Exhibit," Sohl visited the set. "Here I am standing with Chuck Beaumont," he recalls, "and John Brahm, the director, comes up, puts his arm around him with the script that *I* did and says, 'Chuck, you've done it again!' And here I am, standing right next to Chuck, unable to say a word!"

"ON THURSDAY WE LEAVE FOR HOME" (5/2/63)

James Broderick and James Whitmore

Written by Rod Serling
Producer: Bert Granet
Director: Buzz Kulik
Director of Photography:
George T. Clemens
Music: stock

Cast:
William Benteen: James Whitmore
Col. Sloane: Tim O'Conner
Al: James Broderick
George: Paul Langton
Julie: Jo Helton
Joan: Mercedes Shirley
Jo Jo: Daniel Kulick
Lt. Engle: Lew Gallo
Hank: Russ Bender
Colonist: Madge Kennedy
Colonist: John Ward
Colonist: Shirley O'Hara
Colonist: Anthony Benson

"This is William Benteen, who officiates on a disintegrating outpost in space. The people are a remnant society who left the Earth looking for a Millennium, a place without war, without jeopardy, without fear—and what they found was a lonely, barren place whose only industry was survival. *And this is what they've done for three decades: survive; until the memory of the Earth they came from has become an indistinct and shadowed recollection of another time and another place. One month ago a signal from Earth announced that a ship would be coming to pick them up and take them home. In just a moment we'll hear more of that ship, more of that home, and what it takes out of mind and body to reach it. This is the Twilight Zone."*

The planet is a nightmare place of two suns, unending day and terrible meteor storms. Despair prevails among the 187 survivors of the original colony and suicide is not uncommon. Their thirty-year survival is attributable to one source: the iron leadership of Benteen, their self-appointed Captain. He has maintained order, told them tales of the wonders and beauties of Earth, and convinced them that rescue is imminent. Problems arise, however, when a rescue ship finally *does* arrive; Benteen has become so accustomed to absolute power over "his" people that he cannot relinquish command. When the survivors disobey his orders by pressing the crew of the rescue ship for stories of the Earth and then playing a baseball game with them, he begins to feel his power slipping.

He is determined that they all stay together on Earth, with him as their leader, but when he tells them of this they rebel. He becomes desperate; he tells them that Earth is *not* the paradise he'd told of—it is a *hell*—and they will all die if they go there. They *must* stay here on the planet with him. Colonel Sloane, commander of the rescue ship, tells Benteen to let his people put it to a vote. Unanimously, they vote against Benteen. Raging, Benteen attacks the ship with a length of pipe. When he is pulled away, he angrily states that *he* intends to remain—the rest of them can go or stay. As the ship prepares to depart, the crewmen search for Benteen but he hides from them, ignoring them when they say that if he doesn't leave *now* he will be stranded permanently. Deep in a cave, Benteen pretends that he is still surrounded by his people and recites again the litany of the glories of Earth. Suddenly, the *meaning* comes clear to him; for the first time, he actually remembers his home world. Frantically, he rushes outside, pleading not to be left behind. But it is too late: the ship is gone. Condemned by his own rigidity, Benteen is alone.

"William Benteen, who had prerogatives: he could lead, he could direct, dictate, judge, legislate. It became a habit, then a pattern and finally a necessity. William Benteen, once a god—now a population of one."

Serling's best effort on the hour-long shows came with "On Thursday We Leave for Home," a science-fictional examination of the positive and negative uses of power.

Directed by Buzz Kulik, "On Thursday We Leave for Home" is a marvelous, engrossing story. As Benteen, James Whitmore is intelligent, gentle, commanding, and—ultimately—thoroughly blind and self-centered. His is an intense, riveting performance. In the beginning, before the arrival of the rescue ship, we see that Benteen actually *is* responsible for keeping the others alive, that were it not for him they would have given up long ago. Serling's writing is elegant and precise, and it is clear that he knows his character very well.

A marvelous example of Serling's writing comes following a meteor storm, as the colonists huddle in an enormous cavern. They are a wretched lot, hopeless and despairing. Then, gently, quietly, Benteen begins to tell them of the Earth, something he has done many, many times before. The one he is supposedly telling the story to is a little boy named Jo Jo (Daniel Kulick), but in reality he's speaking to them all:

BENTEEN: . . . I was just a boy when we arrived here, I was fifteen years old, but I remember the Earth. I remember it as . . . a place of color. I remember, Jo Jo, that in the autumn . . . the leaves changed, turned different colors—red, orange, gold. I remember streams of water that flowed down hillsides, and the water was sparkling and clear. I remember clouds in the sky, white, billowy things, floated like ships, like sails . . . And I remember night skies. Night skies. Like endless black velvet, with stars, sometimes a moon—hung as if suspended by wires, lit from inside.

JO JO: What's night, Captain?

BENTEEN: Night. Night is a quiet time, Jo Jo, when the Earth went to sleep. Kind of like a cover that it pulled over itself. Not like here, where we have the two suns always shining, always burning. It was darkness, Jo Jo, darkness that felt like a cool hand just brushed past tired eyes. And there was snow on winter nights. Gossamer stuff. It floated down and covered the Earth, made it all white, cool. And in the mornings we could go out and build a snowman, see our breath in the air, and it was good then, it was *right*.

JO JO: Captain, why did you leave there?

BENTEEN: Well, we thought we could find another place like Earth, but with different beauties, Jo Jo, and we found this place. We thought we could escape war, we thought we could—well, we thought that we could build an even better place. And it took us thirty years to find out that we left our home a billion miles away to be only visitors here, transients, 'cause you can't put down roots in this ground.

The most poignant moments in the episode comes at the end. As the rescue ship is taking off, Benteen is alone in the cavern. He pretends to be speaking to the colonists one by one, reciting again the old litany, assuming the roles of leader, guide, father confessor. As he reaches Jo Jo (pretends to reach Jo Jo, that is) he begins to rhapsodize about the Earth. At first, it is like before. Benteen has been so busy telling fairy stories and (when he didn't want them to leave) horror stories about the Earth, that he hadn't bothered to listen, hadn't *really* remembered. But suddenly, the reality of Earth, its beauty, its variety, hits home, and Benteen realizes the awful consequences of his decision to remain. Too late, he rushes out of the cave. "Don't leave me here!" he shouts. "Don't leave me *here*!" Suddenly, all the fury leaves him. All along, Benteen has been a man powered by rage; rage against the terrain and, when they turned against him, rage against the colonists. But now, his anger has run out. With a crushing softness, Benteen pleads, "Please . . . I want to go home." The camera pulls up and back, revealing Benteen for what he is: a tiny and solitary figure in an uncaring landscape.

It was a shot that almost didn't come off. The set consisted of planetary terrain and a number of metal shacks in which the colonists live. Director of photography George T. Clemens recalls, "Buzz said, 'Tomorrow we'll start with a really high camera.' I said, 'Wait a minute. Let's get a ladder in here and see how this looks.'" When they did, they got a shock—none of the shacks had roofs! "Sets normally don't have roofs," explains Clemens, "because you have to put lights in there. So there was a hurry-up job at night to put tack and canvas over the tops of these shacks. We really had to do this overnight."

SEASON'S END

In the spring of 1963, CBS renewed *Twilight Zone* for a fifth season, shortening it back to a half hour. The network's experiment had failed: *Twilight Zone*'s expanded size had not made for an expanded audience.

"Our shows this season were too padded," Serling concluded at the end of the run. "The bulk of our stories lacked the excitement and punch of the shorter dramas we intended when we started five years ago and kept to for a while. If you ask me, I think we had only one really effective show this season, 'On Thursday We Leave for Home.' . . . Yes, I wrote it myself, but I overwrote it. I think the story was good despite what I did to it."

Objectively, Serling's assessment was *too* hard. There had been a number of fine hour-long episodes, among them "On Thursday We Leave for Home," "The Bard," "Death Ship," "In His Image," "Jess-Belle," "Miniature" and "The Incredible World of Horace Ford." The series had not disgraced itself.

But, clearly, by the end of the fourth season, the show was winding down. Increasingly over the next season, it would find itself trapped within its own clichés. After four years and 120 episodes, *Twilight Zone* was showing its age.

THE FIFTH SEASON: 1963–1964

Producers: Bert Granet and William Froug
Production Manager: Ralph W. Nelson
Directors of Photography: George T. Clemens and Robert W. Pittack
Assistant Directors: Marty Moss and Charles Bonniwell, Jr.
Casting: Patricia Rose and Larry Stewart
Art Directors: George W. Davis, Malcolm Brown, Walter Holscher and Eddie Imazu
Editors: Richard Heermance, Thomas W. Scott and Richard W. Farrell
Makeup: Bob Keats
Special Effects: Virgil Beck
Sound: Franklin Milton, Joe Edmondson and Phillip N. Mitchell
Theme Music: Marius Constant
Set Direction: Henry Grace, Robert R. Benton, Frank R. McElvy and Jerry Wunderlich
Titles and Opticals: Pacific Title
Mr. Serling's Wardrobe: Eagle Clothes
Filmed at Metro–Goldwyn–Mayer

VII / THE FIFTH SEASON

"There was this knock on the door of my office—I had this huge office—and Rod came in on his knees, he walked in on his knees like Toulouse-Lautrec, see. . . . And I said, 'What have you done now?' He says, 'Well, I've just blown *Twilight Zone*, that's what I've done!'"

—WILLIAM FROUG

In its transformation from half hour to hour to half hour again, *Twilight Zone* had lost a great deal of its vitality. Several fine episodes still lay ahead, but the thoughtfulness and innovation of the first three seasons was, for the most part, sadly lacking. Gone too were some of the show's best directors: Douglas Heyes, Buzz Kulik, Montgomery Pittman, Lamont Johnson and Don Medford. Worst of all, the quality of writing—always the show's strongest asset—slipped badly. As Serling himself said, "Toward the end I was writing so much that I felt I had begun to lose my perspective on what was good or bad."

Nevertheless, Bert Granet still had a show to get out. "You're at the mercy of the fates, of what is available to you," he notes. "You're always looking for something better than what is waiting on your desk, but frequently the source is not there. It might be someplace in the world, but you're not fortunate enough to get your hands on it at that moment when you need it." For all its faults, however, *Twilight Zone* was *still* vastly more interesting and entertaining than the majority of television programs. If it had faded, it had faded only in comparison with itself.

"IN PRAISE OF PIP" (9/27/63)

Jack Klugman and Billy Mumy

Written by Rod Serling
Producer: Bert Granet
Director:
Joseph M. Newman
Director of Photography:
George T. Clemens
Music: composed by
Rene Garriguenc; conducted by Lud Gluskin

Cast:
Max Phillips: Jack Klugman
Pip: Billy Mumy
Pvt. Pip: Bob Diamond
Mrs. Feeny:
Connie Gilchrist
Moran: John Launer
Doctor: Ross Elliott
Surgeon: Stuart Nisbet
George Reynold: Russell Horton
Lieutenant: Gerald Gordon
Gunman: Kreg Martin

"Submitted for your approval, one Max Phillips, a slightly-the-worse-for-wear maker of book, whose life has been as drab and undistinguished as a bundle of dirty clothes. And, though it's very late in his day, he has an errant wish that the rest of his life might be sent out to a laundry to come back shiny and clean, this to be a gift of love to a son named Pip. Mr. Max Phillips, Homo sapiens, *who is soon to discover that man is not as wise as he thinks—said lesson to be learned in the Twilight Zone."*

After learning that his beloved son Pip, now a soldier, has been critically wounded in South Vietnam, alcoholic bookie Max Phillips feels a tremendous remorse for not having been a better father. Out of kindness, he returns three hundred dollars to a luckless bettor—an action that earns him a bullet from one of his boss's gunmen. Stumbling to an amusement park he used to visit with his son—now closed for the night—Max is amazed to see Pip appear before him, magically transformed into a boy again. The park comes alive and the two relive past pleasures. Suddenly, Pip grows solemn and runs away. When Max catches him, Pip explains he's dying and disappears. Sobbing, Max offers God a trade: himself for the boy. He dies. But his sacrifice is not in vain—Pip survives.

"Very little comment here, save for this small aside: that the ties of flesh are deep and strong, that the capacity to love is a vital, rich and all-consuming function

of the human animal, and that you can find nobility and sacrifice and love wherever you may seek it out; down the block, in the heart, or in the Twilight Zone."

"Pip is dying. My kid is dying. In a place called South Vietnam. There isn't even supposed to be a war going on there, but my son is dying. It's to laugh. I swear it's to laugh."

So says Max Phillips in Serling's sentimental and gripping "In Praise of Pip," the premiere show of the fifth season. Very possibly, this marks the first mention of an American casualty in Vietnam in any dramatic TV show, and it seems remarkable for its perceptiveness. But curiously, Serling originally placed the action in Laos. This was changed when de Forrest Research went over the script for inaccuracies and reported:

> The Geneva Treaty on the neutrality of Laos stipulated that all foreign troops be removed. At present the only U.S. military in Laos is a small mission with the Embassy. There are officially no combat or special forces in Laos. The implication that the U.S. has troops fighting in Laos (even in The Twilight Zone) could be an embarrassment and might cause repercussions. U.S. Special Forces are fighting ("in an advisory capacity") in South Vietnam. Suggest South Vietnam.

Also, Serling originally had Phillips say "There isn't even a war there." De Forrest Research:

> In South Vietnam it is common knowledge that there is a Civil War, but U.S. troops are not supposed to be fighting there. Suggest "There isn't even supposed to be a war there."

"In Praise of Pip" doesn't have much to do with politics, though; in reality, it's simply a touching drama about a man's love for his son. Jack Klugman's absolutely dead-on portrayal of Phillips keeps the episode from sinking into bathos. Particularly moving is his death scene, in which he offers to make a trade with God: his life for his son's. Sobbing, he falls to the ground and dies. The amusement park is empty and dark. A wind comes up, scattering papers over the body. It is a moment of eerie beauty, solemn and sad.

Skillfully directed by Joseph M. Newman (whose movie credits include *This Island Earth*), "In Praise of Pip" was filmed at Pacific Ocean Park during two consecutive nights when the park was vacant. "It was real spooky," says Billy Mumy. Particularly disconcerting to him was a scene in which he had to run through a house of mirrors while being chased by Klugman. Although some of the closeups were shot in-studio, most was done in the amusement park's actual house of mirrors. "They had the floor taped with markers that would lead you to the right turns," Mumy recalls, "but they had to get it the way they wanted to get it, in the sense that I had to run through the house of mirrors, and I remember that was pretty scary."

"UNCLE SIMON" (11/15/63)

Constance Ford and Cedric Hardwicke

Written by Rod Serling
Producer: Bert Granet
Director: Don Siegel
Director of Photography: Robert W. Pittack
Music: stock

Cast:
Uncle Simon Polk: Cedric Hardwicke
Barbara Polk: Constance Ford
Schwimmer: Ian Wolfe
Police Officer: John McLiam
Robot: Dion Hansen

"Dramatis personae: *Mr. Simon Polk, a gentleman who has lived out his life in a gleeful rage; and the young lady who's just beat the hasty retreat is Mr. Polk's niece, Barbara. She's lived* her *life as if during each ensuing hour she had a dentist appointment. There's yet a third member of the company soon to be seen. He now resides in the laboratory and* he *is the kind of character to be found only in the Twilight Zone.*"

Barbara and her Uncle Simon, an inventor, thoroughly detest each other, but she has cared for him for twenty-five years because he is rich and *she* is the only heir. When he tries to strike her with his cane, she grabs it from him and he falls down the basement stairs to his death. Barbara thinks she is free of her uncle at last, but she is mistaken. His will provides that she will inherit his estate only if she agrees to look after his latest invention: a robot. As the days go by, the robot takes on the mannerisms of Uncle Simon, including a desire for closed drapes and a craving for hot chocolate. When the robot assumes Uncle Simon's *voice,* Barbara pushes it down the basement stairs—which only succeeds in giving it a limp identical with

Rod Serling and Robby the Robot

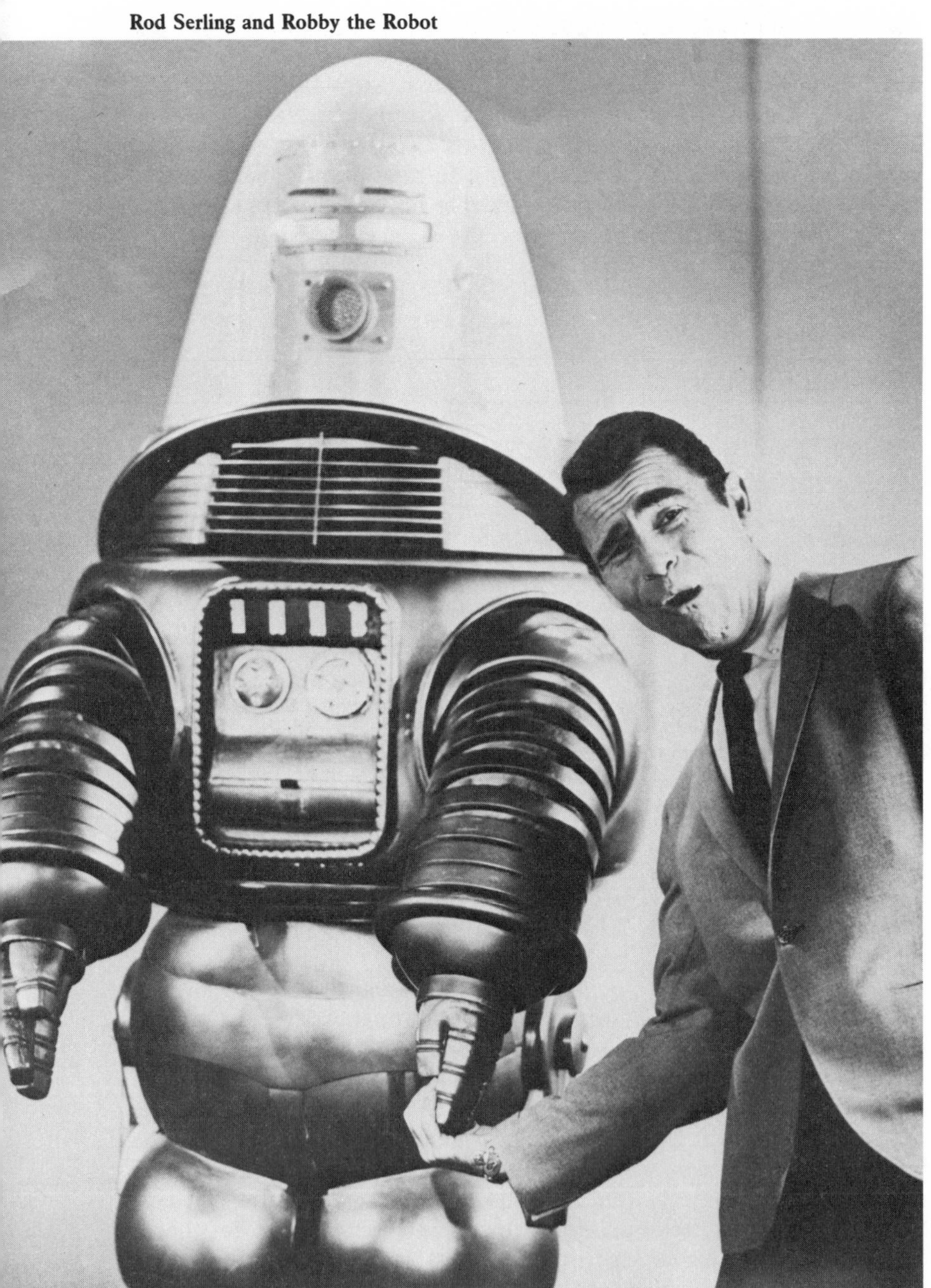

that of her late uncle. It is crushingly clear to Barbara now that she will *never* escape Uncle Simon.

"Dramatis personae: *a metal man, who will go by the name of Simon, whose life as well as his body has been stamped out for him; and the woman who tends to him, the lady Barbara, who's discovered belatedly that all* bad *things don't come to an end, and that once a bed is made it's quite necessary that you sleep in it. Tonight's uncomfortable little exercise in avarice and automatons—from the Twilight Zone.*"

Although directed by Don Siegel (whose movies include the original *Invasion of the Body Snatchers, Dirty Harry* and *Escape From Alcatraz*), "Uncle Simon" remains talky, badly acted, and badly staged. It's a sordid story about two sordid people, both of whom make it a point to say *everything* that's on their minds, to the point of simple-minded absurdity. Neither character is terribly likeable; consequently, the fact that Barbara never escapes the clutches of her uncle doesn't seem very important.

"A KIND OF A STOPWATCH" (10/18/63)

Richard Erdman

Written by Rod Serling
Based on an unpublished story by Michael D. Rosenthal
Producer: Bert Granet
Director: John Rich
Director of Photography: Robert W. Pittack
Music: Van Cleave

Cast:
McNulty: Richard Erdman
Potts: Leon Belasco
Mr. Cooper: Roy Roberts
Joe the Bartender: Herbie Faye
Secretary: Doris Singleton
Attendant: Ray Kellogg
TV Announcer: Sam Balter
Charlie: Richard Wessel
Man: Ken Drake

"Submitted for your approval or at least your analysis: one Patrick Thomas McNulty, who at age forty-one is the biggest bore on Earth. He holds a ten-year record for the most meaningless words spewed out during a coffee break. And it's very likely that, as of this moment, he would have gone through life in precisely this manner, a dull, argumentative bigmouth who sets back the art of conversa-

tion a thousand years. I say he very likely would *have, except for something that will soon happen to him, something that will considerably alter his existence—and ours. Now you think about that now, because this is the Twilight Zone."*

After being fired from his job, McNulty goes to a bar where he makes the acquaintance of a slightly potted foreigner named Potts, whom he treats to a beer. In gratitude, Potts gives McNulty a most extraordinary stopwatch: when its button is pressed, the watch stops everything in the world except McNulty! Eager to show off his new acquisition, McNulty tries to demonstrate it to his ex-boss and to the people in the bar. Unfortunately, when he uses it the people are *also* frozen, and thus are unaware of anything having occurred. McNulty is stymied only briefly, and then gets a brainstorm; he stops time and strolls into a bank vault, intending to make a sizeable withdrawal. But when he wheels a cart filled with cash outside, he drops the stopwatch and it breaks. McNulty is trapped permanently in a timeless world—with *no one* to talk to.

"Mr. Patrick Thomas McNulty, who had a gift of time. He used it and he mis*used it, now he's just been handed the bill. Tonight's tale of motion and McNulty—in the Twilight Zone."*

As with "Uncle Simon," a feeling of watching uninteresting characters go through the motions predominates in "A Kind of a Stopwatch." The writing here is slapdash, uncaring. Who, for instance, is Potts, and why does he give McNulty the incredible stopwatch? The dialogue doesn't give us many clues; it's supposed to make Potts seem the kind of eccentric character who *might* give a total stranger a mysterious and magical device, but it plays very flat. Potts is no more than a plot device, the intention being to get the watch into McNulty's hands as quickly as possible.

The one bright spot in "A Kind of Stopwatch" comes when McNulty, a man who *loves* to talk, realizes the one major drawback in a watch that freezes people dead in their tracks. "How about that?" he says (to himself). "The greatest conversation piece in the world . . . and what does it do? It stops conversation!"

"THE 7th IS MADE UP OF PHANTOMS" (12/6/63)

Ron Foster

Written by Rod Serling
Producer: Bert Granet
Director: Alan Crosland, Jr.
Director of Photography: George T. Clemens
Music: stock

Cast:
Sgt. Conners: Ron Foster
Pfc. McCluskey: Randy Boone
Cpl. Langsford: Warren Oates
Captain: Robert Bray
Lieutenant: Greg Morris
Scout: Wayne Mallory
Sergeant: Lew Brown
Corporal: Jacque Shelton
Radio Operator: Jeffrey Morris

"June twenty-fifth, 1964—or, if you prefer, June twenty-fifth, 1876. The cast of characters in order of their appearance: a patrol of General Custer's cavalry and *a patrol of National Guardsmen on a maneuver. Past and present are about to collide head-on, as they are wont to do in a very special bivouac area known as . . . the Twilight Zone."*

During National Guard wargames near the Little Big Horn, a three-man tank crew hears gunfire, then discovers a teepee and a canteen marked "7th Cavalry"—the outfit led to their deaths by General Custer in 1876. Next morning, driving along Rosebud Creek, the men see smoke signals and hear Indian war cries. Private McCluskey fires blind into a dust cloud—and a riderless Indian pony runs by. Both McCluskey and Sergeant Conners believe they somehow are pursuing the past and that soon they will find themselves in the middle of a massacre. Corporal Langsford thinks they are crazy, but then he stumbles upon a deserted Indian village—and McCluskey gets an arrow in the back! Discarding their tank, the three struggle across Rosebud Creek to the scene of the battle and charge into the fray. Later, their superiors find the tank but no sign of the men . . . until they check the names of the dead listed at the Custer Battlefield National Memorial.

"Sergeant William Conners, Trooper Michael McCluskey and Trooper Richard Langsford, who on a hot afternoon in June made a charge over a hill—and never returned. Look for this one under 'P' for phantom, in a historical ledger located in a reading room known as the Twilight Zone."

The premise of "The 7th Is Made Up of Phantoms" is an intriguing one, as the three-man tank crew encounter physical evidence that they are in the past (empty wigwams, a riderless horse, and so on) but see no human beings until the very end. There is the feeling that they are pursuing an elusive historical event—one they eventually catch up with.

Some things in the episode aren't so easy to swallow, though, such as the fact that two of the three men are conversant in the most minute details leading up to the battle. "McCluskey," the sergeant asks, "do you remember what it was that Reno found before the battle?" "Sure," the other answers, as though it were the most obvious thing on earth, "the village."

More disturbing is the fact that the episode takes it for granted that Custer's men are on the side of Good, and that giving them a modern tank to even up the odds would be a swell idea. It is a cavalry versus "Injuns" mentality, and it seriously damages an interesting idea.

"THE OLD MAN IN THE CAVE" (11/8/63)

James Coburn

Written by Rod Serling
Based on the short story "The Old Man" by Henry Slesar
Producer: Bert Granet
Director: Alan Crosland, Jr.
Director of Photography: Robert W. Pittack
Music: stock

Cast:
Mr. Goldsmith: John Anderson
Major French: James Coburn
Jason: John Marley
Evelyn: Josie Lloyd
Harber: Frank Watkins
Douglas: Lenny Geer
Man: John Craven
Woman: Natalie Masters
Furman: Don Wilbanks

"What you're looking at is a legacy that man left to himself. A decade previous he pushed his buttons and, a nightmarish moment later, woke up to find that he had set the clock back a thousand years. His engines, his medicines, his science were buried in a mass tomb, covered over by the biggest gravedigger of them all: a Bomb. And this is the Earth ten years later, a fragment of what was once a whole, a remnant of what was once a race. The year is 1974, and this is the Twilight Zone."

A tiny community has survived for ten years by following the instructions of the mysterious "Old Man in the Cave," as relayed to them by Mr. Goldsmith, their leader. But then a small band of armed soldiers commanded by the violent Major French drives into town and takes over. Against Goldsmith's vehement objections, they distribute food and liquor branded contaminated by "the Old Man." Resentful over their past privations, the townspeople force Goldsmith to open the cave. "The Old Man" stands revealed—as a computer! Enraged, the townsfolk destroy the machine. Later, though, they pay the price for their faithlessness: the food *was* contaminated, and all but Goldsmith die.

"Mr. Goldsmith, survivor, an eye witness to man's imperfection, an observer of the very human trait of greed and a chronicler of the last chapter—the one reading 'suicide.' Not a prediction of what is to be, just a projection of what could *be. This has been the Twilight Zone."*

Two episodes in the fifth season were based on short stories by Henry Slesar, a leading mystery writer and for many years a staff writer on *The Edge of Night*.

Based on Slesar's "The Old Man" and scripted by Serling, "The Old Man in the Cave" dwells on a small group of Atomic Holocaust survivors whose status quo is maintained by an unseen computer. James Coburn, John Anderson and John Marley all perform their roles well, but there are several issues raised by the episode that are hard to ignore. For instance, Goldsmith views the computer as a deity-like authority, and when the people demand to know the identity of "the Old Man" and disregard his instructions, this is considered the ultimate act of faithlessness—the punishment being death. But, in actuality, a computer is *not* a god, it is a man-made tool, and the townsfolk's insistence to know the true nature of their leader seems less an act of faithlessness than a natural human curiosity for vital information, a desire for democracy, for self-determination.

On a more prosaic level, there is yet another question: what has been powering the computer during the ten years since all-out nuclear war—and *how* did it get in that cave in the first place?

"THE SELF-IMPROVEMENT OF SALVADORE ROSS" (1/17/64)

Gail Kobe and Don Gordon

Written by Jerry McNeely
Based on the short story "The Self-Improvement of Salvadore Ross" by Henry Slesar
Producer: Bert Granet
Director: Don Siegel
Director of Photography: George T. Clemens
Music: stock

Cast:
Salvadore Ross: Don Gordon
Leah Maitland: Gail Kobe
Mr. Maitland: Vaughn Taylor
Old Man: J. Pat O'Malley
Albert: Doug Lambert
Mr. Halpert: Douglass Dumbrille
Jerry: Seymour Cassel
Bartender: Ted Jacques
Nurse: Kathleen O'Malley

"Confidential personnel file on Salvadore Ross. Personality: a volatile mixture of fury and frustration. Distinguishing physical characteristic: a badly-broken hand which will require emergency treatment at the nearest hospital. Ambition: shows great determination toward self-improvement. Estimate of potential success: a sure bet for a listing in Who's Who*—in the Twilight Zone."*

When Leah Maitland, his former social worker, rejects his romantic overtures, Ross angrily punches a door and breaks his hand. Admitted to a hospital, he makes the acquaintance of an elderly patient suffering from severe bronchial congestion. Facetiously, Ross suggests they trade ailments; the old man agrees. Later that night, Ross finds to his amazement that it has worked—he now has a cold but *no* broken arm! Utilizing his bizarre talent, Ross trades forty-six years of his life to an aged millionaire in exchange for a million dollars and a posh apartment. He then buys back his youth from a variety of young men, a few years at a time. His vitality restored, he sets about courting Leah in style. But it's no use; Leah wants a man with *compassion,* a trait her crippled father has in abundance. Although Mr. Maitland objects strongly to him, Ross convinces him to sell him his compassion for $100,000. The next day, Ross—now filled with compassion—easily wins Leah's love. But when he tells her father of his plans to marry her and asks his blessing, the compassionless Mr. Maitland pulls a gun and kills him.

"The Salvadore Ross program for self-improvement. The all-in-one, sure-fire success course that lets you lick the bully, learn the language, dance the tango and anything else you want to do—or think *you want to do. Money-back guarantee. Offer limited to . . . the Twilight Zone."*

Scripted by Jerry McNeeley (*Something for Joey, Streets of San Francisco, Marcus Welby, McMillan and Wife,* and others) from "The Self-improvement of Salvadore Ross" (appearing in the May, 1961, issue of *The Magazine of Fantasy and Science Fiction,*) the episode bears both the same title and plotline.

In the lead is Don Gordon, in his first *Twilight Zone* appearance since "The Four of Us Are Dying." The character here is similar—cocky, slightly cruel, short-tempered—and, for the most part, Gordon does a good, credible job of it. Fine too is Gail Kobe as Leah Maitland, the gentle social worker who won't give Salvadore Ross a tumble—until he mysteriously acquires a kindly disposition.

Although competently directed by Don Siegel, the episode suffers from a sloppiness of production, a lack of attention to detail.

One problem is the improbability of the idea that Leah could go from a rigid conviction not to have anything more to do with Sal to a state of complete infatuation in a single day. No matter how overwhelming his change in personality, this just isn't plausible. It would take time for him to convince her of his sincerity and to heal the wounds caused by his previous behavior.

Worst of all is the scene in which Sal, having traded his youth for a million dollars and an elegant bachelor pad, is supposed to look and act like a man of seventy-two. The age makeup on Gordon looks like something out of a high-school play.

"STOPOVER IN A QUIET TOWN" (4/24/64)

Barry Nelson

Written by Earl Hamner, Jr.
Producer: Bert Granet
Director: Ron Winston
Director of Photography: Robert W. Pittack
Music: stock

Cast:
Bob Frazier: Barry Nelson
Millie Frazier: Nancy Malone
Mother: Karen Norris
Little Girl: Denise Lynn

"Bob and Millie Frazier, average young New Yorkers who attended a party in the country last night and on the way home took a detour. Most of us on waking in the morning know exactly where we are; the rooster or the alarm clock brings up out of sleep into the familiar sights, sounds, aromas of home and the comfort of a routine day ahead. Not so with our young friends. This will be a day like none they've ever spent—and they'll spend it in the Twilight Zone."

After getting drunk at the party, Bob and Millie wake up the next morning, fully dressed, in bed in a strange house, with no idea where they are nor memory of how they got there. Finding themselves alone, Bob tries to use the kitchen phone—it comes off the wall in his hand. Odder still, the foods in the refrigerator are inedible props; the drawers nailed-down facades. Suddenly, they hear the giggling of an unseen little girl. Investigating outside, they find a town completely devoid of people. The mystery grows: a squirrel on a branch is stuffed; a tree falls over when leaned on; grass is made of papier-mâché; a car has a dummy at the wheel and no engine. Hearing a train whistle, Bob and Millie hurriedly board a train, which chugs out of town, makes a big circle, and returns them to the same station! Suddenly, a huge hand reaches down and grabs them. The town is merely a toy. Bob and Millie have been abducted by a giant alien and taken to its home world—where they are now the playthings of its daughter.

"The moral of what you've just seen is clear. If you drink, don't drive. And if your wife has had a couple, she shouldn't drive either. You might both just wake up with a whale of a headache in a deserted village in the Twilight Zone."

Earl Hamner, Jr.'s, "Stopover in a Quiet Town" bears a number of similarities to Serling's "Where Is Everybody?" The genesis of the story was similar, too. "I got that idea walking around the backlot at MGM once," Hamner recalls. "Everything was made of papier-mâché and was a false front. It suddenly came to me, what if someone woke in this surrounding and there was nothing but false labels on everything, and if you dropped a lighted match on the grass it would catch fire, and if you got on a train it would come all the way around to where you started from?"

The greatest weakness in "Stopover in a Quiet Town," beside the fact that it's fairly predictable, lies in its two main characters. The lead in "Where Is Everybody?" although seemingly none too bright, is at least likeable. But Bob and Millie Frazier have almost no redeeming qualities. They're short-tempered, quarrelsome, and blame each other for their predicament. The wife tends toward hysteria and the man is brutishly insensitive. Clearly, neither has much regard for the other. A marvelous exchange occurs when Bob sarcastically remarks, "You're the one who drove us into this nuthouse in the first place!" When Millie takes exception to this, Bob replies, "I'm sorry I said that. It's all my fault for being too tight to drive." Some apology; the implication is clear: had *he* been driving, they wouldn't be in this mess.

"A SHORT DRINK FROM A CERTAIN FOUNTAIN" (12/13/63)

Ruta Lee and Patrick O'Neal

Written by Rod Serling
Based on an idea by Lou Holtz
Producer: Bert Granet
Director: Bernard Girard
Director of Photography: George T. Clemens
Music: stock

Cast:
Harmon Gordon: Patrick O'Neal
Flora Gordon: Ruta Lee
Dr. Raymond Gordon: Walter Brooke

"Picture of an aging man who leads his life, as Thoreau said, 'in quiet desperation.' Because Harmon Gordon is enslaved by a love affair with a wife forty years his junior. Because of this, he runs when he should walk. He surrenders when simple pride dictates a stand. He pines away for the lost morning of his life when he should be enjoying the evening. In short, Mr. Harmon Gordon seeks a fountain of youth, and who's to say he won't find it? This happens to be the Twilight Zone."

Desperate to keep up with his gold-digger wife, wealthy Harmon Gordon begs his doctor-brother to inject him with a highly experimental youth serum. Initially, the doctor refuses, but when Harmon threatens suicide he reluctantly agrees. At first, the serum's effects seem miraculous; Harmon is restored to vigorous young manhood. But the formula continues to work—and Harmon regresses into an infant. As his wife starts to walk out, Harmon's brother makes a threat that compels her to stay: raise Harmon to adulthood, staying with him every minute—or be cut off without a penny.

"It happens to be a fact: as one gets older, one does *get wiser. If you don't believe it, ask Flora. Ask her any day of the ensuing weeks of her life, as she takes note during the coming years and realizes that the worm has turned—youth* has *taken over. It's simply the way the calendar crumbles . . . in the Twilight Zone."*

Poetic justice of a sort is served at the end of "A Short Drink From a Certain Fountain" but it would be more satisfying were it not for the uncomfortable realization that a helpless child is being left entirely at the mercy of someone who was an unfit wife and will almost certainly be an unfit mother. For reasons which are cloudy at this late date, this is one of four half-hour episodes which are not in syndication. Considering its wordiness and predictability, however, this is no great loss.

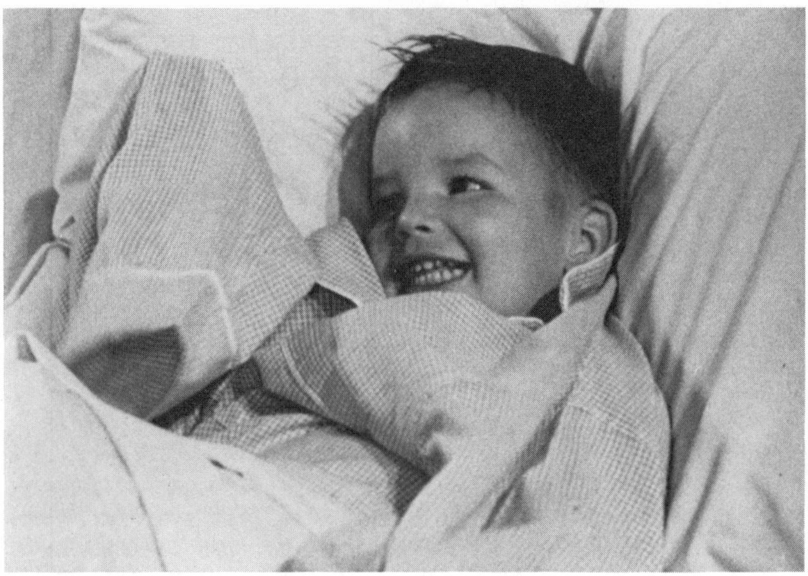

"The way the calendar crumbles . . . in the Twilight Zone"

"THE MASKS" (3/20/64)

Virginia Gregg, Milton Selzer, Alan Sues and Brooke Hayward

Written by Rod Serling
Producer: Bert Granet
Director: Ida Lupino
Director of Photography: George T. Clemens
Music: stock

Cast:
Jason Foster: Robert Keith
Emily Harper: Virginia Gregg
Wilfred Harper: Milton Selzer
Wilfred, Jr.: Alan Sues
Paula Harper: Brooke Hayward
Doctor: Willis Bouchey
Butler: Bill Walker

"Mr. Jason Foster, a tired ancient who on this particular Mardi Gras evening will leave the earth. But before departing he has some things to do, some services to perform, some debts to pay—and some justice to mete out. This is New Orleans, Mardi Gras time. It is also the Twilight Zone."

Knowing he is about to die, Foster summons his heirs—with whom he shares no affection—to his mansion for a bizarre Mardi Gras ritual. A Cajun has fashioned grotesque masks for him that reflect the true inner natures of his family: the whining self-pity of his daughter Emily; the avariciousness of his son-in-law Wilfred; the vanity of his granddaughter Emily; and the dull cruelty of his grandson Wilfred, Jr. Foster demands that they wear the masks until midnight; as for him, *he* will wear a death's-head. They refuse—until he informs them that they'll be disinherited unless they comply. Their greed overcomes their disgust; they all don the masks. As the hours slowly tick by, Foster's kin beg to be allowed to discard the masks, but Foster is steadfast in his determination. As midnight tolls, Foster dies. Overjoyed to be rid of him and to have gained his wealth, his family throw off their disguises—and are horrified to see that their faces have taken on the hideous physical characteristics of the masks.

"Mardi Gras incident, the dramatis personae *being four people who came to celebrate and in a sense let themselves go. This they did with a vengeance. They now wear the faces of all that was inside them—and they'll wear them for the rest of their lives, said lives now to be spent in shadow. Tonight's tale of men, the macabre and masks—on the Twilight Zone."*

"The Masks" is both well written and well directed (by Ida Lupino, making her the only woman to direct a *Twilight Zone* episode *and* the only person to both star in an episode—"The Sixteen-Millimeter Shrine"—and direct one). But much of its success must be credited to the masks themselves, and to the artistry in the heavy makeup applied to the faces beneath. As in "The Eye of the Beholder," there is a compelling beauty in the ugliness, an alluring repulsiveness. Designed by William Tuttle and crafted by Tuttle, Charles Schram and others, they are works of art, grotesqueries which reflect all the cruelty, ignorance, vanity and avariciousness described in the characters. And best of all, they bear enough resemblance to the actors' faces to seem like hideous, degenerate alter selves.

"SPUR OF THE MOMENT" (2/21/64)

Diana Hyland

Written by Richard Matheson
Producer: Bert Granet
Director: Elliot Silverstein
Director of Photography: Robert W. Pittack
Music: composed by Rene Garriguenc; conducted by Lud Gluskin

Cast:
Anne Henderson: Diana Hyland
Robert Blake: Robert Hogan
David Mitchell: Roger Davis
Mr. Henderson: Philip Ober
Mrs. Henderson: Marsha Hunt
Reynolds: Jack Raine

"This is the face of terror: Anne Marie Henderson, eighteen years of age, her young existence suddenly marred by a savage and wholly unanticipated pursuit by a strange, nightmarish figure of a woman in black, who has appeared as if from nowhere and now at driving gallop chases the terrified girl across the countryside, as if she means to ride her down and kill her—and then suddenly and inexplicably stops, *to watch in malignant silence as her prey takes flight. Miss Henderson has no idea whatever as to the motive for this pursuit; worse, not the vaguest notion regarding the identity of her pursuer. Soon enough, she will be given the solution to this twofold mystery,* but *in a manner far beyond her present capacity to understand, a manner enigmatically bizarre in terms of time and space—which is to say, an answer from the Twilight Zone."*

After being chased by the black-clad figure on horseback, Anne rushes home to where her parents are waiting with her fiancée Robert, a young stockbroker. Suddenly, in bursts David, to whom Anne was once engaged, but of whom Anne's parents disapprove. He begs Anne to marry *him,* whom she loves, and not be forced by her father into a marriage with Robert. Anne's father won't hear of this; he forces David to leave at gunpoint. Twenty-five years pass. Anne is now a bitter alcoholic of forty-three; her drunken bum of a husband has gone through her family's entire fortune. It is *she* who, dressed in black, chases her younger self, trying in vain to warn her not to marry the wrong man. But the wrong man was *not* Robert—it was David!

"This is the face of terror: Anne Marie Mitchell, forty-three years of age, her desolate existence once more afflicted by the hope of altering her past mistake—a hope which is, unfortunately, doomed to disappointment. For warnings from the future to the past must be taken *in the past; today may change tomorrow, but once today is gone tomorrow can only look back in sorrow that the warning was ignored. Said warning as of now stamped 'not accepted' and stored away in the dead file in the recording office of the Twilight Zone."*

Richard Matheson's final four *Twilight Zone* scripts run the gamut from mildly disturbing to outright horrific. In "Spur of the Moment," the romantic situation is a familiar one: Anne's family wants her to marry the proper-but-dull stockbroker, but she is in love with the romantic, headstrong young fellow of whom they disapprove. We all make the assumption that the older woman is warning her younger self not to allow her family to force her to marry someone she doesn't love, but here Matheson gives the story a delightful twist. Anne runs away with her true love—who turns out to be a thoroughgoing wastrel who goes through all of her money and utterly ruins her life. The warning was to *not* marry for love!

"I liked the idea," says Matheson. "It's like J. B. Priestley, the British playwright who wrote all these plays about time travel, the convolutions of time. He wrote a book called *Man in Time,* too. I like that type of story where you play around with time and show, with things that you meant to do, how badly they worked out."

In the lead, Diana Hyland is convincing, both as a naive, impetuous eighteen-year-old and as a cynical, wretched woman of forty-three. Not so capable is young Roger Davis, who obviously found it far beyond his ability to play the middle-aged derelict his character ultimately becomes.

"I didn't like the way it was done, particularly," Matheson says of the episode. Especially galling are certain closeups in the teaser which clearly show that the girl and her middle-aged pursuer are one and the same. "I felt the director gave the whole thing away in the beginning. You could see it was the same girl, and you weren't supposed to know that until the end."

"STEEL" (10/4/63)

Lee Marvin

Written by Richard Matheson
Based on the short story "Steel" by Richard Matheson
Producer: Bert Granet
Director: Don Weis
Director of Photography: George T. Clemens
Music: Van Cleave
Makeup: William Tuttle

Cast:
Steel Kelly: Lee Marvin
Pole: Joe Mantell
Maynard Flash: Chuck Hicks
Battling Maxo: Tipp McClure
Nolan: Merritt Bohn
Maxwell: Frank London
Man's Voice: Larry Barton

"Sports item, circa 1974: Battling Maxo, B2, heavyweight, accompanied by his manager and handler, arrives in Maynard, Kansas, for a scheduled six-round bout. Battling Maxo is a robot, or, to be exact, an android, *definition: 'an automaton resembling a human being.' Only these automatons have been permitted in the ring since prizefighting was legally abolished in 1968. This is the story of that scheduled six-round bout, more specifically the story of two men shortly to face that remorseless truth: that no law can be passed which will abolish cruelty* or *desperate need—nor, for that matter, blind animal courage. Location for the facing of said truth a small, smoke-filled arena just this side of the Twilight Zone."*

Battling Maxo, an outmoded B2 model, breaks down before the bout. Desperate for the five-hundred-dollar fight money to repair Maxo, his manager, "Steel" Kelly—so-named because, as a heavyweight, he was never knocked down—decides to disguise himself as a robot and fight the Maynard Flash, a brand-new B7, in Maxo's place. Predictably, Steel is beaten to a pulp in the first round, but his ruse is not detected. He is paid *half* the promised money—not a great deal, but it will help to effect the needed repairs.

"Portrait of a losing side, proof positive that you can't outpunch machinery. Proof also of something else: that no matter what the future brings, man's capacity to rise to the occasion will remain unaltered. His potential for tenacity and optimism continues, as always, to outfight, outpoint and outlive any and all

changes made by his society, for which three cheers and a unanimous decision rendered from the Twilight Zone."

"Steel" is Richard Matheson's faithful adaptation of his own short story, originally published in the May, 1956, issue of *The Magazine of Fantasy and Science Fiction* and collected in *The Shores of Space*. It is his favorite of all his *Twilight Zone* episodes. Like many of his scripts, this too has a title with a double meaning. "Steel was his nickname and that was his character, his backbone, that he was so determined," Matheson explains. "When you have a monomaniacal character like that, it's easier to handle. Captain Ahab is like that, too. He has no grays; he just wants to kill the whale."

As Steel Kelly, Lee Marvin turns in a strong and single-minded performance. Matheson was there during the rehearsals. "I remember Lee Marvin making crowd noises and street noises to get himself into the feeling," he says. "Even though there was no set or anything, he was psyching himself into feeling the moment, which I found impressive, that an actor would go to that trouble."

Equally impressive were the two robots, Battling Maxo and the Maynard Flash, played by Tipp McClure and Chuck Hicks. Massive and muscular, they look completely human but for two things: their fluid mechanical movements (cleverly directed by Don Weis) and their utterly immobile faces, complete with shiny black eyes.

The two robot faces were crafted by William Tuttle. Lifemasks were taken of the actors, atop which the robot faces were sculpted in clay. Foam rubber and latex copies were cast of these, which were then glued onto the actors' faces. As for the inhuman, expressionless eyes, those were sections of ping-pong balls, painted black, with pinpoint eye holes through the center.

If there is a problem with "Steel," it would have to lie in the area of the main character's motivation. Steel goes into the ring in order to get money to repair his robot. Yet Pole pleads with him not to do it, explaining that there are safer—although more time-consuming—methods of getting the necessary money. Rather than seeming an act of courage, on the face of it Steel's actions seem the result of a near-suicidal bullheadedness.

"I saw the Lee Marvin character as the sort of man who never liked to ask anyone for help but chose, in the old-fashioned way, to take care of things for himself, however mad," says Matheson. "To him it was a straight line progression: to get the money to put Maxo back in condition, he had to get that fee—*now*. So he got it in the most obvious way he could as he saw things. He couldn't see Pole wiring for money. That would take time. Worse, it would be begging. The money might not come anyway. What if Pole's sister said no? What if the work in Philadelphia did not eventuate? Much too complex for Steel. Go in the ring and hang in there and get the money and leave. Even when he got his brains beaten out and only a small percentage of the money, he did not give up. Not the brightest man in the world but, in many ways, pretty admirable, pretty brave."

"NIGHT CALL" (2/7/64)

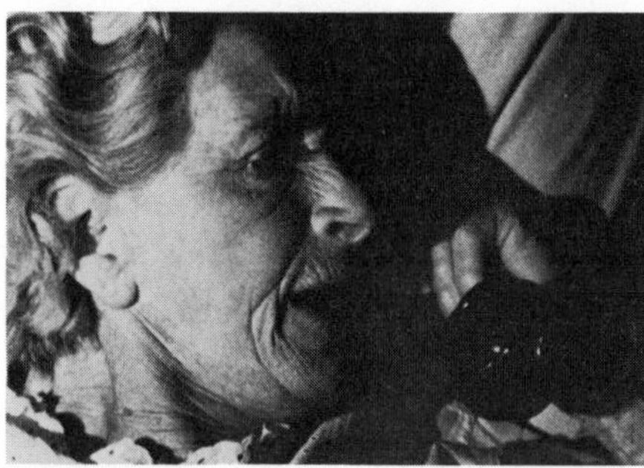
Gladys Cooper

Written by Richard Matheson
Based on the short story "Long Distance Call" by Richard Matheson
Producer: Bert Granet
Director: Jacques Tourneur
Director of Photography: Robert W. Pittack
Music: stock

Cast:
Miss Elva Keene: Gladys Cooper
Margaret Phillips: Nora Marlowe
Miss Finch: Martine Bartlett

"Miss Elva Keene lives alone on the outskirts of London Flats, a tiny rural community in Maine. Up until now, the pattern of Miss Keene's existence has been that of lying in her bed or sitting in her wheelchair reading books, listening to a radio, eating, napping, taking medication—and waiting for something different to happen. Miss Keene doesn't know it yet, but her period of waiting has just ended, for something different is about to happen to her, has in fact already begun to happen, via two most unaccountable telephone calls in the middle of a stormy night, telephone calls routed directly through—the Twilight Zone."

Over a period of several days, Elva receives a number of mysterious phone calls, culminating in a dull voice saying, "Where are you? I want to *talk* to you." In reply, the terrified Elva screams, "Leave me alone!" But then the next day she discovers that the calls are originating from a fallen wire lying atop the grave of her long-dead fiancée Brian, who always did what she said—including letting her drive on the occasion that she crashed the car, crippling herself and killing him. Elva is filled with joy; with Brian to talk to, she won't be lonely anymore! Rushing home, she lifts the receiver and speaks his name. His sole reply: "You said, leave you alone. I always do what you say." Then he is gone.

"According to the Bible, God created the heavens and the Earth. It is man's prerogative—and woman's—to create their own particular and private hell. Case in point, Miss Elva Keene, who in every sense has made her own bed and now must lie in it, sadder, but wiser, by dint of a rather painful lesson in responsibility, transmitted from the Twilight Zone."

Based on his short story "Long Distance Call" (which is included in his collection *Shock!* and which originally appeared in the November, 1953, issue of *Beyond* under the title "Sorry, Right Number"), Matheson's "Night Call" is a wonderfully creepy tale, a triumph of atmosphere in which the horror grows ever so slowly, bit by bit. It is directed by Jacques Tourneur, a master of subtlety, in whose finest films (notably *Cat People* and *Curse of the Demon*) what is unseen remains always more terrifying than what is seen. Here, he applies the same techniques. Aided by director of photography Robert W. Pittack, "Night Call" is filled with exquisite detail, suggestively malevolent, such as when the shadows of the branches of a tree play over the old woman's face as she sleeps.

It was upon Matheson's recommendation that Granet hired Tourneur (Granet had worked with Tourneur before, on the 1948 film *Berlin Express*). "There was some doubt at the time as to whether to use Tourneur, because they thought he was a movie director and couldn't handle the scheduling," Matheson recalls. "As it turned out, he, to my knowledge, shot the shortest shooting schedule for a half hour—I think it was twenty-eight hours."

For the most part, the episode remains close to the original short story—with one notable exception. The original ends gruesomely: after the operator has mentioned Miss Elva's home address on the line and then informed her as to the source of the curious calls, the phone rings. On the other end a cadaverous voice says, "Hello, Miss Elva. I'll be right over."

The alternate ending of the episode might seem somewhat cruel. Miss Elva initially reacted out of fear, as any normal human being would. To have permanent solitude visited on her as a result of a perfectly natural frailty seems extremely unjust. Still, one can't deny that it's better than having a corpse come 'round the house, as in the original.

"NIGHTMARE AT 20,000 FEET" (10/11/63)

Nick Cravat and William Shatner

Written by Richard Matheson
Based on the short story "Nightmare at 20,000 Feet" by Richard Matheson
Producer: Bert Granet
Director: Richard Donner
Director of Photography: Robert W. Pittack
Music: stock
Makeup: William Tuttle

Cast:
Bob Wilson: William Shatner
Ruth Wilson: Christine White
Gremlin: Nick Cravat
Flight Engineer: Edward Kemmer
Stewardess: Asa Maynor

"Portrait of a frightened man: Mr. Robert Wilson, thirty-seven, husband, father, and salesman on sick leave. Mr. Wilson has just been discharged from a sanitarium where he spent the last six months recovering from a nervous breakdown, the onset of which took place on an evening not dissimilar to this one, on an airliner very much like the one in which Mr. Wilson is about to be flown home—the difference being that, on that evening half a year ago, Mr. Wilson's flight was terminated by the onslaught of his mental breakdown. Tonight, *he's travelling all the way to his appointed destination which, contrary to Mr. Wilson's plan, happens to be in the darkest corner of the Twilight Zone."*

Looking out his window while the plane is in flight, Wilson sees a bulky, furred creature land on the wing. At first, he doubts his own sanity, but soon he comes to believe the evidence of his eyes. The creature is a gremlin, and it means to sabotage one of the engines. Unfortunately, it flies out of sight whenever Wilson summons his wife or the stewardess—and the flight engineer refuses to heed his warnings to keep a close watch on the wings. Wilson realizes he must act alone and—seeing that the gremlin has already forcibly torn back one of the cowling plates—he must act quickly. He removes a pistol from a sleeping policeman, then throws open an emergency door and empties the gun into the gremlin. Mortally wounded, it is swept off the wing. Later, Wilson is taken off the plane in a straitjacket. "It's all right now, darling," his wife reassures him. "I know," he replies, "but I'm the only one who *does* know—right now."

"The flight of Mr. Robert Wilson has ended now, a flight not only from point A to point B, but also from the fear of recurring mental breakdown. Mr. Wilson

has that fear no longer, though, for the moment, he is, as he has said, alone in this assurance. Happily, his conviction will not remain isolated too much longer, for happily, tangible manifestation is very often left as evidence of trespass, even from so intangible a quarter as the Twilight Zone."

Richard Matheson's ingenious "Nightmare at 20,000 Feet," starring William Shatner and based on the short story of the same name, was originally published in the anthology *Alone by Night* (Ballantine, 1961) and included in Matheson's *Shock III* (Dell, 1966). In setting up the situation, Matheson deftly avoids the cliché—oft-repeated on *Twilight Zone* itself—of the otherwise normal character who witnesses or experiences something out of the ordinary and then is unable to convince others of it ("You must believe me! I'm *not* insane!"). Here, the first person Bob Wilson must convince of his sanity is himself, and in telling others of what he has seen he risks far more than their disbelief—he almost certainly guarantees his recommitment. In the end, Wilson succeeds in killing the creature and gaining the assuredness of his own sanity. It is a double triumph.

For Matheson, the idea came from a simple source. "I was on an airplane. I looked out the window and said, 'Jeez, what if I saw a guy out

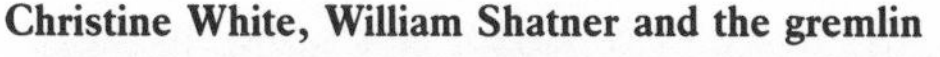

Christine White, William Shatner and the gremlin

there?' In the story, I spent some time in setting up the main character as a businessman who really *was* having a nervous breakdown, to the point where he was considering suicide and had a gun in his handbag and was thinking of shooting himself. But of course you couldn't do that on television."

As Wilson, William Shatner is complex, intelligent, insecure. He is a man on the brink, trying desperately to hold on to his recently regained normalcy. "Shatner's performance was really marvelous," says Matheson. "I remember the particular moment when the flight engineer [Edward Kemmer, previously the star of TV's *Space Patrol*] is trying to reassure him, saying, 'We see it, too,' and the look that crossed his face when he realized that they were putting him on."

Playing the gremlin on the wing is Nick Cravat, Burt Lancaster's acrobatic partner (he appears in a number of Lancaster films). As the monster, Cravat wears a mask made by William Tuttle and a furry suit from Wardrobe. Although initially scary (particularly to small children), at close inspection the monster seems all too transparently a man in a furry suit wearing an immobile rubber mask. Matheson was not at all pleased. "I didn't think much of that thing on the wing. I had wished that Jacques Tourneur had directed it, because he had a different idea. The man who was inside that suit looked exactly the way I described him in the story. All they had to do was use him the way he was. Tourneur was going to put a dark suit on him and cover him with diamond dust so that you hardly saw what was out there. *This* thing looked like a panda bear."

The man hired to direct the episode was young Richard Donner (later to direct *Superman* and *The Omen*), at the time a television director who had no experience with special effects ("I don't know why the hell they hired me," he says). Despite this, he did a wonderful job, and the episode is skillfully acted and shot.

The logistics involved in filming "Nightmare at 20,000 Feet" were enormous. The set consisted of the interior of an airline passenger cabin with the left airplane wing attached to the outside. This was all suspended over a huge water tank, in order to contain the water from the rain effect. Donner remembers the shooting as one big headache. "Because you were suspended up, you had no stage floors. Every movement was a bitch." He lists the factors that had to be considered in virtually every shot. "A man flying in on wires. Wind. Rain. Lightning. Smoke, to give the effect of clouds and travel and speed. Actors. You couldn't hear yourself think because of the noise of the machines outside. And fighting time, all the time. It was just unbearable. If any one of those things went wrong, it ruined the whole take." All of this consumed lots of time. "We were supposed to take a fourth day in the tank set with the airplane," Donner remembers. "Then they found out that the studio had committed it to another company. We had to work all night to finish it up. We went overtime till early the next morning."

In spite of all the difficulties, Donner has only praise for the finished product. "I love it, I do love it. It's just such an unusual thing for television, really, to see that much energy go into a little half-hour film. And the story was good, too."

The final story on "Nightmare at 20,000 Feet" occurred several months after the shooting. "Matheson and I were going to fly to San Francisco," Serling recalled in 1975. "It was like three or four weeks after the show was on the air, and I had spent three weeks in constant daily communication with Western Airlines preparing a given seat for him, having the stewardess close the [curtains] when he sat down, and I was going to say, 'Dick, open it up.' I had this huge, blownup poster stuck on the [outside of the window] so that when he opened it there would be this gremlin staring at him. So what happened was we get on the plane, there was the seat, he sits down, the curtains are closed, I lean over and I say, 'Dick—' at which point they start the engines and it blows the thing away. It was an old prop airplane. . . . He never saw it. And I had spent hours in the planning of it. I would lie in bed thinking how we could do this."

TRANSITION

With thirteen of the half hours produced and another thirteen in development, Bert Granet received an attractive offer from CBS. "They were doing a series called *The Great Adventure* with John Houseman, and John, God bless him, is one of the most talented men in the business, but he made three shows and was something like $600,000 over budget. CBS had a serious problem, and I think they gave me a quarter of a million dollars for the year to finish the series out." There was no way that Serling could offer Granet an equal salary, so in the middle of the season, *Twilight Zone* was abruptly without a producer. "He was very angry with me when I left," Granet says of Serling, "because he felt I was letting him down. But I wasn't doing what anybody else doesn't do in the picture business: protect their own hide for the most money."

Hired to replace Granet was William Froug, a writer-producer-director on radio with *Hallmark Hall of Fame* and *The Columbia Workshop* (on which he oversaw production of a radio version of Aldous Huxley's *Brave New World)* and a writer-producer on television with *Alcoa-Goodyear Theater, Adventures in Paradise, The Dick Powell Show, Playhouse 90,* and *Mr. Novak* (later, he would have production chores on *Bewitched* and *Gilligan's*

Island). Froug was an extremely good-natured man who got along well with Serling (he remembers his stint on *Twilight Zone* as "Fun! Wonderful fun!"). Froug: "When I came on the show, Rod . . . wanted me to start clean as producer." A number of scripts that Granet had in development were abandoned, including ones by Matheson, Beaumont, Jerry Sohl (under Beautmont's name) and Arch Oboler (noted for his work on radio's *Lights Out).*

The cancelled scripts were: Matheson's "The Doll," about a lonely, middle-aged bachelor who falls in love with a beautiful, handmade doll, searches out the model—and finds that she has fallen in love with a doll that looks like *him;* Beaumont's "Gentlemen, Be Seated," about a future society in which laughter has been outlawed and a humor underground flourishes; Oboler's "What the Devil!" about a couple of murderers who are chased along a highway by a dynamite truck driven by Satan; and two by Sohl—"Who Am I?" about a man who wakes up, looks in the bathroom mirror and finds that his face has changed utterly (a fact that only *he* seems to recognize); and "Pattern for Doomsday," in which a tremendous asteroid is on a collision course with Earth and a computer selects eight people—a bacteriologist, a psychologist, a philosopher, an auto mechanic, an artist, a singer, a con man and a shady lady—to escape on the lone spaceship. Curiously, Froug himself wrote a script that was never produced. In "Many, Many Monkeys," an epidemic breaks out that causes folds of flesh to cover people's eyes (the "monkeys" in the title refers to "see no evil," etc.). A nuclear bomb explosion is blamed, but one character thinks the disease is merely a physical manifestation of the hate within people. After buying it, the network shelved it. Says Froug, "I think they had the feeling it was too grotesque."

A quote from Froug as reported in *Daily Variety,* August 30, 1963, laid out the game plan for the rest of the year: "We're not only going way out on stories but in casting as well. One of our stories would be perfect for Jack Benny and another for Lena Horne. One of the segs will be directed by Mickey Rooney and we're hopeful of getting Judy Garland for the lead. It would be great teaming with vast promotional possibilities." Ultimately, neither Horne, Benny nor Garland appeared on *Twilight Zone.* Mickey Rooney did not get his chance to direct, but he did star in one episode, "The Last Night of a Jockey."

In the middle of its fifth season, *Twilight Zone* was more and more reliant on gimmicks. This was the year that Virginia Trimble, a nineteen-year-old UCLA astrophysics major—supposedly with an IQ of 180—toured the country as "Miss Twilight Zone" in order to promote the show.

Director of photography George Clemens found working conditions far different from those he had enjoyed during the first three seasons. "I got along with Froug like any cameraman, but we didn't have the relationship

I had with Buck and Rod. Occasionally, I'd go in with ideas on how I'd like to do things and he didn't see it my way, so I just gave up. I did less and less of them when he got in there."

While Froug himself felt great enthusiasm for the show, others who had labored longer on it were finding their inspiration flagging—including Serling.

William Froug recalls an incident regarding Serling's "Probe 7—Over and Out" that was fairly typical: "The script arrived and it was forty-five pages. I said, "Rod, it's a half-four show, pal. You above all people know we can't use more than thirty or thirty-two pages." He said, 'Don't worry, just cut whatever you think we don't need.' There were these speeches that went on and on for pages. So I remember taking ten pages out of the script, and it didn't affect it in the least."

With twenty-three episodes yet to go, the end was in sight.

"THE LAST NIGHT OF A JOCKEY" (10/25/63)

Mickey Rooney

Written by Rod Serling
Producer: William Froug
Director: Joseph M. Newman
Director of Photography: George T. Clemens
Music: stock

Cast:
Grady: Mickey Rooney

"The name is Grady, five-feet short in stockings and boots, a slightly distorted offshoot of a good breed of humans who race horses. He happens to be one of the rotten apples, bruised and yellowed by dealing in dirt, a short man with a short memory who's forgotten that he's worked for the sport of kings and helped turn it into a cesspool, used and misused by the two-legged animals who've hung around sporting events since the days of the Coliseum. So this is Grady, on his last night as a jockey. Behind him are Hialeah, Hollywood Park and Saratoga. Rounding the far turn and coming up fast on the rail—is the Twilight Zone."

After being banned from the track for horse doping, Grady sits alone in his run-down room, contemplating the ruin of his career and his life. Suddenly, a sardonic inner voice speaks to him, asking him his dearest wish. Grady doesn't have to think about it: he wants to be *big*. When he wakes from a nap, he finds that the wish has been granted: he's over eight feet tall! Grady is elated, until he gets a call from the racing commissioner telling him he's been given another chance, he can ride again. The horrible realization comes crashing in on him: he's grown even larger—and ten-foot-tall giants *can't* be jockeys.

"The name is Grady, ten feet tall, a slightly distorted offshoot of a good breed of humans who race horses. Unfortunately for Mr. Grady, he learned too late that you don't measure size with a ruler, you don't figure height with a yardstick and you never judge a man by how tall he looks in a mirror. The giant is as he does. You can make a parimutuel bet on this, win, place or show, in or out of the Twilight Zone."

The first two of Froug's episodes to be aired were strong shows, exceptions to the rule.

In 1958, Froug had won an Emmy for producing "Eddie" on *Alcoa-Goodyear Theater,* a half-hour, one-character tour-de-force starring Mickey Rooney as a two-bit gambler desperately trying to raise some cash. Serling's "The Last Night of a Jockey" must have seemed like old home week to him.

As Grady, Mickey Rooney runs a gamut of emotions from rage to grief to a terrible self-loathing, and is credible throughout. Serling's script displays both intensity and understanding, but ultimately it is Rooney's acting that carries the show.

"LIVING DOLL" (11/1/63)

Written by Jerry Sohl
Plotted by Charles Beaumont and Jerry Sohl (show credited solely to Beaumont)
Producer: William Froug
Director: Richard C. Sarafian
Director of Photography: Robert W. Pittack
Music: Bernard Herrmann

Cast:
Erich Streator: Telly Savalas
Annabelle: Mary LaRoche
Christie: Tracy Stratford
Voice of Talky Tina: June Foray

"Talky Tina, a doll that does everything, a lifelike creation of plastic and springs and painted smile. To Erich Streator, she is a most unwelcome addition to his household—but without her he'd never enter the Twilight Zone."

Erich is displeased when his wife Annabelle buys an expensive doll for his step-daughter Christie—and even more displeased when the doll *tells* him it doesn't like him. Initially, he suspects trickery, but as the doll repeatedly vocalizes its hatred of him—though only when the two of them are alone—he comes to believe it really *is* alive. He throws it in the garbage, but it escapes and phones him with a death threat. To save himself, Erich tries to burn the doll and saw off its head, but both attempts fail. He throws it back in the trash, trapping it with weights. But his actions have convinced Annabelle he's insane; she's taking Christie and leaving. In order to placate her, Erich—by now doubting his own senses—agrees to return the doll to Christie. But late that night, investigating a sound, Erich trips on the doll and falls down the stairs to his death. Horrified, Annabelle rushes to him and picks up the doll. "My name is Talky Tina," it tells her, *"and you'd better be nice to me!"*

"Of course, we all know dolls can't really *talk, and they certainly can't commit murder. But to a child caught in the middle of turmoil and conflict, a doll can become many things: friend, defender, guardian. Especially a doll like Talky Tina, who* did *talk and* did *commit murder—in the misty region of the Twilight Zone."*

The "Living Doll" is a most unusual talking doll that says things like "I hate you" and "I'm going to kill you" (as supplied by the voice of June Foray, who is also the voice of Rocky the Flying Squirrel). Masterfully written and superbly directed, acted, photographed and scored, it is an episode that can stand with the best of any season.

Based on an idea by Charles Beaumont and written in one day by Jerry Sohl (although credited entirely to Beaumont), "Living Doll" sets up a diabolical situation. Erich Streator is trying desperately not to alienate his wife (Mary LaRoche, previously Mary in "A World of His Own") and her young daughter (Tracy Stratford, previously Tina in "Little Girl Lost"). When the child brings home a doll that makes clear its murderous intentions—but only when it's alone with him—Erich is in one hell of a bind. If he tries to tell his wife of it, he sounds like a lunatic, and if he tries to protect himself by attempting (unsuccessfully) to destroy the doll, his actions seem those of a twisted mind striking out resentfully to hurt a helpless little girl. Poor Erich; it is clear early on that he hasn't much of a chance against this ruthless doll.

"You really sympathize with the guy," says Jerry Sohl. "If that goddamn doll kept saying those things, I'd feel the same way myself: throw it in the damn trash can!"

"SOUNDS AND SILENCES" (4/3/64)

John McGiver

Written by Rod Serling
Producer: William Froug
Director: Richard Donner
Director of Photography: George T. Clemens
Music: stock

Cast:
Roswell G. Flemington: John McGiver
Mrs. Flemington: Penny Singleton
Psychiatrist: Michael Fox
Doctor: Francis Defales
Secretary: Renee Aubrey
Conklin: William Benedict

"This is Roswell G. Flemington, two hundred and seventeen pounds of gristle, lung tissue and sound decibels. He is, as you have perceived, a noisy man, one of a breed who substitutes volume for substance, sound for significance, and shouting to cover up the readily apparent phenomenon that he is nothing more than an overweight and aging perennial Sea Scout whose noise-making is in inverse ratio to his competence and his character. But soon our would-be admiral of the fleet will embark on another voyage. This one is an uncharted and twisting stream that heads for a distant port called . . . the Twilight Zone."

Flemington, the owner of a model-ship company, is enamored of nautical jargon and *very* loud noise. At home, he relaxes by playing phonograph records of naval battles. When his wife of twenty years walks out on him (for a little peace and quiet), Flemington feels only joy—now he can enjoy the din without having to put up with complaints! But that night, he undergoes a bizarre transformation: trivial sounds—water dripping, the ticking of a clock—become deafening to him. The next day, his employees are astounded to hear him demand *quiet* in the office! This doesn't work, though; the thundering of squeaking shoes and typewriter bells drive him to a doctor, then to a psychiatrist—who convinces him the problem is all in his head. Returning home, Flemington encounters his wife, there momentarily to retrieve her jewelry. Using his new-found willpower, he shuts out the sound of her voice until it is a tiny squeak—then finds to his horror that *everything* sounds this way to him.

"When last heard from, Mr. Roswell G. Flemington was in a sanitarium pleading with the medical staff to make some noise. They, of course, believe the case to be a rather tragic aberration—a man's mind becoming unhinged. And for this they'll give him pills, therapy and rest. Little do they realize that all Mr.

Flemington is suffering from is a case of poetic justice. Tonight's tale of sounds and silences from . . . the Twilight Zone."

In May, 1961, a script was submitted to Serling entitled "The Sound of Silence," concerning a man who could not hear the sounds around him. Serling rejected it, then forgot all about it. Two years later, he wrote "Sounds and Silences." As soon as it aired, the writer of the original script filed suit. Because of the similarities of title and plot, the writer was paid $3500 and the matter was settled. Unfortunately, because the suit was in litigation when *Twilight Zone* was put into syndication, "Sounds and Silences" was not included. The episode was aired only once—and then put away in the CBS vaults.

"RING-A-DING GIRL" (12/27/63)

Maggie McNamara

Written by Earl Hamner, Jr.
Producer: William Froug
Director: Alan Crosland, Jr.
Director of Photography: George T. Clemens
Music: stock

Cast:
Bunny Blake: Maggie McNamara
Hildy Powell: Mary Munday
Bud Powell: David Macklin
Ben Braden: Bing Russell
Mr. Gentry: Hank Patterson
State Trooper: Vic Perrin
Dr. Floyd: George Mitchell
Cici: Betty Lou Gerson
Pilot: Bill Hickman

"Introduction to Bunny Blake. Occupation: film actress. Residence: Hollywood, California, or anywhere in the world that cameras happen to be grinding. Bunny Blake is a public figure; what she wears, eats, thinks, says is news. But underneath the glamor, the makeup, the publicity, the build-up, the costuming, is a flesh-and-blood person, a beautiful girl about to take a long and bizarre journey into the Twilight Zone."

Preparing to leave on a flight to a movie location in Rome, Bunny—"the ring-a-ding girl"—receives a present from her home town fan club. It is the latest addition to her ring collection, but *this* ring is unique: in its gem, Bunny can see the faces of people she knew back in Howardville, telling her she's needed there. Dropping in on the home of her sister Hildy, Bunny discovers it's the day of the annual Founder's Day picnic. Seemingly on a whim, she asks Dr. Floyd, chairman of the Founder's Day committee, to postpone the picnic for a day; he refuses. She then goes on TV and announces she will be performing her one-woman show in the school auditorium *today only*—the people of Howardville must choose between going to the picnic or seeing her. Hildy can't understand Bunny's actions, seeing them as merely the selfish acts of a spoiled Hollywood star. Just prior to her performance, though, Bunny disappears. All becomes clear. A jet airliner, bound from Los Angeles to New York, has crashed on the picnic grounds. Thanks to Bunny, most of the people in Howardville are safe in the auditorium. But Bunny herself is dead—she was a *passenger* on the plane!

"We are all travellers. The trip starts in a place called birth—and ends in that lonely town called death. And that's the end of the journey, unless you happen to exist for a few hours, like Bunny Blake, in the misty regions of the Twilight Zone."

Earl Hamner, Jr.'s, final four *Twilight Zone* episodes came nowhere near the drama or poetry of "Jess-Belle," his previous contribution. Unfortunately, "Ring-a-Ding Girl" is much like the stone in the ring Bunny Blake receives: interesting, but no gem.

"YOU DRIVE" (1/3/64)

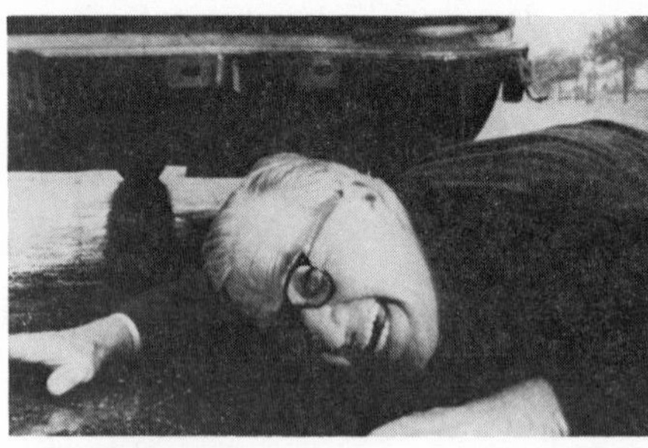

Edward Andrews

Written by Earl Hamner, Jr.
Producer: William Froug
Director: John Brahm
Director of Photography: George T. Clemens
Music: stock

Cast:
Oliver Pope: Edward Andrews
Lillian Pope: Hellena Westcott
Pete Radcliff: Kevin Hagen
Policeman: John Hanek
Woman: Totty Ames

"Portrait of a nervous man: Oliver Pope by name, office manager by profession. A man beset by life's problems: his job, his salary, the competition to get ahead. Obviously, Mr. Pope's mind is not on his driving . . . Oliver Pope, business-

man-turned-killer on a rain-soaked street in the early evening of just another day during just another drive home from the office. The victim, a kid on a bicycle, lying injured, near death. But Mr. Pope hasn't time for the victim, his only concern is for himself. Oliver Pope, hit-and-run driver, just arrived at a crossroad in his life, and he's chosen the wrong turn. The hit occurred in the world he knows, but the run will lead him straight into—the Twilight Zone."

Pope is determined to keep his guilt a secret—even after the boy dies from his injuries and his co-worker, Pete Radcliff, is mistakenly identified as the hit-and-run driver. But Pope's car has *other* ideas: late at night, it honks its horn, flashes its lights and blares its radio. When Pope's wife takes it out for a drive, it steers itself to the scene of the accident, then stalls. Finally, when Pope decides to walk to work, the car pursues him, coming within inches of running him down. Realizing he's beaten, Pope gets in the car—and lets it drive him to police headquarters.

"All persons attempting to conceal criminal acts involving their cars are hereby warned: check first to see that underneath that chrome there does not lie a conscience, especially if you're driving along a rain-soaked highway in the Twilight Zone."

For Earl Hamner, Jr., "You Drive" was little more than an extension of his own relationship with such devices. "All mechanical things frustrate me. I'm like my friend, John McGreevey, the writer, who once cut himself with a sponge. I am afraid of and inept with all mechanical devices. It's kind of a love-hate relationship. I drive a Corvette which I love because it is so at odds with the image of John-Boy Walton as an old man. And of course it is a stunning machine. But at the same time, I do not trust it. It seems to have a life of its own, and sometimes when it will not start I suspect it is because it has some personal grudge against me."

Although not a particularly effective story, "You Drive" does have some good effects, such as when the determined automobile follows Edward Andrews (last seen in "Third From the Sun") down the street.

"We had a man under the dashboard with a tiny periscope that stuck up through the hood of the car, and he drove with special controls," explains William Froug. "I remember watching it, because I was on location when it was filmed, and I was astonished. This car would come driving by and it was spooky, because you couldn't see this little periscope sticking up."

The most impressive shot occurs in a scene in which the car chasing Andrews increases its speed. Running madly, Andrews stumbles and falls. Cut to a closeup as the car roars to within inches of his head—and stops. "You do it in reverse," explains director of photography George Clemens.

"Start the car right at him and pull it back. Those things always work well when they're done right."

"BLACK LEATHER JACKETS" (1/31/64)

Written by Earl Hamner, Jr.
Producer: William Froug
Director: Joseph N. Newman
Director of Photography: George T. Clemens
Music: Van Cleave

Cast:
Scott: Lee Kinsolving
Ellen Tillman: Shelley Fabares
Steve: Michael Forest
Fred: Tom Gilleran
Stu Tillman: Denver Pyle
Martha Tillman: Irene Hervey
Sheriff Harper: Michael Conrad
Mover: Wayne Heffley

"Three strangers arrive in a small town, three men in black leather jackets in an empty rented house. We'll call them Steve and Scott and Fred, but their names are not important; their mission is, *as three men on motorcycles lead us into the Twilight Zone."*

Steve, Scott and Fred are actually part of the first wave of an invasion force from another planet. They set up an antenna to receive instructions, a side effect of which is neighborhood disruption of electricity and radio and TV reception. When neighbor Stu Tillman complains, Steve uses his superior mind to brainwash him into believing that the three are no more than "nice boys." A week later, Stu's teenage daughter Ellen misses her bus and Scott gives her a ride. A romance soon develops, the result of which is that Scott is considered a traitor by Steve and Fred. When he overhears them receiving orders to poison the water supply, Scott tries to warn Ellen, but he succeeds only in convincing her that he's lost his mind. He then pleads with his leader to spare mankind, but his pleas are wasted. Rushing back to the Tillman house, Scott finds that Stu, worried about Scott's sanity, has called the sheriff, who has brought with him several men in white coats. The men grab Scott and hustle him away. In reality, the sheriff and the men in white coats are aliens—and they want nothing to interfere with their plans.

"Portrait of an American family on the eve of invasion from outer space. Of course, we know it's merely fiction—and yet, think twice when you drink your next glass of water. Find out if it's from your local reservoir, or possibly it came direct to you . . . from the Twilight Zone."

"Black Leather Jackets" might more aptly be titled "*The Wild One* Meets *It Came From Outer Space*." The episode is filled with wild implausibilities, such as the fact that these creatures, attempting to blend into the background as much as possible so that they can surreptitiously poison the water supply, assume disguises guaranteed to attract the eye of every nervous suburbanite. Then there's the matter of one of them falling in love with a pretty little native girl. Although he has telekinetic powers (with which he can open windows and such), the smitten alien makes no effort to prove his claim that he's from outer space by demonstrating his otherworldly abilities. Naturally, with nothing more than his slightly hysterical word to go by, the young lady assumes he's crazy and our well-meaning but stupid young invader is hauled away.

"THE BEWITCHIN' POOL" (6/19/64)

Tim Stafford, Kim Hector, Georgia Simmons and Mary Badham

Written by Earl Hamner, Jr.
Producer: William Froug
Director: Joseph M. Newman
Director of Photography: George T. Clemens
Music: stock

Cast:
Sport: Mary Badham
Jeb: Tim Stafford
Aunt T: Georgia Simmons
Whitt: Kim Hector
Gloria: Dee Hartford
Gil: Tod Andrews
Radio Announcer: Harold Gould

"A swimming pool not unlike any other pool, a structure built of tile and cement and money, a backyard toy for the affluent, wet entertainment for the well-to-do. But to Jeb and Sport Sharewood, this pool holds mysteries not dreamed of by the building contractor, not guaranteed in any sales brochure. For this pool has a secret exit that leads to a never-neverland, a place designed for junior citizens who need a long voyage away from reality, into the bottomless regions of the Twilight Zone."

Jeb and Sport are playing in their back yard, trying to ignore the continuous bickering of their parents, when Whitt, a boy resembling Huckleberry Finn, suddenly appears in their swimming pool. He beckons the children to follow him. Intrigued, they dive in—and surface in a swimming hole adjacent to a backwoods paradise populated by happy children. This is presided over by Aunt T, a loving, matronly old woman who tells them that this is a sanctuary for children of unworthy parents. Sport explains that *their* parents love them. Thinking their arrival has been a mistake, Aunt T sends them back home. But next morning, Jeb dives in the pool and returns to Aunt T. Sport pursues him and convinces him to come back home, but when they return their parents tell them that they're getting a divorce—and the children must decide which parent they want to live with. "We don't have to stay with neither one of ya!" says Sport, and she and Jeb plunge into the pool, magically returning to Aunt T—for good.

"A brief epilogue for concerned parents. Of course, there isn't any such place as the gingerbread house of Aunt T, and we grownups know there's no door at the bottom of a swimming pool that leads to a secret place. But who can say how real the fantasy world of lonely children can become? For Jeb and Sport Sharewood, the need for love turned fantasy into reality; they found *a secret place—in the Twilight Zone."*

"That was my reaction to California, where there seemed to be a startling divorce rate at that time," says Hamner of "The Bewitchin' Pool," "and being somewhat puritanical, I felt that must have a terrible effect on children. And living, as I still do, in the San Fernando Valley, I saw affluence affecting people who were not accustomed to the California lifestyle, transplanted Eastern people who come out and suddenly start making a great deal of money but don't know how to deal with it and don't have social grace; 'surface' kind of people. Then I was struck by the number of swimming pools. Back where I grew up, there was never a swimming pool. We would consider such things sissy. But there were marvelous wide places in the creek that, over generations, had become the traditional old swimming hole. So I put all of those together and thought how marvelous it would be for children not to have to hear parents quarreling if to escape it they could simply come up in the arms of some Earth Mother–type person."

"The Bewitchin' Pool" had more than its share of problems, though. "I didn't like that old woman who played the Earth Mother," says Hamner. "There are real Earth Mothers, like Patricia Neal, women who can impart love without it being cloying. I thought that old woman was sort of 'cute.'"

In the lead as one of the children was Mary Badham, fresh from her role as Scout in *To Kill a Mockingbird* (for which she received an Oscar nomination). Unfortunately, in all but her scenes with Aunt T, her voice is actually that of June Foray. "We had backlot noise, but that wasn't entirely the trouble," explains William Froug. "She had such a thick Southern accent, combined with some bad noise, that between that and the voice levels, we were forced to loop her. It wasn't good. The others we got around, and it was sloppy and we hated it." What remains is a scarred-up version of what was, for which Froug blames the director. "I never worked with him again. I just didn't like what he did with her at all. It was all overplayed and corny, I thought, even granted it was a children's story."

In coming to the close of Hamner's contributions to *Twilight Zone,* it is interesting to observe that throughout his eight scripts, country folk are generally presented as honest, warm, and well-balanced, while city folk are for the most part bitchy, self-centered, and neurotic. "What I was going through was a psychological adjustment to a city that did not seem to care for me," says Hamner. "A psychiatrist might say that I was working out some hostility toward city people. But I think that all along in my work, because I'm so attuned to country folk, that unconsciously if I'm looking for a villain it probably triggers in my mind that the city person would be a more likely candidate to be evil—which shows you how provincial I was, and am."

"NUMBER TWELVE LOOKS JUST LIKE YOU" (1/24/64)

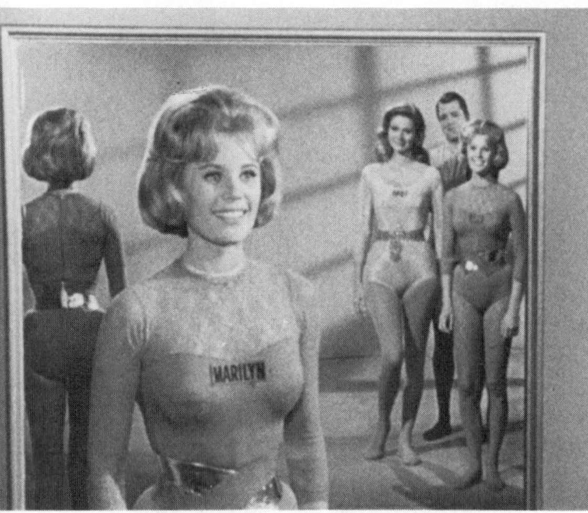

Pam Austin, Suzy Parker and Richard Long

Written by John Tomerlin (credited to Charles Beaumont)
Based on the short story "The Beautiful People" by Charles Beaumont
Producer: William Froug
Director: Abner Biberman
Director of Photography: Charles Wheeler
Music: stock

Cast:
Marilyn Cuberle: Collin Wilcox
Lana Cuberle/Simmons/Doe/Grace/Jane/Patient/#12: Suzy Parker
Uncle Rick/Dr. Rex/Sigmund Friend/Dr. Tom/Attendant: Richard Long
Valerie/Marilyn (after operation), #8: Pam Austin

"Given the chance, what young girl wouldn't happily exchange a plain face for a lovely one? What girl could refuse the opportunity to be beautiful? For want of a better estimate, let's call it the year 2000. At any rate, imagine a time in the future when science has developed a means of giving everyone the face and body he dreams of. It may not happen tomorrow—but it happens now *in the Twilight Zone."*

At the age of nineteen, people in this world of the future undergo the supposedly voluntary Transformation, which makes them beautifully identical to millions of others. But eighteen-year-old Marilyn Cuberle, whose free-thinking father committed suicide after *his* Transformation, thinks the operation is merely a way of enforcing conformity—she wants to keep her *own* face. Her mother Lana, her Uncle Rick and her friend Valerie all view this as an aberration. Marilyn is sent to a doctor, then to a psychiatrist—who puts her in the hospital. Marilyn tries to escape, but finds herself in an operating room—with a doctor and nurse waiting for her. She emerges with nothing but joy in her mind, looking and *thinking* just like Valerie. The Transformation has been a complete success.

"Portrait of a young lady in love—with herself. Improbable? Perhaps. But in an age of plastic surgery, body building and an infinity of cosmetics, let us

hesitate to say impossible. These and other strange blessings may be waiting in the future—which after all, is *the Twilight Zone."*

"Number Twelve Looks Just Like You" is a companion piece to "The Eye of the Beholder." This is a world where books are outlawed, people drink a cup of Instant Smile when they feel blue, and concerns are only skin-deep. Supposedly, the transformation surgery is entirely voluntary. But it soon becomes clear that it represents far more than the miraculous cosmetic boon of a beneficent society. Rather, it is a rite of passage into a rigid physical and mental conformity. The rebellious girl quotes her father (who committed suicide after the transformation): " 'When everyone is beautiful no one will be, because without ugliness there can be no beauty.' . . . They don't care whether you're beautiful or not, they just want everybody to be the same!" But her protests fall on deaf ears.

Based on Charles Beaumont's short story "The Beautiful People" (originally published in 1952 in *If* and included in his collection *Yonder*), the episode is credited to Beaumont and Tomerlin. By this time, however, Beaumont's mind was failing rapidly. "By 1963 he was still able to sell stories, but he was neither conceiving nor writing them," says Tomerlin. "The short story, of course, was his, but I wrote the script entirely myself. I wrote it in New York, as a matter of fact, consulting with him on the phone as to deadlines and things of that sort. He just called and said he had an assignment and asked if I would do it, and I said, 'Sure.' I needed the money and was delighted to do it."

Tomerlin's script is an improvement over the original short story, in which the teenager is put on trial and the verdict forces her to submit to the operation. Here, things are more subtle. Everyone seems to be trying to help. Marilyn doesn't *want* to be beautiful? Unthinkable. She must be ill.

Playing all of the adults in the episode in multiple roles are Richard Long (previously in Beaumont's "Person or Persons Unknown") and Suzy Parker. "Suzy Parker was at that time the most famous model in the country," says producer William Froug. "She was the superstar of models. She wasn't much of an actress, but she was gorgeous to look at. It was my notion that if you were going to do a show about everybody looking as beautiful as possible to use *her.*"

In the lead, Collin Wilcox is excellent. Intelligent, intense, pretty-plain but by no means beautiful, she is ideally suited to the role. Her anguish when she realizes that she is utterly alone, that no one can understand her feelings, seems very genuine.

In the end, she emerges looking *and* thinking exactly like her best friend

Valerie (Pam Austin). As she stands admiring herself in the mirror, she says, "And the nicest part of all, Val—I look just like you!" She has been utterly crushed by a society intent on conformity. It is a chilling finale, made all the more so by its uncomfortable—and deliberate—similarity to our own society.

"QUEEN OF THE NILE" (3/6/64)

Ann Blyth

Written by Jerry Sohl
Plotted by Charles Beaumont and Jerry Sohl (show credited solely to Beaumont)
Producer: William Froug
Director: John Brahm
Director of Photography: Charles Wheeler
Music: composed by Lucien Moraweck; conducted by Lud Gluskin

Cast:
Jordan Herrick: Lee Philips
Pamela Morris: Ann Blyth
Viola Draper: Celia Lovsky
Krueger: Frank Ferguson
Mr. Jackson: James Tyler
Maid: Ruth Phillips

"Jordan Herrick, syndicated columnist whose work appears in more than a hundred newspapers. By nature a cynic, a disbeliever, caught for the moment by a lovely vision. He knows the vision he's seen is no dream; she is Pamela Morris, renowned movie star, whose name is a household word and whose face is known to millions. What Mr. Herrick does not *know is that he has also just looked into the face—of the Twilight Zone."*

Arriving at her house to interview her, Herrick finds Pamela Morris as lovely and youthful-looking as when she starred in the 1940 film, *Queen of the Nile.* Upon leaving, he is confronted by seventy-year-old Viola Draper, a woman he takes for Morris's mother but who tells him she is actually her *daughter*! Intrigued, he does some investigating and finds that Constance Taylor—a *femme fatale* from the early years of the century who looked exactly as Morris does now—starred in a silent version of *Queen of the Nile,* then disappeared. Suspecting that, somehow, Morris and Taylor are the same woman, Herrick confronts Pamela. She drugs his coffee, then admits she really *was* a queen of the Nile—in ancient Egypt! Using a live scarab, she drains all of Herrick's life force and transfers it to herself. Just then, the doorbell rings. A handsome young man enters—soon to be yet another in a long line of victims.

"Everybody knows Pamela Morris, the beautiful and eternally young movie star. Or does she have another name, even more famous, an Egyptian name from centuries past? It's best not to be too curious, lest you wind up like Jordan Herrick, a pile of dust and old clothing, discarded in the endless eternity of the Twilight Zone."

The final *Twilight Zone* script credited to Beaumont was "Queen of the Nile," which deals with an immortal movie queen who lures men to her mansion and transfers their life force to herself via an Egyptian scarab. (One curious item that is never explained in the show is why Ann Blyth, as the immortal "Queen of the Nile," speaks English perfectly while her daughter [Celia Lovsky, later to play ruler of the planet Vulcan on *Star Trek*], now an aged woman, speaks with a heavy Viennese accent.)

Beaumont had already made his statement regarding immortality four years earlier with "Long Live Walter Jameson." Why do it all again, and not as well? The answer is that Beaumont had little to do with "Queen of the Nile."

"He was in bad shape at this time," explains Jerry Sohl. "It was I who suggested it. I had a scarab ring many years ago and knew that the scarab was the symbol of fertility and immortality in Egyptian times, so I said, 'Chuck, let's have this woman wear this scarab ring, it gives her immortality.' After about half an hour we had the story worked out. I just went home and did it, sent it in, and they shot it exactly the way I wrote it."

"THE FEAR" (5/29/64)

Hazel Court and Mark Richman

Written by Rod Serling
Producer: William Froug
Director: Ted Post
Director of Photography: Fred Mandl
Music: stock

Cast:
Trooper Robert Franklin: Mark Richman
Charlotte Scott: Hazel Court

"The major ingredient of any recipe for fear is the unknown. And here are two characters about to partake of the meal: Miss Charlotte Scott, a fashion editor,

and Mr. Robert Franklin, a state trooper. And the third *member of the party: the unknown, that has just landed a few hundred yards away. This person or thing is soon to be met. This is a mountain cabin, but it is also a clearing in the shadows known as the Twilight Zone."*

Trooper Franklin visits the cabin of Miss Scott, a frightened woman living in seclusion following a nervous breakdown, to investigate her reports of lights in the sky. Suddenly, there is a blinding light outside, following which Franklin sees his patrol car roll away and crash. His radio is broken, and Miss Scott's telephone no longer works; the two are stranded. But later, Franklin finds his car has been righted—and huge fingerprints cover the side of it. Next morning, the two of them discover a tremendous footprint. Terrified, Miss Scott runs blindly away—and directly in front of a gigantic, one-eyed, spacesuited figure. Franklin draws his pistol and tells Miss Scott to run; he'll try to fend the creature off. But she's found new courage—she's staying with the trooper. Franklin fires several shots at the giant. Hissing, it collapses on top of them—it's no more than a balloon! The real culprits stand revealed: two minuscule aliens in a tiny flying saucer. Frightened by the size of the humans, they hurriedly depart, their campaign of terror a failure.

"Fear, of course, is extremely relative. It depends on who can look down and who must look up. It depends on other vagaries, like the time, the mood, the darkness. But it's been said before, with great validity, that the worst thing there is to fear is fear itself. Tonight's tale of terror and tiny people on the Twilight Zone."

In the seven remaining shows written by Serling, his fatigue was clearly evident in the writing. Most of the scripts were clichéd, maudlin and melodramatic. Often, the plots were so thin that the episode consisted of people standing around stating and restating the obvious. Everything had to be made verbal; characters either defined themselves or each other at tedious length. And because Serling dictated his scripts—and because his verbal style as narrator was easily recognizable—if he wasn't cautious his characters ended up speaking in a manner that was exclusively his. In "The Fear," much of the dialogue sounds like two Rod Serlings talking to each other.

"THE BRAIN CENTER AT WHIPPLE'S" (5/15/64)

Richard Deacon

Written by Rod Serling
Producer: William Froug
Director: Richard Donner
Director of Photography: George T. Clemens
Music: stock

Cast:
Wallace V. Whipple: Richard Deacon
Hanley: Paul Newlan
Dickerson: Ted de Corsia
Technician: Jack Crowder
Watchman: Burt Conroy
Bartender: Shawn Michaels
Robot: Dion Hansen

"These are the players, with or without a scorecard: in one corner, a machine; in the other, one Wallace V. Whipple, man. And the game? It happens to be the historical battle between flesh and steel, between the brain of man and the product of man's brain. We don't make book on this one, and predict no winner, but we can tell you that for this particular contest there is standing room only—in the Twilight Zone."

Callous factory owner Wallace Whipple automates his plant, putting thousands of men out of work—much to the dismay of Hanley, the chief engineer, and Dickerson, the foreman, both also rendered obsolete. Dickerson drunkenly storms into the plant late at night and confronts Whipple, then attacks one of the computers. Frantically, Whipple grabs a gun from a security guard and shoots Dickerson, wounding but not killing him. Next day, Whipple is back at work, feeling totally self-justified. When a technician complains of the mechanized plant's sterility, Whipple discharges him. But once he's alone, Whipple's machines play back the criticisms of Dickerson, Hanley and the technician. Sometime later, Whipple seeks out Hanley in a bar. He laments that the board of directors has fired *him*—and replaced him with a robot!

"There are many bromides applicable here—too much of a good thing, tiger by the tail, as you sow so shall ye reap. The point is that too often man becomes clever instead of becoming wise, he becomes inventive but not thoughtful—and sometimes, as in the case of Mr. Whipple, he can create himself right out of existence. Tonight's tale of oddness and obsolescence from the Twilight Zone."

In "The Brain Center at Whipple's," there are two kinds of people: ones who make speeches, and ones who make speeches while shouting. Typical is the scene in which Dickerson, the foreman made obsolete by automation, returns to the factory and loudly confronts Wallace V. Whipple, the owner:

DICKERSON: I've worked here for *thirty* years! And I've been a foreman for *seventeen* of 'em! In my book that gives me some rights, Mr. Whipple!

WHIPPLE: Well, you've got the wrong book, Dickerson. My book reads as follows: you're drunk, disorderly, and trespassing on private property, and therefore subject to arrest!

DICKERSON: *Tell* me something, Mr. Whipple! *When you're dead and buried, who do you get to mourn for you?!!*

WHIPPLE: Shall I tell you the difference, Mr. Dickerson, between you and *it*? That machine costs two cents an hour for current. It gets no wrinkles, no arthritis, no hardening of the arteries. That one machine is a lathe operator, a press operator. Two of those machines replace 114 men that take no coffee breaks, no sick leaves, no vacations with pay! And that, in my book, Mr. Dickerson, is worth considerably more than you are!

DICKERSON: They shoulda stopped you a year ago! Somebody oughta held you down and put a bit in your head and poured in some reminders that men have to eat and work! And you can't pack 'em in cosmoline like surplus tanks or put 'em out to pasture like old bulls!! I'm a *man,* Mr. Whipple, ya *hear* me!? I'm a *man*—and that makes me better than that hunk of metal!! *Betterrrr!!!!!*

(Dickerson attacks the machine. Whipple grabs a gun from a security guard and shoots him)

DICKERSON (*As he falls*): Ya see, machine? It took more than *you* ta beat me—It took a man!

"THE LONG MORROW" (1/10/64)

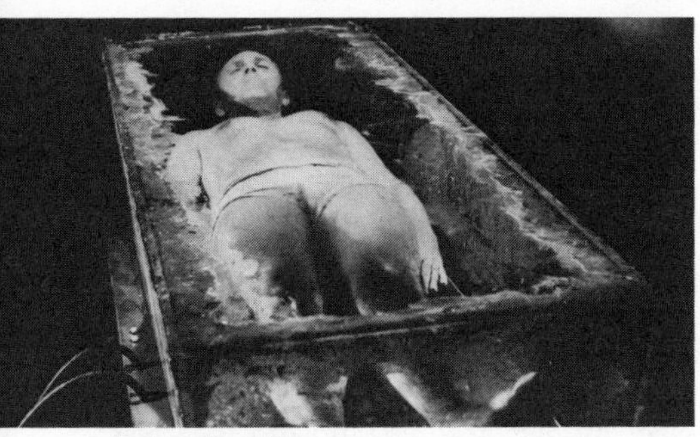

Robert Lansing

Written by Rod Serling
Producer: William Froug
Director: Robert Florey
Director of Photography: George T. Clemens
Music: stock

Cast:
Commander Douglas Stansfield: Robert Lansing
Sandra Horn: Mariette Hartley
Dr. Bixler: George MacReady
Gen. Walters: Edward Binns
Technician: William Swan

"It may be said with a degree of assurance that not everything that meets the eye is as it appears. Case in point: the scene you're watching. This is not a hospital, not a morgue, not a mausoleum, not an undertaker's parlor of the future. What it is is the belly of a spaceship. It is en route to another planetary system an incredible distance from the Earth. This is the crux of our story, a flight into space. It is also the story of the things that might happen to human beings who take a step beyond, unable to anticipate everything that might await them out there. . . . Commander Douglas Stansfield, astronaut, a man about to embark on one of history's longest journeys—forty years out into endless space and hopefully back again. This is the beginning, the first step toward man's longest leap into the unknown. Science has solved the mechanical details, and now it's up to one human being to breathe life into blueprints and computers, to prove once and for all that man can live half a lifetime in the total void of outer space, forty years alone in the unknown. This is Earth. Ahead lies a planetary system. The vast region in between is the Twilight Zone."

A month prior to leaving for deep space, Stansfield meets Sandra Horn, a warm and attractive Space Agency employee. The two fall in love, but both realize that it is a tragic affair. When Stansfield returns from his mission—kept in suspended animation for most of it—he will still be in his early thirties, but Sandra will be an old woman. Soon after Stansfield departs, however, Sandra has herself put into hibernation. When Stansfield returns she is revived, still a young woman of twenty-six. But General Walters has some bad news for her: six months into the mission,

Stansfield—for love of her—came out of suspended animation. He is now an old man of seventy!

"Commander Douglas Stansfield, one of the forgotten pioneers of the space age. He's been pushed aside by the flow of progress and the passage of years—and the ferocious travesty of fate. Tonight's tale of the ionosphere and irony, delivered from—the Twilight Zone."

Although "The Long Morrow" has quite a memorable payoff, the episode also has its share of problems. Robert Lansing and Mariette Hartley portray their characters with sincerity, but the lines they are forced to speak are often uncomfortably purple. Additionally, the age makeup applied to Lansing—crucial to the plausibility of the ending—is embarrassingly bad.

Lansing recalls the scenes in suspended animation with humor. "I was a little reluctant to do the semi-nude thing in the ice block, but it was such a good idea, so visual, that I bypassed my own feelings and did it. I was wearing a pair of mini-trunks which today I'd wear on a beach."

"I AM THE NIGHT—COLOR ME BLACK" (3/27/64)

Michael Constantine

Written by Rod Serling
Producer: William Froug
Director: Abner Biberman
Director of Photography: George T. Clemens
Music: stock

Cast:
Sheriff Charlie Koch: Michael Constantine
Colbey: Paul Fix
Jagger: Terry Becker
Deputy Pierce: George Lindsey
Rev. Anderson: Ivan Dixon
Ella Koch: Eve McVeagh
Man #1: Douglas Bank
Man #2: Ward Wood
Woman: Elizabeth Harrower

"Sheriff Charlie Koch on the morning of an execution. As a matter of fact, it's seven-thirty in the morning. Logic and natural laws dictate that at this hour there should be daylight. It is a simple rule of physical science that the sun should rise at a certain moment and supercede the darkness. But at this given

moment, Sheriff Charlie Koch, a deputy named Pierce, a condemned man named Jagger and a small, inconsequential village will shortly find out that there are causes and effects that have no precedent. Such is usually the case—in the Twilight Zone."

On the day Jagger is to be executed, a number of people wonder why it's still pitch black throughout the midwestern town. Jagger is an unpopular idealist whose conviction—for killing a "cross-burning, psychopathic bully"—had a number of questionable elements: during the trial, Deputy Pierce perjured himself on the stand; Sheriff Koch failed to bring up facts that might have led to acquittal; and Colbey, editor of the town paper, printed only articles naming Jagger guilty, although he personally believed him innocent. On the gallows, Rev. Anderson asks Jagger if he *enjoyed* the killing—Jagger did indeed. Anderson pronounces him guilty to the bloodthirsty crowd, and Jagger is hanged. The darkness closes in, a darkness created by hate . . . and it's spreading to other parts of the world.

"A sickness known as hate; not a virus, not a microbe, not a germ—but a sickness nonetheless, highly contagious, deadly in its effects. Don't look for it in the Twilight Zone—look for it in a mirror. Look for it before the light goes out altogether."

In "I Am the Night—Color Me Black," pretentious writing overwhelms fine acting. In its intent, the script was meant to rank with "The Monsters Are Due on Maple Street," but is done in by its own pomposity. An example is when the preacher tells the crowd gathered around the gallows that the man *is* guilty. Sneering, the prisoner says, "It's important to get with the majority. . . . That's a big thing nowadays, isn't it, Reverend?" Slowly, with great meaning, the clergyman replies, "That's all there is, is the majority. *The minority musta died on the cross, two thousand years ago.*"

"PROBE 7—OVER AND OUT" (11/29/63)

Antoinette Bower and Richard Basehart

Written by Rod Serling
Producer: William Froug
Director: Ted Post
Director of Photography: Robert W. Pittack
Music: stock

Cast:
Col. Adam Cook: Richard Basehart
Eve Norda: Antoinette Bower
Lt. Blane: Barton Heyman
Gen. Larrabee: Harold Gould

"One Colonel Cook, a traveller in space. He's landed on a remote planet several million miles from his point of departure. He can make an inventory of his plight by just one 360-degree movement of head and eyes. Colonel Cook has been set adrift in an ocean of space in a metal lifeboat that has been scorched and destroyed and will never fly again. He survived the crash but his ordeal is yet to begin. Now he must give battle to loneliness. Now Colonel Cook must meet the unknown. It's a small planet set deep in space, but for Colonel Cook it's the Twilight Zone."

After Probe 7 crashes, Cook receives a transmission from home telling him that a nuclear war has destroyed his planet—and that Cook, therefore, is stranded . . . permanently. Exploring outside his ship, he discovers a footprint. He invites whoever made the print to come out and be friendly, but all he gets for his trouble is a rock hurled at his skull. Eventually, however, the stranger *does* emerge; she is Norda, a space traveller, the sole survivor when her own planet went out of its orbit. The two of them will start new lives together, on a first-name basis: his is Adam; hers is Eve. As for the planet, Eve gives it a name: Earth.

"Do you know these people? Names familiar, are they? They lived a long time ago. Perhaps they're part fable, perhaps they're part fantasy. And perhaps the place they're walking to now is not really called 'Eden.' We offer it only as a presumption. This has been the Twilight Zone."

"Probe 7—Over and Out" sets up a situation filled with a number of dramatic possibilities. An astronaut is stranded on an alien planet; meanwhile, his home world is devastated by nuclear war. Colonel Adam Cook (Richard Basehart, pre-*Voyage to the Bottom of the Sea*) is a Robinson

Crusoe in space—with no hope of possible rescue. He has a lifetime ahead of him with an unknown world full of strange beauties and horrors to explore. What waits for him beyond the door of his wrecked spacecraft?

Unfortunately, what waits beyond the door is one of the oldest science-fiction chestnuts known to man: Colonel Cook is Adam, the woman he discovers is Eve and the planet—let's just call that Earth. What could have been a marvelous adventure instead becomes something that, had it been written as a short story, would have been rejected by every science-fiction magazine at the time, because it had been done to death many years earlier.

"THE JEOPARDY ROOM" (4/17/64)

Martin Landau

Written by Rod Serling
Producer: William Froug
Director: Richard Donner
Director of Photography: George T. Clemens
Music: stock

Cast:
Major Ivan Kuchenko: Martin Landau
Commissar Vassiloff: John vanDreelen
Boris: Robert Kelljan

"The cast of characters: a cat and a mouse. This is the latter, the intended victim who may or may not know that he is to die, be it by butchery or ballet. His name is Major Ivan Kuchenko. He has, if events go according to certain plans, perhaps three or four more hours of living. But an ignorance shared by both himself and his executioner is of the fact that both of them have taken a first step into the Twilight Zone."

Major Kuchenko, a defector from the Eastern bloc, waits in a hotel room in a neutral country for passage to the West. Commissar Vassiloff is assigned to kill him, but he intends to do it with an artistry approaching that of a ballet. He visits Kuchenko and knocks him out with a glass of drugged wine. When Kuchenko regains consciousness, a tape recording informs him that Vassiloff has planted a bomb in the room. If Kuchenko finds it and disarms it within three hours, he is free to go. If he triggers the bomb, it will explode—and if he stops searching, turns out the light or tries to bolt from the room, Vassiloff's assistant Boris will shoot him from a room across an alley. Frantically, Kuchenko searches for the bomb—without result. In reality, the bomb is in the telephone, and it will explode if Kuchenko picks up the receiver after it rings. Vassiloff dials Kuchenko's number. Kuchenko reaches for it, stops, then runs out the door, ducking a spray of bullets. Later, Vassiloff and Boris stand in Kuchenko's room, speculating on *how* he guessed the bomb's location. Suddenly, the phone rings. Without thinking, Boris picks it up—and detonates the bomb. On the other end is Major Kuchenko, calling from the airport and certain that, although no one spoke, he *reached* his party.

"Major Ivan Kuchenko, on his way west, on his way to freedom, a freedom bought and paid for by a most stunning ingenuity. And exit one Commissar Vassiloff, who forgot that there are two sides to an argument—and two parties on the line. This has been the Twilight Zone."

"The Jeopardy Room" is a gripping little political thriller, acted with intensity by John vanDreelen and Martin Landau (last seen in "Mr. Denton on Doomsday"). Like Serling's previous "The Silence," this has no fantasy element in it at all; nonetheless, the battle of wits between predator and prey is fascinating.

The major weakness of "The Jeopardy Room" is in its finale. It is simply preposterous that a Soviet assassin would knowingly enter a room containing a live bomb which he himself planted, after he has *seen* his intended victim escape. This is done merely so his none-too-bright assistant can accidentally set it off, killing both of them and providing the piece with a happy ending.

"MR. GARRITY AND THE GRAVES" (5/8/64)

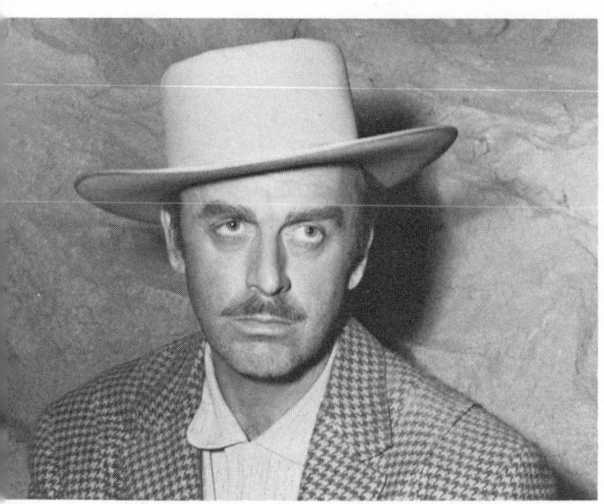
John Dehner

Written by Rod Serling
Based on an unpublished story by Mike Korologos
Producer: William Froug
Director: Ted Post
Director of Photography: George T. Clemens
Music: Tommy Morgan

Cast:
Jared Garrity: John Dehner
Gooberman: J. Pat O'Malley
Jensen: Stanley Adams
Lapham: Percy Helton
Sheriff Gilchrist: Norman Leavitt
Man: Patrick O'Moore
Lightning Peterson: John Cliff
Ace: John Mitchum
Zelda Gooberman: Kate Murtagh

"Introducing Mr. Jared Garrity, a gentleman of commerce, who in the latter half of the nineteenth century plied his trade in the wild and wooly hinterlands of the American West. And Mr. Garrity, if one can believe him, is a resurrecter of the dead—which, on the face of it, certainly sounds like the bull is off the nickel. But to the scoffers amongst you, and you ladies and gentlemen from Missouri, don't laugh this one off entirely, at least until you've seen a sample of Mr. Garrity's wares, and an example of his services. The place is Happiness, Arizona, the time about 1890. And you and I have just entered a saloon where the bar whiskey is brewed, bottled and delivered from the Twilight Zone."

After bringing back to life a dog run over by a wagon, Garrity promises to resurrect, at midnight, all 128 of the town's dead—all but one of whom died by violence. As the hour draws near, the townsfolk grow apprehensive at the prospect of the deceased returning, notably the sheriff, who ambushed an unarmed gunman; the barkeep, who shot his no-good brother in the back; and the town drunk, whose 247-pound wife broke his arm *six* times before she died. Garrity agrees to reverse the resurrection—for a price. The townsfolk pay him off handsomely. Much richer, Garrity leaves Happiness, but not before retrieving his dog *and* the man who supposedly ran it over—both Garrity's accomplices in a most imaginative con game. But as they pass the cemetery, they fail to notice that the dead *have* risen, appreciative of Garrity's ability—and extremely eager to get back into town.

"Exit Mr. Garrity, a would-be charlatan, a make-believe con man and a sad misjudger of his own talents. Respectfully submitted from an empty cemetery on a dark hillside that is one of the slopes leading to the Twilight Zone."

The best of Serling's final episodes was "Mr. Garrity and the Graves." John Dehner is marvelously dry as a con man in the Old West and there is a good deal of humor as he goes about his business in the town of Happiness, Arizona, with 128 dead, all but one victims of violence ("That was my dear wife Zelda, rest her soul," the town drunk explains, "a fine, healthy, strapping woman of 247 pounds—but not unattractive, mind you"). But even here there is a sloppiness of conception. For instance, when Garrity reveals that those with him in the saloon will have to pay him to *not* resurrect their less-than-dearly departed, everyone, including the town drunk, has between five hundred and twelve hundred dollars on their person. Clearly, this was intended as an expedient to keep the plot moving along as quickly as possible, but it is just not plausible.

Then there is the matter of Garrity's accomplice, who impersonates the barkeep's dead brother and limps slowly down the town's foggy, moonlit dirt road. The instant that the bartender coughs up Garrity's requested *un*resurrecting fee, the man disappears, right in front of the astounded townsfolk's—and our—eyes. What's never explained, though, is just how the fellow accomplished this seemingly-supernatural trick.

"NINETY YEARS WITHOUT SLUMBERING" (12/20/63)

Carolyn Kearney and Ed Wynn

Written by Richard deRoy
Based on an unpublished story by George Clayton Johnson
Producer: William Froug
Director: Roger Kay
Director of Photography: Robert W. Pittack
Music: Bernard Herrmann

Cast:
Sam Forstmann: Ed Wynn
Marnie Kirk: Carolyn Kearney
Doug Kirk: James Callahan
Dr. Mel Avery: William Sargent
Carol Chase: Carol Byron
Mover #1: Dick Wilson
Mover #2: Chuck Hicks
Policeman: John Pickard

"Each man measures his time; some with hope, some with joy, some with fear. But Sam Forstmann measures his *alotted time by a grandfather's clock, a unique mechanism whose pendulum swings between life and death, a very special clock that keeps a special kind of time—in the Twilight Zone."*

Although he is sent to a psychiatrist, Sam Forstmann remains unshakable in his conviction that when the grandfather clock he has owned all his life comes to a stop, he will die. Nevertheless, in order to appease his granddaughter Marnie and her husband Doug, he sells the clock to their neighbor Carl, with the proviso that he can make regular maintenance visits. But when Carol and her husband leave on vacation, the clock begins to wind down. On the verge of hysteria, Sam tries to break into the house in order to wind it, only to be stopped by the police. Back home in his bed, he is resigned to the fact that he will die momentarily when the clock stops. The pendulum slows, then is still. Sam's spirit leaves his body, informing him it's time to depart. But Sam has other ideas. He doesn't believe that nonsense about the clock—*he's* been to a psychiatrist! The spirit—no more than a figment of Sam's imagination—disappears. Sam has triumphed over himself. Or, as he tells Marnie, "When that clock died, *I* was born again."

"Clocks are made by men, God creates time. No man can prolong his allotted hours, he can only live them to the fullest—in this world or in the Twilight Zone."

While Bert Granet was still producer, George Clayton Johnson submitted a story entitled "The Grandfather Clock." He was given the go-ahead and enlarged it to a full teleplay with the title "Tick of Time." In the sensitively written original, Johnson once again returned to the themes of old age and fear of death. An old man who lives with his pregnant granddaughter and her husband believes he will die if his grandfather clock ever stops. Pressured by the young people to get rid of the clock, the old man gives it to an antique dealer. But later, he changes his mind and tries to struggle the huge clock home in a child's wagon with the assistance of a neighborhood boy. It is an exhausting and hazardous ordeal, made doubly so by the knowledge that a grandfather clock, in order to keep ticking, must remain absolutely upright. When the old man tries to lift the clock out of the wagon, it falls on top of him. It stops ticking and he dies. Several bystanders set the clock upright. At the same moment that it begins to tick again, the man's granddaughter gives birth to her baby. The cycle begins anew.

By the time this script was done, William Froug had taken over. Serling told Froug of the script and, as Froug recalls, "asked me to meet with

[Johnson] and, as politely as possible, tell him we were not going to use [it]." Johnson was paid and Richard deRoy hired to revamp the script. Sadly, little was gained and much was lost.

In the finished episode, "Ninety Years Without Slumbering," both the family situation and the central obsession remain the same. Although he is sent to a psychiatrist, Sam Forstmann remains unshakable in his conviction that his mortality is inextricably intertwined with that of his clock. Back home in his bed, he is resigned to the fact that he will die momentarily when the clock stops. "It is better this way," he says. "It has to come sometime, and I want it to come for me here."

Then, something extremely peculiar happens. Sam's spirit leaves his body and begins to beckon him to depart:

SPIRIT: . . . Your time has come, Sam. After all, you *are* seventy-six.

SAM: Don't give me that "spirit of seventy-six" stuff. And who says it's my time to go?

SPIRIT: Have you forgotten what your father told you and your grandfather?

SAM: About what?

SPIRIT: Didn't they always tell you that when the clock winds down you'll die?

SAM: Yes, and you know something? I used to believe that stuff!

SPIRIT: Well, you should have. They told you often enough.

SAM: But that's silly, don't you know that? I do. I've been to a psychiatrist!

SPIRIT: So what?

SAM: So he told me he didn't think I needed the clock—and he didn't think I was crazy! And you know something? *He* was right and *we're* wrong.

Imagine, Sam Forstmann has staunchly held to his belief in the face of all logic to the contrary, trumpeted it to a psychiatrist, even attempted breaking-and-entering in order to keep the clock ticking—and what does he do at the last possible moment? Blithely talk himself out of his most strongly held belief of over seventy years. As Forstmann, Ed Wynn is about as disarming and lovable as one could hope for, but not even he can sell *this* bill of goods.

Not at all happy about all this is George Clayton Johnson, who rightly views it as an inept alteration of something he originated. "It makes the plot trivial. If you're going to get involved in his problems you've got to *believe* in his problems, and if *he* doesn't believe in them you feel cheated."

NEWCOMERS

Including "Ninety Years Without Slumbering," six episodes produced by William Froug—fully one-fourth his output—were written by newcomers to the series. As the results demonstrate, most of them just did not understand the form.

In previous seasons, virtually all the better episodes had running through them a sense of cosmic justice, of people getting their just deserts, often with a full helping of irony. The fantastic element that *was* the Twilight Zone was there for a reason: if the main character was a rotter, it would give him his comeuppance; if he was a decent sort it would give him a second chance, a magical opportunity to set his life right. On the rare occasion that someone inoffensive ended up badly (as in "Time Enough at Last"), there was a deliberate sense of tragedy. A moral code was being applied.

In the six episodes by the newcomers, such is not the case. Instead, there is a feeling of things gone tilt. Consequences are often unfairly meted out. Rather than a cosmos in which every action brings about an equal reaction, this is a universe ruled by chaos.

"CAESAR AND ME" (4/10/64)

Jackie Cooper

Written by A. T. Strassfield
Producer: William Froug
Director: Robert Butler
Director of Photography: George T. Clemens
Music: Richard Shores

Cast:
Jonathan West: Jackie Cooper
Susan: Susanne Cupito
Mrs. Cudahy: Sarah Selby
Mr. Smiles: Olan Soule
Pawnbroker: Stafford Repp
Watchman: Sidney Marion
Detective: Don Gazzaniga
Mr. Miller: Ken Konopka

"Jonathan West, ventriloquist, a master of voice manipulation. A man late of Ireland, with a talent for putting words into other people's mouths. In this case, the other person is a dummy, aptly named Caesar, a small splinter with large ideas, a wooden tyrant with a mind and a voice of his own, who is about to talk Jonathan West into the Twilight Zone."

Unable to get bookings because his act just isn't funny, West has no money to pay for food or rent. After bombing out at an employment agency, West follows Little Caesar's directions and commits several petty burglaries. During a theater robbery, West is spotted by a night watchman. His landlady's niece Susan, a vicious brat, overhears him discussing the bungled job with Caesar and calls the police. West is hauled off to jail, but Little Caesar—being viewed as merely inanimate wood—gets away scot-free. Caesar tells Susan he likes her style and suggests they team up. They'll go to New York—but first they'll have to get rid of her aunt.

"Little girl and a wooden doll, a lethal dummy in the shape of a man. But everybody knows dummies can't talk—unless, of course, they learn their vocabulary in the Twilight Zone."

The basic theme of "Caesar and Me" had been done many times before, including in Serling's "The Dummy." "The Dummy," however, focuses on a specific dramatic issue: a battle of wills between an anthropomorphized piece of wood and a ventriloquist whose tenuous hold on reality is rapidly slipping. "Caesar and Me" is merely pointless. The mild-mannered ventriloquist is framed by his dummy (with the aid of the vicious little girl) and taken away by the cops. Little Caesar, certainly the villain of the piece, never pays for his deeds, and the hapless ventriloquist gets much worse than he deserves. It would be tragic were it not for the fact that the ventriloquist is such a dull-witted patsy, so utterly unable to defend himself, that he elicits little sympathy.

William Froug reveals one distinction peculiar to this episode. Credited to A. T. Strassfield, it is the only episode of the series scripted by a woman. "Adele T. Strassfield was actually my secretary," he explains. "She was an exceptionally bright woman, and she said to me, 'I can show you I'm a writer. I want to write a *Twilight Zone*.' So she came up with a notion. She'd never written a script before and has never written one since. In effect, I sort of wrote it with her. I wanted her to have the credit, and she got a great thrill out of it."

"FROM AGNES—WITH LOVE" (2/14/64)

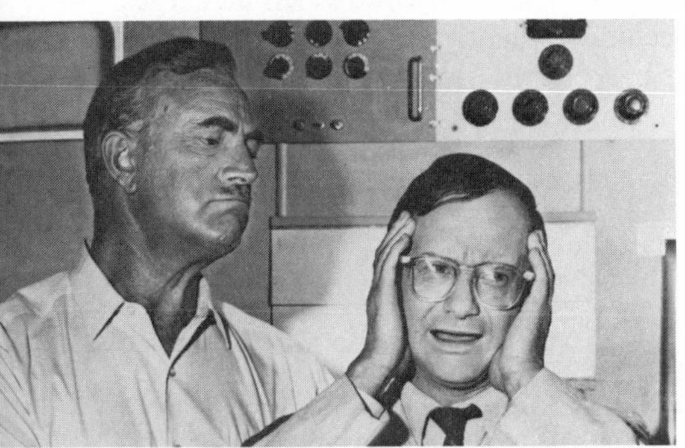

Raymond Bailey and Wally Cox

Written by Bernard C. Shoenfeld
Producer: William Froug
Director: Richard Donner
Director of Photography:
George T. Clemens
Music: Van Cleave

Cast:
James Elwood: Wally Cox
Millie: Sue Randall
Walter Holmes: Ralph Taeger
Supervisor: Raymond Bailey
Fred Danziger: Don Keefer
Secretary: Nan Peterson
Assistant: Byron Kane

"James Elwood, master programmer, in charge of Mark 502–741, commonly known as 'Agnes,' the world's most advanced electronic computer. Machines are made by men for man's benefit and progress, but when man ceases to control the products of his ingenuity and imagination he not only risks losing the benefit, *but he takes a long and unpredictable step into—the Twilight Zone."*

When Agnes breaks down, Elwood is called in to replace Fred Danziger, a programmer whose mind has cracked trying to deal with Agnes. All goes smoothly until Elwood asks Millie, a pretty secretary, for a date—and Agnes begins to make suggestions. On the machine's advice, he takes Millie to his apartment, which ends in Millie storming out. Then—again on Agnes's advice—he introduces her to Walter Holmes, a dashing co-worker who sweeps her off her feet. Elwood demands to know why Agnes has sabotaged his relationship with Millie. He gets a shocking answer: Agnes is in love with him! Elwood can't accept this; his mind snaps. Next morning, Walter Holmes is brought in as his replacement. Laughing insanely, Elwood tells him he doesn't stand a chance against Agnes, the computerized *femme fatale.*

"Advice to all future male scientists: be sure you understand the opposite sex, especially if you intend being a computer expert. Otherwise, you may find yourself, like poor Elwood, defeated by a jealous machine, a most dangerous sort of female, whose victims are forever banished—to the Twilight Zone."

The problem in "From Agnes—With Love" lies with the main character. James Elwood is enormously inept and unforgivably dense. When he takes his date back to his apartment, he reads to her from a book of

Einstein. When she turns off the light he says, "Millie, I can't read this chapter to you without proper lighting." Upon the advice of Agnes, he introduces her to a handsome playboy and then is amazed when he barges in on them and finds they've become romantically involved. Elwood doesn't need a computer to ruin his life; clearly, he's capable of doing it on his own.

"WHAT'S IN THE BOX" (3/13/64)

Joan Blondell

Written by Martin M. Goldsmith
Producer: William Froug
Director: Richard L. Bare
Director of Photography: George T. Clemens
Music: stock

Cast:
Joe Britt: William Demarest
Phyllis Britt: Joan Blondell
TV Repairman: Sterling Holloway
Dr. Saltman: Herbert Lytton
Woman: Sandra Gould
Judge: Howard Wright
Russian Duke: John L. Sullivan
Panther Man: Ted Christy
Car Salesman: Ron Stokes
Prosecutor: Douglas Bank
Announcer: Tony Miller

"Portrait of a TV fan. Name: Joe Britt. Occupation: cab driver. Tonight, Mr. Britt is going to watch 'a really big show,' something special for the cabbie who's seen everything. Joe Britt doesn't know it, but his flag is down and his meter's running and he's in high gear—on his way to the Twilight Zone."

After loudmouth Britt insults a TV repairman working on his set, the man abruptly closes up the television and says that it's fixed—for free. Britt thinks nothing of this until he sees that the set is able to pick up channel ten—something it's never done before—and that the screen shows Joe in the company of his mistress! Joe is desperate that his shrewish wife Phyllis not see this. Things rapidly get worse, however; the TV now shows a scene in which Joe argues with Phyllis and punches her through their apartment window to her death—a scene which only Joe seems able to see and hear. Frantic to avoid this tragedy, Joe admits his past adultery and begs Phyllis to forgive him. This only serves to infuriate her; the two argue and Joe, enraged, punches Phyllis through the window. As the police lead him away, the repairman appears. "Fix your set okay, mister?" he asks Joe. "You *will* recommend my service, won't you?"

"The next time your TV set is on the blink, when you're in the need of a first-rate repairman, may we suggest our own specialist? Factory-trained, prompt, honest, twenty-four-hour service. You won't find him in the phone book, but his office is conveniently located—in the Twilight Zone."

"Marty Goldsmith had written a *Playhouse 90* for me years before," says William Froug, "so I sought him out. He had written a number of movies and wasn't that anxious to work—still isn't, really. But I knew he was just a wonderful writer and I said, 'Please, write a *Twilight Zone.*' And he came up with this notion of the guy looking at the boob tube and seeing his own extramarital activities and trying to turn it off before his wife could see it."

Martin M. Goldsmith's "What's in the Box" has a marvelous cast of old-time actors (William Demarest, Joan Blondell, Sterling Holloway), but that's not enough to carry the show. The problem lies with the two main characters.

Britt and his wife are a loudmouthed, bickering couple, but neither of them deserves to die. Had Britt's wife forgiven him, then the show would have had some moral to it. The fantasy element would have allowed an unhappy couple a second chance, it would have been there for a reason. As it is, one is left with a tremendous sense of purposelessness, of things happening with no object in mind.

Goldsmith himself is no fan of the episode. "I didn't like it," he says. "It lacked all subtlety the way it was done. I think Joan Blondell and William Demarest overplayed it. It was just too broad."

"THE ENCOUNTER" (5/1/64)

Neville Brand

Written by Martin M. Goldsmith
Producer: William Froug
Director: Robert Butler
Director of Photography: George T. Clemens
Music: stock

Cast:
Fenton: Neville Brand
Taro: George Takei

"Two men alone in an attic: a young Japanese-American and a seasoned veteran of yesterday's war. It's twenty-odd years since Pearl Harbor, but two

ancient opponents are moving into position for a battle in an attic crammed with skeletons—souvenirs, mementoes, old uniforms and rusted medals—ghosts from the dim reaches of the past that will lead us into . . . the Twilight Zone."

Fenton, a middle-aged World War II veteran, is rummaging around in his cluttered attic when young gardener Arthur Takamuri appears, saying he'd heard from a neighbor that Fenton needs his lawn trimmed. Fenton offers him a beer, then says he'll pay him to help clean up the attic. Arthur, whose real name is Taro, is extremely sensitive about his Japanese-American heritage, and Fenton, a bigot, enjoys needling him with racist slurs. Alone in the attic for a moment, Taro picks up a samurai sword Fenton claims to have taken off a Japanese officer in battle, a weapon bearing the inscription "The Sword Will Avenge Me"—and is astounded to hear himself say he's going to kill Fenton! After some strained conversation, Fenton begins to reminisce about the war, reliving it as he tells it. Taro is drawn into the fantasy and—believing himself a Japanese soldier—raises the sword to decapitate Fenton. Just in time, he comes to his senses. He then has a sudden realization: Fenton *lied* about the sword; he murdered a surrendering enemy officer, then took the sword off the body. Made uncomfortable by this knowledge, Taro tries to leave, but finds the attic door—which has *no* lock—inexplicably stuck; the two of them are trapped together. Taro then tells of *his* past, at first saying that his American-born father, a construction worker who built the docks at Pearl Harbor, was a hero who died trying to warn sailors during the Japanese attack. But soon the truth comes out: his father was actually a *traitor* who signalled the enemy planes where to drop their bombs. Fenton then makes a revelation of his own: in the last week, he's lost both his job and his wife as a result of his heavy drinking; he has nothing left in him but hatred and he *wants* Taro to kill him. He lunges at Taro. There's a scuffle, and Fenton falls on the sword and dies. Overwhelmed by his tremendous guilt, Taro grabs up the sword, yells "Banzai!" and leaps out the attic window to his death . . . after which the attic door gently slides open.

"Two men in an attic, locked in mortal embrace. Their common bond and their common enemy: guilt. A disease all too prevalent among men, both in and out of the Twilight Zone."

Pleased with "What's in the Box," William Froug again contacted Martin Goldsmith. "He asked me to do another one, and I had an idea but it wasn't really a *Twilight Zone* idea," says Goldsmith. "I had been playing with the idea of two people confronting each other over an issue that's long dead and really has nothing to do with either one of them. In this particular thing there's this aging Marine and this young Japanese gardener. I didn't know quite what I was going to do with this whole idea until Froug mentioned *Twilight Zone* and I said, "Well, why not?"

Cast in "The Encounter" were Neville Brand, the fourth-most-decorated U.S. Army soldier of World War II, and George Takei, later to play Lt. Sulu in *Star Trek*.

Goldsmith recalls that troubles began when the director read the script. "He was a young guy and he was quite unhappy about the whole thing. He didn't like it, he didn't understand it. He told Froug that he would have great difficulty directing it. So I said to Froug, 'Look, you're going to need a director. *I'll* direct it.' He said, 'No, no, we have to pay this guy whether he does the job or not. Serling wouldn't hear of it.' "

Goldsmith was out of the country when "The Encounter" aired, so he never saw it. But he notes, "I started getting strange letters from people who *had* seen it. They saw a lot of existentialism in it and things of that nature."

Like "Miniature," "A Short Drink From a Certain Fountain" and "Sounds and Silences," "The Encounter" is not in syndication. The reasons for this are not clear. Very possibly, CBS received complaints from Japanese-Americans. The ex-Marine mouths a number of tirades against the Japanese and Japanese-Americans, filled with a variety of racial epithets. Also, there's the matter of the private guilts the characters carry. The Marine killed a Japanese officer who had already surrendered. But the young gardener's guilt stems, not from an action of his, but from one of his father: "I grew up in Honolulu.... My father and mother lived in Hawaii all their lives. My father worked for the Navy as a civilian.... He helped build the docks at Pearl. He was foreman of a construction gang.... He signalled the planes. He showed them where to drop the bombs!.... My old man was a traitor!"

In reality, there was no Japanese-American traitor at Pearl Harbor guiding the enemy planes. In fact, there is no case of sabotage by a Japanese-American during all of World War II. The suggestion of such an action—even in a fictional context—could easily have brought protests.

"COME WANDER WITH ME" (5/22/64)

Gary Crosby

Written by Anthony Wilson
Producer: William Froug
Director: Richard Donner
Director of Photography: Fred Mandl
Music: Jeff Alexander

Cast:
Floyd Burney: Gary Crosby
Mary Rachel: Bonnie Beecher
Billy Rayford: John Bolt
Old Man: Hank Patterson

"Mr. Floyd Burney, a gentleman songster in search of song, is about to answer the age-old question of whether a man can be in two places at the same time. As far as his folk song is concerned, we can assure Mr. Burney he'll find everything he's looking for, although the lyrics may not be all to his liking. But that's sometimes the case—when the words and music are recorded in the Twilight Zone."

Floyd Burney, "the Rockabilly Boy," journeys to the backwoods in search of authentic folk songs to appropriate. Questioning an old man in a store filled with musical instruments, he hears someone humming a haunting ballad. Searching outside, he fails to notice a tombstone with *his* name on it, but he *does* notice the singer: shy but lovely Mary Rachel. Although she is betrothed to Billy Rayford, Floyd romances her in order to convince her to sing her song into his tape recorder. Suddenly, Billy appears, carrying a rifle and telling Floyd that he and his brothers know what to do with *him.* But when Billy is momentarily distracted, Floyd hits him with a guitar, killing him. The tape recorder begins to play back Mary Rachel's song—but now there's a lyric about Floyd's murder of Billy! Mary Rachel pleads with Floyd not to run, that the Rayford Brothers will catch him *again,* as they always have before. Floyd doesn't know what she's talking about, and he's horrified to see that she is now inexplicably dressed in mourning garb. Hysterical, he rushes back to the music store. There, the old man refuses to help him; Floyd strikes him down. But by then the Rayford Brothers have arrived—and they *do* know what to do with him.

"In retrospect, it may be said of Mr. Floyd Burney that he achieved that final dream of the performer: eternal top-name billing, not on the fleeting billboards of the entertainment world, but forever recorded among the folk songs of the Twilight Zone."

"Come Wander With Me," by Anthony Wilson (creator of *Land of the Giants* and *The Invaders,* and the man who developed *Planet of the Apes* for television), has various twists and turns that render it virtually incoherent. At the beginning, Burney walks past a grave reading "Floyd Burney/The Wandering Man"—we see it again at the end of the show. There are *two* Mary Rachels seen throughout: one dressed in everyday clothes, the other in black mourning garb. The song she sings to Burney predicts events to come. Repeatedly, when events occur, Mary Rachel explains that they happen in that way because they "*always* happen that way." And when Burney contemplates flight in order to avoid the Rayfords' vengeance, she pleads, "If you run they'll catch you. You know that. . . . Maybe if you didn't run this time, if I hid you, maybe it could be different." Naturally, Burney disregards this, and flees—to his death.

Obviously, what all these obscure clues are meant to indicate is that this story is an eternal cycle. What's more, Mary Rachel *understands* what is going on—unlike Burney she remembers going through all of it before—but she is unable to alter events.

What is not at all clear is *why* this is a cycle. What exactly are we witnessing? Indeed, is there *any* point to it?

" 'Come Wander With Me' was too soft, and Dick Donner and I knew it," says William Froug. "It was a script that read good but, Jesus, it just didn't work. I wouldn't do it today."

Froug's choice of script wasn't the only curiosity to be found in the show. He recalls an incident during the casting of Mary Rachel: "One of the people I interviewed was this nervous, frightened little girl whose hands shook and who was covered with sweat, and I said, 'She'll *never* make it.' Her name was Liza Minnelli. And *I* chose Bonnie Beecher, and we all know what became of Bonnie Beecher!

"I'll never forget Liza Minnelli sitting there and her agent saying, 'This girl can really sing.' I said, 'I'm sure she can,' but I thought, Oh, she is so nervous! She's scared out of her mind. To picture her as a hillbilly singer: no way. And I must tell you—and this is the truth—at the time, I sat there thinking, Well, I'll probably kick myself for this but I can't see this girl playing the part—but she'll probably be a big star. I still don't regret it, but it was really classic stupidity."

"AN OCCURRENCE AT OWL CREEK BRIDGE" (2/28/64)

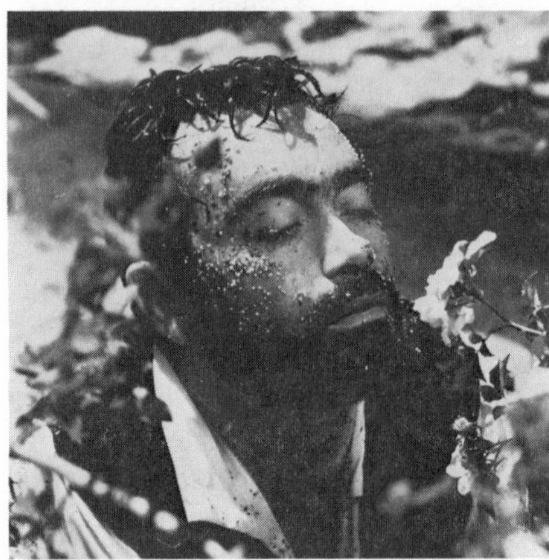

Roger Jacquet

Written and Directed by Robert Enrico
Based on the short story "An Occurrence at Owl Creek Bridge" by Ambrose Bierce
Producer: Marcel Ichac and Paul de Roubaix (*Twilight Zone* opening sequence produced by William Froug)
Director of Photography: Jean Boffety
Music: Henri Lanoe

Cast:
Confederate Spy: Roger Jacquet with Anne Cornaly, Anker Larsen, Stephane Fey, Jean-François Zeller, Pierre Danny and Louis Adelin

"Tonight a presentation so special and unique that, for the first time in the five years we've been presenting The Twilight Zone, *we're offering a film shot in France by others. Winner of the Cannes Film Festival of 1962, as well as other international awards, here is a haunting study of the incredible, from the past master of the incredible, Ambrose Bierce. Here is the French production of 'An Occurrence at Owl Creek Bridge.'"*

It is the American Civil War. Union soldiers stand on a railroad bridge, preparing to execute a Confederate spy. They set a plank out from the bridge, stand the man upon it, make the noose tight around his neck. The plank is pulled out from under him, he falls through space—but miraculously, the rope breaks! Dodging bullets, the man swims for his life. Reaching the shore, he manages to evade the enemy troops. He has one goal in mind: to get *home*. Struggling over the terrain, he eventually reaches his plantation. His wife—beautifully dressed, every hair in place, seemingly untouched by war—comes running toward him. But as her hands go round his neck, he seizes up. In an instant, he is back at Owl Creek Bridge, hanging by his neck—and very much dead.

"An occurrence at Owl Creek Bridge—in two forms, as it was dreamed, and as it was lived and died. This is the stuff of fantasy, the thread of imagination . . . the ingredients of the Twilight Zone."

With thirty-five episodes completed and one left to go, William Froug found *Twilight Zone* significantly over budget. The solution he came up with was unique.

Some time previously, he had seen *An Occurrence at Owl Creek Bridge*, a French film that had won first prize for short subjects at the 1962 Cannes Film Festival. Based on the story by Ambrose Bierce, it told the story of a condemned Confederate spy who, during the instant that he's falling before the rope breaks his neck, imagines an involved and successful escape.

"It was almost entirely silent," Froug recalls of the film. "There were maybe a half-dozen lines in it, and there was one brief ballad—in English, of all things. CBS was very reluctant—'A French film on television? Who ever heard of such a thing?'—but I convinced them, because we bought all TV rights for $10,000. With that one airing, we immediately took care of the whole year's overage. It brought us out at the end of the year under budget."

The film was shortened by several minutes and an introduction by Serling was added. "An Occurrence at Owl Creek Bridge" was aired February 28, 1964, and repeated September 11, 1964. (It was shown as a *Twilight Zone* episode only these two times and was not included in subsequent syndication packages.) A coup for the show, it was well-received. *Variety*'s reaction was typical: "This French short film, which has been nominated for an Oscar, undoubtedly received more exposure than any such candidate in Oscar history when aired on Rod Serling's *Twilight Zone* Friday. A fascinating and eerie Ambrose Bierce tale . . . it fits perfectly into the *Zone* format."

Subsequently, the film won its Oscar—another first for *Twilight Zone*.

At the end of January, 1964, CBS announced its fall schedule. *Twilight Zone* was not included.

"For one reason or another, Jim Aubrey [then president of CBS] decided he was sick of the show," says William Froug. "He claimed that it was too far over budget and that the ratings weren't good enough." In truth, *Twilight Zone* was still rating well, although not in the top ten, and "An Occurrence at Owl Creek Bridge" had put the show back under budget.

Nevertheless, on February 5, *Daily Variety* reported that Serling considered the odds of a sixth season "unlikely." Serling: "I decided to cancel the network."

Serling's agent, Ted Ashley, felt that since the show's ratings weren't bad he might be able to sell it to a rival network. NBC passed, but Tom Moore, president of ABC, was interested. Since CBS had rights to the title *Twilight Zone,* Moore proposed a new name for the show: *Witches, Warlocks, and*

Werewolves (taken from *Rod Serling's Triple W: Witches, Warlocks, and Werewolves,* a 1963 paperback anthology edited by Serling).

This did *not* sit well with Serling. On March 11, he submitted a proposal for a series more to his liking. It began:

> ROD SERLING'S WAX MUSEUM
>
> We would open the series in the following manner:
>
> A helicopter shot of Heart Island with a series of slow dissolves to a closer angle of Boldt Castle. The latter is the "haunted house" of the world. It is a vast multi-spired stone mausoleum with hundreds of bare rooms (its construction was stopped three quarters of the way through completion and never recommenced). The camera moves closer to the Castle in a series of dissolves until finally we're inside its gigantic echoey front hall. Lining the long stairway are a series of shrouded figures that extend into the darkness. Down the steps walks Serling past these figures and ultimately past the lens of the camera to a vantage point (now we are on a stet Metro set) where stands another shrouded figure. Serling removes the wrapping and we are looking at a wax figure of that particular episode's leading character.
>
> SERLING: A hearty welcome to my wax museum. For your entertainment and edification we offer you stories of the weird, the wild and the wondrous; stories that are told to the accompaniment of distant banging shutters, an invisible creaking door, an errant wailing wind that comes from the dark outside. These are stories that involve the citizenry of the night. In short, this museum is devoted to . . . goose flesh, bristled hair and dry mouths.
>
> *(He moves over to the wax figure now uncovered)*
>
> Now this gentleman is . . .
>
> NOW SERLING LAUNCHES INTO A BRIEF BACKGROUND COMMENT ABOUT TONIGHT'S EPISODE)

Moore, however, was still locked-in to his "Triple W" concept. On March 18, the two men met. Things apparently did not go well, for the next day Serling told *Daily Variety* that Moore "seems to prefer weekly ghouls, and we have what appears to be a considerable difference of opinion. I don't mind my show being supernatural, but I don't want to be hooked into a graveyard every week." He added that he thought Moore's conception of the series would result in "walking dead and maggots . . . I don't think TV can sustain C-pictures every week."

The next day, Moore, after reading Serling's comments, told the papers (with apparently no pun intended), "We have buried the project."

Twilight Zone had reached the end. After five years and 156 episodes—ninety-two of them scripts by Serling—Cayuga Productions closed its doors.

In 1962, when it looked like *The Twilight Zone* was about to be cancelled, Serling summed up his participation for a newspaper article. He said, "We had some real turkeys, some fair ones, and some shows I'm really proud to have been a part of. I can walk away from this series unbowed."

Two years later, his words were just as appropriate.

VIII / AFTER THE TWILIGHT ZONE

Over the eleven years following the demise of *The Twilight Zone*, Rod Serling was a busy man.

Shortly after the series went off network, Serling sold his rights to CBS for a considerable lump sum. "One reason that my husband ultimately sold out," notes Carol Serling, "was that the show often went over budget and CBS said they would never recoup the costs. Needless to say, they have, many, many times."

Even more regrettable to Serling was having to watch what was done to

Props set up at Cayuga Productions' farewell party, following the cancellation of *Twilight Zone*.

Twilight Zone in syndication. Catching "Walking Distance" on a local station, he commented, "You wouldn't recognize what series it was. Full scenes were deleted. It looked like a long, protracted commercial separated by fragmentary moments of indistinct drama."

Serling, however, didn't have time to dwell on *Twilight Zone*. In 1964 he won his sixth Emmy, for "It's Mental Work," an episode of *Bob Hope Presents The Chrysler Theatre* starring Lee J. Cobb as the owner of a bar who has a heart attack, Harry Guardino as a bartender and Gena Rowlands as a cocktail waitress.

In 1965, Serling embarked on another series. *The Loner,* an extremely nonconformist Western, starring Lloyd Bridges as a former Union cavalry officer. With its emphasis on character and motivation rather than gunplay, the series was generally well-received by the critics, who particularly applauded Serling's unconventional scripts.

Not so pleased were the higher-ups at CBS, and Serling began to get pressure from above to tailor *The Loner* to the measure of Westerns that had gone before it. Serling went to the newspapers, charging that the CBS vice president in charge of programming had demanded he put in more violence. In response, the V.P. countered that he had meant "action"—"chases, running gun battles, runaway stagecoaches, etc."

Serling was not happy with the end product. "Some weekends I wish Friday would move into Sunday and skip Saturday so there wouldn't be any *Loner,*" he said. Halfway through the season, *The Loner* was cancelled.

In the years that followed, Serling was involved in an amazing variety of projects. He served a two-year term as President of the National Academy of Television Arts and Sciences, overseeing the 1965 and 1966 Emmy Awards. A popular celebrity, in 1969 he presided over the game show *The Liar's Club;* in 1970 he served as host for *Rod Serling's Wonderful World of . . . ,* a local Los Angeles program examining such human failings as prejudice, gluttony, snobbery and so forth; and in 1973 his mellifluous voice could be heard presenting *Zero Hour,* a syndicated dramatic radio show. In addition, he narrated the Jacques Cousteau specials, as well as a number of programs dealing with ancient astronauts, UFOs and similar speculative subjects. He acted as spokesman for dozens of products on television and radio.

And, of course, there was the writing: in 1968, "Certain Honorable Men," a political drama starring Van Heflin, Peter Fonda, Pat Hingle and Will Geer; in 1969, the debut script of *The New People,* a short-lived ABC TV series; in 1970, "A Storm in Summer" on *Hallmark Hall of Fame,* detailing the confrontation between an elderly Jewish delicatessen owner (Peter Ustinov) and a black youth (N'Gai Dixon, son of Ivan Dixon). Although "A Storm in Summer" received extremely mixed notices, it won Emmys for Ustinov's performance and as best dramatic program.

There were also a number of screenplay adaptations, including *Planet of the Apes* (1967), based on the novel by Pierre Boulle. Serling wrote the first three drafts of the script which, like the book, depicted a technologically-developed ape society. When it was decided that this would be too expensive to produce, Michael Wilson was hired to rewrite Serling's script to present a more primitive simian world. Wilson and Serling shared on-screen credit.

Serling's work was in evidence on big screens and little screens. His face and voice were everywhere. But he was far from satisfied.

"Rod was much less than a happy and contented man in the last ten years of his life, I think there's little doubt of that," says his close friend, producer Dick Berg. "His own self-esteem had deteriorated. I don't think this depressed him, but I do think it made him less comfortable here and somewhat disenchanted with the business. Because you must understand that he enjoyed an exalted status in those first three to five years, it was a rarefied situation. Serling and Chayefsky were the two major names from the golden era of television. And to move from that to becoming a member of the army of working journeymen writers was a great comedown. In Hollywood, he was a guy taking assignments. Quite frustrating, particularly for a man of such spirit."

Serling was a man being pulled in many different directions, trying to fill many roles: serious writer, TV star, media commodity. Often, his decisions left him with ambiguous feelings, particularly regarding his work on commercials. "How could I turn those offers down?" he asked a reporter rhetorically. "I spend eleven months on a screenplay but get about the same money for a one-minute commercial."

Serling also had mixed feelings about his writing. Although still capable of skillful, incisive writing, he was aware that often his work fell well below his own standards—a fact he acknowledged with honesty and humor. "Every now and then, you write something that you think at the moment is quite adequate and then many years later you suddenly realize you have given birth to a turd," he once said.

Some things, however, could not be viewed with humor. On December 13, 1966, NBC aired *The Doomsday Flight,* a TV movie written by Serling. The plot concerned a mentally-disturbed former-airline mechanic (Edmond O'Brien) who plants a pressure bomb set to explode below 4,000 feet aboard a commercial airliner. Ultimately, the scheme is foiled when the plane's pilot (Van Johnson) lands the aircraft in Denver, which is situated at a height of 5,300 feet. To all initial appearances, the show was a tremendous success, gathering the second-highest rating of the 1966–67 season (surpassed only by the network showing of *The Bridge on the River Kwai*).

The first bomb threat came at 10:45 P.M., while the show was still on the air. In the days that followed, TWA, Eastern, American, Pan Am and Northwest Airlines all received similar threats. Within six days, the total rose to eight—and each of these had to be taken seriously.

Serling was devastated. "I wish to Christ I had written a stagecoach drama starring John Wayne instead," he told the papers. "I wish I'd never been born."

Fortunately, *The Doomsday Flight* was the low point for Serling. Other projects might disappoint him, but none would equal this for nightmarishness.

On November 8, 1969, NBC aired *Night Gallery,* a TV movie consisting of a trio of bizarre stories by Serling, two of which were adapted from his 1967 book *The Season to be Wary.* (These were *The Escape Route*, about a

Rod Serling on *Night Gallery*

former Nazi [played on the show by Richard Kiley] hiding out in Buenos Aires, and *Eyes*, about a wealthy blind woman [Joan Crawford] who ruthlessly tries to purchase another person's sight. *Eyes*, incidentally, marked the professional directorial debut of Steven Spielberg.) A pilot for a possible series, it was the highest-rated program of the evening. For his writing, Serling was awarded a special Edgar Allen Poe award by the Mystery Writers of America. NBC gave the show the go-ahead.

Rod Serling's Night Gallery, produced at Universal by Jack Laird, debuted during the 1970–71 season as a group of six episodes that rotated with three other series—*McCloud*, *The Psychiatrist*, and *San Francisco International*—under the umbrella title *Four-in-One*. Each episode consisted of several stories, interspersed with comedic vignettes—all with a supernatural bent. As he had on *Twilight Zone*, Serling acted as host and major contributor. In 1971, the series aired on its own, opposite *Mannix* on CBS. In 1972, its final season, *Night Gallery* was cut from an hour to a half hour.

In agreeing to do *Night Gallery*, Serling made a sizeable error in judgment. From the outset, he had no intention of having anything to do with the production end of the series (in 1969 he'd said, "There's not enough money in the world to take a guy over forty and make him go through that grind again—that is, at least not me"), but he did assume that the producers would defer to him in matters of policy, seeing as how the show *was* billed as *Rod Serling's Night Gallery*.

Such was not the case. Time and time again, the producers sacrificed quality for shock value. *Night Gallery* quickly became exactly what Serling had so desperately tried to avoid when he had rejected Tom Moore's *Witches, Warlocks, and Werewolves* proposal five years earlier. "On *Twilight Zone* I took the bows but I also took the brickbats, and properly, because when it was bad it was usually my fault," Serling said. "But when it was bad on *Gallery* I had nothing to do with it—yet my face was on it all the time . . ."

For all its problems, *Night Gallery* did have its occasional successes. In "The Dead Man," a chiller written and directed by *Twilight Zone*'s Douglas Heyes, a doctor (Carl Betz) fails to bring an experimental subject back from an induced state of rigor mortis only to discover, months later, the error in his methods—a bit too late for the now decaying (but ambulatory) corpse. In Serling's horrifying little tale, "The Doll," a British Empire officer (John Williams) must confront his young niece's particularly hideous—and murderous—doll. In "Green Fingers," adapted by Serling from the short story by R. C. Cook, a strong-willed old woman (Elsa Lanchester), proud of her gardening abilities and determined not to sell her property to a conscienceless industrialist (Cameron Mitchell), has her fingers hacked off by a thug but manages to plant them in her garden before bleeding to death—with terrifying results. In the end, Mitchell, thoroughly mad, his hair turned white, peers at the camera from out of the bushes and rasps, "You know what grows from little old ladies' fingers? . . . *Little old ladies!*" In "The Caterpillar," an effective and disgusting piece adapted by Serling from Oscar Cook's short story "Boomerang," a scoundrel (Laurence Harvey) plans to kill a beautiful woman's husband by using an "earwig"—an insect that will enter the man's ear and eat its way through his brain—but falls afoul of his own scheme. The conclusion is particularly grisly, as the villain, after miraculously surviving the agonizing ordeal of having the earwig journey across his entire head, discovers that the insect, a female, has laid its eggs in his brain!

Without doubt, *Night Gallery*'s high point came with its two Emmy nominations, both for thoughtful, original pieces by Serling. In "The Messiah of Mott Street," a nine-year-old boy seeks out the Messiah to aid his ailing, Jewish grandfather (Edward G. Robinson). In "They're Tearing Down Tim Riley's Bar," a lonely widower (William Windom, in a brilliant performance), on the twenty-fifth anniversary of his association with a plastics firm, discovers the ghosts of his past beckoning to him from a vacant bar about to be demolished.

In particular, "They're Tearing Down Tim Riley's Bar" represents Serling at his best, writing with an insight and power the equal of anything he had done before. Interestingly, the episode forms a curious triad with two of Serling's previous works, each of which forcefully reflected an aspect of the author's personality at the time. In 1954, Serling—twenty-nine and full of ambition—wrote "Patterns," about a rising young executive facing a future full of challenges and success. In 1959, Serling, older, more thoughtful, crafted "Walking Distance," in which a similar executive, having achieved a certain degree of success, is so overwhelmed with nostalgia that he attempts to escape into the past of his childhood. His past rejects him, but when he returns to the present—albeit sadly—it is clear that he will survive. In 1970, Serling—forty-five, with his greatest triumphs fully a decade behind him—set down "They're Tearing Down Tim Riley's Bar." Here, the executive is a tired man on the way down, his only joys memories of times long gone. Of the ghosts calling to him from his past, he says, "They're the best friends I've got. I feel a lot more comfortable with them—than I do with all those warm, living flesh-and-blood bodies I ride up and down the elevators with!" His is a life of unfulfilled expectations, eloquently described to a friendly cop in this manner:

> I rate something better than I got. Where does it say that every morning of a man's life he's got to Indian-wrestle with every young contender off the sidewalk who's got an itch to climb up a rung? (*Voice suddenly softer; smiles, cups*

> *policeman's face in his hands*) Hey, Flaherty . . . Flaherty . . . I've put in my time. Understand? I've paid my dues. I shouldn't have to get hustled to death in the daytime . . . and die of loneliness every night. That's not the dream. That's not what it's all about.

For this man, the present is one long gut-ache—and the only hope for salvation lies in reclaiming the past. For a brief moment, this seems a possibility as the man finds himself at a ghostly re-creation of his 1945 homecoming (like Serling, he too was a paratrooper during the war). But as the demolition on the bar begins, the phantoms start to fade away. He pleads with them:

> Wait a minute . . . Listen to me . . . I can't stay here. I don't have any place here. I'm an antique . . . a has-been. I don't have any function here . . . I don't have any purpose. (*Halts, holds out his hands, fists clenched*) You leave me now and I'm marooned! (*Points toward window*) I can't survive out there! Pop? Tim? They stacked the deck that way. They fix it so you get elbowed off the earth! You just don't understand what's going on now! The whole bloody world is coming apart at the seams. And I can't hack it! I swear to God . . . I can't hack it!

The story is bleak but accurate—and a long sight from a tale whose sole point is to jump out at you and yell, "Boo!" It does have a fairy tale kind of ending: although the ghosts disappear, the executive's devoted secretary convinces his boss—who has just fired him—to rehire him and *also* throw him a surprise party, demonstrating that the present is not the empty, terrible place it had seemed. However, this was *not* the original ending. William Windom recalls: "They added a sweetener. The way it ended was just like it says in the script: 'Where Tim Riley's bar had stood there was now an empty lot. The construction workers are just putting away their equipment. And in the middle of this empty, rain-swept square stands Randolph Lane, all by himself, the rain pouring down on him.' They didn't have the guts to do it."

Unfortunately, those involved with *Night Gallery* didn't see things Serling's way. Over the course of its second year, the show was being consistently bested in the ratings by *Mannix*. Both NBC and Universal were determined to do something about this—by making the series more like its competition. They rejected scripts by Serling in favor of more conventional fright stories by other writers and embarked on a campaign to turn *Night Gallery* into (as Serling put it) "*Mannix* in a cemetery."

Serling protested vehemently—to no avail. "When I complain, they pat me on the head, condescend and then hope I'll go away."

He summed it all up in a letter to Universal: "I wanted a series with distinction, with episodes that said something; I have no interest in a series which is purely and uniquely suspenseful but totally uncommentative on anything."

In spite of his feelings, Serling was contractually bound; he remained the host of *Night Gallery* until its cancellation.

In spite of such disappointments, Serling was still witty, full of fun—and committed. Throughout the late sixties and early seventies he taught writing, both in Los Angeles and Ithaca, New York, and lectured at colleges across the country, coming out against the Vietnam War and generally speaking his mind on political issues.

"He gave so much of himself to other people," says director Ralph Nelson. "I met a woman who recalled that once a guest speaker dropped out at the last minute, and she called Rod and said, 'I'm desperate and I can't pay you anything.' He said, 'Well, let me think it over and I'll call you back in thirty minutes.'

"He called her back in *fifteen* minutes and said, 'I'll be on the next plane.'"

In May, 1975, Serling was admitted to a hospital after experiencing a mild heart attack. One month later, he was re-admitted for a coronary bypass operation. Complications arose after ten hours of open-heart surgery, and he died on June 28, 1975, in Rochester, New York. In all, he had lived fifty years, six months and three days.

Most who had known him met the news of his death with shocked surprise. "Rod was built like a rock," says director Buzz Kulik. "Even as he got older, he was always very lean, very muscular. The shrapnel wound was there—it was visible, you know—but if anyone had said, 'Who is your least likely candidate for a bad heart?' it would have been him."

To those closest to him, it was not quite so unexpected. "His death reminded me of an airplane crash," says Rod's brother Bob, "in the sense that there is never any single cause of a crash; it's always a culmination, a combination of circumstances that build, each on top of the other, and climax in the accident. There was no single reason for Rod's death. I think it started with heredity: he had a family history of arteriosclerosis from my dad's side of the family, of high blood pressure from my mother's. The second adverse circumstance was his smoking four packs of cigarettes for God knows how many years—like twenty, twenty-five years. This had to have an effect on him. Third was his personality. He was so dynamic, so volatile, so intense about everything that—although we don't know everything about the effects of personality on a heart attack—I suppose he was just literally an accident going someplace to happen."

"He was truly a gentleman and a gentle man," actor Don Gordon ("The Four of Us Are Dying," "The Self-improvment of Salvadore Ross") says of Serling. "He was soft-spoken and very kind. He always had a smile, and it wasn't a fake smile either—he *liked* you. He was a terrific man. You miss somebody like that very much."

Memorial services for Serling were held on July 7, 1975. Part of producer Dick Berg's eulogy defined Serling in this way: "He was eternally the new boy on the block trying to join our games. And he penetrated the circle by regaling us with those many fragments of his Jewish imagination . . . intellectual stories, fantastic stories, hilarious stories, stories of social content, even one-liners about man's lunacy. However, they were always seen through his prism, becoming never less than *his* stories. And because he came to us with love . . . seeking *our* love . . . we invariably let him tell us a story. And how much richer we are for it."

Gene Roddenberry, the creator and producer of *Star Trek,* said of Serling, "The fact that Rod Serling was a uniquely talented writer with extraordinary imagination is not our real loss. These merely describe his tools and the level of his skill. Our loss is the man, the intelligence and the conscience who used these things for us. No one could know Serling, or view or read his work, without recognizing his deep affection for humanity, his sympathetically intense curiosity about us, and his determination to enlarge our horizons by giving us a better understanding of ourselves. He cared and, I suspect, perhaps too deeply too much of the time. He dreamed of much for us and demanded much of himself, perhaps more than was possible for either in this place and time. But it is that quality of dreams and demands which makes the ones like Rod Serling rare . . . and always irreplaceable."

In his last interview, several months before his death, Rod Serling said, "I just want them to *remember* me a hundred years from now. I don't care that they're not able to quote a single line that I've written. But just that they can say, 'Oh, he was a writer.' That's sufficiently an honored position for me." To leave Serling on this note would be to do him a disservice, for as usual he had underestimated himself and his works.

A far more fitting statement could be found in something he said to a college audience in 1970. "There is just one thing I would like on my headstone," he told them. "A line that read only, 'He left friends.'"

When Serling died, he had no way of estimating his friends—for they numbered in the millions. With his passing, their number has not diminished.

EPILOGUE

"On *The Twilight Zone,* there was an attempt to keep it literary, to keep it bright, to keep it good. No one in the show ever suggested at any time that something would be good enough—although that's commonplace today in commercial television, just to do it good enough, what the hell. Quality doesn't count now, but quality counted in *The Twilight Zone.*"

—GEORGE CLAYTON JOHNSON

"Even if I had done, say, six more *Twilight Zone* episodes that were of a lesser nature, still I had that much respect for that series that I couldn't feel anything but saying, 'Well, that's one of the things I've done along the way that wasn't just junk.'"

—CHARLES AIDMAN

In an interview given in 1972, Serling said, "As I grow older, the urge to write gets less and less. I've pretty much spewed out everything I have to say, none of which has been particularly monumental. I've written articulate stuff, reasonably bright stuff over the years, but nothing that will stand the test of time. The good writing—like wine—has to age well with the years and my stuff is momentarily adequate." As so many times before, his assessment was candid and hard. But fortunately, both for him and us, it is an opinion that time has proven wrong.

Today, *The Twilight Zone* is a perennial television favorite around the world. Serling's three *Twilight Zone* collections have over two and a half million copies in print; the *Twilight Zone* comic book over ten million. A rock version of the *Twilight Zone* theme climbed into *Billboard*'s Top Thirty. And since 1981, *Rod Serling's Twilight Zone Magazine* has been enjoying a broad national circulation, featuring articles about the series as well as short fiction by such authors as Stephen King, Peter Straub, Robert Silverberg and Joyce Carol Oates.

The series continues to be regularly satirized on television shows and comedy albums, in comic books, and on TV and radio commercials.

Early *Twilight Zone* parodies on television include a *Jack Benny Show* in which Jack gets lost in a fog, only to arrive at his house and find that no one knows him. The owner of the house (played by Rod Serling) introduces himself: "I'm the mayor of this town. In fact, they named it after me. I'm Mr. Zone. . . . You can call me Twi." Benny flees his house, yelling for help. Serling turns to the camera and says, "He'll be back. . . . Any man who claims to be thirty-nine as long as he has is a permanent resident of the Twilight Zone." On *The Dick Van Dyke Show* Robert Petrie (Dick Van Dyke) once found himself trapped in the "Twilo Zone," in which humans suddenly lose their thumbs and an invading alien being resembles Danny Thomas. More recently, *Saturday Night Live* has kidded *The Twilight Zone* several times, most notably in a humorous skit in which guest-host Ricky Nelson, trying desperately to get home to Ozzie and Harriet, journeys through the sit-com dwellings of *Leave it to Beaver, Father Knows Best, Make Room for Daddy* and *I Love Lucy.*

"It's a hell of a credit," says George Clayton Johnson. "I can just feel people back away from me when I say I wrote episodes of *The Twilight Zone*. They don't believe me, it's just like, 'How could he do that? Those things come from the dawn of time. . . .'"

"I can tell you, for all of us concerned it was a very special time," says actor John Anderson ("A Passage for Trumpet," "The Odyssey of Flight 33," "Of Late I Think of Cliffordville," "The Old Man in the Cave"). "The scripts, of course, were invariably superior to the general run of shows around then—in addition to which you had a day of rehearsal. Rod was almost always on hand for an hour or two to take suggestions growing out of the rehearsal and would 'fix it' during lunch break. Looking back on it, it was like a dream—when you consider today's pell-mell, hurly-burly approach."

"Rod was extremely proud of *The Twilight Zone*," says his brother Bob. "You can watch them now and see how professional they were, what a beautiful thing, compared to some of the other anthologies. So many of them really had a message, very subtle—it was a pill with sugar all over it—but you swallowed it and you learned something."

"There was a magic to the show," says actor Don Gordon, "and I think there still is and I think there always will be. It had the quality—and has the quality—of making us children, being frightened and saying, 'Ooh, what's going to happen next?' It has the quality, really, that radio used to have before television, and it's one of the few programs that does. Your imagination is allowed to work on *Twilight Zone*. You're invited in—to think. They're not bombarding you and saying, 'You're stupid, we're going to tell you what this is all about.' You're a participant, and that's very important."

Perhaps the most telling statement comes from Earl Hamner, Jr. "*The Twilight Zone* was an embodiment of great storytelling," he says. "Back when we all sat around fires and had animal skins for clothing, there were great stories told around campfires, and those same principles are at work in *The Twilight Zone*. So it doesn't surprise me at all that it has universal and lasting appeal. They're great stories well told."

If, in his darkest moments, Rod Serling felt his accomplishments on *The Twilight Zone* were of a transient nature, these were only the passing fears of every writer that his life's work has been of no consequence. The shining product of his imagination still flourishes, reborn each time a person turns on a television and sits before the glowing screen, caught in the spell. To those already acquainted, each new meeting is a reunion filled with delight. To those coming to it fresh, it is a revelation full of wonder and mystery and awe.

The Twilight Zone has endured. And like all lasting art eventually must, it has outlived its creator.

Addendum / The Eighties

"The operative word is that basically nobody understood what made *The Twilight Zone* work except Rod."

—BUCK HOUGHTON

Rod Serling had said, "I just want them to remember me." Since *The Twilight Zone Companion* first appeared, he's been remembered with a vengeance—day-long *Twilight Zone* marathons on stations across the country, record albums, cassettes, CDs, videotapes, T-shirts, buttons, magazines, books of short stories and trivia, even a toy called "the Zone Box," on which a button is pressed to play back Serling's opening narration. Serling himself has been inducted into the Television Academy of Arts and Sciences Hall of Fame, had retrospectives of his work at the Museum of Broadcasting in Los Angeles and New York, and has gotten a star on Hollywood Boulevard.

Richard Matheson's fine script "The Doll," bought but unproduced during *Twilight Zone*'s fifth season, was published in *Twilight Zone Magazine* and ultimately filmed as an episode of *Amazing Stories,* winning its star, John Lithgow, an Emmy and Matheson a Writers Guild Award nomination. In the fall of 1984, stations across the country aired a holiday special consisting of three previously unsyndicated *Twilight Zone* episodes: "Miniature," "A Short Drink From a Certain Fountain" and "Sounds and Silences," with Patrick O'Neal, star of "Short Drink," hosting. (The versions aired were substantially altered, with the dollhouse sequences in "Miniature" colorized and the entire special subtly speeded up via computer to allow for more commercials.) And for eight years, *Rod Serling's Twilight Zone Magazine* filled a unique niche before finally ceasing publication in June 1989.

Most significant of all, the eighties found many attaining prominence who had been nurtured on Serling's tales—and who longed to add to them. It was they who would provide the most intriguing footnotes to the history of *The Twilight Zone*.

Twilight Zone—The Movie

When, in 1982, it was announced that Steven Spielberg would be making a *Twilight Zone* movie, the news was greeted with excitement. More than any other individual, Spielberg seemed the true heir to Serling's crown. While still in his early twenties, he had directed the "Eyes" segment of Serling's *Night Gallery* pilot and Matheson's classic TV movie *Duel*. Over the ensuing decade, he had been responsible for a string of wonderful fantasy films. *E.T.*, *Close Encounters of the Third Kind*, and *Poltergeist* all seemed like two-hour-long *Twilight Zone* episodes, with their emphasis on average people stumbling into astonishing events (many particularly noted *Poltergeist*'s similarity to Matheson's "Little Girl Lost").

Years earlier, Serling himself had tried numerous times to get a *Twilight Zone* feature mounted. In 1963, while writing the screenplay for *Seven Days in May*, he met with Kirk Douglas, the film's star, to discuss such a project, which he then envisioned as consisting of several short tales linked together, à la *Dead of Night*. Some years later, taking a different approach, he wrote a full-length adaptation of Jerome Bixby's short story "It's a Good Life," which he had crafted so skillfully into a *Twilight Zone* episode in 1961. Despite his best efforts, nothing came to fruition.

When Spielberg decided to make *his* movie, he chose the anthological approach; four short tales, each about as long as an episode of the series.

His initial choices seemed in the right direction. He hired *Twilight Zone*

Kevin McCarthy, Kathleen Quinlan, William Schallert, and Patricia Barry in the movie segment "It's A Good Life"

alumni Richard Matheson and composer Jerry Goldsmith ("Nervous Man in a Four Dollar Room," "The Big Tall Wish") and recruited three top young directors, Joe Dante (*The Howling, Innerspace, The 'Burbs*), John Landis (*Coming to America*) and George Miller (*The Road Warrior*).

"I was a third wheel on that picture," notes Dante. "Landis and Spielberg had already planned it, and I just happened to be involved with Spielberg on *Gremlins* at that time. It was sort of like, 'Oh, Joe's here, why don't we ask him?' And that was what happened with George Miller. He visited Spielberg at a meeting that I happened to be attending, and everybody said, 'Oh, there's George Miller. Why don't we get him to do an episode?'"

Landis would write an original story for his segment; the other three would be remakes of *Twilight Zone* episodes to be adapted by Matheson. For his segment, Spielberg—fresh on the heels of *E.T.,* with its focus on children—wanted strongly to direct a story dealing with the elderly. He considered a number of stories, including Serling's "The Trade-Ins," before settling on George Clayton Johnson's "Kick the Can." Joe Dante, whose films *Gremlins* and *Piranha* focused on adults being terrorized by small, deadly monsters, was handed "It's a Good Life" and George Miller, so skilled at edge-of-the-seat suspense, was pegged for Matheson's "Nightmare at 20,000 Feet."

The decision to do a majority of remakes rather than new stories was a commercial one. Joe Dante: "The original concept that I guess sold the idea to the studio was that we'll do these great old stories that everybody loves. It's guaranteed surefire."

It was an approach that Richard Matheson had his doubts about. "Since *The Twilight Zone* has been shown so many times on television, there may have been an inordinate familiarity with those stories."

Such familiarity turned out to be only one of the film's many problems. Narrated by Burgess Meredith (star of four *Twilight Zone* episodes), *Twilight Zone—The Movie* opens with a prologue written and directed by Landis. In tone more similar to a *Night Gallery* blackout than something from *The Twilight Zone,* it features Dan Aykroyd and Albert Brooks as a pair of affable couch potatoes on a long drive, amusing themselves by guessing TV themes and reminiscing about old *Twilight Zone* episodes. Brooks and Aykroyd are appealing and funny, their banter natural (Brooks—recalling "Time Enough at Last," in which Burgess Meredith breaks his only pair of glasses after a nuclear war—comments, "That freaked me out. When I was seven years old, I bought another pair of glasses, just in case that would happen"). But the climactic moment, in which Aykroyd is revealed as a monster, falls painfully flat.

The first segment, Landis's untitled story, deals with an American bigot

(Vic Morrow) who finds himself on the receiving end when he leapfrogs back and forth through time between Nazi-occupied France, a Southern lynch party and Vietnam, finally being shipped off to a concentration camp. The work holds echoes of such relatedly themed Serling episodes as "Four O'Clock" and "Death's-Head Revisited" and the *Night Gallery* segment "Escape Route" (in which a fugitive Nazi escapes into a painting). But it quickly pales in comparison, seeming a thin, movie-derived quick sketch, uninformed by depth of insight or firsthand experience.

Spielberg's version of "Kick the Can" stars Scatman Crothers (*The Shining*) as a mystical, whimsical old man who breezes into the lives of a group of worn-out rest-home lodgers and gives them the gift of youth—a gift that turns out not as appealing in actuality as in daydream. In the end, all but one (Murray Matheson, the clown in "Five Characters in Search of an Exit") opt to return to old age, having learned to appreciate their years.

Such a finale was a radical departure from the original, in which the oldsters-turned-kids disappear into the night. The idea originated with George Clayton Johnson. "You're provoked into a lot of thought once you see these children running off into the night. What are they going to do? The story has really just opened when that happens. That had been on my mind for years, so I had worked out another half-hour teleplay that took off at the end of that." Johnson submitted a suggested outline to producers Frank Marshall and Kathleen Kennedy.

What eventually was filmed emerged as a sticky-sweet insult to seniors, overwrought and insincere, full of easy homilies and broad caricatures. Where the original had offered sentiment, this provided little but sentimentality. (Enough shards of Johnson's original teleplay remained that he was granted co-screenplay credit with Matheson and "Josh Rogan" [*E.T.* screenwriter Melissa Mathison's nom de plume].)

"When I went to see the film, I was charmed in a couple of places that were actually quite sweet," says Johnson. "The old lady and her late husband, Jack Dempsey—not the fighter—and her wedding ring falling off when she becomes a child. But the *rest* of it, making Scatman Crothers into the Tin Can Fairy or whatever. I called Richard Matheson and said, 'What about this? It's the damnedest script.' He said, 'Well, it's got nothing to do with what I wrote.'"

Unbeknownst to Matheson, once he'd turned in his draft of "Kick the Can," it had been extensively overhauled by Melissa Mathison. "I just don't write like that," he explains. Regarding the finished segment, he adds, "I didn't care for it. It had the gloss and it had the look, but it was a bit too soft for my taste. My script had a little more bite to it."

George Clayton Johnson did note that the movie utilized his new ending . . . and he contacted the Warner Brothers lawyers. "I said, 'Since you used my ending, you oughtta pay for it.' They said, 'Well, how do we know that we used your outline?' I said, 'Just go ask the producer. He's not gonna lie to you.'" In the end, Johnson was duly paid.

Of all the remakes, Joe Dante's "It's a Good Life" proved the most far removed from the source material—by choice. "My personal view was that it was a mistake to remake episodes of *The Twilight Zone,*" says Dante. "I thought it would have been far more interesting to do new stories that were in the *Twilight Zone* tradition that people hadn't already seen."

But Dante had no say in it; he had been assigned "It's a Good Life." Dante: "It was done very well on television . . . I didn't see how doing an updated version of it was going to get me anywhere. So I just took the basic premise of what would happen if there was a kid who could do *anything* and tried to make something as new as possible out of it."

In Dante's version, Anthony (Jeremy Licht), a lonely little boy with terrifying psychic powers, entraps a group of adults in a weirdly distorted house, forcing them to be his "family" and live a horrific child's-eye view of reality, complete with peanut-butter-and-ice-cream meals and round-the-clock cartoons.

Richard Matheson: "It was very close to what I wrote, and I liked what Joe did a lot. The visuals were largely his ideas, the way the house looked and everything. It was so grotesque, and the performances were good. It was my favorite segment of the movie."

A brightly colored oddity with a Venus-flytrap allure, the piece is engaging and disquieting, full of shrewd in-jokes (Cliffordville, Beaumont, Willoughby, Homewood, Helen Foley) and delightful performers from the series (Kevin McCarthy, Patricia Breslin, William Schallert and Billy Mumy, star of the original, with a cameo by Buck Houghton). Loaded with sight gags and extreme reactions, the tone is that of a living cartoon, with Dante making clever use of the TV sets' animated images to punctuate both the humor and the horror. Most of this footage was gleaned from old cartoons, but one sequence, in which Anthony sends his "sister" to her death in Cartoonland (reminiscent of Max Fleisher by way of Salvador Dali), was the work of premier animator Sally Cruikshank.

Dante's choice of style did not prove to everyone's taste. "When I saw the set they were working in, with the doorways aslant and curlicues across the furniture and all this, I knew that Joe Dante and the art director didn't understand *The Twilight Zone,*" says Buck Houghton. "We never had a bizarre set in our lives. We made that story about the little boy who controls everybody with the power of his glance comprehensible, because he lived in a house just like you and I do, and the people he bossed around looked exactly like you or I.

"But on *this,* they said to themselves, 'With a bizarre little guy like this, he'd probably bizarre up his house, then he'd bizarre up his friends by sealing their lips. . . .' It was bizarre in every way they could think of. As soon as I saw that, I said, 'Oh ho, these guys don't get it.'"

Most upsetting to some was the story's finale, a finale quite different from the one Dante initially considered. "Originally, mine was the last segment," says Dante, "and it ended with Dan Aykroyd picking up Kathleen Quinlan on the highway. That was also based on a draft where the house blew up. Anthony got killed, everybody got killed. This was long before I had shot it, and eventually we decided to abandon that completely. I didn't think it was very satisfactory."

Instead, Dante opted for an absurdly cheery ending in which the young teacher (Quinlan) takes the sadistic, murderous monster under her wing, to the accompaniment of flowers blooming along the roadway.

It didn't go down well. "The whole beauty of the original story was that it's impossible to put a happy ending on it, because once the kid is corrupted, he's corrupted completely," says George Clayton Johnson. "Joe Dante and I were on a panel at a convention, and I asked him, 'Whose idea was that to put the happy ending on it?' and he said it was his. And I said, 'Well then, too bad, Joe. You blew it.'"

It's an evaluation Dante himself rejects. "I don't think it *is* an upbeat ending. Who knows what that kid is gonna do? I don't believe for a minute he's gonna be a Goody Twoshoes, just because he does it at that moment. . . . I thought of it as a what-could-happen-around-the-corner ending."

Most effective of all is George Miller's remake of "Nightmare at 20,000 Feet." John Lithgow (*Harry and the Hendersons,* and also the lead in the short-lived Broadway version of *Requiem for a Heavyweight*) turns in an adrenaline-rush of a performance as an airline passenger terrified of flying, who spies a monster sabotaging the jet's engine in flight (with Carol Serling in a bit role as a fellow passenger). Matheson: "Lithgow was absolutely brilliant, starting from one hundred percent and building from there." From the first frame, it's a roller-coaster assault, with Miller lending it the same breathless pacing as *Road Warrior.* And *this* monster—a lean gargoyle designed by Ed Verreaux—is no lumbering Panda bear. "I thought the creature on the wing was infinitely superior," says Matheson. "Of course, they spent a lot more money on it."

The story went through many changes to get to the screen. Matheson: "Initially, they were going to have three major stories and a little filler [about] ten minutes long. I never understood how they were going to do it. Then, at another point, I was told they were going to put Gregory Peck in it, so I was trying to think in terms of the character from *Twelve O'Clock High*—a much older man remembering World War II and going through the same experience. Then Miller decided he wanted to go back to the basics. It wasn't as it was in my story, where he'd had a nervous breakdown. He was just a nervous guy, going on an airplane and seeing this thing."

As in the other segments, sacrificing character complexity for an onslaught of effects proves a grave flaw. In the original, William Shatner played a man freshly released from a mental hospital and desperate to prove his sanity. When he defeats the monster on the wing, he also conquers his own inner demons; no longer will he fear for his mind. His journey through the Twilight Zone has been for a *reason*.

But in the remake, Lithgow's character has no such history; he merely survives a totally inexplicable experience. In the end, he's carted off in an ambulance driven by the monster seen in the opening segment, presumably to his death—a comic tag that serves only to trivialize both Lithgow's character and his triumph.

Matheson reveals that Miller drastically altered his script. "It was like he was starting from scratch, as if it had just occurred to him. It didn't have any kind of depth to it. As so many pictures are today, it was just pizazz, visual skill, good camera work . . . and underneath, something missing."

Twilight Zone—The Movie premiered in June 1983 to poor box office and generally negative reviews. In the end, however, an event that occurred during shooting overshadowed any other consideration of the film. In John Landis's original screenplay for his segment, the Morrow character overcomes his bigotry by saving two Vietnamese orphans (Myca Dinh Le and Renee Chen) during an American attack in the jungle. As this sequence was being filmed, a ground-based explosion damaged an airborne helicopter. The copter crashed, killing Morrow and the two children.

Le and Chen had been hired illegally, as a way of circumventing child labor laws. The Directors Guild reprimanded Landis for "unprofessional conduct." The California Labor Commission fined Landis, associate producer George Folsey, Jr., unit production manager Dan Allingham, and Warner Brothers $5,000 each, the maximum possible fee, for violating child labor laws, and the California Occupational Safety and Health Administration issued 36 citations and levied $62,375 in fines (later lowered to $1,350, as the organization was being dismantled).

Most serious of all, Landis, Folsey, Allingham, special effects coordinator Paul Stewart and helicopter pilot Dorcey Wingo were charged with involuntary manslaughter—the first time a Hollywood director was ever indicted on criminal charges stemming from a fatality during filming. During the next five years—a period marked by endless legal delays and a tempestuous trial—a storm of controversy split the Hollywood community. While some held that it was merely an unforeseen freak occurrence, others felt that Landis, as director, bore direct responsibility.

In the end, all five defendants were found not guilty. Wingo never again worked in Hollywood. Landis continued his career as America's most successful comedy director. It was an outcome that many found disturbing and that resulted in two books critical of Landis: *Outrageous Conduct*, by Stephen Farber and Marc Green (Arbor House/Morrow, 1988), and *Special Effects*, by Ron LaBrecque (Scribners, 1988).

Twilight Zone—The Movie, which began as an honest attempt by aficionados of the series to beguile a public hungry for diversion, ended in notoriety and anguish, one of the grimmest pages in cinema history. Or as George Clayton Johnson says, "A tragedy, just a bloody tragedy."

CBS Returns to the Zone

Regarding the failure of *Twilight Zone—The Movie*, Richard Matheson speculated that such stories "only work best in short bursts," and that therefore television provided a more favorable arena. He was not alone in such thoughts. Over the years, several attempts had been made to return *Twilight Zone* to the small screen.

Buck Houghton: "When Rod was alive, we tried to revive *The Twilight Zone*, and the rumor down at the computer was that it would never be popular, so we could never get it going." In 1980, Francis Coppola also tried unsuccessfully to interest CBS in such a production.

But by the mid-eighties, the network's position was changing—guided by economic reality. TV rights to *Twilight Zone* were owned by CBS, and that meant that the profits to the network from a potential remake could far outstrip those from a series produced by an outside company.

"There had been quiet pressure to do in-house projects," explains Carla Singer, then CBS Vice President of Drama Development. "*Twilight Zone* was a series I'd always liked as a kid, it was one of my favorites . . . and at that point it sounded like an interesting challenge for me personally."

As executive producer, Singer recruited Phil DeGuere, creator-producer of *Simon and Simon* and no stranger to science fiction and fantasy, having previously written and directed the pilot for an unsold series based on the *Dr. Strange* comic book and having adapted Arthur C. Clarke's *Childhood's End* for an unproduced miniseries. DeGuere brought with him James Crocker, a talented writer-producer he had worked with many times. Before long, CBS approved the project. *Twilight Zone* was off and running. (At the same time, Steven Spielberg was thinking along similar lines; his *Amazing Stories*, a *Twilight Zone* clone heavy on effects and light on story, debuted the same season on NBC.)

DeGuere gathered together a writing staff with knowledge and expertise in the genre: executive story consultant Alan Brennert, fantasy novelist and previously story editor on *Buck Rogers;* story editor Rockne O'Bannon, later to script *Alien Nation;* creative consultant Harlan Ellison, a brilliant, fiery fantasist with a host of award-winning books and classic episodes of *The Outer Limits* and *Star Trek* to his credit (later, they would be joined by Hugo and Nebula winner George R.R. Martin; comic book writer, Martin Pasko; and newcomer Rebecca Parr). Well-known science fiction and horror writers were hired to provide scripts, including Ray Bradbury, David Gerrold, Steven Barnes, Richard Matheson (under the pen name Logan Swanson), Ed Bryant, and Michael Reaves. Classic short stories were purchased for adaptation from Bradbury, Ellison, Clarke, Sturgeon, Silverberg, Zelazny, Stephen King, Joe Haldeman, Henry Slesar, and William F. Wu. DeGuere also actively sought out prominent feature directors: genre heavyweights William Friedkin (*The Exorcist*), Wes Craven (*Nightmare on Elm Street*), and Joe Dante, in addition to John Milius, Robert Downey, Martha Coolidge, Claudia Weill, and Allan Arkush.

From the first, there was agreement as to what the show would *not* be. "None of us were going back into the series grind and the terrible hours *that* entailed just to do a rehash of somebody else's show," says Alan Brennert. "We all had stories we wanted to tell, that no one had ever allowed us to do on television before, and we saw this as a rare opportunity to do something different. We were following in Serling's footsteps but not mimicking his style. It was very much a conscious decision not to do that show—because that show had been done already."

Clearly, this would be a series far removed from the one penned by Serling and company, a *Zone* in color and stereophonic sound, an hour in length (each made up of two to three segments), with a new logo and theme music courtesy of the Grateful Dead.

And what of the host? "Originally, when they did the first presentation cuts, Phil did the narrations himself," explains Brennert. "And Carla Singer came out of the meeting and said, 'Very nice,' and then, as an afterthought, added, 'Oh, and get a *real* narrator, would you?' And Phil pantomimed an arrow going into his heart." A number of others were tested, including Ellison. Ultimately, the off-screen narrator chosen was actor Charles Aidman, star of "And When the Sky Was Opened" and "Little Girl Lost." Brennert: "We needed somebody who could just as easily do a very warm, sensitive story as a very hard, dark story, and Charlie was the only one who had the range . . . plus I think at the back of our minds there was a little bit of that link to the old show."

The new *Twilight Zone* debuted at eight P.M., September 27, 1985, against ABC's *Webster* and *Mr. Belvedere* and NBC's *Knightrider.* Initial audience response was good; *Twilight Zone* won its time slot four of the first five weeks. Then ratings started to slide. (Brennert: "You have not known humiliation until you have been beaten by *Webster* and *Mr. Belvedere*.")

It was soon obvious that *Twilight Zone* was losing ground with the viewers. Michael Cassutt, a staff writer on the show and later executive story editor on *Max Headroom,* comments, "I can see why people who were expecting *The Twilight Zone* were disappointed with it. The original series was pretty much Serling's point of view, with Richard Matheson and Charlie Beaumont imitating or transcending Serling's point of view. There was very much a style of storytelling and narrator presence that we never had. So our show always seemed uneven to me. There were episodes perfectly in keeping with *The Twilight Zone* spirit, and then others that could have been from *The Outer Limits* or from anything."

Twilight Zone managed a second-season renewal by the skin of its teeth. In what Brennert calls "a haunting echo of what happened to *Night Gallery,*" the show was cut down to a half hour. Brennert: "It aired for about five or six weeks as a half-hour, was completely killed, just run over by the *Cosby Show.*" CBS withdrew the series, then later put it back on briefly at an hour length, two half hours back-to-back. But by then, as writer-director J. D. Feigelson commented, "The stink of death was on it."

As the network representative overseeing the show, Carla Singer had been democratic and fair-minded. But after the first thirteen episodes, she moved on to other projects—and the show went under the scrutiny of CBS's Current Programming Department. And as ratings declined, the network's "notes" increased.

On the original *Twilight Zone,* network meddling had been minimal. "We never had a script rejected on any grounds," says Buck Houghton. "Scripts were sent to CBS immediately, but failing to hear from them we sailed right along. And we seldom heard from them."

Not so with the new series. Every premise, every outline, every script, every draft, had to be approved by Current Programming and then the scripts passed by Program Practices, the network censors. It was an approval often mercurial and difficult to obtain.

Brennert recalls an incident during the filming of an episode entitled "Tooth or Consequences," in which Program Practices temporarily shut down production, at a cost to CBS of about $100,000. "One of the characters tries to commit suicide by hanging himself with the cord of a dentist's drill, and they said, 'Imitable behavior.' And we said, 'Oh, come on. Children across the country are going to creep into their dentists' offices and try to hang themselves with the drill!?'" Ironically, by the time shooting resumed, costar Kenneth Mars could not be located to alter the sequence. "So it went on the air anyway."

Although such events were largely trivial, they bespoke a pervasive network attitude. "If you take something that's the slightest bit controversial and you try to mask it in fantasy terms, the way that Serling did so successfully, they see through it now—because *they* grew up watching *Twilight Zone,* too," notes Brennert. Reasons for rejection were often seemingly contradictory, but a pattern soon emerged. "It was anything unusual, that's not the expected, that isn't proven. It can be a story in which you have two characters talking for forty minutes. It can be a story that they think is too dark or esoteric. They want *safe* shows . . . and by its very nature, *Twilight Zone* cannot be a safe show."

Events came to a head over "Nackles," a script by Harlan Ellison, based on a short story by Donald Westlake (under the pseudonym Curt Clark), about a bigot who gets his comeuppance one Christmas when "Nackles," a monstrous anti-Santa he's made up to scare some minority children, turns out to be very real . . . and very *black.* West Coast Program Practices had approved the script, and Ellison was preparing to make his directorial debut, having already cast Ed Asner in the lead.

Brennert: "And then, a few days before shooting, somebody in New York pulled the plug, saying, 'It's an offensive story. We can't do this.' In effect, it was the East Coast preempting the West Coast." In protest, Ellison resigned from the series.

"There was a lot of noise about it," Ellison later wrote in *Twilight Zone Magazine.* "I don't suffer in silence. It was in *The New York Times, TV Guide, Variety,* dozens of newspapers all over the country, on *Entertainment Tonight* and, ironically, *CBS News.* But they wouldn't back down."

Halting the episode cost the production company somewhere between $150,000 and $300,000, and another segment had to be slipped into the slot originally intended for "Nackles." (Later, the network agreed to a compromise rewrite offered by Ellison, then once again reversed itself.)

In spite of network static, a handful of imaginative, lovingly rendered tales emerged, including:

- "Paladin of the Lost Hour," written by Harlan Ellison and directed by Gilbert Gates. A perceptive, unforgettable piece in which a dying old man (Danny Kaye) must find a successor to guard a timepiece containing Earth's last hour. Glynn Turman is superb as the tormented Vietnam vet who at first rejects, then embraces the responsibility, and in turn finds salvation. This marked Kaye's last dramatic performance and won Ellison a Writers Guild Award and (in its short-story version) a Hugo.
- "Her Pilgrim Soul," written by Alan Brennert and directed by Wes Craven, in which a scientist (Kristoffer Tabori) captures the spirit of a little girl inside a holographic field and, as the girl rapidly ages, falls in love with her. A heartfelt examination of love and loss spanning generations, the teleplay earned Brennert a Writers Guild Award nomination. Richard Matheson: "The writing was good, the plot was clever, and the performances were great. Now that, to me, was an ideal *Twilight Zone.*"

• "Nightcrawlers," scripted by Phil DeGuere, from a story by Robert R. McCammon. A harrowing, lavishly produced story of a crazed Vietnam vet's (Scott Paulin) arrival at a roadside cafe—and the dead buddies he abandoned who appear and wreak havoc whenever he falls asleep. Paulin's performance is a taut piano-wire, Friedkin's direction masterful and Bradford May's cinematography spellbinding. And the pulse-pounding score by Mel Saunders and the Grateful Dead (with Huey Lewis on harmonica) grabs you by the jugular and doesn't let go.

• "But Can She Type?" by Martin Pasko and Rebecca Parr, directed by Shelly Levison. A charming, humorous piece, in which a beleaguered secretary (Pam Dawber) finds herself miraculously transported to a parallel world where being a secretary is the most glamorous and prestigious job imaginable.

• "Dead Run," teleplay by Alan Brennert from a short story by Greg Bear, directed by Paul Tucker. An unemployed truck driver (Steve Railsback) accepts a job transporting people to hell—only to find that the administration of hell has been subcontracted to the Moral Majority and that a number of the "damned souls" (including a gay man and an addict) don't deserve the fate allotted to them. In the end, the trucker chooses to continue driving the Hellbound Road, surreptitiously releasing those he feels have been unfairly judged. A courageous story that received a commendation from the Alliance of Gay and Lesbian Artists.

• "The Road Less Traveled," by George R.R. Martin, directed by Wes Craven, in which a guilt-ridden draft dodger encounters the legless, dying vet he would have been had he gone to war. Although more than ten minutes were excised to fit it into a second-season half-hour slot, what remains is a thoughtful, touching, and effectively scary piece, with the versatile Cliff DeYoung astonishing in twin roles as the gentle young draft evader and his bitter, wasted alter self.

Three additional stories received Writers Guild nominations—Rockne O'Bannon's "The Storyteller," Virginia Aldridge's "The Junction," and George Miller's "The Last Defender of Camelot" (from a Zelazny story)—and others were notable for their imagination and skill. But for each episode that soared, many stayed firmly rooted to the ground, victims of misfired writing or execution. Remakes of old episodes generally came across as tired retreads, while many of the new tales missed the mark. Matheson: "A lot of them were weak . . . attenuated, based on just a little surprise ending that wasn't really that much of a surprise."

Often, there was a sense of distance, of condescension. The original *Twilight Zone* had been populated with a multitude of distinctive and memorable souls: Martin Sloane in "Walking Distance," Wanda Dunn in "Nothing in the Dark," Janet Tyler in "Eye of the Beholder." We recog-

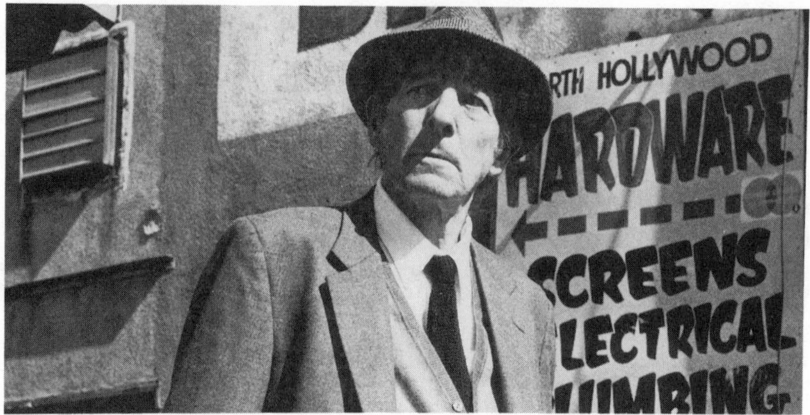

Danny Kaye in "Paladin of the Lost Hour," an episode from the revived CBS series

nized their reality; the colorations of personality and experience added conviction to the stories. But in the new *Zone,* characters frequently tended to be generalized, simplified, familiar TV cutouts giving voice to exposition without subtext.

Still, for all of that, the series was an earnest attempt by hardworking professionals. Says Alan Brennert, "If there were clunkers, by God, they were *our* clunkers, at least that first season. We could always say, "Yeah, we shouldn't have done that one. Oh, well, on to the next story."

Adds Michael Cassutt, "I didn't find anybody on the show who didn't have a lot of respect for the original *Zone* . . . I think the motive was there to try to honor Serling's memory by doing the kind of shows he might have done in the mid-eighties. I just don't think it worked. . . ."

Following cancellation of the new *Twilight Zone,* the logical step for CBS to recoup its investment would have been to place the series in syndication. But there was a financial equation that militated against this: The shows most successful in syndication were those that could be "stripped"—aired five times a week. Common wisdom held that the minimum number of episodes a series needed to be successfully stripped was around ninety, so that individual episodes wouldn't repeat so often as to lose viewer interest. The new *Twilight Zone* had produced only seventy-nine stories, many of which had running times that didn't fit into the half-hour syndication slot. In all, only sixty-four were suitable.

The conclusion was inescapable; in order to syndicate the new *Twilight Zone,* CBS needed to make more episodes, yet they definitely did *not* want *Twilight Zone* back on the network lineup.

Their solution was ingenious.

A New Zone

In the fall of 1988, a new syndicated show debuted on over two hundred local stations—a *third* version of *The Twilight Zone,* thirty brand-new episodes, broadcast for the first time anywhere . . . produced solely to round out the syndication package. MGM/UA had approached CBS with an appealing proposal: They would foot the bill for the new episodes and pay off the deficits left by the network show, in exchange for domestic syndication rights (leaving CBS all foreign distribution). What emerged was a joint venture by CBS International and MGM/UA, in association with London Films and Atlantis Films.

The personnel hired to guide the show had solid credentials on television, though little experience in fantasy: executive producers Mark Shelmerdine (*I, Claudius*) and Michael MacMillan, and story editors Paul Chitlik and Jeremy Bertrand Finch, a writing team that had done sitcoms and had written the "Aqua Vita" episode of the recent network *Zone*. The sole exception was story editor J. Michael Straczynski, horror novelist, coauthor of the *Night Gallery* episode guide in *Twilight Zone Magazine,* and previously story editor on *Captain Power* and *The Real Ghostbusters*.

Straczynski had literally grown up in the Twilight Zone. "We traveled a lot, my family and I, because my father had a unique economic philosophy: Blow into town, run up lots of bills, and split. Consequently, I never really had any friends. Books were my friends, and science fiction movies and, of course, *The Twilight Zone*."

Although he had written "What Are Friends For?" for the recent network *Zone* (about a man's imaginary playmate reappearing years later to be a companion to his son), Straczynski was less than enthusiastic about the series. "Many of the stories were marginal, at best. Some of the humanity, I think, was lost. The morality-play aspect of the original series was missing in a lot of them."

Shelmerdine agreed with Straczynski's assessment and was determined to return to what he perceived as the structure and tone of Serling's series, to do the sort of "little people" stories that Serling so valued. Still, they had no desire to ignore material that might be rewarding. "When we came onto *Zone,* we got about two hundred leftovers from *TZ* II," Straczynski recalls. "They had overdeveloped to an astonishing degree—outlines, stories, scripts, premises, everything in between. And we read it all."

In the end, most of this material was jettisoned. An exception was Alan Brennert's script "The Cold Equations." Adapted from Tom Godwin's classic short story and originally intended for the network run, it emerged as a high-water mark for the syndicated show. In it, a spaceship stowaway (searingly portrayed by Christianne Hirt) learns that the unyielding mathematics of fuel consumption decree that the ship can't reach its destination with her added weight—and so she must willingly sacrifice herself by stepping out the airlock.

When executives at MGM read the script, *they* nearly went out the airlock. Finding the dark, suicidal ending unsuitable, they suggested two possible "fixes"—that the captain of the ship amputate his own legs and dump them out the airlock to get rid of the extra weight and save them both, or that he blow the girl's brains out and shove her into space, so that she wouldn't have to commit suicide. Straczynski: "They wanted 'The Lukewarm Equations.'" CBS backed up Shelmerdine and Straczynski, and the script was shot unchanged.

A number of those who had contributed to the network series were commissioned to write scripts, including Harlan Ellison, Michael Reaves, and Michael Cassutt. Other skilled writers were sought, but as Shelmerdine notes, "It is incredibly difficult to come up with original ideas for *The Twilight Zone*." Straczynski: "Most of the writers we went to who had the big reps just weren't available, and often they didn't have the background in the genre or they weren't conceiving *Zone*-type stories." Straczynski himself ended up writing ten scripts, fully one third of the entire series (one of them, "Our Selena Is Dying," adapted from an original unproduced *Twilight Zone* outline by Serling, about a dying old woman with the power to leech the youth out of others).

The decision to go back to the basics of *The Twilight Zone* was more than an aesthetic one. "It was my understanding from Mark Shelmerdine when I first met with him that it was an economic imperative," says Alan Brennert. "They were going for more low-key shows with only a few sets and a few actors." The budget was stringent—$350,000 per half hour, barely half that of the network show. Or, as Brennert termed it, "The Diet Zone."

Shelmerdine and company would have to cut corners at every turn. The network episodes had been filmed in thirty-five millimeter; the syndicated would be in sixteen. Shooting would be in Canada, where costs were lower and the currency exchange-rate favorable. Additionally, Canadian tax laws allowed benefits for shows that met "Canadian content" requirements, notably that fifty percent of the writers and directors be Canadian.

Unfortunately, suitable Canadian writers proved virtually impossible to find. As a result, all the writers on *Zone* were Americans, and—to meet Canadian content—*all* the directors Canadian. "Many of them were very, very good," says Straczynski. "But a few of them would best be suited for directing cod fishing in northern Ontario." The cast also had to be Canadian, save a recognizable American in the lead (these included Henry Morgan, Ted Shackleford, Louise Fletcher, Timothy Bottoms, William Sanderson, Michael Moriarty, Colleen Dewhurst, Bud Cort, Paul LeMat, Charles Haid, Dean Stockwell, Janet Leigh, and Karen Valentine).

Story-editing offices were in Los Angeles, while the episodes were filmed three thousand miles away at the Atlantis Film Studios in Toronto, with no writer on the scene to make last-minute changes. Straczynski: "There was no rewriting done up there. There were cuts that were made, but they never knew *what* to cut, because they weren't writers."

The budget pinch created other problems. "I very much wanted Charles Aidman to narrate our episodes, too," says Straczynski, "but his costs were far beyond what we could afford." Robin Ward was hired instead. "Unfortunately, he doesn't do as well. There's a sort of car-commercial voice he uses every so often."

It didn't end there. Alan Brennert explains, "Some pinhead at MGM/UA made the decision, because they wanted the entire package to have 'uniformity,' of going back and redubbing all of the episodes made on network. So Charlie Aidman's voice was stripped and replaced with Ward's. All of us—Harlan, Phil, Jim, Rock—were on the looping stage with Chuck Aidman, directing him for those narrations. We put *care* into the thing—and suddenly this *stranger's* voice comes in. It's the verbal equivalent of colorizing."

Shelmerdine and his colleagues also assumed the thankless task of reediting the network shows to fit the twenty-two-minute running time required for syndication. Although they took great pains to alter the episodes with sensitivity to the intent of the original, a few stories presented special problems. Alan Brennert's "Her Pilgrim Soul" and "Message From Charity" (based on a short story by William M. Lee) required that discarded footage be added back in to pad them out to two-parters.

Of "Message From Charity," Brennert recalls, "They were trying desperately to expand it, and I kept saying, 'There's this scene that'll do it, just put this scene in.' Mark would say, in his proper, patient tone, 'We can't find that scene, Alan, it doesn't seem to exist anymore. The only one we have is of Peter running.' So they put in a sequence of Peter running toward Bear Rock for what seems like half an hour."

Most lamentable of all was the fate of "Paladin of the Lost Hour"—the high point of the network run in Shelmerdine's view—in which nine of its thirty-one minutes were lopped off, creating what Brennert terms "a jerky, jarring simulacrum of the original." Harlan Ellison responds, "The people who did this are the direct lineal descendants of those who took mauls and hammers and bashed off the nose of the Sphinx. These are the sort of people who can justify anything in the name of business . . . It's what drives people who have talent away from writing for television."

On occasion, budget constraints led to questionable decisions. At one point, Straczynski recalls, "a curious thing happened—we ran out of money." A script was needed, but there were no funds to pay for it. In 1964, during the original *Twilight Zone*'s last season, William Froug had written "Many, Many Monkeys," about a worldwide outbreak of blindness. It had never been produced. "We did a check on it and found it still belonged to CBS," Straczynski adds. "I said, 'Please, pay this man an additional fee if we're going to be doing a script.' I don't know whatever happened to that."

Then, in the midst of production, the five-month-long Writers Guild Strike hit. Straczynski: "The bulk of the production was done during the strike, on scripts that were finished prior to then." As a Guild member, he could not participate in any way, nor could any other Guild writer.

As the strike wore on, the backlog dwindled, until a new script was desperately needed. Not wanting to use scab writers, the producers decided to remake George Clayton Johnson's "A Game of Pool," utilizing the original, unfilmed ending in which Jesse *loses* the game. Shelmerdine contends that the choice was due more to the quality of the script than to production pressures. Whatever the reason, filming began, without paying or even telling Johnson.

Johnson got wind of it from a friend. "I laid low, just to see how long it would take for them to tell me, and they weren't *going* to tell me. They just thought they'd have themselves a free script." Shelmerdine responds, "It's a complex situation . . . these things are fairly gray, enormously sensitive areas . . . I'm sure CBS did not act outside any rights they had." As of this writing, the matter is being arbitrated by the Guild. But whatever the outcome, as Buck Houghton notes regarding the incident, "That's not very good moral thinking."

Without input from the writer on "Game of Pool," the results were dismaying. "They turned it from something that I liked to utter shit," says Johnson. "They changed every important line, took all the suspense out of it. I tried to find the reason for it. I think it's that, if you make one key change, if you don't watch yourself, you have to change everything else. And after a while, you just lose your place."

Over its initial run, the syndicated *Zone* demonstrated a commendable tendency toward exploring fresh, intriguing concepts. Straczynski's "Dream Me a Life" was a poignant love song set in an old folks home, with Eddie Albert and Barry Morse contributing fine performances. Tom Palmer's "Extra Innings," with Marc Singer as a crippled ex-ballplayer who travels back to the turn of the century to win the World Series, proved affecting and surprising. Christy Marx's "Cat and Mouse," about a shy woman (Pamela Bellwood) finding sexual liberation with a werecat, had one hell of a kicker. And Harlan Ellison's "Crazy as a Soup Sandwich" explored the confrontation between a Mafia don (Anthony Franciosa) and a demon from hell with pungent wit.

But for all of that, the series overall proved a disappointment. Uninspired direction and acting, bargain-basement production and superficial writing repeatedly sabotaged thought-provoking concepts.

Generally ignored by the critics and given little publicity, the syndicated *Zone* nevertheless managed to gain respectable ratings. With most series, such a response would have guaranteed another season, but not so here. "MGM just wanted thirty more half hours to fill out the package," says Straczynski. "The fact that it's rating well and very positive letters are coming in is irrelevant to them. They wanted their financial considerations taken care of. And now they can forget about the whole damn thing, because producing it is a pain in the ass."

Looking Ahead . . . And Behind

In truth, one shouldn't judge the new *Twilight Zone* stories too harshly. The creative individuals involved worked with sincerity and dedication. If they failed more than they succeeded, it wasn't for lack of trying. It was a tribute to Serling and his legacy that they tried at all.

In 1959, when Rod Serling created *The Twilight Zone,* he little dreamed that thirty years later those enamored of his work could insert a tape in a machine and view "Eye of the Beholder" or "The Lonely" or any of the other dozens of marvelous tales whenever they wished. Though this would have surprised him, the world we live in would not. It is a world of gleaming wonders and bleak horrors, a world in which the impossible corners of the Twilight Zone no longer seem quite so impossible.

The network executives and advertising men who first viewed the *Twilight Zone* pilot found it a curiosity and a mystery, a bizarre, unnatural creature first cousin to the Minotaur and the Chimera. Born before Dachau, before the Bomb, these men lived lives that were coherent to them, bracketed within certain rational, limited boundaries.

Our lives are not.

If *Twilight Zone*'s popularity has grown, it is because *we* have grown, and not always in ways we intended or desired. The dark places of the Twilight Zone are familiar to us, and comforting. The nightmare is a friend, the darkness a sanctuary.

We are the children of Serling's vision.

INDEX

About the Author

Marc Scott Zicree was born in Santa Monica, California, but his family soon migrated to Los Angeles. He is an alumnus of the Clarion Writers Workshop and has a B.A. in painting, sculpture, and graphic arts from UCLA and an M.F.A. from Lowell Darling's Fat City School of Finds Art. His short stories, articles, and photographs have appeared in a variety of newspapers, magazines and anthologies, including *Omni*, *Video Review* and *Twilight Zone Magazine* (on which he was a contributing editor). He is an American Book Award nominee for *The Twilight Zone Companion* and has five screenplays and over seventy-five teleplays to his credit, including contributions to the recent network *Twilight Zone*, *Beauty and the Beast* and *Star Trek—The Next Generation*. He has been a guest on more than a hundred radio and television shows, including *The Today Show*, *Entertainment Tonight* and *All Things Considered*, and has lectured at UCLA, USC and the University of Colorado. Currently, he divides his time between story-editing TV series, writing network pilots, crafting movie scripts, and serving as a regular commentator on National Public Radio's *Morning Edition*. He lives in Hollywood with a marvelous wife and two vile dogs.